The Lisle Letters

An Abridgement

EDITED BY

Muriel St. Clare Byrne

Selected and Arranged by Bridget Boland

Foreword by Hugh Trevor-Roper

Secker & Warburg · London

The University of Chicago Press · Chicago

First published in England 1983 by
Martin Secker & Warburg Limited
54 Poland Street, London W1V 3DF

Foreword © 1982 and 1983 by Hugh Trevor-Roper

British Library Cataloguing in Publication Data

The Lisle letters.
  1. Lisle, Arthur Plantagenet, *Viscount*
  2. Statement – Great Britain – Correspondence
  3. England – Social life and customs – 16th century – Sources
  I. Lisle, Arthur Plantagenet, *Viscount*
  II. Byrne, Muriel St. Clare
  III. Boland, Bridget
  942.05   DA335.L5

ISBN 0-436-07905-4

Printed in the United States of America

Contents

Illustrations

Foreword

HUGH TREVOR-ROPER

The English historian G. M. Young once wrote that the historian should read
the documents of an age until he could hear the people speak. That was all
very well for the Victorian age of which he wrote, but how can we penetrate,
in that depth, those earlier periods for which private correspondence hardly
exists? Fifteenth-century England seems to us infinitely remote, its anarchy
almost unimaginable, until we read the Paston Letters and see the daily
problems of a Norfolk family during the Wars of the Roses. Publicly, an age
may be well documented; but it is by its private character, by the attempts of
individuals to lead conventional lives even in the midst of revolution, that we
sense its reality and seem, while we read, to share its life.

The public character of the reign of Henry VIII is well documented. That
too was an age of revolution. Not anarchy, as in the fifteenth century, but
controlled revolution, revolution from above. The seven-year period from
1533 to 1540 – the seven years of Thomas Cromwell – witnessed the breach
with Rome, the dissolution of the monasteries, the Pilgrimage of Grace, the
creation of a new state church and a new 'despotic' state. Politically, the
process was continuous, legalized in regular institutions, but it was accompanied, and indeed driven forward, by a reign of terror. All who opposed or
obstructed it, even involuntarily, were ruthlessly eliminated: More and
Fisher, Anne Boleyn, the Carthusians, the Pilgrim leaders, the Pole family,
finally Cromwell himself; and even after him the process would go on,
though more untidily: 'The Tudor revolution in government' had the true
character of a revolution: it devoured its children.

Are there any documents which reveal the private character of this hectic
period as the Paston Letters revealed that of Henry VI? There are, and
thanks to a lifetime of devoted study, some two-thirds of them have been
edited and presented in readable form, with a copious running commentary,
by Miss Muriel St. Clare Byrne, and published in six ample volumes,
beautifully printed, by the University of Chicago Press. They are the Lisle
Letters, and they cover exactly those seven years in which Thomas Cromwell

With the exception of the final paragraph, this material is taken from the author's review of the six-
volume edition of *The Lisle Letters* (Chicago, 1981), published in *The American Scholar* 51, no. 3 (Summer,
1982): 410–23.

both ruled and transformed England in the name, and at the mercy, of Henry VIII.

The Lisle Letters are not a new discovery. They were calendared long ago, in the great nineteenth-century collection, *Letters and Papers of Henry VIII,* begun by John Brewer and continued by James Gairdner (who also edited *The Paston Letters*). Historians have always used them, picking out what they wanted, but it was left to Miss Byrne to see that they had a coherent unity, which was lost by such piecemeal use: that they could be used not merely incidentally and individually to illustrate the course of politics, but collectively in their own right, to bring back to life the self-contained human world which had created them – the world of a prominent but essentially unpolitical family which chance had involved (and in the end nearly ruined) in this formidable Cromwellian revolution.

Who was Lord Lisle? He was the illegitimate son, by the daughter of a Hampshire gentleman, of King Edward IV. As such, he was a Plantagenet, the only male survivor, after 1485, of the White Rose dynasty in the Wars of the Roses; but his illegitimacy, which debarred him from the throne, made him politically harmless. His own character, like that of his father, was agreeable and easygoing, and Henry VII, having married Lisle's legitimate half-sister in order to appropriate her Yorkist claims, could afford to be indulgent to this unambitious and inoffensive kinsman. Henry VIII continued the indulgence. Under him, Lisle became keeper of the royal forests of Clarendon and Bere, Privy Councillor, and Vice-Admiral of England. Finally, in 1533 when he was about seventy (if we accept Miss Byrne's calculations, which seem here to be questionable), he was appointed the King's Deputy, or Governor, of Calais, the last relic of English rule in France. His predecessor had been Lord Berners, the translator of Froissart. Lisle took over his official residence, the old Staple Inn, and his private furniture and plate. With him went his second wife, Honor.

Lisle's first wife, by whom he had three daughters, had been a Grey, baronness Lisle in her own right (hence his own choice of title), widow of Edmund Dudley, the minister of Henry VII and first victim of Henry VIII. He was thus stepfather of John Dudley, afterward duke of Northumberland, who would be executed for seeking to place his family on the throne. Through her, he acquired land in ten counties. His second wife was a Grenville, of a famous and dynamic Cornish family. She too had been married before, to a West Country gentleman of very ancient family, Sir John Basset, and her Basset children were still young when she went to Calais. She was then in her early forties and still hoped to bear a male heir to the name of Plantagenet; but in this she would be disappointed. Her continuing ambitions were to preserve and enlarge the ample Basset estates in Devon and Cornwall and to ensure the worldly success of her Basset children.

Lisle's government of Calais has generally been dismissed as lax and inefficient. This view was expressed categorically by the American historian R. B. Merriman, the biographer of Cromwell, and has been repeated since. It irritates Miss Byrne, who protests – perhaps too much – against this 'Merriman myth'. Lisle's correspondence does not suggest a forceful personality, but let us concede that he was a conscientious official, worried by his duties and his debts – he was always short of cash, and lived, as was expected of him, far beyond his means – and that the compliments which he received from Henry and from Cromwell were genuine. Certainly everyone agreed that he was 'gentle'; 'the gentlest heart living', said the king; 'of a most gentle nature', wrote the Protestant martyrologist John Foxe. Lady Lisle was not gentle. Some thought her a termagant, others a busybody, others (like Foxe) a popish bigot. She knew what she wanted and was determined to get it. She knew all the details of her own estates and of her husband's business, which she did not hesitate to mind. Those who wanted something from the Lord Deputy either enlisted her aid or, if she were unwilling, got at him alone.

Lisle's duties at Calais were to ensure the defense and provision of the town, to see that the soldiers' wages were paid, and – most difficult of all – to keep the peace among the English officials, all of whom were on the make and some of whose families had been entrenched there for generations. In time of war between its neighbors, the king of France and the emperor, he had to preserve the neutrality of Calais, and of course he had to entertain visiting grandees on their way to or from England: the Admiral of France, for instance, on his embassy in 1534, or the Elector Palatine, coming to fix the Cleves marriage in 1539. To assist him in these tasks he had a council of officials and a retinue, whose officers were known as 'Spears'. Commissions as Spears were highly valued – they provided the basis for profitable sidelines – and local officials coveted them for their sons. So did courtiers in England. This competition was not the least of Lisle's worries.

Theoretically such commissions were in the gift of the Lord Deputy, but in fact well-placed young men, with powerful backing, were always seeking to jump the queue. Lisle's greatest trouble came from Sir Richard Whethill, mayor of Calais. He came from an old Calais family and claimed priority for his son, Robert. When Lisle resisted, there was a long quarrel in which all Calais took sides. Sir Richard abused Lisle in the Deputy's own garden, and Lady Whethill made a disgraceful public attack on Lady Lisle in church, screaming insults at her 'in Pilate's voice' (Pilate and Herod, Miss Byrne explains, were the two shouting partners in mystery plays). The dispute was carried to London where the Whethills boasted of their influence, and young Robert exhibited himself at court 'in a coat of crimson taffeta, cut and lined with yellow sarcenet', velvet breeches and shoes to match, and a scarlet cap with red and yellow feathers. The king was thoroughly bored with the whole affair, but the two ladies kept it going, at the highest level, for years.

Another great Calais battle involved Sir Robert Wingfield. He, too, came from an entrenched official family and was on Lisle's council. He had used his position to invest in a marsh, which he had 'improved', but which the king now insisted should be reflooded in the interest of defense. This battle, too, was carried to London and went on for a long time. In the end Lisle prevailed; 'Wingfield's Marsh' was successfully 'drowned' and, although Wingfield vowed revenge on Lisle, it remained drowned.

To drown Wingfield's marsh in Calais in the interest of defense was one thing. To pull down Lady Lisle's weir on the river Tawe at Umberleigh in Devon in the interest of navigation was, of course, quite different. In 1535 the Crown ordered a general destruction of weirs on navigable rivers. Landlords, whose weirs enabled them to corner the fish, were indignant, and none so indignant as Lady Lisle. She demanded, first, that the weir be spared, then, when it was down, that it be rebuilt. Like Lady Whethill, she became a great bore on the subject, but the weir, like the marsh, was not restored.

Although a royal commission in 1535 vindicated Lisle's government, he soon realized that he had made a mistake in accepting it. The local troubles were endless and were being inflamed by religion. At home, his interests and his wife's estates were being threatened, and he was not allowed to leave Calais except by royal license. He was also missing great opportunities at home – opportunities in which his rivals were investing. It was all very depressing, especially when Cromwell, who was now clearly in command of everything (he was Mr. Secretary, Master of the Rolls, and Lord Privy Seal), reproved him for troubling him with trifles. The man who was changing the structure of England did not wish to be bothered by the internal squabbles of a garrison town.

Fortunately for Lisle – and for us – there was John Husee. Husee is Miss Byrne's hero, and rightly so. But for him, the correspondence would be an amorphous mass. He is 'the unifying, energising agent who is ultimately to weld the material into a whole, and to give it momentum and direction.' For Husee was Lisle's agent, his secretary, his universal factotum, the man who watched his interests, served him at every turn, knew everybody, had the entrée everywhere, was prepared to do anything: to buy supplies, order clothes, argue with lawyers, transport children, arrange travel, deliver presents, handle creditors, and, above all, to report regularly in writing.

Husee was a young man of thirty at the time. He had begun as a London merchant – 'citizen and vintner' – and Lisle evidently found him in Calais where he was already a member of the retinue although clearly he was not tied to his post. He reveals himself as a man of great energy and charm, and infinite resourcefulness. He is the sharpest of observers, quick to note who is moving up or down at court, and generally the first to report it. Everyone knows him, welcomes him, speaks freely to him. 'Here cometh my Lord Lisle's man', says Cromwell to the king, smiling benevolently as Husee en-

ters the presence chamber with his master's New Year's gifts in 1533. He
has no enemies – except perhaps the abbot of Westminster, a lordly and
exacting creditor, and Sir Richard Rich, of whom no one has ever said a good
word. He is a natural diplomat, and warm and sympathetic too. How dis-
armingly he protests when his employers (for Lady Lisle, of course, treats
him as her servant: she is the real boss), in their anxiety, rebuke him for
unavoidable delays! How sympathetically he consoles Lady Lisle when the
expected Plantagenet heir, for whom he has obtained everything – a cradle, a
display bed, 'a holy-water stock with sprinkler and casting bottle' – turns out
to be a 'phantom pregnancy', or rallies Lord Lisle when the frustrations of
Calais politics drive him into melancholy or despair! And then, to crown all,
he is a marvelous letter writer, with a sharp eye for detail, a nice sense of
humor, a pretty turn of phrase, a delightful irony. He is the most memorable
character in the whole story, for it is he, above all, who brings all the rest to
life.

As we read these letters, we are staggered by Husee's ubiquity and resourcefulness. But Husee, we soon find, is not alone. He is the organizer of
intelligence, but there are other agents too: 'fee'd men', or 'privy friends', as
they are called, men who are formally and officially employed by other great
men at court or in the country, but to whom Lisle pays regular secret
'fees' – generally £10 a year – to keep him informed whenever his interest is,
or might be, involved. Lisle had at least two fee'd men in Cromwell's
service – William Popley, Cromwell's man of business, and Ralph Sadler,
one of the ablest of Cromwell's young protégés – and several in the country.
In Devonshire, he had Sir Richard Pollard, the surveyor general and sheriff.
But the most dramatic coup was achieved by Hugh Yeo, the agent for the
Basset lands in the west. Through two privy friends in the employment of
Lord Daubeney and one in that of the earl of Hertford (afterward the Protector Somerset), he discovered the secret plot that these two were hatching,
whereby the Basset heir would lose a substantial estate for their benefit:
Hertford to have the property and Daubeney to pay for an earldom with the
proceeds. This plot nearly succeeded, and Daubeney, in expectation of
triumph, came up to London accompanied by eighty horsemen all dressed in
'new liveries of my Lord Privy Seal's colour'; but Husee, thus warned, was
able to get to Cromwell in time, and Cromwell (at a price) got the king to
intervene and save the property. All great men, it seems, kept these privy
friends in other great men's service: that, after all, was how Cromwell built
up his marvelous intelligence service, so envied by the French ambassador,
and how Shakespeare's Macbeth secured his own interests:

> There's not a one of them but in his house
> I keep a servant fee'd.

Apart from such outright espionage, there was another no less necessary method of self-protection which is vividly illustrated by these letters. This is the regular, almost ritual, distribution of gifts in kind. Here again Husee is the central figure. It is he who advises who should receive gifts, and what they should receive – how large a gift will suffice, what would be most acceptable, or perhaps has already been hinted; he who collects and delivers. The most frequent gifts are of game or wine, hawks or hunting dogs. The best wine is claret from Gascony, but tastes differed. Whereas the earl of Suffolk would only look at 'mighty great wines', Henry VIII, who had simple tastes (he was 'wondrous pleased' with Lady Lisle's homemade marmalade), was content, like Lisle himself, with 'hedge wine', which was apparently 'a good *vin ordinaire*'. Among the items of game are boars' heads and wild swine, baked cranes and sturgeon, venison of red and fallow deer, storks, egrets, guinea-fowl, herons and snipe, herrings, salmon, sprats, partridges, dotterels, peewits, quails and puffins. Sometimes they are distributed alive, like the quails, which were bought wholesale in Calais or Flanders and killed on arrival at Dover, or the dotterels, of which Anne Boleyn was very fond, and which were put in her garden in Greenwich until it was time to eat them. The fish came in barrels, as did the congers supplied by a Cornish parson and the puffins (which were regarded as fish, owing to their taste) sent regularly from the Basset estates in the west. Sometimes the game was made up into pasties or pies, like the lamprey pies, 'baken after our Cotswold fashion', sent by a Gloucestershire gentleman, or a partridge pie which was unfortunately misshapen by immersion in the Channel, 'but they found good meat in it'. Once Lisle sent a porpoise, of which a section was gratefully acknowledged by Cromwell; but the more prestigious gift of a seal proved less successful. It was destined for the Lord Admiral, perhaps as an aquatic symbol, but Husee had great difficulty in delivering it. He had to keep it alive for five weeks at Wapping, where it cost him sixpence a day in fish 'and yet she had not dined'. When he finally presented it, the Admiral said that he had nowhere to keep it, and told him to kill it and have it baked and sent to his wife, 'and so it is done'.

Traffic in game entailed traffic in the means of catching it; so the gifts include every kind of hawk and dog: goshawks, gyrfalcons, merlins, greyhounds, lanyers, water spaniels. Red-and-white spaniels passed from France to England; English greyhounds and mastiffs were in great demand in France. The birds were liable to all kinds of accident en route: Hawks escaped, or were stolen; an unspecified bird sent to Lord Hertford survived shipwreck only to be eaten by a cat at Billingsgate, 'which my Lord of Hertford took right grievously'. Sometimes we find more recondite gifts. The Lord Admiral of France sent Lisle two miniscule marmosets from Brazil and 'a long-tailed monkey, which is a pretty beast and gentle', with instructions for care and feeding. Lady Lisle thought to gain favor by sending one of them on to Queen Anne Boleyn, but this proved a gaffe: 'the Queen loveth no such beasts', Husee reported, 'nor can scant abide the sight of them'; on the other hand she appreciated a linnet, which delighted her with its incessant song. Lisle loved birds, and he and his wife seem to have kept a small menagerie: a monk of Canterbury sent Lady Lisle, by the hand of 'a singing child' for whom he sought patronage, an unspecified 'beast, the creature of God, once wild but now tame, to comfort your heart at such time as you be weary of prayer'. One does not get the impression that Lady Lisle wearied herself much with prayer.

This constant flow of gifts is the most striking feature of the correspondence. Some of them, of course, were real gifts, in our sense of the word. Such, no doubt, was the touching present which Lady Lisle sent to the Elector Palatine after he had been her guest at Calais. She had noticed that he had picked his teeth with a pin, so she sent him her own toothpick, which she had used for seven years. Some were commissioned purchases. But most of them were an essential part of the system of patronage. Gentlemen did not give bribes. Of all the officials whom we meet, only one – Sir Thomas Pope, treasurer of the Court of Augmentations, which handled the sale of monastic lands (and afterwards founder of Trinity College, Oxford) – declined 'wine or other pleasure', saying bluntly that he wanted 'ready money . . . yea, and doth look for the same'. But there was no undue delicacy in defining what would be acceptable, and whether it gave satisfaction when it came. Cromwell let it be known that 'a pretty dog' would not come amiss. Others specified particular kinds of hawk. The king complained that Lisle's quails were not fat enough. Husee insisted on this again and again: 'Let them be very fat', he wrote, 'or else they are not worth thanks.'

Lisle specialized in quails, buying them up in vast quantities. They were 'a prime delicacy' and could be used to sweeten requests, to attract attention, to turn away wrath. Husee was continually advising that such and such a person be remembered with wine and quails. Mr. Skut, for instance, the king's tailor, with whom Lady Lisle ran up huge bills, and who sometimes became impatient for payment, received a regular tribute of quails. On one occasion Husee did not dare call on him with twelve yards of satin to make up for Lady Lisle 'because the quails be not yet come'. This of course merely shifted the debt: there is a plaintive letter from the Calais poulterer begging payment long overdue, for forty-three dozen quails. But the operation was worthwhile, as one episode emphatically proved.

Lady Lisle, naturally, wished to do the best for her daughters, Katherine and Anne Basset. After the usual beginner's course under the eye of a local abbess, they were sent to live with a grand French family near Calais. This entailed some agreeable correspondence and a constant commerce of hawks, dogs, salmon, marmalade, etc. It also introduced a French cousin, an aristocratic abbess whose disciplined army of nuns knitted vast quantities of

nightcaps, male and female, in elegant lozenge patterns. She supplied Lady
Lisle with a steady and copious flow of nightcaps and family gossip. After
that, the girls were on the market. Then Lady Lisle's competitive instincts
were aroused. On hearing that two of her Arundell nieces had been accepted
as maids of honor at court, she decided to launch Katherine and Anne in the
same warm water. So she mobilized two dexterous dowagers, the countesses
of Sussex and Rutland (the latter a great oracle on court and society) and set
the quails in motion. The moment to strike came when the two countesses
were in waiting and the queen was actually dining off Lord Lisle's quails. The
concurrent pressure of the ladies and the birds was irresistible, and the
queen agreed to see both girls and choose one of them. She chose Anne,
whom the king so fancied that at one time she was tipped for the dangerous
honor of being the fifth queen of Henry VIII. Katherine stayed on with Lady
Rutland.

Lady Lisle also had Basset stepdaughters. They, of course, were older. The
most enjoyable is Jane, a spinster in her forties. She had no great love for her
stepmother's family, but she loved her old home at Umberleigh and begged
for two rooms in it, and pasture for one cow, in order to live there with her
unmarried younger sister, Thomasine. Once established there, she found
herself at loggerheads with the vicar, an elderly man who acted as Lady
Lisle's agent. Each wrote to Lady Lisle denouncing the other. Jane accused
the vicar of embezzling the fish; the vicar retaliated by intercepting and
suppressing her letters. Finally, sister Thomasine decided that she had had
enough and bolted. Rescued before dawn by a raiding party led by the vicar,
she fled to Cornwall leaving her clothes behind. When we last see Jane, she is
still at Umberleigh with one maid, two cows, and a horse. 'Also she hath a
greyhound lieth upon one of the beds day and night, but it be when she
holdeth him in her hands and that every time when she goeth to the door.'

Most important, of course, were the three Basset sons. The eldest, John,
was sent to Lincoln's Inn, and then, being married to the eldest Plantagenet
daughter in order to secure the lands, was on the way to being 'the diamant
of Devonshire'. Miss Byrne describes him as 'a dull dog'. The second,
George, was first placed in an abbey, then briefly crammed, with his younger
brother, at Saint-Omer, and sent, in the usual English fashion, to 'wait' in the
house of Lisle's intimate friend and ally, Sir Francis Bryan, before dis-
appearing into Cornwall, where he founded a long-lasting branch of the
family. He is described as 'self-effacing'.

So we come to the youngest son, James. He was not self-effacing. On the
contrary, he was 'a precocious little horror', spoiled, charming, sophisticated,
and, like his mother, determined to get his way – as he generally did. After
Reading Abbey, he was sent to Paris, to the Collège de Calvi. The president
of the Parlement of Paris, who had met Lisle in Calais (he had come in the
train of the ambassador-admiral), had promised to look after him in Paris,

but once there, he soon forgot his promise and James was taken over by a group of English scholars at the university, of whom the principal was John Bekynsaw. They took care of him and later, when he returned to Paris from the crammer in Saint-Omer, placed him, with a tutor, in the house of a kindly French merchant, Guillaume le Gras. But James had no taste for private tuition: he was determined to go to the university, to the fashionable Collège de Navarre. There, he explained, he would get to know the sons of the duc de Vendôme and the duc de Guise and such persons; and of course he went. Once there, he got what he wanted in other ways too. Lady Lisle in Calais, Le Gras and Bekynsaw in Paris, were all manipulated by a determined boy of ten.

Since he was the youngest son, his parents had destined James for the Church, and the Lisles, with their old-fashioned notions, naturally assumed that a fat benefice would be found for him, with all necessary dispensations for tender age, nonresidence, etc. He was to end, no doubt, as a grand worldly bishop, like Lisle's friend (and creditor) Bishop Sherburn of Chichester who, at the age of ninety-five, astonished his fellow commissioners for the valuation of church lands by giving them a Good Friday fish dinner for seven hundred persons – 'such a dinner of fish', said one of them, as none present had ever seen 'for the quantity and goodness of them'; or like Bishop Veysey of Exeter whom we see arriving in London to call on Cromwell accompanied by eighty horsemen in livery, and scattering twenty nobles in tips. They reckoned without Archbishop Cranmer, who absolutely forbade any cure of souls for a child, however well connected. So James had to be content with minor orders and the income from a prebend in Cornwall. He never went further in the Church. He was, as Husee noted, 'meeter to serve the temporal powers than the spiritual dignities' – as indeed, in the end, he did, passing from the household of Bishop Gardiner to that of Queen Mary. But he was not entirely worldly. Marrying Mary Roper, the granddaughter of Sir Thomas More, he was absorbed into that devoted Catholic circle; and perhaps it was for his sake that his father-in-law, William Roper, afterwards relieved the wants of his old protector John Bekynsaw, and through his influence that his great-nephew Sir Robert Basset (if he is correctly identified) wrote one of the many family biographies of Sir Thomas More.

Such were the main interests of the Lisles in Calais. But what, we naturally ask, about the revolution going on in England? Did they not notice it? Yes, when they had to. They could hardly fail to notice the execution of Anne Boleyn, for Lisle, in effect, provided the executioner. She was to be beheaded by the sword, not the ax – a skill that was practiced only by the French – so an expert was sent from Calais. Also, the affair had, for the Lisles, an unfortunate consequence. One of those who was framed and executed with the queen, as her supposed lover, was Sir Henry Norris, Keeper of the Privy Purse, who had been Lisle's chief informant and 'faithful assured friend'. All Lisle's interests at court had been managed for him by Norris, whose services, constantly extolled by Husee, had been recognized by valuable gifts – a superlative falcon, the best horse that ever came out of Flanders, etc. When he was charged, the Lisles were dismayed. Putting first things first, they tried – without waiting for their 'very friend' to be hanged, drawn and quartered – to get a grant of his confiscated lands. But how could one put in a bid without an immediate successor to Norris himself as friend at court? Husee at first suggested Sir John Russell for this office, but then, finding Russell in earnest colloquy with Lisle's enemy Whethill, feared that he 'had taken the wrong pig by the ear' and recommended Sir Thomas Heneage. Eleven dozen quails and a hogshead of Gascon wine were quickly delivered to Heneage, and snipe and wine were sent off to Cromwell. All was of no avail. Lisle was told that he had applied too late. Russell smugly said that he could have secured something if only he had been asked in time, and it was thought prudent to recognize his retrospective goodwill with wine and quails.

Norris's execution was doubly unfortunate for Lisle, because he was at that moment seeking to pick up another windfall. His spies had given him early notice of the impending dissolution of the monasteries, and he had naturally mobilized Norris. He also wrote direct to Cromwell. The abbey of Beaulieu was his first choice, being conveniently close to the Lisle lands in Hampshire; but that was asking too much – the greater abbeys were not yet to be dissolved, and anyway one of Cromwell's young men had his eye on it. So Lisle's fee'd man in Cromwell's service discreetly suppressed the letter. But Lisle was not to be restrained. He wrote direct to the king, begging him 'to help me to some old abbey in mine old days'. If not Beaulieu, there was Southwick. Waverley, too, he was told, was 'a pretty thing'. Finally, he decided that it was necessary to accept the advice given to Lady Lisle: that she should come over in person, bringing her husband in tow, in order to sue for 'one of the abbeys, towards the maintenance of my Lord's and your good Ladyship's charges'.

In the end, thanks to this visit, and a new and closer relationship with Cromwell, who was determined to cut out intermediaries, Lisle did get an abbey: the priory of Frithelstock in Devonshire, conveniently close to the Basset home at Umberleigh; but the officials of the Court of Augmentations saw to it that there were many obstructions before he could call it his own. The chancellor of the court was the dreadful Rich, immortalized by his perjury at the trial of Sir Thomas More. 'He is full of dissimulation', Husee reported: 'I fear that he will so handle himself that he will deserve neither thanks nor reward. He passeth all that I ever sued to.' However, in the end (Rich having received a velvet gown) all was well, and in August 1537 Husee could tell Lisle that his 'long tracted suit is finished' and 'your Lordship is now prior and Lord of Fristock'.

So far so good. In 1537 the Lisles were still living splendidly in Calais, entertaining as lavishly as 'the best duke in England'. There are indeed some difficulties. The unpaid grocer is getting impatient and threatening to cut off credit; the bishop of Chichester is discreetly, the abbot of Westminster stiffly, demanding repayment of their debts; the weir at Umberleigh is down and all Lady Lisle's efforts cannot rebuild it. But the property is still basically intact, its future assured by marriage; the children are placed; and although Thomas Cromwell has now apparently established a complete monopoly of power, relations with him – perpetually sweetened with quails and wine, hawks, dogs, hunks of porpoise, etc. – seem particularly close. Thanks to that special relationship, Lisle's 'back friends' in Calais – false friends who go sneaking up to London – are frustrated. Husee is constantly alert, always ready to wait on the Lord Privy Seal when he is not too busy with 'the Carthusians' or 'these matters' (that is, state trials and executions), and the Lord Privy Seal is invariably solicitous, invariably reassuring: he is 'your Lordship's unfeigned friend'. 'As long as the King's Grace doth live, and he together', he assures Lisle, 'you shall remain the King's Deputy at Calais . . . you shall die Deputy of Calais.' And Lisle believed it. Cromwell, he wrote, was his 'special good Lord', 'my only and most assured friend and last refuge in all my suits'.

Alas for all these promises. Politics never stand still, and in revolutions the changes can be very fast. From 1537 the terms of life shift, and a course of events begins, which turns these hitherto purposeless annals into a fast-moving drama – and which, incidentally, has preserved these records for us. For without it they would have been dissipated long ago; our knowledge of the public events of the reign of Henry VIII would then have been diminished; and the Lisles, the Bassets, and all their family circle would have been – as they are after 1540 – mere names in genealogical records, without human identity or voice or the breath of life.

How did things go wrong? Why did Cromwell, in the last weeks of his power, call Lisle back to London, confiscate his papers, and have him thrown into the Tower, from which he would never emerge, and from which he was expected to emerge, like so many others, only to grace the scaffold? Why indeed did Cromwell himself fall, moving, with such shocking suddenness, from apparently unchallenged authority to a traitor's death? The answer, as Miss Byrne shows, with meticulous scholarship, is to be found in three converging courses of events: the treason of Cardinal Pole; the struggle for power between Cromwell and his conservative rivals; and the religious developments in Calais.

Reginald Pole was the king's cousin on the Yorkist – that is on Lisle's –

side. He had been expensively educated and amply beneficed by the king
and had lived in Venice on his bounty, the center of a Platonic circle, in
contact with Thomas More and other humanists at home. Henry had hoped
to have him as his archbishop of York, after Wolsey; but the king's divorce,
his marriage with Anne Boleyn, and the breach with Rome put an end to all
that, and in 1536, after the execution of More and Fisher, Pole did the
unforgivable thing: he recited to the king, in writing, the full catalogue of his
crimes. From that moment Henry would pursue Pole with all the hatred
which he felt toward those – like More and Anne Boleyn – whom he had
once loved and who, in his view, had betrayed him; and Pole, on his side,
became a bitter enemy in deeds as well as in words: as cardinal and papal
legate, he appealed to foreign powers to unite and dethrone the heretic king.
Henry sought to have Pole kidnapped in Liège, 'trussed up and conveyed to
Calais'. He was resolved to lay hands on him and destroy him. Nor was that
all: with his hatred of Pole was joined fear for the succession, still hanging by
a slender thread, and hatred of all the remaining members of the rival house,
the White Rose. That meant the Poles and the Courtenays: the cardinal's
mother, the aged countess of Salisbury, his elder brother Lord Montague,
and his cousin, the marquis of Exeter. As Henry told the French ambassador,
he was 'resolved to exterminate this house of Montague, which is still of the
White Rose faction, and also the family of Pole, to which the Cardinal
belongs'.

At that cannibal court, where, as Husee said, every man was for himself,
two great men at least believed sincerely in what they were doing: Thomas
Cromwell and Archbishop Cranmer. Cromwell might be helping the king to
build up the machinery of tyranny, but it was a tyranny that was to be used
for a specific policy: the reform of the Church. In 1539 that tyranny, and that
policy, had isolated Henry in Europe and had almost isolated Cromwell and
Cranmer in England. With the rulers of Europe combining from without,
and Pole calling for revolt from within, the politics of the English court were
polarized. On one side, Cromwell urged Henry further on the path of defiance and reform, proposing an alliance with German Protestantism and
marriage with a German princess, Anne of Cleves. On the other side, more
conservative men – men who were happy to see monasteries dissolved and
papal authority rejected but had no love of religious or social change –
declared that reform had gone far enough: that it must now be stabilized on
a Catholic base, and defended externally, not by confronting, but by splitting
the Catholic powers. The leaders of this party were Thomas, duke of Norfolk,
now back from suppressing revolt in the north, and Stephen Gardiner, bishop
of Winchester, now back from his embassy abroad.

Between these two parties the king occupied a middle position. On one
hand, he was conservative, opposed to 'Lutheran' heresy. On the other hand,
he appreciated Cromwell, the architect of his new power, the best servant (as

he would afterward admit) that he had ever had. The conservatives therefore did not openly attack Cromwell: they attacked heresy, which the king, too, hated; and Cromwell did not openly attack religious conservatism: he concentrated his fire against the king's enemies, the Papacy and the traitor Pole. The king preserved a judicious balance, and emphasized it by sending, in almost equal numbers, Catholics as 'traitors' to the scaffold and Protestants as 'heretics' to the stake.

How could Lisle avoid being drawn into this battle? Calais was itself in the center of it. Internally divided, geographically 'exposed to all the winds of doctrine that blew', it was a refuge for heretics from France, Flanders, and Germany, and religious differences inflamed all the existing discontents. The established families who dominated the council were orthodox, but Cranmer's 'commissary', who controlled the clergy, supported heresy. As a secular-minded official, untouched by new ideas, or indeed by any kind of ideas, Lisle followed the royal line. So long as Cromwell was going slowly, destroying only monasteries, and the authority of Rome, there was no difficulty. The dissolution of monasteries, after all, could be useful. So could the condemnation of Pole: Lisle tried hard to get one of his rich livings for young Master James. But by 1537 the Protestants were in trouble with the council, and the archbishop's vigorous new commissary, their supporter, was complaining that 'much papistry doth reign still, and chiefly among them that be rulers'. Cromwell and Cranmer took up the cause of the heretics. At one time, a colleague reported to Lisle, Cromwell 'swore by God's Blood we were all papists . . . and I swore by God's heart it was not so'. When Lady Lisle interceded for a priest whom the commissary had denounced for popish observances, Cromwell let fly. If the councillors winked any longer at such abuses, he wrote, the king would dismiss them all, for it was against all reason that they should heed 'the prayers of women and their fond flickerings' rather than 'his just laws'. No wonder Husee was alarmed and begged Lisle to walk warily. As Lisle had hopes of benefits still to come – the dissolved friary at Calais and a pension of £400 – he did.

Next year there was a crisis provoked by the arrival from Germany of a young English priest called Adam Damplip. He was a 'Sacramentary', that is, a Zwinglian, who denied the Real Presence in no uncertain manner: a mouse, he said, 'would as soon eat the Body of God as any other cake'; and other such heresies. These doctrines split the council, and both parties appealed to London. When Damplip himself fled to London, Lisle thought it time to act. He hurriedly sent a water spaniel to Cromwell, and in response to a hint, poor Master Basset had to surrender his favorite hawk – 'a merlin for patridges as good as flies'. Unfortunately the hawk, on its first flight under its new owner, was pricked by a thorn and died. After that an uneasy calm returned to Calais.

It did not last long. Next year the Sacramentaries returned to the charge, more insolent than ever, and Lisle, realizing that they were being secretly supported by Cromwell and Cranmer, began cautiously to change sides. One man to whom he appealed was Sir Anthony Browne, the Master of the Horse. Having secured Battle Abbey for themselves, the Brownes would become one of the mainstays of English Catholicism. 'I beseech you,' Lisle ended his letter, 'keep this my letter close, for if it should come to my Lord Privy Seal's knowledge or ear, I were half undone'. Perhaps it did come to the Lord Privy Seal's ear: who knows whether he had not a fee'd man with the Master of the Horse? In any case, Cromwell must, by now, have suspected. Meanwhile, in London, the struggle had become even more intense. The conservatives secured the passage of the Act of Six Articles declaring Catholic doctrine, while Cromwell was staking all on the German marriage. At the end of 1539 the German bride, Anne of Cleves, stopped at Calais on her way to London and was stuck there by bad weather. Fortunately – since she stayed for fifteen days, with a train of 263 attendants and 238 horses – the cost of her entertainment did not fall on Lisle. When she arrived in London and the king met her, his heart sank. He went through with the marriage, but with inward reluctance, and almost immediately began to seek a means of release by annulment.

The first task was to break up the foreign coalition that had necessitated the marriage. For this purpose the duke of Norfolk was sent on a secret mission to France. He performed his task well. The king of France was perfectly willing to agree with his brother of England – if only his brother of England would get rid of that dreadful heretic, the cause of all the trouble, Thomas Cromwell. This of course was just what the duke wanted too. Nor was this all. Both coming and going, the duke, as Miss Byrne has shown, stopped in Calais and evidently concerted action with Lisle. On his return, a commission was set up to investigate the religious troubles in Calais. Rather surprisingly (since he was a party to the dispute), Lisle himself was on it. Less surprisingly, its report was a condemnation of the Sacramentaries. Thus on all sides, it seemed, the enemy was closing in on Cromwell; and Lisle was with the enemy.

Even so, Cromwell did not see himself as defeated. Admittedly, the Cleves marriage had been a mistake, but it was a mistake that could be rectified; and although he was hated in the country, no doubt he thought himself indispensable to the king. His confidence, in this dark hour, is extraordinary: we find him reassuring the Sacramentaries who had been sent in chains from Calais, promising them that they would go free (in fact they would be burnt). But then he had managed it before. Religious radicalism and royal divorce had brought him to power; why should not the same means keep him in it? What was needed, while he arranged the divorce, was an external enemy. A new conspiracy must be discovered, originating, if possible, with 'the traitor Pole'.

Luckily, just at this time, such a conspiracy presented itself. A priest, one Botolf, known as Sir Gregory Sweetlips, had bolted from Calais to France, and had afterward told his associates that he had been to Rome, had seen the Pope and Pole and had conspired with them to surrender Calais to the French. His story was suspect, but it served its purpose. Also, Botolf had once been Lisle's chaplain. How convenient! Of all the conservative enemies of Cromwell, Lisle was the most exposed. He was the enemy of reform in Calais, which was now revealed as 'a nest of papists'. He was a member of the White Rose faction and the family of Pole which Henry was resolved to destroy. Now he could be directly implicated with Pole himself. His destruction would be a warning to the conservatives not to join the party of Norfolk and Gardiner; it would show who was master of the king's government; and it would be a blow struck for religious reform.

Such, it seems, was Cromwell's plan. It nearly succeeded. In the spring of 1540 Lisle was summoned back to London. He set out confidently. In Calais it was thought that he was going to be made an earl. In London, he attended the House of Lords. He was present at a chapter meeting and feast of the Knights of the Garter. Then the blow fell. He was arrested and disappeared into the Tower. His documents, his goods and plate were seized. Cromwell it was who was made an earl.

Meanwhile, what about the royal divorce? Alas, it was here that the master plan came to grief. The duke of Norfolk had a young niece, Katherine, daughter of his brother Lord Edmund Howard, comptroller of Calais, recently deceased. At the house of his ally, the bishop of Winchester, this seductive girl was placed before the royal eye. The operation was successful. From that moment, Cromwell was doomed; for he was faced with an insoluble dilemma. If he did not achieve an annulment of Henry's marriage, he would have failed, as his master Cardinal Wolsey had failed, and, like him, would be cast aside. But now, even if he secured an annulment, he would have failed no less: for as the husband of Katherine Howard, the king would be in the camp of an enemy from whom Cromwell could expect no mercy. So, at the last moment, the tables were turned. It was game, set, and match to the duke and the bishop.

If Cromwell had won that last desperate round in the struggle for power, Lisle would no doubt have gone to the block along with his equally innocent kinsmen, the Courtenays and the Poles. In the Tower, he must have expected no less. That he did not suggests that Henry himself thought him innocent. Perhaps the execution of the last of the Pole family, the octogenarian countess of Salisbury in 1541, slaked the king's thirst for blood. The faction of the White Rose was now dead, and although the Tudor succession was not yet firm, the Tudor despotism had little fear from the last of the Plantagenets. Even so, Lisle remained in prison for eighteen months. It was only after the execution of Katherine Howard that the king, being now at leisure, issued his pardon. Lisle was so delighted by the news that he died next day, still in the Tower, 'through too much rejoicing'.

Such is the story told by the Lisle Letters – a story which was quite unappreciated until Miss Byrne, by some intuitive flair, recognized the unity and vitality which animated that mass of confiscated paper, and set out to restore it. It was an act of faith, and of courage, which in the end has been rewarded. The six large volumes in which her edition first appeared have been greeted with enthusiasm by historians and laymen alike. This is largely because the editor has known how to combine great scholarship with great art, and indeed tact. That is, she allows the letters themselves to tell the story, with as much explanation and commentary as she thinks necessary for that purpose. The commentary is copious, but it is sustained by an infectious enthusiasm which carries even the most recondite explanation. The scholarship, gathered in a lifetime, extends to every subject: it neither holds up the story nor weighs it down, and the reader hardly notices the range of editorial skill which has been necessary to overcome recalcitrant problems of orthography, palaeography, dating, interpretation. Above all, I am impressed by the editor's invariable freshness and enthusiasm, which permeates the whole work. At first the pace is slow, for we must get to know the scenario and the persons; but soon it quickens: we come to know the characters and find ourselves in the middle of a fascinating family saga, a sixteenth-century *War and Peace* or *A la Recherche du Temps Perdu*.

However, even Tolstoy, even Proust can be abridged. The original edition of *The Lisle Letters* requires and rewards an ample leisure. It was my companion for many enjoyable weeks. But no one should be ruled merely by authority or example and I hesitate to command a costly assent. Not everyone has all those weeks at his disposal; nor can everyone afford the necessarily high price of those splendid volumes. Therefore I prefer to recommend, at least as a beginning, this abridged version which, while quickening the movement, preserves the admirable balance of the whole work. Here, at a more modest price, and in a briefer space of time, the reader can enter into the charmed, or rather bewitched, circle of Lord and Lady Lisle and their friends; having become intimate with them, he will suddenly find himself swept up into the most revolutionary years of Tudor England; he will see how, even in the midst of revolution, conservative social habits and family interests prevailed; and insensibly he will find himself becoming personally involved in a drama which is no less vivid and exciting for having been enacted over four centuries ago.

Preface to the Selection

This selection from *The Lisle Letters* (6 vols., University of Chicago Press, 1981) is designed for the pleasure of the general reader, rather than as a handy textbook for the student. There are three things the letters have to offer such a reader: to me the most important is a superb, slow-building human drama, culminating in the sending to the Tower of Arthur Plantagenet, Viscount Lisle. If we remember that all these letters, covering seven years, were originally collected together in search of evidence to be used in a trial for treason, we can watch for the makings of that situation in each new character who is introduced and in each development of the story. The second great contribution of the letters is to give a unique picture of life in a family of the early Tudor period so that we can live it with them, from the education of their children and the management of their estates and the legal battles that dogged them, down to the sports they indulged in and even the pets they kept. Thirdly, they provide a picture, again unique, of Calais when it was an outpost vital to England; and there, as on a slide under a microscope, we can watch the growth of the religio-political virus that infected human lives. The letters also contain gems in the form of style and of characters whom the reader must meet at all costs. All these elements have to be included to give a fair sampling of the treasures that Miss Byrne's collection of over 1,900 letters contains, while keeping the continued delight of the reader always essentially in mind.

I must defend my decision to arrange the letters I have chosen in groups according to their subjects rather than in chronological order (though I have retained that order within the groups). When so much of both letters and commentary had to be cut out, it became impossible to follow the threads in the different elements unless they could be isolated, with any necessary explanations, and presented in separate chapters. Thus the material concerning Calais will be found in one chapter for a given period, with political and religious developments in England during that period in another, until politics and religion take over Calais and Calais moves, from an isolated outpost, into the centre of the English political scene. In the same way, the complexities of the Lisles' business affairs can only, in their truncated form, be followed if they are concentrated upon in isolation. But because the whole story is a consecutive one, I have arranged the subjects in relation to each other in blocks of two or three years at a time, so that developments in one may not too far outstrip events in another. The reader is to imagine having access to a filing system into which the Lisles might have dropped the letters they received, and the copies or drafts of those they sent.

Though I have had to compress hundreds of pages of commentary, I have quoted from it where I can, and the 'I' who appears in it is Muriel St. Clare Byrne and not Bridget Boland. My hope is that this edition will serve as a taster for the real thing.

B.B.

The letters which concern the business of the Crown are Crown copyright and are reproduced with the permission of the Controller of Her Majesty's Stationery Office, London.

Permission to reproduce illustrations has been granted by the Archbishop of Canterbury, British Museum, Camden Society, Church Commissioners for England, Courtauld Institute of Art, National Portrait Gallery (London), Newberry Library (Chicago), Public Record Office (London), Royal College of Surgeons, Society of Antiquaries (London).

Genealogy charts were prepared by Bridget Boland and the University of Chicago Press staff.

Publication of the original six-volume work, *The Lisle Letters,* upon which this abridgement is based, was made possible in part through grants from the Joseph and Helen Regenstein Foundation, Her Majesty Queen Elizabeth II, the family of Robert Metzenberg, and others.

1

Introduction

The Letters and Their World

Those who delight in being lured backwards through time by their sense of the past very quickly become aware of two dominant themes – the way things change, the way things do not change. So much detail remains, so many documents, so much information about meals and manners, customs and costumes, that it is comparatively easy to grope one's way back, holding on to the chairs and tables, while the intelligence pieces it all together.

Rebuild their houses, furnish their rooms, store their larders, lay out their very garments for them; but not so will you persuade the past to send back one individual ghost. You must seize upon the speech, the character, the way of life, the experience of whatever century is your personal starting-point, catch the quality, temper, and colour of its modes of thought and feeling. My starting-point was the Tudor century, so that it was only a matter of time before I encountered the Lisle Letters. Here is the very earth – not the background, but the soil itself. In this great national collection I had found what I wanted – the lost moment that was Tudor England.

I say 'moment' advisedly, for it is by virtue of their intensity that the Lisle Letters are unique. There are some three thousand of them, but they cover a period of only seven years. It is moment-to-moment life, sensation, and thought, that is recorded in them – the almost unbelievable dailyness of life. For the amount of varied character interest that is to be found in them they are unrivalled; and besides this they have what one has no logical right to expect of letters – namely, a concentrated and sustained narrative interest, with a tragic and dramatic climax.

The story told by the Letters is centred in three people – Arthur Plantagenet, Viscount Lisle; his second wife, Honor, a daughter of the Cornish Grenvilles; and their man of business, John Husee, gentleman, of London. Arthur Lisle was the illegitimate son of Edward IV, the last Plantagenet king. On the mother's side he came of respectable Hampshire gentlefolk,

I

established as considerable landowners since the fourteenth century. Anstis in his *Register of the Garter* describes him as the son of Elizabeth Lucy, daughter of Thomas Wayte. But for his illegitimacy he was, in fact, the last of the Plantagenets in the direct male descent.

His royal blood was as openly acknowledged as the fact of his illegitimacy. By blood he was half-brother to Edward V and Elizabeth of York; he was uncle to a king and two queens, Henry VIII, Margaret Tudor, wife of James IV of Scotland, and Mary Tudor, once Queen of France; the great-uncle, consequently, of two queens and two kings, Mary and Elizabeth, Edward VI, and James V of Scotland, and of Margaret Douglas, the mother of Darnley, and Frances Brandon, Duchess of Suffolk, mother of Lady Jane Grey. Outside the royal family his nearest blood relations were the Poles and the Courtenays. Margaret Pole, Countess of Salisbury, the daughter of Edward IV's murdered brother, 'false, fleeting, perjur'd Clarence', was his first cousin. Her second son, the Cardinal, to whom Lisle always refers as 'my cousin Reynold Pole', became a vitally important figure in his story. He was consanguineous to the house of Tudor, descended from John of Gaunt, and to the Howards, Dukes of Norfolk, descended from Thomas of Woodstock. He flourished as one of the personal attendants and boon companions of Henry VIII, and held high office under him. Had he lived out his days peacefully he would be little more than a name to us – a Knight of the Garter, a gentleman who accompanied Henry VIII to the Field of Cloth of Gold, Vice-Admiral of England, Lord Deputy of Calais. But the unhappy chance which at one blow deprived him of rank, titles, possessions, and liberty meant also that the whole of the family correspondence which had accumulated in his house for seven years was seized by order of the King, and has, in consequence, been preserved ever since amongst the State Papers.

The commissioners responsible for the confiscation of the correspondence were looking for items of treasonable import. They did not discriminate, but seized upon business letters and personal letters alike; upon begging letters and dunning letters; children's letters, letters from friends, doctors' prescriptions, marriage proposals that came to nothing, notes refusing invitations to dinners that had cooled on the tables five years before, bills for shoe leather long since worn through. Not theirs to select or to discard, fortunately for us; and so, in these letters, this moment of time lives again.

As his second wife Arthur Plantagenet married Honor Grenville, whose brother Roger was the great-grandfather of the famous Sir Richard Grenville of Elizabeth's reign. She was then a widow, with a family of seven children by her first husband, Sir John Basset of Devonshire. Whether the alliance was originally entered into by both parties as the usual Tudor business arrangement we do not know. What we do know, from the letters they wrote as husband and wife, is that either before or after their marriage they fell as whole-heartedly in love with each other as the most romantic modernist could wish. The letters they exchanged, when absent from each other in 1538 and 1539, are, as a group, incomparable: the sixteenth century has nothing else of the kind to touch them. The intimacy of the writing is intensified rather than obscured by the formal phrasing. In the midst of what is apt to seem to us the bewildering and terrifying brutality of the age, these letters make, as it were, a point of rest, reassuring us of ultimate values. That the quality of their love shone through their lives and in their daily intercourse is witnessed by that most shrewd and cynical of observers, the notoriously dissolute Sir Francis Bryan, who, in a letter to Arthur Plantagenet, sends commendations to Honor, and writes, 'unto whom and to your lordship, because ye be both but one soul though ye be two bodies, I write but one letter'.

Until 1533 Arthur Plantagenet and his family lived the life of the English nobility and gentry of their day. In 1533, however, he was appointed to the office of Lord Deputy of Calais – a position somewhat resembling that of a modern Governor-General. Accompanied by his wife he took up his residence there in June, and remained in office until summoned back to England in April 1540.

It is to these seven years that the Lisle Letters belong. These are years of vital significance in the history of England   the years of Thomas Cromwell's rise to power, and of his ascendancy and fall. Throughout, the personal story of the Lisles and their fortunes is set against the larger background of events of national and international importance. Just before he left England for Calais Lisle officiated at Anne Boleyn's coronation banquet; and the years that follow see the completion of Henry's breach with Rome, the ensuing religious settlement, the dissolution of the monasteries, the Pilgrimage of Grace, and the continued success of the 'judicious meddling' in foreign affairs which was Henry's method of ensuring that France and the Empire should not combine against England. In terms of more individual significance, they are the years which see the tragedy of Anne Boleyn, the rise of the Seymours, the birth of Edward VI, the executions of Sir Thomas More and Bishop Fisher, and the ruthless butchery of the Pole family and their friends. In terms of the personal rule of Henry VIII they are the crucial years which begin and accomplish that hardening of character which made the French ambassador in 1539 describe him as 'the most dangerous and cruel man in the world'.[1]

The picture which emerges, of a society that while undergoing in less than seven years a series of revolutionary changes nevertheless retains its essen-

---

1. Castillon to Montmorency, *L. & P.* xiv i 144.

tial solidarity, is extraordinarily vivid, when seen in these individual terms. The breach with Rome, the destruction of the monasteries, the emergence of Parliament and the reorganizing of finance and administration, strengthen rather than weaken its autocratic, authoritarian, dictatorial, and privileged structure. We catch the voices of gossip and rumour, echoes of the individual and national hopes and fears of gentle and simple, and of the trend and sway of opinion; but the most vivid impression conveyed is that of a more or less general acquiescence, in so far as the reactions of the average man to events and policy are concerned. As always, under any form of dictatorship, it was admittedly dangerous to express opinions at variance with those officially held; and the Letters make us very conscious of the extent of that danger. Nevertheless, when all allowance has been made for the fear and the discretion of individuals, the fact remains that the attitude of the average man is ostensibly complaisant.

The Tudor plan, from Henry VII to Elizabeth, was the first great political plan of the modern world. Its aim was the security of the State, at whatever cost to the individual and to existing institutions, all of which were tried nominally by moral, legal, and religious standards but actually by the simple standard of what was expedient for the consolidation of power. To the Tudor rulers and their helpers and servers, and above all to Henry VIII, this meant the establishment of the Tudor succession and the concentration of wealth and authority in the hands of the prince to assure control from a central absolutism, exercised in the name of the State and for the State. The plan won its own 'moral' victory when it secured the Anne Boleyn marriage, the breach with Rome, and the legalized murder of Fisher and More, without incurring disaster. The men at the top and the man in the street had acquiesced in the abandonment of the accepted ethical and religious values and the substitution of the new morality of expediency.

For the casual and almost accidental brutality of weak government and civil strife there is substituted in these years the brutality of organization and plan – the State plan to which everything must give way. It was not Henry's plan, it was Cromwell's, tailored to fit the monarch for whom it was made, and dictated by the political needs of its day. Its automatism was mitigated to some extent by the character of the King, who could and did intervene on behalf of the individual, as long as it did not cost him anything. But against this occasional relaxation must be set that terrifying fixity of purpose which was the fundamental activating quality in the King's character – the thing, as we would say, that makes the man tick. Much of the planning was good, and it was vital to have the Tudor succession ensured. The brutalities of imprisonment, torture, and execution were no more excessive in England than elsewhere in the sixteenth century. But the calculated use of terrorism – State trials with foregone conclusions and condemnation without trial, the apparatus of tyranny and the suppression of free opinion and judgement – is the familiar pattern of deterrence which we have recognized with horror and detestation in our own time.

'News here are none, but that the abbeys shall down', writes Thomas Warley to Lady Lisle in 1536, as one of the most far-reaching changes in European history, disruptive of the older social order, is decided upon. How often do not we ourselves write 'No news here', in times of equal crisis, simply because for the greater part of his life the average man extends his imaginative reach hardly at all beyond his own concerns, his own profits, his own safety, or at most the concerns, profits, and safety of his family.

It is significant in the absolute sense, and also in the specific context of Lisle's career, that the first event of the new reign to which most histories draw attention was the trial and execution of the rapacious and detested tax-gatherers, Empson and Dudley, who had enabled that frugal monarch, Henry VII, who had conquered a bankrupt kingdom in 1485, to leave it with an annual income of some £142,000 a year and a reserve of treasure worth nearly two million pounds. After a decent interval, Edmund Dudley's widow, Elizabeth Grey, became the wife of Arthur Plantagenet, bringing him a substantial share of the Dudley lands and, before long, the Lisle lands that came to her as Baroness Lisle *suo jure,* together with the bestowal by the King of the title of Viscount Lisle. It is the first instance readers of the Lisle story encounter of the way in which men near to the King, who stood well in his favour, benefited by the deaths of those condemned for offences against the State; and they will be reminded of it when Lisle himself tries to join the scramble for confiscated lands before the victims in the Anne Boleyn affair are even brought to trial.

The Letters and the Editing of the Text

The bulk of the Lisle collection is in the Public Record Office, in the eighteen volumes known as the Lisle Papers (S.P. 3, Vols. 1–18); but a considerable number of the letters are in the chronologically arranged State Papers of Henry VIII (S.P. 1, Vols. 8–242, *passim*), and a few items have strayed to the British Museum, into the Cotton, Harleian, and Royal MSS. The letters have been calendared in *Letters and Papers, Foreign and Domestic, of the Reign of Henry VIII* (ed. Brewer and Gairdner, Vols. I–XVII, and Addenda), abbreviated *L. & P.* in footnotes to this selection.

The letters are in an amazingly fine state of preservation. Injury from dirt, damp, or other causes is the exception. In a few cases the conclusion of a document or the writer's signature has been torn off – in the latter case a pathetically futile expedient, one would have thought, if done by Lisle or his wife or a member of their household; but the contents of these mutilated letters and the insignificance of some of the writers suggest a contemporary rather than the later amateur collector of autographs. Many of the letters have been sealed with wax, and some, consequently, have been slightly torn when opened by their recipients. In some instances fragments of string, used in conjunction with the seal, have also been preserved. Only in rare cases has the ink faded badly, or have edges become friable or torn. The paper in general is of good quality, and has yellowed or darkened only very slightly. The ink is as a rule of a good colour, generally of the brownish tone. With the usual irony of such things, the really atrocious writers like Sir Thomas Palmer tend to use the worst paper and the worst ink.

Most of the letters are addressed. The formulas vary considerably. In some, the style of the recipient is given in the fullest possible manner; others are semi-formal; and a few pleasantly informal. The destination is not infrequently omitted. A number of them bear the well-known instruction to the messenger who carried them: 'Haste! Haste! Haste! For thy life.' Many were endorsed with the sender's name, and sometimes dated, before being folded and filed for reference. Some of these endorsements are in Lisle's own hand, but mostly in his secretary's. Many of the purely personal letters, as well as the business ones, were treated in this way.

The decision to print a modern text was based primarily upon a wide experience of the reactions of the ordinary reader – and also of the average student who is not necessarily the born scholar – to similar texts where the original spelling and other peculiarities have been preserved. For any but the specialist who takes them in his stride, these things undoubtedly distract attention from the more to the less important – from matter to manner, from the essential to the accidental. Amusement caused when the Pope figures as 'Pop' can easily distract the mind from the proper excitement of the letter in which 'Pop' appears. Its entertainment value may be harmless, but it is neither more nor less amusing than the phonetic or illiterate or inaccurate spelling which is always with us in all ages; and a few specimens will be found in the footnotes.

If we allow that the occasional inconsistent or old-fashioned or peculiar spelling is always a normal feature of ordinary contemporary letter-writing in any age, it follows that phonetic spellings and dialect forms or any tricks of country speech must also be retained in the text, or noted. For example, the countrified style of the local vicar and of Jane Basset's various Devonshire amanuenses has been recognized by preserving in the text such verbal forms as 'be' (been) and 'byth' for is and are, together with the Devonshire trick of referring to Lady Lisle's evidences or her jointure or the weir on the river at Umberleigh as 'her' or 'him'.

It is not so easy to know whether to modernize 'ne', 'or', and 'mo(e)' throughout, as nor, ere, and more are almost equally common. Husee definitely prefers the old forms. Enough examples have been left in to remind the reader of their coexistence. With some words, to call attention to the few writers who use a modern form, I have avoided consistent modernization in order to stress these exceptions, as in the use of Madam and Madame. Husee has both, but he uses the French form much more frequently, and it is more usual in the letters in general. Where a writer employs both 'ye' and 'you' they have been preserved, as also the possessive 'his' (hys), but not the 'ys', 'is' forms which are modernized, as I think the ordinary reader takes 'his' = 's in his stride but may be momentarily confused by the others. Freak spellings are noted, if not retained in the text. Deputy is frequently 'Debite', and James Hawkesworth's pair of 'Depewtty' and 'Dewputty' tell the double tale of an uncertain speller and his pronunciation. I have also retained certain French words or phrases that disappear by the end of the century. Lisle and his various secretaries use 'contynew(ue)' for contents, as do all his French correspondents. The phrase 'in gree' (gre) – meaning to take something kindly, in good part, with good will (prendre en gré, de bon gré) – is common to Lady Lisle and her French correspondents, and is used by other English writers.

This, however, is by no means the end of the modernizer's spelling troubles. Proper names and place names, which had seemed a simple enough matter at the start, soon developed into a major headache. They present not one but several problems, confronting us, in the case of family names, with a choice between the writer's own signature, the variants used by his contemporaries, and alternative modern forms.

Where we write Lisle, Grenville, and Basset for the three family names of most concern in these Letters, Arthur Lisle signs himself Lyssle but is addressed or written of as Lile, Lyly, Lylie, Lysle, Lyssley, Lisley, Lysley, Lisle, etc. Husee generally prefers Lyssle to Lysle; James Hawkesworth uses lysley, lyssley, leysley, leyssley. The Grenvilles, who have now reduced the family variants to Grenville, Granville, and Grenfell, but are of course still surrounded by Greenfields, were addressed by every possible variety of the Grayn(e)felde, Grenfild, Greenfilde forms, though Sir Richard and all the rest of the family letter-writers stick to Graynf(f)cld(e) or Graynfyld. Sir Richard invariably signs himself Ryc. Graynfelde. Basset, then as now, has one *t* or two, at the writer's individual pleasure. Cromwell signs himself Crumwell. Christian name spellings can also vary. John Bekynsaw, a scholar, writes William, Guyliam, Guylyome, and Guylyam in one short letter. It seemed that the best way to reflect this diversity was to use the modern, accepted form in the letter-heads, commentaries, and notes, but to preserve the writer's own signature. This is admittedly *ad hoc* treatment, but it should not interfere with easy reading or cause any genuine confusion, and I believe that the best way of meeting a difficulty of this kind is simply to keep the reader reminded that it exists. All Lisle and Graynfyld spelling variants are

preserved throughout the text; otherwise, the assumption is that most
readers will prefer the accepted modern forms, and will take the occasional
reminders as sufficient token of the underlying diversity.

Place names are equally if not more troublesome. The obvious interest of
Calles, Caleys, Calays, Cales, Callis, Calis, Callys, etc., is the assurance these
forms give that the English pronunciation was the normal one. It would be
feasible to modernize all the Womblegh, Womberlegh, Womberley, Om-
barley, and similar spellings as Umberleigh, but I have left some of them in
as local colour when they occur in letters from Devon.

When, in the original, punctuation is non-existent, inadequate, or mis-
leading, I have tried to make the sense clear and directly apparent with the
minimum of pointing, so as to preserve the natural rhythm and pace of the
writing. I have illustrated the use of the fifteenth-century virgula, or diagonal
stroke, in several letters where it is the only form of punctuation used. It was
not used for clauses, but it noted short pauses in reading and also ends of
sentences. It is definitely old-fashioned after the end of the century, but it is
common in these letters, and is similar in function to the comma, which came
into English writing in the sixteenth century, and into printing about 1521.
Paragraphing also has its problems for the modernizer. The average letter of
this period, whether short or long, tends to be written in one solid block,
presenting a very daunting appearance to the modern reader; and though
this visual continuity can give both punch and speed to reasonably brief
specimens, in the long, packed letters which abound in this collection it is
unpleasing to the eye and can make it more difficult for us to grasp the
content. It has been suggested that this lay-out was a precaution to avoid any
tampering – hence the use, by some writers, of a curlicue to fill up the end of
a line. When the letter is short enough for this solid construction to offer no
obstacle to our ready understanding and enjoyment, it has been preserved.

The treatment of numbers developed into a problem as I worked. At first
sight it appeared obvious that the consistent use of roman figures asked for
an equally consistent use of arabic in the modern text, and was particularly
desirable when accounts and sums running into hundreds and thousands
were involved. That usage was inconsistent seemed a fact worth registering,
so the most practical method was obviously arabic for arabic, roman for
roman, and words for words when dealing with numbers.

Having made it possible to read these letters at the same speed and in the
same way as we read those we ourselves receive, I hope that the preservation
of enough of their natural inconsistencies will help to convey the impression
of individuality and the engaging freshness and occasional happy absurdities
such as we enjoy when we read the outpourings of our own less sophisticated
correspondents.

Each letter is preceded by its number in the sequence in this edition
(hereafter called the selection), and followed by its volume and number in

the six-volume edition (hereafter called the collection); references to the manuscript source and to its place in the *Letters and Papers* calendar may be found following each letter in the collection. Letter-heads and dates have been supplied for convenience; and the names are given in modern spelling. Letters written throughout in the writer's own hand are described as holograph, indicated by *Hol.* According to its position, *Signed* means either that the subscription and signature are both holograph, or else the signature alone. Insertions above the line or in the margin have been incorporated in the text between caret marks, ∧as thus∧. Round brackets (parentheses) are those used by the writer; square brackets indicate words or letters supplied by the editor, either because there are lacunae in the manuscript or because it is clear they have been omitted by mistake. Where there are traces of letters in the mutilated passages, these are printed in roman, and words or letters conjecturally supplied in brackets. Omissions due to failure to read the original are noted, and so are conjectures, however obvious or plausible.

Characters in Order of Appearance

ARTHUR PLANTAGENET
'The gentlest heart living'

There is no extant portrait of Arthur Plantagenet – not even a conventionally sculptured tombstone effigy to hint at his appearance. In the remarkable painting of the Field of Cloth of Gold, Sir Arthur and his companion knights ride too far behind the great dukes and earls and bishops for any attempt to have been made by the painter to catch a likeness. It may be that in the thirteenth figure, representing Viscount Lisle, in the engraving of the procession of the Garter knights, we have warrant for the cut of his beard and type of countenance, as neither is wholly conventional (see Pl. 18).

Lisle was a descendant of those Angevin kings whose strongly marked physical characteristics survived in generation after generation. Distinctive in build and feature, the large frame, the fair florid countenance, and the graceful strength came to a typical perfection in Edward IV, the last Plantagenet king, reputed to have been the handsomest monarch who ever sat on the English throne. 'Princely to behold' is Sir Thomas More's description, 'of visage lovely, of body mighty, strong and clean made'. When his seven-foot coffin was opened in 1788 his skeleton measured 6 feet 3.5 inches. If I am right in believing that it was during his summer progress in the south in 1461 that the nineteen-year-old Edward IV first met and seduced Elizabeth Lucy, I think the portrait reproduced here (Pl. 1) is possibly a better likeness of Lisle's youthful father than the much more interesting and well-executed painting in the royal collection of the king in later years. What is of particular interest, however, is the undoubted facial resemblance established between

1. Edward IV
Courtesy of the Society of Antiquaries of London

ELIZABETHA · VXOR
HENRICI · VII ·

2. Elizabeth of York, daughter of Edward IV and wife of Henry VII
Courtesy of the National Portrait Gallery

Edward and his daughter Elizabeth of York, Lisle's half-sister, the ancestress of the Tudor line (Pl. 2): the family face persists. Its persistence is also shown by the portraits of Margaret Pole and her son Reginald, the Cardinal, daughter and grandson of Edward's brother, George, Duke of Clarence (see Pls. 19 and 20). The auburn hair and fair skin that is marked in four generations of Lisle's royal relations may justify us in a fair guess at his colouring as well.

There is just one piece of evidence which I believe gives authenticity to this conjectural portrait. At the end of 1533, when there was some reason to believe that war might break out, Lisle asked the King to give him a 'hosting-harness' or field armour. On 20 January 1534 Sir Francis Bryan wrote to say he had moved the King's Highness for this harness, and that 'at his Grace's next repair to Greenwich ... he will look out one for you himself'. Lisle did not possess a complete field armour and in his position as the King's Deputy needed one that was handsome, serviceable, and appropriate; so his nephew chose out one of his own Greenwich armours and sent it to him. If this is so, Lisle must have been of approximately the same height as Henry VIII, that is, 6 feet or more; and of similar build either to Henry as he was then or, more likely, as he had been earlier in life.

Lisle's handwriting is simple, confident, easy, as though he could dash off a letter at speed. It is strikingly superior to that of nearly all his noble or gentle contemporaries, the legacy perhaps of a childhood education at his father's court though his youth was spent among his Hampshire kinsfolk. He writes easily because he writes as he would speak – forthright and direct, at times abrupt in the manner of speech, at other times, especially when reciting his troubles, voluble in the unconsidered manner of speech. Nevertheless he can compose an excellent official letter when necessary, and can take considerable pains – resulting in several drafts – to pull the composition into the best shape possible.

There are certain traits of character in Arthur Lisle reminiscent of Edward IV, such as the King's preference for bourgeois society, which was reflected in his son's easy and familiar ways with men of all conditions and his hearty, friendly manner with his inferiors. When one of the King's trumpeters wants to ask a favour he does so 'by the same token that your Lordship took me by the hand through the grate at the Lantern Gate', and 'by the same token I sent you a dog by the farrier of the town, which dog's name is Wolf, and I heartily thank you for my dog you gave me'. An affable, easy-going man: affable and easy to a fault, according to his enemies; so that his friend Sir Francis Bryan warns him, 'Keep all things secreter than you have been used', for 'there is nothing done nor spoken but it is with speed knowen in the Court'. 'Take more upon you', he recommends, and 'be knowen for the King's Deputy there'. He was out of his natural element when plunged into the personal and private jealousies, local and official feuds, and petty squabbles that were the running accompaniment to the task of governing a frontier town, complicated as this was by wire-pulling, privilege, and vested interests; but bombarded as he was with contradictory orders, and advice and requests from the various persons of influence who had friends to prefer or some axe to grind, whatever he did was bound to offend or victimize someone. When, however, he is concerned with straightforward, administrative business, as in the autumn of 1533, his letters are well calculated and the measures he advocates are practical and necessary. Victualling and repairs to the fortifications were the essentials of the situation that he took over, and he goes on pressing for the town's needs as firmly as only a man with experience of top-level inertia on the part of the bureaucracy at home and of confidence in his own authority and his duty could do.

Recognizably his father's son, in a general sense, as to character and tastes, to Lisle's princely disposition all alike bear witness. Henry himself speaks of him as 'the gentlest heart living'. 'Ever called the pleasantest-witted man in the world', according to Husee, he was essentially a good-natured, social being, a good host and a popular guest, and very ready to enjoy life, if it would only let him. He does not ask much more, in these last years, than that it should provide him with his 'gentle bedfellow', his good food, the specially chosen wine 'for his own drinking', and enough money. To Honor Lisle, less extravagant by nature, there fell the task of endeavouring to curb this lavish spirit, and many of the letters requesting payment of the debts are either sent direct to her or come as duplicates of the letters to her husband. The Lisle of the Letters was an ageing man, if, as I believe, he was born *c.* 1462 and was about seventy when he went to Calais in 1533. Small wonder, therefore, if his powers and his health may have deteriorated, under Calais conditions, towards the end of his seven years of office. But in 1533 he was still able-bodied and energetic, ready to don a 'hosting harness' again.

A brief summary of his life before we come to know him is necessary. There are conflicting theories about the date of his birth, but 1462 seems the most acceptable. His mother, Elizabeth, born Wayte, was already the widow of one of the Lucy family when at the age of nineteen she met Edward IV. It would seem that Arthur was brought up at first by his mother at Court, where she may have had another child, Elizabeth, by the King. From the age of about ten, he was with his mother's family at one of their manors in Hampshire, possibly Soberton. In 1501 he joined the household of his half-sister, Elizabeth of York, and in 1503 he joined that of Henry VII. He kept his place at Court when Henry VIII succeeded to the throne, and was known as a close companion to the King. In 1511 he married his first wife, Elizabeth Grey, widow of the executed Edmund Dudley, and the King returned to her the Dudley lands forfeited by her first husband. The following year, Arthur became, and remained for many years, a member of the Commission of the Peace for Hampshire. He was a Gentleman of the Privy Chamber, and in 1513 was made a Spear of Honour, member of a crack corps of men of noble blood. He was in high favour at court, and given various ceremonial and semi-diplomatic jobs. In the same year he held a command in the naval forces in the war against France, with responsibility for the seas between the Thames estuary and Brest. In 1519 his wife succeeded to the rest of the Dudley lands and became Baroness Lisle in her own right. In 1520 he accompanied the King to France for the peace celebrations that became known as the Field of Cloth of Gold. In 1523 he was created Viscount Lisle, and the following year a Knight of the Garter. It was probably in 1525 that his wife Elizabeth died. In 1529 he married Honor Grenville, widow of Sir John Basset. From 1525 until he was appointed to Calais in 1533, Lisle was Vice Admiral of England, a post requiring considerable administrative ability, which would not have been given to a man without it by Henry VIII, who took the navy he was building up very seriously indeed.

HONOR GRENVILLE
'My Lady Deputy'

If we are right to believe that Lisle took after his father in height it would be tempting to guess that Honor Grenville was one of those small women who generally marry tall husbands – a neat, compact, and dignified little person, cleverer than Lisle and a born manager. All that we know for certain is that she was 'of a cold complexion', or what contemporary physiology called a phlegmatic constitution – with a delicate skin and colouring. Her friend Sœur Anthoinette de Saveuses speaks of her 'tender and delicate person'; and Sir John Wallop's none-too-veiled compliment to her physical charms suggests the plump well-made figure. As in Lisle's case, there is no known portrait of her. She is one of the two identically clad, conventionally featured wives who stand on either side of Sir John Basset on his monumental brass in the Church of St. Mary at Atherington (Pl. 3). We know that her daughter Anne had the good looks that commended her to the King and secured her a place at Court, and that her youngest daughter Mary was acclaimed as something of a beauty. We can probably take it for granted, therefore, that she herself was personable and good-looking in the contemporary style, if nothing more, as she was one of the six ladies chosen to accompany Anne Boleyn to the 1532 Calais interview between Henry and Francis I. When they danced with the French King and his lords, 'in the dancing the King of England took away the ladies' visors so that there the ladies' beauties were shewed'.

3. Monumental brass of Sir John Basset and his two wives, Church of St. Mary, Atherington, Devonshire

Drawing reproduced from W. R. Crabbe, 'monumental Brasses of Devonshire', *Transactions of the Exeter Diocesan Architectural Society*, Vol. VI (1856), Pl. 2; courtesy of the Newberry Library, Chicago

We know that she dressed well, as befitted her station in life. Her choice of colours to wear, with her preference for the fashionable 'lion tawny', is very much the conventional taste of the day. We can add, too, some individual touches – the 'beads of coral with a heart of gold' of which she was particularly fond, and which she was accustomed always to wear about her arm; on her fingers, three rings with 'turkases', an emerald ring, a sapphire ring, ruby rings. We see her functioning in all the characteristic relationships – at home as wife, mother, and mistress of the household, and as hostess providing hospitality and entertainment. She is the business woman, dealing with the affairs of all the members of the family and fully empowered to act for her husband, his 'dearest partner of greatness', using her influence with him on behalf of all kinds of petitioners, and her own influence or their joint influence with both men and women in great place. She reflects in quite a remarkable manner the difference between the theory of woman's place in the scheme of things, as set forth in the mass of sixteenth-century treatises on the subject, and the reality as we encounter it both in the lives of noblewomen and gentlewomen and in their letters.

From the very first contact we realize the force of her character, and can watch it being gradually revealed and established as the letters pile up detail after detail. We realize her decidedly religious bent, her housewifely competence, her knowledge of physic, her love of pets of all descriptions, her social accomplishments such as dancing, card-playing, shooting with the bow, and the more practical ones such as reading and riding. She is more typical than a Margaret Roper: Honor Lisle is the norm in her attainments and her education, or rather, her lack of education. She knew neither Latin nor French, and curiously enough does not appear to have picked up this latter tongue even by the end of her seven years' stay in Calais. She could read, and she could sign her own name, but she always dictated her letters, even those to her husband; and her signature suggests that she handled a pen with difficulty.

It was easier to get round Arthur Lisle than his wife. As one of their acquaintances boasted, 'with a few words and a present of a penny he would have his lordship's good will, so that my lady was not in the way'. But if more than good will was required, in some matter of business or preferment, it was to Honor that most of their correspondents wrote. They knew, then, that something would be done about it. Husee nearly always repeats in his letters to Honor the business details he has just written to Lisle, and on one occasion at least makes the specific complaint that his lordship 'doth never make me thorough answer of my letters'. It is obvious from the tone of her letters that Honor possessed to a high degree the family characteristics that were to bring the Grenvilles into prominence during the Tudor and Stuart reigns. She has something even of the fierce pride and domineering spirit that legend and fact associate with the famous Sir Richard. There is a dynamic energy behind her utterances that accords well with the glimpses we get in other people's reports. She ran things. She could never have helped running things.

That she was a devout woman, and punctual in her observance of all the rites and ceremonies of the older faith in which she had grown up, is evident throughout the correspondence, and more especially in the later years, when such devotions as she was accustomed to use were in danger of being frowned upon as 'papish'. Cromwell obviously thought Honor Lisle had too much influence over her husband, but it looks as if he objected to it because he knew her to be inconveniently attached to the older mode of worship, and because in matters of business her judgement was shrewder than Lisle's. Also, she was more pertinacious in soliciting the family interests. Lisle would always let himself be put off by fair words and specious promises, while she had more than a touch of Cromwell's own quality of tireless persistence. She obviously read some of her husband's official correspondence. Some of the writers particularly ask him to make my lady privy to their letters; a few address them to the Lord Deputy, 'or in his absence to the gracious lady his bedfellow'.

From thanks and comments in letters from others we know that she must have been an energetic correspondent, for from these alone we can estimate some six hundred letters that have vanished, but in all only forty-five from her remain. Yet her style is so unmistakable that even a letter in French translates itself almost automatically into her very idiom. There are no letters written in her own hand; but it is obvious from the consistency of the style that she herself dictated whatever she signed as hers. It is a good style – clear, flowing, measured, and dignified; and so full of natural speech cadences and rhythms that we may, without being fanciful, allow ourselves the belief that we know something of the individual manner of her talk. She obviously enjoyed 'pastime with good company', good food, good entertainment, was at her ease, socially, with men and women of all ranks in life. She could tell merry tales to the ship's master and the men of her escort while they waited for their supper, and a few nights later be as delighted as a child when bidden to a special banquet at Court given by the King – 'the best that ever I was at', she writes to tell her husband, 'and was partly made for me'. It was reported – by her enemies, perhaps – that Honor Lisle was 'very sharp and hasty'. Whether in speech or in action, is not specified; probably, on occasion, in both. She was obviously perturbed by this criticism, but it contains that residuum of truth which is generally to be found in such remarks when applied to vigorous, fearless people who do not hesitate to 'speak their minds'.

Honor was about forty when Arthur was appointed Lord Deputy, and had seven children by her first marriage – Philippa, John, Katharine, George, Mary, Anne and James. Arthur had three by his first wife – Frances, Elizabeth and Bridget. They both had several stepchildren.

Nothing reveals the Lisles' relationship to each other better than a few words in a letter from Arthur on one of the rare occasions when they were apart: 'I had never better health, but I think so much on you I cannot sleep i' the night. When I think on you, in two hours after there was never child thought so long for his nurse as I do for you.'

JOHN HUSEE
'My Lord Lisle's man'

Of all the other personalities who insinuate their way into the reader's affections the most engaging is certainly John Husee. He held one or two official positions in Calais, and is generally described as a 'gentleman of the King's retinue'. On one occasion Rokewood, a member of the Calais Council, refers to him as Lisle's 'steward': in fact, he was offered this position but refused it. Although he came and went between Calais and England, he spend a very considerable part of his time in London, often making the Red Lion at Southwark his headquarters. Lisle entrusted his most complicated legal, financial, and personal concerns to his care, with the result that Husee was always dealing with people of importance like Cromwell or Fitzwilliam or Wriothesley in his endeavour to secure justice or favours for the Lord Deputy, or the Lady Deputy, or their various families. He knew exactly how the system worked, and had the whole business of 'suits', and the art of 'waiting' upon the great ones of the earth at his finger tips, combining tact, pertinacity, and patience in his dealings to an almost superhuman degree. He knew, as well as anyone outside the inner circle of power could know, what was likely to happen, and could often see one move ahead so that a 'petitorie' epistle could arrive at the crucial moment. He was prepared to hang about for days, attending Mr. Cromwell's pleasure – ready to wait and choose the moment that was 'propice and meet'. Husee had a cool head and a warm heart. He knew when to lose his temper and when to keep it, when to assert himself and when to temporize, when to work through a subordinate and when the only possible course was to 'refer all to God'. He had – or else won very quickly as 'my Lord Lisle's man' – the confidence of such influential friends as Bryan, Norris, and Fitzwilliam. And he knew the terms on which he had to deal with their confidential servants and the useful men on the lower levels. He knew what tips to give, and when letters of thanks or presents were required from his lord or lady. Altogether a jewel of a man – one of those young-old men who always profit from and learn by any experience the first time it is encountered. Almost, one is tempted to say, the only man for Honor and Arthur Lisle.

As the years go by, his relations with both Honor and her husband become more personal, more affectionate and confidential; but he never takes advantage of the increasing intimacy to bate one jot of the respect due from 'your ladyship's own man', 'your lordship's most bounden'. To the end he is the perfect family retainer, his own life and interests genuinely identified with the lives and interests and needs of those whom it was his pride to serve. He subscribes himself to Lady Lisle as 'he that will be your ladyship's during life, whether your ladyship will or no'; 'thinking every day a hundred till I be with you again'. There is no letter from Honor to show in what manner she reciprocated this devotion, but we may take it that Lisle speaks for them both when he calls him 'my friend John Husee', and begins the draft of a letter in his own hand, 'Gentle Husee, I commend me to you'.

A few years' experience of handling the family affairs quickly taught Husee more worldly wisdom than his many years of court life and administrative work ever taught Viscount Lisle. When, as frequently happens, he offers his 'poor advice', it is always sound: never more so, incidentally, than when he counsels Lisle how to deal with Henry VIII. If he *must* write to the King, then the fewer lines the better, 'for I have heard say that his Grace loveth not to read long letters'. His lordship's easy-going ways gave his lordship's man many anxious moments, but when the required letter is forthcoming Husee never forgets the word of praise: 'As concerning your lordship's letter sent unto my Lord Privy Seal, the same was a very good letter.'[2] His scheme of values is always nicely graded: in the important matter of gifts, the recipient's rank and services rendered are estimated and appraised:

> Garter looketh that your lordship should remember him with some pleasure. A hogshead of Gascon wine were not ill-bestowed on him, for he is a much honester man than the last was.[3]

> My Lord Privy Seal maketh much of his piece of wine your lordship sent him. He keepeth it for his own drinking. You could not have done him greater pleasure. The boars' heads are not come; but at their coming I shall deliver them accordingly. It had been a goodly present for the King, for my Lord Privy Seal setteth no great store by them.[4]

The one person who really baffled Husee was Cromwell. It is as if his instinct told him this man could never be quite as other men in his values, and that he had better be distrusted on instinct, though without reason. 'By my faith', he writes in 1534, 'I cannot see the contrary but Mr. Secretary beareth my lord good mind and heart'. In his perpetual reassurances to Lisle

2. Vol. 5, No. 1090.
3. Vol. 4, No. 942.
4. Vol. 5, No. 1260.

he is obviously trying to reassure himself: 'By utter appearance he showed that time to be your lordship's faithful friend, trusting in God that you shall so find him'.

Despite his common sense, Husee was a soft-hearted fellow when it came to dealings with the young Bassets. He obviously felt himself responsible for their manners and morals, as well as their finances, their clothing, and their general advancement in life. His pride in all of them, their looks, their achievements, and their successes, becomes more and more personal year by year.

Besides looking after her children Husee did nearly all Lady Lisle's shopping for her in London. He knew her ladyship's tastes to a nicety, and was always a close bargainer on her behalf: 'And where your ladyship writeth that the riband was dear, I bought it as I would have done for my life; and I am sure there is none better to be had in London of that price'.[5] When he has to apologize for not sending the cloth-of-silver she wants, he explains that there is none of the right quality to be had, and 'I know well the low price silver is not for your ladyship's wearing'. And his advice on the question of dyeing is obviously reliable: 'The old damask gown your ladyship sent will never be good tawny. It will take a good black.'

Husee wrote and worked always under pressure. In his letters he skips from subject to subject with all the speed and disregard of transition that speaks the harassed and over-busied mind. But despite the haste apparent behind his writing he is no mean stylist, and he has often enough a pretty choice of words. He can quote his Latin tags on occasion, and he has a shrewdly humorous turn of phrase for summing up a situation or a man's character. And he can be admirably direct: 'The King inquired how the man was slain, and I answered that one of them, or both, was drunk'. In the letters an individual expresses himself, realizing for us as completely as possible one of the most attractive personalities that the century can boast.

To complete the introduction of the Lisles to the reader, half a dozen letters are given here to illustrate something of their characters before the main stream of the selection starts. The following characteristic letter shows Lady Lisle interceding with Cromwell for an offender, undaunted by a rebuke about meddling lately administered by him.

1   LADY LISLE TO CROMWELL   7 October 1533

Right worshipful Sir, in my most hearty manner I commend me unto you, thanking you for your special goodness towards my lord and me at all times,

5. Vol.4, No.857.

which we are not well able to deserve; yet for my part I am so bold once again to be a suitor unto you; tenderly desiring you to be good master unto this bearer, who is like to have much wrong by the Abbot of Bruton, if you be not his singular good master, for that by chance, and himself defending, as is very well known, he killed a man, and therefor he hath his pardon. The Abbot would put him clearly from his living, and in especial it is for my lord's sake and mine he would so uncharitably do. Yet if you knew how much my lord hath done for the Abbot, you will think he useth the right part of a churl abbot, as Leonard Smyth at your pleasure can tell you. Sir, I beseech you, know thoroughly the matter; then I am sure pity will move you to be good master unto this honest man, the rather, I trust, at my poor request, though you know me unable to deserve it. You shall have my good will and service, glad if it might lie in me to do you pleasure, as our Lord God knoweth, who preserve and keep you, with long life, good health, and to attain your gentle heart's desire.

At Calais, the vij^th day of October, by your ever assured.

Signed   Honor lissle   (Vol. 1, No. 57)

Lisle's French neighbour, the Seneschal of Boulogne, writes as one who expects from him an equally charitable response to distress.

2   OUDART DU BIES TO LORD LISLE   *27 October 1533*

My lord Deputy, my good neighbour and entire friend, I recommend me to your good grace. My lord Deputy, I am informed by one of my *mortepays*, this bearer, that a stepson of his, of the age of fifteen years, being still under the tutelage of the Court of Justice of Tournay, he being native thereof, is at your town of Calais in the lodging of Père Brisselet, where I am told he hath been for some time. And because the poor youth hath no money to defray his expenses, he hath been kept prisoner these six or seven months, where he remaineth yet in great poverty, and as it appeareth, must so continue, because neither the youth nor his mother can pay that which is demanded of him. Wherefore, my Lord Deputy, I pray you in favour to me to have the poor child recommended to you, for it is great pity thus to maltreat a child of such age as he is of, and also it is not reasonable. At which point, my Lord Deputy, my good neighbour and entire friend, I conclude; praying our Creator to give you good life and long.

From Boulogne, this xxvij day of October,

Entirely your good neighbour and assured friend,

Signed   Oudart du Bies   (Vol. 1, No. 65)

A fellow courtier of Lisle's youth gives us a glimpse of what at least at one time was another side of his character.

3   SIR FRANCIS BRYAN TO LORD LISLE   *24 October 1533*

My good lord, after my hearty recommendations, this shall be to advertise you that I have received your letter, by the which I do not only perceive that ye would be glad of my return but also my ∧Lady∧ your bedfellow, whom I do heartily thank. Sir, whereas in your ∧last∧ letter I perceive that in Calais ye have sufficient of courtezans to furnish and accomplish my desires, I do thank you of your good provision, but this shall be to advertise you that since my coming hither I have called to my remembrance the misliving that ye and such other hath brought me to; for the which, being repented, have had absolution of the Pope. And because ye be my friend, I would advertise you in likewise to be sorry of that ye have done, and ask my lady your wife forgiveness, and that forgiveness obtained, to come in all diligence hither to be absolved of the Pope, who I think will not tarry here much longer than Hallowmas, ere which time shall be married the Duke of Orleans to the Pope's niece, who arrived as yesterday in this town, accompanied with xij or xiiij gentlewomen, which gentlewomen nor mistress be not as fair as was Lucrece. And thus heartily fare ye well, my good lord. From Merseles, the xxiiij^(th) day of October.

The above is dictated, the remainder written in his own hand.

I beseke youe this Lett*er*
may co*m*mende me to m*r*.   *you*r lovyng brother
p*or*ter & my Lady his wif   of wold
                                  ffranssys Bryan   (Vol.1, No.66a)

4   JOHN KITE, BISHOP OF CARLISLE,   *23 November 1533*
       TO LORD LISLE

My Lord, I commend me much heartily unto your good lordship. . . .
And my lord, I am very glad to hear the high report that is of your lordship, in that ye use yourself so like a Captain and the King's Lieutenant ministering justice so indifferently, with your much liberality besides, to your great honour and no small comfort to your friends in these parts to hear the same, which I promise you are many. Also I require you to let me see other whiles your letters whereby I may know how ye do, with my good Lady your bedfellow, nothing, I assure you, more my comfort; and to whom

I desire you have me most heartily recommended. . . . And any pleasure here that I may do for you or yours, to use me after the old wont manner; and to my power I will not fail you, God so willing, who evermore preserve your good lordship as myself.

Written at Carlisle Place the xxiij^th day of November

Signed   Yo*ur* own w*ith* his.

Jo. Karl*iol*   (Vol.1, No.82)

Sir Thomas Elyot, diplomatist and one of the leaders of the classical renascence in England, gives us a glimpse of Honor Lisle ruling the household in Calais.

5   SIR THOMAS ELYOT TO LADY LISLE   *3 December 1533*

My singular good lady, in most humble manner I recommend me unto your good ladyship. And where by the report of your servant Thomas Raynsforde I perccive that he hath founden you alway his special good lady. . . . I am moved to desire your ladyship heartily to continue his good lady, according as I doubt not but that ye shall find his merits in doing his service and duty unto my good lord and your ladyship. Albeit forasmuch as I consider that he hath too much delighted in dicing, whereby he hath been an ill husband in providing for that which might now honestly furnish him in serving my lord and you; and as it seemeth he now much repenteth, with other loss of time, recounting to me how much he is bounden to your ladyship for your honourable and most gentle advertisements, I . . . do humbly desire your ladyship to preserve your honourable and most charitable favour towards your said servant; and in doing his diligent and true service to my lord and you, on my part I beseech your ladyship to recommend him unto my lord's good remembrance for his advancement. And as your ladyship have done, when ye shall perceive any lack in him touching his service, or excess in gaming, of your goodness and wisdom withdraw him with your sharp admonition and commandment, which I perceive he doth much esteem and dread. . . .

Our Lord send my good lord and you long life in much honour.

writon at London, the iij^d day of December,

At y*our* co*mm*aundement

Hol.   Th*os.* Elyot. Kt.   (Vol.1, No.90)

When a cousin sends Lisle a rumour that the clergy are to be allowed to marry we have another glimpse of the past.

6   LORD LISLE TO ANTONY WAYTE   *23 November 1535*

Cousin Wayte, I commend me unto you, and have received the letter you
sent to my wife, and well perceive the contents of everything therein,
thanking you of your news concerning priests, which I would a'been gladder
of xx^{ti} year gone, that I might a'made one priest cuckold. To your other
matter concerning payment now, I ensure you I never had such charges in ij
year. It hath cost me this year iij$\mathcal{C}^{li}$ sterling more than it did the first year, by
reason of the ambassadors coming and going, and at the last interview of the
Duke of Norfolk and the Admiral and Grand Ecuyer of France, which had
with them L gentlemen. I know the good heart of my lord towards me. When
you shew him ∧my great charges∧ I trust there shall not redound to your
displeasure. If that should, I had liever take great pain on me, and my wife
also, who hath often called on me for the matter. Trusting to see you this
summer. . . .
Hol.   (Vol.2, No.479)

Lisle's jest about making 'one priest cuckold' twenty years ago is presumably a particular reference: '*one* priest' is an individual, not any priest. Twenty
years ago Wolsey, then a man of forty-four, Archbishop of York, Lord
Chancellor, and Cardinal, with a couple of bishoprics and other ecclesiastical
sinecures, was the wealthiest, the most powerful, and the most unpopular
man in the kingdom, and was the father of two bastard children.

2

Calais 1533–1535

To the question, Why was Arthur Lisle originally given the appointment of Lord Deputy of Calais? there is only one possible answer – that in the given circumstances of the year 1533 he seemed to Henry VIII to be the most suitable man available for the job. He was about sixty-nine or seventy years old, but 'I have heard his Grace say', writes John Rokewood to Lisle in 1534, 'that you were and are the most meetest and best for that room that he knoweth in his realm.'

Calais was an important post, and a difficult one: it required a man of varied experience, preferably as soldier and as civil administrator; a man of good social standing, accustomed to command, capable of sustaining the dignity of the office, dispensing hospitality on a generous scale, and keeping on good terms with the representatives of other nations. It required, moreover, a man of whose personal loyalty at this particularly critical moment Henry had no manner of doubt. The loyalty of Arthur Plantagenet was unquestioned; that of his legitimate Plantagenet cousins was suspect. He belonged to the circle of the King's intimates but he was not among the number of those whose business or diplomatic talents made them of prime use as councillors or ambassadors. In spite of several efforts on his part to be relieved of his office, both Henry and Cromwell saw to it that he retained his position for seven of the most crucial years of English history. It must be admitted that Calais remained in the hands of the English during these years, not thanks to the foresight and wisdom either of Thomas Cromwell or Arthur Lisle, but simply because neither the King of France nor the Emperor made any attempt to wrest the town from them, and because Henry's foreign policy was sufficiently realist and well calculated. When, at last, in 1557–8, the attempt was made, it succeeded at once.

Keeping always in mind that the drama of the Lisles is a developing story, what we must look out for in the early years in Calais are portents of potential trouble where as yet there is none. Any fault in the bureaucratic structure of the city's government or of the military establishment, any

defect in the system of relations with London, any tension between the
inhabitants, may unobserved be playing a vital part. There is a power struggle in England, there may be a "fee'd man" of the other side in any household, a whisper in Calais may be heard at Court, and these are dangerous
times.

The pictorial map of the town in the Cotton manuscripts gives quite a vivid
impression of its appearance and of the surrounding countryside (Pl. 5). The
drawing shows a seemingly well-fortified town, the space within the walls
forming a parallelogram about twice as long as its own width and apparently
completely filled with buildings. Actually, of course, these were intersected
by a network of streets. The market, as the plan shows (Pl. 4), though the
centre of the life of the town, with the town hall, Staple Hall, and Staple Inn
on its southern side, was situated towards the north-east, due south of the
Lantern Gate and approached directly from the north by Lantern Gate
Street, Staple Street, and Calkwell Street. The old Staple Inn is of importance to us because the house became the home of the Lisles. Next to
Lantern Gate Street, on the west was Whethill Street: the family owned a
considerable amount of property in this area. The Deputy's Council
Chamber was on the lower floor in the north-east corner of the town hall. It
was in the market-place that the daily trade in victuals was carried on, and
here the Retinue assembled before dispersing to their duties of watch and
ward.

In the picture (Pl. 6) we can identify the churches of Our Lady (left) and
St. Nicholas (right), also the town hall and the Staple Hall standing out
against the skyline. In the foreground the fine natural harbour, lined with
quays and jetties, is shown in a somewhat telescoped manner, the approach
guarded by the Castle of the Rysbank. To the right is the Watergate, beside
the Search Tower which guards the entrance to the inner harbour. In the
middle is the Lantern Gate, the principal gate of the town; to the extreme
left stands the Beauchamp Tower, flanked by the Beauchamp Bulwark. Following the circuit of the walls we would then come to four smaller towers; on
the south-east corner the Devlyn or Dublyn Tower. The two most important
towers on the south side were Pryncen Tower and the Northumberland
Tower, with the postern exit between the Dublyn Bulwark and the Pryncen
Bulwark, and the Boulogne Gate towards the south-west corner. Finally,
after the Snayle Tower, the Castle with its moat guarded the whole of the
south-westerly approach.

A mile outside the town, on the road to Boulogne, lay the well-fortified
outpost of Newenhambridge, which had its own small garrison. It controlled the sluices which regulated the flow of the Hammes river. About six
miles inland, due south of Calais, lay the castle and town of Guisnes, the
nearest outpost to the French frontier, and between Calais and Guisnes lay

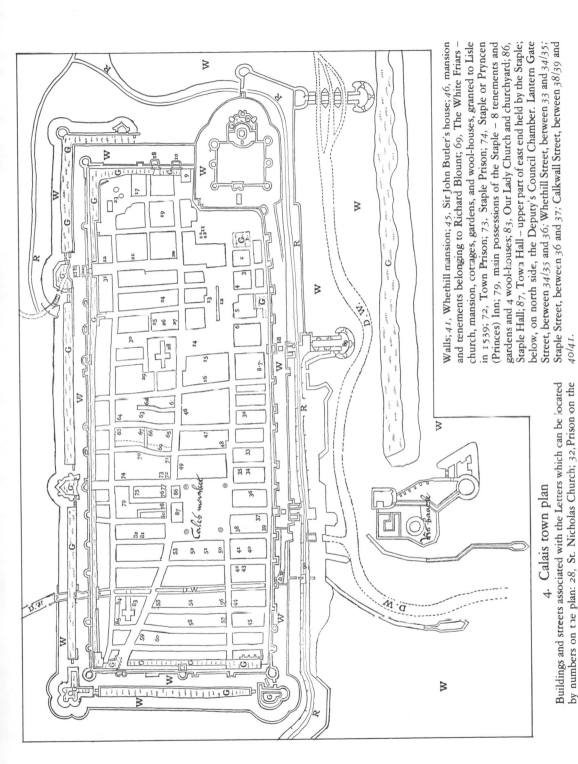

4. Calais town plan

Buildings and streets associated with the Letters which can be located by numbers on the plan: 28, St. Nicholas Church; 32, Prison on the

Walls; 41, Whethill mansion; 45, Sir John Butler's house; 46, mansion and tenements belonging to Richard Blount; 69, The White Friars – church, mansion, cottages, gardens, and wool-houses, granted to Lisle in 1539; 72, Town Prison; 73, Staple Prison; 74, Staple or Pryncen (Princes) Inn; 79, main possessions of the Staple – 8 tenements and gardens and 4 wool-houses; 83, Our Lady Church and churchyard; 86, Staple Hall; 87, Town Hall – upper part of east end held by the Staple; below, on north side, the Deputy's Council Chamber. Lantern Gate Street, between 34/35 and 36; Whethill Street, between 33 and 34/35; Staple Street, between 36 and 37; Calkwall Street, between 38/39 and 40/41.

Reproduced by permission from Viscount Dillon's 'Calais and the Pa e', *Archaeologia* Vol. LIII (1892), and taken originally from Cotton MS. Aug. I ii 71

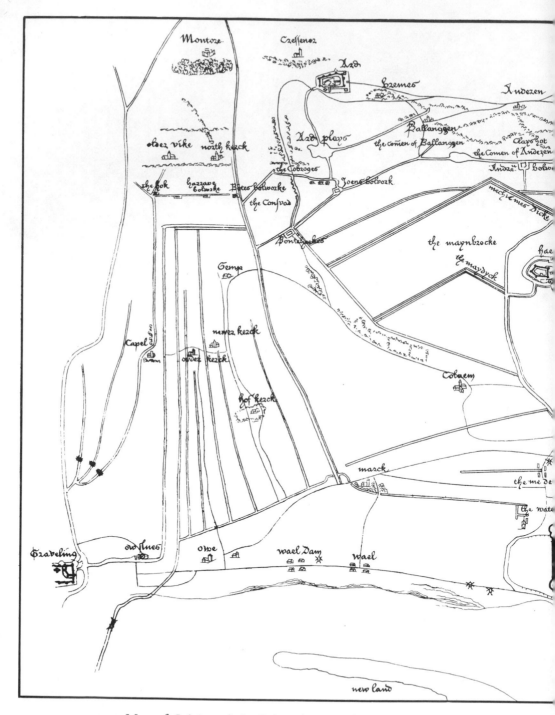

Montoze
Czessenoz
Azd
hzemes
Andezen

ober vike noith kezck
Azd plays
Ballanggen
the comen of Ballanggen
Clays zot
the Comen of Andezen
Andz   bobroc

the bok bazzazq bobwake
Bozeo bobwake
the Cobzoges
the Confzad
Joens bobwozk

mecti mes Dicke

Ponte   kee
the maynbzoche
the maydyck

hae

Gemp

newez kezck
Capel
obdez kezck
Cobaem

bof kezck

mazck
the me de

the wate

Gzabeling
ow slues
obwe
wael Dam
wael

new land

5. Map of Calais and the Pale (1/5 size of original)

Reproduced by permission from the Camden Society's *Chronicle of Calais*, edited by J. G. Nichols (1846),
and taken originally from British Museum, Cotton MS. Aug. I ii 71

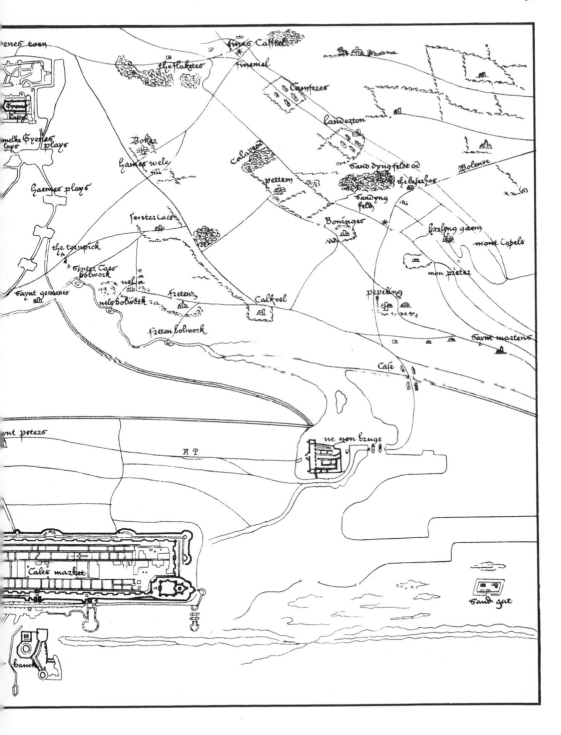

Guynes toun
the Flaketes
Fures Calfket
tinemel
Oentezes
Oenetpes
Landexton
Byenes
Calp
melke Oyenes plays
Oyenes plays
Boker
Calaues
Sand zyng feloe oꝛ
Bolenne
Hames wele
pettem
the baserhos
Guemes plays
Sandyng feld
Boninges
harlyng gaem
mont Copels
Ienfter Laes
mon pietaz
the toumpick
Ienfter Caes bolwork
nel on
pepeling
Saynt germeres
Freten
Calkuel
nelo bolwork
Freten bolwork
Savnt martens
Cale
ynt peters
ne non bruge
A P
Cales market
Sand gat
land

6. View of Calais
From Cotton MS Aug. I ii 70

the smaller castle of Hammes. To the south-east was the town and the ruinous castle of Ardres, belonging to the French, and some ten miles along the coast to the east was Gravelines, the Emperor's frontier town. Boulogne lay about twelve miles to the south-west. This was 'the Pale', the town and marches of Calais, first occupied by the English in 1347 – some hundred and twenty square miles of territory, low-lying ground to the west, higher ground to the east, where little hills and wooded valleys with tiny villages nestling half-hidden in them give us such a delightful impression of rural life in the Field of Cloth of Gold painting. The low ground to the west, between Calais and Guisnes, originally marsh-land, had been drained, cultivated, and built upon during what had been nearly two hundred years of the English occupation. The network of water-courses, dykes, and canals which had successfully converted so much of the marsh into arable or grazing was costly to maintain, but the whole elaborate system was controlled, and by the closing of the sluices the country immediately surrounding the town could be inundated in the event of an enemy attack. What it looked like, when flooded, can be clearly realized from the Field of Cloth of Gold painting.

The house first occupied by Lisle was on the southern side of the town, just inside the city walls, towards the south-east corner. From the tower they would look inland across the marches towards Hammes and Guisnes. It had been the residence of Lisle's predecessor, Lord Berners, so was presumably a house of considerable size, suited to the dignity of its official occupant, who had maintained a household of forty servingmen. Its garden or gardens, in which it was possible to rear pheasants, would probably have been enclosed by the buildings, making one or more central courtyards, judging from the lay-out of most Calais houses. The Calais gardens, in fact, were almost as much a feature of the town's life as those of sixteenth-century London.

To conclude this sketch of the Calais background something must be said about the town's inhabitants. It was no longer as predominantly English as in the fifteenth century, when the Staple, the governing body of the wool trade, had first been established there, and it had been the only channel for all English exports, with the Staplers receiving all tolls and customs and in return paying the Retinue's wages and for the upkeep of the fortifications, money for which had now to be found somehow from the Crown. With the decay of the wealth and influence of the Staplers in Henry VIII's time came the material decay of the town. Its prestige and that of its posts had decreased further since it had ceased to be the base for Henry's wars, as in the opening years of the reign. Cromwell's rapidly evolving Civil Service attracted the better educated and more ambitious at home, and though there was still great pressure to obtain posts in the Retinue for the less well qualified, the English in the town as a whole began to be outnumbered by 'strangers' from France and Flanders. Left in Calais in Lisle's time were elderly men like Sir Richard Whethill and Sir Robert Wingfield, who had inherited or acquired a considerable amount of property or spent most of their lives there, had their roots in the town and its government, and stayed on in their fine mansions with their pleasant gardens, enjoying rents from their properties and the society of Government House and of their old friends and relations in this little English colony, big fish in a small pond, who would have felt at a loss in the new England of the 1530s.

Lisle received a yearly rent of £100 from the royal manors of Marke and Oye and also £104 'for money which here is commonly called Spyall money'. His wages were 2s. a day, plus a 'reward' of 20 marks per annum. For his 'own proper retinue' he was allowed thirty-eight soldiers, plus one horseman

called a Spear and two called archers. A Spear received 18*d.* a day, the
archers 8*d.*, and the soldiers 8*d.* or 6*d.*, from which sums were deducted
'one day for the king' and the eighteenth part of their wages for victual
money. Lisle had the right also to appoint and discharge officers and men of
the garrison of about five hundred, including twenty-four Spears for whose
posts the letters teem with applicants. They were men of good family, and as
often as not had either seen service at Court or held minor Court appointments at the same time. John Russell, afterwards Earl of Bedford, had been a
Spear for a brief period early in his career.

Controlling matters other than military was the Council, which, in order of
precedence, consisted of the Deputy, the Lieutenant of Guisnes, the High
Marshal, the Lieutenant of the Castle, the (Vice-) Treasurer, the Lieutenants
of the Rysbank and Hammes, the Comptroller, the Knight Porter, the
Lieutenant of Newnhambridge, and the Under Marshal. The Lieutenants, as
often as not, are referred to as Captains; Lord Sandys, Lieutenant of Guisnes,
is generally known by the title of his highest office as 'my Lord Chamberlain'.

The very first letter in the collection, chronologically speaking, is so typical of many that follow that it seems a suitable choice to lead this chapter too.
The writer is Sergeant-at-Arms of Calais.

7   JOHN ROKEWOOD TO LORD LISLE   *16 March 1533*

My singular good Lord, In my most humble manner I recommend me
unto your good lordship, certifying you that my Lord Deputy is departed to
God, whose soul Jesu pardon; understanding that your lordship comes
hither to furnish the room of the said Lord Deputy. My lord, so it is that here
is an honest man called Robert Donyngton, one of the soldiers of the King's
retinue here, who keeps a beer brewhouse, and brews as good beer as any
man doth within Calais. And he hath served my Lord Deputy that is departed
ever since he came to Calais: beseeching your good lordship to be so good
lord unto the said Robert Donyngton that he may likewise serve you of your
beer; and the sooner because he is a soldier: beseeching your lordship, at this
my poor suit made unto you, that my friend may have your favour in this
matter. All pleasure and contentment that you shall please to desire of me
shall be at your lordship's will, as knows God, who preserve your lordship.

At Calais the xvj day of Marche xv cxxxij^ti
Signed   by yow*r* louyng ffrynd John   (Vol.1, No.1)
                        Rokewood

Brewing was one of the chief industries of Calais, and beer – half a gallon
of it for a penny – was an important item in the soldiers' rations. When, after

playing an official role in the celebrations for the coronation of Anne Boleyn, Lisle reached Calais in June, a nephew of Honor's with a post in the
Lord Chancellor's office and another under the Admiralty on the east coast
was in a good position to report on the gossip at home about his reception
there.

8   JOHN GRENVILLE TO LORD LISLE   *21 June 1533*

   Right honourable and my most especial good Lord, my duty remembered,
I commend me unto you and to my right honourable good Lady, praying to
Jesu long to continue you in honour. Pleaseth it your lordship that all your
friends in these parts be merry and all your affairs do as well as you will
desire, thanks be to Jesu. I trust you and my lady and all yours be merry, for
the report was made in the Court that there was never captain better welcome to Calais, the hearing whereof was much to the comfort of me, your
poor man. I pray your lordship if any mewed goshawk come to your hands
reward me with it, and I shall provide you like pleasure. I pray your lordship
speak to my Lord of Norfolk for my poor office in Essex, that I may continue
therein. And thus Jesu preserve your good lordship and my good lady.
   Written the xxj day of June
                Your faithful
Hol.   John Graynfyld   (Vol.1, No.9)

   As an example of the spelling of a gentleman of the period, and of a
standard frequently found in these letters, here follows that in the original of
the above:

Ryght honerabill and my moste especiall good Lord My dewty remembred I
commend me vn to yow And to my Ryght honerabill good Lady praying to
Jhesu longe to contenew yow in honor · plesitht hit yowre lordschypp that
all your fryndis In thes partis be mery and all yowr afferes doo as well as yow
woll dessyre · thanke be to Jhesu · I trest yow And my lady and all your be
mery for the Reporte wasse mad in the curt that theyr wase neuer captyn
better welcome to calys · the hyryng where off wasse myche to the confort
of me your pour mane I pray your lordschyp yf any Mued gosshocke come to
your handis reward me w*ith* hit and I schall provid yow lycke plessur I pray
your lordschyp specke to my lord of Norfoloke for my poure ofys In essexe
that y maye contynw theyr yn and this Jhesu pre*ser*ve your good lordschyp
and my good lady wryttyn the xxj daye of June
                Your faytfull
                John Graynfyld

Requests for jobs in Calais continue to pour in, and the following from one of Lady Lisle's estates in England provides as good grounds as many.

9   THOMAS GILBERT TO LADY LISLE   8 August 1533

My honourable and worshipful good lady, In most heartiest manner I commend me to your good ladyship, thanking you of your great and benevolent goodness. . . .

. . . I shall entirely desire your good ladyship, of your special goodness, to be good lady and gracious lady to William Rose, the bearer hereof, where that as the whole parish will testify of his behaviour and of his goodness: Good madam, the cause of his departing from us is that his wife will not suffer him in ease no manner of way, where that he came to my master with weeping tears for because she is so unreasonable a woman. She is more liker a woman of Bedlam than liker any other woman, where that he desireth your good ladyship of your benign goodness to be good unto him, as your ladyship hath in times past:

Good lady, remember me of something, that I may pray for you dai [ly;] and so ∧I do∧, nevertheless, for my good lord, and you, good lady, and all yours. You be in my memento, and ever shall be, as knoweth God, who ever preserve you to his mercy.

Wryton att Bysshoppswaltha*m* the viij^th daye off august
          By yo*ur* obedyant & dayly orato*r*
Hol.   Thom*a*s gylbert Curat ther   (Vol.1, No.25)

The state of affairs in Calais when Lisle was sworn in on 10 June was chaotic. His predecessor had complained to London in February of fallen walls and 'ruin and decay', and the victualling of the troops and authorization of appointments were in complete confusion. It should be noted that in writing to the King on 21 June Lisle draws attention to the fact that 'all matters concerning this town be resumed into your Highness' hands and the Council'. He cannot act without their approval from England.

10   LORD LISLE AND THE COUNCIL OF   21 June 1533
       CALAIS TO HENRY VIII

Pleaseth it your Grace / to be advertised / that on Wednesday last past / one William Marche and Robert Donyngton / soldiers / of your Retinue here / also being farmers / of the soldiers' garner / did put up a bill / unto me your Highness' Deputy and Council here / which bill your Grace / shall receive / joined to these / also the copy of their indenture / with the copy of a commission / which was granted / unto the said farmers / by the Lord Berners / whose soul God pardon then being your Deputy here / with others of your Council / to the intent that your Highness may cause / your Council / to look upon the said writings / also to consider / how the case stands / so that quick remedy / may be found / for as appeareth / in the before-mentioned bill / the before-named William Marche / and Robert Donyngton be utterly determined / to leave it / after such form / as is expressed / in the said bill / And because that all matters / concerning this town be resumed / into your Highness' hands and Council we (though there be many things / which were most needful / to be quickly reformed) / dare not meddle / with them / and rather because / that by a long season / we have looked / and hoped / to have had knowledge / of your high pleasure / in all such things / as were contained / in a book of Articles / first sent by Mr. Cromwell / to the Lord Berners / then being your Grace's Deputy / and the Council here / And after / that the same / was somewhat reformed / by your said Deputy / and Council / they sent it again / unto the said Master Cromwell and so remaineth / Wherefore in most humble wise / we beseech your Highness / that we may know your Grace's pleasure in the premises / with as goodly haste as may be / for surely the necessities / which be now / in this town / for lack of convenient liberties which this town / hath always enjoyed / until your Grace's restraint / be so many and great / that they require quick remedy / as our Lord knoweth / whom we beseech / to preserve your most gracious Highness / in prosperous health / with long and most joyful life / to his pleasure

Written at Calais the xxj^ti day of June 1533
>By your most humble servants
Signed   Arthur Lyssle
                Edmund Howard
                Wyngffeld R Sir
                Edward Ryngley
                Crystofer Garneys *Sir*   (Vol. 1, No. 37)

It was not, as these first months make only too clear, ability to see what was necessary, to send prompt warnings, requests, notifications, and to prod both King and minister by the word in season that was lacking. It becomes more and more obvious, as the months and years go by, that Cromwell left many urgent letters unanswered, and guarded himself at times either by ambiguity or generalization, so that he could, if necessary, protest that he had been misinterpreted. When convenient he could also, in his letters, ignore the fact that he had already been sent information and rebuke Lisle and the Council for not sending it, or give orders for measures which had already been taken.

This is not to say that he was wrong to give Calais affairs a low priority when he was engaged in reconstructing the whole English political system. In the circumstances, Calais, to a certain extent, could and did look after itself and muddle along as usual; and until the confiscated wealth of the monasteries began to flow in, there was not enough money available for repairs.

11   LORD LISLE TO CROMWELL   *12 August 1533*

Right honourable Sir, in my heartiest manner I commend me unto you, signifying you that this present day John Fletcher of ∧Rye∧ arrived here, which came from thence with a hoy laden with wood; and by the way they saw xj sail of great ships of iij tops and ij tops ∧every∧ ship, which ships ∧be∧ fully furnished with men; and from one of the said ships came a boat aboard ∧to∧ the said hoy, which seeing, the said Fletcher, when the boat came towards them, he went under hatches, as he confesseth with his own mouth. And the said men of war asked the hoy men of whence they were, which said that they were of Dunkirk: to whom the foresaid men of war answered and said, 'Thou art of Calais, and carriest this wood thither'. Then answered the hoy men, 'Of whence soever we be, we have war with no man'. To whom then answered the said men of war, 'We have war with none but with the Hollanders and Englishmen', as the said Fletcher and hoy men testifieth. And more, they say that there be xvij sail. I have also tidings that the Hollanders armeth out xxx sail of great ships against the Lubeck[er]s. Further, Antony Morys, pursuivant of the Staple, which came this day from Bruges, saith that there cometh a ₵ men of war to Gravelines: to what ∧intent∧, as hitherto, is unknown.

And as I was writing of this present, there came iiij sail of French ships into the haven of Calais to take succour, which saith that the foresaid ships hath robbed an Englishman in the Downs. Other news I have not at this present to advertise you of, as knoweth God, which preserve you and send you as well to fare as I would myself.

From Calais, the xij^th day of August, A°. 1533.   (Vol. 1, No. 40)

12   LORD LISLE AND THE COUNCIL OF   *?July or August 1533*
        CALAIS TO CROMWELL

After our most hearty recommendations, forasmuch as we have always seen and known the good mind and zeal ∧that you∧ accustomably have borne towards this the King's town and us his Grace's servants here, we thought it expedient to advertise you what poverty and penury the same is in, assuring you never so poor since it was first English, for the King's servants here were never so bare ne needy; insomuch those same amongst themselves consulting, have determined and concluded to send over unto you the bearers hereof, presuming verily ∧and∧ having full hope and confidence by your good mediation and assistance (∧as∧ in whom their whole trust lieth) to be relieved thereof or at the least somedeal eased. And they, thinking verily that at this our poor instance and request unto you made in their behalf to speed something the better, have with one voice desired us to write unto ∧you∧ this present, . . . as Christ knoweth, who send you long life in health, to your most gentle heart's aggradation.

    From Calais etc.   (Vol. 1, No. 43)

While appointments to places, or 'rooms', in the Retinue were officially in Lisle's hands, they were often promised or sold by retiring incumbents, a practice so long established that it was proving impossible to put a stop to it. Lisle had asked for Russell's intervention with the King in the matter.

13   Sɪʀ Jᴏʜɴ Rᴜssᴇʟʟ ᴛᴏ Lᴏʀᴅ Lɪsʟᴇ   *29 August 1533*

    Right honourable and my singular good Lord, in my heartiest manner I recommend me unto your good lordship, certifying you I have received your letter and also a goshawk by your servant, whereof I most heartily thank your lordship, assuring you have done me a great pleasure therein. . . .

    And where you write unto me that George Browne intendeth to sell his room to Pole, as Mr. Hall sheweth me that since his coming over he is informed that it is past and gone to another man, so that Pole shall never have it; in this thing I am and have been always against, as much as any man, for by reason thereof the King shall never be well served nor the town well furnished; for such shall buy it for money that shall not be able to serve the King when they have it, nor none for them. Wherefore if there be not remedy the shortlier, I think it will be part of the decay of the town. . . .

    My lord, I am sorry that I am not at the Court, whereby I might do you some . . . service, which you shall be assured of during my life. . . . As knoweth Our Lord, who preserve your lordship and send you good, honourable and long life.

    From Mylton, the xxix^ti day of August.

Signed   Your owen to com*m*ande

        J. Russell   (Vol. 1, No. 44)

14   Cʀᴏᴍᴡᴇʟʟ ᴛᴏ Lᴏʀᴅ Lɪsʟᴇ   *1 September 1533*

    After my right hearty recommendations unto your good lordship; This shall be to advertise the same that I have received your letters wherein ye and the Mayor of Calais do desire to have new provisions concerning the restraining of corn otherwise than hath been used in times past. I ensure your lordship the King's Highness is not a little displeased with that your desire, but supposeth your business to be very small that will in any wise importune his Highness with any such matters, Saying that before this time the Town and marches of Calais hath been well maintained, and prospered without any such new devices. And I assure your lordship, as your friend to my power, that I have great marvel that ye will so soon incline to every man his device and [counsel and . . .][1] specially in matters of small impor[tance . . .   ] yea, and as [it is] reported [unto me   ] [. . .]causes as meseemeth th[at . . .   ] nothing to [. . .] ne gentlewomen. For although my lady be right honourable and wise, yet in such causes as 'longeth to your authority her advice and discretion can little prevail; wherefore I pray your lordship to consider the same, and to importune the King's Highness with none other matters than that of necessity ye ought to do. And thus the blessed Trinity preserve you,

  At London, the first day of September.
Signed   Your lordshyppes assuryd
                       Thom*a*s Crumwell   (Vol.1, No.46)

  Personal criticism apart, it was a dusty answer to the three-fold woes of Calais, as set forth up to this point – the decay of the fortifications, the unsatisfactory arrangements for victualling, and the buying and selling of rooms.

15   JOHN GRENVILLE TO LORD LISLE   *16 October 1533*

  Right honourable and my most singular good lord, my duty remembered as your own faithful servant and bedeman, . . .

  Pleaseth it your lordship to be ascertained that the Parliament is prorogued till the xvth day of January next coming. Also in most humble wise I beseech your goodness to be shewed to me that where one John Highfield, spear of Calais, lieth in jeopardy of death, and a very old man as report is made here; if it fortune the said Highfield to die, that it may please your lordship to stop a passage and that I may there of your goodness be ascertained by your letters of his death before any man by post. The pains of the bringer and your goodness shall be highly deserved, for I am very desirous to have a friend of mine to obtain a room of a spear of Calais: which I doubt not, if I may have knowledge that a room is void, but that I shall obtain it. If my said friend may obtain any of the said rooms I promise your lordship by this my letter that your lordship shall have xx marks for your pain, and my honourable good lady your wife a kirtle of velvet or the value therof. And

  1. MS. torn in two places, lines 14–17, with traces of letters.

thus Jesu preserve your lordship and my singular good lady always to continue in honour.

> Written at London the xvjth day of October,
> > Your most humble and faithful to his power,
> > > John Graynfeld   (Vol. 1, No. 60)

That the sum Grenville offers for this favour is the same as the 'reward' Lisle received annually as a bonus on his year's salary is a vivid reminder of the code which took the *quid pro quo* for granted in all ranks of society.

Brusset was Captain of the Emperor's town of Gravelines, near the edge of the Calais Pale.

16   ANTHOINE BRUSSET TO LORD LISLE   *19 November 1533*

My Lord, As humbly as I can I recommend me unto your good noble favour. My lord, I beseech you in the cause of justice, and as reason would, that it would please you to command your bailly, your sergeants and officers of justice of your town of Calais to take and apprehend the person of a Spaniard, one that calls himself Ylayre or St. Ylayre, that has the nose on his face very red and thick with little pimples like a leper. The aforesaid is the companion and accomplice of another Spaniard called Espinosse, which two are homicides. They have villainously and traitorously slain my lieutenant of the marches of this town. And incontinent upon that they shall be in the hands of justice, I beg of you that I may be advertised thereof, when I will send you the evidence to inform the judge, to the end that his head may be cut off according to his demerits; and in so doing ye shall do me a singular pleasure, the which I shall requite you in like case; and to conclude, praying God, my lord, that he will give you health, and good life and long.

> From Gravelines, this 19th day of November, 1533.
> > Entirely your good neighbor and friend,

Hol.   Anthoine Brusset[2]   (Vol. 1, No. 76)

Though Lisle constantly complained to Cromwell that he could get no replies from him to letters asking for authority with regard to works or the victualling of the town, in October the latter wrote him a stern rebuke for his neglect of these matters, quoting the displeasure of the King and Council. Lisle's response is an admirable example of his best official manner.

17   LORD LISLE TO CROMWELL   *c.7 October 1533*

After my right hearty recommendations, pleaseth it you to be advertised that this day I received your letter of this instant month, dated the iiij[th]

2. French.

day. . . . You may be sure that if the King's Highness hath been so informed, the truth is otherwise; for it shall be surely found that such mandates as I by the advice of the King's Council here have made out do not extend but only to bring victual into this town, which ordinance, as I esteem, was both goodly and necessary, considering the common bruit that goeth in these parts. For though the King's Highness and his Council hath the perfection of knowledge, yet I, having the charge of this town under his Grace, and having no manner of knowledge but such as is bruited abroad, I trust it cannot be thought but I and the King's Council here hath done as becometh us to do, in consulting and commanding that such victual as may goodly be had within the King's pales here to be brought into this town successively as it may conveniently be brought, considering that and any sudden chance should happen it were much more meet that the said victual should serve this, the King's town, which hath been long in great necessity for lack of victual out of England, than I and the King's Council here should negligently leave it in prey for the King's enemies.

And where, in the said article, you like my special good friend *do advertise me* in most familiar manner concerning *the vigilant eye and await* which you will me to have to see *the sure defence and fortification of this the King's town and marches here,* and *that I should do nothing to the enbolding of the King's enemies, or putting in fear the King's subjects, more than needeth* – as to that part of your said article, I trust I have used such vigilance and await for the sure defence of this the King's town as hath been possible for me to do, having no more knowledge from the King's Highness than I have had, though I have written many times unto you in divers causes which I and the Council here count both great and urgent, of which, as yet, we have had no manner of answer.

And furthermore, as to the perfecting of the premises, I and the King's Council here do think that, among many necessaries, nothing may be more necessary than victuals. For, blessed be our Lord, if this town were in necessity and peril of enemies, if it shall please the King to cause it to be provided of men and victual, it needeth not to fear the Great Turk, and he were as nigh neighbour as France or Flanders is. Howbeit, where you writ in the latter end of your said article that *undoubtedly it is thought to the King's Highness and his Council that my practices and doings be very ill and not circumspectly considered,* yet I trust that when the King's Highness shall be advertised of the very truth those notes shall be clearly wiped out, or else I would be very sorry. As he which alway to his power shall eschew to do anything that may be to his high displeasure.[3]

(Vol. 1, No. 91b)

---

3. Fair copy in Husee's hand at its neatest and most formal; not signed.

Further requests to Cromwell for a free hand with the victualling proving fruitless, and with fears of war growing through the autumn, Lisle finally wrote to him that unless existing restraints are lifted and 'this town may be victualled in general from all parts of the realm as we have been in time past, that we shall be at an extreme point and in manner undone, if it should chance us to be put to any brunt or affront which we daily look for: praying you most instantly that remedy with speed may be had in the premises, or else we must be fain to write to the King's grace for remedy of the same.'[4] This at last produced the requisite authorization. Meanwhile, part of Lisle's business being the provision of intelligence, he sent Cromwell packets of 'such news as were brought to me this day by mine ordinary spies,' and a copy of the papal decree excommunicating the King being circulated in France. But now relations were not too secure with the Emperor either, and the border with Flanders was perilously near to Calais.

18   THE DUKE OF NORFOLK   *16 December 1533*
      TO LORD LISLE

My very good Lord, with hearty recommendations these shall be to advertise the same that after I had declared unto the King's Highness such matters of credence as ye sent by the herald Ryscbank, which his Grace heard at good length, his Highness commanded me to write unto you that his pleasure was ye should have a vigilant Eye and respect to the fashion of the Emperor's subjects in the Low Countries, and to signify unto his Grace from time to time as ye shall perceive good matter or cause why.
    Thus our Lord have you in his most assured tuition.
    From Hampton Court the xvj day of December
                Your owne asseuredly
Signed   T. Norfolk   (Vol.1, No.100)

19   JOHN ROKEWOOD TO LORD LISLE   *3 June 1534*

My singular good lord, In my most heartly manner I recommend me unto your good lordship and to my singular good lady your wife; advertising your lordship that the day of the date hereof I took my leave of the King, whose Highness commanded me to make his commendations unto your lordship and to my lady. Further, to shew you that his pleasure is, you should, if any Contagious or dangerous Sickness were within the town of Calais, that you should cause them so diseased to be avoided out of the town; so that as much

4. Vol.1, No.92.

as you may you shall save the town from dangerous Sickness; and that you
should cause the town and all the streets and other places thereabouts to be
kept as clean as may be, to the intent that the town in anywise may be kept
clean and sweet. For His Grace, God willing, intendeth to be there within a
short space after this date to meet with the French King. So his Grace
commanded me to show your lordship; and that he would not yet have it so
reported on that side the seas. Also that your lordship should see the town
very well victualled against that time. My lord, I have such business here for
iiij or five days that I cannot well come over; wherefore I send this bearer
unto your lordship with these my letters to certify you of the King's pleasure
with speed, as his Grace commanded me. As our Lord knoweth, who keep
you, with long life and much honour.

    From London, this iij^d day of June
             By your assured
Signed   John Rokewood   (Vol.2, No.206)

Sir Edward Ryngeley was marshal of Calais.

20   SIR EDWARD RYNGELEY TO LORD LISLE   *11 June 1534*

    My lord, In my most humble manner I recommend me unto you, certify-
ing you that the King's Grace and the Queen['s] Grace be in good health,
thanks be unto Almighty God. Sir, I came to the Court on Tuesday last
about iij of the clock. I was not there half an hour but his Grace sent for me
into a garden which his Grace hath new made, and when I came I did your
recommendations to his Grace, which asked me heartily how you did; and
the first thing that he asked me was whether the town were clean without
sickness, and whether that it were clean kept: which I told him was clean
without sickness, and also clean kept; wherewith his Grace was very well
contented. Wherefore, sir, if you would speak to Mr. Mayor for the mending
of the ij gutters that goeth from the Market to Our Lady Church, I think he
should do a marvellous good deed to mend them. And if he lack paviours let
him send me word, and I shall send them to him from London, as many as he
will have; for the King is very well contented that his works go so well
forward, and I have declared unto him, Master Treasurer being by, how
much is done more in thickness than did appear by his book, as well in two
towers as in the wall; the which the King's Grace doth accept very well, and
could tell me himself what pains you have taken in the oversight of them,
and what pains you have likewise taken for the sandhills, wherein he is as
well contented as with anything that was done there this many years, and
rejoiceth much in his Retinue that hath taken pains therein, which I think

they shall well perceive when that his Grace cometh thither. Sir, my poor 'vice shall be unto your lordship that the drags and plows shall go still upon the sandhills till such a time that you may shoot level over them from the mount at Beauchamp Tower. . . .

From Hampton Court, the xi^th day of June.

By your assured to his little power

Signed   Edward Ryngeley

My Lord, I pray you be contented with my meaning, for my inditing is but reasonable.   (Vol.2, No.212)

21   JOHN HUSEE TO LORD LISLE   *15 July 1534*

Humbly advertising your Lordship that incontinent upon my hither coming I presented Mr. Cromwell with your baken crane and with the sturgeon, which was thankfully received on his behalf; further saying that for your lordship's affairs he should that afternoon take some pain, as he did indeed, as your lordship shall perceive plainly by Mr. Windsor's and Smyth's letters, which this bearer hath; and by utter appearance he shewed that time to be your lordship's faithful friend, trusting in God that you shall so find him; but the matter is yet deferred until the next term, but I cannot perceive but that finally your lordship must depart with possession, and for to abide their arbitrament they will have new obligations. I have attended till this day upon Mr. Cromwell for the answer of your letter touching the new works, and he hath promised me verily to be despatched, but nothing can I get, trusting tomorrow to have it, for so he hath faithfully promised me; which if he so do shall be sent to your lordship with diligent speed. . . .

Your lordship will not believe the importunate suit that Mr. Cromwell daily hath, which continually increaseth. . . .

. . . If your lordship write anything to me against my coming from Soberton, let it be left with the good man of the Red Lion in Southwark, for my father is seldom within, and then men know not where to deliver your letters, as God knoweth, who preserve your lordship in long life with health and honour increasing, to your most noble heart's desire.

From London in haste the xv of July,

Your lordship's most bounden during life,

Hol.   John Husee the younger   (Vol.2, No.229)

Husee's extreme discretion in his next letter is typical of his and all Lisle's other correspondents at this time on all matters involving the King: they will tell him what is behind the news when they meet.

My humble duty premised, this is to certify your lordship that I have been in Hampshire and reckoned with Nicholas Person according unto your lordship's commandment, which reckoning your Lordship shall be perfect in at my coming to Calais, which had been ere this time but Mr. Cromwell hath commanded me the contrary, ∧and∧ till such time as he hath further commoned with me, or given me answer in writing, that I in no wise depart. And I think hourly to be despatched, doubting nothing but my tarrying shall be to your lordship's contentation. And as this day, Mr. Cromwell commanded me to write you that the King's Highness is now determined to tarry, and will not over this year; and it hath been much the rather stayed at his labour and motion, by reason of certain considerations, ∧as∧ partly your lordship shall understand at my coming, which I now will not declare by writing. And touching the ending or achievement of the works, I think there shall be no great haste made in the performance of the same till after March, further than that which is now requisite and must needs be done. . . .

From London, the xxix^th of July,
          Your lordship's most bounden during life,
Hol.   John Husee the younger   (Vol.2, No.240)

Lisle is almost constantly at loggerheads with the whole Whethill family in Calais. The current dispute is over a son of the house bringing pressure to bear for a post in the Retinue.

23   JOHN HUSEE TO LORD LISLE   *20 September 1534*

Pleaseth it your lordship, . . .

Also, notwithstanding the importunate suit of young Whethill I doubt not but your lordship shall have the most part of your desire. Howbeit, Whethill hath great friends. . . . But Mr. Norris and Mr. Bryan both willed me to write you that yet all times you should obtemper[5] the King's letters; to whom I answered ∧that∧ no man living would gladlier fulfil his gracious desire than your lordship. Further, Mr. Secretary marvelled that your lordship should write to Mr. Norris that in case Whethill had the room your lordship would rather give up your room and wait upon the King in England ∧than abide∧; and he said in case the King had seen that letter it would not a' pleased his Grace. I perceive a man had need take heed what he write, but truly both Mr. Norris and Mr. Bryan are your lordship's unfeigned friends, wherefore they are both to be highly thanked and to be remembered.

5. i.e. obey.

. . . Also Mr. Bryan willed me to write further to your lordship that you must keep all things secreter than you have used, and saith that there is nothing done nor spoken but it is with speed knowen in the Court. And further he willeth your lordship to take more upon you and to be knowen for the King's Deputy there, and not to use company of mean personages, nor to be conversant ∧with∧ some persons which he saith useth daily company with your lordship sounding highly against your honour. I trust your lordship will take no displeasure with me because I write so plainly, as I was desired, but I take God to record, I would your lordship as much good as my own heart. And at my coming I know well Mr. Bryan will advertise you largely of that, with all others.

Also I showed Mr. Secretary that you would send him a mewed hawk that should be special good, and he thanked your lordship for that, with all others. Further he would fain have a little spaniel, and I perceive by Palmer the spear he hath told him of my lady's spaniel, which I know well her ladyship would in no wise depart withal. If your lordship may get any proper one I would you did send it him while I were here, but I perceive Palmer intendeth to have the thanks. Thus our Lord preserve your lordship in long life, with health, to your most noble heart's desire.

From London, the xx^ti day of September anno 1534,

   Your lordship's most bounden during life,

Hol.   Jn° Husse   (Vol.2, No.260)

24 JOHN HUSEE TO LORD LISLE   *23 September 1534*

My duty humbly premised, this shall be advertising your lordship that with Corbet I wrote you what till that time was requisite. And this is certifying the same that I received of Mr. Vice-Treasurer a letter which your lordship sent to Mr. Cromwell, and incontinent upon the receipt of the same I went immediately unto Mr. Secretary, who is now Master of the Rolls, and delivered it unto his own hand, who incontinent after he had read it asked me for a commission that your lordship wrote you had sent therewith, and I answered that I received it of Mr. Vice-Treasurer and that he delivered me no such commission; but and if any such there were sent that the said Vice-Treasurer had it; and so I departed from him, who then lay at Canonbury. And the next day following, which was St. Matthew's Day, I attended upon him, desiring to know his pleasure; and coming from my Lord Chancellor's, where he then dined, he called me to him and said, 'My Lord hath sent a letter and would have a redress, and hath not sent the commission'. To whom I answered and said that I thought Mr. Vice-Treasurer had it, and he said he knew right well that he had it not, and commanded me to write your lordship with all speed to send the said commission, so that it shall be necessary your lordship convey the same hither with all speed and celerity. And then I moved him for my despatch in the rest of your affairs, who said after that he had perused both yours and Mr. Whethill's I should know the King's pleasure therein, commanding me to wait upon him on Thursday next to the Court, which is then at Grafton.

I further moved him how unjustly my Lord Chamberlain had complained on your lordship, who then said that you should not care therefor, for no man should do you wrong. Then he reasoned further with me of your letter sent unto Mr. Norris, and said if the King had seen it he would have taken your offers, which was that your lordship had liever render to the King your patent than that Whethill should enjoy that room against your will by the way of conquest; and that, his Highness being good and gracious Lord unto you, you would rather attend upon his Grace to wait and serve him here in England, than to be there so handled. And I shewed him how ungoodly Sir Richard Whethill handled you in your own garden, and then he said, if your lordship had shewed yourself as the King's Deputy you should have set the father and the son in prison and have punished them according unto their desert; and in so doing, bearing yourself with the right, he feared nothing but the King's Highness and he, with the Council here, would have maintained you therein. Further, he saith, your lordship is led there by some which although you take them for your friends are but feigned, and they do nothing but lead you to have you in some snare and then let all the burden rest in your neck; and some of those he named, which I now overpass till my thither coming.

And he and I being thus in communication he met coming against him Turney, and said further to me in my ear, 'Yonder cometh a man whom my lord hath put out of wages, wherein he hath not done well.' And I answered that as far as I knew it was not so, but that your lordship with the Council there sent him to my lord of Canterbury to be examined. Then he said, 'Well, I would you advised my lord to meddle in no such like matters, for what is passed, by books or otherwise, by the King's privilege, must be common, and it is lawful for every man to occupy them; and that all such books are set out for the furtherance of the King's matters in derogation of the Pope and his laws.' Notwithstanding, the said Turney is commanded to speak with my Lord of Canterbury ere he depart. Wherefore, after my poor advice, it shall please your lordship to admit him again, but in case he hath offended the ordinance, the punishment is remitted to your lordship and the Council there.

He further touched me for the wheat that you wrote for, and said if your lordship did accustom to impeach the King and his Council here with such slender causes you would make all your friends weary for you. And something he moved touching my lady, to whom I answered as my poor wit did serve me. But it hath been here said, as it hath been showed me, that the most part of those of Calais which cometh hither should report that if any man had aught there ado that he should shew unto my lady and that he should speed. This, with much more, hath been told me by them that are nigh about Mr. Secretary. It is to be doubted that much of this clamour hath been raised by means of the discharging of Turney and the banishment of Wolfe, for divers hath told me that my lady is very superstitious and that she with Mr. Marshal and Mr. Porter, as it hath been here reported, should be chief causers of the same. And in my lady's behalf I answered as it becomed me to do, let the rest shift for themself. But thus my lady hath for her goodness and entreating for offenders; but I can in no wise know the parties' names particularly, but I have a shrewd judgement. But one thing your lordship is assured of, that Mr. Secretary is your friend to the uttermost of his power, and I ensure your lordship for that I have found in him for your affairs he shall have my heart while I live.

I require your lordship to keep what I writ unto you secret, as ever you will have my poor service; for now by the means of some I have had the sight of Sir Richard Whethill's libel,[6] wherein he first complaineth of Thomas Fowler for the coney clap, and on his brother, and further of him again, and of the Marshal for the admittance of Gillam Brawderer, and after for bearing of the man the Knight Porter smit in the gate. And in all the premises he taketh unkindness and ingratitude against your lordship forbearing. Then cometh he in with the copy of his patent, but all this is iij sheets of paper, and after he complaineth of your lordship for giving the room from his son and for stopping of his passage, and for ungodly words you should give him; and he openeth in the same much of such words as passed betwixt your lordship and him on St. Thomas's Day, but not all wholly but it is ill enough. Then cometh he in with such words as he spake to your lordship in your garden, but he changeth them to another hue.

Also this day by chance I met with Clywtton, my Lord Chamberlain's steward, whom I debated the matter withal, marvelling that my lord his master should complain against your lordship without any cause or good ground; who answered that it was not only by Waterton's report, but also that one of the crediblest persons of Calais had written to my lord his master thereof, and that credible letter should be at all times his discharge; so that I perceive your lordship hath privy dissimuled friends and familiar enemies. I doubt not but they shall be knowen, for Clutton saith, when time shall require, his master will not be afeared to show the letter. And I said plainly that whatsoever and whosoever was written or did write falsely belied your lordship. And then he said, if it were so proved he would thereof be right

6. Libell, small book.

glad. And now that I have opened unto your lordship the circumstance of what I was commanded and what I do know, I trust your lordship will in the premises take pain to be your own secretary, for so it doth behove you to do, and else you may be deceived. And what you write or send, let it be left in my absence with the wife of the Red Lion in Southwark, for I know not how long I shall remain at the Court.

I would God there might be some pretty dog found for Mr. Secretary, for it would be highly esteemed, as God knoweth, who preserve your lordship with my lady to your most noble heart's desire.

From London, the xxiijrd of September,

Your lordship's most bounden during life,

Hol.   John Husee the younger   (Vol.2, No.260a)

The 'Turney' mentioned above was Henry Tourney, a member of the Retinue, and Wolfe was Wolfe Alarde, banished from Calais. In both instances the main gravamen of the charges appears to have been the 'publishing' of 'heretical' books – that is, reading, speaking of them, and circulating them – and in both cases the defence was that the books in question had now been allowed by the King and were therefore privileged. In view of the effectiveness of the intervention made on behalf of Henry Tourney it is difficult to see why no similar action was taken on Wolfe Alarde's behalf, unless, indeed, the simple answer is that he was not an Englishman, had no influential friends, and did not address his appeal direct to Cromwell and Cranmer. Whatever the reason, Tourney was reinstated, and Wolfe Alarde just disappears.

25   SIR FRANCIS BRYAN TO LORD LISLE   *1 October 1534*

My Lord, I heartily commend me unto you. And where it is so as I do understand ye do doubt that Wynnebank should not enjoy the office which that Whettyll doth make suit for, I do advertise you that you have such friends here in the Court that I think his labour shall little prevail him, and that the said Wynnebank shall obtain by force of your gift. Wherefore I would advise you to take no fantasy in this matter, but be merry. And of ij things I would be glad to move you of: first is, that you consider in what office the King's Grace hath deputed and set you in, that you do shew yourself to be the King's officer and be not afraid of no man in doing right and justice: The second is, as I am informed, you are no good husband in keeping of your house, which is a great undoing of many men; therefore I would advise you to look upon it, and to consider that in taking good heed you may do yourself pleasure and your friends also. I trust you will think none unkindness in me in writing after this manner unto you. I promise you, amity bindeth me to do it. I desire you to have me heartily commended to my good lady your wife, and also Sir John Russell hath him heartily commended unto you. Thus the Holy Trinity preserve you and yours.

From Grafton the first day of October,

Signed   Yours assuryd to my pow*er*,

ffranssys Bryan   (Vol.2, No.263a)

---

26   JOHN HUSEE TO LORD LISLE   *18 October 1534*

Pleaseth it your Lordship to be advertised that since my letter sent with the King's letter I have not heard from your lordship; and notwithstanding that I had thought long ere this time to have been with your lordship, yet as soon as I heard of Sir Richard Whethill's coming I made a stay, as not knowing the pretence of same, which not undoubted was nothing, as far as in him lay, for your honour and profit. But thanked be God, a shrewd cow hath found short horns,[7] yea the very stumps, as your lordship shall more largely know at my coming, which shall be within this iij days at the farthest. . . .

There hath been here a little murmur of the gift of Turney's room. I hope well your lordship hath fulfilled Mr. Secretary's request according to the King's pleasure in that behalf, or else undoubtedly you shall conceive high displeasure and lose some of your best friends. As God knoweth, who preserve your lordship with my lady in long life and health to your most noble hearts' desire.

From London, the xviij[th] day of October 1534.

Your lordship's most bounden during life,

Hol.   John Husee   (Vol.2, No.269)

Lisle had been asking at intervals for nearly a year for authority to return to its former state of flooded marshland an area within the Pale essential to its defence, now held and built upon by an important local family.

---

27   THOMAS CROMWELL TO LORD LISLE   *29 October 1534*

In my right hearty manner I commend me unto your good lordship. And whereas of late the King's Highness hath directed his commission unto your lordship and other for pulling down and reformation of certain anoysaunces made and done by Sir Robert Wingfield within the Marches of Calais: the

---

7. Proverbial; 'shrewd' is used as in 'shrewish', bad tempered. Cf. 'God sendeth a shrewd cow a short horn', Chaucer, *Eight Goodly Questions;* 'God sends a curst cow short horns, but to a cow too curst he sends none', Shakespeare, *Much Ado,* II.i.24.

King's pleasure is that ye and the other Commissioners shall circumspectly view and oversee the same: and that that of necessity ought to be reformed for the wealth, strength, and commodity of the said Town and marches according as it was thought at my last being there to be amending, and the residue that [ne] damageth ne hurteth the same town to stand still, as ye see reasonable cause after your discretion, and as ye shall seem good. And thus the Blessed Trinity preserve your lordship,

At London the xxix day of October

Signed   your lordshippis assuryd freend

Thomas Crumwell   (Vol.2, No.274)

More trouble was brewing. Richard Hunt, another member of the Retinue, had been dismissed. Every man in Calais now knew it was always possible to defy the authority of the Deputy and Council by appealing to Cromwell, and this Hunt promptly did. Cromwell sent him lack to Lisle with a letter which has disappeared, as has Lisle's reply of which the following is the draft.

28   LORD LISLE TO CROMWELL   *18 November 1534*

After my right hearty recommendations, these shall be advertising you that this xviij day I received your letter of the last of October which was opened ere it came unto my hands. And where you write that Richard Hunt alledgeth him to be an old servant of the King's and that it is a strange case that he which hath of long continuance served his Grace should in his old days be put from his room or living for any light cause, what service he hath done is notorious. And first, he hath so well behaved himself there is none here can afford him one good [word], and his here abode hath been to the great losses of divers, and to the destruction of some others. And [a] few years past he caused ij men [to] come out of England hither and here to forswear themselves in his behalf, willingly, as it is here well known to all the inhabitants of this town. And they both, like perjured persons, wore papers and stood openly upon the scaffold and were then banished this town and marches, and so should he then have been ordered, had it not been by Mr. Compton's letters stayed. And now since that time, these few days past, he willingly forswore himself before the Under Marshal for the value of x^s, although he was the same time 'monished by [a] witness, standing then by him, which deposed to the contrary that he should not so do, as it doth appear by the depositions against him deposed. And then, being not content, but desired to have the spiritual law deposed; and when the Commissary did give him xx days respite to bring in his proofs, he stole away making no answer, without my licence, wherein he offended the ordinaries and was also falsely forsworn. So that I now remit it to your judgement, whether such a person be meet here to have wages and inhabitation or no; for surely, if he had not this last time stolen away, he had been banished according to the ordinance, and so should he now have been had he not brought your letter. And thus I rest, as willing to accomplish your desire as any man this day living.

Along left margin] Sir, what surmise or information soever he hath made you, his demeanings and doings are right well here known for naught, and detestable both to God and man, as shall evidently appear whensoever it shall please you to write or send for the trial thereof.

(Vol.2, No.285)

Hunt was not reinstated.

At the end of 1534, what were the relations between Lisle and his masters in London? So far as the royal favour went, he was known to stand high, as was indicated over the curiously important ceremony of the King's New Year gifts, when there was 'high and importunate suit' and more labour made for the privilege of taking the King's gift across the Channel to the Lord Deputy of Calais 'than for any one New Year's gift'.

In view of the complaints, rebukes and threats of royal displeasure with which Lisle found himself confronted during his first eighteen months in office, was this justified by the facts? When the King sends special messages of approval throughout the year, why then is there a critical and admonitory tone in several of Cromwell's letters, why the delay in dealing with Lisle's own suits and the Deputy's business, why the interference in matters of discipline where Lisle is clearly acting correctly and within his rights in the cases of Richard Hunt and Henry Tourney?

To all these questions, which must occur to anyone reading the correspondence and Husee's reports of his interviews with Cromwell without prejudice, there is a plain enough answer. His trouble was, he had been too much of a success; he must be made to realize he was vulnerable, must be put in his place. 'Never was Captain better welcome to Calais.' Excellent – as long as the Captain realized that Mr. Cromwell was in command. He must be made to toe the line and accept his dependence upon Mr. Secretary's personal support, both in his own affairs and the business of his office, by being kept in a state of continual uncertainty and anxiety about both. There are few better illustrations of the art of Cromwell's methods for managing men in important positions and manœuvring them into dependence upon himself than his letters to Lisle, annotated by Husee's accounts of their conversations about his master's affairs.

29   LORD LISLE TO CROMWELL   *27 March 1535*

Right honourable Sir, After my most heartiest recommen[dations][8] . . .
In mine humble wise I desire you to be so good master to the garrison
here, that they may be paid at their day or shortly after. I dare take it on mine
oath made to the King that there be a C not able to buy their dinner against
this time, and pay their house rent. Sir, for my discharge, I shall desire you in
my most humblest wise to regard it; and thus I pray God send you well to
fare, with much honour, to your heart's desire, as I would have myself. I do
write plainly, for my discharge, for penury causeth many things.[9]

                                                          (Vol.2, No.357)

Religious (which means also political) affairs were at least as important as
the state and morale of the garrison. Archibishop Cranmer's commissary,
John Butler, reported from Calais about this time:

> At divers times heretofore I have openly declared unto my Lord Deputy,
> the Mayor, and all other of the King's Council here, the oath of renounc-
> ing the Bishop of Rome's pretenced power, which was stablished in the
> last Parliament . . . but such oath is there none taken, used, or spoken of
> among them, for lack whereof much papistry doth reign still, and chiefly
> among them that be rulers.

He wants Cranmer to secure a commission to the Deputy,

> with some other to be joined with him . . . that were not of the papistical
> sort (which were hard to be found among the Council here) to see the said
> oath put in execution from time to time, as oft as any officer shall be
> admitted, according to the King's statute. And then I suppose some would
> alter to another fashion. But in the meantime I suffer much trouble of
> some of them, insomuch that they have sought and yet daily do seek ways
> to undo me, and all for maintaining of the truth, and yet to my face do
> speak fair, I pray God forgive them and give them grace to know him.[10]

30   LORD LISLE TO CROMWELL   *2 July 1535*

Right honourable, after most hearty recommendations, this shall be to
advertise you that I understand you should be not a little discontented with
me, not only for the rumour that was here of war, by reason that Mr.
Whethill's son brought in his father's stuff to this town, whereof I did advertise you. Which rumour or bruit I could not a 'letted if my life had lien in it.

---

8. MS. torn.
9. Rough draft. Endorsed: the copye of my lord*es* letter sent to Mr. Secretary
10. Vol.3, p.470.

And such news as are brought me, I shall desire you to take them in gree:[11] though all be not true, yet I am bound to advertise, for I know not the contrary. . . .

It may please you to understand that I was forth with my wife and others at a place of mine iij mile out of Calais for my recreation; and that time left the keys of the gate with the High Marshal; so that he, knowing such carts of stuff coming in to the town, sent word unto me of the rumour that was in the country: insomuch as my Lord Edmund and my Lord Grey Wilton came unto me and showed me of the same, my Lord Grey willing to have gone to Hammes with all speed. And I counselled him the contrary, shewing him that there was no necessity of such things, but bade him send word home commanding his jurisdictions of the country not to use no such business; and so I did send in likewise commandment throughout all the country, whereby they were peacified and no more was done. Whereupon the rumour rose I cannot tell, nor how the same proceeded first. . . .

And as for the writing of news unto you, I think myself of duty bound to do the same, for and if I should not I know not how you would take it. Nevertheless, in that it shall please you to ordain, I shall be glad to follow the same, or any other things that you shall command ∧me∧. . . .

And thus the blessed Trinity preserve you, with the increase of honour, long life and prosperous health to his pleasure.

Written at Calais, the ij^{de} of July.

Signed   Yo*ur* owen to commaund,

Arthur Lyssle   (Vol.2, No.411)

Henry Tourney, dismissed by Lisle from the Retinue in the previous October and reinstated by Cromwell's orders, subsequently fell foul of the civic authority and was banished from Calais by the Mayor. In June Lisle received the King's authority to appoint Edward Clifford to his vacant post. Tourney now seeks with Cromwell's help to get the post again.

31   LORD LISLE TO CROMWELL   [*n.d.*] *c.20 July 1535*

Right honourable, after my hearty recommendations, This shall be to advertise you that I have received your letter dated at Stepney the xvij day of this instant month touching Henry Turney which was banished by the ordinance of this town, who afterward made suit unto you for his admission again into his room, as appeareth by your letter: whereupon I wrote to you a letter that Master Treasurer at his coming hither might have the hearing of the matter; and thereupon by your next letter he and his colleagues heard the matter at length, the report whereof I am in doubt that Master Treasurer hath not yet shewed you: beseeching you to take no displeasure although I

11. in good part.

stay the matter until such time as I hear from you again that Master Treasurer have informed you the truth thereof.

Sir, it toucheth the ordinance here two ways. One is, that I cannot put out
Clyfford, who is admitted into the said room that Turney had by the King's
commandment and yours. Secondly, I am sworn upon the holy evangelist to
observe and keep the ordinances of this town, the copy of which oath I do
send you herewith. And there is no man living would be gladder to fulfil and
do everything ye shall command than I would be, saving mine oath and poor
honesty, willing ye knew my mind as much as God doth. But in case there be
no remedy, and that the King's pleasure and yours shall be that he shall be
restored to a room again, then it may please you to send ∧hither∧ the King's
pardon, as well for his banishment as for the discharge of mine oath, or else
great rumour and exclamation shall be made upon me, and I should never be
able to serve the King in executing any ordinance, but that every man hereby
would be encouraged to speak at large, so that I were better be out of the
world than bear office, if the ordinances be once broken. And Sir, for any
rancour or malice that ever I bare unto him, if he be a just man he will say
that I gave him as good counsel as I would have done my brother before he
incurred this danger, if he would have followed it. And thus I beseech the
most blessed Trinity to send you prosperous life and long, to his pleasure.

At Calais, etc.[12]   (Vol.2, No.424)

From the point of view of Calais people, townsfolk and Retinue alike, the
event of the year was the setting-up of a royal commission to inquire into the
state of the town and the garrison and to remedy the abuses about which
Lisle and his fellow Councillors had been complaining since the summer of
1533. As far as one can judge, it was this insistence from Calais upon the
need for drastic reforms in administration, and finally the report prepared
this year by Ryngeley, and Lisle's representations to Cromwell about this
report, that actually secured the commission of inquiry. It is also worth
noticing that in a letter from Fitzwilliam to Cromwell, there is a distinct
implication that it was the King himself who took the initiative in the matter.
That the King and his ministers in the preamble to the Act that resulted from
the report should lay the blame for the troubles of Calais upon everybody
except themselves was, of course, only common form. Not a word, needless
to say, of the fact that it was the parsimony and neglect of the central
authority which had created a situation in which every kind of abuse and
official graft was bound to flourish.

The commission worked in Calais from the end of August through Sep-

12. Endorsed 'Copie'; not signed.

tember. Before it sat, Ryngeley had virtually accused Lisle of taking bribes and selling places in the Retinue; but Lisle does not seem to have done more than accept the sort of gratuity customarily offered for securing an appointment. Fees and rewards on an acceptable scale were the concomitant of the low wages and salaries system, and everyone, from the Secretary of State downwards, operated accordingly. Calais posts and the men who sought them, on the evidence of the correspondence, were on the whole likely to have brought more profit to those who tried to use their influence with Lisle than they did to the Deputy. We hear nothing more of Ryngeley's charge, and Lisle emerges from this ordeal by commission with great credit.

The commission recommended, and an Act the following year confirmed, the strict regulating of appointments, numbers, wages, and duties of the Retinue. Pluralism and absenteeism were forbidden, and also certain work that we should call moonlighting. Old regulations regarding the town, particularly in respect of foreigners, which had become a dead letter, were given the force of law. All of this, if no one overrode him, should give Lisle far clearer authority within which to act.

Fitzwilliam, who had been one of the commissioners, wrote of the reception of the report at Court.

32   SIR WILLIAM FITZWILLIAM TO LORD LISLE   *4 October 1533*

My very good Lord, in my most hearty manner I recommend me unto your good lordship, advertising the same that I have made your humble recommendations as well unto the King's Highness as to the Queen's Grace; and also have made such report unto the King's said Highness of the good conformity which I have found in your lordship and other of his servants in those parts as surely is to his Grace's good contentation. And doubt ye not but that his Highness is and will be good and gracious lord unto you all, and intendeth to establish and do such things for the weal and surety of the town and marches as was never done nor heard of before. And in the mean season the pleasure of his Highness is, that your lordship, specially and above all things, do see not only that the proclamations made by me and my colleagues at our late being with you be duly executed and kept, but also that the town with all diligence be victualled for half a year according to the order I and my said colleagues took in that behalf.

I have spoken to Master Secretary for money for the payment of the Retinue wages, who would have taken the same unto me if I had had any man which might have received and conveyed the same. Nevertheless his pleasure is that Master Vice-Treasurer shall send over unto him a man for the said money, whom he will incontinently dispatch therewith accordingly.

And thus after my right hearty recommendations made unto my good
Lady your bedfellow I will bid your Lordship as right heartily to fare well as I
would do myself.

At Southampton, the iiijth day of October,
Signed   Y*our* hovne Asevred
                 Wyll*iam* ffytzwyll*iam*   (Vol.2, No.456)

So even the pay and the authority for the victualling which Lisle had so
long pleaded for was forthcoming at last.

The following letter is endorsed by Husee 'the form of a letter devised by
the Archbishop of Canterbury to be sent to the Deputy of Calais for Henry
Tourney'. It is difficult to see how it came to be preserved with the Lisle
correspondence. Did Cromwell simply enclose it, to substantiate his own
order for Tourney's restoration in his now-missing letter which Lisle ac-
knowledges in No. 34? Had it, in fact, ever been submitted to the King, or
did Cromwell only say Tourney was to be restored by the King's commandment, and were he and Cranmer responsible for this neat bit of pressure? In
other words, 'Restore Tourney, or else . . .' Their support for him was
understandable, in that he had friends among the extreme Reformist group
in Calais; but meanwhile Lisle had filled his post.

33   HENRY VIII TO THE DEPUTY, TREASURER, AND COMPTROLLER

To be written in due form
            To our Deputy/Treasurer and Comptroller
                of our town and marches of Calais

Right trusty etc. We let you wit, That forasmuch as we have ∧heretofore∧
ij divers times caused our will / pleasure and commandment to be signified
unto you our Deputy / by our right trust and faithful Councillor etc. for to
restore Henry Tournay, one of our soldiers there of viij^d st. by the day /
unto his former warrant and wages from the which he was expulsed and
is kept out / by you: And yet ye have not hitherto / obeyed and accomplished
the same. Wherefore we let you wit / that we ourself do readmit and
give unto the said Henry his said warrant and wages: To have occupy
and pursue the same from that day that you put and expulsed him last
out of the same during our pleasure, without any check or controlment:
And that ye our Treasurer reenter him into his old place of your books /
and pay him his wages at all payments accordingly: And also that ye our
Comptroller / allow the payment thereof from time to time. Provided
always that he find an able man within our said town / to keep his skry /
larum / watch / and ward. And ∧that∧ ye fail not hereof / as ye will avoid

our high displeasure: And these our letters shall be unto you a sufficient warrant and discharge: Any law / act / custom / or ordinance of our said town and marches in any wise notwithstanding. Given etc.

(Vol.2, No.474)

34   LORD LISLE TO CROMWELL   *7 November 1535*

Sir, in the humblest manner I can I commend me unto you, and have received your letter dated the iiij[th] day of this month[13] and well perceive the contents thereof, which is no little grief to my heart; but I shall accomplish your commandment though it touch mine oath and ordinance, and so would I not have done for none within the realm of England except the King's my most dread sovereign lord's commandment. This man never served the King, and for his duty done here I am sure he kept not his watch iij nights since I came to Calais. And for my scrupulosity of conscience I would ye knew it as well as myself. Notwithstanding, I would be loath to lose the honour that God and the King hath called me unto, to be perjured. I take God to record I never did nothing to Tourney for malice, and that he should not deny if he and I were both present before you. I trust the King's Highness will be good lord unto me. And next him my trust is in you to maintain me in execution of justice to keep the retinue in obedience, causing them to do their duty with as good circumspection and with the advice of all the Council and with as much charity as in me lieth; and that I do it by all their advice putting myself to the trial of them all. And where it pleased you to write to me of matters more to be banished and that men have winked at it, I know not what ye mean in it. And also for the long delay of him, your own letter shall save me, for ye commanded me in your said letter to be good unto Clifford and that it was the King's pleasure he should have Tourney's room, which 'couraged me in the doing that I have done.[14] Clifford is the King's sworn servant, and it becometh me not to take him to my service. Praying you to be good master unto him, for I have no room void as yet; and thus I pray God send you as well to fare as I would myself, with much honour and long life. Written with the hand of him that had never a heavier heart. At your commandment, the vij[th] day of November.[15]

(Vol.2, No.475)

We gather from a letter of Husee's on the nineteenth that Clifford returned to London with a gift of 20*s.* from Lisle and the prospect of 8*d.* a day

---

13. Missing. Perhaps written to accompany No.33.
14. Cromwell's letter in Clifford's favour is missing.
15. Draft; not signed.

'extraordinary' till the next vacancy occurs in the Retinue; but this is not the end of Clifford.

Here follows a draft of a letter that gives a better picture of everyday official life in Calais than any royal commission could.

35   LORD LISLE TO SIR WILLIAM   *after 25 December 1535,*
      FITZWILLIAM   *before 6 January 1536*

Right honourable, after my most heartiest manner I commend me unto [you]. This shall be to advertise you that on Christmas Day last past, which is a day for the Council and all the retinue here to wait on ∧me∧, the King's Deputy here, as the order is, the Council ∧came∧. All except Sir Robert Wingfield and Sir Ric[hard] Whethill was at my house, and Saint George's priest, who came and gave me warning that the hour of my coming to church was come and that the guard tarried for me. And upon that I went to church, and tarried a quarter of an hour and more, and as yet the Mayor [had] not come. Then I commanded the curate to go in procession; and the procession past, the Mayor came in with his aldermen, very sore grieved that I tarried not for him. And I made him answer, if there should be any tarrying he ought to tarry for ∧me∧. Sir Robert Wingfield made me answer that the Mayor was capital Justice here and the King's Lieutenant, and I but the King's Deputy. I made him answer that the King's Highness hath made me his Deputy here, without any superior above me, during his pleasure; and so I would keep it till his Grace's pleasure were known; trusting his Grace will be my good lord, for come Twelfth-day I and the Council will go, and my fellows of ∧the∧ retinue together for I had liefer beg my bread for one year than to tarry for the Mayor, to show an example that was never seen in time past, and the Mayor and his jurisdiction, and he will, by themselves.

Sir, I have entertained the Mayor more than it hath become me, but Sir Robert Wingfield his malice for the drown of the marsh will not be forgotten. He said to me this Christmas that he would have me ∧and the Porter∧ in action for the drowning thereof. I made him answer, he that commanded me should save me harmless. I said I marvelled he would sit with the Mayor and leave me and the King's Council chamber. He made answer he was sworn to the Mayor and burgesses, and that he would keep. And then I said, 'for your first oath, I am sure you have a dispensation'; and so I departed. Beseeching you I may know your pleasure at your most convenient leisure, as you promised me at your last being here.
Hol.   (Vol.2, No.509)

3

Everyday Life in Calais
1533–1535

The sports that enlivened the countryside round Calais also helped to cement Lisle's excellent relations with his nearest important neighbour in France, the seneschal of Boulogne.

36   OUDART DU BIES TO LORD LISLE   *2 September 1533*

My lord Deputy, my good neighbour and excellent good friend, I commend me right heartily to your good favour.

My lord, I was informed yesterday of a wild boar the which was sighted a league hence; and took thither my greyhounds which did take the same, and it killed me two of the best of them. I send you the head thereof, praying you to take this my poor gift in good part. I shall take pains to procure other greyhounds; and if you find the said boar's head to your taste I pray you inform me, and if I take more you shall have your part therein.

My lord Deputy, my good neighbour and my very good friend, I bid you farewell, recommending me to your good grace, and praying God to grant you good, prosperous life and long.

From Boulogne, this ij day of September,
                    Entirely your good neighbour, and assured good friend,
Signed   Oudart du Bies[1]   (Vol.1, No.48)

Leonard Smyth became the Lisles' agent in London when they first went to Calais, and his business included the sending of all clothes and provisions required.

37   LEONARD SMYTH TO LADY LISLE   *22 November 1533*

Please it your ladyship to be advertised I received your letter by Swyfte your servant, and since have spoken for a lettice bonnet for Mrs. Frances,

1. French.

59

which will cost xiij^s iiij^d. As the skinner saith, you shall have it within vj days. Also I have written to Kyne, who is in his country, for your cloth, by a kinsman of the Bishop's. . . . Your scarlet[2] is ready, and you shall have it shortly after the date hereof. . . .

. . . I have also this day received ∧your letter dated the xviij day of this month∧, and delivered your frontlet to the Queen's broiderer, who saith you shall have one of other fashion shortly after Christmas, to be at your pleasure and commandment. Also I delivered the measure of your neck for your partlet collar, which you shall have within x days he saith. . . .

Madame, I cannot cause Holt by no means to send unto my lord and your ladyship more cloth before Christmas than for xx or few more as his own cloth will extend unto, yet Mr. Windsor hath spoken with him, since he came, for the same; yet did speak unto him at Bartholomew time as you commanded me, and he promised to provide for your liveries without fail; and now he saith he cannot provide so much cloth of one colour before Christmas without ready money, and yet it should be very ill. But after Christmas, he saith, he will send to my lord the residue of cloth to furnish up your whole number.

. . . as our Lord God knoweth, who ever preserve the noble estate of your ladyship, and grant to you your heart's desire.

At London, the xxij day of November.
By your servant during life,
Hol.   Leonard Smyth   (Vol.1, No.81)

The lettice or lettuce cap or bonnet, ordered for Lisle's eldest daughter, was a neat little fur hood with three corners, favoured by young women and worn for domestic rather than formal occasions.

Sir William Fitzwilliam had been, with Lisle, one of the commanders of the fleet at Brest in 1513. He was now Comptroller of the Household and one of the most influential men at Court.

38   SIR WILLIAM FITZWILLIAM TO LORD LISLE   *25 November 1534*

My very good lord, In my most hearty manner I recommend me unto your good lordship, advertising the same that according to your request mentioned in your letter, which I have received by your servant this bearer, I have in such wise informed the King's Highness and his Council of the Customer, which, as ye write, of late not only arrested certain Oxen provided in England for the provision of your household, but also sold the same as goods forfeited. As order is given, the said Customer shall be sent for to

---

2. Scarlet was a very fine worsted cloth, expensive and of various colours. In crimson it was restricted by sumptuary law to royalty, nobles, and officials.

appear before the said Council to answer thereunto, where doubt ye not but that he shall be in such wise punished and ordered as his demerits in that behalf shall appear he hath deserved.

My lord, after ∧my∧ most hearty recommendations unto my very singular good lady, your bedfellow, with most hearty thanks unto your lordship for the wild swine it pleased you heretofore to send unto me; This shall be only to advertise your lordship that if ye could get me a wild Sow and close her in a coffer, or in some other thing to be made for her, and to send her unto me alive, ye should do me as singular and as high a pleasure as is possible to devise. Your kindness wherein I shall be glad to deserve in my power. I suppose Monsieur de Bies could help you to one, who useth much hunting of the wild Swine. As our Lord God knoweth, who have your lordship in his blessed preservation.

At Westminster the xxv[th] day of November,
Signed   yo*ur* hovne
            Wyll*ia*m ffytzWyll*ia*m   (Vol.2, No.280)

Warley is a member of Lisle's household, and writes from London of a useful find.

39   THOMAS WARLEY TO LADY LISLE   *13 August 1534*

Right honourable and my most special good lady, my duty evermore remembered. . . .

. . . pleaseth it your ladyship to understand that here is a priest, a very honest man, which would gladly do service to my lord and your ladyship. And these properties he hath: he writes a very fair secretary hand and text hand and Roman, and singeth surely, and playeth very cunningly on the organs; and he is very cunning in drawing of knots in gardens, and well seen in graffyng[3] and keeping of cocomers[4] and other yerbes.[5] I judge him very meet for to do my lord and your ladyship service. If I did know your ladyship's pleasure I would make him answer accordingly. . . .

Written at London, at the house of Robt. Spicer in Lombard Street, the xiij day of August,
            By yo*ur* humble s*er*vant
Hol.   Thomas Warley   (Vol.2, No.245)

40   ROBERT ACTON TO LADY LISLE   *19 September 1534*

Madam, in my most humblest wise I have me recommended unto your good ladyship, signifying to you that my lord hath sent Christopher the

3. i.e. grafting.   5. herbs.
4. cucumbers.

yeoman of his horses unto me to cause certain stuff to be made for your ladyship. He cannot ascertain me whether that your ladyship will have your saddle and harness fringed with silk and gold or not, and in likewise whether your saddle and harness shall be of Lucca velvet or Genoa velvet. Madam, other lords' wives hath their saddles and harness of Lucca velvet, fringed with silk and gold, with buttons of the pear fashion and tassels quarter deep of silk and gold. And whether ye will have a stirrup parcel-gilt, with a leather covered with velvet, or else to have a footstool according unto your saddle; and also your pleasure known what device ye will have given in your saddle head of copper and gilt? It may please your ladyship that I may be ascertained of your pleasure with speed, and I shall be ready to do you all the service that lies in my little power, as God knoweth, who ever preserve you,

from Sowthwarcke the xix day of September

By your owne assuryd to hys lytell power

Hol.   Robart Acton   (Vol.2, No.257)

The Lisles' hospitality to the Lord Admiral of France during his stay in Calais recently, on his way as special Ambassador to a meeting with the King in London, gives rise to warm thanks through a member of his suite.

41   JEHAN DE MOUCHEAU TO LADY LISLE   *29 November 1534*

Right honourable lady, I humbly beseech you that I may be recommended to your good grace, not forgetting my much honoured lord; advertising you that my lord the Admiral hath charged me to write to you to make his humble recommendations for divers your good favours, and equally to my lord. And I promise you that there was never man made such good report unto the King as my lord the Admiral hath done, and doth hold himself the most bounden of any man in the world to your ladyship and to my lord; certifying you that my lord loveth you and will so long as he shall live.

Further, there hath been brought to him out of France certain small beasts, the which are come from Brazil; and Mr. Bryan, who is your proper friend, was with him, to have him give them to the Court. But I was in presence when my lord the Admiral said that without respect of persons, none should be served by him before he had served Madame de Lisle; by the which you may perceive whether very cordially he loveth you or not. And the said beasts are called two marmosets, the smaller ones; and the larger is a long-tailed monkey, which is a pretty beast and gentle. And you must understand that the said beasts eat only apples and little nuts, or almonds, and you should instruct those who have the charge of them that they give them only milk to drink, but it should be a little warmed. The larger beast should be kept near the fire, and the two other small ones should always be hung up for the night close to the chimney in their *boite de nuit,* but during the day one may keep them caged out of doors. I send you the said three beasts by a merchant of Rouen, who is this bearer, and a man of substance. . . .

All the gentlemen of my lord the Admiral recommend them humbly to your good grace. No more, Madame, worth penning, but that I pray Our Lord to give you good life and long, to my lord and to you.

From London, this Sunday, the xxix[th] day of November mv[C]xxxiiij,

> By him who is entirely your humble and obedient servant,
>> Your servant, humble and obedient,

Hol.   Jehan de Moucheau[6]   (Vol.2, No.290a)

Falconry was certainly the most popular sport in Calais, and the gift of birds to and from England was an important part in the ritual of obtaining a *quid pro quo,* as is seen in the next letter, from a landowner in Somerset.

42   THOMAS SPEKE TO LORD LISLE   *28 November 1534*

Right honourable and my singular good lord, my duty always remembered, I humbly recommend me unto your good lordship, heartily thanking you for your great gentleness shewed unto [me] at all times: and also for the hawk that you sent me of late. I have nothing to recompense you withal. Nevertheless, I have sent your lordship a brace of bandogs[7] and a cast of lanards,[8] by my servant the bearer hereof, the which I shall desire you to accept as a poor gift of your own assured as long as I live. If that all promises had been kept I had sent your lordship hawks long or this time, but of truth hawks hath failed much this year. And what these are I cannot perfectly inform you, for the lanard was never proved; but the lanneret flew well the last year, as I am informed. I am always bold upon your lordship; and now I shall desire you again to be so good lord unto a friend of mine, whose name is Richard Appowell, as to grant him your letters of protection in as ample manner as you think most convenient. And in this doing ye bind me always to be at your commandment for any friend or servant of yours: as knoweth God, who ever preserve your good lordship.

From London, the xxviij[th] day of November

> by all yours to his poer

Hol.   Thomas Speke   (Vol.2, No.291)

6. French. Paragraphs indicated by large capitals projecting into margin.
7. bandogges, i.e. probably mastiffs or bloodhounds: fr. band dog, a chained-up or guard-dog.
8. cast = couple: lanard (lanner) was the female falcon and lanneret the male.

43   WILLIAM NEWMAN TO LORD LISLE   *6 February 1535*

Right honourable and my singular good lord, my duty remembered. I commend me unto your good lordship, trusting in Jesu that you be merry, and heartily require your lordship to help a brother-in-law of mine to a warrant for a protection, whose name is Thomas Layer of Ovington in the County of Essex, yeoman, otherwise called Thomas Laer of the aforesaid county, husbandman: by the same token that your lordship took me by the hand through the grate at the Lantern Gate at my last being with you, and moreover by the same token I sent you a dog by the farrier of the town, which dog's name is Wolf; and I heartily thank you for my dog you gave me. And thus the Holy Ghost preserve your lordship.

> from London the vj^th day of ffebruary
> > your old ser*ua*nte William newman
Hol.   one of the kynge*s* trumpett*es*   (Vol.2, No.324)

44   JACQUES DE COUCY TO LORD LISLE   *12 March 1535*

Monsieur, last Sunday I betook me to the fields where I lost a saker[9] which belongs to my lord the Seneschal, the which I have been unable to recover. And I think that he hath flown towards your quarter; wherefore, Monsieur, if you have any news of him, or if it is in your power, you will do a very great pleasure to my said lord the Seneschal and to me to have him recovered. The said saker is easily recognizable, because he has three feathers missing in his tail and the imping of the said tail broken, and hath no varvels.[10] If you have no knowledge of him, you have nevertheless the power to be a mean to your neighbours, if that he is in any place near to you, being recognized, to be informed thereof, of the which I would heartily desire you. And wheresoever you may perceive that I could do you service I shall therein employ myself with all my heart, with which I recommend me humbly to your good grace. And I beseech our Creator, my lord, to send you good life and long.

> From Boulogne, this xii^th day of March,
> > Your humble neighbour, ready to do you service,
Signed   Jacques de Coucy[11]   (Vol.2, No.343)

Husee's letters continue to contain, frequently sandwiched among weightier matters, notification of materials and items of apparel that he is sending, usually for her ladyship. There is a long bill for Lord Lisle from a shoemaker in London that is interesting in that it gives us a good idea of the rate at which an elderly though still active Tudor gentleman wore out his

---

9. i.e. the larger lanner falcon.
10. Varvels are the rings for the leash attached to the jesses or straps round the bird's legs.
11. French.

shoes. Besides two pairs of boots, two pairs of buskins, and five pairs of Spanish leather shoes, in nineteen months Lisle got through twenty pairs of 'quarter shoes'. These were presumably the characteristic early Tudor flat pump or slipper, in which the upper consisted of practically nothing but a very square toe-cap. It was secured over the instep by a strap or ribbon-tie, and could be made in leather, but was more often of velvet, cloth, or some other material to match the garments. It went out of fashion after 1540, though the shoe or slipper remained a fragile affair till the end of the century. The shoes were made separately, and the cork soles attached afterwards. They can be very clearly seen in monumental effigies. For the student of Shakespeare it has further significance as yet another instance of that almost unconscious assimilation, in the speech of his characters, of the minutiae of everyday existence, as in Hamlet's exclamation upon his mother's precipitate remarriage:

> But two months dead, nay, not so much, not two . . .
> A little month, or ere those shoes were old
> With which she followed my poor father's body.

45   SIR ANTONY WINDSOR TO LADY LISLE   *26 March 1535*

Right honourable, After my most hearty manner, my duty remembered, I recommend me unto your Ladyship. Pleaseth you to understand that now of late Peter Norton, a very young man, one of Mr. Richard Norton's sons, came to my house at East Meon a' Sunday was sennight, and so desired a servant of mine to go with him to Hambledon, the which servant came to me and desired me that he might so do and so to go home to his wife; and so I gave him leave. And the truth is, they went straight to the Forest of Bere, where my lord hath rule, and so inrushed in the said forest and missed, and as they went by the highway homewards a buck roused, and so with their greyhounds killed him; and by reason of such persons as looked upon the marks the keeper had word of it, and because my servant was known, he and Hayeward came to East Meon to my house at ix of the clock in the night, drawing with their hounds, insomuch that all the town did perceive it; and where that I nor none of my house, on my faith and truth, had no more knowledge of their being in the forest, nor of no deer killed at that time than the child tonight born. Howbeit, within ij hours after, the deer was brought into the town, and it was in the morning ere I had knowledge thereof, and so Peter Norton brought it into my house. And when I saw that it was in by chance, without consent of me or any of mine but only he that asked me leave to go to his wife, I took the one half of his gift and the other half he had home to his father. And I dare say for his father, [he] was as ignorant of the deed doing as I was. Also I thought the flesh as meet for us as for the keepers.

I know right well they will make a grievous matter to my lord of it and
otherwise than the truth. Madame, as I will answer before God, this is the
very truth of the killing of this deer. Good Madame, though my servant and
this young man hath done lewdly and have deserved punishment, I beseech
you, Madame, to desire my lord to be good lord to them, for if old Mr.
Norton know it his son shall need no other punishment; and as for my
servant, if it shall please my lord that I shall have the punishment of him, I
trust so to order him that he shall never offend his lordship again, and
though having been lewd before time I trust to bring him to goodness. And
thus the Holy Ghost preserve your ladyship with much honour. Written in
haste the morrow after our Lady Day.

            Your own assured with my service
Hol.   Antony Windsor

Madame, I beseech your ladyship to send me an answer of this letter. I
pray God that your keepers and the officers may be found as true unto my
lord in all other things concerning the forest, both in word and deed, as they
be in this. You shall know more hereafter if you keep this article secret.

                                                    (Vol.2, No.356)

The intermittent complaints in these letters about hunters at Umberleigh
and this little affair reported by Sir Antony Windsor to her ladyship, to be
passed on as tactfully as possible to Lisle, were indeed very minor incidents
compared with certain armed raids elsewhere for which the law had exacted
savage penalties. But the importance of Windsor's account lies in the seriousness with which the matter has to be taken, trivial as it is, which is
stressed by the way it goes on reverberating in the Hampshire letters for
several months. The importance of deer to the domestic economy of landowners was a fact, and in Clarendon and Bere Lisle had overall responsibility
for the safe-keeping of the King's herds.

46   THOMAS CULPEPER TO LADY LISLE   *5 May 1535*

Madam, in my lowliest manner I most humbly salute your good Ladyship,
much desiring your prosperous ∧health∧ which I pray Jesu long to continue
to his pleasure and your most heart's desire, ever thanking your good
ladyship of all goodness shewed unto me. If it lie in me to do you pleasure, I
am at your commandment. Madam, I have written to my Lord for a spaniel in
Calais, which I hear good report of, wherein I desire your ladyship's furtherance.

Thus the Holy Ghost have you in his tuition.

From the Court the vth day of June,

            By yours to his power,

Madam, I have sent you by my servant a buck. If there were any novelties to be gotten, I would send your ladyship part; but good Madam, when you send over some time, let me hear from you if there be anything to do a' this side the sea for yourself or your friends. Send to me as sure as to your own son: so shall you find me during my life.

Thomas Colpeper   (Vol.2, No.382)

47   JOHN HUSEE TO LORD LISLE   *8 May 1535*

Pleaseth your Lordship to be ascertained that I have sent you by this bearer, Harry Drywry, first vj pair of hosen for your lordship; item, ij caps with ij under-caps, one of velvet another of satin, locked in a new cap-case whereof he hath the key; more, a yard and a half violet frisado for Mr. James; item iiij dozen staff torches; ij dozen quarriers; more, a chest containing therein j£j lbs. fine sugar in xij loaves; ij lbs cinnamon; ij lbs ginger; j lb cloves; j lb maces; j lb sawndres;[12] x lbs pepper; j lb tornsel; ∧half lb∧ isingglass. I think all the before mentioned is as good stuff as ever was occupied. And for the viij dozen counterfeit[13] dishes, if it be possible to have them in all London, I will have them this day, for yesterday Hugh Colton and I were about all London for them, but we could not speed above j dozen, and within a house which your pewterer hath, and he is surely no honest man But I trust this day to be sped of them and so to send them with Gardner, who is freighted with the King's stuff out of the wardrobe for the apparelling and trimming of the ambassadors' lodgings. But I must needs pay ready money for the vessel, which I would, and so have done for all the rest, though Mr. Windsor be not come, who I think will be here this night, or else he doth not well, seeing I sent to him. As soon as he come I will see the liveries laden and the money made over to your lordship with speed. . . .

From London the viij[th] of May.

By your lordship's during life thereto most bounden,

Hol.   John Husee   (Vol.2, No.387)

The eight dozen counterfeit dishes are referred to by Husee in other letters as banquet dishes, and when he actually sends them he gives the information that two dozen of them were 'pounced', i.e. embossed or ornamented by chasing. Taken in connection with the delay in procuring them, this raises two interesting questions. Does 'counterfeit', in this instance, mean that they were not made of a base metal but were made according to pattern? And ought we to understand that, in a noble household, the 'ban-

---

12. i.e. saunders = sandalwood.
13. Can mean either made of base metal, or made according to pattern.

quet' which followed the meal and consisted of fruits, sweetmeats, cheeses, and wine, and was generally served in another apartment, was graced by specially handsome dishes, instead of the ordinary pewter plates bought by the garnish?

48   LADY RYNGELEY TO LADY LISLE   *18 May 1535*

Right honourable and my singular good lady, After all due recommendations, I have me heartily recommended unto your good ladyship, evermore thanking you of your manifold kindness toward me at all times. Madam, please it you to be advertised that I received your bedes of coral, with a heart of gold, which was to me a great comfort, I knowing that you loved them so well, for you were wont to wear them about your arm. And madam, by him that I love best, and your ladyship next, I send you your said token again; which bringer of your said token I heartily pray your ladyship to cherish and make much of now in my absence, called Master Marshal by name. Madam, I beseech you that I may, with the most part of my heart, be recommended unto my singular good Lord ∧Deputy∧, and that done I pray you that I may be recommended to my Lady Clynton and to my Lady Banester, and to all the young gentlewomen pertaining unto your ladyship there; also to my husband, Mr. Secretary. And I put you, Madam, in trust to see that my Lady Banester have not all the love away, I being not present there; wherefore I pray you, madam, to be a mean in it, and that I be not all forgotten in Calais. Madam, I have sent your ladyship a ring of gold, with a flat stone, a diamond, which I pray you, Madam, well to accept, by Perres, my servant, which shall be married as on Sunday come se'night. And thus the Holy Ghost have your ladyship in his keeping.

From my poor house at Knolton, the xviij day of May, by your poor bedwoman, whiles life in her remaineth, to her little power.
Hol.   Jane Ryngeley   (Vol.2, No.390)

The master Marshal and Mr. Secretary to whom Lady Ryngeley refers are both her husband: at present he is the one, and hopes on his return to become the other. The dangers of Lady Banester's charms were evidently a standing joke, for she has mentioned them before.

Lord Edmund Howard was the youngest brother of the Duke of Norfolk. Always in debt and the despair of his family, he held the office of Comptroller of Calais. He was the father of the future Queen, Katharine Howard.

49   LORD EDMUND HOWARD TO LADY LISLE   [*n.d.*]

Madame, so it is I have this night after midnight taken your medicine, for the which I heartily thank you, for it hath done me much good, and hath caused the stone to break, so that now I void much gravel. But for all that, your said medicine hath done me little honesty, for it made me piss my bed this night, for the which my wife hath sore beaten me, and saying it is children's parts to bepiss their bed. Ye have made me such a pisser that I dare not this day go abroad, wherefore I beseech you to make mine excuse to my Lord and Master Treasurer, for that I shall not be with you this day at dinner. Madame, it is showed me that a wing or a leg of a stork, if I eat thereof, will make me that I shall never piss more in bed, and though my body be simple yet my tongue shall be ever good, and especially when it speaketh of women; and sithence such a medicine will do such a great cure God send me a piece thereof.

        all youres,

Hol.   Edmund Howard[14]   (Vol.2, No.399)

In a letter to Cromwell on 2 July 1535, explaining his absence from the town of Calais when a false rumour of war started, Lisle wrote:

It may please you to understand that I was forth with my wife and others at a place of mine iij mile out of Calais for my recreation.

This was presumably the farm mentioned in the 1540 inventory of his possessions. The sixteenth-century gentleman or nobleman lived in the country. When he was at Court he either stayed in his London house or in lodgings, unless he was officially lodged in whatever palace the King was occupying. It is endearing to find Lisle and his wife, like ourselves, week-ending for recreation at that little place in the country. Even three miles distance from the garrison town made a difference, and the contents of the farm suggest genuine, functional, rural simplicity, including 'two new bee-hives and a spinning wheel' and a candle-mould. In the hall there were six pieces of 'paynted hangyng' – stained cloth to us – a table on trestles, a coarse carpet, a cupboard with an old carpet on it, a long form, and two small andirons. The parlour was hung with six pieces of red and green saye and had 'a curteyn to the wyndowe', two carpets, six cushions, two chairs and two forms, six joined stools and four footstools, a long table and two small tables 'with a foot'. There was a bed in the little chamber by the parlour, with a feather bed, a tester, and a ceiler, another bed in the little chamber by the kitchen, and a mattress, with bolster, blanket, and coverlet in the loft over the kitchen. Seven pairs of sheets, four plain table cloths, nine plain napkins, two plain towels, and one napkin and one towel of diaper suggest that it was possible for Lisle and his lady to live the simple life there for a night or two.

14. Addressed: To the ryght honerable the Vycountes lysle this be delyuerd has post hast hast / for thy lyffe. See Pl. 7.

Madame so yt is I have this nyght after mydnyght
taken yor medysyn for the whyche I hertely thanke
yow for yt hathe done me myche good and hathe
cawsyd the stone to breke so that now I voyd myche
gravell but for all that yor sayd medysyn hathe
done me lytyll honeste for yt made me pys my
bed thys nyght for the whyche my wyffe hathe
sore beten me and sayinge yt ys chyldernes partes
to be pyst there bed / ye have made me suche a
pysser that I dare not thys daye go abrode wherfore
I besech yow to make myne excuse to my
lorde and master tresurer for that I shall not
be wt yow thys daye at dyner / madame it
ys shewyd me that a wynd or a leg of a storke
yf I ett therof wyll make me that I shall
never pysse more in bed / and thoughe my
body be symple yet my tong shalbe euer good
and specyally whom it speketh of women
and seyinge ~~~~ suche a medysyn wyll do
suche a ~~~~~~~~ therfore god send
me a pece therof.

all yors so
Edmund Howard

7. Lord Edmund Howard to Lady Lisle (No. 49)

S.P. 3/11, f. 24

The kitchen was well furnished, but the notable thing is the provision for handling the farm's dairy produce – churns, bolting vats, cheese tubs, butter tubs, two cheese presses and a cheese-rack, baskets for butter, cheese cloths and butter cloths, two maunds for chickens, racks for the feeding of sheep and bullocks, dung forks and spades. There were 'nineteen hurdles for the fold' and twenty-three ewes and a lamb to put in it, a bull and sixteen cows and 'a pole and five pails' for the milk, and two boars and three sows for breeding. Where the farm was situated is not mentioned, nor does Lisle in his letter indicate the whereabouts of 'this place of mine'; but as it was only three miles out of Calais it would not be surprising if it was near Landretun, which would help to account for the family's acquaintance with 'the lady of Landertyn', Jenne de Quieret.

The position of a gentlewoman in a noble household was very much that of a friend and companion, and the finding of one to suit Honor Lisle took Husee an immense amount of time and trouble. He uses the word 'liketh' here in its sense of 'pleaseth'.

50   JOHN HUSEE TO LADY LISLE   *21 June 1535*

Pleaseth your ladyship to be advertised that I have received your sundry letters. Answering first touching your gentlewoman, I am sorry she liketh your ladyship no better. Randall and I will do our best in procuring of such one as your ladyship desireth, which will be hard to come by. . . .

. . . And as touching your monkey, of a truth, madam, the Queen loveth no such beasts nor can scant abide the sight of them. . . .

Madam, I do humbly thank your ladyship for the offer of your stewardship, but surely it is no room for me, for I have no such knowledge nor experience in that office, whereby I might do such service as should be to my lord's profit and honour, and your ladyship's, and ∧to∧ my poor honesty. It is a room for some wise man being exercised and learned of continuance in the same, having great experiences, for such one my lord and your ladyship lacketh, and if you might have such a man of knowledge for the ordering and redress of your household but one year it should be a precedent for ever. And xx^{li} or xl marks were well bestowed on such one, being expert, for his year's wages. I do write your ladyship my mind in this behalf. I would God I had as much knowledge therein as any man hath in England, and then should your ladyship know that I would do my lord and your ladyship good service. As God knoweth, who send your ladyship long life, with much honour.

From London, the xxjth of July,
          to your ladyship most bounden while I live,
Hol.   John Husee   (Vol.2, No.421)

Luckily, Lady Lisle's eldest son, John Basset, now studying law at Lincoln's Inn, is a serious and by no means extravagant young man, for the financial situation grows worse daily.

51   JOHN HUSEE TO LADY LISLE   *29 November 1535*

Pleaseth your ladyship . . .

As touching Mr. Basset, your ladyship may send him what money it please you, but a C shillings would be the least. And as touching the draper, your ladyship oweth him the content of the bill herein closed, for he hath delivered now since my last coming over a coat for Bremelcum and a cloak for Mr. Basset and the rest almost xij months agone, as appeareth by the account I gave your ladyship at my being at Calais. Further, I owe the pewterer money for making and changing your vessel, and Mr. Lock demandeth money, and the broiderer. Madam, the grocer is unpaid, whereby I have lost a friend. As touching your ladyship's kirtle, I shall not forget it. As touching Mr. Brian Tuke, I have given one of his clerks a piece of money to search for to know whether your ladyship's sureties be in suit or no; and of truth, they are not. Therefore it shall be requisite your ladyship remember him with a loving letter, with thanks, and some gentle pleasure besides. Madam, the debit of your receipt is lxxxviij^{li}, as Smyth showed me; which, ∧if∧ it had been delivered to me according to my lord's letter, had been with your ladyship long ere this time. As God knoweth, who send your ladyship long life with much honour.

From London, the xxixth of November,

By your ladyship's assured thereto bounden,

Hol.   John Husee   (Vol. 2, No. 492a)

4

Politics and Religion
1533–1535

At this time the problems of Calais were Calais problems, and life there can be more clearly envisaged if it is looked at in its own context; but we need some picture too of the outside world, and of the tensions that were building up in England and would eventually grip Calais as well.

In a postscript to a letter of 21 June 1533, John Grenville wrote to Lisle: 'This day there was judged to death ij heretics, one named Frith and one Tayler, which shall be burned on Wednesday. And one was abjured.'[1] The two heretics mentioned were John Frith and Andrew Hewet. Frith, a young Cambridge scholar, a friend of Tyndale's and formerly a pupil of Bishop Gardiner's, was the first to die for maintaining the doctrine of the sacrament as it was eventually to be set forth in the Book of Common Prayer. He had been imprisoned for denying the doctrines of Transubstantiation and Purgatory. Already the difficulty of knowing exactly what was the current official stance on such doctrinal matters was becoming apparent, and was to lead over the next seven years to Lisle's major problem in Calais. In the political sphere as well, both diplomatic relations and the struggle for power at home were inextricably involved with religion. Norfolk had been dispatched to France just before Anne Boleyn's coronation to persuade the French King to adhere to his alliance with England in spite of Henry's defiance of the Pope, and to dissuade him from keeping his agreement to meet the Pope in September, thus coming out openly on Henry's side over the divorce. But Francis was too wily for Norfolk, and without breaking with his brother of England refused to break off his coming meeting with the Pope. Henry immediately recalled Norfolk, who was back in England by the end of August. Cromwell was not yet in entire command, Norfolk an influence to be reckoned with; and thereafter Lisle writes to both of his troubles, carefully informing both of the fact, hoping that in their jockeying for power in the

1. Vol. 1, No. 9.

73

King's Council he may gain what he needs for Calais. The excerpts from two
letters that follow give an excellent example of this necessary technique.

52   LORD LISLE TO THE DUKE OF NORFOLK   *?early September 1533*

Pleaseth it your Grace to be advertised the xxx day of the month past I
writ my last letter unto you; and whereas continually I have folks abroad,
both east and west, by which I have knowledge weekly of such sayings as be
abroad, insomuch that yesterday one of them hath been with me and hath
shewed such things as be comprised in a bill which your Grace shall receive
joined to this. And whether the said things be true or not, I do send them
unto your Grace for my discharge. And also I require you to have this poor
town in your remembrance, for surely there be many more necessities in this
town than be well knowen, wherefore my very trust is that such advertisements as I have made to the King's Highness, as well for artillery as such
other things as lacketh, hath been looked upon and shall be provided for.

Also I and the King's Council hath divers times advertised the King and
his Council in what estate the soldiers' garner of this town standeth in. . . .

(Vol. 1, No. 47)

53   LORD LISLE TO CROMWELL   *?early September 1533*

Sir, after due recommendation, pleaseth it you to be advertised that I have
divers folks, both east and west, to advertise me of such news as is abroad,
the which I have written a letter unto my Lord of Norfolk and enclosed them
therein. Whether they be true or no yet I have sent them for my discharge.
Further, requiring you to regard this poor town what case it is in, as I and the
Council here have advertised you sundry times; for surely there be many
more necessities in this town than be well known, and what estate the
soldiers' garner is in. . . .

(Vol. 1, No. 47a)

In the first session of 1534, an Act for the Succession declared the King's
marriage with Katharine invalid and his marriage with Anne Boleyn valid,
asserted the illegitimacy of the Princess Mary, established the succession
upon the issue of Henry and Anne, and made it high treason maliciously to
deny or attack the Anne Boleyn marriage. Rokewood reports:

54   JOHN ROKEWOOD TO LORD LISLE   *8 March 1534*

Right honourable and my singular good Lord, in humble wise I recommend me unto your good lordship, and to my singular good Lady your wife.
. . .

Also the Lady Dowager's jointure is clean taken away by Act of Parliament, and she is restored to other lands in the name of Prince Arthur's dowager, and the saying is that the Queen's Grace shall have the said lands for her jointure. And as concerning the Pope there is taken from him by Act of Parliament that he shall have no more out of the land, neither Peter's Pence nor yet none other thing. All his authorities be clean disannulled here, and daily doctors and great clerks maketh new books, and writeth again his pomp and other his inordinate living. And as upon Thursday last past all the whole Parliament house were with the King at York Place in his gallery the space of iij hours, and after that all the Lords went into the Council House at Westminster and there sat till x a'clock at night. And by my next letters I trust to advertise your lordship some of that business which is not yet come to light. And as for preaching, in these quarters the preachers accordeth meetly well, for here preacheth none but such as be appointed [by the King]. Beseeching God that all may be well, for there is many men much desirous to hear them preach, and the most famous doctors of Oxford and Cambridge, with the Vicar of Croydon and many other good clerks faileth ∧not∧ to be at their sermons and marks the opinions and articles, as well of Latimer as of such as preaches. And it is thought that when the matter shall come to disputation amongst them, that the business and inconvenience thereof shall come to great trouble when the contrary parties may be suffered to dispute with them. . . .

. . . as our Lord knoweth, who preserve you to his pleasure.

From the Court, the viij day of March,

Signed   by yo*wr* most bownd,

John Rokewood   (Vol.2, No.138)

In the second session, November to December, the Act of Supremacy was passed: another act made first fruits and tenths payable to the Crown; and the Act of Treason puts words expressing treasonable intentions on a par with treasonable action. By the end of 1534 the power of the Pope in England had been completely abolished, and in the following January the King added the title of 'Supreme Head of the Church of England' to his style. He still, of course, remained 'Defensor fidei', and though there was much sympathy everywhere for Katharine and Mary and active dislike of Anne Boleyn, there was no real parliamentary opposition to the ecclesiastical policy thus carried to its logical conclusion.

But foreign policy was definitely a more tricky affair. The French alliance of the 1520s worked well enough until the end of 1533, but as Francis I began to grasp the full implications of England's religious policy, the danger was that he might turn away from the English alliance towards Spain, from which a European-Catholic and anti-English redeployment of power might develop. Hence the English negotiations, all fruitless as it turned out, with Lutheran Germany.

The continual rumours in the letters to Lisle throughout 1534 that the King was minded to go over to Calais spring from the fact that he was anxious to do everything possible to keep the French alliance alive by another personal interview with Francis and that he even envisaged trying to get his nephew James V of Scotland to make a third at their meeting. Its continual postponement was at least partly due to the fact that Anne Boleyn was expecting another child in the early summer and that Henry was afraid to leave her in England in case his absence might create an opportunity for a rising in favour of Katharine and the Princess Mary, aided possibly by invasion from the Emperor. The country as a whole was far from accepting the King's religious moves as placidly as Parliament, and Lisle's correspondents frequently inform him, though carefully without comment, of this or that important man having visited the ex-Queen or her daughter. Equally without comment, Husee tells him on 17 April: 'The Bishop of Rochester is in custody of my Lord of Canterbury and Sir Thomas More in the keeping of the Abbot of Westminster and Doctor Wilson in the Tower.'[2] Three days later he writes:

> This day the Nun of Kent, with ij Friars Observants, ij monks, and one secular priest, were drawn from the Tower to Tyburn, and there hanged and headed. God, if it be his pleasure, have mercy on their souls. Also this day the most part of this City are sworn to the King and his legitimate issue by the Queen's Grace now had and hereafter to come, and so shall all the realm over be sworn in like manner. The bishops of Durham, Winchester, and York are now sent for, to what intent God knoweth. Some thinketh they shall to the Tower.[3]

Husee appears as well informed as anyone of the arrests which resulted almost daily from the administering of the oath to the Act of Succession, although Bishops Tunstall, Gardiner, and Lee were not imprisoned, as all three, needless to say, subscribed to the full oath. More was willing to swear to the succession but not to subscribe to the oath as offered to him, which meant repudiating the Pope's authority and acknowledging Katharine's marriage invalid, and he and Fisher were sent to the Tower. The French Ambassador wrote home that the great majority of the people took the oath, which they resented, under pressure of fear.

Lisle evidently needed constant reassurance of the King's goodwill, particularly when his affairs were going ill with Cromwell.

2. Vol.2, No.168.   3. Vol.2, No.171.

55   JOHN ROKEWOOD TO LORD LISLE   *8 May 1534*

My singular good Lord, my duty preferred, I have me recommended unto your good lordship. And my lord, I am very glad that your lordship sent your steward to make answer to Master Cromwell in such things as he found himself grieved with your lordship, which I trust now that ye be at a good point, for he was in no little umbrage before your steward coming. And if your lordship follow my poor opinions ye shall weigh such things but light, for words be taken here but for wind, for there is such matters here every day. And my lord, as concerning news, at this time here goeth a great voice of the King's coming over. But my lord, as yet there is no certainty of that matter; but within this viij or x days the Bishop of Paris or the Great Master of France is and cometh in post, at which time the certainty of everything shall be knowen, at which time I will advertise your lordship of these same, as I shall see cause.

And my lord, as concerning the Scots, there have been many great days between the Council and them, but here is but little concluded as yet. And there is an abbot of Scotland that is riding in post to the King of Scots and shall return in post hither again with the King of Scots' answer. My lord, I will you ensure ye are much bound unto Master Treasurer for the gentle report he made to the King's Highness of your lordship, not only for the good cheer that ye made, and good entertainment at his last being there, but also for your diligent service as concerning reparations and casting down of sandhills, and also other thing concerning your lordship['s] office and charge there. Which time that Master Treasurer made the same report, I was by, and heard the King's answer. And I will ensure your lordship his Grace said that your lordship had a will to do well as any gentleman living, and then desiring Mr. Treasurer to present his hearty thanks to your lordship. And I will ensure you, my lord, the King's grace is your singular good lord. And that Mr. Treasurer may do, your lordship is ensured thereof. . . .

My lord, I desire your lordship that I may be humbly recommended unto my singular good lady, and if I can do your lordship any pleasure here, or my good lady, I beseech your lordship command me, of whom you may be 'sured to the uttermost of his power. Written the viij day of May.
Signed   by yow*r*ys duryng lyff
                      John Rokewood

                                                      (Vol.2, No.186)

In Rokewood's next letter the Lord Dacre he mentions is William, Lord Dacre 'of the North', so called to distinguish him from Thomas, Lord Dacre 'of the South'. Suspected of conspiracy with the Scots, his case became important.

56   JOHN ROKEWOOD TO LORD LISLE   *15 May 1534*

My singular good lord, according unto my duty in my most heartly manner I recommend me unto your good lordship. . . .

. . . The Lord Dacre, his uncle and his bastard son be committed to the Tower; and some men think that they be in great danger. Also the Prior of the Charterhouse of London, and the Prior of the Charterhouse of Sheen, they be both in the Tower. And on Wednesday there was a great fray between Master Wyatte and the serjeants of London, where one of the serjeants was slain and divers of them hurt, whereupon Mr Wyatt is committed to the Fleet.

Moreover, my lord, the ambassadors of Scotland departeth home this ∧next∧ week, and there is a general peace taken between the King's Grace and the King of Scotland during both their lives. Howbeit, my lord, many men have small trust in the continuance thereof. Other news as now here be none, but and any come to my knowledge while I am here I shall send you with speed such as shall come to knowledge; but I trust to bring your lordship the first news myself after this. My lord, if there be any service or pleasure that I may do for your lordship while I am here, I beseech you command me as boldly as any friend that ye have, and I shall as gladly accomplish it to the best of my little power. As Almighty God knoweth, who preserve your good lordship with long life to his pleasure.

From London, the morrow after Ascension Day,

By ∧your∧ own assured to my poor power

Signed   John Rokewood   (Vol.2, No.195)

Dacre seems to have been the victim of a conspiracy of enemies, and when he was tried on 9 July the verdict returned was Not Guilty – according to the Imperial Ambassador, 'one of the most novel things that have been heard of for a hundred years, for no one ever knew a man come to the point he had done and escape'. For a whole day, he writes, 'there was never seen such universal joy shown in this city as there was at his liberation'.[4] He believes that the peers acquitted him because they were already beginning to fear that Cromwell, like Wolsey, was preparing to attack the nobility, and so rallied to the defence of their own order. On the 10th Ryngeley advised Lisle of his acquittal, with the comment that he is sure he has already heard about it.

The trend of events in England in 1534 had alarmed the Emperor for the safety of his cousin, the Princess Mary. Realizing the necessity for working by indirect means and through Henry's nominal ally, France, Charles had made overtures to Francis I for a general settlement of their rivalries, and

4. Vol.2, p.205.

had instructed his ambassador to insinuate into the King's mind the idea of an alliance between his third son, the Duke of Angoulême, and the Princess Mary, as a means of bargaining for the remitting of the annual pensions paid to England. With this proposal de Brion was instructed to couple a demand for an acknowledgement of Mary's legitimacy and a plea that the King and his realm should return to their spiritual allegiance to Rome. Henry made his reply in unequivocal terms. If Mary and Angoulême were to marry, then they must renounce all right to the English crown. Angoulême might have the hand of the Princess Elizabeth, his legitimate heir, and Henry would forgo his claim to the title of King of France and would remit the pensions: but that was all. The embassy had failed of its ostensible purpose. Not, however, of its deeper intention—the intention of Charles V. There was no marriage treaty, and no acknowledgement of Mary's legitimacy: but his ally's offer had been a practical demonstration to Henry that a European value was set upon the life of his elder daughter. Important to Lisle was a side effect of this embassy: the Ambassador said repeatedly to the King that he could not speak too highly of his reception in Calais, and the Lord Deputy made several abiding friends among the mission.

The negotiations with France at the end of 1534 had achieved nothing: the situation, indeed, was less satisfactory than it had been, and might even lead to some combination against Henry. At home, moreover, there was greater discontent than ever before at the King's treatment of Katharine and Mary. Henry's reaction to this state of internal disaffection and uneasy equilibrium in foreign affairs was characteristic. He redoubled his efforts to secure a permanent peace with Scotland; he saw to it that the fortifications at Calais, and on the Border, and along the south coast were put in good repair and strengthened; and before the year was out he had subdued the Geraldines' rebellion in Ireland. At the same time, Cromwell's plans for consolidating the royal power were pressed on without intermission. Finally, everything was set in motion for the visitation of the monasteries, beginning, of course, with the lesser and more vulnerable houses, and preceded in January by the commission for the valuation of all ecclesiastical property. Within six months the results, now embodied in the famous *Valor Ecclesiasticus,* were in Cromwell's hands, and he and his master knew the real value in pounds, shillings, and pence of their intended spoils. In 1534 the Crown had acquired the Church's first fruits and tenths, generally reckoned to have been worth some £40,000 per annum. With all the facts at last ascertained, they now knew that the revenues of the monasteries totalled something like £140,000, and those of the spiritualities some £320,000. And they also knew that, provided they had their share of the loot, the nobility and gentry, as a whole, would acquiesce in confiscatory measures. Everything was set for the final move which would make the Supremacy the most important factor in the new conception of sovereignty. The pattern of the remaining twelve years of royal despotism was now irrevocably established.

The first rumblings are now heard of what are to become major storms over the authorization of preachers. Henry still uses the papal title of Defender of the Faith, but exactly what the tenets of that faith are now supposed to be in England has never been defined; and the King is considerably less reformist, doctrinally speaking, than many important churchmen who have taken the Oath of Supremacy, and, importantly, less so than Cromwell. This is to become a vital issue in Calais. Husee's letter announcing the King's reception of Lisle's New Year gift introduces the subject:

> . . . I have been with my Lord of Canterbury's ∧grace∧, who now lieth at Knole, and I have delivered him your lordship's letters and have opened unto him your full mind, who is very willing to see everything redressed. . . . You shall shortly have there ij preachers of his Grace's own appointing. And some thinketh his Grace will be there this Lent himself. Howbeit, he hath yet no licence of the King. I have hitherto nothing further to write your lordship, but that I do herein send the abridgement of the Statutes, for the Statutes are not yet out. As soon as they may be had I will not fail to send your lordship the book. . . .[5]

The statutes to which Husee refers included some of the most momentous enactments, with the most terrible consequences, of any that were ever passed by even an Henrican parliament. While establishing the Royal Succession and Supremacy, they enabled the state 'to repress, redress, reform, order, correct, restrain and amend all such errors, heresies, abuses, offences, contempts and enormities whatsoever they be', including words or writing.

It was part of Lisle's business to keep a watchful eye upon the activities of his neighbours on the frontiers of the Low Countries and to report anything that looked like preparations for war. The draft that follows retains the scribe's use of the virgula.

57   LORD LISLE TO CROMWELL   *1 February 1535*

After my most hearty recommendations / this shall be to advertise you / that / in my information how th'Emperor should be ∧in High Almayn∧ with three score thousand men. / And all the Captains of the frontiers here / be at Mechlin at a Council there. / And further the mariners along the coast of Flanders / as Armuyden, Campvere, Flushing, Middleburgh, Sluys,

Ostend and all along the coast / is warned that none shall depart / and the common bruit is / they shall row iij galleys in the narrow sea. Further I have received a letter / sent to the Secretary here / that the King's money out of France will be here / in short time[6] / Which letter I send unto you closed in this / to th'intent / you shall perceive the contents of the same / And further as you shall have knowledge of this news / I may be advertised / for th'assurance of this my charge here / from you / Thus the blessed Trinity / have you in his tuition.

From Calais, this first day of February / 1534

(Vol.2, No.320)

Actually, the Emperor had no intention of meddling in English affairs at the moment. He was preparing his great campaign against the Turk, and was himself even more suspicious of Henry's designs.

New arrivals in Calais had been using a story of the change of heart of the strongly reformist Bishop of Worcester for counter-reformist propaganda, and Lisle needs to be sure he does the right thing about it.

58   LORD LISLE TO CROMWELL   *27 February 1535*

After most hearty recommendations, This shall be to advertise you that the xxvj day of this present month I received a letter from Sir John Wallop, which I send you herein enclosed. Further, touching news occurrent here, is that Doctor Latimer hath turned over the leaf, for on Wednesday in the Ember week last he preached before the King's Highness, 'knowledging the Pope's authority to be the highest authority upon earth, and if he shall misuse himself he ought to be reformed by a General Council and none otherwise. He also confessed our Lady and holy saints most necessary to be honoured and prayed unto and that pilgrimage is very acceptable unto Almighty God and profitable for the wealth of man's soul. I beseech you I may know your pleasure whether there were any such sermon or no, whereby if it be contrary the party which hath brought such tidings may be punished in ensample of other, here or elsewhere, as it shall please the King's Highness and you. News about the Borders here is, that the Emperor hath made proclamation at Dunkirk, Burborow, and Sainct Omers that no horse shall pass out of his dominion to no Englishman nor Frenchman. Also, Turneyhem was sold to the Frenchmen and the buyer and seller as well the Frenchman as Fleming, taken, and be in the custody of Monsieur du Bever.

---

6. i.e. Henry's annual pension of 100,000 crowns, agreed on in 1525, which by 1543 was one million crowns in arrears.

Moreover, the Captain of Turwyn was at a point with an Archer of the Emperor's guard for Arye and it was discovered, so the said Archer is hanged, drawen and quartered, insomuch that all the towns on the frontiers kept never better watch in time of war than they do now. And as it is said proclamation is made through the Emperor's land, that every man being under his obeisance within vj weeks to come and be resident within his dominion. And thus I pray Jesu preserve you, with prosperous life and long, to his high pleasure.

From Calais, the xxvij day of February,

Signed   Yo*ur* own to com*m*avnd,

                        Arthur Lyssle   (Vol.2, No.334)

59   CRANMER TO LORD LISLE   *27 April 1535*

My Lord, in my most hearty wise I commend me to you, and in likewise to my good Lady, your wife, thanking you both for the well and gentle entreating of my chaplains which of late were with you at Calais. And where you wrote unto me that you have been noted a papist by some of my house (as you be informed) and that unworthily, inasmuch as you have everywhere spoken against the acts and living of the Pope, and thereby the less have deserved to be accounted his fautor:[7] my lord, it is not the person of the Bishop of Rome which usurpeth the name of the pope ∧that∧ is so much to be detested, but the very papacy and the see of Rome, which both by their laws suppressed Christ and set up the Bishop of that see as a god of this world. . . . And this is the chief thing to be detested in that See; that it hath brought the professors of Christ into such an ignorance of Christ. And besides this, he hath consumed and wasted innumerable goods of all Christendom for the maintenance of that estate, to the intolerable impoverishment of all Christian realms; which said dominion and power, with other corrupt doctrines by them invented, is the thing rather to be abhorred than the person; yea, and the person also, if he prosecute to maintain the same. Therefore, albeit that some, paraventure, have partly suspected you to have favoured this his said usurped power by ignorance, yet nevertheless, inasmuch as I perceive that both you, of your gentle nature, and the great towardness of that your good lady, be so inclined to promote the word of God, it shall from henceforth enforce me, from time to time, to stand in this behalf for your defence, as well to the King's Highness and his most honourable Council as to other: requiring your lordship, as you do now favour the word of God, so to persever to the end, whereby you shall not alonely deserve of God immortal reward for the same, but also be sure of me to do unto you such pleasure as I may.

7. i.e. favourer.

... And thus to make an end I pray you to have me most heartily commended unto my good Lady. Thus our Lord preserve you both in prosperity.

At Otford, the xxviij day of April,

　　　Your loving friend,

Signed 　　　　　Thomas Cantuar 　　　　　　　　(Vol.2, No.376)

Politico-religious news from England usually comes, if at all, carefully without comment. At the end of a long letter about business affairs, Husee writes to Lisle on 4 May: 'This day were drawn, hanged, headed, and quartered iij monks of the Charterhouses, j of the brethren of Sion, and a priest. And the Vicar of Thistleworth[8] hath his pardon.'[9] And on the same day he writes to Lady Lisle: 'News here are none, but of certain which were put to death. But I know your ladyship so pitiful that such are little pleasant unto your ear.'[10] Anyone steeped in the atmosphere of the Letters may even feel that Antony Wayte is taking a risk when he writes to Lady Lisle on the 27th: 'These be our news. It is amongst the people rumoured that one should be committed unto the Tower because he hath said that this month shall be rainy and full of water; the next month, death; and the third month, wars; there to be kept until experience may instruct us the truth of his prophecy.'[11] Lest we mistake Wayte for an altogether modern minded satirist, however, it must be added that he then goes on blithely to relate the arrest of twenty three refugee Anabaptists from Flanders of whose beliefs he strongly disapproves. Later, fourteen of them were condemned, one man and a woman being burned at Smithfield and the rest at other towns about the country.

60 　　—— TO LORD LISLE 　　　　　　　[n.d.] c.2 *June 1535*

Monsieur, There went into England on Tuesday at night a man sent by the Pope to the King with a red hat for the Bishop of Rochester that is prisoner in the Tower of London, and with it a bull of excommunication to be uttered against the King if he will not set the said Bishop at large and if he should prevent him from the acceptation of the hat. The said messenger arrived on Tuesday, as did Monsieur the Admiral.

Monsieur, whatsoever the said Admiral may conclude with you, the Pope will utterly destroy it and would excommunicate the King of France if he depart not from your alliance. And if that you will not be reconciled to the Pope, the King of France and the Pope, with whom come great forces, will ruin and destroy you utterly.

Sir, I beseech you for the love of God that it may please you of your grace to despatch me, and it is now fifteen days that I have been here; and further,

8. i.e. Isleworth. 　　　　　　　　10. Vol.2, No.380.
9. Vol.2, No.379. 　　　　　　　　11. Vol.2, No.396.

if you no longer desire my service, that it may please you to pay me my wage for the service I have given. Praying God, Monsieur, to give you good life and long.

By your obedient servant[12] (Vol.2, No.397)

To understand the political motivation behind the religious persecution of the Catholics it is only necessary to remember the King's dominant obsession with the security of the Royal Succession: the long chaos of the Wars of the Roses must not return. The concept of any child of Anne Boleyn's as a bastard, held by the Papacy and the European powers, must be stamped out in England. No oath of allegiance to the Crown was enough without rejection of the Papacy as well. Hence the condemnation of Catholics was for High Treason, and the sentence was partial hanging, the heart and intestines being drawn out while the victim was still alive, and the body then quartered so that parts could be displayed in different places for the discouragement of others. Heretics, on the other hand, were a threat to the new, and Henry hoped unifying, royal supremacy of the English Church as such, and heretics were burned. In the case of the Anabaptists there may have been an additional political element: the sect had been prominent in the start of the Peasants' Revolt in Germany, and these members of it had been expelled from the Low Countries as a danger to the State.

On 28 June Husee sends Lisle in one line the news that Sir Thomas More is expected to be arraigned at the end of that week, and then never mentions him again.

12. No signature; French original; described by *L. & P.* as 'in the hand of Lisle's spy'; not addressed.

5

Educating the Children

In popular opinion Tudor parents have a bad reputation. The cue is taken from Lady Jane Grey's description of her own childhood, the – to us – shocking account of the way Frances Brandon, daughter of Henry VIII's younger sister Mary, brought up her entirely admirable little Jane with cuffs on the ear – 'didn't she realize she might permanently injure the poor child's eardrum?' – we start with an accumulation of prejudice, and a self-satisfied conviction of our own humanitarianism and educational wisdom. Tudor parents took their responsibility seriously, and did their utmost to civilize their offspring. They knew their own world, and were anxious to prepare their children for it as adequately as they could.

Whatever we may feel about their methods, their aim was a discipline calculated to produce young people with pleasing manners, a knowledge of how to behave in whatever company they might find themselves, and a capacity for making themselves useful and acceptable to their elders and betters so that influential people should be ready to forward their interests and advance them to position and office. Nobility, gentry, and the professional and wealthier middle classes all alike accepted the idea that in giving their children this training in manners they were doing the best thing for them. It was no want of affection that made parents send their children away to some great household even before they were ten years of age, nor was it done to save money, for in many cases to 'find' children in another person's establishment must have cost parents more than it would to have kept them at home. The whole idea of the system was to give the children thus 'preferred to service' the best possible chance in life, by securing for them the best social training available.

By the standards of their own time Honor and Arthur Lisle would not have been considered excessively 'charged with children'. Her father had had ten children, her brother Roger nine, and her nephew Diggory and her niece Philippa were in process of acquiring, respectively, thirteen and sixteen. Moreover, in the case of Lisle and Honor, the stepchildren of their first marriages were already settled in life by 1533. Lisle's eldest stepson, Sir John Dudley, was a man over thirty, pursuing a promising career; and at no time does Lisle appear to have taken any responsibility for the two younger brothers, Andrew and Jerome. Of Honor's four stepdaughters, two were already provided for in marriage, and the other two stayed in England when she left Soberton. There remained, in consequence, only her seven Basset children and Lisle's three daughters; and of these latter only one resided in their household.

Throughout their seven years' stay in Calais the advancement of her children was one of Honor Lisle's chief concerns. Children and stepchildren were regarded as one family by everybody. The Abbess of St. Mary's writes to Lady Lisle of Bridget Plantagenet as 'your daughter'; the Paris merchant, Guillaume Le Gras, writes to Lisle of James Basset as 'your son'; and all the Basset children refer to Lisle as 'my lord my father'. They were all of them Honor's responsibility rather than her husband's. It is she who sends instructions about them to Husee and to their various guardians; and it is to her that the bills come in for payment. From time to time Lisle bestirs himself and writes to some influential friend on behalf of one or other of the Basset boys; messages about lettice bonnets for the girls find their way into his business correspondence; and several of the letters from the French friends who took charge of Anne and Mary Basset are addressed to him. The outstanding feature of this section of the correspondence, however, is the masterly demonstration given by her ladyship and Husee of the gentle art of wire-pulling and of the strategy and tactics required for the successful 'placing' of a family of children.

Lisle's eldest daughter, Frances, and the four Basset girls went with their parents to Calais in June 1533, and Frances, Philippa, and Katharine had the somewhat unusual experience of living at home and enjoying the society of Government House and its opportunities for festivity. In normal circumstances they would probably have gone to the households of friends or relations of superior rank as waiting-gentlewomen, until suitable marriages could be arranged for them. That they went to Calais because it was considered the most advantageous thing to do may be taken for granted; but the possibility that both Lisle and Honor liked having their children about them need not therefore be ruled out. The two younger Basset girls, Anne and Mary, went to live with noble French families, where they were accepted as the daughters of distinguished parents sent to learn the language and to be 'finished'. Elizabeth Plantagenet was left in the care of her half-brother, Sir John Dudley, and apparently remained with him throughout these seven years.

Philippa must have been about seventeen when she left England, and Frances was probably about the same age. There is nothing to suggest that either of them had been placed in service before Lisle's appointment to Calais, and the only accomplishment of which they give evidence is needle-work. Frances may have been able to write, but there are no letters from Philippa. She could apparently read, as Mary takes the trouble to write her two special letters, while the rest of the family are only sent messages. The saddles ordered for my lady's daughters in 1533 show that they could ride, but there are no hints of musical abilities except for Mary, who played the lute, the virginals, and the spinet. It is impossible to generalize about the extent of literacy among women of gentle birth in the early sixteenth cen-tury: one can only examine the evidence for the individual case. Many of them – like Honor Lisle or Dame Alice More – obviously learnt to be com-petent business women. It is equally obvious that the education given to the princesses of the Tudor royal house and to Lady Jane Grey was as much the exception as that given by Sir Anthony Coke to those learned ladies his daughters, or by Sir Thomas More to Margaret Roper and his other daughters, which was exactly the same as his son's.

Everyone of importance sent abroad on diplomatic missions passed through Calais, and was entertained by the Lord Deputy and 'my lady de-bite'. Their daughters could be seen, spoken with, reported on; matrimonial alliances might well have been expected to result. Opportunities, the Lisles must have argued, would be considerably greater on the other side of the Channel than in most private households in England; but the curious fact is that the only negotiations set on foot came in every case either direct from England, or from England in reply to some such approach as the following, made by Lisle on behalf of his second daughter, Elizabeth. Although the proposed match fell through, the letter gives a good idea of the way in which negotiations for a suitable marriage were undertaken. The Lovells of Barton Bendish in Norfolk were a rich, East Anglian landowning family.

61   SIR FRANCIS LOVELL TO LORD LISLE   *14 September 1534*

My especial good Lord, In my right hearty manner I recommend me unto your good Lordship and unto my Lady your wife, and so do my wife recom-mend her unto you both in her most loving and lowly manner, thanking your good Lordship of your great kindness which I perceive as well by your favourable letter as by your good gift and loving words reported by your faithful chaplain Sir Oliver Brown. And whereas it pleaseth your good Lordship to bear unto me so entirely love and favour, not deserved on my behalf nor of none of mine, that your noble blood and my poor stock shall be by the grace of God confedered together in lawful marriage, there should be no thing more comfortable to me, as knoweth God. And as concerning a clear declaration of my mind in this behalf, it is thus: if your good lordship be

1. *The Plantagenet Connection*

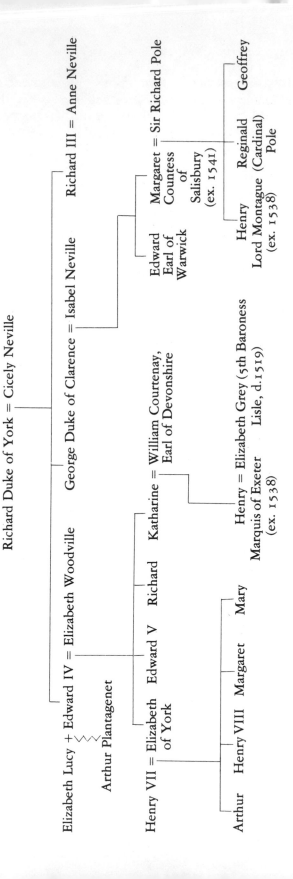

Richard Duke of York = Cicely Neville

Elizabeth Lucy + Edward IV = Elizabeth Woodville

Arthur Plantagenet

George Duke of Clarence = Isabel Neville

Richard III = Anne Neville

Edward
Earl of
Warwick

Margaret = Sir Richard Pole
Countess
of
Salisbury
(ex. 1541)

Henry
Lord Montague
(ex. 1538)

Reginald (Cardinal)
Pole

Geoffrey

Henry VII = Elizabeth
of York

Arthur   Henry VIII   Margaret   Mary

Edward V   Richard

Katharine = William Courtenay,
Earl of Devonshire

Henry = Elizabeth Grey (5th Baroness
Marquis of Exeter   Lisle, d. 1519)
(ex. 1538)

2. *The Lisle-Dudley Connection*

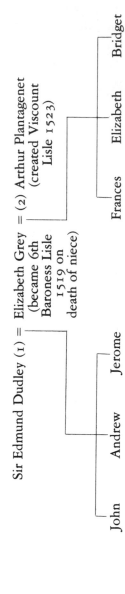

Sir Edmund Dudley (1) = Elizabeth Grey = (2) Arthur Plantagenet
(became 6th   (created Viscount
Baroness Lisle   Lisle 1523)
1519 on
death of niece)

John   Andrew   Jerome

Frances   Elizabeth   Bridget

3. *The Basset Connection*

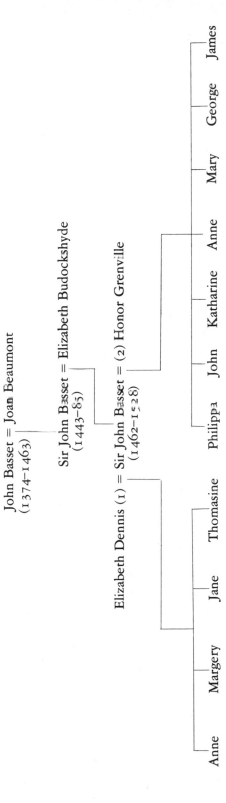

John Basset = Joan Beaumont
(1374-1463)

Sir John Basset = Elizabeth Budockshyde
(1443-85)

Elizabeth Dennis (1) = Sir John Basset = (2) Honor Grenville
(1462-1528)

Anne   Margery   Jane   Thomasine

Philippa   John   Katharine   Anne   Mary   George   James

pleased therewith, to have my eldest son (Thomas Lovell), and heir, to marry with your second daughter, Lady Elizabeth Plantagenet, upon this condition ensuing, that it shall please your good lordship to pay unto me or to mine assigns seven hundred marks of lawful money of England, to be paid in form and manner at such days as your said Chaplain and mine, Master Ralph Sparke, shall instruct your lordship. And as touching her jointure, I am content to bind myself to make her assurance of one hundred pounds sterling by year, during her life natural, out of my lands, with as good assurance as your learned Counsel and mine shall devise. Desiring your good lordship that I may be advertised by your letter in this behalf of your whole mind and pleasure with as great speed as may be: and furthermore to give form and entire credence unto your said Chaplain Sir Oliver and to Mr. Sparke my Chaplain also. And what order and direction they shall take in this matter, I shall be at all times well content and agreeable to it. And if I may do your good lordship any pleasure in the country where I dwell in, or otherwhere, I desire your good lordship be as bold of me as of the dearest friend you have. And thus Almighty God preserve your good lordship to his pleasure.

At East Harling, the xiiij[th] day of September.

By your own to his power,

Signed   ffrancys louell K.   (Vol. 3, No. 510)

In any Tudor family, gentle or simple, a girl's upbringing was designed to fit her for marriage, and service in a noble household or with any family of higher social standing than her own could enlarge her experience and perhaps bring her to a better match. For girls of noble families, and exceptionally for a favoured few of gentle birth, there were two further possibilities. They could be taken into the royal household in their teens as maid of honour to the Queen; or, in some cases, while they were still young children, they could be attached to the separate establishments set up by the King for his daughters, to serve them and act as their companions. As Anne Basset's career will show, her mother judged shrewdly when she made Court preferment her objective for this third daughter who was still young enough to be educated specially for it.

The Tudor social system was still basically feudal, hierarchical, and patriarchal and therefore personal and individual, and the idea of 'service' was central to it. Service was at once education for life and a way of life. The system says to the boy or girl, Serve your apprenticeship to the state of life to which you have been born, learn well to the end you may do better service to your prince, your country, and help your parents, yourself, and all yours. Service is the social contract, inherited by the sixteenth century from medieval thought, which gives security to the individual by recognizing the concept of order that places all men as equals or superiors or inferiors. It gives every man his place in the scheme of things. He belongs. To some extent, perhaps, it had once solved the structural problem of the small society. But as always, whenever some formula is accepted which alleviates the natural inequality of the human lot, the system was already beginning to decay from within, even by the 1530s, as the steadily rising tide of inflation began to erode the foundations of this particular form of the welfare state. The great noblemen and the wealthy prelates were being forced to cut down their enormous households which they could no longer afford to maintain, and to try to place their redundant gentlemen-servingmen and also yeomen servants with better-off friends; and this meant that the gently born who had hitherto accepted service with their equals or their superiors, either as an assured livelihood for their working life, with an annuity in old age, or else as a stage or successive stages in their advancement in some career, found that this social security was definitely at risk.

The system still works: it is still alive in the 1530s, not yet a nostalgic relic of the good old days. But these seven years provide a significant prelude to its ultimate decay. There was a new spirit stirring: there were new ideas abroad about education, and men in positions of authority were planning a different kind of upbringing for their sons. The more we see here of the qualifications traditionally required for service, the more clearly do we realize that this new kind of education which Lisle plans for his two younger stepsons did not envisage the old kind of service as an end in itself, but only as a means – the first step in a career.

When the move to Calais was made, the Soberton household dispersed gradually during the summer of 1533. Jane Basset had an inventory made, left the house in charge of William Seller and his wife, two of Lisle's servants, and early in July took herself off to her native Devonshire. John Basset was supposed to go to the household of a neighbour at East Tisted, some ten miles north of Soberton; but the letters suggest that he put off going there until the autumn, possibly for fear of 'the sickness' – either plague or sweating sickness – which was reported in the neighbourhood. What he did with himself in the meantime does not appear, and there is nothing to tell us how he had been educated before the family left England. George and James Basset and Bridget Plantagenet were entrusted to the care of three of the Lisles' clerical neighbours – George to the Prior of the Abbey of Hyde at Winchester, where their friend John Salcot, the Abbot, kept a more or less casual eye on him; James to Hugh Cook, the Abbot of Reading; and Bridget to Dame Elizabeth Shelley, the Abbess of St. Mary's, Winchester, while Anne Basset and her sister Mary strike out into an unknown world and provide us with what is, I believe, though not a unique experience for that time, a unique account of two English girls being 'finished' in good French society.

JOHN BASSET

The arrangements made by the Lisles for the guardianship and upbringing of the children who remained in England were obviously thought out with care. Richard Norton's household was in every way a suitable establishment for John Basset, the fifteen-year-old heir. Norton was a justice of the peace, a near neighbour, and a prosperous gentleman of a good Hampshire family which had been established at East Tisted since 1308. He was a man of Lisle's age. Whether the arrangement made for his stepson's residence is to be attributed to Lisle's rank, or whether it was considered more suitable for such a well-endowed young landowner as John Basset, it would appear that he lived with the Nortons not on the basis of 'service' but as a youthful friend and guest whose formal education still needed supervision before he could proceed to the Inns of Court. While there, as later on when in residence at Lincoln's Inn, he had with him a man-servant, William Bremelcum, who had either moved with the family when they went to Soberton, or else came from Umberleigh after the departure to Calais in order to wait upon 'the young master'. There is nothing to indicate Bremelcum's station in life. He wore his master's livery coat, but so did Husee and other gentlemen. He wrote a good hand, and appears to have known Latin.

62   RICHARD NORTON TO LADY LISLE   *11 October 1533*

Please it your good ladyship to understand that Master Basset, your son, came ∧to me∧ on Friday last past, and is in good health and merry, and he right humbly commendeth him to my good lord his father and to your good ladyship, and likewise so doth both I and my wife, most heartily thanking my lord and your ladyship for your good wine, which I have in my house, and also for your manifold kindness to me and mine always showed; and your most gentle son humbly desireth you of your daily blessing, which I know well he so hath.

I shall to the best of my little power for the Savegarde of your said son, and also for his learning; wherefore I have required the parson of Colmer[1] to be with him at my house every day in the week to instruct him in his learning, which he will so do, and I doubt nothing but he will make him a very good grammarian. Further ascertaining your ladyship there is no Comen Syknes within v miles of me, save only at Faringdon, thanks and laud be to God. There was none sick in the said Sickness ∧in∧ the parish that I dwell in this ix weeks past and more. Wherefore, Madam, I heartily and humbly desire you nothing to doubt but that I shall do the uttermost that may lie in me for your most gentle son, in any ∧thing∧ that may do him good and pleasure, as knoweth our Lord God, who preserve my singular good lord and your good ladyship together with prosperous health and long life.

1. Peter Bentley.

At East Tisted xj[th] day of October, with the rude hand of him that is yours, with his service, at your commandment.

Hol.　　　　　　　　Ric*us* Norton, thelde*r*　　　　　　(Vol.3, No.525)

John's first letter from East Tisted in the collection is in Latin. Whether the Latin gives us the measure of John's scholarship, or his tutor's, or even William Bremelcum's, it doubtless satisfied his mother. The handwriting is neither John's nor Bremelcum's: is it, perhaps, Peter Bentley's? Bremelcum thoughtfully enclosed a translation for Lady Lisle.

63　　WILLIAM BREMELCUM TO LADY LISLE　　　　*12 March 1534*

Madam, this is the English of my master's epistle only for your ladyship: –

The third day of February, worshipful lord and lady, I received from Calais your loving letters, by the which I do perceive my good lord and you and all your whole household (which is to my great comfort) be in good health. Since I sent you my last epistle, these tokens I have received from you; half a crown of gold and a purse of crimson velvet and shirt band, and for Master Norton a pouch of russet velvet, and for Mistress his wife a pair of beads, with all other tokens to be divided after your gentle mind. And whereas as your ladyship did require and move me by your last letters that I should write again more epistles to your pleasure and to my profit, the labour and pain of this simple epistle I take upon me with my young wit, the which I pray you take it now lovingly as a kind mother to her child. And hereafter with the grace of God ye shall have more at your pleasure. Thus fare ye well.

From Tystyd the xij[th] day of March.

　　　　　By yo*ur* se*r*uant

Hol.　　　　　Wyllya*m* Bremelcum　　　　　　　(Vol.3, No.527)

64　　WILLIAM BREMELCUM TO LADY LISLE　　　　*4 July 1534*

Right honourable and worshipful lady, my especial good lady, I have me recommended unto your ladyship, in likewise so does my Master, and heartily thanking your ladyship for a crown that ye sent him by Master Kyrton, which had my master's best velvet cap for Master George in your ladyship's name. Also my master has need of so much crimson satin to stock him a doublet, and so much black satin for another. Moreover I heartily thank your ladyship for my good coat cloth sent by Sir Robert and iij skins.

Thus fare ye well,

From Tystyd the iiij day of Julius

　　　　　By yo*ur* se*r*uant to his powre,

Hol.　　　　　Wyllya*m* Bremelcu*m*　　　　　　(Vol.3, No.528)

65   RICHARD NORTON TO LADY LISLE   *6 July 1534*

After all humble and due reverence had unto your good ladyship, . . .
Please it your ladyship to have knowledge that my master your ∧son∧ was
merry and in good health at the making hereof. . . .

Madam, ye have ∧cause∧ to yield thanks to God greatly that ye have so
towardly a son, for assuredly there is in him many good qualities, like a
gentleman concerned to wisdom and learning, and is fully replenished with
courtesy, gentleness and kindness. And he shall lack nothing to his comfort
and pleasure at all times that may lie in me. I thank your ladyship for your
kind remembrance and provision for venison, mews and wine, which mews[2]
I have received from James your servant. . . . And anything wherein I may do
your ladyship service or pleasure I shall be right glad to do it, at your
commandment.

As knoweth our Lord God, who preserve your good ladyship with prosperous health and long life. ,

Scribbled the vj day of July, by him that is all yours at your commandment
Hol.   Richard Norton the eld*er*   (Vol.3, No.529)

66   WILLIAM BREMELCUM TO LADY LISLE   *18 October 1534*

Right honourable and worshipful lady, I have me recommended unto your
ladyship: in like case so doth my Master, Mr. Norton and Mistress his wife.
. . . And whereas your ladyship writ to me that your ladyship was informed
that my Master should be sick and keep his chamber iij or v days, and I
would let no man to see him; surely, madame, if so that any man can prove
that my Master was sick or diseased iij or ij days or one day, since the time
that Mr. Norton did write unto your ladyship (and that was about May), let
me never be betrust more, that will I be judged by my Master, Mr. Norton,
his wife, and all his, but as lusty and so merry as any gentleman can be,
thanks be to God! Forsooth, madam, whosoever showed your ladyship so,
he said contrary, and so I desire your ladyship to take it. . . .

As for a chamber in the Inns of Court, Mr. Norton did send one of his
sons purposely for, and can get none, but Mr. Holles of Winchester has one
there, and he does come there but seldom and he may spare him very well,
except certain times. . . . I desire your ladyship to send my Master some
cloth for hosen, and so much to make me a pair, and a shirt cloth for me, and
some money for my Master to make merry withal. Thus fare ye well.

from tystyd the xviij^te daye of Octtober,
          By yo*ur* se*r*uant,
Hol.   Wyllya*m* Bremelcu*m*   (Vol.3, No.530)

2. i.e. sea-mews, the common gull.

Bremelcum's letter is the first indication we have that John was to proceed to the Inns of Court. No one seems to have felt any particular sense of urgency about it, except perhaps his mother, who had obviously written to make inquiries, and nothing more was heard of the matter until December, when Husee took charge. On the 29th he wrote to say that John ought to come up before the next term started; but John himself does not appear to have been in any hurry to leave Hampshire, and it was not until 26 January 1535 that he actually arrived in London.

GEORGE BASSET AND BRIDGET PLANTAGENET

George Basset in 1533 was probably old enough to have been put to service in a noble household, just as his Grenville cousin Nicholas, one of Diggory's sons, was put to service in Lisle's household in Calais. The fact that, although he was old enough, he was not thus disposed of, makes it plain that a different kind of education had been definitely planned for him, as for his brother James, when the family left England. The arrangements made for them suggest that their stepfather was fully alive to the advantages conferred by a more modern education upon younger sons, who would have their own way to make in the world.

George seems to have been one of those happy creatures who know what is proper to their station in life, are content with their lot, and keep instinctively to the way mapped out for them. His self-effacement is that of the model second son; he is never any trouble, and nobody ever troubles very much about him.

When we first hear of him it is practically as an afterthought. His guardian, the Abbot of Hyde, begins by 'advertising' Lord Lisle that 'Master James, your young gentleman . . . is in good health and very well exercised in his learning', despite the fact that James had been left in charge of the Abbot of Reading. After this, as if gravelled for lack of matter, he falls back upon the English weather and the death of an acquaintance to eke out his 'no news'. And then he remembers his own charge, the unobtrusive George:

> Master George, your son, is in good health, and daily encreaseth in his learning, and is as good child as may be. I have sure trust he shall prove a great wise man.[3]

Bridget Plantagenet, Lisle's youngest daughter, was about seven or eight when she was left at Winchester. Besides the Abbess there were twenty-six nuns, thirteen poor sisters, five chaplains, and twenty-nine officers and servants. Dame Elizabeth's own household consisted of a gentlewoman, a servant, and a laundress; and twenty-six 'children of lords, knights and gentle-

3. Vol. 1, No. 28.

men' were being educated there, including Bridget and her cousin Mary
Pole. We know that she learned to read, though not whether she could write,
and if she could not it would not have been unusual in her station. She would
have learned to sing, if only for church purposes, and sewing and embroidery
would have taken up much of her time. Above all she would have learned
Manners.

Though separated from their parents, the children were not left friendless
in England, as witness the involvement of Christopher Plummer, a canon of
Windsor and sometime fellow-courtier of Lisle's, in the high drama of a
certain bonnet for Bridget.

<h2>67   CHRISTOPHER PLUMMER TO LORD LISLE   27 March 1534</h2>

My most singular good lord, Where my evil scribbling pen with lack of
cunning to give your lordship such thanks as I were bound to do ∧be not
sufficient∧, I humbly beseech you to accept my most humble recommendation to your lordship, and to my singular good lady your wife: and certifying
her ladyship that Waynam's wife, ∧that∧ when she knew my lady's grief,
then she was not a little bashed therewith, and therefore she gat a'horse and
rode to Sir Antony Windsor, for to his wife, as she said that little Lady
Bridget's bonnet was sent by a man that she knew not, but that he said he
knew the said Sir Antony and the lady his wife well, and so she sent the
bonnet by him. And as she saith, she sent to the said lady xl^s that she did owe
unto her, which xl^s she feareth is lost. Then, at her coming to the said Lady
Windsor, this bonnet was not come. Then, as she saith, there was search
made where the man that ∧had∧ the bonnet was lodged; and with a woman a
box with the bonnet ∧was∧ found; and then was present my lord's servant,
one Robert Anmer, and he did promise her ∧to∧ bring the bonnet to Winchester from Southwick, which had been no great journey if she had ∧had
any∧ great mind to have visited either St. Swithin or any else. And thus I do
certify my said singular good lady can learn how by her wisdom it shall please
her to allow with credence the premises. I remit all to her pleasure, for
further excuse than her saying I cannot write. . . . .

By your humble servant and bedeman,

Hol.   *Christ*ofor Plum*mer*   (Vol. 3, No. 533)

Although George had been left in the charge of the Abbot of Hyde and
the more active care of the Prior, several references to money for his 'hostess' at this time might conceivably imply that he did not live, as the custom
had been for such boys, in the Abbot's own house, but lodged in the town of
Winchester and perhaps attended the College as an oppidan, or townsman.

The next letter introduces the Abbess of St. Mary's.

68   ELIZABETH SHELLEY TO LADY LISLE   *26 February 1535*

After due recommendation, pleaseth it your good ladyship to know that I have received your letter, dated the iiij^th day of Februarii last past, by the which I do perceive your pleasure is to know how Mistress Bridget your daughter doth, and what things she lacketh: Madame, thanks be to God, she is in good health, but I assure your ladyship she lacketh convenient apparel, for she hath neither whole gown or kirtle but the gown and kirtle that you sent to her last. And also she hath not one good partlet to put about her neck, nor but one good coif to put upon her head. Wherefore, I beseech your ladyship to send to her such apparel as she lacketh, as shortly as ye may conveniently.

Also, the bringer of your letter shewed to me that your pleasure is to know how much money I have received for Mistress Bridget's board, and how long she hath been with me. Madame, she hath been with me a whole year ended the viii^th day of Julii last past, and as many weeks as is between that day and the day of making of this bill, which is xxxiij^tl weeks; and so she hath been with me a whole year and xxxiij^ti weeks, which is in all four score and five weeks. . . . I have received in all, since she came to me, toward the payment for her board, lxx^s. Also, madame, I have laid out for her, for mending of her gowns and for ij matins books, iiij pair of hosen, and iiij pair of shoes, and other small things, iij^s v^d. And, good madame, any pleasure that I may do your ladyship, and also my prayer, you shall be assured of, with the grace of Jesus, who preserve you and all yours in honour and health. Amen.

Written at Winchester, the xxvj^ti day of Februarii, by her that is at your commandment,

Elisabeth Shelley   (Vol. 3, No. 539)

It would have been unusual for a child in an abbey school not to pick up at least a modicum of Latin, and here we see that Bridget was expected to be able to read a matins book.

69   JOHN ATKINSON TO LADY LISLE   *July–24 August 1536*

Right honourable and my singular good lady, in my most heartiest manner I recommend me unto your good ladyship. . . .

Mr. George your son hath been sick in an ague and lay at his hostess', where they sent to me word thereof; and as evyll as I might ride I was with him, and comforted him the best I could; and took the wife money to buy such gear with as was needful for him. And she desired money for his lodging and washing since Magdalene tide, which at that time I had not ready, but promised her to send it her at Easter or soon upon. And as I understand, Edward Russell fett[4] Mr. George away from Winchester upon Easter Eve; and since I heard not of him. But the poor woman shall be contented her duty. And Mrs. Bridget is merry, and her lady desireth ij partlets ∧for her∧, which your ladyship may please to send. . . .

Written in haste, at Mottesfont, by the hand in haste of your assured bedeman and chaplain,

Hol.   John Atkinson, priest   (Vol. 3, No. 540)

By the autum of 1536 the plans for the next stage of George's education have been made: he is to perfect his French, in the house of a priest in St. Omer where James and the son of one of the Spears of Calais are already living. The devoted Husee is making the final preparations.

70   JOHN HUSEE TO LADY LISLE   *1 November 1536*

Pleaseth your Ladyship to be advertised that I received your letter by Clifford, and where your ladyship writ touching Mr. George's coat, the velvet was bought long since, ∧but∧ because the tailor's man was sick I would not suffer it to be made till such time I knew what would become of the tailor's man, in whom, indeed, at length proved that there was no parcel of sickness: for if it had not been for this cause he had had the same at the King's being there, for that was wholly my mind and pretence; but I thought it better he to be without a new coat than to abide the danger of the plague. Madam, his coat is made, and sent him by the receiver of Hyde, both long and large, and no fear but it shall serve him any day this v years with little reparation, for it is very good velvet, and (being not Lucca velvet) there is no better worn. I had it of Christopher Campion – it cost xijs. the yard – whom at St. Andrew's tide your ladyship must needs have in remembrance; and likewise the draper for such stuff as Mr. Basset and his man hath had, for the which I am bounden. And where your ladyship willed me to make Mr. George a coat of damask or of some other silk, truly, a coat of damask or silk were skant to serve him one year, and is much sooner worn than this will be. I think I have done most for your ladyship's profit and honour in this matter. . . .

From London this All Hallow's Day.

By him that is your ladyship's during life,

Hol.   John Husee   (Vol. 3, No. 544)

4. i.e. fetched.

71   JEHAN DES GARDINS TO LORD LISLE   *28 November 1536*

My right honourable and renowned lord, humbly beseeching you that I may be taken as of your most humble servants and of my right honourable and very good lady your wife, I am very glad that it hath pleased you to send to us your son George Basset, to be instructed as well in the French tongue as the Latin, in company with his brother James, who studies and profiteth well, and I find him a child of gentle conditions and of a very good understanding, also obedient. I trust that his said brother is of like sort; and with the help of God, without which nothing is possible, I shall take pains to instruct them both in good manners and in learning, as I hope you have confidence in me. . . . And thus my right honourable lord, I make an end, praying Our Creator to give you whatsoever of good you may ask of him in faith.

Written the xxviij[th] day of November by
          your humble and lowly servant,
Hol.   Jehan des Gardins[5]   (Vol. 3, No. 545)

However, James was sent for back to Calais a fortnight later, and, as rumours of impending war between France and the Emperor grew ever stronger, so was George in April.

72   JEHAN DES GARDINS TO LORD LISLE   *19 April 1537*

Right honourable and renowned lord, I humbly beg that I may be recommended to your good grace, and to my honoured lady, my lady your bedfellow. According to the contents of your letters and in furtherance of your command, I send you your son George, whom I have found a good child, obedient and diligent in his study, and right discreet for his years. May God grant him grace so to persever.

I had hoped that he might have tarried longer, so that he could have mastered his grammar, but the times will not suffer it. I am comforted that you have commanded him home in good time. I had intended, had the French approached unto St. Omer, to have taken him back to Calais by way of Flanders.

Furthermore, my honoured lord, I humbly thank you for your good liberality. If it had happened that the danger had been greater, I should have taken refuge with you, trusting in the good offer and conditions that it hath pleased you to make me, all undeserving though I am, howbeit my willingness and desire to do you service be great, and to your gentle son. At the

5. This and the following letter from des Gardins are in French.

same time, fearing lest some evil may overtake us, I have delivered to your good friend a little packet, in the which is a little sum of gold pieces and of silver, and vj little goblets of silver; the which, of his good favour, he hath promised me to deliver at your lodging, so that it may remain in safety until such time when we may hope to see things go better.

And as concerning that which is owing to me, James came to me the xix[th] day of August, and George leaveth us the xix[th] of April, which is viij months. I have expended for the two of them xl[s], but I would not willingly have the money, because it is safer in your hands.

Thus I conclude, praying humbly that I may be of the number of your lowly servitors, and may God preserve you.

Written the xix[th] of April
    Your servant,
Hol.   Jehan des Gardins, priest   (Vol. 3, No. 548)

George may have returned to St. Omer, as des Gardins hoped, when international tensions eased in the autumn; but by the following March the third stage of his educaiton had begun: he had been 'preferred' to Sir Francis Bryan, with an eye to the public service. The only two letters he wrote which survive both belong to this year. As letters they are purely formal: the boy has nothing to say, and says it in the approved Tudor manner. But as specimens of handwriting they are really beautiful, and as the work of a boy of about fourteen they well deserve commendation (see Pl. 8).

73 GEORGE BASSET TO LORD AND LADY LISLE   *1 July 1539*

Right honourable and my most dear and singular good lord and lady, in my most humble manner I recommend me unto you; beseeching to have your daily blessing and to hear of your good and prosperous health, for the conservation of which I pray daily unto Almighty God. I certify you by these my rude letters that my Master and my Lady be in good health, to whom I am much bound. Furthermore, I beseech your lordship and ladyship to have me heartily recommended unto my Brothers and Sisters. And thus I pray God to conserve your lordship and ladyship ever in good long and prosperous health, with honour.

From Woburn, the first day of July,
    By your humble and own Son,
Hol.   George Bassette   (Vol. 3, No. 549)

So there was George, readied for his world – an ordinary little boy, less noticed than his elder brother the heir, and his younger brother the bright

Right honorable and my moste dere and syngler goode lorde
and ladye/ in my most humble manir I recomaunde me vnto your
besechynge to haue yor darlye blessynge/ and to here of yor goode
and prospus helth/ fore the consideracione of whiche/ I praye
darlye vnto almyghty godde. I certifye yowe by thyes my
rude lres that my Maistr and my ladye be in goode helthe/
to whome I am myche bounde. ffurthemore I beseche
yor lordeshepe and ladyshepe to haue me hertelye recomendid
vnto my brothr and systers. And thus I praye godde to conserue
yor lordeshepe and ladyshepe evr in goode/ longe/ and
prosperus helthe wt honor. ffrome woobnam the
firste daye of Julye

By yor humble and
owne son George
Basset

8. George Basset to Lord and Lady Lisle (No. 73)

lad of the family, but ultimately the sturdy stock 'from whom the Bassets of Cornwall'.

JAMES BASSET

'That sweet babe' is the description applied to James Basset, then aged seven, by the good-natured English scholar Antony Barker, who helped to take charge of him in Paris: 'much meeter to serve the temporal powers than the spiritual dignities', was Husee's head-shaking comment, when James was taken into the service of Bishop Gardiner. The childless Wallops, Sir John and his lady, were enchanted by his pretty manners, and his precocious fluency in the French tongue; and everybody seemed delighted to take endless trouble over his affairs. Only Husee was never taken in by little James and his facile charm. It was fortunate, therefore, that James's career was the one with which he had least to do.

James always had opinions of his own: about his education, about his creature comforts, about his clothes, about Lenten fish. And he had his wants: a gold chain and slashed, square-toed, velvet shoes, to be in the fashion; and a bed to himself – an unheard-of indulgence, this last, for a mere schoolboy . . . did not the younger scholars at Winchester and Eton sleep two to a bed? James knew how to look after himself from the very beginning. Not only was he the outstanding letter-writer among the Basset children: he was also the cause of much letter-writing on the part of others. There is ten times as much correspondence about James and his affairs as there is about his brother George; and it is noticeably upon behalf of James that Lisle really exerts himself.

It looks as though James, then aged six, arrived at Reading in the summer of 1533. Alexander Aylmer, the steward of Kingston Lisle, was evidently sent to check on his welfare.

74   ALEXANDER AYLMER TO LADY LISLE   *4 November 1533*

Right honourable and my singular good lady, In my most lowliest manner that I can I recommend me unto your good ladyship, certifying your ladyship that I have received your letter. . . . Certifying your ladyship that Master James is in good health and merry, and as well ordered as any gentleman may be; and as much my Lord of Reading maketh of him; and playeth[6] him to his learning, both to Latin and to French. And as for shirts and hoses and all other gear, a' shall lack none. And moreover my Lord of Reading desired my

---

6. pleythe. Baskerville in *English Monks and the Suppression of the Monasteries* reads 'plieth'. Aylmer began to write 'ply' and then crossed it out.

Lord and your ladyship to put no mistrust in him for keeping of Mr. James, for he is as tender of him and were the King's son. No more to your ladyship at this time, but Jesus preserve you long to his pleasure.

wryttyn At kyngston lyle the iiij day of this mone

Hol.   Yo*u*r Seruaunt Alexander Aylmer   (Vol. 3, No. 551)

75   HUGH COOK, ABBOT OF READING,   *20 November 1533*
      TO LORD LISLE

My singular good lord in my most hearty wise I have me recommended unto your good lordship // Rendering unto you most hearty thanks for the manifold & continual gentleness toward me shewed / & have received your lordship's letter // And as concerning your young gentleman // because I would he should be well seen unto by a woman for his dressing and ordering / for because as yet he is too young to shift for himself // I have set him with William Edmunds my under-steward / where I warrant you he is well ordered. And I assure your lordship he is the most towardly child in learning and other his qualities that I have knowen // And where it pleaseth your lordship to write to me / that if I need any wine or herring // your lordship will prepare for me // My lord if it shall be your pleasure that I may have iiij^{or} tun of Red & Claret I shall see your lordship there for contented // And also shall be very glad to take of your lordship's gift one barrel of herring for mine own eating / how dear so ever they be // And as your own ye shall so find me, As knoweth Almighty God / who increase your lordship with much honour to his pleasure //

At Redyng the xx^{ti} day of Novembre //

        ffrom hym that is At yo*u*r lordshypes Co*m*maundement. . . .

Signed   Hugh Abbatt
        ther /   (Vol. 3, No. 552)

The stay of the special embassy from France in Calais in November 1534 was seized upon for the benefit of James. The advantages of speaking French really well – an accomplishment still somewhat rare among the English nobility and gentry – must have been in Lisle's mind when his education was begun by the Abbot. The plan was, accordingly, that James should be sent to school in Paris without further delay, and to this end the help of one of the members of the embassy, Guillaume Poyet, President of the Parliament of Paris, was enlisted. He was to see whether James was sufficiently advanced to benefit by such tuition, and if so, to bring him over to France on his return journey. From the next letter it seems that the Oxford scholar Antony Barker was called in to put him through his paces.

76   ANTONY BARKER TO LORD LISLE   *12 December 1534*

My very honourable and singular good Lord, Please it you to be advertised
that I spake here with little Mr. James Basset, your son, and according to
your commandment I proved his wit and towardness, which is far beyond the
praise and esteem your lordship hath made of it. Ye need not to doubt but
that he is as apt to send to France as any young thing that went thither this
many years; and specially forasmuch as your lordship hath commended him
to the tuition of so worshipful and so substantial a master, who is my singular
good friend and shewed me you had moved him therein at Calais. But when
he saw the child, and had heard him commune, he was as glad of him as he
could, which I right well perceived by his words had to me of him. If you had
sought all France ye could not a' procured him so notable a man, nor that is
able or more willing to do him good than he is. If I should choose a friend in
a whole realm I would gladly light upon him. Wherefore I do greatly rejoice
both for the quietness and contentation of your most noble mind and my
especial good lady's, and for the profit of that sweet babe, who shall have
both a master and a father of this gentleman. If it be my fortune to see France
again I will do him all the good I can, howbeit, I nor ten such cannot do the
least part that he may.

Such news as we have here I would write to your lordship if I knew ye had
them not, from time to time, as I am sure ye have of those that know them
better than I. There is in France very sharp execution of heretics, as I think
your lordship hath heard; and I pray God continue them in that good purpose. Thus I commit your goodness to the tuition of Almighty God.

　　from London the xij^{th} of December,
　　　　By yours moste obediently,
Hol.　　　　　　Antony barker   (Vol.3, No.553)

The embassy returned via Calais on 7 December and on the 27th Poyet
wrote from St. Germain-en-Laye, 'I beg you will not forget to send me my
little man, as you promised, and I will take pains to do with him as you wish.'
He may have taken the boy over with him and left him with his parents for
Christmas. That James was certainly in Calais on 19 January 1535 is evident
from a letter of Husee's of that date, in which he says he has sent over a
saddle for him.

In spite of the President's eagerness to take charge of him, Honor Lisle
seems to have been loath to part with her seven-year-old, and letters which
follow suggest that she was bent upon securing for him the care and attention
of some of her fellow countrymen, just to be on the safe side. John Bekynsaw, Thomas Rainolde, and Walter Bucler, to whom she turned for
assistance, were Oxford scholars who had, like Barker, been drawn to Paris
by the reputation of its great University.

77 JOHN BEKYNSAW TO LADY LISLE   *8 April 1535*

Right honourable and my singular good lady, my duty humbly used, please it your good ladyship. . . . I am very sorry my first letters came not to your ladyship's hands, with whom ye should have received a letter of Mr. Thomas Raynoldes, priest, whose name you desired to know of me in your first letters, who will be (doubt ye nothing) as diligent for his part as is possible to see to your son whensoever it shall please you to send him hither, if it would please you to certify us by your letters how and with what condition ye put your son to him, and whether he should be at school within his house or whether he shall ride with him when he rideth about his progresses. To the which, I think, your ladyship will not agree, for his age is too tender. Whatsoever your mind be, we will see him ordered according, and continually certify your ladyship by the grace of Jesus, whom I shall pray continually to augment prosperously your noble state to his honour and your heart's desire. Thus I commend me humbly to your good ladyship.

    Att paris the viij^th day of Ap*r*ile

        by yowr humble & dayly bedma*n*

Hol.   Joan*nes* bekynsaw, scholar   (Vol. 3, No. 554)

78 THOMAS RAINOLDE TO LADY LISLE   *19 April 1535*

My honourable and singular good Lady, after most humble commendations to my honourable good Lord and you, this is to advertise your Ladyship that the ix^th of this present month I received your kind letters dated at Calais the ij^de of the same, whereby I understand that . . . ye mind shortly to send my master your son to Paris as ye did before: at whose coming I shall lament nothing else but that my power shall not be according to my will to do him such pleasure and service as my good lord and you hath bound me unto by such high kindness as ye showed unto me at my last being in Calais with you, which unfeignedly was such as I never found before in persons of your estate and dignity.

    Doubt ye therefore no more of me in this point to my little power than ye would of him that ye most trust, for beside this your inestimable goodness, the old familiarity and gentleness of your brother Mr. John Grainfild,[7] the singular benefits of Mistress Grainfild to whom ever I have been much beholden, would compel me to the thing and I had never seen nor heard of your highness. Moreover I am a poor countryman of his, which thing naturally as ye know engendereth a certain love towards such as we were never beholden unto. I desire thereto no more but that at his coming ye send

---

7. Lady Lisle's half-brother, John Grenville, Rector of Kilkhampton near Bude.

instructions what ye will command me to do, and by God's grace it shall be fulfilled with the advantage, if I can.

And thus the grace of our Lord be ever with you, with long prosperity in your honourable estate.

ffrom Paris the xixth of April
                    Your power bedisma*n*
Hol.   Thom*a*s Rainolde priste   (Vol. 3, No. 555)

Despite Poyet's eagerness to have the boy, and the response made by Bekynsaw and Rainolde, it was not until August 1535 that James was dispatched to Paris in the charge of John Worth, a member of the Retinue.

79   JOHN WORTH TO LADY LISLE   *13 August 1535*

Right honourable and mine especial good lady, My duty done, I lowly submit me to my good lord and your good ladyship as your poor bedeman during life /// Pleaseth your ladyship to be advertised that my master, your son Master James, ca[me] to Paris in good health and merry, thanks be to God. An[d the] Lord President was very glad of his coming, and s[o was] Master Bekynsaw and Master Rainolds, and hath them recommen[ded unto] my good lord and your ladyship; and to the uttermost of [their] ij powers they will do to the furthering of my master [your son] in his learning and good manners, for his profit: and [my] lord's honour and your ladyship's: Howbeit they wi[ll take] no charge of his apparel, to receive it by bill: but they [desire] that there may be one continually waiting upon h[im], to keep his apparel and to make answer for it, and to 'ray him in the morning, and to see him to have his meat and drink in a due time, and to wait on him wherever he go: for they say it were dangerous that he should go alone and nobody to wait upon him: for there are so many ungracious lackeys in Paris that he may soon have a displeasure amongst them: if he have not one waiting on him: and so they desired me to write to my lord and your good ladyship: · // And for that cause, this vj weeks I will wait on him myself: for so long I may be from Calais without any check of my wages: to my own cost and charge I will tarry so long: praying your ladyship in that mean time that I may have a letter from my lord and your ladyship of your pleasure: and I trust as long as I am with him to attend and wait upon him as duly as any servant shall wait on his master: · and to write daily to my lord and your ladyship how he doth in his learning, and how he is entreated with them, and whether there be any sickness here or not: or else any wars towards, whereby that there might any danger happen to him if that he should tarry there, whereby ye might the sooner send for him again: · But I trust in God it shall not so need ///

... No more to your good ladyship, but Jesu preserve my good lord and your ladyship to his pleasure and to your hearts' ease.

at p*a*rys the xiijth day off Agust,

yo*ur* pow*re* bedman,

Hol.   John Worth   (Vol. 3, No. 556)

80   THOMAS RAINOLDE TO LADY LISLE   *14 August 1535*

My honourable and singular good Lady, most humble commendations premised to my singular good Lord and you. This is to advertise your ladyship that the xijth of this month my master your son came to Paris in health and merry, thanks to God; by whom I received from you letters and also a cramp ring of gold, wherefore most humbly I thank you.

And as touching your request for your son, doubt ye nothing but that I shall rather forget myself than him, in all things that I may do him pleasure or shall appertain to my duty, as concerning counsel or furtherance in his learning. Howbe[it], after that Mr. Bekynsaw and I had opened your mind to Monsieur Poyet to whom ye send him, he determined to put him into a College. What he meaneth thereby I cannot yet well perceive, and therefore I judge the best. The truth is, he gave as great a charge to the Principal of the College, which is called the College of Calvy, and also to the man which shall teach him, as he had been the King's son, declaring also the honour of my Lord and you, and how greatly he was bound unto you.

After this we went to the College, where we saw the chamber where he shall be, which is not to be contemned, after the manner of Paris. He shall have his bed alone. He shall dine and sup with the Principal of the College. And because the child is tender and come into another manner of air than he hath been herebefore accustomed unto, his diet also must somewhat be altered. And principally because he is forth of Monsieur Poyet his house, and in a place whereas be many rude and wild children, we thought it right necessary to retain your servant Mr. Worth with him, for the time at the least, if ye mind not that he shall not continue. This far we are, and if anything mislike us, as I will be plain with you I do somewhat suspect the manner of the College will, ye shall soon be informed thereof. For as for Mr. Bekynsaw or me to meddle in that point we thought it not best: nor ye gave us no such commission.

Monsieur President commanded the Principal to provide all things necessary for him, and he would content him therefor. Your servants Smith and Goodale would fain have sooner returned than they did; but to see all things discharged, and to bring you a full and a determinate answer, it was not possible; as knoweth Our Lord, whose grace continually be with you, with daily increase of your honour.

from Paris the xiiijth of Auguste
          Your holy to his litell power,
Hol.   Thom*a*s Rainolde p*ri*st   (Vol. 3, No. 559)

The Collège de Calvi at which Poyet placed James was one of the few colleges in the University of Paris intended only for what we might call primary education, or, perhaps more properly, education in the rudiments of grammar.

81   JOHN BEKYNSAW TO LADY LISLE   *30 August 1535*

Right honourable and my singular good lady, my duty humbly used to my lord and to your ladyship. It may please your ladyship to accept my short writing unto you at this time of Mr. James your son, because your own servant can certify your ladyship of all things concerning him more plainly than I can; which I promise you hath shewed himself a trusty and loving servant (as he declareth himself to be bound) to my lord and you. He hath paid for his own commons here, waiting on Mr. James himself, and given the pedagogue ij crowns for the dressing of the chamber of Mr. James. For although that Monsieur le President commended him (as I wrote) very heartily and tenderly to the Principal and the Regent, saying they should tenderly and nobly regard him / and that for his expenses, they should have no recourse to no man but only to him, yet the Principal, and specially the Regent, knowing sufficiently his fair words and little deeds, will not stand to his promise. For they say they must (because they be but scholars them-selves) have money beforehand. And he will give them none, neither before nor after, but with shameful asking. Wherefore they will not have to do with him. Howbeit the Principal denieth not to furnish him his commons (how, this bearer can tell) at the President's word. Mr. Raynoldes and I durst not far to meddle / seeing the child was sent to him to be found at his cost. Your ladyship's pleasure knowen, we shall, to the uttermost of our power / accomplish it, as long, for my part, as I shall be here, which I know shall not be long. Wherefore I am sorry I cannot in this part no longer tarry to do your ladyship such service as my heart would. Thus humbly I commend me to my lord and your ladyship, desiring Jesus to have you in his keeping.

Att paris the xxxth day of August 1535
          by yowr one humble bedman
Hol.   Joan*nes* beky*n*saw   (Vol. 3, No. 560)

My honourable and singular good Lady, after my most humble commendations to my honourable good Lord and you, this is to advertise your Ladyship that Master James, your dear son, is in health, thanks to God. As touching his governance *he lacketh nothing necessary.*[8] But as *for learning, or the French tongue, he* prospereth not so well as I would he did; which I assure you grieveth me, both for that he is (by as much as I can ye perceive) apt to learn: and also for that ye put your trust in me, which to the most of my power I would be loath to see it frustrated.

The impediments hereof, as I better perceive now than I did at the beginning, be this. The children of the college as he is of, and more also, by their statutes are compelled to speak Latin, so that he cannot get the tongue there neither so well neither so soon there as he might do, being in some honest house of the town, *with a small reward given to some* person there to take pains ∧with∧ him. For by mine advice he should be utterly from the company of English men, or else it will hinder the learning of the tongue very much, *which I think most necessary first* to be learned. *And therefore if* he spendyd this year in that and writing, with a little induction to his grammar, if I be not deceived, it would be most to his profit. *For until he perceive* the tongue he shall get little learning at any Frenchman his hand. *And again, it will* never be so well taken as now, at the beginning. *And* ∧*that*∧ *once* a little had, he cannot choose but daily increase more and more in it.

Master Poyet is not yet returned, nor, as they say, will not return this month; but as soon as he cometh I will *know his mind concerning your re*quest in your letters. But in the meantime, if ye write a letter to me, to be delivered to him, expressing that ye would have your child where he might principally for this year learn to speak, read and note the French tongue, I think it would do well. *And if he will* not accomplish that, and you be at the charges of his finding, as I suppose ye are, if ye take him from him I doubt not but he shall be better seen unto for his profit than he is now. *Neither for this (my trust* is) that ye will not be aggrieved with me, for it is no honesty to be too busy in another man his cure. And to take him thence I have none authority, *neither it were not convenient until such* time as it may be known what Mr. Poyet will do; for he seemed that he would have him most honestly and profitably handled, *which now I know* well cannot be where as he is now.

If ye put him into the town, all charges counted, he will cost you little less than xx^li sterling the year, as I have experience by such as are committed to me already; for as much costeth a child's commons as a man's, yea, they be more dangerous to take a child than a man, because they require more attendance, and also are more apt to sickness.

---

8. The italicized passages underlined in the MS.

Thus I trouble your ladyship ∧with∧ long tedious letters, but I hope the sooner to obtain your pardon for that I do it of good zeal and love that I have towards your son; as knoweth our Lord, whose grace ever be with you, with long continuance of your honourable estate.

from Parys the vth of Octobre. I wrote vnto yow the xxvth of Septembre I truste my *lett*res came to yo*ur* hands.

                    Yo*ur* Orator
Hol.   Thom*a*s Raynolde priste   (Vol. 3, No. 563)

It looks as if this suggestion of Rainolde's took effect; and whether or not James was removed from the College it is obvious that from now on the priest was in charge of him. Poyet vanishes from the scene as abruptly as he appeared. Throughout the spring and early summer there were rumours of impending war between France and the Empire (both coveting the duchy of Milan and Francis I having annexed Piedmont and Savoy), and constant talk of removing James to the safety of Calais. When Rainolde left the city, apparently early in June, Barker took over, with Bekynsaw and Walter Bucler acting as a kind of advisory committee in the background; and finally, some time about 11 July 1536 James rode back to Calais with a member of the Retinue.

He seems to have had a brief summer holiday with his parents at Calais, and was then dispatched to a crammer's to prepare for his return to the university. When next heard of, he has been since 19 August 1536 in the care of Jehan des Gardins at St. Omer. Early in December he returned to Calais.

ANNE AND MARY BASSET

In November 1533 Anne Basset, then a girl of twelve or perhaps nearly thirteen, was sent to live with a well-connected French family at Pont de Remy, some few miles along the River Somme from Abbeville. Thybault Rouaud, or Rouault, Sieur de Riou, was a gentleman whom Lisle had met on the occasion of his Garter embassy to the French king in 1527, and whom he describes in 1538 as one of his best friends. He was known as a fine soldier, and came of a family established in Poitou since the fourteenth century. His ancestors for many generations had been distinguished servants of the Crown, and his own grandfather, Joachim de Riou, was a Marshal of France who had helped to defeat the English in 1453.

Thybault's wife, Jeanne or Jenne de Saveuzes as she always signs herself, came of an even more distinguished lineage than her husband, being the only child and heiress of Ferri, Seigneur de Saveuzes, of an ancient family of Picardy. By her first marriage in 1511 to Antoine de Créquy, 'dit le Hardi', she became allied to one of the most illustrious houses of Artois and Picardy, and it was in her right as de Créquy's widow that the lordship of Pont de Remy was held. Madame de Riou's daughter, Anne de Créquy, and her husband Guillaume du Bellay are the Monsieur and Madame de Langey referred to in various letters. Thybault de Riou's sister, Anne Rouaud, married Nicholas de Montmorency, Seigneur de Bours, in 1512. It was to the household of Madame de Bours in Abbeville that Anne Basset's younger sister, Mary, was sent in August 1534, when she was about eleven or twelve years old.

Both girls were apparently 'at the finding' of their guardians, but their clothing and their pocket-money were supplied by their mother, and the situation was adjusted by the usual gifts from Honor and Arthur Lisle. Polite letters and presents were exchanged at frequent intervals, and both ladies, together with their daughters and daughters-in-law and sons and cousins, gradually built up an acquaintance with the Lisle family which outlasted the stay of the two girls and was apparently broken only by the abrupt termination of Lisle's tenure of office.

The motives which prompted Lisle and his wife to send Anne and Mary to these distinguished households, in the given circumstances of 1533, were quite simple. Honor's two eldest daughters, aged between eighteen and sixteen, could be expected to make the suitable matches which were normally arranged for a knight's daughters whose upbringing had been homely and whose features and accomplishments were apparently the same. But Anne and Mary, who were obviously extremely good-looking and were not yet in their teens, given the right background and training during the next few years, might surely aspire to something considerably more ambitious – to preferment in their stepfather's world. There were many links with France. Henry's sister Mary had been its Queen, and his new queen had been brought up in the French court. French culture, good looks, and influence might well bring a stepdaughter of the King's uncle to an honourable position at Court and some great marriage.

Madame de Riou and Madame de Bours both write in French,[9] and both go straight into the matter of the letter in refreshingly direct terms. The women always sign themselves by their family names.

83   MADAME DE RIOU TO LORD LISLE   *15 November 1533*

Sir, your daughter whom it hath pleased you to send me is here arrived on Thursday night, who is so much the more than very welcome to me that I know not how to yield you sufficient thanks for the confidence you have in

9. Except for the letters from Lady Lisle, all letters in this section, including those from Anne and Mary Basset, are written in French.

me, entrusting her to my keeping. Sir, I ensure you that, God aiding me, I shall cherish her, entreating her every way as she were my natural daughter. And as for the recompense of which it hath pleased you to write to me, neither Monsieur de Riou nor myself desire none other recompense saving only your friendship and good favour. The young gentlewoman is of such good conditions that it will not be difficult to instruct her; and as for such gear as she needeth, the gentlewoman that brought her can inform you what will be necessary, as will John Smyth also. Until he doth return again, I send you no commendations from Monsieur de Riou, because he is not here; but on his behalf I thank you as much as possibly I can for the dogs which it hath pleased you to send him. And to conclude I heartily recommend me to your good favour, praying God, Sir, to grant you good life and long.

From Pont de Remy, the xvth day of November.

Signed   By her who right heartily desireth to
     do you pleasure and service,
      Jenne de Saveuzes   (Vol.3, No.570)

We have no means of knowing whether the following letter from Anne is actually her first, and was written because, during the six months that had passed since her arrival at Pont de Remy, she had by then become proficient enough to dictate in French to Madame de Riou's usual secretary the gist, if not every word, of what she wanted to say. The reference to 'the second reader' ('second lisour') in the postscript would seem to mean Lady Lisle's secretary, who would have to translate the letter to her.

84 ANNE BASSET TO LADY LISLE   *11 May 1534*

Madame, I was very glad of the coming of John Smyth, being greatly desirous to hear good news of you. Madame, I must not omit to advertise you of the goodly entertainment made me by Monsieur and Madame. Had I been their natural daughter they could not better nor more gently have entreated me. I very much wish that my sister might be here with me in these parts.

Madame, and it might please you, I would heartily desire you to send me some demi-worsted for a gown, and a kirtle of velvet, and also some linen to make smocks, and some hosen and shoes. I send you back again the gold ornaments which I brought with me, because I know not how to make use of them here. I heartily beseech you that it may please you to send me some others. I have need of three ells of red cloth to make me a cloak, with a hood of satin.

Madame, commending me very humbly to your good favour, I pray our Lord to grant you in health very good life and long.

From Pont de Remy, the xjth day of May.

I beg the second reader of this my letter to recommend me very humbly to the good grace of my lord. I have promised a mastiff to a certain gentleman here. I beseech you, madame, that you will have one sent to me, to the end that I may acquit me of my promise.

Your most humble and very obedient daughter,

Signed   Anne Basset   (Vol. 3, No. 571)

85   ANNE BASSET TO LADY LISLE   *10 June 1534*

Madame, I recommend me most humbly to your good grace. It is now eight days since Madame de Riou gave me leave to come here to visit. I came with the daughter of Madame de Bours. This bearer who has come hither will more at large tell you of my news; and I greatly desire to know yours, and I beseech you that it may please you to send me word by the first messenger who cometh from those parts. Madame, I beseech Our Lord to give you very good life and long.

From Bours, the xth day of June.

Your most humble and obedient daughter,
Anne Basset

I beseech you that I may be recommended to the good grace of my lord my father, not forgetting the good remembrance of my brothers and my sisters. Madame de Bours recommendeth herself to your good grace.

(Vol. 3, No. 573)

It is more probable that Anne's visit in June was arranged in order to give Madame de Bours the opportunity to see for herself that the Basset daughters were acceptable, well-brought-up girls. Mary arrived at Bours at the beginning of August, or possibly in July. She herself, as far as the correspondence shows, did not write home until November.

86   MADAME DE BOURS TO LORD LISLE   *9 August 1534*

Monsieur, I have read the letter which it hath pleased you to write me, and I humbly thank you for the honourable proposal which you make me. Unworthy as I am, I would fain be so happy as to be able to do you service, and to take every care of the young gentlewoman your daughter. She hath been merry and in good health since she came into these parts. I find her of such an excellent disposition that I love her as if she were my daughter, and she is beloved of all them that see her. It maketh me not a little proud that they should say she is fairer than Mistress Anne. I shall be very glad when soon she can understand the French tongue, for then she will have greater pleasure than she now hath. If this bearer might have remained here longer he could have helped her much in the understanding. Nevertheless she hath begun well and with a good will. No more at this present, after having me humbly recommended to your good favour.

Monsieur, I pray our Lord to preserve you in health, with good life and long.

From Bours, the ix^th day of August.

By her who is more [than yours] to do you se[rvice],
Signed   Anne [Rouaud]   (Vol. 3, No. 574)

Mary writes in her own hand. Was the dictation by, rather than to, the secretary?

87   MARY BASSET TO LADY LISLE   *8 November 1534*

Madame, I recommend me very humbly to the good favour of my lord my father, and to you. Madame, I am very glad that this bearer goeth to you, so that I may have news of your welfare. I beseech you, madame, that you will be so good lady unto me as to send me word thereof, for it is the thing in the world of which at all times I have the most desire to hear. Madame, this bearer hath procured me a gold ornament. He would not let me have it for less than five crowns for the making, but Madame de Bours hath given him three crowns only; and that I may secure it I have promised him that you will give him a gold crown on the behalf of Madame de Bours. If it shall please you to do me this kindness madame, I shall study to requite you. I hope to write to you further when the time doth allow. Madame de Bours sendeth you some goshawks. To conclude I pray our Lord, Madame, to give you very good life and long.

From Bours, the viij^th of November.

Your very humble and obedient daughter,
Hol.   Marie Basset[10]   (Vol. 3, No. 575)

10. French original:

Madame Je me recommande tres humblement a la bonne grace de monsieur mon pere et de vous Madame Je suy bien aise que le porture va de vers vous affein de savoir de vos bonnes nouvelles. Je vous suplye Madame me vouloir faire le bien que de men mander car set le chose de se monde que Je desyre le plus que deen avoyr bien souvant Madame le porture ma baylle ung dorure. Il na point voulu baille a moin de synx ecux de la fason mais Madame de Bours ne luy a baille que troes ecux et affein de lavoir Je luy et promys que vous luy donnere ung ecu an darure de Madame de Bours sy vous plet Madame luy vouloir faire le bien Je seroye bien bonne a vous Je espere de vous escrire plus a loyty mecque Madame de Bours vous envoie des outours quy sera la fien Je prie nostre singour Madame vous donner tre bonne vie et longue de Bours le viij^e de Novembre Votre tres humble et obesante file Marie Basset.

88   THYBAULT ROUAULT, SIEUR DE RIOU,   *11 August 1535*
       TO LORD LISLE

Monsieur, I have received the fine present which by this bearer it hath pleased you to send me and I ensure you they are the finest birds that I have seen here this long time. I hope within a short while to be able to recompense you for them with some hawks which I shall send you, of which sort, as I think, you have hardly any in those parts. My wife and I have been very sorry that Mistress Anne hath been taken with a certain sickness, but thanks be to God she is now wholly recovered from it, for the which we have been greatly comforted, and shall be much distressed if it should again fortune to come upon her here. But if so, we shall see to her entirely as if she were our natural child. As for Mistress Marie, who is with my sister, she is merry, and is indeed the fairest maiden in the world to look upon. To conclude, heartily recommending me to your good grace, as in likewise doth my wife, who desireth me to thank my Lady Deputy for the goodly present that she hath sent her. Praying God, Monsieur, to give you good life and long.

From Pont de Remy, the xj[th] day of August.
Signed   He who desires to do you service
                  Thybault Rouault   (Vol. 3, No. 577)

James evidently stopped at Pont de Remy on his way from Calais to Paris.

89   ANNE BASSET TO LADY LISLE   *17 August 1535*

Madame, I commend me to your good favour as effectually and in the most humblest wise that I can.

Madame, I was very glad to receive good news of you, as also of the coming of my brother, whom Madame findeth handsome and of good conditions and that he knoweth enough to converse. Madame, I would most earnestly entreat you that if I am to pass the winter in France I may have some gown to pass it in, as I am all out of apparel for every day. Madame, I know well that I am very costly unto you, but it is not possible to do otherwise, there are so many little trifling things which are here necessary which are not needed in England, and one must do as others do. Madame, I have received some shoes and some hosen which are too small for me: I beseech you of your goodness to send me some others. And thus I make an end, praying God to preserve you in health with prosperous and long life.

From Pont de Remy, the xvij[th] day of this month.
              Entirely your humble and obedient daughter,
                  Anne Basset[11]   (Vol. 3, No. 578)

11. In one hand throughout, not the hand of Mme de Riou's usual secretary.

After a pregnancy that occasioned some concern, Madame de Riou gave birth to a child at the end of October. It is perhaps worth noting that her two youngest daughters were called Anne and Marie.

The notes that follow have been jotted down on the back of a letter from Madame de Bours by Lady Lisle's secretary. They could be either the summary of what the speaker wished the writer to expand with some elegance, or, at the least, to translate into normal syntactical form, or else the form which the writer knew that the speaker usually employed. That Lady Lisle intended them to be transmitted in their abbreviated form I do not believe.

90   LADY LISLE TO MADAME DE BOURS   *after 4 November 1535*

To make recommendations to ∧my lord your husband, M. d'Agincourt, and my lady∧ your daughter there is married, and to my lord her husband, and to the good gent that maketh so much of my daughter, and to my lord your son that maketh so much of my daughter. My said daughter hath written to one of ∧her∧ sisters to be mean for her to me for money to play. I am content that she play when ye shall command her; but I fear she shall give her mind too much to play. It will come soon enough to her. I would she should ply her work, the lute and the virginals, but I refer it all to your goodness. Thanking her for the oultour.[12] My servant showeth me that ye have made my daughter a robe furred with white. I pray you send me word what it cost, and I shall send you.   (Vol.3, No.583a)

In the spring Madame de Riou took Anne on a journey of some two hundred and forty miles to Vendôme for the lying-in of her daughter, Madame de Langey, and to visit relations and friends en route.

91   MADAME DE RIOU TO LADY LISLE   *12 March 1536*

Madame, having secured this bearer, I would not let him depart towards you without sending you my news, which is that I returned on Friday at night to this place from our journey, the which was accomplished without any mishap, thanks be to God; and throughout Mademoiselle your daughter hath been merry, unto whom I have shown many parts of the country, and also honest company, by all of whom she hath been esteemed very fair and of good conditions. She and I are greatly desirous to hear from you, and if I had not found this bearer I had been minded to send a man to you on purpose that I might be informed. I pray God that you fare as well as I can desire it. . . .

From Pont de Remy, the xij[th] day of March

Signed   She who from her heart would do you pleasure and service,
Jenne de Saveuzes   (Vol.3, No.585)

12. i.e. outour = goshawk.

There was increasing tension now on the Franco-Flemish borders; war between France and the Empire was realized to be inevitable, though in fact it was not declared till 17 June.

92   MADAME DE BOURS TO LADY LISLE   *13 March 1536*

Madame. . . . The gentlewoman your daughter is merry. I shall procure for her that which she hath need of as you write me, and you may trust to it that I shall do for her as she were mine own daughter. She is of such excellent conditions that she well deserveth to be cherished. I would that for an hour of each day I might be with you, as she doth also.

It is now x or xij days since I was obliged to bring Monsieur de Bours and all our household to this town for fear of these evil times, as more at length this bearer can report. It falleth out very ill for me, whether we are defeated or whether we succeed, as I shall lose all our goods. I had never greater need of the help of Our Lord, to whom I pray, madame, to give you good life and long, recommending me humbly to the good favour of Monseigneur the Deputy and you.

From Abbeville, the xiij^{th} day of March.

She that is always ready to do you service,

Signed   Anne Rouaud   (Vol. 3, No 586)

93   MARY BASSET TO LADY LISLE   *13 March 1536*

Madame, I commend me most humbly to the good grace of my lord my father, and to yours. Madame, I am greatly rejoiced that Madame de Bours is sending you to know of your welfare. I most humbly thank you for the seven score pearls, and for the crown that it hath pleased you to send me. I send you a pair of knives for to put in your cabinet, because I think you have none of such fashion. The spinet-player who taught me at Guechart Madame de Bours hath contented for that which he hath done; and she hath taken another in this town. Also, I have given the schoolmaster who taught me to read and write ten sols only, while waiting to hear from you. My said lady of Bours as yet hath not had my dress of satin mended, because to this hour she hath been right occupied with her affairs. She will have it repaired for Easter, and also will look about her to find some good spinet. I am greatly indebted to the said lady, who taketh always much pains for me. She doth not send you the items, what she hath spent for me; but when you shall send here one of your own servants the sum thereof will be given him to bring you.

This bearer who goeth now to you is one of the servants of this house. When we go into the country he attendeth the chariot of Madame. I have always promised to give him some present: I commend him to you. This day I have been to see my sister at Pont de Remy. I have brought letters, which I send you. No more, madame, but praying our Lord to give you health, good life and long.

From Abbeville, this xiij[th] of March.

Your very humble and very obedient daughter,

Signed   Marie Basset[13]   (Vol. 3, No. 587)

94   MARY BASSET TO PHILIPPA BASSET   *13 March 1536*

My good sister and friend, I greatly desire to hear good news of you and of my other sisters. If I might have my wish I would be every day an hour with you, that I might teach you to speak French. I enjoy myself so much here in this country that I should be right well content, if that I could often see my lady my mother, never to return to England.

I send you a purse of green velvet, and a little pot for my sister Frances: also, a gospel to my sister Katharine, and a parroquet to my lord my father, because he maketh much of a bird. I beg of you, my sister, to have the goodness to present it to him, and to entreat him to send me some pretty thing for this Easter. He hath yet not sent me anything, although I have never forgot him.

There is a gentleman here who is called Philip, and for love of your name he sendeth you a little basket. I have promised him a bow. I pray you to be a mean to my lady that she send it him by this bearer. I owe a pair of shoes to the gentlewoman who seeth to my wants which I lost at play with her. I greatly wish that my lady my mother would send them to her. I have not yet given any present to the chamberer of Madame. I were right glad to have something to give to her.

Recommending me as well and as humbly as I may to your good favour, to the good favour of my sister Frances, and to that of my sister Katharine, and to all the gentlewomen of my lady my mother. I beg to be recommended to Jan Semy.[14] I would fain know whether he be healed. I pray our Lord to give you a good husband, and that very soon.

Madame de Bours commends herself as heartily as she may to your good favour, and to my other sisters.

From Abbeville, the xiij of March,

Your most loving sister, ever your friend,

Signed   Marie Basset   (Vol. 3, No. 588)

That both Anne and Mary should write to their mother in French to demonstrate their progress is understandable – their letters, like those of their hostesses, would be translated to her. But why should Mary do so to

---

13. In the hand of the usual de Bours secretary.
14. John Smyth.

Philippa, who could not speak French, when she could have written in her own hand in English? There must have been a 'house rule' that while French was still not perfect no English should be spoken, read, or written. Letters from the girls' mother may have been an exception, but these rough notes were dictated, possibly for translation.

95   LADY LISLE TO MARY BASSET   *after 16 April 1536*

Sending God's blessing and mine, willing you to serve God and please my lord and lady; and so doing I think the cost of you well employed. I send money by this bearer, John Smyth, to my lady, that ∧thereof of the money that I owe her∧ she shall buy you such ∧sleeves∧ as ye shall need. I send you also hose-cloths because the hosiers here, for lack of measure of your leg, cannot make them meet for you. I will that ye make mine excuse unto my lady that she be not discontent that I have not sent her money or this time. I had such business that I could send it no rather. And any other thing that ye lack, show your mind unto John Smyth. And if ye can perceive what thing my lady lack –   (Vol.3, No.590a)

96   LADY LISLE TO ANNE BASSET   *after 16 April 1536*

And I send you God's blessing and mine charge, you to please my lord and lady, and that ye keep you a good maiden.

I send you by the bearer money to buy you smocks, because ye say that which I sent you was too thin. I send you also hose-cloths, because the hosier here knoweth not the bigness of your leg. I have sent my lady a needle-case. And because I have had no leisure to work ∧it∧ as I would have done, I pray my lady to take it gree.[15] And shortly I will send her better.

                                                   (Vol.3, No.592a)

Anne spent nearly three years in the de Riou household, but in the early summer of 1536 her family were beginning to make plans for her future career and her 'preferment unto the queen'. By the end of September she was back in Calais and remained at home while the plans progressed, but the Lisles remained in friendly touch with Madame de Riou.

97   MADAME DE BOURS TO LADY LISLE   *17 November 1536*

Madame, I humbly thank you for the fine ox you have sent me, and in likewise for the gracious letters you have written me. And I am very glad to hear of your welfare, and greatly wish that I might more often be with you.

15. i.e. kindly, in good part.

This shall be to advertise you that the young gentlewoman your daughter is merry, nor would you believe how fair and tall she is become. She commendeth herself in humblest wise to your good favour. She hath received the velvet that you did send to her to make her a gown, also the six crowns, and the border that before you sent her. I promise you she rejoiceth much to have some pretty thing such as I saw she had need of. I have admonished her according to your commandment, and this you can be sure of in me, that I shall entreat her as if she were my daughter.

I beg of you to procure me a couple of lanners as I have been requested by one of my good friends to get them for him. I address myself first to you, trusting you will not take it amiss. I have given Monsieur de Gamaches my brother the horn that you sent him. He humbly thanketh you, and recommends him to your good favour. My daughter recommends her humbly to your good favour, and thanketh you for the shoes and hosen that it hath pleased you to send her. She was married eight days ago. If it might please you to send her husband an English greyhound you would do him pleasure, as he taketh great delight in the chase. And if there be anything in these parts I beseech you to be so good to me as to advertise me. Monsieur de Riou telleth me that he could send one of his people to you from here in eight to ten days time. Pray send me word at large of all your news. Thus to conclude, after recommending me to the good favour of my Lord Deputy, and to you, I pray our Lord, Madam, to grant you good life and long.

From Bours, the xvij^th day of November.

My son Montmorency recommends him humbly to your good favour.
She that is more than yours to do you service,

Signed   Anne Rouaud   (Vol. 3, No. 596)

98   MARY BASSET TO LADY LISLE   *23 December 1536*

Madame, as humbly as I can I recommend me to the good grace of my lord my father and of you.

Madame, I most humbly beseech you that it will please you to pardon me that I have so many expenses to write you of: to make my peace with you I send you a little melon. I pray you to take it in gree.

I send you the account of the expenses that Madame hath incurred for me. I shewed Jensemy the expenses to which I put the angel that you sent me. I would heartily desire you that it will please you to send me a little money, for I have none for my small pleasures. I was very glad of the lanner which you sent to Madame de Bours, which incontinent she hath presented to the captain of this town, in the which he taketh great pleasure, and saith that if you have any matter, so that it is in his power, he is at all times ready to do you pleasure and service. It was a great pleasure to me to have seen my brother before he departed to Paris. He waited upon Madame de Bours at Gamaches. Monsieur de Gamaches was greatly rejoiced to see him. He made him right good cheer, as this bearer will more at large inform you.

Madame de Bours was sick the last time that the merchant departed hence, which was the cause that she wrote not to you. My brother hath sent me a chain for the neck. I would fain desire you to be glad of the gentle remembrance and good friendship that he showeth me. To conclude, praying our Lord, madame, to give you very good life and long.

From Abbeville, the xxiij^d of December.

     Your very humble and most obedient daughter,
Signed   Marie Basset   (Vol. 3, No. 597a)

Both the Basset girls had been happy in homes where they had been loved and really treated as daughters of the house. Only now do we learn of the secret unhappiness of one of their hostesses. Madame de Riou had a cousin, Anthoinette de Saveuses, a nun at a convent in Dunkirk, who had become a friend and constant correspondent of Honor Lisle. She had recently often asked, pressingly, for the latter's latest news of the de Riou household; and though up to now she had been uncharacteristically discreet she at last comes out with her reason. She tells the story of Madame de Riou from the death of her first husband, from whom she had inherited the Pont de Remy property where Anne Basset has spent the last three years. We have had a glimpse of Thybault de Riou in letter No. 88, though only as a keen sportsman with an eye for a pretty girl.

99 ANTHOINETTE DE SAVEUSES TO LADY LISLE *10 September 1537*

Madame, my Lady Deputy, as humbly as I may I recommend me most affectuously to your good favour, beseeching you, madame, in my heartiest wise, that I may be commended to the good grace of my lord your husband. Madame, I have received your letter, and have right well understood the contents thereof. . . .

Madame, you have written to desire me briefly to declare to you the secrets of these poor people, and that you will most gladly mediate therein, for the which your benignity most humbly with all my heart I thank you. Nevertheless, my intention was not to speak of no worldly poverty but of a spiritual need, entreating you, madame, by the good estimation I have that God will not refuse you anything that you ask of him, for I trust that you are wholly stablished in true charity. But to ensure you, madame, that I would never distrust you, so it is that I advertise you privily, that Madame de Riou carries as much grief in her bosom as any lady in the realm of France. The good lady, who is of noble descent and of a very great house, possessed by year an income of 15,000 livres, in spite of many who show daily, after getting their evil counsels put into execution, that what they seek in her is nothing but the enjoyment of her property. So it is, Monsieur de Riou was a very impoverished gentleman of a very good family, and Madame de Bours, the sister of this aforesaid gentleman, the which during the lifetime of the late Monsieur du Pont de Remy was often at the house, as Madame had the up-bringing of one of the children of the aforesaid lady of Bours. After the death of the aforesaid Monsieur du Pont de Remy, Madame de Bours very slily tried to persuade the good widow to take in marriage her brother de Riou. She, being young, and well-disposed to have her pleasure, took him, to the displeasure of all her own relations, because she might have matched with two gentlemen of considerable standing, one of whom could spend 20,000 livres of income, and the other 30,000. Madame, I cannot express to you the distress that I have endured for the three weeks which I spent with her; for she told me so much of her grief that I could not listen without freely shedding tears with her. And it is great marvel to me how she hath had of this second marriage as many as twelve children, having suffered such distress as she hath told me. So much so, that she has even proved to me that one day Monsieur broke open a great coffer that had belonged to Monsieur de Saveuse, Madame's father, which was full of fine vessels, the which he placed on a table and staked at dice to the value of 14,000 livres in one afternoon; not to mention all his other follies and the great gifts which he hath made to his own near relations, as if he wished totally to destroy likewise his own children, of whom he makes as little account as if they were nothing to him.

The good lady doth consider the great charge of her six little children, of whom the eldest is not more than ten years old, and that all that they can have cometh from her, and that daily she sees thus pitifully wasted the goodly estate that the late gentleman her father left her – so much so, Madame, that she made her moan to me that during these twelve years that she had been married to him, he has diminished her inheritance by the value of more than 50,000 livres, for in her youth one could hardly have found a gentlewoman of her sort in all the realm of France; and as for wishing to return to any of her own relations, she can find in them neither loyalty nor the aid of good counsel in this cause. Beseeching you most humbly that of your kindness it may please you by means of your most discreet counsel to help in the necessity in which this good lady at this present finds herself, for she laments to me that she doth not know to whom to turn; but since the last letter received from you I have determined to apply to you in confidence, to know, Madame, whether one cannot prevent the said gentleman so that he may no longer give rein to such prodigality with her possessions and those of his children; because if he continues these expenses much longer, without brooking any hindrance, however much she resists, the good lady will, I fear, be obliged in the future to sell her lands.

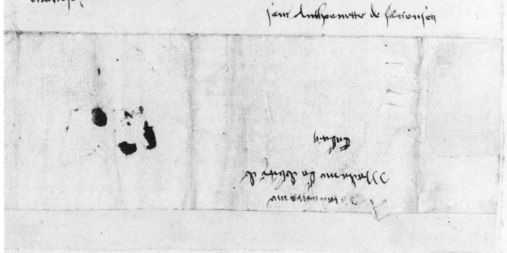

9. Concluding page, with address, of Anthoinette de Saveuses
to Lady Lisle (No. 99)

Madame, I trouble you much, and in especial your good secretary, but the good hope I have to obtain of you some good counsel impelleth me to return by way of you, beseeching you, madame, that the report of this affair may not be any further divulged than of your good favour, madame, you have promised me by the contents of your letter. . . . thus praying God to grant you, Madame, the entire accomplishment of your virtuous and most noble desires.

    From Dunkirk the tenth of September,
              by your humble servant, ever your good friend,
Hol.   Seur Anthoenette de Saueuses[16]   (Vol. 3, No. 605)

Lady Lisle offered to put Madame de Riou's situation before the King of France via the English Ambassador, a prospect that possibly reached the lady's husband, who thereupon suddenly became a reformed character, 'as from night to day' according to Sister Anthoinette.

    And what are we to think of her sister-in-law, Madame de Bours? Is she really a Henry Jamesian villain-of-the-piece, somewhat in the style of Madame Merle; or is she just what she seems in her letters – a sensible, kindly lady, to whom Mary Basset became much attached? Did she really scheme the marriage between her impoverished brother and the rich young widow? And did she know, all the time, of the goings-on in her own household and the fondness which was developing between her son and Mary Basset? Did she secretly encourage it, in the belief that such a match would be a good one for Gabriel de Montmorency, future Seigneur de Bours?

    Mary was sent in February 1537 to Amiens for a brief holiday with Madame d'Agincourt, Madame de Bours's daughter, because her hostess's mourning for her brother meant that 'she would have had but little pleasure here'.

100   MADAME DE BOURS TO LADY LISLE   *22 February 1537*

Madame, I was very glad to have good news of you. I thank you as heartily as I can for taking pains to write to me. Your servant Jehan Semy has been here since Sunday. . . . And he tells me that there are horses of all prices in Calais, and that there is a roan which it seems to him would serve well for Montmorency. . . . I have given him lx crowns of the sun, but if it cannot be had for this price, and if it amounteth to no more than another x crowns, I beg you to obtain it and I will repay you.

    Mademoiselle your daughter is very well. Those in whose company she hath passed her Shrovetide hold her in high esteem, and consider she is very handsome. Mademoiselle de Gamaches and I have been at Amiens, and by

16. See Pl. 9.

reason she was in her chariot I asked her to take her home with her, and she was to have sent her back to me here, the which she could not do by reason there are so many mercenaries in the fields, as my servant will more plainly declare to you. . . . I pray our Lord, Madame, to give you good life and long.

From Abbeville, this xxij day of February.

More than ready to do you service,

Signed   Anne Rouaud   (Vol. 3, No. 612)

There have been requests for news of Lady Lisle's pregnancy in previous letters from both the Basset girls and their hostesses, but only in a line or two here and there. As the time for her mother's confinement approaches, Mary writes of it at greater length.

101   MARY BASSET TO LADY LISLE   *17 March 1537*

Madame, I most humbly recommend myself to the good favour of my lord, and to you.

Madame, I beseech you to pardon me that I have not written to you to thank you for the crown that was delivered me by a gentleman who passed by Amiens where I was. Madame de Bours had sent me there to spend Lent, where I have had much good honest company. And as concerning the border costing twenty crowns which you desired Madame to procure for me, she hath sent to Paris for it for me, and she saith she will have a gown made me for this summer. Mademoiselle d'Agincourt begs me to make you her humble recommendations to your good favour. I have seen my Lady Wallop when she passed through this place, whom I besought to remember me to my lord for the gown which he promised to give me. If it will please you to do me the kindness to remember him I would beg you to do so.

I pray that it may please our Lord to send you your heart's desire, with safe deliverance of your child, and that he may send you a good hour, even such as I desire for you. If I might have my wish I would be with you when you shall be brought to bed, to warm his swaddling clouts for the babe. I have besought all my good friends to pray God for you, and chiefly I have commended you to the good prayers of my schoolmaster when he sayeth his mass, who recommendeth him to your good grace.

I pray our Creator, madame, to give you very good and long life.

From Abbeville, the xvijth of March.

Your humble and very obedient daughter,

Marie Basset   (Vol. 3, No. 615)

On 5 April Mary sends her mother the news that Monsieur de Bours has died, and asks if she may wear mourning. In the next letter, the reader may wish to be reminded, the 'Mademoiselle' d'Agincourt is always so called, though she is Madame de Bours' respectably be-husbanded daughter.

102   MARY BASSET TO LADY LISLE   25 *April 1537*

Madame, I recommend me most humbly to the good favour of my lord my father, and to you. Madame, I was very glad that this gentleman hath taken pains to come here, in order that I might write to you. I greatly desire to hear good news of you, and when you shall be brought to bed. I pray our Lord to give you a good hour. I began oft times to write to you, but Madame de Bours has had much trouble which has been the reason that I have not more often sent you my news. I thank you most humbly for the laces which you have sent me, and the little piece of border has been given to the little son of Mademoiselle d'Agincourt. Whilst the Queen was in this town, Madame de Bours made me take off my mourning apparel to go to see the Court. I always went there with Madame de Riou. I will not write you a long letter, madame, at this present, trusting another time to inform you more at length of my news.

Mademoiselle d'Agincourt hath her most humbly recommended to your good favour. Madame, I have promised a pair of hosen of kersey to a man, if it would please you to send me the same, for the which I most humbly thank you. I pray our Lord, madame, to give you very good life and long.

From Abbeville, the xxv[th] of April,
          Your very humble and most obedient daughter,
                    Marie Basset   (Vol. 3, No. 619)

In replying to Lady Lisle's letter of condolence, Madame de Bours had assured her that the French Queen had found 'the gentlewoman your daughter to her good liking'. She says later, 'As I think, you would scarce recognize her, she hath grown so tall and she is considered by all who see her to be of excellent conditions, and I love her as she were my daughter.' One cannot help wondering whether 'the man' Mary refers to in this letter and 'the gentleman' in the next were both Gabriel de Montmorency.

103   MARY BASSET TO LADY LISLE   5 *September 1537*

Madame, I recommend me most humbly to the good favour of my lord my father and to you.

Madame, I am right heavy at being so long without tidings of your welfare. And glad am I indeed that Madame de Bours now sendeth to you. It was told me at Abbeville that you had sent me a letter; but the messenger lost it, which grieveth me sore. Madame, I most humbly thank you for that which you sent me by Jehan Semit. I am waiting till he must pass again by Abbeville in order that I may send you tidings of myself.

Madame, I entreat you to be so good lady to me as to send me a pair of sleeves to give to Madame, and a pair for me. She hath very little that is from England. If it please you to send her something I should be very glad. There is a gentleman, who is a good friend of mine, who hath begged a pair of me, and a pair of shoes. I should be very glad to make him a present of them. This bearer will tell you who he is. . . .

Mademoiselle dagincourt recommendeth her very humbly to your favour.

Your very humble and most obedient daughter,

Hol.   Marie Basset[17]   (Vol. 3, No. 622a)

In January Madame de Bours agreed that Mary should be allowed to go to Calais for her brother John's wedding 'provided that you send her back to me soon after'.

104   MARY BASSET TO LADY LISLE   *28 January 1538*

Madame, I most humbly recommend me to the good favour of my lord and you.

Madame, I was very glad to have your good news, for to me it is the greatest happiness in the world thus to hear from you very often. I perceive from this that you will shortly send to fetch me, within ten or twelve days, to be at the wedding of my brother. I beg of you, madame, and also of my lord, that you will be so good unto me to permit me to return [to be] with Madame; for indeed I should be very sorry to leave Madame de Bours as she hath done me so much honour and hath showed me so great friendship that I can never forget how well I am entreated of her. I have received by Le Jolier the buckram and the shoes that you sent me. I most humbly thank you for them and in likewise for the gloves and laces which you sent me by this present bearer. I beg of you, madame, to be so good lady unto me as to send me some pretty thing to make a present to the gentlewoman of Madame de Bours, for she doeth for me as much service as she may, and yet I have not given her anything, save that she thinketh her much beholden to you for the two ells of worsted that you sent her when I came first into this country. To conclude, I pray our Creator, madame, to give you very good life and long.

From Bours, the xxviij[th] of January.

Your very humble and most obedient daughter,

Hol.   Marie Basset   (Vol. 3, No. 623a)

17. See Pl. 10.

Madame je me recommande treshumblement a la
bonne grace de monsr. mon pere et de de vous
madame i mengre bien de estre se long tampz sans
auoir de vos bonnes nouuelles jay este bien ayse de se
que madame de bours vous enuoye leora il
ma este dyt a abbeuylle que vous mengpes lettres le
messagere le pardon de quoy jay este fort marye madame
je vous remerçye treshumblement de l le en que vous marye
enuoye par jehan je ma fande que dit serpere
pas abbeuylle adin que je vous eue escripre de mes nouuell
Madame je vous supplye me voulons fande se bien de
mennorer vne pere de marlye de lene a madame et vne
pere pour moy elle na pn de se dangleterre je vous
pleset iny en amouere je seroye bien ayse il ia vng gentslome
de me boys iny que ma prye de nauoro vne pere et vne
pere de souples je seroye bien ayse que vng en sese present
se prome vous dyroi que i est les je prye que madame
de bonras vous diret escripre pour quelque tyous romant
pour monsr dagnemont et vng ternore blau pour soy fret
tout l le lettre que je vous escripre souet terrianes que vous
pour vous demandero je boono vng sorm que l pasosero tant demande
et me fon tant de onoeno que je ven bien recommaçre
lle bonne edraoy que llont a moy me fet prandre
tant de hardyelle de vous demandero que sera l la fin de
sproreso nostre seyr madame vous donnero tres bonne et longe
longue vye de bonnes se vo de sosebare

Mademoselle dagnemont se recommande
treshumblemet a rostre grace

rostre treshumble et tres
obeisante fylla mason basset

10. Mary Basset to Lady Lisle (No. 103)

For some reason, though John Basset's wedding took place in the third week of February, Mary did not reach Calais until the first week in March. Presumably Lady Lisle had sent the escort she had been waiting for, but Madame de Bours says in the letter she sent with her: 'I send the lackey with the gentlewoman your daughter because she is not accustomed to ride a hackney, and so that he can keep by her and can report to me how she shall sustain the fatigue of the journey. I greatly fear lest she may take cold.' Later she was able to write: 'I was very glad to learn that she was merry on all her journey. I often wish she were with me, and it is marvel how much I miss her.'

Mary did not return to Madame de Bours. Like Anne, at fifteen or sixteen she was ready for the world.

6

Estate and Legal Business
1533–1535

Lisle had inherited a life interest in certain lands in Somerset from his first wife, Elizabeth Grey, and these caused him more trouble than the rest of his estates put together. They had been acquired by Sir Edward Seymour (later Earl of Hertford), and legal disputes over the terms of the agreement and payment of rents went on interminably. What mattered most was that Lisle's need for bringing the case to an end made him more and more dependent on the goodwill of those who alone could get the agreement officially ratified, and we shall see later how valuable this dependence became to Cromwell.

105   EDMUND WINDSOR TO LORD LISLE   *12 July 1533*

Right honourable and my singular good Lord. . . . It hath pleased your lordship to admit me with my uncle one of your attorneys in your absence, as unworthy. Certifying your lordship that Sir Edward Seymour hath been divers time with your Counsel and his at divers meetings concerning the bargain of all such lands as he hath bought of your lordship in Somersetshire, and saith that your lordship hath not kept your covenants because your lordship hath entered into your lands again, which is contrary to your covenant and against the law.

Unto whom Master Densell and Master ∧Marvin∧, your Counsel, answered and said, that if the law were according as his counsel had said, that he would not of his worship take both your lands and your money, saying that the meaning of the Indenture was otherwise, and also that he was bound to make your lordship a lease for term of your life of a Cxl^li within a month next after the estate and assurance made according to the word of the Indenture, wherefor he had forfeit five m^d marks. And Master Seymour's Counsel answered that your lordship had not discharged it of all incumbrances, wherefor he hath forfeit no bond neither is not bound in the law to make your lordship a lease, by reason that the land is not discharged. And further saith, that your lordship shall not have lx^li of it, because it is left

130

out of your recovery, and your lordship hath been a wrongdoer, for because my Lord of Norfolk and other that were feoffees neither made your lordship a state but were seised unto the use of Sir John Dudley, whose right he had. And then your Counsel answered that Sir John Dudley and his friends were bound unto your lordship in the sum of ten m^d li that your lordship should enjoy all such land that my lady your wife had during your life: which Indenture, if your lordship do not agree before this and the next term, your Counsel must have a sight of it.

And when your Counsel and his had debated all these matters, he asked them what they would do, and then they took day to answer, which was on Friday last. And their answer was this: that your lordship will be content that if you might keep your possession, or else to be made sure of your annuity during your life according to the true meaning of the Indenture. And further they would not go in your lordship's absence; and that your lordship should take no extremity of your part and he to do likewise on his part, whereunto he would not agree, but would have the possession of the land. And then they prayed him to determine his mind, what he would do, in writing; whereupon he was content; which shall be sent unto your lordship as shortly as may be. . . .

Also that if it may please your lordship to write unto such as be your friends in that country, that if he make any business[1] with your tenants, that they may resort to them for help in your absence. For he intendeth to make business, as you shall perceive by his writing more plainly hereafter, when it shall come. He hath promised your Counsel to do nothing until he hear word from you again, as God knoweth, who preserve you.

ffrom London this Saterday att Night the xijth daye of Julye

by your assuryd to his lyttell power

Hol.   Edmond Wyndesore[2]   (Vol. 1, No. 17)

From the man left in charge of Lisle's manor of Soberton in Hampshire comes a letter typical of a constant stream of such, concerned with the day-to-day affairs of the properties in England.

106   WILLIAM SELLER TO LADY LISLE   *5 November 1533*

Right honourable and my singular good lady, my duty lowly remembered to my good lord and your ladyship, please it to you to understand that this day Nicholas Person paid to Thomas Miller xvj^{li} viij^s iiij^d. Also the said Thomas demanded vj^{li} xiij^s iiij^d for Michaelmas rent, which Nicholas Person would not pay without my lord's pleasure further known therein. Also my

---

1. i.e. if Seymour makes trouble.
2. Addressed: To the Right honorable lorde lisley att Caleys this lettre be delyered yn haste.

lord left at his departing with me a bill to deliver John Hyntton of Portsmouth xx^{ti} quarter of barley, wherein Nicholas Person will know more of my lord's mind afore the deliverance. Also the 'erschedowe' is sowed for my lord and x acre in the 'gafton' for your ladyship. All other grounds were let out. The sum of wheat sown is xij quarter; moreover xxiiij^{ti} pound of fine yarn is put to weaving for your flannel, which shall be sent as soon as it is ready. Your board is ready and good. It may please you send for the swans and the peahens, for the fox hath killed your crane. I have killed iiij of your hogs; the salt cost ij^s. It may please you send salt for the residue; they be fed at home for fault of mast. Six be put to Rumsden. Please it your ladyship to send word how the rest of your wool shall be used. Madame, we live hardly now, but in Lent, without your good help ∧of herrings or some other fish∧ we shall take more penance for our sins against our will. Your good neighbours were glad to dress your land; praying to the Blessed Trinity my lord and your ladyship would come hither to eat it, who have you both in his blessed keeping.

    fro Subberton the vth day of nouember
           by your bed[e]man,
               Wyll*ia*m Seller   (Vol.1, No.71)

Honor's brother-in-law, married to Mary Grenville, keeps an eye for her on her Cornish estates, including the rich tin mines inherited from her first husband.

107   THOMAS ST. AUBYN TO LADY LISLE   *23 November 1533*

To my very good brother and sister,

My duty done with most loving and hearty recommendations, I recommend me to your good Ladyship and so doth your loving sister my gentle bedfellow. . . .

And as touching your right in any tin-work within the Sanctuary ground, the custom of Stannary giveth you no more than any man will give, for the said custom giveth liberty to any tinner to work in all waste ground without licence, as well in the waste of any Sanctuary as elsewhere; but whether it be lawful to any incumbent to license any tinner to work within his closes without the assent of his patron or no, I refer that point to your learned counsel in both laws. And hereupon the setting of any man for you is forborne till my said lord's further pleasure and yours be known therein. And further of my simple mind herein this said bearer can shew you at length, for tinners at St. Uny Sanctuary worketh now as well within close as without; the workers without worketh by the custom and within by licence of the parson, and else they could not there work.

Also, good Madame, all the works in Carnkey and Carnbrea been all in good peace, thanks to Almighty God, and have had no better likelihood this iij years to be ∧so∧ good as now; and at every wash I have been at ∧it∧, both early and right late, and have seen to the uttermost of your profit as it had been to mine own, and have done my diligence about in your courts and at your audit, and instead of a better place it was kept at Clewens. . . .

ffrom Clewen in Cornwall w*ith* lytill leys*or* the Sonday byfore sentt Kat*er*nes daie w*ith* the rude hand of me yo*ur*s Assuredly Thomas *Hol.*   Seyntaubyn   (Vol. 1, No. 80)

108   Lord Lisle to Sir Anthony Windsor   *17 November 1533*

Master Windsore, I commend me unto you, and have received your letters with the foot of your account signed by mine auditor. And as touching the difference between Sir Edward Seymour and me, you shall understand that I gave mine instructions and mind unto my servant Leonard Smyth at his departing. . . . yet my whole trust was and is specially in Mr. Marvin and Mr. Densill, and others of counsel, and wholly, yea and entirely, in your good information and following the said my causes in general as though I were there myself: most heartily praying you to look upon the letter herein closed, and according as you with my counsel shall think most meet, so it be not for my utter dishonor, I shall and will always be content to be ordered. But one thing I will advertise you, that seeing I have kept possession till this day of the lvj^{li} by year: I intend, till I see and know better right and reason to the contrary, to possess and also to continue the same as long as the law will bear it, yea and as much more as my friends and I can make to the mainte-nance of the same. And as soon as you have commoned with my counsel in it and know the extremity what the law will bear in it for the continuance of my said right and my most advantage, I most heartily pray you that I may be advertised with all speed of the same and that you keep this my letter secret and close unto yourself, with the letter here enclosed, as my special trust is and always hath been in you; for I promise you I have the said Smyth in a jealousy by reason that his brother married Sir Edward Seymour's sister.

Also I marvel that Mr. Seymour claimeth now more for his right the lvj^{li} than the lxxx^{li} ∧there resteth∧ of the whole Cxl^{li} that he demandeth, for I have as much right to the one as to the other, and I also intend to keep the one as well as the other during my life and after, till all covenants be fulfilled. And where he offereth me v C^{li} to release clearly the whole Cxl^{li}, I have lived too long to make so simple merchandise. . . .

From Calais the xvij day of November Anno 1533.   (Vol. 1, No. 85)

A document on the Seymour and Dudley dispute was drawn up by Lisle's lawyers for submission to the Lord Chancellor and Cromwell of which the following is a summary. John Dudley, Sir Edward Guildford, and Lord La Warr were bound to Lisle in recognizances of £10,000 for the performance of covenants that Dudley, after coming to his full age, should assure to his stepfather, for term of life, the lands which he would eventually inherit from his mother, Elizabeth Grey. Lisle had always peaceably enjoyed these lands, during the life of his late wife and since her decease, 'except certain lordships which the said Sir John Dudley had immediately after the death of the said lady,' until 'of late' Sir Edward Seymour bought from Dudley the reversion of certain manors of the yearly value of £140. Trusting Seymour when he brought the indentures made out to his own specifications to be signed, Lisle signed them without advice from his own counsel and without even reading them. Nor was this all: Sir Edward had asserted that Lisle had no rights at all in certain lands to the annual value of £60. Documents proving Lisle's right to these (at Painswick) were obtained from Oliver Pole – and then lost. The tenants, for fear of Seymour, meekly paid the whole of their rents to him.

The lawyers admitted that on paper Seymour now had the better claim because Lisle had never 'recovered' these lands and therefore they had never been his in law since the deal was made, and Seymour could therefore refuse to pay Lisle his life interest. The presumption is that the indentures had been drawn up so that this recovery could and did affect the legal position. The lawyers assert, however, that because Sir John Dudley, when he came of full age, did not fulfil the covenants to which he was bound, his stepfather had not merely a life interest but a better estate than the stepson, and could by the covenants originally drawn to protect Lisle and his wife, will or determine the use of the lands himself, so that the bargain made between Dudley and Seymour was, in fact, 'voyde and of none effecte'. This is the substance of the case to which constant reference is made throughout the letters of 1534, and which was not finally settled until 1535.

Small matters happily counterbalance the great legal disputes in the Lisle correspondence over their estates. William Wayte, of the next letter, is a distant kinsman on Lisle's mother's side and a near neighbour in Hampshire.

109   WILLIAM WAYTE OF WYMERING   9 *July 1534 (?1533)*
      TO LORD LISLE

Right honourable and my singular good lord, I recommend me unto you, and to my good lady also, trusting that you with all yours be in good health. My lord, according to your bill I have caused your keeper ∧to∧ serve your lordship's ij warrants, the which were killed both in my ground at the Bere at one standing, by mine own appointment. But my lord, your keeper, with other of Mr. Uvedale's servants, were before that time in the ground, I being there, and had made their standings and shaken off their hounds, wherewith, my lord, I was not best content, telling Marks that it had become them best there never to have made me a counsel, seeing that they knew me there. Whereupon, after that I departed from them, they went unto the Bere again and hunted in despite of me and had of me afterwards werry[3] opprobrious words, the which your lordship shall have further information of hereafter. Wherefore I shall desire your good lordship to command your keeper to walk well his own walk, for I think he shall have enow with that.

My lord, whilst your lordship and my lady were in the country I was glad to see game therein for your pleasures; but my lord I would be loath to cherish game for mine enemies or for lewd fellows. The one of your bucks is through baken and the other is in dry salt. My lord, James hath done as much as in him lieth to the performance of your warrants for your birds. If any lack there is no fault in him, for he hath served as many as sent in any due time; but my Lord Chancellor sendeth now, the which your lordship knoweth well is far after the time. And my lord, I have sent you two barrels of salt.

I pray your lordship let not your company of your ship come too hastily to your presence, for I assure your lordship they never died so sore in Porchester since I had understanding. And thus Jhesu save you, my lady, with all yours.

At Wym*e*ring by you*rs* to hys litill pow*re* the ix day of July,

Hol.   William Way*t*te   (Vol.2, No.225a)

110   SIR ANTONY WINDSOR TO LORD LISLE   [*n.d.*] *c.15 July 1534*

Right honourable and my singular good lord, After all due recommendations, my duty remembered, pleaseth your lordship to be advertised, the Tuesday next after the breaking up of the term Mr. Smyth and I were commanded to be before my Lord Chancellor and Mr. Secretary for your lordship's matter, and that time all your Counsel learned were departed the City, the which we showed to Mr. Secretary and he made himself very angry and said that it was but a delay. I perceiving the matter so taken, I said to him, So that Mr. Seymour would relinquish his Counsel, we were content, for your lordship's part, to have no Counsel, but only refer the matter wholly to the discretion of my Lord Chancellor and of his mastership. And he was very well content with that motion, and so commanded us to be at my Lord Chancellor's immediately after dinner, where this matter was well and substantially handled by Mr. Secretary for his part, for he left all the rigour of the laws and took the very true meaning of both parties accordingly as the book maketh mention. And where that Mr. Seymour requireth iij^{xx}li by the year, the which your lordship have no title to by the law, insomuch it is out of the recovery, notwithstanding the knowledge thereof he did bargain with your lordship for the whole ₡ ij^{xx}li. This matter Mr. Secretary did lay to his

---

3. William Wayte is not the only sixteenth-century speaker to anticipate Sam Weller.

charge, that he should handle you so craftily, and you intending no deceit. In so using himself it sounded greatly to his dishonesty. And further, Mr. Seymour saith, to fortify his title the better, that when he did bargain with Sir John Dudley for the reversion, that the said Sir John did show him of the feoffment, so that he should know that your lordship had no right to that iij^{xx}li. And Mr. Secretary answered, 'If Sir John Dudley $_\wedge$be$_\wedge$ a true gentleman $_\wedge$that$_\wedge$ is untrue', for he did examine him thereof and he denied it utterly. In good faith, I shall love Mr. Secretary the better while I live in my heart, for the substantialness that I perceive in him toward your lordship, not for no maintenance, but only that you shall take no wrong, being absent, but that the true meaning of your book shall be taken. I fear me they will judge your whole rent to be paid your lordship from time to time and Mr. Seymour to have the possession, and that is the true meaning of the indentures, and by likelihood it was your very purpose at the bargain-making, no doubt.

My lord, the law is against you for the iij^{xx}li. Howbeit your remedy for that is against Sir John Dudley. Wherefore, if you may have your rent according to your indenture, and your tenants not be interrupted of such holds as they have taken of your lordship herebefore, but that they may enjoy them during your life, that end shall stand with reason and good conscience, if it may be had, as I trust it shall, and I perceive no other. Howbeit, if it shall please your lordship to write your letters of thanks to my Lord Chancellor and specially to Mr. Secretary for their pains, so desiring them, if you shall needs depart from your possession, as you trust not, that it may please them to award your lordship some recompense for your possession; for you may allege that you have sustained a $\mathcal{C}$ li loss by his bargain and $_\wedge$by$_\wedge$ his loan money that he lent your lordship. . . .

Yours with my seruyce

Hol.   Antony Wyndesore   (Vol. 2, No. 232)

Windsor's glimpse of Cromwell deliberately putting on a calculated display of anger to get what he wanted is perceptive and revealing. It will be worth while to remember how he 'made himself very angry' when reading Honor Lisle's accounts of her interviews with him in 1538.

In thanking the Lord Chancellor, Lisle asked particularly 'that some good way may be taken for the poor tenants and avoiding the exclamation of the poor people'.

Thomas Broke was an Archer of Calais.

III   THOMAS BROKE TO LORD LISLE   *17 October 1534*

After most due humble recommendations unto your good lordship and to my singular good lady, it may please you to know that on Friday last, your lordship's counsellors, and likewise Mr. Seymour's, were all before the King's Council at Westminster, where I assure your lordship Mr. Secretary answered and pleaded on your lordship's behalf as much and as friendly as was possible. Insomuch that he said himself thus, 'Perchance, my lords, you do think that I speak thus for affection that I bear my Lord Lisle, by reason of some great rewards or gifts. But I assure you, on my faith, it is not so; nor I never received of his lordship anything, unless it were a piece or ij of wine, or a dish of fish or wild fowl. But yet I assure you I would be glad to do him pleasure; and moreover I do know so perfectly well this matter, that I must needs speak in it.' Then at last one of Mr. Seymour's counsel required that it might please the Council to refer the matter unto the trial of the common law; whereunto one of your lordship's counsellors answered, that the King's Grace being your lordship's good lord, it should be all one to your lordship wheresoever it should be in trial of the law. With that answered Mr. Secretary in this manner, 'The King's Grace being his good lord, say you? Yes, marry, I warrant you, he is and will be his good lord. His good lord, quod a! Marry, ye may be sure he is and will be his good lord. Doubt ye not of that.' And thus he repeated it, iij or iiij times, that the King's Highness was and would be good lord unto your lordship, which hearing was great comfort to me and other your poor servants and friends to hear, and that caused me to write unto your lordship thereof, to the intent that you may know the assured good mind and loving friendship that Mr. Secretary doth bear unto your lordship: and that also it may please you (now knowing it) to shew like cause of thanks, if at any time hereafter his mastership shall fortune to attempt or prove your lordship for any servant or friend of his; and that your lordship may in the mean time give him thanks by your letters. And thus I commit your lordship to the tuition of the Blessed Trinity, beseeching you to command me to do your lordship any service that may lie [in] me to do whilest that I tarry here, as boldly as any other servant that your lordship hath. For during my life, to my little ∧power∧, though it be ∧small∧, I am your lordship's own assuredly, with faithful heart.

Written this xvij^th day of October,

Your humble assuryd at commandment,

Hol.   Thomas Broke   (Vol.2, No.267)

112   JOHN HUSEE TO LORD LISLE   *6 February 1535*

Pleaseth it your Lordship to be advertised that the last day of January was fully ended your difference with Sir Edward Seymour, which is that he shall pay your lordship vj^xxli yearly and that your lordship shall discharge the statute by All Hallow tide next coming. God knoweth how this matter hath been handled, but surely if my Lord Chancellor had not been, you had had xx^{li} by the year more than is now judged. Notwithstanding, till this day Mr. Seymour will not receive the award. I cannot say what he meaneth: I think but dissimulation, for if he refuse this award it shall not be the worst bargian that ever your lordship made. I can no more say in that behalf, but it is hard trusting this wily world. . . .

From London the vjth day of February 1534.

Wholly to your lordship bounden during life,

Hol.   John Husee   (Vol.2, No.323)

113   JOHN HUSEE TO LORD LISLE   *4 March 1535*

My humble duty unto your lordship premised, . . .

As touching the award made betwixt your lordship and Sir Edward Seymour, Smyth hath written you thereof at large, but the effect thereof is that Sir Edward Seymour shall pay your lordship yearly vj^{xx}li.[4] at ij sundry payments, and for the surety thereof and accomplishment of the said payment, your lordship shall have as good ∧assurance∧ as your learned counsel can devise, which now cannot be done before the next term, for I have been with Mr. Densill for the same, who is now ridden into Cornwall and saith when all your counsel shall the next term meet, he will with their help ∧then∧ devise such writings for your assurance in the premises as shall be requisite. Further, your lordship shall receive herewith an obligation the which your counsel saith is requisite to be signed and sealed by your lordship, or else the award shall take none effect, forasmuch as it was not delivered within the day limited within the compromise. It shall be needful the said bond be sent with all celerity, because the day is the xxvth of this month; unless your lordship would refuse the award, which if you so should do, would not be well taken, seeing your lordship remitted the matter wholly to Mr. Secretary. I trust your lordship will not be displeased that I write you my poor advice, for your lordship may do your pleasure, that notwithstanding. If your lordship send your obligation I will be sure that Mr. Edward Seymour shall deliver me like bond ere your bond go out of my hands. Also it shall be very well done that you write Mr. Secretary a letter with thanks for the pains he hath taken for your lordship in that matter, and how, although your lordship be thereby a great loser, yet if he had awarded you less you would have bidden his award. It shall be good to please all parties: notwithstanding, I am well assured it is one of the unprofitablest bargains that ever you made. And also, if your lordship be pleased, with the award to send

4. i.e. 6 score pounds.

me word whom you will have to receive your part of the award and what you
will therewith have done. . . .

> By him that is to your lordship most bounden during life,

Hol. John Husee (Vol. 2, No. 338)

Here follows another letter typical of the many minor matters of a land-
lord's business. Grenville Hall, near Soberton, is still marked on modern
maps.

114 SIR ANTONY WINDSOR TO LORD LISLE *7 March 1535*

Right honorable and my singular good lord, after my lowly recommendations, my duty remembered, pleaseth your lordship to be advertised
. . . I have spoken with the Warden and his tenants of Meonstoke as touching
Grenfylde, where they will not suffer Twynnam neither to haye nor ferret;
but they have hedged and diked it after such fashion that Twynnam can take
little profit of that farm; and also they will not suffer him to use it as he hath
done when your lordship was there abiding: wherein I reasoned with the
Warden and them, and alleged great unkindness ∧in them∧ toward your
lordship that they would make such maistrie in your absence, with other
commands, and so at length I brought them to this pass that they would be
content to give Twynnam a reasonable day to destroy the game there, or
else, if it shall please your lordship to compound reasonably with them, that
you shall have your pleasure of it. One of these ways your lordship of good
conscience must needs take with them, insomuch the land is their own and
no parcel of your manor. An' your lordship intend neither of these ways,
then your lordship had need to abate Twynnam part of his rent, or else he
shall have a very hard bargain, having no liberty in that ground as he hath
had. My lord, I reckon if it shall please ∧you∧ to send a loving letter to the
Warden of your lordship's pleasure in this behalf, ∧I think∧ by reason of that
same, with mediation of your friends, that some good reasonable way shall
be taken therein.

Also, my lord, Mr. Uvedale and I shall appoint a time shortly to view the
forest, according to your commandment. Also, where it pleased your lordship to remember [me] with a hogshead of wine I heartily thank your lordship of your gentle remembrance. At the writing of this letter I had no word
of it, as knoweth our Lord, whom I beseech of his mercy to send your
lordship long and prosperous life.

Written upon mid-Lent Sunday, at East Meon,

> *Yours with* my *seruyce,*

Hol. Antony Wyndesore (Vol. 2, No. 340)

The problem of the weir at Umberleigh, Honor Lisle's manor in Devon, filled a great deal of the correspondence at this time. It played an important part in the domestic economy of the manor, and its supplies of fish, particularly the salmon that was one of the most popular of salted fish for winter consumption; and control of the waters of the Tawe at this point also affected the working of water mills. Weirs and fishgarths had begun to be a nuisance by the time of Edward III, and statutes made against them were reaffirmed by Edward IV because they hindered the passage of ships and boats, and also in order to safeguard the fry of fish spawned in the rivers. Henry VIII, whose movements around the country were not, as sometimes seems, entirely devoted to hunting, had recently 'ridden all about Hampshire' to see for himself whether the statutes were being obeyed.

115   DIGGORY GRENVILLE TO LORD AND   *17 November 1535*
       LADY LISLE

Right honorable and my singular good lord and lady my [duty] done, thanking you for your great goodness to me shewed, which as yet undeserved, but you be sure of my poor service during my life. Further, ascertaining you that I was with Master Courtenay the Wednesday after St. Martin his day, desiring him, in your names, that he would be so good to you that your weirs of ∧Umberleigh∧ might stand before Christmas; and then he shewed me that he dare not, for he had privy letters for the same matter ∧from the King∧, and when he was in the Court he dare say no other but all the weirs were down in Devonshire. Then I desired him that there might be but a little hole made in them because if your ∧lordship∧ should obtain licence of the King that they might stand that then it should stand you the less charges the building of them again.[5] Then he answered me that and I would give him a 1000 marks he would not grant me that they should stand one week for fear of the King's displeasure. Then when I saw there was no remedy then I departed from him. I suppose that the weirs were put down that week, for he gave straight commandment to the constable that it should ∧be∧ put down with all haste possible, upon a great pain. . . .
      Written at Exeter, the Wednesday after Saint Martin his day,
              By your poor servant,
Hol.   Degory Graynfyld   (Vol.2, No.482)

Cromwell, of course, is involved if there is to be any hope of a special licence to keep the weir. Husee writes on 19 November: 'I have been

5. *L. & P.* interprets as 'but to leave a small hole in them in the event of Lisle obtaining a licence from the King'.

minded to sue to the King's Highness according to your lordship's writing; but your learned Counsel hath willed me otherwise, for the King sendeth all those that sueth to his Grace in such cases to Mr. Secretary, . . .'[6]

The Lisles were getting chronically short of money, and London trades-men were beginning to refuse them credit, but it is unlike the Honor Lisle of most of the letters to have deserved the next one. The Uvedales were neighbours in Hampshire.

116   MARY UVEDALE TO LADY LISLE   *22 November 1535*

        1535 the 22 day off nouember

Right honourable Lady, my lady Lisle, I heartily recommend me unto your ladyship, glad for to hear of your good welfare. The cause of my writing at this time is this, so that I desire and pray your ladyship for to remember me of my money which I have at this time great need; for now, this time of the year, I must buy brown cloth against Easter. Therefore, Madame, ∧as∧ I do put my trust in you, so I pray your ladyship do unto me. Your ∧ladyship∧ knows full well that it hath been owing a great while, and your ladyship knows that I am a woman alone, and have had great loss, and it is money that I have laid out a' my own purse for my lord and your ladyship. No more at this time, but good Jhesu preserve you and all yours.
?Hol.   Per me marij oudaull   (Vol.2, No.487)

To add to the worries of people abroad, the plague is known to be rife again in London. Whenever the death rate is high, however, Husee sees to it that young John Basset is sent off to stay with friends in the country.

117   JOHN HUSEE TO LADY LISLE   *11 December 1535*

Pleaseth your Ladyship to be advertised that I received by Goodal your letter; and since, by Horsey, your other letter. And touching your ∧weir∧, I am very sorry that it is down; notwithstanding, much I sorrow more that your ladyship should take it so heavily, and my lord both; considering that in case they did more to it than the statute would bear them in with their commission, your ladyship shall have good remedy and be recompensed of them. And in case the statute and commission would bear them in it, then patience to be had is the next remedy. . . .

        . . . And he that shewed your ladyship that Mr. Basset was at London I think dreamed the same by the way: assuring your ladyship that he was not

6. Vol.2, No.483.

here since Bartholomew tide; for the truth is, though he would gladly a' been here, I would never consent the same. . . .

    From London, the xj[th] of December, by him that is
            Your ladyship's and therefore bounden,

Hol.   John Husee   (Vol.2, No.497)

In a letter written to Lord Lisle on the same day, Husee refers to his difficulties with unpaid tradesmen and gives his further opinion on the problem of the weir:

> I had never so much ado, for money is here very scant, and here is nothing to be done without it, for friendship taketh small place when money faileth. And further I have made a very sure promise to see the grocer and chandler paid ere I go. Howbeit I will do the best I can to rid me before Christmas, if it be possible. And as for your weir, I am very sorry your Lordship taketh it so earnestly, and my Lady both, considering that there is but ij things to be judged in it: the one is, that in case it be within the limits of the statute or commission, and that the weir was not lawful, there is no remedy but it patiently to suffer. The other is, that in case it hath been maliciously done, contrary to right, and not offending the statute, then is not to be doubted but that your lordship shall have remedy and recompensation of the ministers and transgressors of the same. And therefore the cause is not so earnestly to be taken, and I shall not let to motion Mr. Secretary in it when I may see that he is pleasantly disposed. And I shall according to your lordship's writing provide some like lodging for my lady as apperaineth; praying God to send your lordship once your own noble heart's desire.[7]

7. Vol.2, No.496.

7

Glimpses of the Court
1533-1535

The Lisles, of necessity, saw next to nothing of Court life at this time, but something of its pattern emerges from the letters, such as the constant moving about the country and the tedium of waiting for audiences. An important feature from the Lisles' point of view was the system of gifts, an integral part of the Tudor economy, whether in return for a service or in hope of benefits to come; they were carefully graded according to the rank and importance of both donor and recipient. In the next letter we see a more routine social exchange in operation. Kingston belonged to the King's intimate circle and had been one of his personal attendants, and his present position as a member of the Privy Council, as well as Constable of the Tower, made him a valuable purveyor of news.

118   SIR WILLIAM KINGSTON TO LORD LISLE   *20 July 1533*

My good lord, I recommend me unto you and unto my good lady, and my poor wife recommends her unto you and my lady both. My lord, I do thank you for my good cheese that your lordship sent me. My lord, as for news we have but few,[1] but as far as I do know we be like to have war with Scotland, for as I hear they be wilful and keeps promise like Scots; but God willing, the King will provide for them. And the King's Grace and the Queen's Grace be in good health and merry, thanked be our Lord, and all the Court, for I came home within this ij day. Your loving friend my Lord of Carlisle[2] is very sick, God amend him, and keeps his bed.

My lord, if I can get any red deer that is good I will send some unto you, but the King is very dangerous[3] of that flesh. I shall desire your lordship that

1. fowy.
2. carlell.
3. In either of its earlier uses: i.e. 'chary of' or 'difficult to deal with'.

143

I may be recommended unto Master Porter and Master Marshal; and God send you all as well to fare as I would myself.

From Wansted, the xx day of July,

By yours duryng my lyf

Hol.   Will*ia*m Kyngston   (Vol.1, No.22)

The news of the King's mood, always vital to Lisle, which the next letter gives, was particularly remarkable in view of its date, and of the effect on diplomatic relations of his recent divorce, his crowning of Anne Boleyn in June, and of his final break with the authority of the Pope less than a month before. John Russell is the future first Earl of Bedford.

119   SIR JOHN RUSSELL TO LORD LISLE   *6 August 1533*

Right honourable and my singular good Lord, in my heartiest manner I commend me unto your good Lordship. And very glad I am to hear of the good report of you, how well you are beloved and how well you use yourself there, which is great comfort and pleasure to your friends here. Howbeit, I would fain know how you like the town and the country there, and the air thereabout. My Lord, news here is none, but that thanked be God the King's Highness is merry and in good health, and I never saw him merrier of a great while than he is now; and the best pastime in hunting the red deer that I have seen. And for cheer, what at my Lord Marquess of Exeter's, Mr. Treasurer's, and at Mr. Weston's, I never saw more delicate nor better cheer in my life. The King was minded to go to Farnham, and from thence to East Hampstead and so to Windsor. And now he cometh not there because of the Sweat, and he was fain to remove from Guildford to Sutton, Mr. Weston's house, because of the Sweat in likewise. And now within this viij days his Grace cometh again to Windsor. And soon after the Queen removeth from thence to Greenwich, where her Grace taketh her chamber.

My Lord, your Lordship was so good unto me at your departing that you promised to provide me of iij tun of wine, whereof I heartily desire your Lordship to be so good unto me as to send me one tun of French wine to Bridewell, to one Gayes, skinner; for I can get none in London that is aught for no money. And I pray you to send me a letter of the price thereof and I shall content the bringer for the same. . . .

If there be any pleasure or service I may do you, you may command me, as he that is your own assuredly, to the best of my little power; as knoweth our Lord, who preserve your lordship and send you good honourable and long life.

From Sutton, the vj^{th} day of August. I pray you that I may be commended unto my good lady your wife.

Signed   Your owen to comande

J. Russell   (Vol.1, No.34)

On 7 September Anne Boleyn's daughter was born. Not one of the Lisles' gossiping correspondents took the trouble even to send them the news. Does it, perhaps, indicate something of the general dislike of the upstart Queen, or disappointment at the sex of the eagerly awaited heir, or simply that most of their friends in England were better friends to Katharine of Aragon than they would ever have dared openly to admit?

120   SIR WILLIAM KINGSTON   *26 September 1533*
       TO LORD LISLE

. . . My lord, to advertise you of news, here be none as yet, for now they be about the peace in the Marches of Scotland, and, with God's grace, all shall be well. And as yet the King's grace hath heard no more from my Lord of Winchester, and so the King hawks every day with goshawks and other hawks, that is to say, lanners, sparhawks, and merlins, both afore noon and after, if the weather serve. I pray you, my lord, if there be any gerfalcon or yerkyn, to help ∧me∧ to both, if it may be; and for lack of both, to have one; and to send me word of the charges thereof, and then your lordship does much for me.

I and my wife both right heartily recommend us unto my good lady, and we thank my lady for my token, for it came to me in the church of the Black Friars and my wife was disposed to have offered it to Saint Loy that her horse should not halt, and he never went upright since. . . .

And thus our Lord in Heaven send you much honour and all your company well to fare.

from Waltham abbay the fryday affore myhylmas ∧day∧
       With the hand of all yours to my power,
Hol.   Will*i*am Kyngston[4]   (Vol. 1, No. 52)

Sir William, it would appear, was not prepared to take his saints very seriously, even in 1533. His more pious wife had offered Lady Lisle's token to St. Eloi or Eligius, the patron of goldsmiths and horses, with a prayer that he would prevent her horse from going lame.

Henry Norris, known to history primarily as one of the victims of the Anne Boleyn tragedy, so far had been one of the King's most favoured companions. Until the very eve of his arrest in 1536 Husee obviously regards him as Lisle's most useful friend at court – the man who, with Bryan, undoubtedly has the King's ear and will gladly put in a word for the absent Lord Deputy.

4. See Pl. 11.

My gud lord I recommende me vnto your gud lordshyp yf it may plece
your lordshyp to vnderstond that master nebell & edward hath
desyred me to wryt vnto you in the fauor of ther seruant harry
and thys berer worcs the brng ye gud lord vnto I
thynke you shall lyke hym well forte hath attendid
in the cort mony yeres with master nebell my lord to
advtyse you of suche fer bewty as yet for now thay be
abowt the pess in the mydce of scotland with godes
grace all shalbe well as yet the kynges grace hath
hardly now wordes from my lord of... the & the
kyng halwet evry day with goshawkes & other sulbe
that ys to say bythe sparhouce & whiche both affore
none & aft yf the wether sue I pray you my lord yf
ther be any gerfaulkes or yergon to helpe to both yf it
may be & for take of both to haue hay is to send me
wordes of the... ther &... they y your lordshyp doce myche
for me I & my wyfe both hertly hertely recommende hus
vnto my gud lady & we thanke my lady for my token for it
came to me in the churce of the blak freres & my wyfe
wase desposed to haue offerd it to sayntbry at... her first
shuld not halt of & now went vp ryght sure & beche your
lordshyp to haue me in yowr remembrance to master port
& my lady & to master marshall & my lady & to master moyes
& my lady & thus o lord in heyben send you myche good
& all yowr company will to fare from waltham abbay
the fryday affore mychelmas with the hand of...
yowrs to my powr

Wyllm Kyngston

121   HENRY NORRIS TO LORD LISLE   *26 October 1533*

Mine honourable good Lord, In my most loving manner I heartily recommend [me] unto you, and to my good Lady your wife, certifying you that I am commanded by the King to write unto you and to show you that the King heard speaking of your spaniel that Robert ap Reynold had. And so his Grace took the said spaniel from the said Robert, and said that he would be bold on you: which spaniel he liketh well, which shall not displease you, I know well, for he esteems him, which is to me pleasure for because he came from you. And thus fare ye well.

From Greenwich, the xxvj day of October,

My lord, I pray you be good lord to Mr. Garncys, for you may appease this matter yourself. Therefore I will not move the King until I hear from you, seeing it is so slight a matter. And if there come any to sue here to the King I shall do well enough. And thus our Lord knoweth, who keep you.
Signed   Henry Norrys   (Vol.1, No.67)

The postscript refers to one of the endemic rows between members of the Calais Council. The experienced courtier knows that the King is bored by such matters. Garneys, quicker than Lisle to recognize where practical power was beginning to lie, wrote to Cromwell and had the matter settled in his favour.

122   JOHN HUSEE TO LORD LISLE   *7 January 1534*

My duty in my right humble wise unto your Lordship premised: . . . Your New Year's gift the King's Majesty received right joyously, and I delivered it to his Grace [with] mine own hand, being present Mr. Bryan and Mr. Kyngston, which preferred it in the best wise, and said to his Grace, 'Although my Lord Lissle be far from your Highness, yet doth he not forget you.' To whom his Majesty answered, 'We thank him.' . . . It hath been shewed me by divers that the rumour was that your lordship should be Earl of Penbrocke, but it is no more noised. . . .

The King's Grace kept this Christmas as great Court as ever I saw. And his Grace is as merry and lusty as ever I see him, God be lauded. With this bearer I do send your lordship a book of the Pope's Articles. I do think your lordship hath seen them ere this time. . . . As God knoweth, which send your lordship long life, with increase of honour.

from london, the vij^th of Janeweary anno 1533
          in hast
                    your Lordshippes most bownden servaunt
Hol.   John Husee   (Vol.2, No.108)

Lisle's New Year's gift to the King was £20 in gold. In return Lisle received the amount of gilt plate appropriate to his rank – in this year a gilt bowl with a cover weighting 28¼ ounces. Husee, presumably, received 20 s. 'in reward' – the sum entered in the Treasurer's accounts for 1529–31 'to the Lord Lisle's servant'. There was a graduated scale of tips, the amount received being determined by the master's rank.

A victim of the custom of exchanging gifts was a certain little dog of Lady Lisle's of which Husee had written to her a couple of weeks earlier: 'In any wise your ladyship must send Purquoy, for Master Bryan asketh me every day ij or iij times for him.' In the next letter we see how Purquoy was received at Court; but that was not to be the end of his story.

123   SIR FRANCIS BRYAN TO LORD LISLE   20 *January* 1534

. . . I beseech your lordship, after my most hearty recommendations made unto my very good lady your wife – unto whom and to your lordship, because ye be both but one soul though ye be two bodies, I write but one letter – that it may please your lordship to give her hearty thanks on my behalf for her little dog, which was so proper and so well liked by the Queen that it remained not above an hour in my hands but that her Grace took it from me. Nevertheless, her ladyship and any friend of hers, for the same, and her kindness therein, shall be assured of such pleasure as in me at any time shall be. As our Lord God knoweth, who have your lordship, with my said good lady, in his blessed preservation.

At Westminster, the xx^{th} day of January
Signed   Yours at commandment,
                    Francis Bryan   (Vol.2, No.114)

Here at last, after nearly six months' delay, is final news of the hosting harness or complete field armour Lisle had asked for at the end of 1533, and which had been the subject of much anxious inquiry in his letters to Husee. The King had said he would select it himself, which suggests that, although it had been 'ready 'pointed long since', no one dared to send it till Henry had seen and approved the choice, and that it was therefore one of his own discarded Greenwich armours which he had outgrown – hence my belief that uncle and nephew were of similar height and originally of similar build. The plate Husee mentions is some left in Calais by Lisle's predecessor which he has been unable to acquire without Cromwell's long-delayed permission.

124   JOHN HUSEE TO LORD LISLE   6 *May* 1534

Humbly advertising your Lordship that this day I received by the King's commandment an osting harness, complete, for your lordship, which I will send with the first ship that goeth to Calais. Lovekyn saith your lordship resteth his debtor of a doublet of satin or xx^s in money. As yet I cannot have answer touching the plate. I trust if Mr. Cromwell go to the Court tomorrow to have a final answer, whereupon I only do tarry. The King's Highness is very well pleased with your lordship, which is to me no little comfort to hear what goodness his Grace hath of your lordship reported. And your lordship is not little bounden to Mr. Treasurer of the King's house, for he of his goodness hath so informed the King's Majesty that his Grace had never your lordship in more reputation, which to your lordship's friends is in this parts no small comfort and rejoicing. . . .

Trusting your lordship will pardon me for my rude and hasty writing. God preserve your lordship and my Lady.

With most haste, in London, the vjth of May

Your lordship's most bounden servant,

Hol.   John Husee the younger   (Vol.2, No.184)

125   SIR FRANCIS BRYAN TO LORD LISLE   *11 May 1534*

My good lord, in my most heartiest wise I commend me unto you, and so desire you that I may be to my good lady your bedfellow. And where your servant is here, attending in the Court in divers your business, in those and all other wherein I may do you pleasure ye shall be as well assured of me as of your next friend. And as concerning the King's coming to Calais, this day the King told me in mine ear that it should be before August next. Wherefore for making of your provisions ye may do as ye shall think good therein. I have not at this time any other writings worth writing. And for the said time of the King's coming, I would not upon this my writing ye should take this for a precise knowledge, whereby ye might take hindrance in your provisions, for ye know the minds of princes sometimes change and times appointed deferred. Where ye delivered me a patent of the keeping of a park in Hampshire, I am informed my lady your bedfellow doth make means to call again the same, wherein I pray you I may know your mind in your next writing. And so at this time shall desire God to send you as well to fare as your gentle heart can best think.

From Greenwich, the xjth day of May,

I pray you kepe thys secrett.

yow*r*s assueryd

ffranssys Bryan

(Vol.2, No.188)

John Brown was one of the Calais Spears.

126   JOHN BROWN TO LADY LISLE   *12 May 1534*

Madam, in my most humble wise, after due recommendation, please it your ladyship to be advertised that I have received your ladyship's token and letter, wherein I perceive the content. And how the Queen's Grace liked your present of dottrels and also your linnet that hung in your chamber, please it ye to understand that her Grace liked them both very well, the one for being a special good dish, and the other for a pleasant singing bird, which doth not cease at no time to give her Grace rejoicing with her pleasant song, that may be comfort to your ladyship. Moreover I know her Grace is good lady to you, as I shall more plainly express to your ladyship at my coming over, that I trust shall be right shortly, by the grace of God, who keep your ladyship with my special good Lord and all yours.

Written at Greenwich the xij day of the merry month of May,
                    By yours assuryd
Hol.   John Brwn   (Vol.2, No.193)

Mrs. Margery Horsman was one of the Queen's gentlewomen whom Lady Lisle found invaluable both for gossip and for influence.

127   THOMAS BROKE TO LADY LISLE   *18 December 1534*

After most humble recommendations to your good ladyship, it may please the same to know that I have delivered your ladyship's token with most hearty commendations to Mrs. Margery Horsman, who saith that she knoweth not the man that she sent to your ladyship, but she saith for truth a nigh friend of hers did heartily require her to write to your ladyship in his favour, wherefore she humbly thanks my lord and you for your goodness toward him shewed. Also she saith that the Queen's Grace setteth much store by a pretty dog, and her Grace delighted so much in little Purkoy that after he was dead of a fall there durst nobody tell her Grace of it, till it pleased the King's Highness to tell her Grace of it. But her Grace setteth more store by a dog than by a bitch, she saith. . . .

Scrybyld rudely in haste. At london. this xviij^th day of dece*m*ber.
                    By yo*ur* humble s*eru*a*nt,
Hol.   Thomas Broke   (Vol.2, No.299a)

128   JOHN HUSEE TO LORD LISLE   *4 January 1535*

My humble duty premised, this shall be advertising your lordship that on New Year's Day I delivered your gift unto the King's Highness, Mr. Norris being present, who furthered the same right gently, his Highness then asking how your lordship and my lady did in his most hearty manner. Touching all other your lordship's affairs, I can yet by no means be of them discharged. Howbeit, I trust ere it be long to have full determination in the most part of them, for this holydays hath been a great hindrance to all suitors, . . . praying God to send your lordship long life and many good New Years.

From London the iiij[th] in January, 1534

Your lordship's most bounden during life,

Hol.   John Husee   (Vol.2, No.301)

The next letter shows the King handling a piece of the day-to-day business of the Court. It concerns Lisle's claim, by custom, to the land and goods of a deceased woolpacker of Calais which had been forfeited to the Crown. Husee had already had three audiences of the King on the matter. No one seemed to know what the value of the property was, but every penny counted in the current financial circumstances.

129   JOHN HUSEE TO LORD LISLE   *25 October 1535*

Pleaseth your lordship to be ascertained that according as I wrote your lordship in my last letter I repaired again unto Mr. Treasurer, he being at Guildford Manor, to know what was presented concerning the lands and goods of late Leonard Mell, woolpacker. And the presentments of the inquests being searched for the same, there was no more found concerning the same than followeth: 'Further find that the lands, goods and tenements of Leonard Packer, Woolpacker of this town, was by the Mayor and Comptroller of this town to the King's use seized, but to what value we cannot tell' ·/. This before mentioned was found and nothing else: the same concerning the which Mr. Treasurer sent by me enclosed in a letter unto Mr. Norris, the King being then at East Hampstead when I delivered the same unto Mr. Norris, the King being present, and Mr. Norris delivered the same incontinent unto his Highness. And after his Grace had the circumstance of the same perused he said that it declared nothing of the just value of the gift; and notwithstanding that his Grace was well pleased that your lordship should the same have, yet would his Majesty know the truth what he giveth. So that it was then there determined, notwithstanding I always said that it was praised to the King's use, according as your lordship wrote Mr. Norris and me both, to the value of v mark lands and v mark goods by the Mayor, then for that time being the King's escheator, that the Mayor that then was, and my lord Comptroller, should by letters by them signed certify Mr. Treasurer and Mr. Norris, ∧Yea∧, by their sundry letters of the just value thereof and how it was to the King's use then praised. And incontinent upon the arrival of these letters I shall have your bill signed without further ado.

I think not the contrary but ∧his∧ Highness hath been informed by some sinister manner the same gift to be of more value and substance than it indeed is. . . .

From London the xxv^th of October, by him that is bounden to your lordship during life,

Hol.   John Husee   (Vol.2, No.467)

In December Husee reported that the land had turned out not to be forfeit anyway and Lisle should tell the widow so, and that Norris advised him not to waste more effort for the tiny value of the goods.

A courtier had to be wherever the Court was, and that (even apart from hunting and hawking) was forever on the move. Our sympathy must go out to the next writer.

130 . SIR WILLIAM KINGSTON TO LORD LISLE   *14 January 1536*

My good lord, I recommend me unto you and also unto my good lady, and my sick wife doth the same. My lord, as youth procures me, I shall desire you to do so much as to help me to some good horse for my money, and that he may be a free[5] horse and able to bear me. And if it may please your lordship to make my friend Richard Blunt privy to the said horse, and that I may have your letter of the price, I shall, with God's grace, make unto your lordship short payment again. My lord, here is much youth, and I am but in the middest of mine age, and I will be a' horseback among them. Sir, I think the King's Grace intends to make his progress northward, and many suppose the King of Scots and his Grace shall meet, God willing. . . . My lord, I shall desire you to take such pain for me touching this horse, and he and I both shall do you service, as our Lord knoweth, who long give you life.

from Greneweche the xiiij day of January. . . .

            By all yours

Hol.   Will*ia*m Kyngston   (Vol.3, No.631)

5. Of a horse, willing, ready to go; *O.E.D.* III 20.c.

8

Politics and Religion
1536

The year 1536 was a momentous one, both in England and on the Continent. March saw the outbreak of war between France and the Emperor; and though England, and therefore Calais, remained neutral, and was not directly affected by the hostilities, there is frequent mention in the Letters of the widely scattered fighting. At home, in the grip of inflation, the general shortage of money was acute: as Husee puts it, 'money was never so scant since this King reigned'. In the desperate effort to raise funds, the dissolution of the lesser monasteries proceeded apace, and already there was a growing conviction that the greater establishments were destined presently to share the same fate. As Hall, the chronicler, writes:

> In this time was given unto the King by the consent of the great and fat abbots, all religious houses that were of the value of CCC marks and under, in hope that their great monasteries should have continued still. But even at that time one said in the Parliament house that these were as thorns but the great abbots were putrified old oaks and they must needs follow; and so will other do in Christendom, quod Doctor Stokesley, Bishop of London, ere many years be passed.[1]

Throughout 1536 we shall see Lisle doing his utmost to secure his portion of these monastic spoils, and largely frustrated by the fact that he was not on the spot to be his own solicitor with the King. The attack on the monasteries, however, was all part of the continuing process of Cromwell's revolution which had got well under way in 1533: the unforeseen dramatic crises of 1536 were, firstly, the trial and execution of Anne Boleyn and her fellow victims in May; and secondly, the outbreak in October of the rebellion which was to be known as the Pilgrimage of Grace, and which was, in fact, the one really serious domestic upheaval of the reign, and the only genuine threat to the policy of the King and Cromwell.

1. Hall, f.ccxxvii^v (1548).

In a sense, up to this point, one has the feeling that in spite of the far-reaching changes which were taking place in England, the Lisles in Calais, though of course affected by these things, were somehow just outside the range of the almost unbelievably rapid extension of the King's power. But by 1536 even Calais has been clutched and drawn in, and this family, like every other, is committed, has become involved. There is no way, now, but the King's way. For the moment, all is well with the Lord Deputy: he has been the King's man all his life. There are favours yet to come. But the shadow of absolutism grows darker and we grow increasingly conscious of the impending menace of the King's implacable egotism, so that even if we were ignorant of what is to come we should be haunted by ominous forebodings. Everyone, noble, gentle, simple, if he had not had his eyes opened before, was awake at last to the reality of these 'grim unlovely years'. The lion, as Thomas More foresaw, had learnt his own strength.

This is not an atmosphere in which political news, let alone opinions on it, were lightly entrusted on paper even to the most trusted messenger. Lisle's urgent demands for it obviously made Husee nervous, until at last he has to protest that he might put himself in danger of his life by compliance:

> there is divers here that hath been punished for reading and copying with publishing abroad of news; yea, some of them are at this hour in the Tower and like to suffer therefor. . . . It is much better that I stay from writing than to put your lordship to displeasure and myself to undoing.[2]

In foreign affairs, on the other hand, news of what Lisle's neighbours in France and Flanders were saying and thinking was valuable to the government, in daily expectation of an outbreak of war between France and the Emperor. Though Francis I had given up his claims in Italy by the Treaty of Cambrai, he had never in his heart relinquished his determination to regain Milan, and Lisle, on the frontiers of both powers, was in a position to learn if warlike preparations were being made.

131   LORD LISLE TO CROMWELL   *2 March 1536*

After my most hearty recommendations / these shall be only to advertise you of such news as are here rumoured. in both the frontiers of France and ∧Flanders∧ which I do write unto you for my discharge, not verifying all the same to be true. ∧Howbeit∧ there is no remedy ∧but∧ I must at some season give like ear to the uncertainty brought ∧to me∧ by my ordinary espies as I would do if the same were of substance and very truth.

First I do send you the copies of such proclamations as hath been published in the frontiers of the Empire herein enclosed. / which is of very

2. Vol. 3, No. 798.

truth / further of certainty, Monsieur de Nyels ∧dwelling∧ upon the frontier of Picardy hath conveyed all his chief stuff to Boulogne, and he himself is in like manner gone thither / And all the chief goods of Ardres are conveyed the same way.

In like manner Monsieur de Cressonyer, a Burgundian dwelling upon the frontier of Flanders is gone to St. Omers /. So that in general. all those that are of any substance of both frontiers, having any place of safeguard to repair unto, are thither gone with the chief of their goods. . . .

Certain pieces of artillery were lately brought to Tourneham / And there shot in triumph upon St. Mathew's Day. . . .

Further on Monday last, being the xxviij[th] of February, certain Frenchmen, to the number of xvj or xx, took the Castle of Ottenges ∧being of the Emperor's∧ lying beside Ardres which keepeth the same, saying they will there remain / but upon what presumption I know not /. Howbeit they found no resistance in the said castle but only ∧one man therein that had the keeping thereof∧. And as yesterday being the last of February certain men of Ardres and others of the borders of Picardy came to Guisnes with xij wagons loden with stuff, which they of Guisnes refused, and would not receive so they were fain to search other places to leave and unload the same in.

Mr. Treasurer of the King's House knoweth the Castle of Ottenges and all the frontiers about the Marches here.

Sir I trust ∧once∧ within this vj days to have further knowledge and I shall not fail to advertise you thereof with speed. And thus I pray Jesu send you as well to fare as I would myself.

From Calais the ij[d] day of March.[3]   (Vol. 3, No. 648)

132   LORD LISLE TO CROMWELL   *6 March 1536*

After my most hearty recommendations / these shall be advertising you that of late divers persons as well of the French King's subjects as of the Emperor's borderers upon both the King's pales here hath required place and sufferance of the officers of the same to convey unlade and leave certain of their goods in / the which as far as I can understand hath neither been granted them ne utterly denied them / so that I thought it right requisite to advertise you thereof. and I would for my discharge gladly know the King's full pleasure therein beseeching you that I may be asartained thereof with all convenient celerity And further where the common bruit in Flanders is that they plainly say. that they will spoil and overrun our marches in a night / forasmuch as the King's Highness (as they saith doth assist the French King with xx[ml] men / Sir loath would I be that it should so chance notwithstanding if I should any way give them warning or monition to have a good eye to

3. This and the following letter are drafts.

their cattle. and goods they are surely of such a nature that the same should be blowen suddenly over both the other frontiers so that I stand therein at a stay till I hear from you what the King's pleasure and your good advice is shall be therein done. for I shall not God keeping me in my right mind attempt to commit anything which should sound any way to the enbolding of our neighbours. be they our friends or foes / And thus desiring your speedy answer in the premises. most heartily I bid you farewell. from Calais the vjth day of March   (Vol.3, No.648a)

Before the end of the month France had invaded Savoy, and on 5 April occupied Turin. But the situation remained confused, as war was still not openly declared. Though such a war, distracting the participants from affairs in England, was precisely what Henry was hoping for, the two English ambassadors to Francis I were scarcely enlightening.

133   THE BISHOP OF WINCHESTER AND   9 *March* 1536
         SIR JOHN WALLOP TO LORD LISLE

In our right hearty manner we recommend us to your good Lordship, and even so thank you for the manifold kindness which ye have shewed to such as have passed by you from us, not ceasing so to do for all our negligence in writing unto you, which we doubt not ye will by your wisdom consider and take in good part accordingly. We can write you no tidings but after such sort as one answered his friend that asked him whether it should rain or no that night. 'In good faith', quoth he, 'the weather is much overcast, and very cloudy'. 'Nay', quoth he, 'I see that myself, but I ask you whether it will rain or no?' The other answered, 'In good ∧faith∧,' quoth he, 'I doubt thereof as well as ye'. And in that case be we here, whether there shall be war or peace. The weather is cloudy, and much preparation there is; and in Savoy hath fallen a few drops of rain; for CCC of the legionaries of France be despatched by men of war of the Duke of Savoy, which issued out of a castle at the town of Montmelian besides Chambery in Savoy. But with the Emperor there is yet no war; and it is not in despair but the sun may shine and put over all these clouds.

We pray you that we may be heartily recommended to my good lady your wife. And even so fare ye most heartily well.

From Lyons, the ix[th] of March.

We beseech your lordship to further the speedy passage of this courier.

                  Your lordship's assured friends,
Hol.   Ste. Winton
Signed   John Wallop   (Vol.3, No.651)

134   LORD LISLE TO CROMWELL   *16 March 1536*

After my most hearty recommendations. . . . I shall not fail, God willing, according to my bounden duty, have a vigilant eye toward the proceedings in both frontiers. They say plainly in Flanders that the war is commenced betwixt the Emperor and the French King. [And of a very surety, on Sunday last, being the xij[th] of this instant, there was war proclaimed betwixt the French King and the Emperor at Gravelines, by sea and not by land. What they thereby meaneth, God knoweth; but][4] the Captain ∧of the castle of Gravelines∧ hath sold two of the King's horse that Parker bought there, and brought iiij horses more of the same home with him to his Castle of Gravelines, and there keepeth them.

Also the saying is plainly that Barbarossa hath resembled above ij[t] m[l] men against the Emperor; and further, of late a band of Robert de la Marche's men hath laid siege unto a castle of the Bishop of Luke,[5] which being demanded whose men they were made answer that they had no master.

The Bishop of Luke sent to the Lady Regent for rescue, but whether it was granted him or not it is yet unknowen, but undoubtedly every man of war was commanded to repair unto his garrison upon pain of death. Notwithstanding, what with Barbarossa, and the Frenchmen on their frontiers here, and for dread that the King our master should assist and take part with the French King, I know certainly they were never so afraid since they knew first what war meant. And thus I pray God send you ever as well to fare as I would myself.

From Calais, the xvj[th] day of March.

Sir, I have written to the King's Highness to be good lord unto me, and am as loath to ask anything out of his coffers as any creatures living, beseeching you to help me to some old abbey in mine old days. I have no trust but God, the King, and you.   (Vol.3, No.653a)

The result of the postscript to the above letter was the peck of trouble that Lisle had over Frithelstock Priory, which will be found under estates and the law (chap. 11).

Although the notes that Lisle enclosed in his next letter have not survived, it is always interesting to see Lisle in his role of spymaster.

135   LORD LISLE TO CROMWELL   *27 April 1536*

Right honourable, after my most hearty recommendations, This is to advertise you that herewith I do send you such news as one hath sent me forth

---

4. Bracketed passage deleted in MS.   5. Liége, in Flanders.

of the French court, whom I retain there, and hath written unto me at this time to amend his pension; yet I will not take upon me the same news to be true, but I require you to accept my true heart and mind, ensuring you he is conversant with many great men and heareth much: and hath of me lx crowns yearly.

Further to advertise you, one of the friars which I wrote of unto you lately, sent unto me this night saying he will show me all that he knoweth, which knowen I shall not fail incontinent to write the same unto you.

Moreover, if it might please you to be so good unto me as to get me licence to come over to see the King's Majesty at his Grace's being at Dover (although I tarried but one hour) I would think myself much bound to God and you, ensuring you what bruit soever hath been made of death here, the most is but viij persons in iij houses, the householders whereof and also servants and children come not abroad, which I will justify and make answer unto before the King's Highness. Beseeching the most blessed Trinity to send you prosperous life and long to his high pleasure.

From Calais this night, being the xxvij day of April.[6]   (Vol.3, No.683)

Lisle wanted to make his plea for an abbey in person to the King.

The dates on which letters were written now become important to our understanding of the drama that was developing behind the scenes. The Queen was to be disposed of, and the King and Cromwell had for some time been making their arrangements accordingly, but in the meantime business must seem to be strictly as usual.

On 24 April Henry signed a warrant to set up a special commission of Oyer and Terminer for Middlesex and Kent, to inquire into every kind of treason, by whomsoever committed, and to try offenders at special sessions. Cromwell had prepared a case against Anne Boleyn and was ready to submit the evidence, and the King knew what that evidence was to be. Thus when Husee wrote on the 27th (and he would have written at once with news of the licence Lisle was waiting for), he could not have known that four days later Henry Norris, Lisle's friend, and even more the King's friend, would be under arrest, and that when the King spoke to Norris about Lisle he had probably no hope on earth of avoiding the fate which must already have been predetermined by the careful planning which had selected the unhappy victims and prepared the details of the official conspiracy.

136   JOHN HUSEE TO LORD LISLE   27 April 1536

Pleaseth your Lordship. . . .

. . . I laboured Mr. Norris for your licence to come over, so that it is obtained, and your lordship may come when it shall please you, for the

6. Fair copy; not signed.

King's Highness granted the same willingly, and said he would gladly see your lordship. I required to have the said licence by writing, but his Grace said it should not need, for his word was thereof sufficient, and that Mr. Norris should bear record thereof. And I shewed Mr. Norris of the wine you sent to Dover, which if it prove well your lordship shall demerit thanks; and if Mr. Norris's Gascon wine prove not excellent good I am shamed for ever, for I made thereof no small boast. He thanketh your lordship for the French wine: it is the best that came this year in England.

The King's Grace will be at Dover in viij days, and now is determined to begin his journey thitherward the iiij[th] day of May. . . . As touching the Abbey your lordship writ of, it shall not need your lordship make further ado therein till such time as they be surveyed. And also now your lordship at your coming over may speak in your own cause. I have no doubt but you shall obtain. . . .

From London in haste the xxvij[th] of April.

          By your lordship's bounden during life,

Hol.   John Husee   (Vol. 3, No. 684)

On May Day the King and Queen attended ceremonial jousting at Greenwich. Among the jousters was Henry Norris. Suddenly, the King departed and rode to London escorted only by six persons, and 'of this sudden departing many men mused, but chiefly the Queen', Hall records. The night before, Mark Smeaton, a musician of the Queen's chamber, had been questioned at Stepney, and that morning taken to the Tower. It was rumoured that he had been grievously tortured before confessing to adultery with the Queen. As Cromwell was at Stepney on 30 April he was certainly Smeaton's examiner, and he would not have hesitated to use torture to extract this essential confession. It is probable that this occasioned Henry's abrupt departure from the jousting and gave the signal for proceeding with the rest of the plan. He never saw Anne again. It was rumoured that when the King rode away from the jousts he took Norris with him and offered him his pardon if he too would confess. Norris refused. He was committed to the Tower that day. Anne Boleyn was interrogated at Greenwich by members of the Council and arrested on the 2nd and brought to the Tower that evening 'in full daylight', her brother Lord Rochford having been taken there a few hours earlier.

There were no letters to Lisle with hot news of any of this. Husee had left London for Calais on 28 April, and would never have trusted such matter to the post at this stage anyway, and Grenville and Warley, who wrote on the 1st and 2nd of May respectively, say only that the King has changed his mind about going to Dover at present.

The Anne Boleyn story is no part of the Lisle story, but the pattern of Anne's tragedy is to be remembered when Lisle's troubles begin. She was

doomed when on 29 January, as Chapuys wrote to the Emperor, she mis-
carried of 'what seemed to be a male child' of less than four months. The
machinery was set in motion, and Cromwell admitted to Chapuys that he was
responsible for manufacturing the plot for her destruction. A number of the
Lisle Letters will be found amongst those which show conclusively that no
care was taken to make possible combinations of dates and places in most of
the charges. In 1534 adultery with Smeaton on 19 May at Greenwich and on
the 20th with Weston at Westminster was alleged, although by the 17th
Anne and the King had already removed to Richmond to keep Whitsuntide
there.[7] She was further accused of adultery with Weston on 20 June at
Greenwich, although the Court remained at Richmond until 26 May and by
3 June had removed to Hampton Court, where on the evidence of dated
letters it remained until at least the 26th.[8] If adultery with Smeaton took
place on 26 April 1536, it certainly did not happen, as the indictment states,
at Westminster. The Court was already installed at Greenwich for Easter by
14 April,[9] where it remained until Anne's arrest. So recent a date as this last,
at least, must have been in the minds of the peers who tried the case in May.
To understand the end of Lisle's story we must identify two emerging patterns in the events of these years in England – the one, a pattern of treason
which accepts the frame-up and the substitution of accusations for evidence;
the other, a pattern formed by the interaction of the characters of the King
and Cromwell and the latter's realistic appraisal of the way Henry could be
worked upon through his egotism, his emotions, his inherently suspicious
nature, and his obsessions and hatreds. If we observe these factors at work
now, we shall appreciate how inevitably they determine Lisle's fate in 1540.
It will presumably always remain an open question whether Anne Boleyn
and any of the men accused with her were guilty, but there is no question at
all that their trials were judicial murder, as many of their contemporaries
were well aware.

That the news of the arrests had reached Calais by 8 May is evident from
the two letters that follow. Lisle was desperate for money, and Calais was
costing him too much; but the reason why he chose this particular moment
to write emerges only in the second letter. It is virtually identical with the
first except for the passage selected here.

137   LORD LISLE TO HENRY VIII   *8 May 1536*

Pleaseth your highness to be advertised that not long since I wrote unto
your Grace, desiring the same to be good and gracious lord unto ∧me∧, for
as much as no man in this town was ordinarily charged with keeping of
household whereunto any daily haunt and resort was made but only I, as well

7. See Vol.2, Nos.193, 196, 199.   9. Vol.3, No.673.
8. Vol.2, Nos.199, 212–12a.

in banqueting and feasting of strange ambassadors and other foreign potestes and great personages as otherwise; which hitherto I have done, although the same hath been further than my power might well extend, knowing that I might no less do than hath so be done, considering the same to stand at all times with your Majesty's honour, and my poor worship; trusting always that your Grace, having some respect thereto, will something dispose toward me for the maintenance thereof, without which I may not well the same continue; which wholly I refer unto your royal accustomed goodness. Praying God to send your Grace long and most joyful life, with suppeditation[10] of your enemies, even as your most royal heart can wish or desire.

From this your Grace's town of Calais, the viij[th] day of this instant month of May, the xxviij[th] year of your most gracious reign.[11]   (Vol.3, No.691)

---

138   LORD LISLE TO CROMWELL   *8 May 1536*

Right honourable Sir, after my hearty recommendations, forasmuch as always my full trust and confidence hath been in you, I thought it most requisite to open my mind unto you. . . . And seeing there are many things now in his gracious disposition and hands, by reason of the most mischievous, heinous, and most abominable treasons against his most gracious and royal crown and person committed, I wholly trust that his Grace, ∧being good lord unto me∧, will vouchsafe to employ some part of those same upon me; which I do well know may so much the rather be obtained by your good mediation and furtherance. . . . And thus I beseech God to send you even as well to fare as I would myself.

From Calais the viijth of May.[12]   (Vol.3, No.691a)

The suits made for the possessions of those whom men expected to be condemned is one of the least pleasant aspects of the Tudor picture. We can only say that these men were all realists, acknowledging one loyalty and one only, and that to the King, who was the State. But for all that, it is somehow reassuring that 'the gentlest heart living', when he writes to the King for help, cannot bring himself to ask that the assistance shall be given from 'the many things now in his gracious disposition'.

Husee must have left Calais immediately after these letters were written.

---

139   JOHN HUSEE TO LORD LISLE   *12 May 1536*

This shall be advertising your lordship that I delivered Mr. Secretary your letter: who hath promised to be your very friend, and commanded me to

---

10. *Rare* or *obs.*, from *suppedito*. Used here with the meaning of overcoming or subduing.
11. In Husee's hand. Endorsed: copy of the King*es* let*t*re.
12. Rough draft, in Husee's hand.

12. Thomas Cromwell, Earl of Essex, by an unknown artist,
after Hans Holbein
Courtesy of the National Portrait Gallery

13. Henry VIII, detail from Holbein's cartoon for 'Henry VIII and the
Barber-Surgeons' (infra-red photograph)
Courtesy of the Royal College of Surgeons and the Courtauld Institute of Art, London

deliver the King's letter. But I in no wise might come unto his Grace's speech, so that I delivered the same unto Sir John Russell, who hath delivered the same to the King's Majesty; and saith further that he will consult with Mr. Secretary, and between them both, if they keep promise, I trust something will rise on your lordship's behalf. But there is no time to make hot suit till time the matters which are now in hand be overblown. And touching the Friar, Mr. Secretary saith he would they were all at the devil. He shall be rid, but it will be tomorrow ere I can have the letter for his dispatch, which Goodall shall bring, who shall depart tomorrow night. And as touching Mr. Treasurer, your lordship may shew Mr. Porter he will meddle with no matter till this business be rid out of hand.

This day Mr. Norrys, Weston, Bryerton, and Markes[13] hath been arraigned, and are judged to be drawn, hanged and quartered. I pray God have mercy on them. They shall die tomorrow, or Monday at the furthest. Anne the Queen and her brother shall be arraigned in the Tower; some think tomorrow, but on Monday at the furthest. And some doth verily think they shall there even so suffer within the Tower, undelayedly, for divers considerations which are not yet known. Mr. Page and Mr. Wyatt are in the Tower, but as it is said, without danger of death: but Mr. Page is banished the King's presence and Court for ever. . . . And thus I beseech Jesu send your lordship once your own heart's desire.

From London, the xij[th] day of May.
                    By your lordship's most bounden during life,
Hol.   John Husee   (Vol. 3, No. 694)

The appointments Husee mentions in the next letter are all to posts held by the arrested men. That of Groom of the Stole was held by Lisle's friend Norris, who was Keeper of the Privy Purse.

140   JOHN HUSEE TO LORD LISLE   *13 May 1536*

Pleaseth your lordship to be advertised that here is no good to be done neither with the King ne with any other of his Council till such time as the matters now had in hand be fully finished and achieved. . . . Also, touching Mr. Treasurer, it prevaileth nothing to sue unto him till he hath more leisure, for he never read letter since these matters begun. If it be as some doth presume, it shall be all rid by the latter end of this next week.

Here are so many tales I cannot well tell which to write; for now this day some saith young Weston shall 'scape; and some saith there shall none die

---

13. Mark Smeaton.

but the Queen and her brother; and some say that Wyat and Mr. Page are as like to suffer as the others; and the saying now is that those which shall suffer shall die when the Queen and her brother goeth to execution. But I think verily they shall all suffer, and in case any do escape it shall be young Weston, for whose life there is importunate suit made. And this day the rumour is that Harry Webbe should be taken in the West country and put in hold for the same cause. By Wednesday all shall be known, and your lordship shall be thereof advertised with speed.

Sir Thomas Cheyney is named Lord Warden: some saith by Mr. Secretary's preferment. My Lord of Richmond is Chamberlain of Chester and North Wales, and Mr. Harry Knyvet is constable of Beaumaris. If Mr. Secretary keep promise your lordship shall have something. This day Mr. Russell was in very sad communication with Mr. Whethill. I fear me that I have taken a wrong pig by the ear. But I shall know more by his preferring of your affairs ere it be long. Mr. Bryan is chief gentleman of the King's Privy chamber and shall keep the table, but there is plain saying the King will assign the Groom of the Stole from time to time at his pleasure.

I trust your lordship will remember Mr. Secretary with wine and letters, and in like manner Mr. Heneage, for as far as I can see they or one of them must strike the stroke. The King cometh not to Dover at ∧this time∧. There shall be both burgesses and knights of the shire for Calais. And that your lordship give credit to what Goodall shall tell you, and that to be kept secret. And thus I pray God to send your lordship your noble heart's desire.

From London, the xiij^th day of May.

By him that is your lordship's while he liveth,

Hol.   J. Husee   (Vol. 3, No. 695)

141   JOHN HUSEE TO LORD LISLE   *19 May 1536*

Pleaseth your lordship to be advertised that I have received your letter, with the spurs; and notwithstanding that I have waited diligently, and made all the friendship that I can make, I can hitherto find no ways to come to the King's presence. His Grace came not abroad (except it were in the garden, and in his boat at night, at which times it may become no man to prevent him) these xiiij days. So that I have been, and yet am, at a bay. I trust ere it be long, seeing that these matters of execution are past, to speak with his Grace, and then deliver your spurs according to your lordship's writing.

The Lord Rochford, Mr. Norris, Brereton, Weston and Markes suffered with the axe upon the scaffold at Tower Hill on Wednesday the xvij^th of this instant, which died very charitably. And Anne the late Queen suffered with sword this day, within the Tower, upon a new scaffold; and died boldly. Jesu take them to his mercy if it be his will.

. . . And now I trust to have more leisure with Mr. Secretary to put him in remembrance to motion the King's Highness even according as he promised to do for the obtaining of something toward your lordship's living. For in case he will be your lordship's friend you should speed the better, undoubtedly, in all your proceedings. I will to-morrow be in hand with him and present him your brews, and then also declare unto him the matter concerning the marsh. Your lordship may be well assured that I will do as much in preferring and soliciting your causes as I may, and that ere it be now x days, to an end your lordship shall know by some likelihood how to speed. . . .

Your hosen shall be sent within this vj days. And touching Mr. Page and Mr. Wyat, they remain still in the Tower. What shall become of them, God knoweth best. The most part of the late Queen's servants be set at liberty to seek service at pleasure. Mr. Aylmer shall show your lordship something by mouth which I will not now write. And thus I beseech Jesus send your lordship once a quiet living to your most noble heart's contentation.

From London, the xix[th] day of May.

I can yet get no answer concerning the friar.

Your lordship's bounden during life,

Hol.   John Husee   (Vol. 3, No. 698)

The news which Husee discreetly sent by word of mouth was presumably concerned with the King's marriage to Jane Seymour, to whom on the 20th, the day after Anne Boleyn's execution, Henry was formally betrothed. He had already secured his necessary divorce when Cranmer on the 17th had pronounced his second marriage void.

142   JOHN HUSEE TO LORD LISLE   *24 May 1536*

Pleaseth your lordship to be advertised that your peascods were thankfully received of the King's Highness for more considerations than I will write of; and as touching your suit to the King, Mr. Russell saith he moved his Grace concerning your lordship's preferment and that his Grace should say that it was too late, for because all things were disposed long since; and that amongst all that were now last in his Grace's disposition and gift there was nothing worth giving for your lordship, except certain offices in Wales, which his Grace said was not fit for your lordship, by reason it was so far from your native country, but that those offices were meet for them that had lands in those parts. Notwithstanding his Highness said that he would gladly that your lordship had somewhat.

The truth is, as I of late wrote your lordship, Mr. Russell is right worshipful and a sad discreet gentleman, but my mind giveth me plainly that he shall never prefer your lordship to anything for your advancement. I pray God take Mr. Norris to his mercy, for you have made an unlike change. But after mine opinion your lordship shall write unto Mr. Heneage some loving and kind letter, desiring him to be your good friend and solicitor to the King's Highness, and to send him some pleasure, as wine or others, as your lordship shall think meet; for I dare depose in my conscience Mr. Russell never spake to the King earnestly for you.

And where your lordship would that I should motion for the priories of Mawdlens and Pylton,[14] if your lordship be so minded, then it shall please you to send me the extent of their lands what either of them may spend, and I shall not let to put it in a proof. But after my mind, if your lordship did name and require some abbey of the suppressed number in Hampshire, Wiltshire or elsewhere being near unto your dwelling place, the same might be so much the sooner obtained. And although your lordship retaining Mr. Heneage, yet though Mr. Russell be assistant, there can be ∧no∧ damage therein. I am advertised, in case your lordship write me not the contrary, when your wine and quails cometh, to distribute the same equally betwixt Mr. Russell and Mr. Heneage. But in any wise your lordship may not forget to write him some loving letter; and likewise unto Mr. Secretary, though he do you little good and promise much. And now that I have written your lordship my mind I shall stay till I know your further pleasure.

Verso] The CC^{li} that the late Lord Rochford had out of the revenues of Winchester returneth to the Bishop's coffers, for the King will in nowise make any grant thereof. Mr. Bryan hath C^{li} that Mr. Norris had out of the same bishopric. I think verily one of the suppressed abbeys or priories shall be your best suit. . . .

. . . News here are none, but that it is presumed that there shall be by midsummer a new coronation: this by conjecture, and not unlikely. The progress shall not this summer pass Windsor. Your Lordship shall receive by Hugh Colton ij pair of hosen. And thus, trusting your L. have remembered me to the Treasurer and his brother, I rest, praying God to send your lordship long life with much honour.

From London the xxiiij[th] of May.

    By your lordship's bounden while he liveth,
Hol.   J. Husee   (Vol. 3, No. 703)

From here on Lisle's attempts to achieve solvency are no longer part of the political scene, and his further pursuit of abbey lands will be found in chapter 11, on business and legal affairs, although Cromwell's tentacles reach into those affairs as well. The death of Norris strengthened Cromwell's position

---

14. i.e. St. Mary Magdalen's, at Barnstaple, and Pilton in Devon.

at Court. Heneage, whom Husee has chosen to replace the former as his chief contact for Lisle with the King, and who becomes Groom of the Stole and gentleman usher of the Privy Chamber, had been in Wolsey's service and was very much Cromwell's 'own man'.

On the continent, months of sporadic fighting between French and Imperial troops had reached a point when, Francis having overrun Savoy and Piedmont and Charles having overrun Provence, Sir John Wallop, ambassador with Gardiner to the French King, writes to Lisle on 10 June[15] that 'the war is now begun, and both princes bent to do all the hurt they can, one to th'other'. On 17 June Lisle writes to Cromwell[16] the news that war has been declared in Boulogne. A royal proclamation of 19 August declares that the King proposes 'so to order and direct himself to his subjects . . . that no manner of suspicion of the leaning more to the one part than the other shall appear in his Grace', who will be 'upright and indifferent' in 'this point of neutrality'.[17]

On 8 July, Husee writes to Lisle, 'This day . . . Mr. Secretary is Lord Cromwell of Wimbledon.'[18]

In foreign affairs, the King remained neutral when the Emperor's troops invaded Picardy in July. It suited Henry's purposes admirably and put him in the satisfactory position of having his friendship solicited from both sides.

At the beginning of October the outbreak of the Pilgrimage of Grace confronted Henry with the one serious domestic crisis of his reign. Apart from the establishment of the royal supremacy in exchange for the papal, no doctrinal stance of a new religion had yet been formulated, nor had any excuse, except for the need of their funds, been presented for the suppression of the monasteries. Widespread discontent had been simmering for months in the North, but there can be little doubt that the spontaneous, popular, unplanned outbreak which took place at Louth in Lincolnshire on 1 October caught both the Government and the local authorities unawares by its suddenness. Henry's boast that he was, within his own dominions, Pope and Emperor had seemed not without reason. And then, suddenly this will to power received an unforeseen check from 'rude and ignorant common people . . . of one shire, and that one of the most brute and beastly of the whole realm', as he told the rebels themselves in answer to their petition.[19] In the first attack on the monasteries, East Anglia, Lincolnshire, and East Yorkshire, being richest in such institutions, had suffered more heavily than the rest of the country, and 87 out of 130 houses were suppressed.

15. Vol. 3, No. 720.
16. Vol. 3, No. 727.
17. Vol. 3, p. 433.
18. Vol. 3, No. 742.
19. See M. St. Clare Byrne, ed., *The Letters of King Henry VIII: A Selection* . . . (1936, 2d ed. 1968), pp. 141–4.

Neighbouring towns joined the men of Louth, and by the 6th their joint forces, numbering at least 10,000, had occupied Lincoln and swept up into their movement many of the local gentry. The King sent troops under the Duke of Suffolk to the area, and proposed to bring a second force himself, but the collecting and moving of an army at such short notice proved difficult. Rumours were spreading that parish churches were to be put down, and rebel forces grew. Had the insurgents pressed on towards London on the 9th or 10th, as was the original intention, they might well have carried all before them. It was the crucial moment, which could have turned a local rising into a civil war. The danger was averted not by the action of Suffolk's forces but by the inaction of the rebels, who waited for the King's reply to their petition while Henry temporized and so gave the royal forces a chance to grow. When the reply came on the 11th, couched in Henry's most majestic style, refusing their demands, ordering them to disperse, and threatening condign punishment, they hesitated and were lost. By the 13th the Lincolnshire rising was over, and the King's vengeance began.

Not a word of all this is to be found in the Lisle Letters, though Husee was at the court at Windsor when he wrote on about the 7th; but of this letter, No.143 below, the final page is missing. It is possible that on that page he gave some hint of what he was in the best possible position to learn.

Before the Lincolnshire rising was over the North was up and the actual Pilgrimage of Grace, to which this first outbreak was only the prologue, had begun. On the 4th the Lincolnshire men had lighted their beacons to warn their fellows on the other side of Humber that they were up; and by the 14th the whole of south-east Yorkshire had risen, animated by a deeper religious fervour than the Lincolnshire rebels. All who flocked to their banner, with Christ on the Cross on one side and a chalice and a host on the other, bound themselves by oath to 'the maintenance of God's faith and Church militant, preservation of the King's person and purifying the nobility of all villein's blood and evil counsellors'. It remained a movement of the people with gentry support rather than the other way about, both proclaiming that their enemies were such men as Cromwell and Riche; and it was the critical moment in these seven years when the Cromwell plan might have foundered.

For months to come, the Lisle Letters must be read against the background of this continuing struggle, but it was a background of which only maddening glimpses reached Calais, with probably garbled rumours from French and Flemish neighbours. Husee's silence, and the general silence that falls upon all who normally write to Lisle and vie with each other to send the first news about English events, makes a contemporary comment which is of real importance and of which, perhaps, no other source makes us quite so vividly aware – a silence, as of censorship, that conveys more effectively than the official correspondence the gravity of the situation and the tenseness of atmosphere which prevailed among those at the centre of affairs. When someone of Husee's volubility, who prides himself on his inside information, shuts up like a clam and refuses to commit anything to paper, and when Lisle cannot understand his reiterated excuses and becomes more and more exasperated by this silence, there is obviously more in it than meets the eye. Thanks to his useful contacts, he probably knew more than was good for him, and realized that the whole situation was much graver than anyone outside the Court circle was aware. If the Lord Deputy inadvertently let slip information of which he had not been officially apprised, it would be his man who took the rap. At the time when Husee writes his letter of 20 October, the King has just under 20,000 men mustered at Ampthill. Troops were still felt to be necessary in Lincolnshire, and he sent 2,000 to the Duke of Suffolk there, while he sent 5,000 north with the Duke of Norfolk, and then 560 extra horsemen. The rest, while temporarily disbanded to save expense, were to hold themselves ready for possible recall.

143   JOHN HUSEE TO LORD LISLE   *20 October 1536*

Pleaseth it your lordship to be advertised that Mr. Scriven with his friends here hath done as much as in them lay concerning the making of this money, which can yet in no wise be brought to pass. For they which should deliver this money will have iiij sundry sureties and will have them such that we can neither get nor find. And others which should deliver money with competent losses will not deal unless they may have those sureties bound in statutes, which we can find no man to do. So that at this time this matter cannot be compassed in no wise. What it will do hereafter, God knoweth, but I assure your lordship Mr. Scriven hath done as much as ∧he∧ might do if his life lay thereon, who can instruct your lordship at large of all things.

Here hath been a busy world, I pray God amend it, for my lord Privy Seal hath been so empeached with the King's matters that he would hear no man speak. I desired Mr. Whalley to deliver your lordship's letter unto him, which he did, and read the same unto him, inasmuch that Mr. Whalley plainly shewed him of the matter; and he said that the Lord Beauchamp should neither will nor choose but receive the money, if it be offered him any time within this month, as Mr. Whalley hath more at large informed Mr. Scriven thereof.

As yet my lord Privy Seal hath not delivered the King's letter, for there is as yet such weighty matters in hand that he will not trouble his Grace with suits. When he seeth time he saith that your lordship shall not be forgotten. My Lord Admiral is at Lincoln, so that I keep his letter still. . . .

. . . As for all news, Mr. Scriven can better inform your lordship than I can write them, for they are not to be written, as wise men hath showed me. I can no more but God better all things at His pleasure, Who send your lordship long life with much honour.

    From London, the xx day of October.

                Your lordship's at commandment so bounden,

Hol.   John Husee   (Vol. 3, No. 776)

We cannot tell how much Husee knew of the chaos that reigned in the King's forces during the next week, with the Dukes of Norfolk and Suffolk and the Marquess of Exeter tying each other in knots, ordering and countermanding men, money, and ordnance, and finally mislaying the latter altogether; but perhaps it is what he means by 'hell' in the next (so very correct) letter.

144   JOHN HUSEE TO LORD LISLE   *27 October 1536*

Pleaseth it your lordship to be advertised that by Mr. Scriven I wrote your lordship how all things passed till that day. And touching the money the Lord Beauchamp should have, my Lord Privy Seal saith that he shall not choose but take it, if it be paid him this xxv days. And as for the Abbey of ffristock, I cannot do nothing therein till such time as these rebels and traitors be subdued, which, God willing, shall be shortly. And as for news I can write none other than Goodal can inform your lordship of, more than of those which came out of hell, which I do send your lordship by this bearer. And thus I beseech Jesu to send your lordship long life and much honour.

    From London, the xxvij[th] of October.

                By your lordship's bounden,

Hol.   John Husee   (Vol. 3, No. 779)

'This bearer' was obviously to convey more information by word of mouth. The suppression of news was important to Henry's policy of making as little as possible of the scale of the revolt, lest it increase adherents to it at home and weaken his standing abroad. In the North, Norfolk, facing vastly superior forces, was advising temporizing, for instead of attacking, the rebels were asking only to be allowed to 'declare their griefs' to the King. He begged the King 'to take in good part whatsoever promises I shall make unto the rebels (if any such I shall by the advice of others make), for surely I shall observe no part thereof for any respect of that other might call mine honour distayned'.[20] The King commended his discretion; and instructing him not to

20. Vol. 3, p. 510.

fight if his forces were insufficient, endorsed his offer to make promises he had no intention of keeping, once it was expedient to break them. Norfolk, with provisions only for less than a third of his little army and their horses, with no fuel, with the plague rampant in Doncaster, his headquarters, and deaths from it already among his men, listened to the demands of the rebels (with two of which, the safety of the monasteries and the removal of 'base councillors', meaning Cromwell, he genuinely agreed), and offered to go to London with two of their leaders and help them present their case. Both armies were meanwhile dispersed. Henry drafted a reply which conceded nothing, but other supporters of the Pilgrimage were meanwhile being raised in Lancashire, Cumberland, and Westmoreland and, growing restless at the delay in London, the original group were only prevented from calling a general assembly at York on 11 November by the news that Norfolk would return on the 18th with the King's reply to their petition.

When Francis Hall, Spear of Calais, wrote the following letter, therefore, the issue was still entirely in suspense, and things were very far indeed from being 'well pacified' in Yorkshire and the North. But his information about the action taken by the Duke of Suffolk to guard 'the passages' was true, and so was his report about the raising of men by Lord Derby and their discharge.

145   FRANCIS HALL TO LORD LISLE   *17 November 1536*

Right honourable and my good Lord, in humble wise I have me most heartily recommended unto your good lordship, and to my good Lady, beseeching Almighty God to send you both your honourable hearts' desire. At my going to Ampthill I wrote unto your lordship, and at this time these be most humbly and heartily to thank your lordship that it would please you to be my wife's gossip and godfather to a mother. If I had been there I could not nor durst not have desired your lordship to have holpen to christen a wench; but now I see my wife will bear but wenches, for divers your goodnesses and specially for this, I and my wife are much bound unto your good lordship and to my good lady, which I pray God we may be able once to deserve.

Further it shall please your lordship to understand that the King and the Queen's grace be ∧both∧ merry, and in good health, lauded be God, and all things be well pacified, both in Lincolnshire, Yorkshire, and in the North parts. I beseech Almighty God to continue it. My Lord of Suffolk, Sir Francis Bryan, Sir John Russell, and Sir Anthony Browne remain yet still at Lincoln. And Sir Ralph Ellerker and Bowes be gone down into Yorkshire with the King's answer to their petitions and requests ∧there∧, so that I trust all things shall be well. My Lord of Suffolk, upon a false report of a spy that

Yorkshire was up again, caused certain passages to be prevented and taken, which caused the Borderers to begin to stir a little, but when the truth was known every man withdrew themself peaceably home again. And where the bruit hath been ij or iij days that Cheshire and Lancashire was up, it is not true; but the saying is that my Lord of Derby had raised a certain number on the King's behalf, and when they should be discharged again, because they were not paid they set upon my said Lord Derby and took such as he had. . . .

From London, in great haste, the xvijth of November 1536.

Your most humble to command in any service,

Hol.   ffrauncys Halle   (Vol.3, No.783)

In a long business letter of 18 November, Husee's only mention of the state of the nation is in his last line: 'How the world here goeth this bearer can inform your lordship.' But we cannot afford to disregard events, because here the two men whose power struggle is behind the drama of Lisle's story are vitally engaged – and only in appearance on the same side. If Cromwell's power, and even his life, is at stake, Norfolk's hopes of establishing himself in Court and Council depend on defeating, if only to an extent and for the moment, his rival's enemies. In spite of his sympathies with the rebels there is no question of his defecting to them: he needs the King's gratitude, which his skill in using his popularity in the North in implementing Henry's strategy must surely earn him. But neither the King nor Cromwell intend that he shall benefit from it.

In foreign affairs at this time, the negotiations of Lisle's great-nephew, James V of Scotland, for marriage with the eldest daughter of the King of France cause disquiet to Henry; in a minor way, the depredations of English pirates have been causing annoyance to France. Stephen Gardiner, Bishop of Winchester, and Sir John Wallop are Henry's Ambassadors to Francis I.

146   STEPHEN GARDINER AND SIR JOHN   *21 November 1536*
       WALLOP TO LORD LISLE

After our most hearty recommendations to your good lordship with like thanks for your last good letters, so full of evil tidings, which be now, thanked be God, well amended, much to our comfort.

I, Sir John Wallop, have heard since of such tidings as I wrote unto ∧you∧ in my letters from Valence concerning the adventurers, which tidings, although they were true, yet because they be sour and displeasant the Frenchmen be not content that any man should boast them abroad. I have had it here laid to my charge.

Now I will leave the matters of France and write somewhat of the King of Scots, who shall shortly be ensured to Madame Magdalene and soon after marry her. He is a man of the fewest words that may be. The ambassador of Venice was with him and spake a long matter unto him, and neither by himself ne any other answered him one word. He spake not to us very many. His wife shall temper him well, for she can speak, and if she spake as little as he the house should be very quiet. We pray you recommend us heartily to our good lady. And most heartily fare ye well. At Blois, the xxj[th] of November.

	Your lordship's assured	
Hol.	Ste: Winton	
Signed	John Wallop	(Vol. 3, No. 785)

Though it is apparent from the above that Lisle risks sending what news he has gleaned from home into France from Calais, the Ambassadors are evidently receiving the official line suitable for dissemination abroad, and Husee still writes with caution on 1 December:

> And touching any news, I trust your lordship will hold me excused, considering that this world is queasy, and I might perchance in writing of some put myself to displeasure and mean no hurt. But as I hear, having an honest messenger, I will declare by mouth that which I shall think to be true.[21]

147   LORD LISLE TO GARDINER AND WALLOP   *6 December 1536*

After my hearty recommendations, this shall be to advertise you I have received your letter dated the xxj day of this present month, wherein ye write that ye have heard again, and how it hath been laid to your charge, the news ye wrote me from Valence. As to that, if there be any in England, either of high degree or low, that can shew my hand to any writing of any news that ever ye should write me (saving once, ij year past, I wrote to my Lord of Carlisle), never trust me for no true man. And rather than my Lord of Winchester or you should suspect me in the same, I pray you never write to me but of your good healths, and I shall do likewise, ensuring you ye never wrote me no news but either I heard them before or within x days after. ∧And thus I beseech∧ our Lord God ∧to∧ send you prosperous lives and long, to his high pleasure.

My wife desireth that this may present her hearty recommendations to you both, and semblably that I and she may be [recommended] to the good Lady Wallop.

From Calais, the ∧vj∧ day of ∧December∧

21. Vol. 3, No. 792.

∧Furthermore to advertise you∧, News I hear that the ∧Rebels∧ be up yet at York, and how the Archbishop there, the Lord Darcy, and all the knights of the country be with them. And the xx day of November my Lord of Norfolk and my Lord Admiral rid thither but with xxx horses, as it is said, ∧to have communication with them. I pray God send a good end thereof. Also the king hath sent to Nottingham Castle vj pieces of ordnance, falcons and sakers. As yet his Grace is at Windsor, and intendeth, as I hear say, to keep his Christmas at Greenwich.∧

Also the Flemings on the sea have robbed certain Englishman; but the Ambassador of Flanders who is in England hath caused restitution to be made, and commandment given to the Admiral, pain of death, to rob nor meddle with no Englishman.

Thus for haste I bid you once again farewell.

From Calais, the vj day of December   (Vol. 3, No. 795)

So those trusted letter-bearers with news to be delivered only by word of mouth had conveyed a certain amount.

The rebels had had two opportunities to strike with vastly superior numbers and alter the course of history, but their loyalty to the King (as opposed, as they saw it, to his advisers), his statecraft, and Norfolk's duplicity had been their undoing. Now, at the beginning of December, they waited, while the King, infuriated by their insisting on an Act of Parliament to confirm their pardon so that they could press their requests, set about secretly trying to persuade their leaders to betray each other. Offers of support were still coming in to the rebels, including, now, from the South.

148   JOHN HUSEE TO LORD LISLE   *11 December 1536*

Pleaseth it your lordship to be advertised that by my Lord Howard's servant George I wrote your lordship of what till then was requisite; and since that time I have had your Counsel with the Chancellor and the Counsel of the Augmentations iij times, but yet we cannot be at no determinate end. . . .[22]

Since the writing of this aforesaid I spake with one that came from your lordship, who told me that your lordship is displeased with me because I write no news. I have written your lordship in my former letters the danger thereof, trusting that your lordship will be therewith pleased; for if I should write it might chance that I thereby might put myself in danger of my life and also put your lordship to displeasure, for there is divers here that hath been

---

22. Business letter finished and signed; then the following postscript added.

punished for reading and copying with publishing abroad of news; yea, some of them are at this hour in the Tower and like to suffer therefor. I have good hope your lordship will hold me excused, for it is much better that I stay from writing than to put your lordship to displeasure and myself to undoing. We trust here that all shall be well, for the King's majesty is piteous and full of mercy, if they that be offenders will submit them unto his mercy, as we have here full hope they will do. . . .

Also, since the writing of this present, news is come that the Northern men are now submitted unto the King's mercy and doth cry peccamus; and they hath obeyed the King's proclamation, so that all is at a very good point, which maketh many joyful hearts. This news my Lord William brought the King yesternight at midnight.   (Vol.3, No.798)

No one could blame Husee for echoing the official line, when driven by Lisle's demands to put something on paper: he was probably aware already of the identity – and the innocence – of the men who were under arrest. They were Sir William Essex and Sir George Throckmorton, both loyal gentlemen who had raised men in their own counties to join the King against the Lincolnshire rising. But the police-state atmosphere of England in the 1530s becomes very apparent from Throckmorton's confession when he was charged with 'certain words spoken at supper' in November, about the northern rising. He remembers sitting at supper, though he forgets where, when someone asked what were the rebels' demands, 'and every man looked upon other, and no man would make answer'. Throckmorton broke that deadly pause himself, saying 'it was in every man's mouth, and we were all true men there, so we might talk of it', and that 'the false knave Aske[23] would rule the King and all the realm'. He 'rehearsed' Aske's demands, as far as he could remember them, without approval of them. Later he lent a copy of the rebels' printed handout to Essex, whose clerk's boy copied it and to whom it was traced back.

Meanwhile, from abroad Wallop sends news of the confused state of Europe, with the French getting rather the worst of the sporadic fighting, but more serious campaigning expected in the summer. To Henry the strengthening of the traditional Scottish-French alliance by the forthcoming royal marriage will be less satisfactory, but Wallop has difficulty in taking King James seriously.

149   SIR JOHN WALLOP TO LORD LISLE   14 December 1536

My Lord, after my most hearty recommendations and this shall be only to make you participant unto the news now in these parts. . . .

23. Robert Aske, leader of the northern pilgrims.

The King of Scots is now in this town to prepare for his marriage, which shall be, as it is said, this Christmas holidays. Great preparations is made here for the same in the palace, in so much that there is no court now kept there, but in the Bishop's palace. The said King lieth at the Tournelles, daily assaying his horse and harness, so I assure you he had need to do, if he intend to get any honour here. He is much praised universally to be very gentle. My Lord of Winchester and I feel little thereof. What he meaneth thereby we know not. His manner of using himself, by that we do perceive, is after the Northern fashion, as the lords of those parts doth use themself when they come first to the Court, now looking over one shoulder and now over the other, with a beck to one and a beck to another, and unto us nothing. He is a right proper man, after the Northern fashion. His being here shall do him much good, and to us little profit, for here he shall learn many things. The French King hath paid him now L m^l crowns in part of payment of D m^l, which he shall have with his wife. What other thing he shall have, as yet I know not. I think he never saw so great a sum of money together before. And thus, my good lord, having no other matter at this time, I heartily bid you farewell, with my wife's most humble recommendations unto your good lordship and my lady, praying you unto my said good lady I may be the like, not forgetting Master Porter, with the rest of the Council,

At Paris, the xiiijth day of December.

        Yours assuredly,

Signed   John Wallop   (Vol. 3, No. 803)

At home, every effort was made to show that all was well, as the Surveyor of Calais here describes.

150   RICHARD LEE TO LORD LISLE   *23 December 1536*

My very good Lord, after my due salutations unto your good lordship and my good Lady your wife, these shall be to advertise the same that I have received your letters dated the xjth day of December. According ∧to∧ the effect and meaning thereof, to the intent I would gratify you if I might, I have moved divers of my friends to borrow so much money for your lordship as ye have need of to pay my Lord Beauchamp. This is the answer they make unto me: they say there was never so little money among them there. The debts, by reason of this business[24] that hath been here, cannot be gathered together. Finally, without sufficient gage or lands for repayment assured, there can be nothing had. . . .

24. i.e. the Pilgrimage of Grace.

My lord, yesterday at afternoon the King's Majesty and the Queen, with all dukes, lords and the ambassador of the Emperor rode through the City of London, whereas they were received so honourably as the like sight hath not been seen ∧here∧ since the Emperor's being here: the streets hanged about with arras and cloth of gold, priests in their copes with their crosses and censers ∧on the one side and∧ the citizens of London, every man in his degree, on the other side. It rejoiced every man wondrously. His Highness is now at Greenwich, where he intendeth to keep his Christmas; which shall be kept, God willing, with as great mirth and triumph as ever was. I pray God keep your lordship and my lady your wife, and make her a glad mother.

From London, the xxiijth day of December.

By yo*urs* to com*m*and,

Hol.   Rychard Lee   (Vol. 3, No. 813)

As a fact, the rebellion was not over, but Henry could well 'rest him merry', knowing he had won. The rebels distrusted the promises that had been made to them, and there were to be fresh outbreaks early in the new year, but the danger to Henry's power and Cromwell's plan was over. Cromwell had been lying low while providing the funds, but it was against him that the Pilgrims' hatred was directed; and it is not wholly fanciful to wonder whether subconsciously Henry never forgave his hitherto hundred-percent successful minister for allowing the Pilgrimage of Grace to happen. The risings in February were easily disposed of. Henry kept none of the promises he had made, and wreaked a terrible vengeance.

9

Calais 1536

It seems appropriate that the new year opens with one of the perennial requests for a job in the Retinue, particularly since it is on behalf of the troublesome Whethill family. Lisle's reply is drafted on the back of it, as though in haste while his resolution lasts, and is here given in his own spelling.

151   SIR THOMAS AUDLEY TO LORD LISLE   *17 January 1536*

After my right hearty recommendations, it shall like your good lordship at this my contemplation to be good lord unto young Whetell concerning the next avoidance of a Spear within your office at Calais: signifying unto you that the King's Highness hath made a grant thereof by his letters patent. Nevertheless, if ye admit him at this my request it shall not hereafter be prejudicial to your office in any wise. Right heartily requiring your good lordship to accomplish this my desire, for divers of my friends hath made earnest suit unto me to write unto your lordship in this behalf. And in this doing for my sake I shall requite your gentleness to my power. As knoweth our Lord, who have you in his blessed keeping. Written at London, the xvij day of January.

Signed   y*our* lovyng ffrend

Thomas Audeley K. Chauncelor   (Vol. 3, No. 633)

152   LORD LISLE TO SIR THOMAS AUDLEY

Ryght honorabyll aft*er* my most humbylyst wyse I co*m*mend me vnto you & have reseyvyd y*our* jentyll let*ter* in the favor of R whethyll co*n*sernyng the next speris rome w*ith*in myn offyce her hit shall plesse y*our* good lordshype that ther is not the trustist s*erva*nt in yo*ur* hovse nother in yngland that shall gladlyer do y*our* co*m*mandment & plessur then I wold w*ith* owght desemylassion as eu*er* devryng my lyffe shall aper toward you & yo*ur*s thys

whethill & his father orderyd me opynly at lantern gate w*ith* word*es* & covntenans that I neu*er* sofferyd so mvche of no degre sens I whas xvj yer old notw*ith*standyng I woll at yo*ur* co*m*mandment forget all
Hol. (Vol.3, No.633a)

---

153   LORD LISLE TO CROMWELL   *14 March 1536*

After most humble recommendations this shall be to advertise you that I received your letter the xij[th] day of this month, and according to your commandment, the morrow after I and Sir Thomas Palmer, Thomas Fowler, Mr. Mason, Mr. Carpenter and their Warden, Robert Shetford, Clerk of the King's Works here ∧and John Lake, Clerk to my Lord Edmund∧, I rode to Guisnes; and there to the best of our understanding have viewed and seen the break of the wall there; and as far as we can perceive and see the said wall will fall daily more and more for great part of it that standeth is cloven, and every day falleth, so that as far as all our wits will serve us there is no remedy but a new wall must be made on the outside of the same, which will contain in length v[c] foot, which wall shall be made diamond point wise, with a great tower or bulwark in the midst of the ∧said∧ diamond point, which ∧shall∧ have a platform in the top of it xxx foot broad, for we consider that that place is most dangerous of the Castle, if any siege should come. And if it may please the King's Highness to have the said new wall made according to a plat made by the warden, bringer hereof, it will cost by estimation xv¢lxxxj[li] iij[s] iiij[d] sterling, as the said bearer shall show you a book of particulars of every thing, which bearer can inform you of every thing thereof as well as all we were with you. And thus we commit you to the Blessed Trinity which ever preserve you with long life and honour.

At Calais, the xiiij[th] day of March.   (Vol.3, No.653)

It was widely believed in Flanders that England would side with France in the current hostilities with the Empire, and the Castellan of Gravelines, just across the Flemish border from the Pale, was perhaps nervous because of two mysterious Englishmen in the vicinity of the castle.

---

154   LORD LISLE TO JEHAN DE TOVAR   *17 March 1536*

Monsieur le capitaine, I commend me unto you. I have this day heard that you have caused to be arrested and held prisoner in your castle of Gravelines one of the servants of the King my sovereign lord and master, called Derrick, and have also taken from him all and sundry the writings that he had with him, and also his money; and besides this, not content therewithal, you have semblably put under arrest another of the subjects of the King my master which was of the company of the said Derrick: which thing meseemeth right strange and illdone, thus to entreat his subjects as ye do, and which is utterly contrary to the good peace and friendship that is betwixt our princes; knowing that if his Majesty the Emperor should be advertised of your conduct in this and in other matters that ye now of late do pretend, that he would be in nowise content with you: wherefore I pray you, Monsieur le capitaine, that it may please you entirely to set at liberty the said Derrick and his companion, together with their writings and all other things to them belonging; and that it may please you to ascertain me by this bearer of the cause of their detention, that I may know what order to take in this matter; and thus Our Creator have you in his keeping.

From Calais, the xvij[th] day of March.

Assuredly yours[1]

(Vol. 3, No. 656)

155   JEHAN DE TOVAR TO LORD LISLE   *17 March 1536*

Monsieur le Debitis, Betwixt vj and vij of the clock I have received from you a letter by the which you advertise me that you have been informed that I have detained a servant of the King your master together with another his subject. And to ascertain you of the truth, I came from the Court between three and four of the clock, and after mine arrival heard that the porters of this town had arrested two Germans, of the which the one whom ye say is called Derrick said he was of Cologne, and the other of Hamburg. And seeing that those who come from Hamburg are not at this present the good servants of the Emperor that they ought to be, and that by proclamation current in these parts everyone must be on his guard against them, my people before mine arrival in this town had here arrested them in an hostelry called the Crown; & upon search made of them to discover what things they carried, had found them to have about them a number of small books of Martin Luther's and others his adherents: the which was cause that they were detained until my coming, and according to my instructions. And when I had put on my harness I spake with them and demanded of them if they had brought such books as was shewed me, and incontinent I had returned to them the said books and other things that were taken from them, and had them put into their hands.

And I have advertised her Majesty the Queen of them, to the end that her Majesty may order these matters according to her good pleasure; for I am assured ye know well his Majesty the Emperor hath proclaimed and given us

1. French. Not signed.

orders to look well to such persons that are full of such errors against the faith of Jesus Christ. Seeing that the said Derrick hath said that he is of Cologne, and that you say he is the King's servant, I shall advertise her Majesty the Queen our Regent of that which you write me. I know she will right well consider it, if things are as you say. And as for that of which you have been advertised, and that you assert by your letter: that I have evilly entreated the subjects of your master; I ensure you that oft times you and others of your parts say that of me which is untrue, always considered that you on your side and other the servants of the King of England should do as much for the good accord and amity which ought to hold betwixt our masters, as daily I do take pains utterly to destroy the wicked inventions that come from your quarter. But I well ensure you that the Emperor knoweth surely how I conduct myself, and that I deserve thereof better than you say. I forbear at this time to write you at more length, seeing that you have not given me answer to others that I have written to you, by the which I have expressed my desire to clear myself before you, and to show you, face to face, that I do not do those things which belong not to a knight like myself, descended of the blood royal, as you do.

From Gravelines, this xvij[th] of March 1535.

Your assured friend,

known as the friend of the Emperor[2]

(Vol. 3, No. 657)

156   LORD LISLE TO JEHAN DE TOVAR   24 *March 1536*

Monsieur le capitaine, I have even now received your letters in reply to mine which I wrote you for the deliverance ∧of Derrick∧, servant to the King my master, whom you have detained prisoner, and also have taken from him all and sundry such writings that he had with him. And I find neither any commodity nor yet the civility of neighbourliness in these your letters in any sort, but in every way a strictness more than becometh you, the which is directly to depart from the good peace and amity that is betwixt the Emperor your lord and his Majesty the King my sovereign lord and master. Wherefore I admonish and pray you to set fully and entirely at liberty this said Derrick together with all his writings and all other things in his charge, and not to make further trial of nor to offend the league and amity betwixt our princes hereafter, but to put yourself in a fair way of reformation to the end that ye may eschew the dangers and inconveniences that might hap by reason of your discourtesy: and ∧henceforth∧ not to provoke thus the King my master, as you have often times done.

---

2. Copy, in French, to be sent to England.

Thus the Deputy of Calais, and thus the copy of his letter as forwarded to Cromwell. But for Jean de Tovar's benefit Arthur Lisle added the following paragraph:

Monsieur le capitaine, where you set forward your birth and nobility by these your letters, few great personages are aware thereof, whereas I know well that all noble princes and honourable gentlemen are surely informed of my extraction. And I verily believe, as do men of all estates, that if you were indeed the issue of a noble lineage, that your conditions and manners would be more honest than they are. This between you and me, to conclude my letter.

At Calais, the xxiijth day of March.
     Assuredly yours,[3]   (Vol. 3, No. 664)

Lisle's anger when he wrote the above may well have stemmed not only from de Tovar's suggestion that he was only an ordinary knight, but also from the fact that, as he told Cromwell, he knew from a spy that de Tovar had already sent the prisoners to the Queen Regent at Bruges without honourably informing him. This he could not reveal without the risk of blowing his agent at the Regent's court.

The facts behind the draft letter to the King that follows are these: Lisle had reluctantly promised Audley on 9 June the presentation of young Robert Whethill to the next vacancy for a Spear *within his own office*. Thomas Prowde's vacancy, which had now arisen, was one which it was not in Lisle's, only in the King's, power to give, and Lisle had refused the Whethills' claim.

157   LORD LISLE TO HENRY VIII   *[n.d.] ? c.10–22 April 1536*

Please ∧it∧ your Grace to be advertised that I am credibly informed that your Highness hath written your letter unto me in the favour of Sir Richard Whethill's son for a Spear's room late being Thomas Prowde's room, which letter the said Whethill doth ∧keep∧ and hath done iij days after he came ∧over, and yet doth∧, not shewing me neither by word nor letter no part of your Grace's pleasure which sounds in my eyne marvellously, fearing by some untrue surmise your Grace should have me in displeasure, which I had liefer I had never been born than to give your Grace any such cause: putting your Grace out of doubt, to be abiden by, I have been handled with Sir Whethill and his wife and his son ∧whom your Grace writes for∧ as I verily believe that the worst groom of your chamber would not a'suffered it. Being

3. French. Not signed.

in the authority that I am in, and because I have not been accustomed ever to hurt no gentleman, hath been the occasion wherefore I did conceal it from your Highness, which I am driven now to declare ∧it∧ to your Grace; and if it may appear that I have done them a groatsworth of wrong but that I have your Grace's letter and commandment for my discharge, then I bind me unto your Grace to give them xx nobles for ever, gratis. And the young man whom your Grace doth write for did declare unto me openly before a hundred of your servants here, ∧in your Gate∧, that he would have a Spear's room here and ask me to leave, and would give me no thanks for the same, which methinks became him evil to say, seeing that I did him no wrong. And within few days after, his father came home to my house, and began to fall out with me maintaining the saying of his son neither wisely nor discreetly but slanderously, and tempted me more than ever I was; and if I had not ∧been∧ your Deputy here he should well a'known his folly! And now, since that, his wife came to my wife in the church, and in Pilate's voice, that all the church heard ∧it, and said∧ I had done her son wrong, and that I had sold her son's room; which if it can be proved that ever I took penny or groat, gold or silver, or any other thing to the value of a penny ∧for the same∧, then I beseech your Grace never be good lord unto me while you live, which I would not lose your favour for all the good in this world: most humbly beseeching your Grace to be so good and gracious lord unto me as to let the matter be heard before your Grace and your Council to the intent you may know the truth, and if he or any other shall handle me on this manner without cause it shall be cause ∧that∧ I shall not be able to serve your Grace as to your honour ∧there∧ which is my desire to do before anything in this world, I take God to be my judge, who send your Highness most long and victorious life to his pleasure.   (Vol.3, No.680b)

Lisle's description of Lady Whethill railing 'in Pilate's voice' remains a vivid image thanks to Chaucer's Miller – 'in Pilates voys he gan to crie'. Herod and Pilate in old religious drama were the outstanding characters for rant and noisy rage – in performance, if not always, in Pilate's case, in the text. But thanks to Hamlet's advice to the players, Herod has out-heroded him and is still a byword.

While Lisle had to wait for a licence to leave Calais for the King's expected visit to Dover (which did not materialize), young Whethill was able to strut about at Court as Thomas Warley delightfully describes him in a letter of 2 May:

Robert Whethill brags freshly in the Court in a coat of crimson taffeta, cut and lined with yellow sarcenet, ∧a shirt wrought with gold∧, his hosen scarlet, the breeches crimson velvet, cut and edged and lined with yellow sarcenet, his shoes crimson velvet and likewise his sword-girdle and scabbard, a cloak of red frisado, a scarlet cap with feathers red and yellow. He hath many lookers-over etc.[4]

To give a true picture of Sir Richard, it is necessary to let him run on and on; and he does give us a striking glimpse of the King, and probably reproduces verbatim his very trick of speech, with its impatient 'once, twice, or thrice' and its characteristic 'Well', at the opening of a decisive comment.

158   SIR RICHARD WHETHILL TO LORD LISLE   *9 June 1536*

My lord, after due recommendation unto you, with my good lady, your wife, I have received your letter dated the ij^d day of this month, wherein it is your pleasure to write me answer as touching a letter I wrote to your lordship in favour of my son Robert, for that he might be admitted to the ∧Spear's∧ room, late Thomas Prowde's, whose soul God pardon, for that I was loath to move the King's Highness further, and thereby his Grace to take displeasure: notwithstanding I perceive by your lordship ye will do as much as in you is to continue Snowden in the same spear's room and for that your pleasure is to advertise me that ye gave it to Mr. Porter and not to your servant, as I and mine hath reported, and will enjoy the said room in despite of your lordship, and also that my wife and son Robert hath behaved them in their words otherwise than it would become them to you and to my lady. I knew not what despitement till I saw your letter nor suppose I go not about after that sort; nor yet that my wife nor son will behave them in their words otherwise than it becomes them; but well I know that Calais tongues in some ∧in∧ reports is not best, nor yet some time with their pens in writing, but lays blocks to do other men displeasure if they could.

But truth with patience shall win at the last; and for truth, after the King's Highness granted me the foresaid Spear's room for my son Robert, I shewed his Grace, if his pleasure was that my son should have the room, his Grace must direct to your lordship his letters to discharge one that was admitted and sworn in the room. His Grace said a'was sure, once, twice or thrice, it was not so. I shewed his Grace it was, of truth. His Grace asked me, Who? I shewed his Grace, one Leonard Snowden, your servant. Then his Grace answered incontinent, 'What? so soon? So soon?' 'Well', said his Grace, 'resort unto us again'. Ten days after I laboured to his Grace to know his Highness' pleasure. His Grace commanded me to cause a letter to be made, which was done, as his Grace's pleasure was, and sent unto your lordship; wherein, as yet, I cannot be at an end. But of your goodness ye offer me the next Spear's room for my son, or else to spend a £^{li} and still to continue in malice towards me, as your letter sounds. My lord, I have given you no such cause, neither in thought, word nor deed. But to suffer Mr. Porter to enjoy his gift given him by the King or your lordship, I trust the King's Highness with his gracious Council will say that my son's gift is best, many ways; first, by the first grant, afore Mr. Porter's, as also his to stand in none effect after he was Master Porter: second, by the ordinance made by Master Treasurer with the other Commissioners that, money given for any room, he to lose the room: further, after the commencement of the Parliament last past, the Acts stayed in stead and effect where by my son's proviso he ought to have the foresaid room, as learned men say. So that I trust not to lose your favour in the obtaining of the same, for considering the gift is out of your hands now, it must be seen whether it shall so stand or not betwixt Master Porter's and my son's grant and Snowden's and my son; wherein I trust that the King's Highness will be my good and gracious lord, as his Grace hath been hitherto. Praying you of your goodness to hold me excused though I follow the King's grant and gift therein; and I shall be always ready to do your lordship that pleasure that in me is. And thus our Lord preserve you, my lady and all yours.

Written at London, the ix day of June.

             Yours

Hol.   S*ir* Ric. Whettehyll   (Vol.3, No.719)

A new Act of Parliament had been designed to regularize once and for all the giving and holding of posts in Calais. The interest in the following letter from Lady Lisle lies in her clear grasp of the way the new Act worked, considerably modifying former practice, the succinctness of her explanation, the practicality of her advice, her refusal of the 'recompense' which it was customary to offer in return for the exercise of influence, her willingness to get round the new restrictions, and her frank avowal of how she proposes to do this by herself 'entreating' the two officials whose consent was necessary.

159   LADY LISLE TO WILLIAM POPLEY   *12 June 1536*

After mine old true hearty manner I recommend me unto you as she that is as glad to hear from you as any living; and as yesterday received your letter dated the vj day of this instant month; and am right sorry it was not your chance to make your request before Michaelmas, and so is my lord, who hath him heartily recommended unto you, for as then my lord might have holpen it better than now; ensuring you although your letter had not come I was minded to have made my moan unto you. For my lord is now in authority without liberty, for since the Commissioners were here, as it is comprised in the Acts, he cannot give no room but after the manner following: first, one in petty wages to the vj^d, and he in vj^d to the viij^d, so that he must first begin in petty wages. Yet my lord hath two overseers, the Lord Comptroller and the Vice-Treasurer. Nevertheless, I pray you send your friend as shortly as ye may. Let him be a tall man and a good Archer. And my lord will admit him incontinent in his wages, and then give him the first vj^d that shall fall; and after, the first viij^d, although the Acts be contrary; for I trust so to entreat my Lord Comptroller and the Vice-Treasurer that they shall be content. And where ye write he shall recompense me, good Mr. Popley, I would not for £^{li} take one penny, nor never did of no man, whatsoever hath been reported; and loath I would be to begin with you. And in anything that I may do I am yours; praying you to give credence unto Husee, who shall shew further of my mind. And thus most heartily fare you well.

From Calais, the xij day of June.

By yours ever assured,

Signed   Honor Lyssle   (Vol. 3, No. 721)

160   LORD LISLE TO CROMWELL   *17 June 1536*

Right honourable, After most hearty recommendations, this is to advertise you that, as yesterday, open war was proclaimed at Boulogne betwixt the French King and the Emperor; and the night following they made intercourse in the Pales adjoining. And as this day, I received a letter of the Captain of Arde, requiring leave for their cattle to be brought within the King's Pales here for succour, which letter I send unto you, ∧Mr. Secretary∧, with the copy of the answer thereof to the said ∧Captain∧ of the Arde. Beseeching you I may be advertised from the same of the King's pleasure, how I shall use myself on every behalf, which shall be done with diligence. And very sorry I am that the marshes here be so dry as they be and so open betwixt both parties, not knowing none answer of all the letters I have written in the same, for I assure you I cannot sleep in quiet to know the same as it is; knowing of a surety that if they make any incurre into any of the parts they may come as nigh as St. Peter's and take away with them what they will, which, rather than I would ∧live to∧ know it, I had liefer lay in perpetual prison during my life, as God knoweth, who preserve you.

Sir, there is ∧no∧ man living knoweth the open way between Arde and Calais better than you do. And now, how dry it is that £m men may come over in a night. I take God to record, I never wrote in displeasure nor malice of Sir Robert Wingfield and so I desire you to answer for me. In the honour of God, set to your helping hand, that I may know the King's pleasure. I have advertised. I trust I am discharged, for ∧all that∧ lieth in my power. I will obey his Grace's commandment to die in the quarrel.[5]

(Vol. 3, No. 727)

5. Copy.

Lisle's reference, here, to Wingfield is to indicate how right he himself had been to oppose the draining of Sir Robert's marsh.

161   LORD LISLE TO THE CAPTAIN OF ARDRES   *17 June 1536*

Messieurs, I commend me right heartily to you and have received by this bearer your letters bearing date of this present day; and do well perceive the contents thereof, of the which ye have fully advertised me.

Sirs, In reply to these your letters, you give me to understand that in the war which has been proclaimed between the Emperor and the King your master, your poor townsfolk have no refuge in your quarters for their own safety and that of their goods, praying me to receive them here in our territory in safety.

Sirs, You must understand that the King my sovereign Lord is indifferent between the two princes, by reason of which he cannot assist either the one side or the other. Notwithstanding, I will advertise the King my master of this your request, and his good pleasure by me being known, will give you thereof full reply. Thus commending you to God, who have you all, Messieurs, in his safe keeping.

From Calais, the xvij day of June
   Le tout votre bon
     Arthur Lysle[6]   (Vol. 3, No. 728a)

Without 'guidance' from England, Lisle had dealt correctly, and expeditiously, with the situation before the news of the declaration of war could have reached London.

The following is the dictated draft of a letter, and the scribe omitted the customary formalities at beginning and end.

162   LORD LISLE TO CROMWELL   *27 June 1536*

And perceiving by the contents of the same that the King's Highness taketh in good part mine answer made to the Bailly of Arde concerning the French King's subjects (which was to my ∧no little∧ comfort); yet to be plain with you, as with my special good master and friend, the residue of your said letters were couched after such sort and ministered unto me such cause of sorrow that never thing grieved me so much in my life hitherto. For I have lived in this world at God's pleasure unto this day, and never went about the bush with any man. And now to hear it laid to my charge ∧and specially by you∧ that I should use myself after that sort towards my most dread

---

6. French. Headed 'Coppie'. Addressed: A messieurs et bon voisins les officiers de Roy en la ville dardre et countie de Guisnes.

sovereign Lord and King, of whom dependeth all my life and living, it is the greatest heaviness that ever fortuned unto me. ∧And surely I had rather be under the ground that either the K.H.[7] or you should worthily conceive any such opinion∧ of me. Wherefore, Sir, I most heartily desire and pray you to interpret my writings and sayings as proceeding for him that meaneth as faithfully ∧and as sincerely∧ to deal with the K.H. as becometh his true liege man; ∧And∧ in all such things as his H. shall commit unto my charge to execute the same with as much truth and diligence as my poor wit can extend unto. And although in my letters unto you I cannot express the same after such sort as my mind and desire is, yet I beseech you of your wisdom ∧and goodness not∧ to impute the same to any default of my truth or good heart towards the King's H. or the execution of his commandments, but rather to the foolishness of my secretary and want of such knowledge as I would God had endued me withal.

And concerning the casting down of the marshes, it may please you to understand that I have according to the K.H. commandment and yours taken such order therein as I doubt not you shall have ∧no∧ cause to impute any negligence unto me in doing thereof; beseeching you, the mean season, to move the K.H. for a warrant to his Vice-Treasurer for the payment of x^{li} or xx marks ∧for the charge∧ thereof, which I doubt will not satisfy the same. And thus I commit ye to the Blessed Trinity, beseeching ye to take ∧this ∧ my writing ∧and all other my letters∧ in the best part, and I shall study, Sir, so to attemper the same from henceforth as shall be to your no molestation, as far as my poor wit will give me leave. Notwithstanding I beseech you to consider how the matters here be many times of such importance that it causeth me, according to my duty, to trouble you as I do, beseeching you to accept my poor heart in the same. Further such news as is in France and Flanders ye shall be participant of them herein.   (Vol. 3, No. 728)

163   HENRY VIII TO LORD LISLE   *19 August 1536*

Right trusty and right well beloved Cousin we greet you well / And forasmuch as revolving in our mind that the wars being open between the Emperor and the French King and great numbers of men of war on either part levied / Albeit we purpose according to our leagues with either party to preserve ourself neuter between them / Yet like as the men of war being desirous of spoil and booty / and commonly of courage to enterprise the achieving of those things that may turn to their greatest advantage and gain / with a renown if they chance to prevail as many times they do where good foresight and provision is not had to resist them / So wisdom would

---

7. Written throughout for 'King's Highness'.

that all men joining upon them should in time make such preparation for defence in all events as might be for the perfect surety of all things as they have in charge in the withstanding of all attemptates that might be advanced against them / Our pleasure and commandment is that immediately upon the sight hereof / you shall not only with such convenient dexterity as no great bruit arise thereof, cause that our town of Calais to be victualled for so many months at the last as our statutes in that behalf do require / but also that you shall see all other things of defence put in such a readiness as not sudden chance may happen of what sort soever it should be that might put you to any notable distress or danger to the peril of our said town and to our dishonour In which part we desire and pray you to foresee the statute and ordinance made for the gunners may be put in execution which as we be informed hath been hitherto neglected to our no little marvel / without failing to see the premisses with diligence accomplished as we specially trust you.   (Vol. 3, No. 756)

The Captain of Gravelines begins a letter with polite (though premature) congratulations on the King of England's having defeated his rebels of the Pilgrimage of Grace at home, but breaks off just as he is about to sign it because some Calais news has just come in.

164   JEHAN DE TOVAR TO LORD LISLE   6 November 1536

. . .

My lord, since this writing I have heard that the French have this night penetrated a considerable distance into the English Pales, to come and pillage this the Emperor's country, or else the country of Langre: beseeching you to undertake to remedy this state of affairs, and to be good enough to inform me in what way you mean to proceed within your Pales if the French pass and are repelled; advertising you that we shall be forced to fight within the said Pales if we encounter the said Frenchmen: further advertising you that we on our side would not engage in any feats of arms that would inconvenience any of the subjects of the King of England. But if it is necessary that our forces should enter upon the said Pales to fight back in this cause, I am very desirous to warn you to as for my part I should be right sorry thus to begin without giving you warning.

Signed   He that is entirely your perfect friend and good neighbour
                        Jehan de Tovar[8]   (Vol. 3, No. 780)

Sir Richard Whethill died in the first week in November. Robert Whethill never obtained his room.

8. French.

10

Careers for the Children

John Basset

The choice of a legal training for the Basset heir was a natural one, not only because it was a useful one for any landowner but because the Basset inheritance was bedevilled by legal complications that dated back to the death of Sir Thomas Beaumont in 1450 and were still unsolved. Letters that chiefly concern these will be found in chapter 17, on business affairs, where they show Lisle's continuing care for the interests of his stepson.

The Inns of Court in the sixteenth century were very much like colleges. Aged seventeen, John is entered in the Admission Register of Lincoln's Inn under date 6 February 1535. He had a 'special admission', which entitled him to certain privileges, such as the right of sitting at Masters' Commons instead of at the Fellows' table before being called. He was also exempted from serving certain offices and from keeping vacations. Of this last indulgence he seems always to have taken advantage; and from Husee's letters it is evident that the conditions governing residence were generally relaxed when the plague or other sickness was prevalent, in order that those who were able to remove into a better air might do so, in the hope of avoiding infection.

John Densell, a senior member of the Inn, and William Sulyard, one of its Governors, both old friends of Lisle's, had promised to keep an eye on John and recommended as his tutor Thomas Lane. Though the latter had been something of a gay dog in his youth, he would now be the most discreet of guardians. John brought William Bremelcum from Devonshire as his servant, and both stayed with Husee on arrival in London.

165   JOHN HUSEE TO LADY LISLE   *27 January 1535*

My humble duty premised unto your good Ladyship. . . .
Madam, Mr. Basset came hither the xxvj[th] of this month, who shall con-

tinue here till the morrow after Candlemas Day. And then, God willing, he shall enter his chamber at Lincoln's Inn. I have spoken with Mr. Hollys this day, but Mr. Lane is not yet come. I doubt not he will be right ∧well∧ pleased to have the young gentleman in his company, who I ensure your ladyship is both gentle, sober and wise. And Mr. Sulyard is contented to see to him in Mr. Lane's absence, and so will Mr. Densell do in like manner. Your ladyship may not fail to send Mr. Tuke and Mrs. Densell the French wine.

Mr. Basset is all out of apparel. He hath never a good gown but one of chamlet the which was very ill-fashioned, but it is now a'mending. His damask gown is nothing worth, but if it be possible it shall make him a jacket, for his coat of velvet was broken to guard his camlet gown. His satin jacket is meetly good, and the other ij nothing worth. His ij doublets will serve; the iij^d is but easy. He hath but j pair of white hosen, and the kersey is not for him, therefore I have sent it by Edward Russell. More, he hath brought with him a feather bed, bolster, blankets, counterpoint[1] and ij pair of sheets. He must have another bed furnished with a pillow, tester, saye[2] or other, with curtains.

Madame, I intend to make him ij pair of black hosen, a new gown of damask faced with foynes or genettes,[3] and a study gown faced with fox pelts of cloth v s. the yard. His damask gown shall be guarded with velvet. And if I can compass it he shall have a gown of fine cloth, furred with bogy,[4] with a small guard of velvet; and his old damask gown shall make him a jacket. And this done he shall be well apparelled for this ij years. He must have wood and coal in his chamber. And less than here written he cannot have, to be anything likely apparelled as appertaineth to his birth.

If your ladyship may send me iij or iiij^{li} more with the next it would ease well to pay for much of the premised, which will cost xx mark at the least. I shall, as much as in me lieth, see him ordered accordingly, and see also that he lack nothing, with the best service that I can do him, as I am bound to do for your ladyship and all yours. Trusting to have your answer shortly. Bremelcum would have a new coat, for he hath but one. I would gladly know your ladyship's pleasure in the premises speedily, as God knoweth, who

1. i.e. counterpane.

2. Saye, spelt by Husee indiscriminately with or without the final 'e', was a finely twilled material, either of silk or wool, much used for hangings, but also for garments.

3. foynes = foins, skins of the foin or beech-marten, of the weasel tribe; genettes = genet, the fur of the civet cat, generally black.

4. bogge, *obs.* form of budge, i.e. white lambskin with the wool dressed outwards. By statute, 24 Hen. VIII XIII (1532–33) John, as the son and heir of a knight, could have worn an imported fur; but ordinary gentlemen were forbidden to wear any but native-grown fur, 'except foynes, genettes called grey genettes and Bogye', unless they were worth more than £100 a year in revenues and possessions.

preserve your ladyship in long life with honour to your most heart's aggradation.

From London, the xxviijth in January,

To your ladyship most bounden,

Hol. John Husee (Vol. 4, No. 826)

166 JOHN HUSEE TO LADY LISLE 7 *February 1535*

My humble duty unto your good ladyship ∧premised∧, . . . where your good ladyship wrote that you sent ij pieces of red say and green, those pieces which was packed with the other stuff are yellow and green; and as far as I can perceive iij pieces more will scant trim up Mr. Basset's chamber, for it is very large; and it shall be necessary your ladyship ∧send∧ the said ∧say∧ with speed, for till it come his chamber cannot well be trimmed. Also it shall be necessary your ladyship send a coffer to keep his apparel, and another for his sheets and linen.

Madam, he must pay weekly for his board and his man's; and also when he list to eat and drink betwixt meals he must buy it for ready money. Therefore he may not well have less left him than xl^s in ready money; and I must pay within this viij days xx^s for his special admittance, and iiij nobles for the admittance in his chamber. And there hath been money spent since he came up for his charges and his man's. But in good faith, he is gentle enow to be ordered; and hath spent soberly, and can keep his money right well. I trust, ere I leave him to see him so ordered as to him appertaineth. . . . and thus I pray God send your ladyship even as well to fare as I can wish, with long life in honour.

At London the vijth day of February,

By him that is wholly your ladyship's during life,

Hol. John Husee (Vol. 4, No. 827)

167 JOHN HUSEE TO LADY LISLE 17 *February 1535*

Humbly advertising your good ladyship that by Edward Russell I have this day received your letter and token, lowly thanking your ladyship for the same; and these days past I received the iij^{li} with your letter sent me, the which I ensure your ladyship came in season, for I was then wholly out of money.

And touching Mr. Basset, I delivered him your ladyship's letter, who was thereof right glad, and in especial to hear that your ladyship is merry, and so was Mr. Skerne his chamber-fellow, who is wholly at your ladyship's commandment. And now Mr. Basset hath his chamber in quiet, but with much ado; for there were ij gentlemen in the same which would not gladly have gone out of it, had it not been both by compulsion and friendship. Howbeit, he is now well, were the ij pieces of say come for to perform[5] his chamber, which I trust will be shortly here.

Your ladyship may be glad that ever ye bare Mr. Basset, for he proveth the towardest and quickest witted young gentleman that ever I knew; and bold enough, which I doubted most in him; but I now dare let him slip to all the house, young and old. He is as well acquainted in that Inn as if he had been there continuer[6] these vij years; and he is beloved of young and old, and nothing too hard for him in learning. I doubt not, if God spare him life, but that he shall prove the diamant of Devonshire, for he is active universally to all things that appertaineth to a young gentleman. Madam, by the faith that I owe unto God, I cannot ∧write∧ the towardness that is in him, but I trust ere I be viij days older to leave him in good order. . . .

As God knoweth, who send your good Ladyship your most noble heart's desire.

From London, the xvij[th] in February, a° 1534.

Your ladyship's during life, and thereto bounden,

Hol.   John Husee   (Vol. 4, No. 828)

Augustine Skerne's uncle, John Danastre, was a senior Bencher of the Inn. He took John very much under his protection in 1535, and Husee considered this sufficiently valuable to make it worth while to divert to him a handsome present – whether with the happy consent of the intended recipients we are not told.

168   JOHN HUSEE TO LADY LISLE   *21 March 1535*

My duty premised unto your Ladyship, advertising the same that I have by Goodal received your letter. . . . Madam, all the wine is delivered according to my lord's commandment and yours. But the piece of wine sent to Mr. Basset ∧and Mr. Skerne∧, I caused them send the same to Mr. Danastre who is Mr. Basset's special friend. . . . Mr. Basset is merry and learneth fast. As God best knoweth, who send your ladyship long life and much honour. From London in haste, the xxj[th] in March.

Wholly your ladyship's during life,

Hol.   John Husee   (Vol. 4, No. 832)

5. Now obsolete in this sense of 'trim', 'furnish', 'decorate'.
6. Denotes one who remains in residence, who, after seven years continuance, can then be called to the utter Bar.

169   JOHN HUSEE TO LADY LISLE   *12 May 1535*

Pleaseth it your ladyship to be advertised that this day by Robert Johnson
I received your letter, with the quails, which are delivered accordingly; and
your Ladyship hath therefore of all parties most hearty thanks. And Mr.
Basset (who lauded be good, is merry and in good health and a great lawyer),
having him humbly recommended unto your Ladyship, desiring your blessing, shall not of those quails lose his part. And the water imperial[7] Bremelcum hath, and it shall be used according to your Ladyship's writing. And
touching the plague or any strange disease, do not your Ladyship mistrust
but Mr. Sulyard and Mr. Danastre will as well see to him as though he were
of their proper kin. And to break his fast he faileth not daily ere he come out
of his chamber. And because Bury is not come, and Mr. Basset goeth to Mr.
Danastre this holidays, I have delivered him iij[li]. . . .

At London, in haste, the xij[th] day of May, in most haste.

Hol.   Your Ladyship's during life, John Husee

(Vol. 4, No. 834)

The legal terms were followed by learning vacations which ran from the
Vigil of Christmas to the morrow of the Epiphany (7 January); from the Vigil
of Palm Sunday, for three weeks; and for two weeks before and one week
after Michaelmas. For the mesne vacations – that is the time left between the
terms and the learning vacations – all students were at liberty. Outbreaks of
plague – 'the death' – frequently caused the cancellation of learning vacations, and sometimes the postponement of term. 1535 was a bad year for
plague in London. On 12 July Husee wrote to Lady Lisle: 'I think by reason
they dieth about Lincoln's Inn Mr. Basset will be all this vacation at Mr.
Danastre's',[8] at Cobham in Surrey. John's country holiday was prolonged by
the postponement of term, and he did not return to the Inn until sometime
after Christmas. The Council decided that 'because of the death and many
other considerations, no "solempne" Christmas shall be kept', so that prolonged absence did not deprive him of the usual week of licensed revelry and
merry-making for which the Inns of Court were famed.

170   JOHN HUSEE TO LADY LISLE   *25 October 1535*

Pleaseth your ladyship to be advertised that I according to your last writing, I have been with Mr. John Basset, who is, lauded be God, at Cobham
with Mr. Danastre, merry and in good health, and humbly having him com-

---

7. *potus imperialis,* 'a drink made of cream of tartar, flavoured with lemons and sweetened' *(O.E.D.).*
8. Vol. 4, No. 836.

mended unto your ladyship, desiring your blessing: ensuring your ladyship that he is there right well entreated; and gladly would be at London; but truly, they dieth yet there, and is nothing clear. And by mine advice he shall not come hither till it be clearer and also till your ladyship commandeth it. He lacketh nothing but hosen; howbeit he is hitherto ∧meetly∧ well stored. And his man lacketh a doublet of saye or fustian, at your pleasure. And that your ladyship remember Mr. Basset with some money when you see time: and also to remember Mr. Danastre with Gascon wine, for he loveth no French wine.

I have made Mr. George a coat of velvet, which shall be sent with the first that goeth to Winchester; and if I thought that John Clement had not made him a frieze coat I would make him a coat here. Others I have not, but that which I advertised my lord of, to write; but that I would gladly be at Calais, as God knoweth, who send your ladyship long life with much honour.

From London, the xxv^th of October.

By your ladyship's and thereto bounden. . . .

Hol.   John Husee   (Vol. 4, No. 840)

As far as his tutor's report and the records of his Society reveal, John ran true to type as the good boy, and kept out of trouble with the authorities during the whole of his time at Lincoln's Inn. At the end of this first year, however, there is a three months gap in our first-hand news of him, as Husee spent the first quarter of 1536 in Calais. Mr. Danastre's hospitality had had the effect upon which, no doubt, he had calculated, for Lisle took him on at a retainer to assist George Rolle with the Basset legal affairs. Presumably he would have charged for any services rendered, and he did well out of gifts of quails and wine, and also recouped himself for the expense incurred by feeding John and his man by charging for their commons at the rate they paid at the Inn.

News of John during his second year at the Inn tends to be limited to such lines as in Husee's letter to Lady Lisle of 1 April: 'Mr. Basset is merry, and would gladly have a horse against he ride into the country; and also money when your ladyship see your time.'[9]

Thomas Warley, calling upon John in his chambers on 2 May, reports on him as 'a toward gentleman and wise'. As the sickness had again broken out in London, he 'motioned Mr. Basset for a season to go to Mr. Danastre's place in the country'; to which John answered that 'he was not feared'.[10] John's mother, however, was feared, and as usual must have written off post-haste to Husee, who sent properly soothing replies. But one reason for John's reluctance to leave London emerges in June.

9. Vol. 4, No. 843.   10. Vol. 3, No. 690.

171   JOHN HUSEE TO LADY LISLE   *24 June 1536*

Pleaseth your good ladyship to understand that this day I received by Corbet your letter and therewith iiij[li] sterling, the which I have delivered unto Mr. Basset, who is now, lauded be God, merry and in good health at Lincoln's Inn, desiring your ladyship's blessing. And this iiij[li] will set him even till this day of all that he oweth and hath borrowed in Lincoln's Inn and elsewhere for his commons and other necessary expenses. And it is not to be doubted but he will be husband good enough, for he is both discreet, sober and wise, and not too liberal in Spending. I pray God send him long to live.

Truth it is, I cannot keep nothing secret from your ladyship. I perceive by gentle Mr. Basset that he hath not been half so well entreated as he was wont to be at Mr. Danastre's, but hath been grontyd and grudged at, and laid in a worse lodging than he was wont to be, which liked him but ill. I perceive by him he is not minded to go no more thither; and the cause is, as it hath been showed me, by reason of a Dun Cow that is in the house, by whom he hath had v or vj calves, so that she thought all too much that was set before him, and would have Mr. Danastre spare, for to bring up her calves, God send them good weaning! But I had little thought that Mr. Danastre had been a man of so vile and dissimuling a nature, for if I had known thereof he should not 'a been so fat-fed as he hath been. But I trust, against the vacation, to 'point him an honest lodging within vij mile of London. But Mr. Skerne and his wife hath showed themselves at all times to be one manner of people . . .

(Vol. 4, No. 850i)

It is eminently characteristic of Husee that even in the heat of his indignation at having wasted so many fat quails and so much good wine upon the undeserving Mr. Danastre he still remembers to bear witness to the right-mindedness of the worthy Augustine his nephew, who shares John's chambers.

The following comments all come from Husee's letters. On 11 July 1536 he writes:

Mr. Basset is, lauded be God, merry, and applieth his learning. Howbeit, there is one or ij sick of the smallpox in the house; but I trust he shall be in no jeopardy.[11]

On 10 August, 'Mr. Basset is in the country, and will into Hampshire. He lacketh a horse. Of Mr. Page none can I get.'[12]

John returned to London in the autumn to keep Michaelmas Term, and the four extracts which follow suggest that he was developing a mind of his own and was deciding for himself, aided by his tutor, just how long he would

11. Vol. 3, No. 746.   12. Vol. 3, No. 753.

or would not tarry at the Inn. Husee reports on 13 November: 'Mr. Basset shall be here within these iij days for so Mr. Sulyard willed Bremelcum.'[13] On 27 November, Mr. Basset

> will tarry at Lincoln's Inn till seven days before Christmas, which is against my mind, for they dieth daily in the City; but Mr. Sulyard must be obeyed.[14]

On 5 December he is 'merry', but has made it plain that 'he would not go so far as Mr. Norton's by his will'.

> It is winter, and foul way. If your ladyship will, I shall provide some other honest place for him.[15]

And on the 11th

> as for Mr. Basset, he is minded to tarry here all this Christmas. I trust all danger of the plague will be well nigh past.[16]

Throughout the spring and early summer of 1537, however, there were constant outbreaks of the plague in London, and Husee was forever chasing John out into 'cleaner air'. Lady Lisle's anxiety about this may have hastened other plans for him, and at the end of April he was warned to be ready to go to Calais as soon as Sir Antony Windsor arrived in London and handed over to him the rents of the Hampshire estates. But Windsor took a month longer than Husee felt he had any right to, especially as May was very hot and 'they die here in every corner'. By 12 June, however, John – and the rents – were safely in Calais.

What had been arranged was his marriage to Frances Plantagenet, Lisle's daughter by his first wife. There is nothing in the Letters to show that John had previously been informed of the plan, but whether or not it came 'as a surprise, pleasant or unpleasant, as the case may be', his mother would have seen nothing humorous in Lady Bracknell's famous dictum, 'When you do get engaged to anyone, *I* or your father, should his health permit, will *inform* you of the fact.' What does appear to be exceptional rather than customary, however, is the postponing of his marriage – and apparently also of his betrothal – until he was already over eighteen years of age. This in itself was late rather than early for the matching of a young gentleman of blood and property.

In January 1538 Husee plunged into active preparations for the ceremony. He was faced with the awkward job of procuring all the bridal finery on credit – a proceeding that irked his frugal soul. The 'longer' the 'day' you

13. Vol. 3, No. 781.   15. Vol. 3, No. 794.
14. Vol. 3, No. 787.   16. Vol. 3, No. 798.

obtained, the more you paid in the end. He had already checked the vital point that the bride, whomever she married, should lose no part of her 'degree' as her Plantagenet father's daughter. Through her mother, a baroness in her own right, she was also descended from Berkeleys, Talbots, and Lisles; the groom was nothing but a plain Devonshire squire – a landed gentleman, of honourable family, and 'well-allied', but still John Basset, armiger. In those days, a good marriage was an important part of a man's career. John was not doing badly. It would appear that the wedding took place on Tuesday, 19 February 1538. One hopes they were as disappointed at Husee's enforced absence as he was himself. It is the measure of his lordship's financial troubles and the urgency of his business that these alone kept Husee in England on such an occasion.

172   JOHN HUSEE TO LADY LISLE   *23 February 1538*

Pleaseth it your ladyship to be advertised that I received your letter by John Teborowe, wherein I do perceive that all thing was well done at the marriage of Mr. Basset, and what pains my lord took that day, which I assure your ladyship doth rejoice my heart not a little, and (would God) it had been my fortune to have been there to do him some service, which I might have been, if I had known Mr. Bonham would have served me thus; for as yet he is not come, nor I never spake with him. Seeing my lord will that he have it, I can see no remedy but I must ride into Wiltshire to him. And where your ladyship writ that there was fault found because Mistress Frances' sleeves was not turned up with tinsel, and that her kirtle was not silver, I followed your ladyship's bill of proportion in it, for if your ladyship had written so to have had it it should not a'lacked. I pray God send them joy and long to live together. . . .

Madam, Mr. Windsor hath moved me to write unto your ladyship to take Sir Peter Philpot's son in service, that shall be his heir. It is neither the first nor second son, but the iij^d and wisest of them, and seemeth to be of a gentle conversation. And his father shall partly give him toward his finding. The eldest son is dead: the second lieth sore sick, not like to recover; but whether he do or no, this shall have the best part, and if the second brother die he shall have all, and inherit, besides his father's lands, v£ marks by the year. And if your ladyship will follow my poor advice he shall not be refused, but he shall not know but it cometh at Mr. Windsor's suit by my means. And if he were once in service and heartily entertained I would hope that such means may be found that Mistress Philip and he may couple together; but this upon liking, and upon your ladyship's pleasure. And I would think it a right good bargain. Your ladyship hath moved me divers times in such like matters, which I have not forgotten, ne yet can spy any like this. And if it be your pleasure to deal with this matter, let me with all speed know your pleasure ere I go into Hampshire, and then will I do my best therein, and cause him to be sent over while his service is offered. And thus I beseech Jesu send your ladyship long life with much honour.

From London, the xxiij[th] of February.

I would also gladly know your pleasure for your Lenten store.

               By your ladyship's own man,

Hol.   John Husee   (Vol. 4, No. 861)

Matrimony was so to speak in the air at the moment, and the more young Bassets who could be disposed of the better. Sir Peter Philpot, the father of the eligible young man, was an old established Hampshire neighbour of the Lisles.

Mercifully, in the Lisle family at any rate, 'liking' could and did enter into this question of marriage; and whether or no it was mutual lack thereof, nothing came of this particular attempt at match-making, which is a relief when we learn that in April 1540 'Clement Philpot, gentleman, late of Calais and servant to the Lord Lisle', was arrested on a charge of treason and found guilty, and was executed on 4 August, being drawn from the Tower of London to Tyburn and there hanged, drawn, and quartered.

For a variety of reasons, including another serious outbreak of the plague in London, John never returned to Lincoln's Inn, except for a few weeks. George Rolle had some time before suggested that he might be put into Cromwell's service with the hope of later progressing to the King's; and when Lisle and Honor saw him in September 1538 it is quite possible that Cromwell himself may have suggested the arrangement, in the hope of making a better all-round profit out of his dealings with the family. The Lisles would probably have been only too ready to be at the expense of John's 'finding' in Cromwell's household, in order to secure such an influential connection for him. By 12 October he had been 'placed', and Husee writes to Lisle:

> Mr. Basset is with my Lord Privy Seal and waiteth daily by Mr. Richard's admission. Howbeit, as yet my lord never spake to him. It were good your lordship wrote some thankful letter unto my lord in his behalf.[17]

John's career had begun, and the great man's own nephew was seeing to it that he was admitted every day to the audience chamber when suitors waited upon my Lord Privy Seal.

17. Vol. 5, No. 1248.

In the first fortnight of May 1539 a child was born in Calais to John and Frances Basset, and christened Honor after her grandmother. Husee, writing on the 12th, mingles his congratulations with the usual Tudor regrets that generally greeted the arrival of a daughter: 'by God's grace at the next shot she shall hit the mark'.[18] John must have been allowed to come to Calais in time for the birth of his child, as when Husee writes again the following day, promising to send over Mr. Basset's spaniel, he asks to be commended to both the young people. John died in England in 1541, leaving a posthumous son called Arthur.

KATHERINE AND ANNE BASSET

It is the third of the Basset daughters who cuts the most brilliant figure. Anne must have been about fifteen or sixteen when she left Madame de Riou and returned to her family at Calais. With an allowance of £6. 13*s.* 4*d.* a year for her 'finding', and a marriage portion of 100 marks (£66. 13*s.* 4*d.*), she was as well provided for as most girls of her class, unless they happened to be heiresses. She was, therefore, as good a match as any of her sisters, but no better: Sir John had provided equally for all his daughters. It is noticeable, however, that Anne is the first of them for whom Lady Lisle attempts to plan a career, from which we may undoubtedly infer that in the general opinion Anne was esteemed the prettiest and wittiest, the beauty of the family, and altogether the best equipped to venture into the more exalted circles to which their mother's second marriage had made it easier for them to find an introduction.

Six days after the execution of Anne Boleyn, five days after the King's formal betrothal to Jane Seymour, Husee had written on 25 May 1536 to say, 'Your ladyship hath two nieces with the Queen, which are daughters unto Mr. Arundell'[19] – meaning, presumably, with the new Queen-to-be, who was married to the King on the 30th. Judging by the letters which follow, it was this news which made Honor Lisle determine to seek similar preferment for one of her own daughters. She must have secured Lisle's immediate support and written post-haste to London, as on 6 June Husee writes:

> As touching the preferment of your ladyship's daughter unto the Queen, I will at the delivering of my lord's letter unto Mr. Heneage, move the same. I trust it will be easily obtained, but what answer I have, and how I do speed your ladyship shall be shortly advertised.[20]

From his next letter, it appears that the daughter she had suggested was Anne.

18. Vol. 5, No. 1409.
19. Vol. 4, No. 847.
20. Vol. 3, No. 717.

173   JOHN HUSEE TO LADY LISLE   *18 June 1536*

Pleaseth your ladyship to be advertised that I have received your sundry letters and have given your tokens and recommendations accordingly. And first, touching my Lord Montague and my Lady his mother, they both hath them heartily commended unto your ladyship, and her ladyship saith that she will do her best to obtain your ladyship's suit for Mrs. Anne; but she saith that it will ask time and leisure, and her ladyship doubts nothing but that Mrs. Anne is too young, and Mr. Heneage putteth the same doubt. And my said Lady of Salisbury thanketh your ladyship for your token, and was right sorry that she had none to send your ladyship yesterday when I met with her at the Court. She made your ladyship's humble recommendations unto the Queen's Highness, whose Grace was very glad to hear from your ladyship. And my Lady of Salisbury thinketh that it should be well done that your ladyship were here at the Coronation.

My Lord of Rutland and my lady his wife hath them recommended heartily unto your ladyship, and they hath in like manner done your humble recommendations to the Queen's Highness. My Lady of Rutland thanketh your ladyship for your token, and sendeth your ladyship another J. Goodall hath, and likewise from Mrs. Arundell and Mrs. Margery,[21] who is in her old room with the Queen. And because your ladyship sent her no token, by the advice of Mrs. Arundell I gave her one in your ladyship's name, a ring of gold worth a vij groats. Mrs. Arundell and Mrs. Margery feareth nothing but that Mrs. Anne is too young. Hereafter as I hear more of this matter I will ascertain your ladyship. . . .

And thus I pray Jesu send your ladyship long life with much honour.

   From London, the xviij[th] day of June.
    By your ladyship's bounden,
Hol.   John Husee   (Vol. 4, No. 863)

It would appear from Husee's next letter that Lady Lisle had decided, under the circumstances, to offer her elder daughter, Katharine, instead of Anne, and was annoyed with him for having pressured too many people already with the earlier idea.

174   JOHN HUSEE TO LADY LISLE   *24 June 1536*

. . . Madame, I shall not fail to know of my Lady Sarum[22] the Queen's gracious pleasure concerning your ladyship's over coming to the coronation, and thereof to certify your ladyship, after her pleasure knowen, with all

---

21. Mrs. Margery was Margery Horsman, maid of honour to Anne Boleyn and Jane Seymour.
22. The Countess of Salisbury.

celerity ... herewith you shall receive my Lord Montague's letter, and thereby you shall know both my lady's and his meaning. My lord showed me that the Queen had all her maidens 'pointed already, and that at the next vacation he would cause my lady his mother to do her best for the preferment of your ladyship's daughter. And this was all the answer he made me. What his letter specifieth God knoweth. And where your ladyship is sorry that I made so many speak in it; truly, madam, there spake no more in it but my Lady Sarum and Mr. Heneage. Notwithstanding, I shewed my Lady Rutland that your ladyship would gladly have one of your daughters with the Queen, and so I showed Mrs. Margery and Mrs. Arundell in like manner, but I am sure none of them never motioned the Queen's grace therein. . . . Now I will show Mr. Heneage that Mistress Katharine is of sufficient age, and do the best I can for her preferment, and therein will work by Mrs. Margery's counsel, and Mrs. Golding's, if I find her your very friend. But if the Queen hath her whole determined number appointed, I suppose this suit will the later take place. Howbeit I will do as much as may be done herein, not forgetting to make your ladyship's excuse to Mrs. Margery, according unto your writing, and to give unto Mrs. Golding your like recommendations, and also to open unto her, as I see cause, the full contents of your ladyship's mind. . . .   (Vol. 4, No. 850ii)

After this, as far as the Letters show, the suit for Anne's preferment was left in abeyance for the rest of the year, but Husee was keeping 'a vigilant eye' for a possible opening, and he writes on 14 January 1537 to inform Lisle that 'this day the Earl of Sussex is married to Mrs. Arundell, my lady's niece', adding 'some are glad of it, and some sorry, for the gentlewoman's sake'.[23] The Earl was already in his fifties and the youthful Mary Arundell was his third wife. Whatever Husee's reservations, Honor Lisle's realist mind recognized that within eight months her sister's daughter had made a great match and was henceforth to be a person of importance and influence at Court. To Court Anne must go, and her cousin's marriage had created a vacancy among the Maids of Honour. Husee obviously received his instructions by the next messenger and at once made the necessary inquiries but the vacancy was already filled.

On 17 February[24] Husee suggested that Katharine should meanwhile become her cousin Lady Sussex's gentlewoman, just as the girl who now had the latter's post had been Lady Beauchamp's, so that she might at least be seen at Court; but in his letter on the 23rd he wrote:

I have been in hand with my Lady Sussex for Mrs. Katharine's preferment, but she will in no wise make grant to have her in her chamber, but she

---

23. Vol. 4, No. 915.   24. Vol. 4, No. 867.

saith that she hath iij women already, which is one more than she is allowed; but if she come she will do her best for her preferment. But I left not this matter so, but went unto gentle Mrs. Margery, who hath made me grant that if your ladyship will write unto Mr.[25] Lystre, she will receive her and lay her in her chamber, or else with young Mrs. Norris, and bring her with her into the Queen's chamber every day. Madam, your ladyship is not a little beholding unto this gentlewoman, for undoubted she hath in this demerited thanks. If Mrs. Katharine come over she must have double gowns and kirtles of silk, and good attirements for her head and neck. And now your ladyship knoweth what hath here been done you may work herein at your pleasure.[26]

The next thing we hear, however, is from Husee on 18 March,[27] that William Coffin has approached the Duchess of Suffolk and got a promise from her to take Katharine. Though the mother of a two-year-old son, the lady in question was only seventeen, having been married at fourteen to her guardian, the Duke; and it may have been only on the grounds of her youth that Lady Lisle hesitated to entrust Katharine to her household. Husee writes on 2 April:

And where your ladyship is not minded that Mrs. Katharine shall be where I wrote last of, my Lady Sussex and Mrs. ∧Staynings∧ thinketh she can be nowhere better. Howbeit your ladyship knoweth best what thereto belongeth. I have given Mr. Coffin hearty thanks for his good mind in your ladyship's behalf. He is a very honest gentleman, and is ready at all times to do your ladyship pleasure.[28]

Nevertheless he goes on gently pressuring her. Meanwhile, Anne's future has not been forgotten, and the Countess of Rutland, who is also at Court, has been approached about her.

175   JOHN HUSEE TO LADY LISLE   *12 May 1537*

Pleaseth your ladyship that by this bearer Agnes Woodroff your ladyship shall receive from the Lady Rutland a token and a letter. And touching Mrs. Anne, your ladyship's daughter, her Ladyship is content to take her at the later end of the progress when all heats and dangers of Sycknesses be past. And as for Mrs. Katharine, the Duchess of Suffolk is not now here, but at her coming Mr. Coffin will be again in hand with her. He doubteth not but that she will keep promise with him, as concerning what hath been already

---

25. Not, I think, a mistake, for Mrs. Margery Horsman is deferring for permission to her newly married husband, Michael Lyster.

26. Vol. 4, No. 868a.

27. Vol. 4, No. 871.   28. Vol. 4, No. 872.

written unto your ladyship in that behalf. Also my Lady of Rutland, at her coming unto the court, will be in hand with my Lady Beauchamp and other of her friends to help (if it be possible) that one of your ladyship's daughters shall be immediately preferred unto the Queen's service at the next vacant, which is thought shall be shortly; and as long as I remain here I will not fail to have her Ladyship in remembrance. . . .

. . . News here are none, but that the Queen's Grace, as the common saying goeth, is with child, which is merry tidings.

As God knoweth, who send your ladyship long life with much honour, and a most fortunate hour.

From London, the xijth of May.

By your ladyship's bounden man,

Hol. John Husee (Vol. 4, No. 875)

With the following brief note of Russell's there begins a sequence that might be called 'A Contribution of Quails'. It runs through the letters for several weeks, and being treated by everyone concerned as a matter of the utmost urgency apparently helps to bring the suit for the preferment of Mistress Anne to a successful conclusion.

176 SIR JOHN RUSSELL TO LORD LISLE *20 May 1537*

Right honourable and my singular good lord, I heartily commend me unto you. My lord, the King commanded me to write to you for some fat quails, for the Queen is very desirous to eat some but here be none to be gotten. Wherefore, my lord, I pray you in anywise that ye will send some with as much speed as may be possibly; but they must be very fat. My lord, I pray you think no unkindness in me that I have not written to you of a long time, for I am as much your friend as ever I was to the uttermost of my power, as knoweth Our Lord, who ever keep you.

At Hampton Court, the xx day of May.

I pray you give credence to this bearer.

Signed Your owen a suryde

J. Russell (Vol. 4, No. 878)

Quails were caught in the low-lying countryside round Calais, or in Flanders.

177 JOHN HUSEE TO LORD LISLE *23 May 1537*

Pleaseth it your lordship to be advertised that this day, at my being at the Court, Sir John Russell called me unto him, and asked me when I heard from your lordship, saying further that he had these days past wrote unto your lordship ij sundry letters by the King's commandment expressly, and how the very effect of those letters was for fat quails for the Queen's Highness, which her Grace loveth very well, and longeth not a little for them; and he looked hourly for your lordship's answer with the said quails, in so much that he did further command me in the King's behalf to write your lordship with all haste expressly again for the said quails; so that his mind is that with most speed your lordship send ij or iij dozen, and cause them to be killed at Dover; and that in anywise that those same be very fat; and afterward, as shortly as your lordship may, to send xx or xxx dozen, as your lordship shall think best. Those that your lordship shall send by land, if they be delivered me, I will speedily see them conveyed unto Hampton Court, for so the said Mr. Russell desired me: and further, in case your lordship can have none fat at Calais, that then you fail not to send with all speed into Flanders for them, for so the King's Majesty willeth, as his only trust is in your lordship. If your lordship may have them by ij or iij dozens in Calais you may send them by every other passage. And I think there is none that will deny the carriage of them hither, and from hence I doubt not but I will use diligence to the Court with them. If your lordship send them by sundry times, and cause them to be killed at Dover, they shall come fat hither, which the Queen greatly desireth. Her Grace is great with child, and shall be open-laced with stomacher by Corpus Christi Day at the farthest. And your lordship send any by water, they must be well tended or else they will wax lean. Mr. Russell caused me incontinent to depart from the Court to write your lordship this present. . . .

     By your lordship's own man bounden,

Hol.   John Husee   (Vol. 4, No. 879)

178   JOHN HUSEE TO LADY LISLE   *24 May 1537*

Pleaseth it your Ladyship to be advertised that I have by this bearer received your letter, with the quails, the which came in season and were very welcome, both to the King's Highness and the Queen's Grace. For immediately as they came unto my hands I rid in post to the court, with ij dozen of them, killed; and so they were anon upon vij of the clock presented unto the King and the Queen's Graces, whose Highnesses, I assure your ladyship, were right glad of them, and commanded the one half of them incontinent to be roasted and the rest to be kept till supper. And those that were alive, Mr. Russell commanded me to kill them on Friday night, and to bring them unto the court upon Sunday. Those that shall be sent from henceforth must be very fat, and killed at Dover, and not to send past ij or iij dozen at once. And as for peascods or cherries, there will be none here, I think, a' this side midsummer. Whensoever they come your ladyship shall demerit high thanks, and so hath your ladyship had for these quails, both of the King and the Queen. . . .

From London the xxiiij[th] of May, with most haste.

By your ladyship's own man,

Hol.   John Husee   (Vol. 4, No. 881)

Plans were now going forward for both girls to come over, one to the Duchess of Suffolk and the other to Lady Rutland. Moreover, Sir John Wallop had mentioned Anne to the King, who had promised to speak to the Queen. Then comes the great news.

179   JOHN HUSEE TO LADY LISLE   *17 July 1537*

My bounden duty premised unto your ladyship, These shall be signifying the same that the Queen's Grace heartily thanketh your ladyship for the quails I brought, and they came very well. Those that your ladyship shall hereafter send, ∧let∧ them be very fat, or else they are not worth thanks. . . .

Madam, upon Thursday last the Queen being at dinner, my Lady Rutland and my Lady Sussex being waiters on her Grace, her Grace chanced, eating of the quails, to common of your ladyship and of your daughters; so that such communication was uttered by the said ij ladies that her Grace made grant to have one of your daughters; and the matter is thus concluded that your ladyship shall send them both over, for her Grace will first see them and know their manners, fashions and conditions, and take which of them shall like her Grace best; and they must be sent over about vj weeks hence, and your ladyship shall not need to do much cost on them till time you know which of them her Grace will have. But ij honest[29] changes they must have, the one of satin, the other of damask. And at their coming the one shall be in my Lady of Rutland's chamber and the other in my Lady Sussex' chamber; and once known which the Queen will have, the other to be with the Duchess of Suffolk, and then to be apparelled according to their degrees. But madam, the Queen will be at no more cost with her but wages and livery, and so I am commanded to write unto your ladyship.

And for as much as they shall now go upon making and marring, it shall please your ladyship to exhort them to be sober, sad, wise and discreet and lowly above all things, and to be obedient, and governed and ruled by my Lady Rutland and my Lady Sussex, and Mrs. Margery and such others as be your ladyship's friends here; and to serve God and to be virtuous, for that is much regarded, to serve God well and to be sober of tongue. I trust your ladyship will not take this my meaning that I should presume to learn your

---

29. Husee's then slightly old-fashioned way of saying they must have two 'respectable' changes of dress.

ladyship what is to be done, neither that I do see any likelihood of ill appearance in them; but I do it only of pure and sincere zeal that I bear to them for your ladyship's sake, to the end I would they should so use themselves that it sound to your ladyship's honour and their worship, time coming. For your ladyship knoweth the Court is full of pride, envy, indignation and mocking, scorning and derision, therefore I would be sorry but they should use themselves according unto the birth and state that God hath called them to; knowing right well, if they order themselves accordingly, it shall be to your ladyship's no little comfort, and all their friends will be glad of them; and doing otherwise, it will be your ladyship's discomfort and discontenation, and their undoing. But undoubtedly a good lesson at their departing, and good exhortations of your ladyship's mouth while they shall remain there, will profit them more than all others here, although they be their nigh kin. For your ladyship's words will stick nigh their stomachs. I doubt not but they will order and show themselves at their coming according unto the praise that I have already given them, for so doing it shall sound to their praise and worship and my poor honesty: which I assure your ladyship would they should do even as well as mine own heart. . . .

. . . In my next letter your ladyship shall know more, as God knoweth, who send your ladyship long life with much honour, making the same a glad mother, when time shall be, of a jolly boy.

From London the xvij^th day of July.

By your ladyship's own man bounden,

Hol.   John Husee   (Vol. 4, No. 887)

Considering all the pressure beforehand, it would seem curious that when the girls could be received at Court there was such a time-lapse before they were sent over; but this was just at the time when their mother's condition was giving concern. On 1 September Husee is still asking for them, for the pregnant Queen will 'take her chamber' for the ritual seclusion on the 20th.

180   JOHN HUSEE TO LADY LISLE   *17 September 1537*

Pleaseth it your ladyship. . . . your ladyship shall understand that Mrs. Anne your daughter is sworn the Queen's maid on Saturday last past, and furnisheth the room of a yeoman-usher. I pray God send her joy. My Lady Sussex would fain have preferred both, but it would not be; so that Mrs. Katharine doth remain with the Countess of Rutland till she know further of your pleasure. Your ladyship may not forget to send thanks as well to my Lady Beauchamp as to my Lady of Sussex and my Lady Rutland, for divers causes.

My Lady of Sussex hath given Mrs. Anne a kirtle of crimson damask and sleeves to the same, and also she hath promised Mrs. Katharine a gown of taffeta, so that she is very good and loving to them; and Mrs. Anne lieth in her chamber, and Mrs. Katharine in my Lady Rutland's chamber. And against Mrs. Ashley's going out, your ladyship must send such bedding as is written in Mrs. Pole's book of reckoning, and that will be within this ij months. And further, Mrs. Anne must have such apparel as is also written in the same book, which was 'pointed by my Lady Rutland and my Lady Sussex. Howbeit, since that time James is come from the court, and saith that the Queen's pleasure [is] that Mrs. Anne shall wear out her French apparel, so that your ladyship shall thereby be no loser. Howbeit, she must needs have a bonnet of velvet and a frontlet of the same. I saw her yesterday in her velvet bonnet that my Lady Sussex had 'tired her in, and methought it became her nothing so well as the French hood; but the Queen's pleasure must needs be fulfilled. I think your ladyship's old apparel would serve this matter for Mrs. Anne, and your frontlets, as well as new, for a time.

And Mrs. Katharine lacketh also such things as is written and appointed for her in the said book of reckonings, and my Lady Rutland would know your ladyship's pleasure whether she should send to my Lady Suffolk to know her pleasure whether she should send Mrs. Katharine there to her or no, or whether she shall keep her still with her till the Duchess' coming, which she thinketh will be long, by reason she is with child and will be delivered ere she return to the Court. . . .

Your ladyship must give thanks to Mr. Porter, Sir Christopher Morys, Antony Antonys, the Surveyor of the Ordnance, Mrs. Hutton and Mr. Lee, who highly feasted your ladyship's said daughters, with right good dishes and great cheer; and so did my Lady Dudley[30] at their going to the Court, wherein she hath demerited thanks. . . .

Further, your ladyship shall understand that Mrs. Mary wrote unto Mrs. Anne her sister for a great mastiff and ij ells of fine holland cloth. And as touching any exhortations or good counsel to be given unto your daughters, your ladyship shall not need fear as long as my Lady Sussex is here; and besides that, the gentlewomen are of a good judgement and hath fine wits, so that I trust there shall be no fault found in them. Mrs. Katharine would gladly be with my Lady Mary and it might be brought to pass. And thus I beseech Jhesu send your ladyship long life with much honour, and a most fortunate hour when his pleasure shall be.

From St. Katharine's the xvij[th] of September.

By your ladyship's man,

---

30. Wife of Sir John Dudley, Lisle's stepson.

I assure your ladyship Mrs. Pole hath taken no little ∧pains∧ at this time in your affairs and hath deserved thanks.

Madam, my Lady of Sussex desireth your ladyship to send her the ring she sent you which is a wreath of gold, for it is the Queen of Hungary's, who would not lose the same for a king's ransom, but maketh much ado for it. The owner is kin to my Lady Paulet. Mrs. Pole knoweth who owneth it.
Hol.   John Husee   (Vol. 4, No. 895)

It was the business of the yeoman-ushers, among other things, to be in attendance in the Chamber by seven or eight o'clock in the morning to guard the door and see that only the right people were admitted; and they gave the necessary orders to the grooms and pages who 'dressed' the Chamber, lighted fires, carried torches and lights, and performed any menial tasks. Gentlewomen attached to the Court had to be apparelled 'according to their degree', by which was meant not the social standing which was theirs by right of birth, but their position in the household. There was one standard for Anne, the Queen's Maid of Honour, and another for her sister Katharine, gentlewoman to one of the Queen's ladies. Perhaps this was a little galling to the elder sister who, despairing now of preferment to the Queen's service, would rather strike out on her own in that of Mary Tudor.

181   JOHN HUSEE TO LADY LISLE   *2 October 1537*

My bounden duty premised unto your Ladyship, These shall signify the same that I have received your Ladyship's sundry letters. And as concerning your daughters, thanked be God they are merry and in good health, and hitherto neither my Lady of Sussex ne other of your Ladyship's friends cannot invent ne compass which way to advance Mrs. Katharine unto the Queen's service. What shall be done hereafter God knoweth. Your Ladyship may be well assured there shall lack no good will in them, but as touching my Lord Privy Seal's help, or Mr. Bryan's, I have no comfort that she shall speed that way. For it is thought by my Lady of Sussex and other your Ladyship's very friends that it is no meet suit for any man to move such matters, but only for such Ladies and women as be your friends. And as touching her preferment unto my Lady Mary, there is plain answer made that her Grace shall have no more than her number. Howbeit, at my coming unto Calais your Ladyship shall know more, for I do partly know both my Lady of Sussex and my Lady Rutland's mind in that behalf. Your ladyship may be assured if it be possible they will help to prefer her. And if not, there is no remedy but your Ladyship must be content. And I doubt not wheresoever Mrs. Katharine be come but that she shall do as well as the other. . . .

Madam, now your Ladyship shall understand that the Queen's pleasure is that Mrs. Anne shall wear no more her French apparel. So that she must have provided a bonnet or ij, with frontlets and an edge of pearl, and a gown of black satin, and another of velvet, and this must be done before the Queen's grace's churching. And further, she must have cloth for smocks and sleeves, for there is fault founden that their smocks are too coarse. . . .

    From St. Katharine's, the ij^d day of September [i.e. October]. . . .

             Your ladyship's own man,

Hol.   John Husee   (Vol. 4, No. 896)

Peter Mewtas, a Gentleman of the Privy Chamber, wrote to Lisle on 9 October:

Sir, the King's Grace, not ij days past, talked of your and your children, amongst which I advertised him of your daughter that last came out of France. Howbeit his Grace thought Mistress Anne Basset to be the fairest, but I said how that your youngest[31] was far fairer. I trust I have not offended in so saying, but if ∧I∧ have I do submit me to my lady's correction.[32]

It is quite obvious that good looks were one of the essential qualifications for the post of Maid of Honour to Henry's queens, and that so far Anne's face had been her fortune. On 12 October Edward VI was born, and Anne was in attendance for the christening; but on the 24th the Queen died at Windsor, only five weeks after Anne entered her service. Anne had her place in the funeral cortège, but then her post at Court was at an end. She was still only about sixteen. Her cousin Lady Sussex took her in, so she remained on the fringe of the Court, and Lady Rutland kept Katharine. Anne's good fortune did not desert her. Husee, writing to Lisle on 14 December, sends the 'welcome news' that 'The King's Grace is good lord to Mistress Anne, and hath made her grant to have her place whensoever the time shall come.'[33]

31. Mary Basset.   33. Vol. 4, No. 1038.
32. Vol. 4, No. 899.

11

Estate and Legal Business
1536

In the spring and early summer of 1536 Lisle was trying desperately to save his financial situation by obtaining the grant of one of the abbeys now being dissolved (see chap. 8). As early as 16 March Thomas Warley was embroidering the conventional ending of a letter to Honor Lisle with the words 'as knoweth our Lord, who send my lord a good abbey or ij for a commendam, and preserve both my lord and your good ladyship in honour, health and prosperity, etc.' But at that time the King's own affairs, disposing of one Queen and acquiring another, made access to him by Lisle himself impossible and by others on his behalf extremely difficult. By the middle of June his quest could begin to depend unimpeded on his own, and Husee's, business abilities. We must presume that Honor, though far more religious than Lisle, could accept this pursuit of Church lands because the monastic Orders were more or less accepting the dissolution of their minor houses in the hope of thereby saving the great ones, not yet condemned, into which they could absorb the dispossessed monks. Lisle had already put in for several without success, including Beaulieu.

182   JOHN HUSEE TO LORD LISLE   *18 June 1536*

Pleaseth it your lordship. . . .

And as touching your suit to the King, Mr. Russell, Mr. Heneage and Mr. Secretary, every of them, saith that they will do their best, etc. Mr. Secretary saith still when I spoke to him that he hath remembered you, but yet I cannot get answer of him ne any of them what the King's pleasure is. Yesterday Mr. Russell and Mr. Heneage delivered the King the spurs and desired his Highness to have your lordship in remembrance: whose Grace made answer that he so would do, and thanked you for the spurs and received the same in thankful part, so that it was then betwixt them concluded that the next time they might see Mr. Secretary with the King in a good mood, they all, with one voice would be suitors for your lordship so that the

King's determinate pleasure should be knowen what he would do for your lordship. I will not fail to call upon them as I see time. Howbeit, I know well Mr. Secretary taketh me for importunate already, and that appeared by the last answer he made, which was more than I now will write. I would God it lay in me to rid it, and then should it not be long adoing.

Mr. Secretary thanketh your lordship for the piece of wine that you sent him. I showed him there was none such in London. . . .

. . . I perceive by your lordship's letter of the xiij[th] day of June that a friend of yours said that I was not with Mr. Secretary in vj days. I think he bare good view of me and watched me well all that space; but under your lordship's correction, your honour reserved, if he be under the degree of a Councillor he falsely belieth me, and to this will I take none other record but Mr. Secretary himself. I further perceive by your lordship's said letter that my lady mourneth in thinking every man shall be sped before your lordship. I am sorry that her ladyship so should do, and that your lordship or my lady should think me to be so remiss or negligent that your suit shall any way be hindered by my slackness. I trust you never found it hitherto in me. But whether your lordship speed well or no, I trust both Mr. Heneage, Mr. Russell and Mr. Secretary will depose for me that I have done my duty, notwithstanding others may imagine and surmise what they list. Humbly beseeching your lordship to accept my doing and proceedings in all your affairs even as I do mean towards you and not to believe all things that is said.

. . . If your friends were now as earnest in your suits to the King as Mr. Norris was, your matters had not slept so long. But your lordship may say the world is altered and that you have lost a friend. . . .

From London, the xviij[th] day of June.

By your lordship's bounden while he liv[eth],

Hol.   John Husee   (Vol. 3, No. 729)

183   THOMAS WARLEY TO LADY LISLE   *1 July 1536*

Right honourable and my special good lady, my bounden duty evermore presupposed. Pleaseth it your goodness to understand that I would be very glad to see your ladyship in these parts for a little season, because I think it should be profitable both to my lord, and your ladyship, though it were somewhat chargeable your coming over. But it is an old saying, Well is spent the penny that getteth the pound. I mean this, because my lord can obtain no licence to come himself, that if your ladyship were here you might move the King's Grace and the Queen for one of the abbeys towards the maintenance of my lord's and your good ladyship's charges, which be not a little. I know this, you should be very welcome to the King and to the Queen, which is as gentle as can be; and now is the time to speak, or never; and the presence of a nobleman or woman may do more than twenty fearful solicitors. Here is Mr. Lovell, Palmer, Corbet, I and Cranwell, Snowden, Clifford, Pykeryng, ∧London∧, and other Spears, which, and we have knowledge of your ladyship's coming, will come to Dover to wait on your ladyship to the Court. . . .

Such news as be here I have written to my lord by this bearer, and how Mr. Secretary is Lord of the Privy Seal. . . . And thus our Lord Jesus conserve my lord and your good ladyship in health and honour, to your gentle and noble hearts' desires.

From London, the first day of Julii.

By your most bounden servant to his power,

Hol.   Thomas Warley   (Vol. 3, No. 737)

Unfortunately Warley's companion letter, written to Lisle on the same day, is missing, but there is no earlier reference than this to Cromwell's grant of the office of Lord Privy Seal, which was actually made on 1 July. Lisle would now be more than ever dependent on his goodwill, in private as well as public affairs.

184   JOHN HUSEE TO LORD LISLE   *5 July 1536*

Pleaseth it your lordship to understand that this day, I being in communication with Mr. Secretary for divers your suits, he made me answer that he had spoken to the King's Highness divers times for you, and said that he had read sundry your letters sent unto the King's Grace and that the King's Grace, as far as he could perceive, would see unto your lordship, but how soon he could not tell, but that from time to time he would not fail to have your lordship in remembrance, and that your lordship should well know he was your very friend. . . . And at my departure from him he called me again and said that he would in any wise that your lordship should meet the King at Dover; and I showed him that your lordship desired nothing so much as to see his Grace and humbly beseeched him to procure your licence for the same. So that, incontinent, he commanded me to go unto Mr. Sadler, who is of the King's privy chamber, in his name, and that he should motion the King's Highness in it: who so did, and his Grace stayed at it and said that he would common with Mr. Secretary and devise farther therein. And so I returned unto Mr. Secretary and showed him the King's pleasure, who said that he would speak to his ∧Grace∧ therein at his next coming to the Court; so that whether your lordship shall come over or no I cannot yet write certainly, but once tomorrow I shall know the truth and then will I advertise your lordship with all celerity.

The King will be at Dover upon Tuesday next, and there remaining

Wednesday and Thursday, and will be on Saturday again at Greenwich, so that it shall please your lordship to be in a'readiness; for if your licence be obtained it shall be requisite your lordship be there a day before the King. And if I can get your lordship's licence I will meet you at Dover. And further, it is now thought Mr. Secretary will over to Calais at this journey. I delivered your lordship's letters, the which the King's Highness read and said it was for a suit and required no hasty answer, but that he would not fail to see to your lordship at leisure.

... and thus I pray God send your lordship long life and much honour. From London, the vth day of July.

By your lordship's bounden while he liveth

Hol., not signed　　　　　　　　　　　　　　　　　　　　(Vol. 3, No. 739)

More lobbying by Husee failed to secure a licence, but as it happened the King's journey was put off.

185　　JOHN HUSEE TO LORD LISLE　　　　　　　　*18 July 1536*

Pleaseth it your lordship to be advertised that I received your last letters of the xiiij^{th} of this instant, and therewith a letter unto my Lord Privy Seal directed, which I immediately delivered unto him, and with much suit have this day obtained your licence to come to Dover, as more plainly shall appear by the letter which I do send herein enclosed; assuring your lordship if that I had known the same to have been so dangerous to come by, your lordship, for so short a space, should never for the same have sued. But I trust now your mind shall be something eased and satisfied. ...

And tomorrow, being Wednesday, the King's Grace, with the Queen, will be at even in Rochester, and Thursday at Sittingbourne, and Friday at Canterbury, and so Saturday to Dover, and there to remain Sunday and Monday. This Mr. Treasurer shewed me, but Mr. Russell saith that he will retu[rn] on Monday to Canterbury, so that it sha[ll be] requisite that your lordship prepare to be upon Friday night at Dover, where I trust to meet your lordship. And I think your lordship and my lady shall have simple lodging if ye bring not provision with you. At my thither coming your lordship shall know more at large how every thing stand. ...

Touching all other matters, your lordship shall the same debate at my Lord Privy Seal's coming unto Dover, who I trust will be your friend, and then shall your lordship speed so much the better. ...

And thus remitting all things to my coming to Dover, I rest, praying God to send your lordship once your heart's desire.

From London, the xviij^{th} of July.

Your lordship's bounden during life,

Hol.　　　　　　　　John Husee　　　　　　　　(Vol. 3, No. 748)

Husee's urgent instructions would have reached Calais in time to enable them to cross to Dover on the Friday, where the King was due to arrive on Saturday the 22nd. There is no direct account of their visit but they were obviously well received both by the King and his new Queen, and Husee's next letter shows that Henry was graciously pleased to bestow on him a gift of monastic property. This was not all. Evidently, in his genial and expansive mood of the moment, Lisle and his wife were honoured with a royal command to accompany the Court when it left Dover, which meant that he extended what had been virtually a forty-eight hours' leave to a week or possibly more. When we watch the interminable delays at Cromwell's hands over ratifying this gift, we may remember how much better Lisle fares when he can get to the King himself.

The Chancellor of the Court of Augmentations, which had been formed to deal with all the business of abbey lands, was Sir Richard Riche, a longtime colleague of Cromwell's who had earned himself the most unsavoury reputation of any Tudor politician, in the eyes of posterity, by giving what is generally thought to be the perjured evidence required in order to convict Sir Thomas More of treason. In his preliminary discussion with Lisle and Honor at Dover he had promised to do everything he could to help them, and apparently at Honor Lisle's suggestion the Priory of Frithelstock in Devon, about eight miles from Umberleigh, was decided upon, being reasonably near in value to the King's gift of land to the value of a hundred marks a year. Husee's second paragraph refers to another case, which has to await Cromwell's co-operation.

186   JOHN HUSEE TO LADY LISLE   10 *August 1536*

Pleaseth it your Ladyship to understand that I have had much ado with the Chancellor of the Augmentations since my coming, in whom I find very small friendship, notwithstanding he hath 'pointed my Lord out of the Priory of ffrystock lxxxvj^{li} by the year, so that, the C marks reserved, my Lord must become tenant to the King for the rest. I have caused ij bills to be made, in the one declaring the gift unto my lord, your ladyship and the heirs of your ij bodies, and the other in like manner and the remainder unto the heirs of my lord's body. Which of these bills he will get signed, God knoweth. I doubt he will speed but the first, for he is full of dissimulation. He would in no wise put Mr. Basset in the remainder, yet I promised him, in your ladyship's behalf, a gown of velvet. And if this bill be shortly sped, my lord shall have this half year's rent. I will do my best in hasting the same. I fear me the Chancellor will so handle himself that he will deserve neither thanks ne reward. He passeth all that ever I sued unto.

Touching the m^{l} marks, I have followed Mr. Heneage for it. He giveth fair words but small comfort. He referreth all to my Lord Privy Seal, so that when this is obtained it must pass by him, there is no other remedy. And whensoever it should come to pass it will be no short suit. So that, as my lord's pleasure is, I can see no remedy but go through with Hide, where Mr. Windsor and I will do our best, as shall become us to do for my Lord's advantage.

. . . And thus I pray Jesu send your ladyship long life and much honour. From London the xth day of August.

By your ladyship's bounden,

Hol.   John Husee   (Vol. 3, No. 753)

187   JOHN HUSEE TO LORD LISLE   *6 September 1536*

Pleaseth it your lordship to understand that I have received sundry your letters, and first one with a letter unto my Lord Privy Seal directed, which I delivered, but answer could I get none by reason of his departing to the Court. . . .

And as for the suit to the Chancellor of the Augmentations, he hath no fellow of all that ever I sued unto; for after I had delivered him your letter I shewed him your lordship's pleasure, to the which he gave little regard, full like a gentleman of his birth; and in no wise the lead will be had, for he saith plainly that the King will have all the lead of the Suppressed abbeys brought to London, and so new tried and fined. And as for the house of ffrisstock and all the lands, are letted for xxj years unto George Carew, so that till that time your lordship, without compounding with the same George, can in nowise the same enjoy, but shall have, after your patent be out, the bare rent of the same yearly paid unto you. And where the said Chancellor promised that your lordship should have the half year's rent due at Michaelmas, he now saith that the house was suppressed since Midsummer, and that your lordship can have no more rent than the King hath, which is since the suppression: and yet he saith that the house and officers must be thereof found till such time as the poor religious may be clearly expulsed, so that by this his reckoning, all things deducted, there will remain nihil. But by this your lordship shall see what constance is in his word and promise. And further, he told me plainly that I should not have your patent out before Michaelmas, because that he saith it may in no wise be. So after much communication I desired him to procure that the same might remain unto your lordship's heirs, which he put into his remembrance with much ado, saying plainly that he could not think the King would thereunto condescend; but he said that he would do his best and further that he would in nowise move the King for the overplus and though your lordship would give him a m^lli. The truth is, I have little trust or comfort in any of his promises. I fear me at length he will get your patent or bill signed but for your lordship's life and my Lady's, his fair behests notwithstanding. I will apply him now at my being at the Court, so that I will know, off or on, whereunto your lordship shall trust. . . .

The plague reigneth here very hot, God cease it when it be his pleasure.

From London, the vj[th] day of September.

By your lordship's as he bounden,

Hol.   John Husee

Mr. Onley is very hot for his money and saith he will no wine, but your lordship send him all at once.   (Vol. 3, No. 765)

Most of the urgency of Lisle's need of money at this time stems from the old Seymour-Dudley dispute. It is to be remembered that Seymour, now Lord Beauchamp, having bought Dudley's reversionary interest, had applied to Lisle for a lease of the property, at the same time also lending him £400, which had been repaid, with interest. Then he had exploited what Husee euphemistically describes as Lisle's 'gentleness' – that is, the downright carelessness of signing an agreement he had not taken the trouble to check. The dispute had been put to the arbitrament of Cromwell and Audley, who awarded Lisle an annuity or annual rental of £120 a year for the term of his life. In spite of this experience of Seymour's methods Lisle had then borrowed £124 from Mr. Hollys, paying interest upon it and pledging as security this annual rental, which would be forfeited if he did not keep his days of payment. Cromwell, having made Jane Seymour's marriage possible, was not likely to do anything that might antagonize the new Queen's brother. Kybworth, mentioned in the next letter, is a property in Leicestershire in which Lisle holds the life interest and on which he could raise money if the reversion of his stepson, John Dudley, were sold.

188   JOHN HUSEE TO LORD LISLE   *12 September 1536*

Pleaseth it your lordship to be advertised that since my hither coming I have had much ado to come to my lord Privy Seal's speech: I mean, not come to his presence but to have him at leisure to common and open my mind unto him; which by Mr. Popley's help I did this day obtain, so that he had me unto his secret chamber where I was with [him] a large half hour. And first, for the offer that I made unto him in your lordship's behalf for the ministration or execution of the office of High Pantership at the Queen's coronation, he giveth your lordship hearty thanks, saying that therein I should know further of his mind ere my departing. Then showed I him your lordship's mind concerning Kybworth, how that to do him pleasure you could be content to part from it for a reasonable sum of money, showing him further that it was xl li by year; and likewise being patronage of the benefice of xl li by year; and how also that the High Pantership did thereon depend on all coronations. To the which he answered me that having communication with Sir John Dudley he would show me further of his mind. Then motioned I him again that your lordship, by reason of charges you have been at, are nothing beforehand, and how that thing that you must do doth require some haste and may not be slacked, for your payments cometh very fast on, insomuch that if iiij^C li and odd be not paid at this side Michaelmas your lordship should forfeit a great portion of your land: to the which he answered that he was sorry that your lordship was no better husband and said that within ij or iij days I should know more of his mind, the which I will diligently apply, but what it shall be God knoweth.

Then I further showed him how the Chancellor of the Augmentations handled you, and how that I could not get out your patent, so that he hath promised me to speak with the Chancellor in it. So that, thus commoning, came in Mr. Heneage, and then he commanded me to void. I trust within this iij days to know his determinate answer, whereupon he will rest. I have also since I spake with him spoke with the Chancellor of the Augmentations, who hath promised to have your lordship in remembrance unto the King: which if he do not, I will, ere I do depart hence, speak unto the King's Majesty myself. I will do my best with my lord Privy Seal, but in case he will not deal nor help I know not what to do, for I see that here is no succour but at the King's hands or his. And what the King granteth passeth all by him. I have moved Mr. Heneage and Mr. Russell but they will deal with nothing unless my Lord Cromwell be privy thereunto.

. . . as God knoweth, who send your lordship with my lady long life with much honour and once your heart's desire.

From Grafton, the xijth of September.

By him that his your lordship's bounden,

Hol.   John Husee   (Vol. 3, No. 767)

Here follows part of a marathon letter from Husee, which is of interest because it shows both his unflagging energy in Lisle's affairs and the extent to which he directed his lordship in his conduct of them. On the personal level the sixth paragraph, in which he answers a letter from Lisle which is unfortunately missing, is particularly moving in the circumstances.

189   JOHN HUSEE TO LORD LISLE   *c.7 October 1536*

Pleaseth it your Lordship to be advertised that by this bearer I received your letters, with the letters obligation and letters of attorney unto Mr. Judd, who was at that time in the country at his house beside Mortlake, so that before the time limited of your lordship's bond there was no help ne recovery. And as for Mr. Hollys he would in no wise condescend unto the stay of payment, ne yet would disburse the money after xx in the C. Howbeit he was content to write his favorable letter unto my Lord Beauchamp, which he indeed did. But it would take none effect, ne yet the letter which I got of my Lord Privy Seal unto the said Lord Beauchamp, which was written as favorably on your lordship's behalf as might well be devised; which, notwithstanding, the said Lord Beauchamp would in no wise condescend unto longer respite nor would grant anything at my Lord Privy Seal's request in that behalf, for I went unto Mortlake myself with my Lord Beauchamp's answer and delivered it unto my Lord Privy Seal, who was not with the same well pleased, but made me this answer: This man will be by no means entreated. Then I desired his lordship to speak unto my Lord Beauchamp himself, who answered that he would right gladly do it, and commanded me to meet him the next morrow at the Court at Windsor, and so I did. And there he was in like manner in hand with my Lord Beauchamp, but no grace would be had at his hand concerning the premise, as my Lord Privy Seal immediately shewed me. So that I would not thus stay, but went unto my Lord Admiral, who I ensure your lordship was a large hour in the King's chamber in hand with my Lord Beauchamp. But at length he made me answer that there was no grace there to be had, which I ensure your lordship brought me almost in despair.

But I left it not thus, but went again unto my Lord Privy Seal desiring him to move the King in it, and so full gently he promised that he would, so that I tarried at Windsor iiij days for his answer; and the last he called me unto him and said that in any wise he will that your lordship should certify by your letter unto the King's Highness the very circumstance of the matter: how he first entered in to this land by buying the reversion of Sir John Dudley and then sued unto your lordship for possession, and how that your lordship, for your gentleness in suffering him to have the possession, is brought in to all this mischief. And as touching the iiij^C li that he then lent your lordship, he had interest for the same and his money repaid him. And yet by the means of that your gentleness, he hath since compassed to put you from the whole, and at length driven you to put it in arbitrament and brought you to the annuity of vj^{xx} li by the year. And how, now lately, that this last shift of Cxxiiij li was made with Mr. Hollys to his use, and that he had for the same large interest in like manner, and that your lordship thought that for xx days, more or less, he would not be extreme upon you, considered your goodness shewed unto him in the possession for his assurance, without which, if Sir John Dudley should have chanced to die, all his money had been in hazard of losing or clearly lost. And, further, that your lordship thought, considering the premise and also the interest that he should have with this money, that it was no great matter to pass upon xx days, more or less, specially considering that your lordship was and is of that side the sea; beseeching his Grace to be good lord unto your lordship in it, trusting that his Grace would not see your lordship thus cruelly handled, and without any conscience to be put from vj^{xx} li by the year for breaking of your day; and how that your lordship is driven to write unto his Grace herein, for as much as he would neither be entreated by my Lord Privy Seal's letter ne yet at his request by mouth, ne yet at my Lord Admiral's desire.

And also your lordship must write that the money is ready at the hour. This letter must be contrived as briefly as may be, even mentioning the very truth. And that your lordship do send the copy of the King's letter unto my Lord Privy Seal, with a letter of thanks for his goodness in this matter and all other shewed unto your lordship, desiring him now to stick to you in this; and a like letter unto my Lord Admiral, and this to be done with all speed convenient, for my Lord Privy Seal saith that he will by this ways find means that he shall take this money. But in any wise the money must be ready ere this letter be delivered, and also that your lordship write me your mind with the copy of all their letters.

Now for the making of this money, I can see no help but that Mr. Skryven must come over himself, and then I trust this matter will be at a point; for here is no remedy but they that shall deliver this money will have ij men of substance of the City to be bound at the least for it. Mr. Judd hath offered to be bound for j^c li, and more he will not enter; and Mr. Whalley for as much. But they that shall deliver this money will have ij men of the City bound every man in the whole, and this is the very truth; and so there is that will deliver for xij in the £ and for xiij^{li} vj^s viij^d in the £ and for xv in the £; but they make much danger for assurance, therefor it shall be much requisite that Mr. Skryven come over himself and that with speed, for this matter may not be slacked. So that concerning this matter here is all that I can devise or imagine to write therein. But I am sure that, setting ij sufficient sureties, citizens, that will be bound every man for the whole, there is no doubt but this money will be made ij or iij manner ways.

As touching the Chancellor of the Augmentations, I have been in hand with him and he maketh me answer that the Commissioners hath not certified yet the house of ffrystock, but as soon as they come I shall have it; I mean your patent. . . .

And now that I have touched all your lordship's causes as much as in me lieth, I can do no less but open unto the same my grieved stomach, which is, that your lordship should report and say that I have had more mind to make banquets and to ride about to my kinsfolk than to apply any of your causes and businesses, which grieveth me not a little. I am sure I have not exceeded in banquets, and to say that ever I came in any kinsman's house of mine this xij month, I dare well justify the contrary, and scant to my brother's house in the town once a month. It sticketh not a little in my stomach and I have always thought that your lordship would have been better lord unto me than to have thus reported.

And also where your lordship writeth that if you had not trusted unto the letter that I sent you by Smyth, that you would have made provision to have kept your day: I wrote your lordship then that my Lord Privy Seal commanded me to tarry; but I did not by that my letter encourage your lordship to trust thereunto, but I wrote you in the same that in case my Lord Privy Seal should not go through, that then your lordship should write me what I should do therein, so that your lordship needed not to trust to my letter, for I knew not what my Lord Privy Seal would do ne what answer he would make me, for there were better men than the best of my kin that were glad to tarry his answer. . . .   (Vol. 3, No. 774)

After a few more lines, recapitulating recent moves, the letter ends at the foot of a page and the next is missing.

Husee's 'Mr. Carow', in his next, is Sir George Carew, a local landowner and High Sheriff of Devonshire, whose lease at Frithelstock turns out greatly to diminish the immediate value of the King's gift.

190   JOHN HUSEE TO LORD LISLE   *18 November 1536*

Pleaseth it your lordship to be advertised that since my last writing I have been with the Chancellor and the Council of the Augmentations concerning your gift and patent of ffristock, insomuch that after long debatement and reasoning of the matter it was concluded that it might in no wise ∧be∧ well and assuredly granted out till such time as the particulars ∧were∧ fully certified according to the extent of the last survey by the commissioners therefor appointed; so that they hath commanded me to send one expressly into Devonshire unto Sir Thomas Arundell and William Tornor for the whole books of the Priory of ffristock; which I have done, with their letter, for because they could do nothing, as they saith, till the same be come. I trust the messenger will be here again within xij days at the farthest, if these men he goes unto be not in Cornwall; and at the coming of the said particulars I trust, if they keep promise, it shall be rid out of hand. They hath caused me to make so many books that I am almost weary, considering the same doth take none effect and the Court is very costly, for it is new begun and no men knoweth the order thereof but they.

Mr. Richard Pollard hath spoken earnestly in your lordship's cause in this matter. I trust he shall do some good. And where your lordship is minded to have the house of ffristock with the demesnes, I have reasoned the matter with divers but they saith is plainly against your lordship's profit, for Mr. George Carow hath the same by lease unto the term of xxj years be expired, so that during that space your lordship shall have no profit but the bare rent of assize, and therefor your lordship must now look upon it, or ere your patent be out, for afterwards it will be too late. That which Mr. Carow hath is xxj^{li} or xxij^{li} per annum. Also if your lordship do mind to have the parsonage you must thereupon find a priest with cure, and for because that your lordship shall know the yearly value of the said priory, I do send you the true book of the whole, as it was surveyed. But there is x^{li} de novo incremented, which is not yet levied. If your lordship do prick in this book such parcels as you will have, I will do my best to make friends to obtaining them, for it is to be known that there is much more profit in lands to be had in possession than in that which is let for xxj years. The very house of ffrystock, as it is now left, by every man's report is scant worth a mean farm, for the house of the priory is pulled down and nothing standing but the house for the farmer. And George Carow hath sold his lease to one Wynslade, and the Chancellor showeth me that your lordship was therewithal contented. It is the busiest matter that ever I had in hand, for there is nothing to be done but at their pleasure. But I think there be not so few as v C as well tangled as I am. Howbeit, if this other business had not fortuned, it had been at a point long ere this time. It shall be therefor requisite that your lordship write me now your determinate pleasure in the premises with speed. I trust it shall take some good end or else I would be sorry to have spent so much time about it.

. . . How the world here goeth this bearer can inform your lordship, as God knoweth, who send your lordship long life with much honour.

From London the xviijth of November.

Your lordship's bounden during life,

Hol.　　　　　John Husee　　　　　　　　　　　　(Vol. 3, No. 784)

By 5 December the particulars for the valuation of Frithelstock were at length secured, the total for the four manors and three rectories leaving a clear annual value of £137. 9s. 1½d. Sir George Carew was only paying £20. 2s. for the priory, the parsonage, and the demesne lands during the 21 years of his Crown lease, these items being valued at £49. 12s. 9d. by the Commissioners.

The duration of the Seymour-Dudley dispute was as nothing compared with that of the Bassets over the Beaumont lands, of which the origins go back over a hundred years. Upon it depended a great part of John Basset's inheritance. Sir Thomas Beaumont of Gittisham, who died in 1450, had two wives. By the first he had five children, by the second, four. The lands in question were left, if his sons by the first marriage died without issue, to his daughters Joan and Alice as co-heirs. Joan married John Basset, grand-father of Honor Lisle's first husband. The wife of the eldest son had had a son during her husband's lifetime by one Henry Bodrugan whom she sub-sequently married, and when Sir Thomas Beaumont died this 'John the Bastard' put in a claim to the lands, but lost, and Sir Thomas's surviving son, Philip, succeeded. Philip's chief concern was that the Beaumont name be left in possession, and, having no children, instead of allowing Joan Basset and her sister to succeed him as his father had wished, he conveyed the lands to his stepbrothers of the second marriage. With the help of Giles Lord Daubeney, our Sir John Basset's father successfully opposed Philip Beau-mont's will. The intention of both families was that Daubeney's son Henry should marry one of the Basset daughters, and in return for his having financed the recovery of the Beaumont lands Basset made over many of the manors, entailed upon the hypothetical heirs of this marriage. Henry, our Lord Daubeney, never did marry a Basset daughter, so he had only a life interest in the properties; and the object of the Lisles' battles with him was to prevent him from either selling them for ready cash or ruining them by mismanagement before our John Basset should succeed to them.

There remained one other small piece of the jigsaw puzzle. When Philip Beaumont had left the lands to the younger sons of his father's second wife he had left out the heirs of the eldest son because he had only a daughter, married to Richard Chichester – and Philip was only interested in the Beau-mont name. A separate deal had been made with the Chichesters by Basset with Daubeney's help at the same time as the main one, and this also could be called into question by the heirs on both sides. No wonder the Lisle correspondence is heavily weighted with matters legal!

Daubeney needed ready money now, and was determined to make all he could by wood-sales from the Beaumont-Basset lands. Everyone seemed to agree that he had the right to make such sales, and that to stop him from despoiling the property in this way Lady Lisle must find the money to re-deem the possession of these lands and hold them in fee farm.

191   GEORGE ROLLE TO LADY LISLE   *27 November 1535*

After the most humble manner I have me commended to your good Ladyship advertising your ladyship I have received your letter by your ser-vant John Borough, by which I perceive the contents thereof, advertising further your good ladyship that ∧I perceive by your letter that∧ ye had been long since contented to have gone through with my Lord Daubeney but for ij causes; one, because men would have thought your son's title the weaker, the ij^nd cause was of the great sum of money to be given for the redemption of the whole inheritance into your hands and possession.

As ∧to∧ the first, the title of your son should nor shall be no weaker nor slighter, but to put everything out of doubt and danger. To the ij^nd cause, he that will win perpetual peace and possession of such an inheritance, ∧being∧ in such one his hand that hath the possession of it, that may transpose it to your son's great displeasure, must take pain both in his purse and his bodily study; and therefore, madam, considering the unstableness of him that hath the possession, I will advise you to take some pain and make some reasonable sum in a readiness against the next term when the Parliament shall be holden. And where my lord that hath possession of the premises will be, that ye send or make provision ready that at least he may have CC^{li} in hand and the residue of such sum as ye shall agree upon to be paid at days. My meaning is, that ye shall have the whole possession of the lands, and to pay my lord the rents of assize and ye to have the casualties. . . .

. . . And thus to our Lord I commit you, long to prosper in honour, by him that is all yours assured.

ffrom London the xxvij^th day of November

Hol.   George Rolle   (Vol. 4, No. 841)

192   GEORGE ROLLE TO LORD LISLE   *4 March 1536*

My duty remembered to your good Lordship, I have me humbly recommended and to my good Lady your bedfellow, likewise advertising your lordship that I have received from your lordship two letters, the one bearing date the viij^th day of February, to which I have made you yet none answer, whereof ye somewhat marvel as appeareth in your second letter dated the xxiij^th day of February last, the tenours of which your letters I do perceive. For answer of your said letters, I have inquired of my Lord Daubeney's demeanour as secretly as I can, and I perceive that at this time he is not determined nor disposed to hurt my lady and Mr. Basset's title; for I have perfect knowledge that he hath made shift with my Lord of Wiltshire for four hundred pounds; and to move him now for redemption of Mr. Basset's lands there is no remedy. But they that knoweth his conditions hath shewed me there shall be no time convenient to move your matter until such time as this money be spent, or else when he shall repay this money again, and then such money as shall be offered must be in a readiness. And my lord, I have moved Mr. John Halse, son and heir of Richard Halse of Devonshire, and a kinsman or ally to my lady your bedfellow, which is now servant to my Lord Daubeney, to whom your lordship may speak, to that intent to give me or any other your friends ∧knowledge∧ when my said Lord Daubeney shall have necessity. He proposeth shortly to be at Calais, who hath promised me to give me warning; and therefore your lordship must be in a readiness of money, for your lordship must take pain if ye intend that matter. He shall be now divorced from my lady by their both assents, and my lady to have now lxxx pounds yearly and her whole jointure after his death, as was appointed the time of their first marriage. I trust to make some further motion by some means, ere I ride into Devon, whereof I shall advertise your lordship.

Also ascertaining your lordship that Mr. John Chichester is departed to God; who had a certain lands in his hands called Dodcott, contrary to the indenture between my Lord Daubeney, Mr. Basset and him. And if his office be found he died seized by right of that parcel, it might and shall turn Mr. John Basset to trouble; wherefore it were necessary Mr. Basset's indenture and writing were here shewed to the jury, and now I think my lady hath her book at Calais, which as methought was not convenient to have been brought to Calais, but to have remained still in the country or here, for your counsel to resort unto in all your needs. And Worth, servant to my Lord Daubeney, showed me yesterday that my said Lord Daubeney hath sold all the timber and wood in Beckingholt to Roger Gyfford and to Thomas Seller, sometime servant to Sir John Basset. What ye will in the premises I pray your lordship to advertise me, and I shall be glad to do that that shall lie in me to do you service. . . .

And thus I commit your good lordship and my lady to Our Lord.

From London, in haste, the iiij[th] day of March.

                    by yo*ur* assuryd,
Hol.   George Rolle

I propose to tarry in London these xvj days. As far as I remember, Mr. Basset's great indenture maketh clear recital that these lands in Dodcott was clearly appointed to Mr. Basset, both by the fine and the indenture between Mr. Chichester and him. Ye may therefore now know the truth. I know not why he was suffered to have the possession of that lands by Mr. Basset.

                                        (Vol. 4, No. 841a)

193   GEORGE ROLLE TO LORD LISLE   *13 July 1536*

Pleaseth it your lordship to be advertised that of late my Lord Daubeney sent to me by a gentleman of his, by mouth, that I should move your lordship that if ye would suffer him quietly to sell and fell Warham Wood he would not fell nor meddle with Bekynholt Wood. But the best way were, in my conceit, that in case your lordship will provide for him xl or L[li], Roger Gyfford shewed me he thought it would satisfy him for the whole, so that he might have in hand at least xx[li], which methinketh were the best ∧way∧, under your lordship's favour, ∧with a gentle letter, which he loveth∧. And what your lordship's pleasure shall be in the premises, your pleasure knowen, I shall be glad to accomplish to the best of my power. And I intend to ride into Devon on St. Anne's Day next,[1] God willing, who have your good lordship and my good lady in his blessed tuition.

> ffrom london the xiij[th] day of Jule
>
>> by yo*ur* assuryd *serv*u*nt*
>
> *Hol.*   George Rolle   (Vol. 4, No. 851b)

These letters from Rolle and Husee about the strategy of the campaign against Lord Daubeney do as much as any in this collection to establish for us the Tudor reality of the 'privy friend' in your enemy's, your patron's, or your friend's household. Though aware of the intelligence services commanded by Walsingham and Burghley and of the competition among Calisiens – and others – to supply Thomas Cromwell with useful information, until these matter-of-fact accounts revealed how gentlemen, as distinct from professional politicians, managed their business affairs, I had never taken the full impact of Shakespeare's 'malice domestic' and Macbeth's

> There's not a one of them but in his house
> I keep a servant fee'd.

Daubeney was a sick man, of unstable temperament, and chronically in need of considerable sums of money. The only sensible course was to 'redeem' the Beaumont lands – to buy them, leaving him in possession for his lifetime but not as owner. For this they must know when his need of money would be great enough to induce or force him to sell.

1. i.e. 26 July.

12

Everyday Life in Calais
1536–1540

In February 1536, the Lisles moved from the house they had taken over from the former Lord Deputy to the very much larger building, one of the finest in Calais, which had previously been the Inn of the Staplers' Company and was still known by that name. From the inventory made in 1540 we can form a perfect picture of the setting of their daily life. There was a Great Chamber and a Great Parlour, 'my Lady's Dining Chamber,' 'my Lord's Chamber', and 'my Lady's Chamber', with 'little' chambers opening off my lord's room and my lady's dining chamber. After these main rooms there was 'the Grooms' Chamber to the Lord's ward', three *garde-robes,* a Counter or counting house, a nursery, 'the Gentlewomen's chamber', 'the Maidens' Chamber', three chambers allotted to named individuals and 'the next chamber', a chapel, and an armoury. There were also all the necessary domestic offices of the typical great household of the sixteenth century – kitchen, ewery, buttery, pantry, storehouse, chaundry, stilling-house, bake-house, spicery, cellar, vault, garner, poultry, fish-loft, and laundry. Wine was stored in the cellar, salt in the vault, wax and tallow in the chaundry, the winter's fish supply in the loft. There were also stables, obviously more than adequate to the normal requirements of the household. When Lisle's establishment was dissolved, fifty men servants and six others – three of them women – were dismissed by the Commissioners, but this list omits three chaplains and members of his personal retinue whom we know were resident, like Edward Corbett, for example, who had his own servant, and Clement Philpot and John Woller. Besides these we must include Lady Lisle and several waiting gentlewomen, her daughers Philippa and Mary, Lisle's daughter Frances before her marriage, and after it, for a time, her husband John Basset, apart from casual visitors of all kinds and of varying degrees of eminence, some of them accompanied by servants and secretaries. At times seventy or more persons must have been housed there, though where those who were not guests slept and ate remains a mystery. Vast quantities of sheets and bedding were listed, a bed of down and two down pillows for Lisle but a feather bed and bolster for her ladyship; eighty-eight diaper napkins, thirty-four fine damask napkins, eighteen plain and five damask table-cloths, five carving towels, and 'arming' towels for the washing of hands at the table.

Like most early sixteenth-century homes it was sparsely equipped with furniture, but the modern Tudor comfort that could be looked for in such a household was well supplied by an abundance of cushions of all shapes, sizes and kinds, and hangings, curtains, tapestries, and carpets – these last nearly all for display on tables or cupboards. The chief rooms were all hung with tapestry. In each of the main rooms there was one chair for the master or mistress or honoured guest, but except in 'My Lady's Chamber' there were surprisingly few stools or forms for the rest of the company. In the Dining Chamber there were two tables, a short trestle and a long one, a chair, a form, six joint stools and a cupboard with a carpet. The chair was covered with crimson velvet, as were a number of the stools in other rooms – which does not mean that they were upholstered. The nine little stools in my Lady's Chamber were variously covered in cloth of tissue, tynsen, crimson satin, crimson velvet, 'needlework with crewel' and 'red cloth embroidered'.

To return to the letters: in the small, closed society of Calais, the arrival of a new member was an important event. Thomas Leygh was a prominent merchant, about to bring home a new wife and laying the groundwork for her reception.

194   THOMAS LEYGH TO LADY LISLE   *13 March 1536*

Right honourable and my singular good Lady, This shall be to advertise your Ladyship that your letter of the vj day of this present month I have received, and perceive by the same, although your ladyship have half a good quarrel to me, by reason I have not advertised you of my marriage nor sent you token nor letter since my coming from Calais, yet your ladyship will not fall out with me for that matter, wherefore I thank your good Ladyship. And the truth is, that I had so good confidence in you that I knew well, albeit that I was so[me]what slothful in doing my duty to your Ladyship, that you of ∧your∧ goodness would right well consider my busyness that I have had of late and to pardon me of never doing my duty. Howbeit, good madame, touching of my marriage, it is of so small a value that I did not only forbear the writing thereof to your Ladyship but also to all other of my friends. And in case I had not liked my wife better than the substance that I had with her I assure you I had returned unmarried again to Calais. And further, your Ladyship shall understand that since my coming from Calais I have received one letter and one small ring from you, for the which I heartily thank you; and other rings nor tokens I have not received as yet. Praying you, madame, to present my most humble recommendations unto my Lord Lysle, my very especial and good Lord. And good madame: thus I bid you most heartily farewell, beseeching Our Lord ever to preserve your ladyship in honour, and send you your heart's desire.

In haste from London, the xiij day of March 1535.

　　　　　　　　by yo*ur* assuryd ser*ua*nt at co*mm*andm*ent*,

Hol.　　　　　　　Thomas Leygh　　　　　　　　　(Vol.3, No.652)

For over a year Lady Lisle had been awaiting a promised gift of a kirtle 'of the Queen's livery' from the Wardrobe, and in the next letter we have a glimpse behind the scenes at Court, and also of the operation of the system of gifts so essential to the economics of society. Mistress Margery Horsman, one of the Queen's gentlewomen, was always a good friend to the Lisles.

195　　THOMAS WARLEY TO LADY LISLE　　　　　*18 March 1536*

My duty most humbly presupposed, pleaseth it your good ladyship to be advertised that I have been attendant at the Court for the kirtle which your ladyship have long looked for. And so much I did that this day in the morning I had a token of Mistress Margery that the kirtle should be delivered to me in the Queen's Grace's Wardrobe, where upon sight of the said token I received the said kirtle, which is of cloth of gold paned, as this other paper here enclosed maketh proportion of, which I did draw out as nigh as I could to the fashion of the cloth of gold. And because Mr. Blunt shewed me of his short departing from hence, and to the intent that he might certify your good ladyship of the same, I shewed to him one of the sleeves of the said kirtle, which is all like etc. After I had received the kirtle I returned to the Queen's chamber to give thanks to Mistress Margery, and to know if she would anything to your ladyship, which as then was returned into the Privy Chamber, so that since I could not speak to her. But, God willing, I intend to be at ∧the∧ Court ∧to-morrow∧, and by the next I know come to Calais I will certify your ladyship what she saith to me, desiring your good ladyship that I may know your pleasure what I shall do with the kirtle; for I dare not be so bold to send it till I know your ladyship's pleasure, ∧and by whom∧: which known, I shall be glad to accomplish the same with all diligence. And if it may please your ladyship to send a letter to Mistress Margery and another to Mr. George Taylor, giving them thanks for their pains, as your ladyship knows better what is to be done than my simpleness can advertise you; if the said letters come to my hands I will not slack the delivery of them. Also, that it may please your ladyship to remember them of the Queen's Wardrobe as shall be your pleasure. . . .

　　written at london the xviij day of m*ar*che

　　　　　　by yo*ur* moste bounden ser*ua*nt to his poer

Hol.　　　　　　Thomas warley　　　　　　　　　(Vol.3, No.658)

196   DAN NICHOLAS CLEMENT TO LADY LISLE   *30 April 1536*

Right honourable and my special good lady, my duty presupposed, I, your daily bedeman, Dan Nicholas Clement, Monk of Christ Church in Canterbury, have me heartily commended unto you, my lord your bedfellow, with all yours, trusting unto Almighty God that you be in prosperity and welfare.

The cause of my writing at this time, is desiring you of your charity to be good lady and to show favour unto a singing child that I have sent unto my lord your bedfellow, pleaseth him of his goodness to take him; the which cometh of an honest stock, and hath besides that many good qualities, as I have informed my lord by writing; trusting through your good word the better I shall obtain of my lord that he may retain with him.

I am very sorry at heart that I have no good thing able to present unto you at this time; but nevertheless I have sent unto you by this child a beast, the creature of God, sometime wild, but now tame, to comfort your heart at such time as you be weary of praying.

No more unto you at this time, but Jesu for his bitter passion preserve you, my lord, with all yours, Amen. Written the last day of April.
?Hol.   (Vol. 3, No. 688)

197   JOHN HUSEE TO LORD LISLE   *27 November 1536*

Pleaseth it your lordship to be advertised that I have received your sundry letters by Warley and Fisher. . . .

Within this vj day we shall hear more out of the North than is yet knowen, whereof your lordship shall be certified. It will not be a little comfort unto all your lordship's friends when they shall hear how my lady hath sped. I pray God send her ladyship a good and fortunate hour, and therewith a son, if it be his pleasure, that that name survive and spring anew, which would make many joyful hearts, as God knoweth, who send your lordship long life with much honour.

From London, the xxvij[th] of November by
          Your lordship's bounden during life,
Hol.   John Husee   (Vol. 3, No. 786)

This letter gives us the first reference in the correspondence to the hoped-for child, preparations for whose birth were to keep Husee so busy in the early months of 1537 trying to borrow or buy all the appurtenances for the lying-in of a noble lady which contemporary protocol decreed as necessary. On the evidence of the letters of congratulation, which began to come in about the middle of December, it would appear that Honor Lisle confided her good news to her devoted Husee a fortnight before it was officially circulated among their friends. By the 15th he was obviously announcing it to everyone he met.

It was probably Husee's inability in the current hard times to obtain goods in London without ready money, especially from long-standing creditors, which he constantly laments, that gave rise to rumours of Honor's displeasure that he seems to have heard just before signing his next letter.

198   JOHN HUSEE TO LADY LISLE   5 December 1536

Pleaseth it your ladyship to be advertised that according unto your commandment I have been with Christopher Campion and have taken of him x yards tawny damask, which is very good; but he will have no less than vij^s and vj^d the yard, so that the whole sum is iiij^{li} xv^s whereof I have made him a bill and am bound for the payment in May next, as I am for the rest; and have delivered the same unto Ric. Harrys. . . .

Further, touching such money as your ladyship will send me, I had never more need of it. Your ladyship hath reckoning thereof long since. Also there is a gentlewoman which is a maiden and unmarried, that lately dwelled with my Lady Waldon, and is of xxx years, a good needlewoman, and also she can embroider very well, and will be content to wash and brush and do anything else that your ladyship will put her to. She demandeth xl s. and a livery. If it be your ladyship's pleasure to have her, she would gladly serve you.

And thus I beseech Jesu send your ladyship long life with much honour and a most prosperous and fortunate hour.

From London, the vth day of December.

Madame, I am informed by divers that your ladyship is heavy Lady unto me. I am therefore right sorry, considering I have not the same demerited, as I do verily trust; notwithstanding it is not a little grief unto my stomach. I think I was born in an unfortunate hour. Notwithstanding, if I have offended your ladyship in anything I am always ready to take such penance for the amends, in recovering your ladyship's good favour, as your ladyship shall will[1] enjoin me. Yet always trusting your ladyship will be my good Lady, or else I have served an ill saint.

> By him that will be your Ladyship's during life, whether your
> Ladyship will or no,

Hol.   John Husee   (Vol. 3, No. 794)

In spite of the tensions on the borders of the Pale during the war between France and the Empire, the Lisles kept up their delightful relations with their friends on both sides as the two following letters show. Ysabeau du Bies (Madame de Vervins) is a daughter of the Seneschal of Boulogne, and

---

1. wyll, meaning 'wish to'.

Ysabeau de Morbecque the daughter, or possibly wife, of the Captain of the Castle of Tournehem in Flanders.

199   YSABEAU DU BIES TO LADY LISLE   *6 December 1536*

Madame, I humbly recommend me to your good grace. Madame, my lord the Seneschal hath on his return made me a present of a little monkey, that knoweth all manner of pretty tricks. I send it to you by this present bearer, praying you, Madame, to accept this poor gift in good part. It grieveth me that it is not more worthy of the regard I have for you. My said lord, and my lady Seneschal, and Monsieur de Vervins have charged me recommend them to your good grace, beseeching you, Madame, in conclusion, to command me to what is your good pleasure that I may obey and do you service therein. Praying the Creator, Madame, to give you good life and long.

From Boulogne, the vj[th] of December,
Signed   Your humble servant,
                         Ysabeau du Bies   (Vol. 3, No. 797)

200   YSABEAU DE MORBECQUE TO LADY LISLE   *20 January 1537*

Madame, I most humbly recommend me to your good grace.

Madame, the bearer of this hath told that it hath pleased you to enquire of me, for the which I most humbly thank you, and also for the cramp ring and the codiniac that it hath pleased you to send me. And I send you a pentar upon which to hang your keys, the which I pray you to accept in gree.

Madame, thus I pray the Creator to grant you the accomplishment of all your virtuous and noble desires.

Written from Bourbour, the penultimate of January.
                         Ysabeau de Morbecque
Hol.   ready to do you service[2]   (Vol. 3, No. 797a)

The 'pentar' which she sends as a present (O.Fr. *pentoir*) means anything upon which to hang things, so that we can add to our imaginary portrait of Honor Lisle a chatelaine for the keys of the household presses and chests and the desk or cabinet in which she kept her letters.

201   JOHN HUSEE TO LADY LISLE   *11 December 1536*

Pleaseth it your Ladyship to be advertised that I received your letter sent by Mr. Marshal's servant. . . .

2. French.

. . . News here are none hitherto so good ne yet that so well liketh me as are those of your ladyship's, which hath so well sped in advancing the name of the noble Plantagenet. If I thought it should not be painful I would never cease praying unto God that your ladyship might have ij goodly sons, as I have full hope that God will show his ∧handi∧work, whose power excelleth all things, to whom I will not fail instantly desiring to send your ladyship a good, fortunate, and most prosperous hour, with long life and much honour. From London, the xj^th December.

By him that is your ladyship's and so will rest during life,
Hol.   John Husee   (Vol. 3, No. 798a)

202   WILLIAM LOK TO LORD LISLE

At London, the xiiij day of December 1536

My singular good Lord, I have me recommended to your good lordship and to my good lady, thanking you ever of your kindness. Sir, you shall receive by the bringer hereof, Mr. Corbett, a stomacher cloth of cloth-of-gold for my lady. I pray Jesu, if it be his pleasure, it may cover a young Lord Plantagenet, as I do understand by divers is well forward, of the which I am very glad, that knoweth Jesu, who preserve you to his pleasure.

By all yo*u*rs to hys powr
Hol.   Will*iam* Lok m*ercer*   (Vol. 3, No. 799)

203   SIR JOHN WALLOP TO LORD LISLE   *18 December 1536*

My Singular [good Lord], After my most hearty recommendations, heartily thanking you for your letter directed unto my Lord of Winchester and unto me, not being a little glad of your news concerning my lady's being with child; first, for both your sakes; secondly, my wife and I conceive great hope thereby, considering not to be so long married as you two, and either of us being younger, man for man, and woman for woman; trusting if we return once quietly to the Castle[3] such good fortune may ensue unto us, and so much the rather if your abode and my lady's may continue at Calais, which I somewhat have heard the contrary, trusting the same not to be true.

And against my lady's lying-in I have sent her two bottles of waters which I brought from Avignon, meet for that purpose, and specially when she draweth nigh the churching time. For she shall be so much the more readier by v or vj days, if she will use the virtue of the same, which is restreynetyve and draweth together like a purse. This secret I remit to your declaration.

3. The Castle of Calais, of which he was Lieutenant.

Furthermore, when a woman's breasts be long, it raiseth them higher and rounder, which peradventure shall be good for some of your neighbours! As for my lady, needeth not.

Your pretty son-in-law,[4] now being here arrived, is the jolliest and wisest that I have seen. My wife and I take great pleasure to hear him so speak, ∧and speaking French∧; and what pleasure we may do to him for your sakes ∧we∧ shall be always most readiest.

All the news I had I sent you by Richard Bird, my servant. And thus fare ye well.

At Paris the xviij[th] of December.

        Yours assuredly,

Signed   John Wallop   (Vol. 3, No. 809)

For the marriage of John Basset and Frances Plantagenet in the Lisles' private chapel all the finery for the bride as well as the groom was bought in England by Husee, although he complained that it would be cheaper in Flanders, probably because it had to be obtained on credit, and it would hardly have been seemly for the Lord Deputy to run up debts just across the border. Husee had even checked on suitable gifts from the groom's mother to the guests: 'My Lady Rutland saith that your ladyship shall need give nothing but gloves.'[5]

204   JOHN HUSEE TO LADY LISLE   *6 February 1538*

Pleaseth it your ladyship ∧to be advertised∧ that by this bearer you shall receive all such apparel ready made accordingly as he came for, made by the tailor's advice according unto your writing. What we had ado with it I remit it unto his relation! And more speed could not have been done therein if the matter had been for our lives. I trust it shall serve the purpose, and come in season, or else I would be right sorry. As yet Coserors hath not delivered the bill of parcels and prices, but your ladyship shall have the same with the next that cometh. Further I do send by him the bonnets and frontlets, which I trust will like your ladyship right ∧well∧. The bill of their prices shall also be sent by the next. I had them of Mrs. Wylkenson, with much ado, because Mrs. Hutton hath not paid her for the last. Also your ladyship shall more receive j ounce iij qtr. of goldsmith's work, with a chain in the same weight, which I had of Mrs. Whalley, and is for to trim Mr. Basset's cap. If your ladyship like them not she is content to take it again. Her price is xlv shillings the ounce.

---

4. James Basset.   5. Vol. 4, No. 858.

I do further send ij pair of clasps, whereof I have caused iij to be new made, and the other new annealed. Mrs. Whalley had liefer have a hogshead wine than a barrel herring. The velvet gown was a'furring ere your last letter came, and as James and Larke can tell, the tailor would have none other fur to the same but luysars[6] and what I have had ado to get them this bearer can tell. And where your ladyship wrote, if it had not been done, to have the same furred with budge, although it had been iiij or v^{li} better cheap yet had it been nothing comely. It had been too ancient for a young gentleman. I have had no time to provide his cap, for where I thought assuredly ∧to∧ have had the same trimmed ready at ∧William∧ Taylor's, when I came for it Larke can tell how he handled me and disappointed me. Your ladyship's honour reserved, he is the veriest knave that ever I met withal, and I put Larke to be judge. But I shall not fail with the next that goeth to send both cap and feather, and all other bills and reckonings, as of tailors and skins. As for Tonge's bill, James hath it with him, and also the licence to marry with once asking. I pray God send me little ado with any spiritual men!

I have seen the front or edge of diamonds. They are all tables,[7] and are xx in number. My Lady Rutland hath seen them, and he will bate no penny of lx^{li}. The uttermost that they are worth is xlv^{li}; and they are not Gerard's of Exeter, but this Gerard of London owns them.

And as for venison, Sir John Dudley hath promised to send iij or iiij does to Dover to Justyce's house. And I do send one warrant which I caused Palmer to get of my Lord Clynton at Folkestone, which is within v mile of Dover. And I trust you shall have some out of Hampshire. . . .

From London, the vjth of February, when I had more will to sleep than write.

> Your ladyship's own man,
>
> *Hol.*   John Husee   (Vol. 4, No. 859)

205   JOHN HUSEE TO LADY LISLE   *10 February 1538*

Pleaseth it your ladyship to be advertised that with this bearer I do send iij does which came out of Hampshire. And I trust ere this time the iij does which Mr. Dudley sent are at Calais, and also the warrant served in my Lord Clynton's park. And another I will send with the first, to be served in Mr. Poynyngs' park. and also by Swift I sent a cap with a white feather in a cap-case for Mr. Basset, which I trust is there ere this time. I cannot yet get the reckoning of Cosers, but on Tuesday he promised me that I shall have it

---

6. i.e. luzernes = lucern = lynx.

7. i.e. cut with a flat top, surrounded by small facets; and, especially, thin diamonds with no facetting on the underside.

without fail, and immediately I shall send your ladyship the same, with all the rest. Mr. Popley lent me xx nobles, whereof I think he doth owe the best part for his rent, which I paid for the furring of Mr. Basset's gown, as your ladyship shall perceive all things plain by my next letter.

There is no man so sorry as I because I cannot be there; but surely, madam, if Mr. Bonham had not 'pointed to be here on Tuesday next, all things set apart, I would not a'failed to have come over. But I know that my lord needeth money, therefore the sooner the matter were ended the more were my lord's profit. . . .

. . . as God knoweth, who send your ladyship long life and much honour.

From London, in most haste, the xth day of February.

> Your ladyship's own man,

Hol.   John Husee   (Vol. 4, No. 860)

206   OUDART DU BIES TO LORD LISLE   *14 February 1538*

The Lord Oudart du Bies, lord of that said place and Knight of the Order, Councillor and Chamberlain, by the King's ordinance Seneschal and Governor of Boulogne, Captain of the town and [castle] of Boulogne, and also Captain of fifty [   ] of the said lord

By these presents, on behalf of my Lord the Governor and Deputy of Calais, we give licence, permission and privilege that his servant or servants or agents may hunt partridges throughout the country in my governance until Lent, to provide for the banquet of his daugher that he is marrying. It is forbidden to all those being under our charge and governance to do any such hunting, or to do or suffer to be done any hindrance or impeachment, on pain of disobedience to us. Given at Boulogne under our hand, the xiiijth day of February, 1537.

Signed   Oudart du Bies[8]   (Vol. 4, No. 860a)

While the Basset wedding went off to everyone's content, Lady Lisle was already engaged on the business of borrowing and buying what was required for the birth of the expected Plantagenet heir. A confinement and a christening were great occasions, and custom decreed that the bedroom in which the child was to be born should be dressed with the richest hangings that could be procured. It was taken for granted amongst friends and relations that such things should be freely lent and borrowed. Those who were highly placed, or sufficiently in favour at court, might even hope to put the royal Wardrobe under contribution.

---

8. French.

207   JOHN HUSEE TO LADY LISLE   *17 February 1537*

Pleaseth it your Ladyship to be advertised that I have received your sundry letters. And first touching such stuff as my Lady Rutland promised, this day Kyne is appointed to see it, and now she saith that she can help your ladyship but with one bed. So that as far as I can hear, there will be therein no help. Madam, they maketh here many promises, and when it cometh to the performance, faileth, as those of the Wardrobe and Closet hath done, of whom there is nothing to be had. But I think of my Lady Rutland your ladyship shall have all things that was written in the bill I sent last, the ∧bed∧ reserved. And in all others my fellow Kyne and I will do as much as we can for our lives; and of all things by the next your ladyship shall know the certainty. And Madam, what was spoken unto Mr. Kingston I spake of my own head, for because the Lord Chamberlain is not here he may command in the Wardrobe. My request was for vj pieces of tapestry, and vj carpets. Whether I shall have them or no I cannot yet tell. I will do the best I can. Also I have spoken unto my Lady of Sussex for a pane. She hath promised to do her best in it. . . .

Madam, your caps of ermines are almost ready, and my fellow Kyne would know what your ladyship will do for waistcoats.[9] They useth them here of white satin or damask, edged with ermine. And as for a cradle, I do perceive that Popley will give your ladyship one ready trimmed, but this must be kept secret till it come. Further, Goodall spake to me for a nightgown of damask. I would know your ladyship's pleasure with the next, what price you will have it of, and whether it shall be guarded with Lucca velvet or no, and what fur that your ladyship would have. Goodall shewed me it was lamb. I am sure your ladyship will wear none. Therefore knowing your pleasure herein, I will do my best to follow it. . . .

. . . And where your ladyship saith that I have good inspeculation to know that your ladyship hath a man child, I would God I were so sure of a m^l li a year as that is true, and then should I live merrily.

And thus I beseech Jesu to send your ladyship long life and much honour, and when time shall be to make the same a glad mother.

From London the xvijth of February.

                   By your ladyship's own man while he liveth, and that bounden,
Hol.   John Husee   (Vol. 4, No. 867)

208   JOHN HUSEE TO LADY LISLE   *23 February 1537*

Pleaseth it your Ladyship. . . .

. . . And as for the order had at christening of the Lady Beauchamp's child,

---

9. The nightgowns and waistcoats were informal, indoor wear, or *négligé.*

I reserve it solely unto this bearer who I know well can do much better than anything was there done.

I have made diligent suit unto my Lady of Sussex, in so much that this day she hath made me grant that your ladyship shall have of her a rich pane for the bed, of ermines bordered with cloth of gold, and a sheet of lawn to cover the same; and more, i or ij pairs of fine paned sheets and a travers, and this is all that she hath promised, and this shall be delivered me xx days hence, for I think the Lady Beauchamp useth part of it, and the rest is in the country. Knowing your ladyship's pleasure, when time shall be, I will reserve it. Also Mr. Kingston hath promised, if George Rolles will answer for the same, we shall have out of the Wardrobe vj pieces arras, and certain carpets, and if need be, a cloth of state. In this I would know your pleasure for this is done of my own head.

My Lady Beauchamp's child was christened in the chapel at Chester Place, and had, I think, the font of the King's chapel. I have shewed my fellow Kyne my mind in this matter. If your ladyship be minded, when God shall ∧send∧ your son, to have him christened in the chapel at the Staple,[10] I think there might be gotten, with my lord's letter, a font at Canterbury, and for need such pieces of arras as shall lack. When this bearer hath declared unto your ladyship his advice, then it shall be in your ladyship to have choice. And touching the ermine bonnets, they are promised to be finished within this x days. He will have ready money. And touching the nightgown, if I knew your ladyship's mind what stuff and of what price to take, I know the best fashion thereof. . . .

. . . And as I shall hear always from henceforth write your ladyship from time to time how I speed in all your affairs, as God knoweth, who send your ladyship long life with much honour, and when time shall be a good, most fortunate and prosperous hour.

From London, the xxiij^th of February, in haste.

        By your ladyship's own man bounden,

Hol.   John Husee   (Vol. 4, No. 868a)

John Hutton was the English agent in Flanders, and the Governor of the Merchant Adventurers.

209   John Hutton to Lady Lisle   *2 March 1537*

Madam, As well the knowledge of your noble heart and most gentle request by writing doth embold me to write unto your ladyship, thinking myself that I should be present with you talking: but when my whole is at an

---

10. Now the Lisles' house.

end, albeit that I am patiently heard, yet the grief is that the answer is absent, so that there is no commodity but only he that talketh alone may say what he will, and so do I; for I have none other matter unto your ladyship but to devise what I may write to cause your ladyship to be merry, and to forget all fantasies by days. As for the nights, my good lord will keep you waking, as I do my wife, whom I sometime make as weary as though she hath watchéd a span.

It may please your ladyship to certify Mr. Surveyor that I do look for answer of your letter and such other as I have written unto him together, for I intend not to bestow any more labour upon him till I hear from him. I trust shortly to be with you at Calais, against which time it may please you to prepare white money[11] that we may play at gleek, for I would gladly be revenged.

To write your ladyship of any news, here is none but all concerning war, which [is] no great pleasure to ladies, wherefore I purpose not to trouble you there with. It may please your ladyship to recommend me to your little boy in your belly, the which I pray God to send into your arms to your comfort and my lord's. And this farewell, my good lady, with much honour and long health. Written this ij[nd] day of March, in Barough,[12] By the hand of him that is all yours to the uttermost of his power,

Hol.   John Hutton   (Vol. 4, No. 869)

Lady Lisle was proving very difficult to please nowadays, and poor Husee writes on 2 April:

> Madam, touching your nightgown and your waistcoats [they] are even in every point made as my Lady Beauchamp's; and it is the very fashion that the Queen and all the ladies doth wear, and so were the caps. But yet I have caused that your ladyship sent me to be new made, which I do send in a box, with such a past as they do now use to wear. Divers of the ladies hath their nightgowns embroidered, some with gold and some with silk.[13]

A 'past' was a decorated border, in some rich material, often ornamented with pearls, precious stones, or goldsmith's work, worn round the front of the French hood, and edged with fine, transparent, goffered lawn.

It would appear that Honor Lisle 'took her chamber' sometime in June.

210   JOHN HUSEE TO LADY LISLE   *23 August 1537*

Pleaseth it your ladyship to be advertised that I have received your sundry letters, greatly to my discomfort to perceive and see that your ladyship

---

11. i.e. silver coins.   13. Vol. 4, No. 872.
12. i.e. Bergen op Zoom.

should take such ways of lamentation and sorrows (and causeless), as my full trust in God is, for your ladyship is not the first woman ∧of honour∧ that hath overshot or mistaken your time and reckoning. But I doubt not but your ladyship, by the grace of God, ∧shall∧ speed as well as ever you have done time ∧past∧; and therefore good madam, in the honour of God, be not so faint hearted, ne mistrust not yourself. For I hope assuredly all is for the best; but I admit that it might chance otherwise (which God forbid), yet should not your ladyship take it so earnestly, but refer all unto God. For where his pleasure is, he will approve and feel faithful hearts, having full confidence in his mercy, which excelleth all worldly judgment. And yet, though your ladyship should chance to miss of your purpose, you should not be the first noble woman that hath been so by God's work visited. For if it be his pleasure he spareth neither Empress, Queen, Princess ne Duchess, but his handiwork must be suffered and his mercy abiden; and whatsoever is said or thought by any creature, God's works cannot be withstand.

Your ladyship can exhort and give others virtuous and good counsel, and now should it best appear in your own person, which both by your ladyship's writing and saying of others approveth for this time contrary. For I have heard of divers that your ladyship weepeth and sorroweth without comparison, which I assure your ladyship grieved me no less than it were my own mother. Therefore good madam, put your whole trust in God, and leave these sorrows, for he will never disdain you. And now it were very requisite that your ladyship did show in your own person and gesture that hope and confidence which your ladyship is wont to exhort and animate other unto, to the end that it may not only be said hereafter that your ladyship doth not only counsel and exhort others to that thing that you cannot observe yourself and utter by outward gesture, but rather that your ladyship did even show the same in your own doings and proceedings that you exhort and counsel others unto. And thus, madam, I am bold to write your ladyship my poor mind, even as he that would you should do no worse than the mother that bare him; and for a truth, madam, there is a woman which took her rights, and reckoned to be delivered before Whitsuntide, which was delivered of a fair daughter within this vj days, therefore I had liever die than your ladyship should despair in yourself. . . .

. . . The signing of my Lord's bill[14] hath not been to me so much comfort as the sorrows your ladyship doth take hath been and are discomfort, as God best knoweth, who send your ladyship long life and much honour, and a most fortunate hour when his pleasure shall be.

From St. Katharine's the xxiij[th] of August.

By your ladyship's own man,

Hol.   John Husee   (Vol. 4, No. 893)

14. For Frithelstock Priory.

If Husee had suspicions of the truth he lets no breath of it escape him, nor, as far as the correspondence tells us, did anyone else; so that, like the unfortunate Queen Mary Tudor after her, Honor Lisle must have continued to cherish her pathetic delusion for weeks, even months, after all real hopes had vanished. On 2 September Husee wishes her 'shortly to be rid out of your pain', and that is the last we hear of the Plantagenet heir. There has survived an undated note[15] to her from a Dr. Le Coop of Paris, who appears to have visited her at about this time. It is a dietary, and in so far as it contains any diagnosis would seem to refer specifically to a phantom pregnancy. We are left to realize from others, dealing with the return of the stuff borrowed from Lady Sussex and Lady Rutland, that all hopes were at an end. If they were ever written, no letters of sympathy have been preserved; but equally the silence of the many friends who had originally been so outspoken in their congratulations, or the destruction of such letters by one who otherwise appears to have destroyed none in seven years, will serve to give us the measure of this personal tragedy.

211   ANTHOINETTE DE SAVEUSES   *after mid-August 1537*
        TO LADY LISLE

                        Jeshus   Marie

Madame, my Lady Deputy, as humbly as I may I recommend me effectually to your good grace, humbly beseeching you, Madame, to be recommended to the good grace of my Lord Deputy. . . .

Madame, some time ago I had a fine piece of the tip of a unicorn's horn that was given me by a great lady, of the which I was very careful on account of the property that the said unicorn doth possess, and of the which I was very jealous when I perceived that by great mischance I had lost it. I was required to lend it to a sick person, the which, when for good friendship I had so done, when I required it of her again I could not recover it, and hath given me answer that she hath been robbed of it. But this little piece was given to me to be mounted. Madame, I have here in this town no jeweller, wherefore I beg of you to enquire if this piece of unicorn's horn can be set, and of your grace, Madame, you will do me a singular pleasure: praying God, Madame, to grant you your desires the which with good discretion you may ask of him.

From Dunkirk, by your humble bedeswoman and good friend. . . .
Hol.   Seur Anthoenette de Saueuses[16]   (Vol.3, No.604)

On 10 September she writes:

I have been much rejoiced to know that the little piece of unicorn's horn

15. Vol.4, No.898.   16. French.

is good, and methinketh, Madame, it might be enchased in silver in a kind of button to the which one attaches a little chain of goldsmith's work, and at your pleasure it will do you much good. And if you have no such thing I beseech you, Madame, keep it for yourself, and you will do me much pleasure.[17]

The tip of unicorn's horn was clearly the gift from a good friend of something she valued to a sick and unhappy lady, but most of those so frequently mentioned in the Letters tend to be the recognized method of paying for services rendered, or given in the hope of benefits to come. Where money would smell of bribery, a horse or a hawk, a side of venison or a baked crane, puffins, or sprats in Lent – all were as seemly as they were practical. But Lisle's gift to the Lord Admiral next described is part of an elaborate deal whereby the latter shall have hunting rights in a 'walk' (one forester's patrol area), pay the forester, and supply Lisle occasionally with venison. Lisle's choice of a gift is clearly his idea of just what an Admiral would want. On 25 July Husee wrote: 'As for the seal, when it cometh I will keep it till my Lord Admiral hath knowledge; and immediately as I hear from your lordship I intend to ride to my Lord Admiral myself. And I trust to procure that your lordship shall have venison ere it be long.' In his mammoth letter of 21 August, the rest of which will be found as No. 262 below, he wrote of the reception of this gift:

> . . . touching my Lord Admiral, he hath him commended most heartily unto your lordship, and thanketh you for the seal. And his lordship saith that he will send your lordship venison shortly. Your lordship shall understand that I kept the seal here at Wapping v weeks and more, for none of my Lord Admiral's men would receive her. She spent me some day in fish vj^d, and yet she had not dined. I could never speak with my Lord Admiral till the King came to Grafton, and there I delivered him your letter. And when his lordship had read the same he said it required no answer, and how that he wist not where to keep the seal, but desired me at my coming to London to kill it and deliver it to Osburne his man and cause him to bake it and send the same to my Lady his wife, and so it is done. I perceive he will keep nothing that shall put him to cost. Further, he willed me to write unto your lordship that he liketh Ralph Rigsby very well, and his lordship is informed that his walk is in good case, but that which Russell hath is nothing like, so that I perceive unless that he may have the oversight of the whole forest he would not gladly meddle, for he will surely have Russell out. I shewed him that your lordship had the whole forest, and that that which my Lord Montague had was but by your lordship's sufferance. It shall therefore please your lordship to write me what answer

17. Vol. 3, No. 605. French.

I shall make him, and whether that he shall have the whole or no, and whether your lordship hath authority of the whole forest or no. For surely, if he have the whole, he will put Russell out. In any wise this must be answered with speed.

Poor Husee, whose own salary as a member of the Calais Retinue was only 8 *d.* a day!
J. de Morbecque is the Captain of Tournehem, in Flanders.

212   J. DE MORBECQUE TO LORD LISLE   *30 December 1537*

My lord, I heartily recommend me to your good grace.

My lord, may it please you to know that yesterday I was at the hunting where there was slain a fine black boar, of the which I send you the head, praying you to accept it in good part. So it is, I have now been for sometime with my Lord de Beures, my master, in Zealand, and if it had not been for this, I would have hoped to serve you in better sort. Further assuring you, my lord, that if there is any pleasure that I can do for you, you shall find me ready: as knoweth the Creator to whom I pray, my Lord, to grant you his holy grace.

From Tournehem, the penultimate day of December,
        by him that will gladly do you pleasure and service
        J. de Morbecque

My lord, I would beg of you that it might please you to procure for me two mastiffs from England and a great dog and I will the more often send you proof of their prowess, what they can do.[18]   (Vol. 4, No. 1041)

Throughout the Letters, interspersed among subjects of importance we find passing allusions from Husee to supplies of every kind that he is sending or trying to obtain for the household in Calais, or is providing for the younger members of the family in England. On matters of dress and fashion he is an expert. Increasingly there is the problem of tradesmen who demand ready money, which occasionally has to be found out of Husee's own pocket. The allusion in the next letter to the Abbot's wine is part of the interminable saga of satisfying that cleric for a debt which Lisle maintains was paid long ago.

213   JOHN HUSEE TO LADY LISLE   *18 May 1538*

Pleaseth your Ladyship to be advertised that by Vernham I sent you the ij pieces sayes. And yet your glasses be not come, but as soon as they come Lawden will see them conveyed. If I have not the traverse against Whitsun-

18. French.

tide I will never speak more for it. The old damask gown your ladyship sent will never be good tawny: it will take a good black. I would with the first gladly know your pleasure in this behalf, for it shall not be dyed till I hear again from your ladyship.

Madam, the Abbot of Westminster will not meddle with the wine my lord sent, so that I have 'pointed his cooper to choose ij tun of wine where he will, and I will pay for it. I pray God never let me have ado with moe monks, for I am too much weary of this. I assure your ladyship the ij pieces wine my Lord sent for his own store is very good, but the other iiij hogsheads are but easy. I have caused them to be conveyed unto Blagg's cellar, your grocer, and there to be new hooped and filled till I may know further of my lord's pleasure, what shall be done with it. . . .

Madam, this matter that I now do move must be kept secret. So it is that I have been enquired of what your ladyship will give with Mrs. Katharine's marriage; and I could not make direct answer, but I thought and said iij$C$ marks. But if your ladyship will find means to make it vC marks I think not the contrary but she shall have an heir which shall spend a m^l marks by year. And I might know your ladyship's full mind I would write further in it. Howbeit, to be plain with your ladyship, I think that money would make her wife to Sir Edward Baynton's son and heir. But this is under Benedicite.[19] I would partly know your mind herein with the first. As God knoweth, who send your ladyship long life and much honour.

From London, the xviijth day of May.

> Your own man bounden,

Hol.   John Husee   (Vol. 5, No. 1164a)

Nothing came of this suggestion.

Dr. Thirlby, Archdeacon of Ely and later Bishop of Westminster, had been with Bishop Gardiner of Winchester and Sir Francis Bryan on their abortive mission to find a French royal bride for the King, and had been lavishly entertained at Calais on their way home. Alas, his reply to the next letter has not survived.

214   LADY LISLE TO ARCHDEACON   *1 October 1538*
        THOMAS THIRLBY

Right worshipful Sir, In my most hearty manner I commend me unto you, thanking you for the great pains that you took when you were here. I was not so glad for your fair passage but I was as sorry for your departing, and that you would tarry no longer at my desire; but my Lord of Winchester and you will do nothing after a woman's advice. I thought surely your horses were not

---

19. i.e. under invocation of a blessing, or as we might say, 'if we are fortunate', 'with luck'.

yet ∧then∧ come. Better it had been your horses had tarried for you, than you had tarried for them. I think verily it was because you were weary here, your cheer was so evil; yet you had it with a good heart. Sir, these shall be to desire you to be so good unto your servant and worst scholar as to write unto me of the thing that you taught me, how many pound of sugar must go to how many pounds of quinces, barberries, and damsons or plums. I have clean forgotten how many pounds of the one and of the other. Now the time of quinces is come, I would fain be doing. It may please you, therefore, to write to me of all this, and of anything more that it will please you to teach me. And thus I shall ever remain your poor scholar, praying our Lord send you your gentle heart's desire.

From Calais, the first day of October.

By your ever assured servant,

Signed   Honor Lyssle   (Vol.5, No.1237)

References to plays and interludes, whether scriptural or secular, are of sufficient rarity in this reign to make two allusions to them from Husee to Lady Lisle of interest to the student of drama, apart from the glimpse they give of social life in Calais. On 3 October he writes:

> And according unto your Ladyship's writing I will be in hand with Felsted, silk dyer, for the players' garments, and also to procure to get some good matter for them. But these new ecclesiastical matters will be hard to come by. Howbeit, I will do as much as lieth in me for the obtainment of them.[20]

By 5 October he has completed the commission:

> I have been with Felsted, and given him earnest for a suit of players garments, which he will keep for you, and an interlude which is called Rex Diabole. Sparke knoweth the matter. I will do my best to get some of these new Scripture matters, but they be very dear; they asketh above xx[s] for an Interlude.[21]

Madame de Bours, Mary Basset's sometime hostess, keeps constantly in touch, and there is usually news of her son Montmorency, and compliments to Mary.

215   MADAME DE BOURS TO LADY LISLE   *13 October 1538*

Madame, The commencement of this present letter shall be to beseech you to pardon me that I have not been able for such a long time to make my

---

20. Vol.5, No.1241.   21. Vol.5, No.1242.

recommendations to you. I am waiting to send you the two goshawks for which you wrote me. I have been able to procure but one, the which hath still an injury to its leg. I understand that there is a certain gentleman who hath made promise to Monsieur de Riou to send a couple to my Lord. It is now six weeks since Montmorency went to the Court. I have required him to take pains to procure them if he could, for me to send you. For the most part of this time I have been continuously away from home, for love of one of my brothers who hath been ill, and whom it hath pleased God to take to himself some fifteen days ago. Ever since my return hither I have been acrased, and do not yet find myself strong enough to be able to write you a longer letter. I beseech you to be so good as to make me partaker at large of your news. By your last letters you tell me that Mademoiselle my good daughter[22] hath been sore sick for a long time and yet is. I am greatly desirous to know how she doth at this present. Madame, after being most humbly recommended to the good grace of my Lord and you, I pray Our Lord to grant you good life and long.

From Bours, this xiij day of October.

Ever most ready to do you service,

Signed   Anne Rouaud

Madame, There is a great personage of this realm who hath prayed me to obtain for him a large English greyhound. I beseech you to do me this favour to procure for me one that will be very good. This is the desire of your very good friend.[23]   (Vol.5, No.1250)

There is a constant interchange across the Channel of food of all kinds, from Calais usually in the form of birds (as well as those for sport), and from England usually of venison. Thus in a business letter from London to her husband, on 28 November Lady Lisle writes:

... most heartily thanking you for your partridges and the baked hare, which I this day received from you, with your two letters. . . . I do send you by Vernam, packed in a barrel, ij does.[24]

On 18 February 1539, Madame de Bours writes to Lady Lisle:

Five days ago I sent you my news by a messenger that Montmorency sent to you. It is a long time, now, since I have seen him. He never moveth from the Court. We expect the King presently at Abbeville.[25]

She writes again on the 23rd:

Madame, Montmorency is returned from Court some time ago, and

22. Mary Basset.   24. Vol.5, No.1290.
23. French.   25. Vol.5, No.1352.

being desirous this long time for tidings of you I send you his lackey to learn your news, beseeching you to take pains to advertise me.[26]

Surely the lackey carried also a note to Mary from his master? It would seem the latter may have visited Calais, for though his mother has not mentioned his health or spirits, Lady Lisle writes at the end of the month:

Of Monsieur your son, who hath returned from the Court merry and in good health, I well perceive you have great comfort; assuring you, madame, that I am as glad thereof as any woman in the world.[27]

The developing relationship between Mary Basset and Gabrielle de Bours, Sieur de Montmorency, is at this stage only part of the domestic background; but it later will become part of the central drama of the Lisles, when we learn what became of letters between them that are missing.

While it has proved possible to exclude some dozen letters from Sœur Anthoinette de Saveuses about the provision of caps for both men and women, and for both day and night, made by her nuns at Dunkirk, the following lines from Husee on 30 September 1539 are irresistible:

I shall according unto your ladyship's writing cause a kirtle to be made for Mrs. Honor and also a lettice bonnet.[28]

Mistress Honor was the daughter of John and Frances Basset, now nearly five months old and therefore out of swaddling clouts and ready to be dressed like any other Tudor lady. Lettice was a whitish-grey fur.

216   ANTHOINETTE DE SAVEUSES   [n.d.] November–December 1539
       TO LADY LISLE

Madame, as humbly as I may I recommend me most affectuously to your good grace. . . .

Madame, I have a great desire to make a poor gift to my best loved Mistress Anne, your daughter; but because she is in England I do not venture to write to her; but truly, Madame, I will send them to you and if you write to her again, if it should be your pleasure, send them to her without making mention of me save very discreetly, for by reason that the *religieuses* there are wholly extirpated I should be very sorry that she should fall into any disfavour if it should be known that a *religieuse* had sent her a pair of gloves. Madame I have had put upon them the name of St. Anne, her patron saint, but if I had known the arms of her father and your own I would have had them put on. When they are dirty one should wash them in cold water

26. Vol.5, No.1353. French.   28. Vol.5, No.1553.
27. Vol.5, No.1354. French draft.

and white Spanish lye. Madame, I know that my first desire would be to send them to your said daughter, if it be your pleasure. Otherwise I am content for you to do with them according to your good pleasure. . . .

. . . Thus praying God to grant you, Madame, the entire accomplishment of your virtuous and most noble desires.

At Dunkirk, from your humble bedewoman, ever your good friend,
Hol.   Sœur Anthoinette de Saveuses[29]   (Vol.5, No.1588)

217   T. DE HARCHIE TO LADY LISLE   *3 November 1539*

Madame, As effectually and as humbly as I may I recommend me humbly to your good grace, and to the good grace of my lord your husband.

Madame, I send you a parrot by Peronne, beseeching you to be willing to accept it in as good part as I right heartily offer it to you. It grieveth me that it is no better and more worthy of your honour, in which I hold it well employed.

Madame, it cannot yet talk, but this is because it hath yet learnt nothing and it is young. As you have one that doth speak it will learn with yours. Madame, if there is any service and pleasure I may do you in these parts, command me and I will therein right gladly employ myself. To conclude, Madame, beseeching the Creator to grant you good life and long.

From Tournehen, the iijrd of November.

From him that is entirely your humble and good neighbour,
Hol.   T. de Harchie[30]   (Vol.5, No.1589)

During most of the Lisles' years in Calais war with France or Flanders, or both, had been expected at any moment, and everybody probably knew that everyone else's spies were dutifully keeping eyes on their fortifications and the strength of their garrisons, yet the family's relations with local officials across both borders remained those of close personal friendship; and when Anne of Cleves was expected with her suite on their way to England, these good friends rallied at once to help.

218   T. DE HARCHIE TO LORD LISLE   *7 December 1539*

My lord, as much and as humbly as I may I recommend me to your good grace, and in likewise to my lady your bedfellow.

My lord, I understand that your Queen cometh to Calais this week, wherefore I well conceive that you will have good company. There is one that hath taken some boars, of the which I send you a head and a side,

---

29. French.   30. This and the following three letters are in French.

praying you to accept them in good part, and sorry that I have nothing better to send you.

Thus to conclude, my lord, praying the Creator to give you good life and long.

From Tournehen, seventh of December.

By your humble to do you service,

Hol.   T. de Harchie   (Vol.5, No.1614)

219   OUDART DU BIES TO LORD LISLE   *13 December 1539*

My Lord Deputy, my good neighbour and singular good friend, in pursuance of what you have written me I send you a mule, enharnessed for your service when that the Queen of England shall come to Calais. If you have need of any other thing that may lie in my power I will gratify you therein. Praying God, my Lord Deputy, my good neighbour and singular good friend, to grant you good life and long.

From Boulogne, this xiij[th] day of December.

Signed   Entirely your good neighbour and singular [friend],

Oudart du Bies   (Vol.5, No.1615)

220   MADAME DE BOURS TO LADY LISLE   *12 February 1540*

Madame, the beginning of this my letter shall be to beg you not to take it ill that I have not for a long time written to you. For a long time I have been unable to remain at Guechard and have been entirely occupied with business matters. Two days ago I came to visit Madame de Riou. For six or seven weeks she has been very sore sick. Since I arrived, Montmorency hath written to me that he is sending this bearer to you to beg you that you will be so good to him as to help him to obtain some good water-spaniels for the cross-bow or for the hackbut. There are some of our good friends who have applied to him to procure these for them. I beg you, if it be possible, that you will send him some. You will do me a very great pleasure to send me a good greyhound, a large one. It may please you to pardon me that I am thus bold upon you, but you shall see that if I can do you any service you will find it employed on your behalf. I beg you to take the pain shortly to send me news of yourself by this bearer. To conclude, after humbly recommending me to the good grace of my lord and to yours, I pray our Lord, Madame, to give you good life and long.

From Pont de Remy, the xij day of February.

Signed   She that doth desire to do you service,

Anne Rouaud   (Vol.6, No.1647)

This is the last letter from Madame de Bours in the collection. As always, when Montmorency sends a bearer to Lady Lisle one is tempted to wonder whether the latter carried also a letter to Mary Basset.

221   LADY LISLE TO MADAME DE BOURS   *28 February 1540*

Madame, You would not credit how greatly I rejoice to learn your good news by your servant this bearer. Very sorry I am for the sickness of Madame de Riou: I pray God may send her comfort. Madame, in accordance with the letter you have written me I send you a greyhound which is one of the best I have been able to procure in this town at present, trusting that in good time I shall be able to send you some others, as also for my lord your son some water-spaniels which I shall send to England to procure, as in this town one can hardly come by them, which is the cause why I send to my lord your son at this present only one such water-dog. But I ensure you, and your son also, that he cannot have had many better in his time. He knoweth well how to retrieve the head or the bolt of a crossbow, as well by water as on land, or such other things as one willeth him to seek, and if one holdeth on high a piece of stuff or a glove on the end of a stick, he will go seek them and hath many another trick that he can perform.

Madame, if there is any other thing in which you would employ me, you will find me heartily ready to know what you desire, entirely commending me to your good favour, to my lord your son, to Monsieur d'Agincourt and my lady his wife your daughter. I beseech our Creator that he will keep you in his safe and blessed tuition.

From Calais, the xxviij[th] day of February.

She who is more than yours, ever ready to do you pleasure and service.[31]

(Vol.6, No.1657)

31. Fair copy, in French, not signed.

13

People Apart

JANE BASSET

In such a collection as *The Lisle Letters* we are likely to come upon characters and stories that exist apart and in their own right, fitting into no category save their own, but demanding a hearing. Such a character is Jane Basset, one of Honor Lisle's stepdaughters by her first husband. There is no way to discover her exact age, but it is not unreasonable to guess that she was in her forties when the Lisles moved to Calais in 1533 and the household at Soberton was dispersed. Unmarried, and with only a pittance under her father's will, she was rich in relations and friends around Umberleigh in Devonshire where she had been born and bred, notably her sisters Margery Marres and Anne Courtenay, and the unmarried Thomasine. Jane went first to stay with Anne.

222   JANE BASSET TO LADY LISLE   *14 July 1533*

My right honourable and singular good Lady, in my most heartiest manner, I commend [me] unto your good ladyship, thanking your ladyship for my gown that ye sent me. Madam, Mr. Doctor sent me his man and his horse, according to his promise, but his man would not carry my male[1] nor suffer his horse to carry it, wherefore I left my male behind me at Soberton, and when I came to Umberleigh I was fain to send John Badcomb for my male, wherein I left your box and the great book. My male was new torned[2] and the box also. Your jointure is come to ∧my∧ hands, but the great book is left behind, for what purpose I have great marvel, seeing that he was fast in my male, wherewith I am not a little sorry; desiring your ladyship to send with speed to Seller for the sure custody of the same book, for before I hear of it again I cannot be merry. I charged Seller and his wife withal and so he keepeth the same book, as I perceive by Badcomb. . . . They that promised

---

1. Trunk.   2. newly torn.

252

14. Jane Basset to Lady Lisle (No. 222)

me horses to ride deceived me, as Thomas can shew your ladyship; as knoweth God, who preserve my good lord, your good ladyship and all yours. From womberleyh the xiiij day of Jule by your doughter

Jane Bassett

Madam, as to my sister Thomasine, she is at a point with my Cousin Elizabeth Paslewe, for at Wynscott she will not be, howbeit my Cousin Anne Barry would fain have her.[3]   (Vol. 3, No. 511)

223   JANE BASSET TO LADY LISLE   *2 August 1533*

Honourable and my singular good lady, In my most humble wise I commend me unto your ∧ladyship∧, doing your good ladyship to understand that I am moved from my sister Courtenay for cause of sickness, and have been at Umberleigh this x days, and now I ride to my brother Marrys with my sister Thomasine. Pleaseth your good ladyship to grant me a lodging at Umberleigh with my sister Thomasine for a season, with such stuff as may be there necessary and the pasture of one cow in the park: for there is no place that I would so fain be in it. And as soon as I may have answer from your ladyship I will return again to Umberleigh. And thus our Lord send your good ladyship long to continue in honour. From womberlegh the morowe vppon saint peter's day by your own to her litle powre

Jane Bassett   (Vol. 3, No. 512)

But alas for Jane and her plans: as always, there was a serpent in the garden – in this case, Sir John Bonde, the vicar of the neighbouring parish of Yarnscomb. Bonde had evidently been left in charge of the house and its contents, probably when Honor remarried, and he was responsible for most of the accounts and for overseeing at any rate some of the business connected with the general upkeep of the estate. He was an elderly man who regarded the Bassets as his patrons and, like John Davy, spoke of the late Sir John as 'my master'. According to Jane he was a bad old man, negligent of her ladyship's interests and always trying to defraud her of the money brought in by the Umberleigh fishing.

224   SIR JOHN BONDE TO LADY LISLE   *2 November 1533*

Right honourable and my especial good lady, My duty in recommendations unto your good ladyship first remembered, I trust my good lord and ∧you∧ byth in good health, I pray Almighty God long to continue to his pleasure. / Madam, I heartily thank your ladyship for my gown, of me

3. See Pl. 14.

undeserved. / As touching your fishing, the water hath be very little all this summer; I trust this will not be the worst year. / As touching Mistress Jane Basset, she came unto Umberleigh the next week before Michaelmas. She lieth in the Corner chamber, and she hath the Buttery, with other houses, at her pleasure, and such stuff as is necessary for her. . . . Item, I have a great loss, I see nothing in that one eye, wherefore I may not stir as I have in time past. / As touching my books, I have made them as true as God hath give me grace; I beseech your ladyship to send unto me some discharge of the same. I pray Almighty God preserve your ladyship.

ffrowe womb*e*rleh the ij^{de} day of Noue*m*ber.

By me yo*ur* bedisman,

Hol. S*ir* John Bonde, p*r*est*e* (Vol. 3, No. 514)

225   SIR JOHN BONDE TO LADY LISLE   [*n.d.*] 1534

Right honourable and my especial good lady, after my duty in recommendations unto your ladyship first remembered, thanking Almighty God of your prosperous health and honour. . . .

Item, as touching Mistress Jane Basset, I wot not what to say of her. She hath be away since Candlemas, but she hath kept a woman servant, I know not to what intent, the which troubleth me much; and will do as pleaseth them. Your ladyship knoweth well that I, simple, have great charge in keeping of such things as be within your place, and special evidence, for the which I have slept unquietly many nights, and have be in great fear, etc. . . .

Item, Mistress Jane['s] servant put up the back door that lieth into park, by some subtle mean, the ∧which∧ put me in great fear to what intent it was done, etc. . . .

Hol. but not signed (Vol. 3, No. 517)

226   SIR JOHN BONDE TO LADY LISLE   2 *May* 1535

Honourable good lady, my duty unto your ladyship remembered. . . .

. . . Also as touching my books, I beseech your good ladyship that they may be well looked upon; if there will be any default I will be very glad to be reformed. Madam, my sight is not as it hath be in time past. . . .

. . . Also as touching Mistress Jane Basset, I have her displeasure in that she may not have the keys of every chamber. Madam, I will get my fingers unto the elbow before she or any other have such keys as beareth any charge, unto the time that please your ladyship command me to deliver &c. And in this behalf, I pray Jesu preserve your good ladyship.

ffrow Womb*e*rleh the ij^{de} day of Maye

By me yo*w*r bedisman

Hol. Sir John Bonde p*r*est*e* (Vol. 3, No. 518)

227   JANE BASSET TO LADY LISLE   *[n.d.] 1535*

Right honourable lady, with all due recommendations I commend me
unto you, glad to hear of your prosperous health and welfare, the which I
pray God daily long to continue to his pleasure and your heart's ease etc. The
cause of my writing unto your ladyship at this time is thus. Honorable lady, it
is so that my cousin Degory Greyndfylde was at Barnstaple, and so desired
Sir John Bonde to commend him unto me and to show me if I would send
any letter or token unto your ladyship he would bring it; and so I had no
manner of answer of Sir John Bonde of that, but there was a tenant of yours
heard when Master Degory spoke the word and brought me word of it, for I
can never have knowledge of Sir John Bonde when any of your servants or
any other come unto you.

Also, madame, as for your feather beds and your testers of silks, they were
not put out this iij quarters of a year until the vj day of June last was, and that
was by the sight of a letter that was come unto him. Whether the said letter
came from you or no, I cannot tell, but I had neither letter, neither word of
the ij letters that I sent your ladyship afore these.

Also, madame, it is your will and pleasure that I shall have a chamber here
at your place; but now I am taken up with Sir John Bonde, and also with
Bremelcum, that I cannot tell what to do, for they had liefer that any
brothel[4] in this parts were here than I, and so the said woman that I wrote
unto you is here daily, and so she said unto me herself and defied also: And
this, good madame, doth grieve me very sore:

Also, madame, as for your fishing, what accompt they make unto you I
cannot tell, but I can prove that when he goeth to market with your fish and
receiveth xx^s a day, they put nothing in the book of accompt but iiij^s; that is
one week with another, and he goes to market lightly, one week with
another, iij times a week, beside that he doth sell otherwise. Also, good
madame, I heartily desire you to send word that all this may be amended and
specially that this foresaid woman come not to your place, for all the country
speak of it; and so Jesu have you in his protection and keeping. Amen.

Also, as I hear say, Sir John Bonde will be with you shortly for to excuse
him and Bremelcum and give you a pig of your own sow.

                    By [your] daughter Jane Bassett
                         in all thing to her small power   (Vol.3, No.519)

That only six of Jane Basset's letters have been preserved lends some
plausibility to the charges she makes in the preceding and in her next two
about lost or diverted letters. One at least has disappeared, namely the letter

---

4. broþell; used in its original sense, which means prostitute when applied to a woman; cf. Margaret
Paston, *Paston Letters* 617.

she first wrote to complain to her stepmother about the lady of shady reputation who had apparently been introduced by Bonde to the sacrosanct premises of the manor house.

228   JANE BASSET TO LADY LISLE   *13 September 1535*

I pray you heartily, good Madam, have me heartily recommended unto my special good lord as a poor maiden may be. . . .

And also ∧it∧ may please you to be advertised, that through the counsel of Mr. Vicar, and divers others, that my sister Thomasine is gone from me unto my brother Marrys, without any manner knowledge given unto me, in the morning early before my rising, and, to say the very truth, asleep; and so there did ride with her the Smith, a little boy, and Mistress Thomasyne, sometime Thomas Seller his harlot, and now God's holy vicar here in earth, as he may be, without devotion, as all the whole country says; and here the said Thomasyne is covered underneath Jone Bremelcomb, the which men think her well near as unthrifty as the other. Wherefore they have rid away my sister in hope and trust to rid me also, because they might the bolder keep forth their bawdy and unthrifty rule without any further trouble. And sithens my sister's departing she hath sent for part of her clothing, the which she left behind her; the which I do retain in my keeping, and will do, until such time that I may know your further pleasure herein.

And also the vicar shewed me that your ladyship had written unto him that she should depart, and go from me whither that she would; and also he says, that I have written many and divers letters unto your ladyship, the which you shall never have knowledge thereof, or else I shall never have answer again: the which I never had indeed, as he hath said. And also he will not suffer me to have the looking upon none of your stuff, the which putrefieth for lack of good governance. And, further, he says that I do covet to have my brother's evidence, and none ∧thing∧ else regarding your profit.

. . . And as for your fishing, he hath utterly dispraised it unto your ladyship and divers others, and Bremelcum also, to this intent that none body should offer for it. And now that they perceive that men will offer for it, they say that your ladyship's mind is turned, and will not sell. Wherefore, if it be your pleasure to sell it, I pray you, madam, to call to your remembrance what ye promised me, that ye willed me divers times to desire one thing of you when I should espy my time; and you of your own goodness promised me that I should obtain therein. Wherefore I heartily pray you, madam, that I may be your farmer thereunto, as there is or shall be offered for with reason, so that I may be somewhat the better therefor, as my special trust is in you. For I ensure you it is very necessary for me, dwelling here under your goodness, towards the augmentation and amendment of my poor living, as in apparelling and welcoming your ladyship's friends whensoever they come, for your sake and honour, the which is very chargeable unto me in buying all things that I shall occupy, as corn, flesh, fish, and other necessaries; unless that ∧it∧ may be through your good ladyship's help. And if your ladyship do mistrust me for the rent of the fishing, I trust to find you three or four sufficient sureties for the payment thereof. . . .

And also, I pray [you] to send me word what your pleasure shall be of your lamp in the chapel, for I ensure [you] he burneth never day in the week, and scant holy days, except that I do light him [my]self. And I pray you send me word whether that I shall maintain your taper in the chapel of our lady of Alston, the which hitherto [I have done]; and as for the cleanly keeping of your house, your servant John Bery can ascertain your ladyship, the which is very uncleanly. As knoweth God, who ever preserve you and all yours in his honour, Amen. . . .

I pray you, good madam, send me some good works.

Written in your manor place of Umberleigh, in the eve of the Holy Cross.

> By your daughter,
> Jane Basset   (Vol.3, No.520)

229   SIR JOHN BONDE TO LADY LISLE   *10 January 1536*

Honourable and my singular good lady. . . .

Also as touching lying in your parlour, I was very sorry that your ladyship [was] somewhat moved for the time. Madam, I lie sometime in one chamber and sometime in another. I move my bed once in every six weeks.

Also, as touching Mistress Jane Basset, I wot not what to say. Her sisters cannot please her. Your ladyship hath commanded me to deliver unto her such things as I thought was necessary for her, yet she will not be pleased. I have delivered unto her 2 feather-beds and 3 pair of sheets, with all that 'longeth thereto. Also she hath 2 kee[5] one horse, with other things. Also she hath a greyhound lieth upon one of the beds day and night, but it be when she holdeth him in her hands and that every time when she goeth to the doors. . . .

From Umberleigh, the 10th day of January,

> By me, your bedesman,

Hol.   Sir John Bonde, priest   (Vol.3, No.521)

230   JANE BASSET TO LADY LISLE   *12 March 1536*

Honourable lady, my duty remembered, &c., advertising you that I have received amiable letters, by the which I perceive the contents of your mind. First, I have received the stuff of Sir John Bonde by a bill, and will do my

---

5. i.e. kine.

diligence in it according unto your mind, God willing. I have received your beds, both flock and feathers, with bolsters and pillows, with cushions and coverlets, as he received them, by his saying: but God knoweth in what case they be; some of them be not able to bide the handling of them to be carried unto the wind.

... And in my next letter I will write unto you an inventory of every thing that I have received, and in what case that every thing standeth, God willing. There is much as yet that I have not received. And as for your cattle in the park, there is iij heifers and iij kee, which kee I have, I thank you. ij of your heifers hath calved, and one the vicar will deliver me for the cow that he sold at Allhallows' tide, and the other heifer he will sell, as he saith. He hath spoken unto the parson to have the tithing-calf already.

Ye shall perceive that your miller hath been with me making his moan. Except that the water be stopped in time the mill shall stand still, which will be to the great hinderance of all your tenements,[6] and others also. The vicar and John Davy saith it ∧must be∧ made; but there is no setting forth in it as yet. In this thing I and your miller will pray you to send your strait answer unto John Davy and to the vicar. The miller hath done his good will, and doth daily, unto his great pains; but it is not one man's work, as ye know. Write ye unto me in your letter of this matter; for if ye write anything unto them that it please them not, it shall be hid long enow from me, because I shall not call on them. There is but few letters that cometh unto me from you but is opened before it cometh unto my hands, and sometime it shall be drowned in Bacus Lane, and if it be not pleasure unto all parties. Write ye unto them by parables, as though ye knew nothing of this, because of the saving of my writer harmless of displeasure.

Your chapel standeth unserved, saving the vicar causeth one mass in the week there to be said, which is of his devotion. But there is an honest priest hath granted to serve there for xl[s] by the year, because he will be quiet to serve God, and he will mend your bedding and other such stuff as is need, if it shall so please you so for to take him; a middle-aged man. I have stayed him unto the time I might know your mind in it. I thank you for your tokens by my cousin Chichester and Ryc. Harrys. I pray you to commend me unto my brothers and sisters, all in general, as well as though I had rehearsed them by name. And thus I leave you and all yours in the keeping of Jesu.

wrettyn att Vmberlay y[e] xij day of marche

By yo*ur*[7] dafther

Jane Bassett

I pray you to pardon me of my rude writing.[8]   (Vol. 3, No. 522)

---

6. This may mean lands, or buildings; or may be a mistake for 'tenants' occupying lands or houses.
7. 'owne' deleted.
8. The phrase is a commonplace and not necessarily proof that she wrote herself.

There are no other letters from Jane. It is difficult to imagine that she stopped writing. Perhaps her stepmother, like Thomasine, had had as much as she could bear of Jane, and simply destroyed her letters. But, Sir John Bonde has the last word, two years later, in their antiphonal hymn of hate.

231   SIR JOHN BONDE TO LADY LISLE   *10 March 1538*

Right honourable and my especial good lady, after my duty in recommendation unto your ladyship first remembered. . . . As touching Mistress Jane, your ladyship commanded me that she should have the pasture of ij kee in your park by the year; now she hath iij head of cattle and one horse. I give your ladyship knowledge of it, and as it shall please your ladyship to be 'vised that I may know better by the next messenger etc. . . . As touching my books, I ∧will∧ send them by John Bery at his next coming unto you. Item, as for ∧Ric.∧ Pitts' fee, I must bestow much money in reparation, for this winter hath be[en] wet, therefore the charges will be much more. As for fish, there is very little take[n], as knoweth God, who ever preserve your ladyship.

From Umberleigh, the xth day of March.

Hol.   By me your bedysman *Sir* John Bonde p*r*est

(Vol. 3, No. 524)

JOHN CHERITON

Cheriton was to Lisle what the Ancient Mariner was to Coleridge's wedding guest, buttonholing him with tales of fabulous disasters at sea. Whether he was something of a seaman as well as an agent for Lisle and a trader on his own behalf it is difficult to tell. In 1536 he writes as if he had been the person responsible for giving orders to cut away all the masts when the ship ran into foul weather, but in his first letter it is clear that he was on board Lisle's ship, the *Mary Plantagenet,* simply as owner's agent.

232   JOHN CHERITON TO LORD LISLE   *24 September 1533*

Jesus. Anno 1533, the 24 September, In Pisa.

Right honourable and my singular good lord, my duty remembered, pleaseth your good lordship to a'know that I have received in Leghorn a letter from your lordship. . . .

. . . I have sold the *Mary* unto Antone de Maryne, according unto your lordship's writing. My lord, he and the master has caused me to spend in this voyage above a m^l¢¢¢ ducats of gold, and in the sale of her he has lost me above lx^li sterling, as it shall appear at my coming to your lordship, by the process of the Court and by testimonies; and as for expenses in victuals, by his negligence, that he would have it or else I should stand in jeopardy of my life, I will promise your lordship, above a £ mark sterling. Wherefore, at his coming home, there will ∧be∧ provision enow found for to make him to pay for it.

My lord, Antone Gethott and James Prevytt has written all the mischief hither that they can. As for the King's ordnance, we were at no point at the making of this letter, for then he could find no sureties for it. . . . And thus I pray . . . that God may send your lordship and my good lady as wholesome air for your health as your lordship had at Porchester Castle, and at Soberton. Amen.

By yo*ur* por / Sarvantc and bedeman

Hol.   John Cheryton   (Vol.1, No.50)

On the same day he wrote again with some wildly garbled gossip of the arrangements in Pisa for the marriage of the French King's second son to Catherine, daughter of Lorenzo de Medici, whom he calls 'the Pope's daughter'. She was in fact his great-niece.

233   JOHN CHERITON TO LORD LISLE   *24 September 1533*

Jesus, anno 1533, the 24 day of September, at Pisa

Right honourable and my singular good lord, my duty remembered, pleaseth your good lordship to a'know part of the news here in Pisa. Your lordship shall understand that the Pope came into Pisa the 23rd day of September; and before him the Corpus Domine and with him 16 Cardinals, and a 100 spearmen and men in harness and hand guns to the value of a 100 more. And he and the Cardinals and the Duke of Florence has in Pisa above 2,000 men, the most part gentlemen; and the Pope is removed out of Rome with most part of all his baggage. My lord, the country says here that he will turn no more again to Rome; and his men says that he will go to a place that is called Nice, in the Duke of Savoy's country. And the Duke of Savoy has sent him word that he shall not land in his country, and there the French King has appointed for to meet the Pope at the said Duke's country in Nice, and the Duke in like wise has sent word to the French King that he shall not come into his land; wherefore the Pope will land at Marseilles in the French King's land. My lord, the Pope's servants says that it is for a marriage betwixt the Pope's daughter and the French King's son; which of them I cannot shew your lordship. But my lord, all the country says here, Pisaneses and Florentines, that he goes into France for to be in areadiness against March for to make an army of men to have war; and some say that it is against the

Emperor, and the more part says here that it is to take the Emperor's part for to come into England.

Wherefore, my lord, here is none other conversation in every man's mouth but that the Pope intends as much good unto England as does a fox among a flock of sheep. Wherefore I beseech Jesus for to save England and send them little power that will it. And yet, my lord, I can have none other passage here but in the same navy that the Pope sails in, the which is 10 galleys and 8 great ships, and all marvellous well appointed, that are sent from the French King to the Pope. And I intend to tarry in Marseilles to a'know more news, and then with all the speed that may be I will send your lordship word, by the grace of God, who ever send your lordship and my good lady long life with much honour, and at the pleasure of God to send your lordship by my good lady a son and heir to make your good lordship and my good lady glad. Amen.

                    By your servant and bedeman,
Hol.   John Cheryton

My lord, as for our Holy Father the Pope, he has 2 the fairest women to his wives that ever I saw out of England, for they are more liken angels than earthly women; and the Pope sends more men for to wait upon them than he did for to wait upon the Corpus Domine.[9]   (Vol.1, No.50a)

234   JOHN CHERITON TO LORD LISLE   *15 February 1534*

Jesus. Anno 1533 the 15 day February, at Bordeaux.[10]

Right honourable and my singular good lord, my duty remembered unto your good lordship as your daily poor bedeman, pleaseth your good lordship to a'know that the second day of December,[11] betwixt Genoa and Savona[12] a ship of Lagos in Portugal that I freighted at Leghorn for to come to Cadiz[13] in Spain, sank in the sea, with as great fortune as ever was seen that any person was saved: wherein, my lord, I lost, as your lordship shall have due proofs of the merchants of Lucca that I bought the silks of for your good lordship and for my good lady, and for my ladies your daughters, and for my Lady's daughters, as much as cost me in presence of Francis di Bardi[14] iiij^C crowns and above, as he shall certify your lordship; and I never saved the value[15] of a penny,[16] and all the rest of goods that I had to her, that was to say galls and alum and cotton and mastic, was worth above ij^C li, and if that God had sent it in safety; and it is all agon, I thank God highly. And lest that your lordship

9. See Pl. 15.   13. Calys.
10. ffebreare at bordes.   14. ffronsis the Barres.
11. 'Maye' deleted.   15. vayler.
12. Jene and Sauone.   16. pene.

15. John Cheriton to Lord Lisle (No. 233)

be good lord unto me I am as a man clean cast away. . . . For my lord, I am put in trust for a man of Florence, the richest merchant that is in all Florence, whose name is Capones; and my lord I have the doing for him in Toulouse[17] for above xij m^l ducats, and at Bordeaux at this hour: and more I am liken to have in my hands of theirs, and if that your lordship will be so good lord unto me as to write me your gracious letter of favour that I may shew it unto them it will bring me into great favour and credence with them,[18] and after that manner, I may with God's grace recover all that I have lost. . . . Wherefore, good my lord, for the Passion of Christ, that your lordship will send your charitable letter unto my poor wife for me, that she may send him to me. And thus Jesus send your good lordship and my good lady long life, with much honour. Amen.

                    By your poor servant and bedsman,
Hol.   John Chereton   (Vol.2, No.128)

For the Mediterranean and Levantine trading voyages merchant shipping was usually equipped with guns for defence against pirates and the Turk. Lisle had apparently lent a number of pieces of ordnance from Porchester Castle for the *Mary Plantagenet*'s voyage; and after her sale to Antonio de Marini this borrowed ordnance became one of Cheriton's worst problems. His reference to the King of Portugal's money is explained by the fact that apparently the captain of his ship had borrowed two hundred ducats from the King and bound Lisle to repay it.

235   JOHN CHERITON TO LORD LISLE   *13 April 1534*

        Jesus Anno 1534 the 13 day of April at Greenwich

Right honourable and my singular good lord, my duty remembered, pleaseth your good lord[ship] to a'know in what case that the King's ordnance is. Your lordship shall a'know that Antone de Marynes did get me no sureties for the ordnance, and therefore I would not lend it to him; and so I have left it at Leghorn, in the hands of one Capones, one of the richest merchants of all Florence. And he is bound by obligation before the Duke of Florence that it shall be safe kept, and for fear of any wars betwixt them and England I caused it to be 'praised by vj merchant men, and for fear of any danger of it homewards, it is valued at ij$C$ ducats of gold, that howsomever that it should chance, that his brother in London shall make good for as much. . . .

Also your lordship shall understand that the King's Grace has given me licence for ij$C$ tun of wines, whereof I have laden already of them lxxx tun,

17. tollose.   18. wetham.

and I do intend, as far as I know yet, for to bring it to London, part of it; and if that I do, I will send your lordship some for your house. I would have sent your lordship iiij tun from Bordeaux by John Perse, your servant, of Weymouth, and he would not carry it neither he would not let me to freight his ship, because that he would not bring your lordship the iiij tun of wine, wherein he did me xl^li of harm, for he promised me that I should have her before any other; and then I might have been at home with the first and a'made my money, and a'been ready for to a'gone again. Wherefore, good my lord, for the passion of Christ, that your lordship send me your commission that your lordship has admitted me for a victualler or for a vintner, that these goods not be arrested, and then I may agree with them to pay every man some, and sooner, and to have a poor living for my wife and me and keep my credence also. . . . And as touching to the King of Portugal's money, the merchant Antony des Marynes has it allowed in the sale of the ship. And my lord, and if that your lordship do not send me this in haste, surely my wines is like to be arrested and then I am clean undone. And thus I pray and daily shall unto the blessed passion of Christ to send your lordship and my good lady long life with much honour. Amen.

　　　　　By yo*ur* pore bedman
Hol.　　　　　John Cherreton　　　　　　　　　　(Vol.2, No.165)

The next two letters, from Cheriton, conclude the story of the voyage to the Mediterranean and the Levant of the *Mary Plantagenet.* Written obviously under stress of considerable mental agitation over his own troubles and the disgraceful behaviour of de Marini and the ship's master, they bristle with eccentric spellings, particularly of proper names, and the awkward syntax makes the meaning of several passages doubtful. As usual, there is no punctuation to help, and both letters allude to matters which would remain obscure if the syntax were above reproach. For the sake of consistency within the letters and because rule of thumb cannot solve the problem, no names have been modernized. Some of the spelling in the first letter is noted.

236　　JOHN CHERITON TO LORD LISLE　　[*n.d.*] *before 29 October 1534*

Right honourable and my singular good lord, my duty remembered, pleaseth your good lordship to a'know when that I came to Hampton I met with John Koper,[19] and he told me that the *Mary* was lost at Bellisle[20] and the *John of Baptist,* the King's ship; and the men that brought[21] the tidings to

19. ?Cooper.　　　　　　　　　21. broffte.
20. byl[lys]le.

Hampton were of Hull,[22] that came from Bordeaux;[23] for the which, my lord, and if that your lordship be not good lord unto me, I am undone for ever, and liken to die for thought,[24] and my wife likewise. Wherefore, good my lord, for the blessed passion of Christ, that your lordship will be so good lord unto me as to provide some living for me in the office of the butlerage with my Lord Chief Baron; or else, my lord, I am clean undone. And Sir Thomas Denys[25] has made John Wat a plain answer, that for no man's pleasure that his servant shall do but take ∧his∧ whole money by and by. Wherefore, my lord, of the great charity that ever has been in your lordship, now let one drop of it fall upon me of your giving, and Jesus send your lordship and me better tidings.

My lord, at Salisbury[26] there was a messenger of the King's that has been at Weymouth and fetched[27] many poor man and woman to appear before the Council, and there they said that Water Porttlond had your commission to make them a general quittance, and so he has done in your lordship's name as they will show it in writing unto your lordship. And more, that they will prove that Water Porttlond has taken above xl^{li} in their company; and Varnam and Torner has used them but ill, as they say. Wherefore, my lord, look upon this matter yourself, for it stands with your honour. And my lord, one of these men is Raynalld, that forfeit his ship unto your lordship for the anchor that he stole.

Written at Salisbury,[28]

By your poor servant,

Hol.   John Cherreton   (Vol.2, No.281)

237   JOHN CHERITON TO LORD LISLE   *5 November 1534*

Jhesus anno 1534 the 5 day of November

Right honourable and my singular good Lord, my duty remembered unto your good lordship and to my good Lady, as your poor and daily orator. . . .

My lord, the cause of my writing unto your good lordship is to certify you that the *Mary* is come home to Hampton. And my lord, I will desire your lordship that you will not for no fair words of Antone Gethott neither of Nyckalyne, neither of Antone de Maryne that was merchant in her, for to take no present of them unless that it be worth a $\mathbb{C}^{li}$ sterling; for he has offended your lordship highly, and he made his boast in Ireland and in Cadiz and in Italy that and if that he had offended your lordship never so highly but with a fair word and a present of a penny that he would have your lordship's

22. hwll.
23. bordes.
24. thofftte.
25. Of Holcombe Burnell, Devon.

26. salles bere.
27. fatt.
28. salles berre.

good will, so that my lady were not in the way. But my lord, and that Antone de Maryne sue unto your lordship for to bring you any present, your lordship may lay unto his charge for his misusing of himself in your ship; and more, for the breaking ope of your letters and the copying out of them before that they come to my hands; and more, he said in Cadiz that the commission that your lordship gave unto me for the ship was too bad, your lordship's honour reserved, for to wipe his shoes; and more, my lord, he carried (and was brought unto him into Ireland out of England) above vjℂ^{li} sterling; more, and beside that, he carried privy letters out of England for the Pope, and had of him a great reward, and he delivered him the letters at Pisa. The same Antone de Marynes, and the master of the ship was of counsel with him, and because that he was of the merchant his counsel he cost me v ℂ ducats the more. And my lord, the master of the ship will be worth xl^{li} unto your lordship and if that your lordship had your office in your hand of the Admiralty, and will be yet and if that it please your lordship for to write to your friends that be in the office, for he made me for to lose iij ℂ ducats of that was his own fault and said that he cared not for it, for your lordship was out of your office and was gone to Calles. My lord, the master's name is Thomas Totyn, otherwise Thomas Gyllam, the falsest wretch in Christendom, bearing so good a face as he does! Wherefore, good my lord, that your lordship give not Antone de Maryne no quittance, neither to Thomas Gyllam, unless that they pay well for it. . . .

. . . and thus Jesus send your good lordship and my good lady long life with much honour, and a son for to be your heir. Amen.

By yo*ur* por Sarvante

Hol.   John Chereton   (Vol.2, No.282)

238   JOHN CHERITON TO LORD LISLE   *24 March 1536*

Jesus anno 1536 the 24 day of March at Marseilles

Right honourable and my singular good lord, my duty remembered unto your good lordship and to my good lady, pleaseth your good lordship to a'know that I am here in Marseilles with a ship that I have bought at Aigues Mortes.[29] She cost me viij ℂ crowns the first penny;[30] and betwixt Aigues Mortes and Marseilles, by chance of foul weathering, I was fain to cut all her masts overboard, and lost all her sails and her tackle, and brast ij cables and lost her rudder, and she ran with the shore, and now she will cost me v ℂ crowns more before that she can make any voyage. Also, my lord, I have gone by land from Marseilles to Leghorn for the King's ordnance, and I have had great business for to recover it, and it has cost me more than the

---

29. a gos mortos.   30. i.e. 'every penny of 800 crowns'.

ordnance is worth; and it is laden in a ship of Marseilles, in one Bylotte's ship, and now I am in worse case than I was before, for there is open war betwixt the Duke of Savoy and the French King, and in Lyons they say that there is open war betwixt France and the Emperor. But my lord, I will not say that it is so, but I fear me that it will be truth, for the Emperor has sent to Nice vj m¹ men: Andrea Doria, for the Emperor there and in his name, has sent them to Nice; wherefore, my lord, I stand in doubt for to lade this ordnance in any ship, because and if that it come in Spain, for fear lest that it should be arrested for the Emperor there. My lord, here is them that will give a 150 crowns of the sun for the xiij pieces of ordnance. There is but ij of brass and a xj of iron. My lord, they be not worth the money, but and if that your lordship may do it with your honour that they may be sold, it were the most surest way; and I will come by land and bring your lordship the money. And if that your lordship think that it may not stand with your honour, that it will please your lordship for to write me your letters to Marseilles whether that I shall sell it or not, for I will not lade it in no ship for to be brought into England, for fear of the Spaniards, for fear of losing, unless that your lordship write me your letters, for it is not for me for to bear the venture, and I cannot find no merchants here in this country that ∧will∧ make no assurance, for I have sought at Lyons and at Avignon,³¹ whereas all the chief merchants be, for to assure it, whatsoever that it cost; and because that the world is so troublous there is none, and if that I will give xl of the hundred; for here is no other provision but all for war, for the bringer hereof can show your lordship that it is of a truth. For at his being here there is nothing but rigging of the galleys and carrying of ordnance to the walls; and the Emperor has sent to Nice vj m¹ Spaniards; and more, they have taken at Nice xxvj great pieces of ordnance of brass out of the ship of Rhodes and have put them into the castle of Nice.

Also, my lord, that it will please your lordship for to be good lord unto the bringer hereof, whose name is Thomas Smythe. He was Captain in the *Trinity of Erith,* and the owners' names ∧Adam∧ Samson and one Spar. My lord, they were betrayed by their pilot, which was a Genoese,³² for he has cast away the ship wilfully, by the reason of him and the Master, James Romney, for when the pilot ran the ship upon a rock James Romney was abed, naked, with a harlot, within the ship.

My lord, this bringer has done his best diligence, as the mariners will testify, and more, as the captain of a ship of Marseilles and all the mariners has testified here, before the best in Marseilles, the which that it will please your lordship to be so good lord unto this bringer, whose name is Thomas Smythe, for to write your lordship's letter unto ∧Adam∧ Samson that for

31. a veneon.   32. Jenevayes.

your lordship's sake that he will be good unto him. For my lord, they might have saved much of the goods, and if that the Venetians[33] had not been, for when that they had saved anything the Venetians took it away from them, as the captain of this ship and all his merchants and mariners has testified here, and as the bringer hereof can show your lordship more largely.

And thus I pray, and daily shall, to God, to send your lordship and my good lady long life with much honour. Amen.

By yo*ur* poor sarvante

IIol.   John Cheryton

My lord, beseeching your lordship for to write me your lordship's pleasure what I shall do with this ordnance with the first that your lordship may possible at Marseilles.   (Vol.3, No.663)

239   JOHN CHERITON TO LORD LISLE   *20 February 1538*

. . .

My lord, since my departing from your lordship I have had great losses. I had my ship here, after time that I bought her, with foul weathering ran withshore and lost all her masts overboard, and sails and cables and anchors, and her bottom rudder, and then she cost me viijC crowns her careen and her masts and apparel afterward; and then after that I was taken with Turks slave into Barbary, and the Baron Syn Blankyrd[34] did ransom me for ij Cl crowns of the sun. I have paid him again, wherefore my lord, and if that your lordship be not good lord unto me I am undone for ever. . . .

And this I pray and daily shall to God, to send your lordship and my good lady long life with much honour. Amen.

By your por sarvante and bydman

Hol.   John Chereton   (Vol.5, No.1105)

240   JOHN CHERITON TO LORD LISLE   *6 December 1538*

Jesus anno 1538 the 6d December at Marseilles

Right honourable and my singular good Lord, my duty remembered unto y[our good] lordship and to my good Lady. My Lord, it shall please your good Lord[ship to] a'know that I have written many letters unto your Lordship as ∧my∧ d[uty is] and I had never no answer of them to a'know your lordship's ple[asure what I shall] do. My lord, the Count de Tando has taken away [my ship and the pieces of] ordnance and all the freight that she has gotten for the voyage to,[35] xj months at ij hundred crowns the month,

33. vyneseanes.
34. i.e. the Baron St. Blankheare (or Blankard), French Admiral.
35. ?for 'too'. There is no room for the destination, i.e. Constantinople.

and he has left me nothi[ng] only j of the brazen pieces that weighs xj hundredweight. And I must pay [ix] crowns before that I can have that piece also. And the other piece was br[oken] all to pieces when the galleys was in Turkey.

My lord, I am undone ever more, for they have imprisoned me so oft and taken from me all that ever I had [with]out justice, and if that your lordship have not compassion on me I am as o[ne] undone for ever. And as for this piece of ordnance that the Count has left [me,] there is no remedy but to sell him; for here is no ship that comes into the [   ]tes[36] and here it is worth but xij francs a hundredweight. My lord [and it] will please your good lordship to send me in writing your pleasure what [I] shall do: for here is sayings that there is open war betwixt England a[nd Spain,] and if that it be so, then will be this country against [En]gland and [so] I go to the galleys in chains, there will be no remedy. Wh[erefore] as shor[tly] as may be possible that I may a'know your lordship's pleasure [a]nd thus I [pray] and daily shall to God to send your Lordship and my good Lady lo[ng life] with much honour. Amen.

By yo*ur* por sarvante and tru bydman

Hol.   John Chereton ////   (Vol.5, No.1308)

241   LORD LISLE TO THE CONSTABLE OF FRANCE   *3 January 1539*

My lord, I most humbly recommend me to your noble favour.

My lord, please it you to understand that there is one of my servants, named John Cheriton, the which was some little time ago cast ashore upon the coast of Marseilles in his ship by a storm upon the sea, in which place he left some xxiiij pieces of ordnance because he could not remove them when that the said ship was altogether wrecked and did perish. And since that time when he has come to claim his pieces of ordnance, my lords the governors of the said Marseilles would not allow him to have restitution thereof. Wherefore I request you, my lord, in the name of justice, that it may please you to send therein your express commandment to the said governors that they shall render to my said servant his pieces of ordnance, and in so doing you shall oblige me to do likewise to those of your country in those parts if it should happen them to require me so to do in like case. Thus to conclude, praying the Creator to grant you in health good life and long.

From Calais, the iij day of January.

He that is always ready to accomplish your commandments.

My lord, I beg you to do me the honour to send me a word in reply touching your good pleasure in this matter.

---

36. He probably wrote 'thes partes' or 'portes', for these parts or this port.

I pray you, my lord, that it may please you to send your commandment to my lord the Count de Tandes, because he it is that hath the said ordnance in his hands.[37]   (Vol.5, No.1320)

As far as the Lisle Letters go – and but for them John Cheriton would be only a meaningless name in an obligation and a mutilated Chancery petition – this, then, is the end of the Cheriton story. Lisle's official position and his personal standing enabled him to intervene as patron, in the traditional manner of 'service', on behalf of his 'poor servant and true bedeman' at top level, by writing a strong and dignified letter to the highest authority, Anne de Montmorency, Grand Master and High Constable of France, his fellow Knight of the Garter. What happened to the famous pieces of ordnance the Letters do not tell us, but there is reason to believe that Cheriton himself returned eventually to his native Devonshire.

GILBERT BURTON AND THOMAS GILBERT

Two irresistible characters come to us from the pen of the Rector of Bishop's Waltham: himself and his sometime curate.

242   GILBERT BURTON TO LADY LISLE   *26 January 1534*

My bounden duty to your good and honourable ladyship remembered, with my daily hearty prayer for my good lord's and your preservation to the pleasure of our Saviour Jesu Christ: Please it your said good and honourable ladyship to understand that William Rose hath informed me that Sir Thomas Gilbert, the which I took into my service at your said good ladyship's request and desire, is come thither to Calais; and hath informed your said good ladyship that I should put him from my service suddenly, and also withhold his wages, and divers otherwise misintreat him, contrary to right and good conscience. The truth thereof, my especial good lady, is that I did not put the said Sir Thomas from my service but by reason of divers and many great offences whereof some I will not write for the honour of priesthood, but defer the same unto such time as I may conveniently speak with your good ladyship myself.

Other causes there be, whereof one is that he regarded not me, but would say that he was as good as I, and better; and as he played at cards with me and other honest company, said I played Jacke napes with him, rehearsing the same divers times under a proud presumptuous and opprobrious fashion before the same honest company, by reason whereof I would suffer him no

37. French draft.

longer to play with me; whereupon he start up in a great fume, saying that he was as good as I and better, and that he set not a straw by me nor my service. I answered and said, 'Sir Thomas, this at night and ye be not well advised'; and thereupon willed him to go to bed and speak with me again the next morning before the said company, and then to show me his mind. At which time he came to me, the said honest company being then present, at what time he defied me and my service, saying further that he would do me displeasures and ring me such a peal that the best in England should speak thereof. By reason thereof, and of divers other matters whereof I had divers and many times warned him of before, touching his unpriestly behaviour divers and many ways; in consideration thereof, [I] willed him to fetch his book of Accounts betwixt him and me, to know whether I were in his debt or he in mine. And the same book cast, and all things reckoned and accounted, I did owe to him for his wages xvd., the which I proffered unto him before your old servant Robert Amner and divers other honest persons. And besides that, for your good and honourable lady∧ship∧ sake, and not for his deserving, I would have given him forty pence more, all which he refused to take. And so under a foolish, proud and presumptuous fashion, without any leave taking, departed.

After which departing he went to divers and many of the most honest persons of my parish, and showed unto them great offences and crimes of me and other good christian people, the which were never done nor thought. . . .

The said Sir Thomas, shortly after his departing from hence, came to London to Mr. Wythers' house, a Residentiary of Paul's, to whom about one quarter of a year before I did put a right honest poor priest, a friend of mine, to be Steward of his house, the which priest for my sake made great cheer to the said Sir Thomas, both in meat, drinking, and lodging. That notwithstanding, the said Sir Thomas played an uncharitable and deceitful and false pagioner[38] with him. That is to say, that the said Sir Thomas had by my means and labour an advowson of the parsonage of Wikeham, of the gift of Mr. Arthur Uvedale, for the next avoidance of the same parsonage. And the same advowson he showed unto Mr. Wythers' said Steward, saying that he would freely give unto him the same for the good love that he owed unto him for my sake, saying and swearing great oaths not only to the said poor priest, but also to Mr. Wythers, his master, that the parson of the said Wikeham the Saturday next before ∧was dead and buried∧. Wherefore he willed the said priest to make all the haste that he could possible, to come to the Chancellor of Winchester for his institution; and caused him also to bring all his stuff with him to his great costs and charges, and moreover, by reason

---

38. Apparently derived from pagond = pageant, and by its connection with acting denoting deception, playing a villain's part.

thereof, caused him to leave his good service. And when the said Mr. Withers enquired of the said Sir Thomas why and for what cause he would not take the said benefice him∧self∧, then he answered and said that my Lord Lyssley and my Lady, to whom he was nigh kinsman, had sent for him to Calais, and had given him St. George Chantry, which was x^{li} by the year, and also two liveries, besides meat and drink, the which pleased him much better than the benefice.

And ere he departed he borrowed under subtle and crafty fashion of the poor priest xiiij^s viij^d, saying to him that I did owe the said Sir Thomas for his wages xv^s ij^d, and he should have a letter to me to pay the same to the said poor priest. As so the said Sir Thomas wrote to me indeed, which letter is to be showed. Albe∧it∧ I did owe no more to the said Sir Thomas but only xv^d, and that I delivered to the said poor priest. . . .

At this time I will not trouble your good ladyship with any longer writing of the behavior of the said Sir Thomas, but defer all other matters unto such times as I may conveniently speak with your said good ladyship myself. As the Father of heaven knoweth, who long preserve my singular good lord and your honourable ladyship in much honour. At my benefice of Bishop's Waltham, the xxvjth day of January.

Yo*ur* good honorable Ladiships true bedeman,

Hol. Gilbert Burton p*res*tc (Vol. 2, No. 118)

ALICE WOLFE

The colourful tale which Grenville now relates began in July, when John Wolfe, a merchant of the Steelyard, his wife Alice, and three accomplices, murdered two foreign merchants in London, having, with Alice's wiles, lured them into a boat on the river, where they stabbed one, broke the neck of the other, robbed them, tied the bodies back to back, and threw them overboard. Wolfe escaped to Ireland, but Alice was imprisoned in the Tower. Now read on. . . .

243   JOHN GRENVILLE TO LORD LISLE   *28 March 1534*

Right honourable and my most singular good Lord, as your humble servant I commend me unto your good lordship, and to my most singular good lady. . . . On Friday about ij of the clock in the morning one Bawde, sometimes the Lieutenant his servant, with counterfeit keys opened the prison door where Wolfe his wife was, and conveyed her out of the Tower with ij ropes tied to the embattlements: and after he had conveyed her down, went down himself ∧to∧ her, and so to∧gether∧ until they came to the Tower Hill or thereabout, whereas stood certain watchmen of London. And the watchmen asked them whither they would, and they perceived that they were suspect persons, demanded whither they went, and they said they would go to Mistress Jenyn's house. Then, as God would, one of the Watch perceived her to be a woman apparelled like a man, took her and Bawde both, and brought them to the Lieutenant. And with him remain they until Tuesday. Wolfe and his wife shall hang upon Thames at low water mark[39] in chains. And Bawde is in Little Ease,[40] and after he hath been in the Rack shall be hanged. My Lord Howard knoweth this Bawde, for Master Lieutenant put him of trust to his lordship. The King's Grace takes great displeasure with Mr. Lieutenant's negligence for suffering the keys of the prison to be counterfeit.

. . . And th∧us∧ the Holy Ghost preserve you, my most singular good lord, and my good lady, and all that I have or may do is wholly ∧at∧ your commandment.

Written the xxviij day of March,
        Your owne faygtfull *seru* nt,
Hol.   John Graynfyld   (Vol.2, No.150)

The story of Alice Wolfe's escape must have been something of a nine-day wonder. John Grenville had picked up quite a circumstantial account within a few hours. But what he has not put on record is the extraordinary power of fascination 'Wolfe's wife' must have possessed, which enabled her to win the pity and help of men and women alike. Interrogated as to why she wore no irons in her prison, she replied it was through 'the goodness and intercession of the Lieutenant's daughters made unto the Lieutenant'. While she was imprisoned in the Coldharbour Tower, William Denys, the Lieutenant's servant, used constantly to visit her, and 'showed her a secret way how she might be conveyed out of the Tower'; but he was discovered conversing with her and was summarily dismissed. Another trusted servant, equally infatuated, at once took his place. Bawde had known both Wolfe and his wife, and he too managed to see her in her prison, and 'when she heard tell that there was no remedy with her but death', she desired him 'for the honour and passion of Christ' to help her to escape. Bawde therefore bought two ropes of hair for 13 *d.*, and like Valentine in *The Two Gentlemen of Verona,* with his ladder 'quaintly made of cords', light enough to be carried 'under a cloak that is of any length', he 'brought the same under his gown into the Tower' and also gave her 'a key which he had caused to be filed and made meet to open the back of the outer prison door'. They arranged to meet that night on the leads of St. Thomas's Tower, overlooking the river. The door of

---

39. Stow says pirates and sea-rovers were hung at Execution Dock, below Wapping Old Stairs, 'at the low water mark, there to remain till three tides had overflowed them'.

40. A minute cell in the Tower in which a man could neither stand nor lie.

the inner ward was 'shut and hasped with a bone put through the staple, which door she saith she did shake and so the bone fell out; and the outer door she unlocked with Bawde's key. At about ten o'clock she climbed out on to the leads, where Bawde awaited her, and 'he cast the said ropes double upon a hook of iron being fastened upon the same Tower wall, and so [they] slid down' to the wharf below where they hid on a lighter for an hour; and then Bawde found a boat, by means of which they got away from the Tower precincts. When they landed by Tower Hill, however, they were stopped by the watch, as Grenville reports, one of whom recognized Wolfe's wife. They were both apprehended. Bawde when

examined what should move him to do this act to help her to escape, knowing for what heinous offence she was prisoner and what danger were imminent upon the same, he answereth that the very love and affection that he bare to the woman moved and constrained him to do it, and nothing else.[41]

41. S.P. 1/83, ff.48 et seq.: the confessions of Alice Tankerfelde (Wolfe's wife) and John Bawde.

14

Glimpses of the Court
1536–1540

Here follows our first glimpse in the Letters of Jane Seymour as Queen.

244   SIR JOHN RUSSELL TO LORD LISLE   *3 June 1536*

Right honourable and my singular good Lord, I heartily recommend me unto your lordship. My Lord, I presented the King with the cherries in my lady's name, which he was very glad of, and thanks you and her both for them. Also, I delivered your letter to the King in presence of Mr. Secretary, the which Master Secretary was caused to read it immediately after to the King's hearing. And he said that he would do anything for your lordship that he could, to the King. Wherefore I do think that you are much bound unto him. My Lord, what effect your letter shall be at, as yet I cannot ascertain your lordship, but I shall be solicitor in it to the best of my power. . . .

My Lord, as upon Friday last the Queen sat abroad as Queen, and was served with her own servants.[1] And they were sworn that same day. And the King and the Queen came in his great boat to Greenwich the same day, with his Privy Chamber and her[s], and the ladies in the great barge. I do ensure you, my lord, she is as gentle a lady as ever I knew, and as fair a Queen as any in Christendom. The King hath come out of hell into heaven, for the gentleness in this, and the cursedness and the unhappiness in the other. Where-[fore], my Lord, me think it were very well done, when you do write to the King again, that you do rejoice that he is so well matched with so gracious a woman as she is, and you hear reported by her; and wherein you shall content his Grace in so doing.

My lord, I thank you for the present that you sent me: And if there be any good or pleasure that I may do you here you may command me as your own assuredly. As knoweth our Lord, who keep you.

From Greenwich this Whitsun even.

Signed   Your owen to com*m*ande,

        J. Russell   (Vol. 3, No. 713)

1. Anne Basset was now a Maid of Honour.

The art of getting what one wanted from the King consisted in getting, if possible, Cromwell's support for the content of a petition, and then the help of someone close to the King (as Henry Norris had been) in presenting it. There followed the interminable waiting about at Court for the right psychological moment. Husee had as yet found no adequate substitute for Norris in this process.

245   JOHN HUSEE TO LORD LISLE   [?17] *June 1536*

Pleaseth your lordship to understand that yesterday I received your letter. And first, concerning the Main Brook, Seyn's Dyke or bank and the whole Marsh, I wrote your lordship what answer Mr. Secretary made me therein; but since that time, whether it were by the means of Wriothesley or some other, he never made me good countenance nor would scant give ear to what I would open or say unto him in that or in your own suit to the King, but said that he had your suit in remembrance. . . .

But touching your own suit, Mr. Secretary is so busied with weighty matters of the King's that he hath no mind to prefer the same, nor leisure, as they about him saith. He may do much, and Mr. Heneage and Mr. Russell remitteth all unto him, saying when they can espy him at any leisure with the King they will speak for your lordship all with one voice. But the truth is, I like none of these coloured[2] dilations,[3] with sweet words and little deeds. I delivered yesterday a bill with names of Quarre and Netley,[4] both to Mr. Russell and Mr. Heneage, desiring them to motion the King therein. They said they would so do, but I have small hope in their promise; but yet will I not let to call vigilantly upon them to know the King's pleasure and what answer his Grace hath made thereunto. But in the meantime I have drawn a letter to the King, which I do send your lordship herewith, so that if the contents thereof do like you it may please your lordship to cause the same to be new written and fair penned, and written in as little space and as few lines as it conveniently may be, being legible, to the end that his Grace may read the same himself; and then your lordship to make up the same and send it me with all speed. And I will not doubt but delivering the same to the King's Highness, at one time or other to know his gracious pleasure myself; and in case your lordship do alter the said letter, or make any other, then to send me the copy thereof, to the end that if his Grace would reason anything therein, I might be prompt and prevented to make him a direct answer. And now that I have written your lordship my poor mind, it lieth in you to follow what best liketh you. . . .

. . . Also the obligation that Benet said was in Mr. Smyth's hands of the Exchequer, wherein Hutton is bound to your lordship, is denied; and Mr.

---

2. Here used to imply deceit.   4. Abbeys in Hampshire.
3. delacyons = delays.

Smyth saith he had never any such bond. If your lordship spoke with Benet he can show you the truth. If I had it, it should be hard but some part should be saved and not to be all lost.[5]   (Vol. 3, No. 726)

Although this next is, at length, a business letter, the interest in it for us lies in Husee's frustration at Court, here extracted.

246   JOHN HUSEE TO LADY LISLE   *18 September 1536*

Pleaseth it your Ladyship to understand that according as I wrote my Lord from the Court by William Smythe, I have there followed and spent all time in vain, for I can there speed of nothing nor have any comfort, as more plainly by my lord's letter it shall appear; one thing assuring your ladyship, unless my lord procure new friends he shall do little good at their hands that he now taketh to be his friends, for here is nothing but everyone for himself. Madame, I am at my wits' end for payment of this money, for unless God help I see no remedy. . . . But in the meantime I will do the best I can. I assure your ladyship this matter grieveth me as much as anything that ever I had in hand; but now I remember my Lord of Rochford's words, who exhorted every man to beware of the flattering of the Court. The Lord Beauchamp will in no wise be entreated, nor give one hour longer respite. . . . As touching the Chancellor of the Augmentations, he hath made me plain answer that the King will in nowise grant the remainder of ffristock to my lord's heirs.

Madam, the Queen's Grace commoneth divers times of your ladyship and giveth your ladyship great praise. I think not the contrary but she beareth your ladyship good mind. They saith plainly that, all things set apart, the Coronation shall be the Sunday before All Hallow Day. . . . And thus madam, having no other ∧news∧ to write your ladyship, I rest, praying God once to send your ladyship your own heart's desire.

From London, in haste the xviij[th] day of September.

   By your ladyship's bounden,
Hol.   John Husee   (Vol. 3, No. 770)

The coronation was twice postponed, and in the end Queen Jane was never crowned at all.

The reception and exchange of New Year's gifts by the King, always important in showing a subject's standing at Court, was particularly so for Lisle after a year in which several of his cousins had been condemned for treason.

---

5. End of page; last page missing.

247   JOHN HUSEE TO LORD LISLE   *3 January 1539*

Pleaseth it your lordship to be advertised that I have received your sundry letters, and have delivered your New Year's gift unto the King's Highness' own hand, his Grace receiving the same very pleasantly, saying, 'We thank him.' And my Lord Privy Seal said, even as he did the last time, as soon as I was within the chamber of presence door, 'This is my Lord Lisle's man.' And on New Year's Eve at noon John Gough brought this cup which the King sendeth your lordship, which is a very goodly cup and well wrought, the which I do send your lordship by this bearer. . . .

Of such things as are bruited here this bearer can partly shew your lordship. Within a day or ij I trust to advertise your lordship how I speed in all your affairs. And thus I pray God to send your lordship long life and much honour, and many good New Years.

From London, the iij of January.
                    Your lordship's own man bounden,
Hol.   John Husee   (Vol.5, No.1319)

Though typical of the Court's regular displays for the people, the details of the religious observances this year were particularly important, for Lisle to know what he could safely permit in Calais.

248   JOHN WORTH TO LORD LISLE   *15 May 1539*

Pleaseth your lordship, so it is this present day, the Holy Thursday eve, the King's Grace took his barge at Whitehall, and so rowed up to Lambeth, and had his drums and fifes playing; and so rowed up and down the Thames an hour in the evening after evensong. And on Holy Thursday his Grace went a procession about the Court at Westminster ∧in the Whitehall∧; and my Lord Cobham bare the sword before the King's Grace, with all other nobles a great multitude. And the high altar in the chapel was garnished with all the apostles upon the altar, and mass by note, and the organs playing, with as much honour to God as might be devised to be done. And they that be in the King's chapel shewed me, and so did Killigrew also, that upon Good Friday last past the King's Grace crept to the Cross from the chapel door upward, devoutly, and so served the priest to mass that same day, his own person, kneeling on his Grace his knees. Also here has been the goodliest musters in London that ever was seen, upon Thursday last past; and the saying is that the King will remove upon Monday next to Greenwich. . . .

    your poer bedman at commandyment
            ffrom london, thys present holly thersday
Hol.   [John Worth]   (Vol.5, No.1415)

A letter from Thomas Warley on 6 July shows us another side of Court life in a list of the King's projected movements.[6]

The Gestes

	The vij[th] day of July to Oatland	vj miles and there iiij days	
	xij day to Woking	v	vj days
Julii	Guildford the xviij[th]	vj	v days
	Farnham xxiij	ix	iiij days
	Petworth xxvij	xiij	iij days
	Cowdray xxx	vij	j day
	Stansted j°	ix	j day
	Bishop's Waltham iij[d]	xii	iiij days
	Wade vj	xiiij	iij days
	Thruxton ix	xii	v days
	Wolfhall xii	viij	v days
Primo Augusti	Donnington xvij	xii miles and there	j day
	Welford xviij	v	j day
	Compton xix[th]	xii	iij days
	Langley xx[ti]	xii	iij days
	Woodstock xxiij	vij	j day
	Buckingham	xiiij	vj days
	Grafton xxix	viij	iij days
	Ampthill iij September	xij	vij days
September	Dunstable vij	viij	j day
	Missenden xij	x	j day
	Windsor xiij	xiij	

Although Jane Seymour had as yet no successor, Anne Basset had continued to hold her place at Court, in great favour with the King, who had given her a horse 'and a saddle for it'. When the ladies made their trip to Portsmouth described below, there had been ninety ships of war counted in the harbour shortly before; and 'the new greate shippe' was the *Harry Grace à Dieu*.

249   THE LADIES OF THE QUEEN'S PRIVY   *4 August 1539*
       CHAMBER, INCLUDING ANNE BASSET,
       TO KING HENRY VIII

Most gracious and benign sovereign Lord, please it your Highness to understand that we have seen and been in your new Great Shippe and the rest of your ships at Portsmouth, which are things so goodly to behold that in

6. Vol.5, No.1475.

our lives we have not seen (excepting your royal person and my lord the Prince your son) a more pleasant sight; for which, and the most bountiful gifts, the cheer and most gracious entertainment which your Grace hath vouchsafed to bestow upon us your most unworthy and humble servants, we render and send unto the same our most humble and entire thanks, which we beseech your Majesty to accept in good part, advertising the same that there rest now but only ij sorrows: the one for lack of your royal presence that ye might have seen your said ships now at this time when we might have waited on you here; the other that we think long till it may eftsoons like you to have us with you, which we all most heartily beseech our Lord God may be shortly; who preserve your most noble person and my Lord Prince, and grant you both to reign over us, Your Majesty many years, His Grace with long continuance but by late succession, as never princes did before you.

From your Majesty's haven and town of Portsmouth, the iiijth of August
        Your Highness most bounden and humble servants and
           bedewomen

Mabyell Sowthampton
  Margaret Taylebois   Margrett Howarde
  Alys Browne   Anne Knevytt   Jane Denny
  Jane Meows   Anne Basset
  Elizabeth Tyrwhyt   Elsabeth Harvy

                              (Vol.5, No.1513a)

Anne had been suffering from some slight but recurrent indisposition for a year or more. Joan (Jane) Denny was a remote Basset connection.

250   ANNE BASSET TO LADY LISLE   *5 October 1539*

Madam, My duty done, I humbly recommend me unto your Ladyship, desiring you of your daily blessing. The cause of my writing unto you at this time is, that I am now with my Cousin Denny, at the King's grace's commandment: for whereas Mistress Mewtas doth lie in London there are no walks but a little garden, wherefore it was the King's grace's pleasure that I should be with my Cousin Denny; for where as she lieth there are fair walks and a good open air; for the physician doth say that there is nothing better for my disease than walking; and I thank God I am a great deal better than I was. Madam, I did hope that I should have seen your ladyship here when my lord came over; but howbeit I trust to God that we shall have a mistress shortly, and then I trust I shall see you here when she comes over, which I hope to God will not be long. No more to you at this time, but I pray God send your Ladyship long life, to the pleasure of God.

From Westminster, the Sunday after Michaelmas day.
        By *your* humbell dowter
           An Basset   (Vol.5, No.1558)

Lisle had hoped to be allowed to escort Anne of Cleves onwards from Calais to the Court, but had been ordered to remain at his post; and his wife had evidently felt that her place was with him, but had asked Anne to let her regrets be known lest this be taken amiss.

251   ANNE BASSET TO LADY LISLE   *22 December 1539*

Madam, My duty done, I humbly recommend me unto your ladyship, desiring you of your daily blessing.

This shall signify your ladyship that I received your letter of Hosse, and according to the contents thereof, I have declared unto the King's ∧Highness∧ all things, as your ladyship willed me to do, so that his Grace took the same in right good part, ∧accepting∧ your good will and toward mind therein as thankfully as though your ladyship had waited on her Grace hither; pondering right well the charges that my lord and your ladyship hath lately been at, ∧and∧ do sustain, specially at this present time. I humbly thank your ladyship of the news you write me of her Grace, that she is so good and gentle ∧to∧ serve and please. It shall be no little rejoicement to us, her Grace's servants here, that shall attend daily upon her, and most comfort to the King's Majesty, whose Highness is not a little desirous to have her Grace here.

And for the good and motherly counsel your ladyship doth give me, concerning my continuance in the King's favour, I thank your ladyship most lowly therefor; trusting God shall no longer spare me life than I shall therein ∧continue∧. For I knowledge myself most bound to his Highness of all creatures: if I should, therefore, in any thing offend his Grace willingly, it were pity I should live. Madam, the King doth so well like the conserves you sent him last, that his Grace commanded me to write unto you for more of ∧the∧ codiniac[7] of the clearest making, and of the conserve of damsons; and this as soon as may be. No more to you at this time, but I pray God send your ladyship long life, to the pleasure of Almighty God.

From York-place, the Monday afore Christmas day.
                    Be yo*ur* humbell And obessent dowter,
                        anne basset   (Vol.5, No.1620)

John Norris was the elder brother of Lisle's good friend, the ill-fated Henry Norris; he was now, in spite of his brother's execution, a gentleman-usher to the King, and had been in Calais with the escort for the new Queen. Anne Basset, as a Maid of Honour, would surely have been present at the arrival ceremonies in England that he now describes, and probably also

7. Quince marmalade.

Katharine (in attendance on Lady Rutland). Honor Lisle hoped to use Norris's influence at Court to secure her an official place with the Queen. Lisle's stepson, John Dudley, was her Master of the Horse.

252   JOHN NORRIS TO LADY LISLE   *c.4 January 1540*

Right honourable, my duty humbly remembered unto my good lord and your ladyship, this shall certify your ladyship in my last letter I ascertained you of the arrival of the Queen's Grace upon the Downs; and so lay at Dover, Sunday all day. Upon Monday her Grace removed to Canterbury with my Lord of Suffolk and my Lord Warden and a great company of ladies and gentlemen; and iij mile from Canterbury there met with her Grace my Lord of Canterbury with iij hundred gentlemen, and at Canterbury in her Grace's Great Chamber there stood iiij [?score] more ladies and gentlewomen. Her Grace took them [   ]. The next day, which was Tuesday, her Grace went to Sittingbourne, and there that night. Upon Wednesday to Rochester, and there met with her Grace, ij miles out of Rochester, my Lord of Norfolk with an hundred horses and a goodly company of gentlemen in [   ] velvet and chains about their necks; and so lay there New Year's Day. And that day the King's Highness came thither prively and banquetted with her Grace upon Friday, and so came prively away again that night. And her Grace went to Dartford and there tarried that night, and upon Saturday, early in the morning, she marched toward Blackheath; and at the foot of Shooter's Hill there was set up a rich pavilion, and there met with her her Grace's Lord Chamberlain, that is the Earl of Rutland, Master Baynton, Vice-Chamberlain, Master Dennys her Chancellor, Master Carew, riding with a great company more; and the Duke of Suffolk's daughter that my Lord Marquess hath married, the Duchess of Richmond, my Lady of Hertford, my Lady Audley that my Lord Chancellor married, with many other ladies that I name not. There is of her Privy Chamber my Lady of Rutland and my Lady Browne and my Lady Edgecombe. These be all the ladies of her Privy Chamber that I know yet. And when her Grace had saluted them, Doctor Day made a goodly oration, and that done, her Grace went into the pavilion and there did shift her wondrous gorgeously in cloth of tissue, made after her own fashion, and a wondrous rich attire upon her head of her own country fashion; and there tarried till the King came within half a mile of her pavilion. And then her Grace took her horse, and afore her a great company of gentlemen and then her own gentlemen that met her there, and then her Council, both English and Cleves, and next her my Lord Chamberlain and Vice-Chamberlain, my Lord of Norfolk, my Lord Great Master, my Lord of Canterbury, my Lord Warden, and then her Grace upon a goodly palfrey or gelding, wondrously rich apparelled, and behind her Sir

John Dudley, Master of her Horse, leading her horse of honour, richly apparelled; and then all the ladies in their degree, and last of all her yeomen and all serving men behind them. This was the fashion of her Grace and her train.

. . . I have not ascertained you of all things so well as it was indeed, but I trust once to tell you all by mouth[   ] of time. This I make an end, and so most humbly fare you as well to do as myself.

By him that is yours to his power. (Vol.6, No.1634)

All but one and a half inches of the rest of the page has been cut off, and with it the signature, but the handwriting and the spelling, as well as its contents claim it at once for John Norris.

15

Calais 1537–1538

From the beginning of 1537, there is no way of tucking politics and religion into a separate section: they begin to become central, if at first only in the background, to the life of the Lisles in Calais. From now on the most casual-seeming mentions of these subjects must be noticed for the significance they may have later on.

Cardinal Pole is a case in point. Son of Lisle's cousin and friend, the Countess of Salisbury, he was also a first cousin of the King, who had educated and favoured him and to whom he remained personally devoted. He disapproved of the divorce and supremacy and left England for Italy, and later, pressed by Henry to state his position, he reluctantly replied with an outspoken attack, particularly on the executions of More and Fisher. Henry feigned forgiveness. He had loved his brilliant young cousin after his fashion, but it was the fashion in which he had loved More. In such people disagreement was treachery, and Henry never forgave. In December 1536 the Pope made Pole a Cardinal, and the breach became open and irrevocable. When, further, it was announced on 7 February 1537 that Pole was to be sent to England as papal legate, to encourage the rebels of the Pilgrimage of Grace, it is not surprising that from henceforth he was regarded as the arch-traitor. He was to be one of the determining factors in Lisle's fate.

Meanwhile the proper business of Calais was to continue its own defence and yet neutrality, as the war between France and the Empire dragged on.

253   OUDART DU BIES TO LORD LISLE   *11 February 1537*

My Lord Deputy, my good neighbour and friend, I have received the letter that you and my masters of the Council have written me. I recommend me heartily to your good favour and theirs.

My Lord Deputy, you write me that daily you have complaints of my soldiers who come within your Pales in such sort that it seemeth to you the rather to be for pillage than anything else. I ensure you, my lord Deputy, that I know nothing of this save that one only man of mine hath done any wrong to the subjects of the King your master; and if you have knowledge of any such, advertise me and I will see to the proper punishment so that ye shall be contented therein, ensuring you that I would not, for nothing in this world, be the occasion to contravene nor break the good peace and perpetual amity of the two Kings, our masters, but would rather employ me to support and observe it by every means in my power, as you may know that I have always done. And as for this that you allege, if you find any of my people within your Pales that you can capture, that you have them executed. As I have before written unto you, I have never heard it said that wherever one shall find his enemy, outside the towns and countries that are neuter, that one may not make war upon him and lead him prisoner or kill him. Because I find you too prudent and wise, and too reasonable to do them any wrong, as I have said to you, if they undertake any enterprise upon the subjects of the King your master, advertise me and I will do good justice in that matter. . . .

My Lord Deputy, I have received the fine oranges that my Lady your good bedfellow hath sent me. I do not know how to thank you or her sufficiently for these fine presents that you bestow upon me. I would fain have some honest thing to send unto you in return, and if such shall come my way you shall have thereof your part; praying you to believe that wherever I may do you pleasure or friendship, if you will inform me thereof, I shall rightly heartily employ me therein. . . .

From Boulogne, the xj[th] day of February.

Your good neighbour and friend,
Oudart du Bies[1]

(Vol. 4, No. 924)

254   JOHN HUSEE TO LORD LISLE   *18 February 1537*

Pleaseth it your lordship to be advertised that this day I wrote the same by Goodal largely, of all things. And since, I received your lordship's packet, which I delivered immediately unto my Lord Privy Seal, and shall not fail with diligence to procure speedy answer thereof. And at my being in the Court there came a messenger from my Lord of Norfolk, who lieth at Barnard Castle in the bishopric of Durham; and thanked be God all things are there quieted and well 'stablished, and all the offenders come in to my Lord of Norfolk, asking mercy, as well the great as the small. And divers hath been put to death of the doers thereof. Bigod is in prison in Carlisle. I think his life is not long, but yet not so short as he hath demerited. The Bishops wax good men and do preach sincerely the word of God. I have

---

1. French.

good hope it shall so continue. As I can hear further news your lordship shall be advertised. As God knoweth, who send your lordship long life with much honour.

From London, in haste, the xviij[th] day of February.

Your lordship's bound man,

Hol.　　　　　John Husee　　　　　(Vol. 4, No. 929a)

The bishops above mentioned were to discuss for the next five months what exactly it was that the new religion was officially to believe – an important matter, since a man's life could depend later on guessing right meanwhile, and Calais was a long way from the centre of theological decision-making.

255　　JOHN HUSEE TO LORD LISLE　　　　*23 February 1537*

Pleaseth it your lordship. . . .

Here are very good news that on Friday last, being the xvj[th] of this instant, Sir Christopher Dacres, uncle unto the Lord Dacres of the North, skirmished with certain of the rebels in the north, and slew vij[C] of them and more, and took the rest in manner as many more prisoners, and hung them up and put them to death upon every bush, insomuch that he hath won his spurs; for I heard my Lord Privy Seal say surely that if it lay in him he would make him an earl for his labour. And thus as I shall hear news your lordship shall be thereof advertised. There was much ado amongst the Council here, ere they could conclude upon this letter, as God knoweth, who send your lordship long life with much honour.

From London, the xxiij[th] day of February.

By him that is your lordship's man bounden,

Hol.　　　　　John Husee　　　　　(Vol. 4, No. 931)

Palmer, though a Calais official, can as a neutral move freely in both France and Flanders, and at present is with the Imperial troops near Cambrai, which is neutral.

256　　SIR THOMAS PALMER TO LORD LISLE　　　　*16 May 1537*

Please it your good Lordship. . . .

Sir, as for news here, the man that you wot of doth not come out of his lodging, nor intends not, as I can learn, for I take the French King too much to be his friend, which I trust he will repent at length. . . .

My lord, this day my lord Great Master of Flanders removed his camp toward Cambray, and is lodged within half a league of Cambray; which is but a small band as yet. I was there with them. If the Frenchmen come near, they intend to enter in to Cambray, as the Great Master did tell me, whom I find an honourable man and makes me very good cheer.

I beseech your lordship to send me Tybalt hither. He shall hear of me at Tournay, at a canon's house named Gabriel Flakeyt. I do send him an angelot to bring him hither by this bearer.

The bruit came this day hither that the French king is at Corbie[2] and intends to come back again into Hainault. I promise your lordship they be not a little afraid. Beseeching your lordship I may be commended to good Mr. Treasurer and to all other my good friends and masters.

From the Camp beside Cambray, the xvj day of May.

By the hand of your own till he be dead,

Hol.   Thomas Palmer   (Vol. 4, No. 953)

'The man that you wot of' is Palmer's way of referring to Cardinal Pole, the first reference we get in the Letters to the English plot for kidnapping him. Originally the King, believing he was coming to England on the Papal mission, had asked both France and the Emperor not to allow him through their lands. Pole, however, had told both the Pope and others he had no intention of trusting his life to Henry. Whereupon Henry realized he *wanted* him in England. He wrote to Sir Francis Bryan on 25 April that 'we would be very glad to have the said Pole by some mean trussed up and conveyed to Calais',[3] and sent him £100 to effect this. Bryan recruited Palmer to make the arrangements locally. The important thing for future reference is that the above letter shows that Lisle knew of and took no action against the plot. When it was realized that Pole (alerted by Englishmen hanging about watching for him to 'walk or ride out') was on his guard, assassination was decided upon; but Cromwell refused to pay the men to be hired for this except by results. There is no indication anywhere that Lisle knew of this development. Pole eventually was given safe-conduct to the security of the bishop's palace in neutral Liége.

On 16 May Husee sent Lisle news of seventeen condemned to death for taking part in the Pilgrimage of Grace, including a woman and six of the clergy. The following brief note was enclosed with that letter.

257   JOHN HUSEE TO LORD LISLE   *18 May 1537*

After the closing of this letter it was shewed me by one that saw the same, which is that x of the monks of the Charterhouse of London were this afternoon had to Newgate. And the Shrieves remained at the writing of this still in the said Charterhouse, and it is thought that the said house shall be

---

2. Corbeyt: a town in Picardy.   3. *L. & P.* XII i 939.

clearly dissolved. And hereafter, as I shall further hear, your lordship shall be advertised.

Hol. (Vol. 4, No. 954a)

The monks were left without food, chained upright to pillars, and on the 29th he writes that eight are dead.

In May the King of Scots, returning home with his French bride and escorted by ten French and four Scottish ships, lay to off the Yorkshire coast for victualling. James Crane, a mercenary in the French service, who seems to have 'left his country for his country's good' but may have in fact been one of Cromwell's spies, had a tale to tell of disaffected persons in Yorkshire he had met on the voyage, which he eventually took to Lisle in Calais. Husee was sent for to bring Crane back fast and secretly to Cromwell.

258   JOHN HUSEE TO LORD LISLE   *10 July 1537*

Pleaseth it your lordship to be advertised that, lauded be God, we had a fair passage, and with much ado we were horsed at Dover, notwithstanding your lordship's commandment in that behalf. Howbeit we made such diligence that we were with my Lord Privy Seal the next day by ij of the clock at afternoon. And his lordship was glad of our coming, and specially of the overthrow of the Frenchmen; so that I do well perceive that any news being good, and in the advancement of the Emperor's host or leaguer, shall be and are unto him right acceptable and welcome. Therefore it shall be requisite that your lordship use such discretion and diligence that your news may be the first, so they be good and pleasant, otherwise I had liefer others had the presentment of such than I.

Since my coming my Lord Privy Seal hath committed James Crane unto my governance and company, so that in manner we have done none other thing than attend his pleasure, which as yet is not known. He deferreth the matter till the coming of his servant from the Court, which hourly we look for. But I judge that James Crane shall northward. Howbeit yet I stand in doubt whether he shall thither or to the Court. This matter is earnestly looked upon, for I perceive what shall be therein done shall be by the King's Highness' assent and the whole Council. What shall further therein be done your lordship shall be by the first thereof advertised. And touching the despatchment of your long tracted suit, my Lord Privy Seal saith that I shall be rid ere he come from the Court. I hope I shall be no longer delayed.

The *Great Bark,* the *Minion,* the *Janet* and the *Swepstake* are prest, and shall forthwith out: but for what purpose it is yet unknown. And my Lady Lawson is dead, God pardon her soul. And as for your lordship's other affairs with your familiar enemies, I doubt not but they shall have the overthrow. Goodal hath received all things according unto Mr. Scriven's writing. I trust

God shall send him in safety, or else would I be right sorry, as God knoweth, who send your lordship long life and much honour.

From St. Katharine's, the xth of July.

By your lordship's own man,

Hol.   John Husee

I had a side of a red deer given me, the which I trust your lordship shall have with the first ship. Harold hath it to bake and Mr. Gonson gave it me.

(Vol.4, No.977)

The first signs of the religious troubles in Calais, which from now on were to increase year by year, began in July 1537, when on the 9th John Butler, Cranmer's Commissary, reported to his master that there were two priests in Calais who were great enemies of the truth, one of whom, Sir William Minstreley, had written a book confirming what had previously been orthodox opinion. Lisle had confined both priests while querying the matter with Cromwell, but Cranmer's report reached him first.

259   CROMWELL TO THE COUNCIL OF CALAIS   *17 July 1537*

After my right hearty commendations, the King's Highness being informed that there be two priests in that town, the one called Sir William Minstreley which is now in ward, the other called Sir William Richardson otherwise good Sir William, hath commanded me to signify unto you that like as his pleasure is that upon the receipt hereof you shall send both the said priests hither as prisoners, in assured custody, so his Grace cannot a little marvel to hear of the papistical fashion that is maintained in that town, and by you chiefly that be of his Grace's Council. Surely his Majesty thinketh that you have little respect, either to him, to his laws, or to the good order of that town, which so little regard him, in a matter of so great weight, which also his Highness hath so much to heart. And willed me plainly to intimate unto you all and every of you, that in case he shall perceive from henceforth any such abuses suffered or winked at, as have been hitherto in manner in contempt of his most royal estate maintained, his Highness will put others in the best of your rooms that shall so offend him, by whom he will be better served. It is thought against all reason that the prayers of women and their fond flickerings should move any of you to do that thing that should in any wise displease your prince and sovereign lord or offend his just laws. . . .

. . . And thus fare you heartily well.

From Sutton the xvij[th] of July,

Signed   Your lordshippis assuryd

Thom*a*s Crumwell   (Vol.4, No.980)

Honor Lisle had tried to intervene on behalf of the priests and did not desist even after Cromwell's warning. When Lisle's delayed letter finally arrived, Husee persuaded Cromwell to write 'gently' to him.

260   CROMWELL TO LORD LISLE   *24 July 1537*

After my most affectuous commendation to your lordship, with like thanks for your news written unto me in your letters of the xv[th] of this month[4] which I have received this morning. And for as much as by the King's Majesty's commandment I wrote unto you and other of his Grace's council there for the sending up of two seditious priests somewhat sharply, to the intent that some of the said council which lean much to their superstitious old observations and Rites might be general warning to you all directed, beware how too much to stand in their obstinate pertinacy and error in some things but be induced to bring their hearts inward to the conformity of the truth. Whatsoever be written in the same, my lord, think none otherwise but that I remain still your perfect and sincere friend and that by such sharpness ye are none otherwise touched to thereby, [than] to take an occasion to be concurrent with me ∧to∧ alter such evil instructed and inclined hearts to [leave] their old ceremonies and observations and exhort them to know and follow the truth declared unto them and to set all obstinacy and hardness of heart apart, not thinking themselves wiser in such things than the most learned and best of the realm.

As I trust so much in your goodness that ye will not fail to do your good office and as much as lieth in your power for the same: And like as therein ye shall administer unto the King's Highness very acceptable pleasure and thankful: So I shall so much esteem your good earnest proceeding thereto as to any other thing as wherein ye could do me most pleasure. And continuing my good affection towards you, will no less earnestly employ myself to the furtherance of your reasonable desires and suits whensoever occasion shall serve me thereto, trusting to get your bill signed at the King's Grace next being at Windsor. Thus fare ye right heartily well.

From Easthampstead this xxiiij[th] of July.

Signed   Your lordshippis assuryd,
                        Thomas Crumwell   (Vol. 4, No. 987)

Husee in his next suggests how such dangerous delays may be avoided in future, and then describes his own meeting with Cromwell.

261   JOHN HUSEE TO LORD LISLE   *25 July 1537*

. . .

And when he had opened his full mind I showed him that your Lordship's

4. These have not survived.

only confidence consisteth in God, the King and him; and how that I was well assured that your Lordship would take no less grief at his writing than at the King's. And further, that if his lordship did not the sooner write some other loving letter unto you that I stood in doubt that your Lordship might take such conceit thereon that might perchance put you in hazard of some disease or peril of your life; to the which he answered and said that he thought your Lordship was wiser than to take it after any such manner; for whatsoever he wrote, he was and is and would remain still your Lordship's sincere and very friend, and so willed me that I should advertise your Lordship. But assuredly he cannot 'bide nothing that soundeth with the papistical laws in any manner wise, for the King's majesty is most earnestly bent against the same. And further, what he wrote last in his said sharp letter, he swore unto me was only by the King's express commandment; but the truth is, he hath divers of the Council there in much more jealousy in those causes than your Lordship. But I, as one that beareth your Lordship no less good heart and mind than to the natural father begat me, that in all causes, and in especial in such as concern the supremacy of the head of the Church, that your Lordship be no less earnest and precise than you would be in causes of high treason, for undoubted, these same are no less abhorred by the King's majesty and those that are in authority about him than very high treason. Howbeit, I showed him that I was well assured that your Lordship never bare no such cause; but I partly suppose this matter springeth of the Commissary and his adherents. Therefore if your Lordship do persecute and search out the same well it cannot be kept secret; and from henceforth in any such cause let not the Commissary be judge ne meddle, but your Lordship and the Council. I cannot perceive since I 'longed unto your lordship that ever you had displeasure but for such and like causes. I would God they would all agree, or else I would the Commissary, and they with him, were in the front of the 'sault of Turwyn,[5] and then I would think they would shortly be despatched. Further, your lordship shall understand that at last my Lord Privy Seal called me to him, and said that he would write your lordship a letter: and I desired his lordship that it might be some gentle letter, and he said that it so should be, for he knew that your lordship would take his writing very earnestly. So that your lordship shall herein enclosed receive his letter. . . .

And surely your lordship needeth not to take it so earnestly, for I think verily my Lord Privy Seal loveth your lordship as well as he doth any man in the realm. And howsoever the world goeth your lordship shall need to take no care, for the King's Majesty loveth your lordship well, and there is no doubt but your lordship shall overcome all at your pleasure; and therefore

5. The assault on Terouenne, then in progress.

me thinketh your lordship should not take everything so grievously, for the world is yours, and I trust shall be better than ever it was; but in no wise it is not for your lordship to take thought, for your lordship hath and shall have wherewithal to maintain your honour while you live. . . .

News here are none, but that the bishops be departed, and I ween not agreed. Whether they be or no there is nothing as yet published, as God knoweth, who send your lordship long life with honour, and once your heart's desire.

From St. Katharine's, the xxv^{th} of July.

Your lordship's own man bounden,

Hol.　　　　John Husee　　　　　　　　　　　　　(Vol. 4, No. 988)

It is the policy of this selection to arrange the letters according to subject, and to cut occasionally less interesting material in a letter altogether, in order to include as much as possible of the best. In the case of Husee's next this policy has been thrown out of the window, in fairness both to Husee and the reader. It is perhaps his masterpiece as a correspondent and a stylist, packing in all the latest news on every subject under the sun. A single paragraph has been extracted and is to be found in chapter 12, on domestic affairs, as it requires some explanation – it concerns the gift of a live seal. The policy of minimum footnotes has also been abandoned, to make the following of so many subjects at once easier.

262　　JOHN HUSEE TO LORD LISLE　　　　　*21 August 1537*

Pleaseth it your Lordship to be advertised that by Henbury's man I wrote the same of the signment of your bill,[6] the which I trust ere this time be come unto your lordship's hands; and I think verily your lordship is no gladder of the whole gift than I was of the signment. Your lordship hath it in fee simple, even to your own desire, and I put no doubt but I shall recover the rent which was due at the Annunciation of Our Lady last past, so that your lordship shall have due unto you at Michaelmas next coming j year's rent and an half. My Lord Privy Seal willed me in any wise to write unto your lordship that you should not sell it, saying that ∧if∧ your lordship so did that you should never have the King good lord unto you, nor him to your friend. And I shewed him that I was well assured that your lordship would not part from it for gold neither silver, considering it was the King's gift. It shall therefore be requisite that your lordship write speedily unto my Lord Privy Seal, giving his lordship most hearty thanks for his goodness: likewise, de-claring by the same that your lordship is not a little bounden unto the King's

6. For Frithelstock Priory.

Majesty for the said gift, and how that your lordship did never think to get nor obtain the same but only by his lordship's mediation and instance: and further how that your lordship is never minded to put it away nor sell it. And the sooner this letter come the better; but it shall be requisite that I have the Copy of the same, to the end that I may so much the better answer my Lord Privy Seal if his lordship chance to reason with me at the delivery of the said letter. And further, Mr. Surveyor's[7] advice is that your lordship should send some loving letter unto Mr. Wriothesley, giving him thanks and desiring him of continuance of ∧his∧ good mind toward you. And if your lordship did send him some gentle remembrance, and though it were not worth past xls. it should be well bestowed. The truth is, the man standeth in place where he may please and displease. It shall therefore be good to entertain him amongst the number of your friends; and this partly Mr. Surveyor's advice.

To write your lordship what hath partly stayed this suit it shall not be best as now, but at my coming I trust to declare that, with others. Now, as touching the dispatchment of your patent, I have been counselled since my last writing, first to go unto the Chancellor of the Augmentations and his fellowship, for divers causes, which I will do, for it must be signed again by all the council's hands of the Augmentations ere it pass the Broad Seal,[8] so that though none of your lordship's counsel be here yet have I had counsel thereto, for a man cannot work too surely in such causes.

Further, as I wrote unto your lordship, I have been in hand with Mr. Fowler, our Vice-Treasurer, for xx^{li}, which with much difficulty he hath lent me, swearing by his faith that he borrowed the same. It shall be good your lordship write him thanks, and how that you do allow the said xx^{li}. Howbeit he hath a bill of my hand in your name, wherein I am bound to repay him the said xx^{li} the last day of September next coming, for otherwise he would not a'delivered me the said money. The charges of the Signet, Privy Seal, and of the Broad Seal of your patent will be xiiij^{li} and odd money besides the Augmentations and what they will have; and ∧what∧ is their duty, God knoweth! Howbeit I shall be the best husband that I can in it. Also Wriothesley's clerk must needs have a reward, for I promised it him, and he hath deserved it, for he hath done as much as in him lay for the furtherance of this suit. I will make Mr. Surveyor privy what I give him. xxs. shall be the most, for it will not be good to depart with too much till such time the money be received, and then your lordship may further reward him and others at your pleasure.

Also in my last letter I sent your lordship a letter from my Lord Marquis[9] to Mr. Poynings for venison for your lordship; and my said Lord Marquis hath him most entirely commended unto your lordship, and thanketh you

7. Richard Lee, Surveyor of Calais.   9. Of Exeter.
8. The Great Seal.

for the last hawk you sent him, which was very toward, but she died in the mew ere she were full mewed, and he said if your lordship could send him a good hawk for partridge and pye it were a great pleasure unto him, and he would requite it your lordship. He careth not whether it be a sore[10] or mewed hawk or else a falcon. He desired me to write your lordship and to procure your answer; and further he desireth your lordship to be good unto his man which shall shortly come over for hawks. . . .

Further, your lordship hath demerited no small friendship of my Lord Privy Seal by reason you have so gently handled Mr. Surveyor and his new-contracted wife, for my lord taketh the same in marvellous good part and thankful. Therefore in any wise your lordship must needs proceed therein as you have begun. And my Lord Privy Seal looketh daily for answer of such letters as he sent unto your lordship and my Lord Chamberlain concerning Mr. Marshal.[11] Your lordship can take no pain therein but it will be recompensed; and if Mr. Marshall will not be ruled he will surely repent it. I think the letter Oliver his man brought him liked him but a little. If your lordship had received such another I am well assured you would not a'slept well in vij nights following! It shall be well done that your lordship, as soon as you know the last of Mr. Marshal's mind, to send your answer therein unto my Lord Privy Seal, so that you may prevent Mr. Marshal, and that your letter may be here before his. I saw the letter Mr. Marshal sent to my Lord Privy Seal, and also the answer my Lord made him, the contents whereof your lordship shall know at Mr. Surveyor's coming over and mind. There can be nothing written nor spoken against your lordship but it will be known, you are so friended; but this must be kept secret.

And touching James Crane, the King hath given him his pardon, and I think he will shortly return. He looketh to have viij[d] a day in Calais. Your lordship hath also deserved thanks for him, for all his sayings hath been found true. And touching any such priests as shall be brought to your lordship by good Mr. Commissary, let them remain in prison, for it is against reason your lordship should be charged with their costs, sending them over. I shall not fail to know my Lord Privy Seal's mind, what punishment they shall have, and how they shall be ordered.

The Abbot of Westminster[12] is sick. I cannot speak with him since your lordship sent me your letter. I would he had a tun of wine, and the cask, in his belly! I think not the contrary but he will have his wine out of hand. Your lordship shall know his full mind by my next letter. And touching the indenture for Huntley, he is content to be bound to give your lordship by bond, besides the indenture, as much for the xij acres as ever they went for.

10. sawre = a hawk of the first year that has not yet moulted; pye = magpie.
11. Sir Richard Grenville.
12. Interminably demanding two tuns of wine in payment of a disputed debt.

And if it be proved that ever it went above ijs. the acre, he will make it good to the uttermost, and if your lordship be not minded that he shall have it, then your lordship may send me the old indenture again. I would not desire your lordship to lose one penny of the accustomed rent.

And where my Lord Comptroller[13] is not contented because he was not admitted Mayor, your lordship shall right well abide his malice. As touching Mr. Porter's[14] coming, I am right glad thereof, for I doubt not but he will speak his mind. And as for the death of the man with the great nose,[15] he dieth oft, but he is not minded to be buried! He will make so long that at length he will go for good and all.

I trust to procure your lordship some venison ere I come from the Court, or else your warrants in Essex. And as for the banding of my Lord Comptroller, Mr. Wingfield, the Marshal and Under Marshal against your lordship, surely they are like to win nothing that way but displeasure, shame and rebuke. And though Mr. Marshal nor his wife will not do their duty unto your lordship and my lady, thanked be God your lordship and my lady may live by them without their help, and I doubt not but at length they will Cry peccavi!

And touching West and his son, I will do my best to stay them of their prepensed purpose. And as for Mr. Richard's[16] horse, John Dolingcourt is come with him, fair and in good liking. I will be at the delivery of him. I trust he will deserve him, time coming, for now at the later end he did little good in it. I trust he will send your lordship some pretty gelding.

Christopher Vyllers[17] is departed; and Sir John Dauncy, Sir John Vyllers and one Wilcox, a man of law, were his executors. They are all out of town and will not be here till Michaelmas. I shall procure to see the testament, and to advertise your lordship of the truth. I spake with Crowder, his man, who shewed me that your lordship is not overseer, but he bequeathed your lordship v marks in money, and a salt of five marks. And he saith that iij hours ere he died he commoned nothing but of your lordship, and after he had made his executors he could never abide the sight of them. If your lordship had been here he thinketh verily that you should have had a great part of his substance, for he had more mind of your lordship than of all world at the hour of his death. When I have seen the testament I will write your lordship the truth of this matter.

News here are none, but that the bishops' books are a'printing, and I think will be out by Michaelmas. And on Sunday next my Lord Privy Seal and the Lord Beauchamp shall be stalled[18] at Windsor. All other I shall advertise

---

13. Lord Edmund Howard.
14. Sir Thomas Palmer, Knight Porter.
15. Francis I.

16. Richard Cromwell.
17. Steward of Lisle's Manor of Kybworth.
18. As Knights of the Garter.

your lordship by Doningcourt at his coming. And thus I pray Jesu send your lordship long life with much honour, and once your most heart's desire.

From St. Katharine's, the xxj[th] of August.

By your lordship's own man bounden,

Hol. John Husee (Vol. 4, No. 1001)

The marriage of Richard Lee to Margaret Grenville, mentioned in this letter, had been violently opposed by her father, Sir Richard, and at Cromwell's request supported by Lisle; which added to the bad relations between him and the Marshal and thence to his difficulties in Calais. That the bishops had agreed on their 'book' might at last help Lisle to know what his religious stance should be. Meanwhile the royal Supremacy made it possible for Cromwell as Vicegerent and Cranmer as Archbishop to press on with their particular brand of reform. On 1 September Husee writes:

> Concerning the priest of Guisnes, or any other which shall offend the King's laws there, my Lord Privy Seal willed me to signify your lordship that the King's pleasure is that they shall be punished by your lordship and the Council there, and not to send them over. And as for the ij priests that be here, my Lord will examine them at his next coming unto London.[19]

That he should entrust the fate of Calais priests to the Council seems strange in view of what Sir Thomas Palmer writes to Lisle on the 7th:

> I promise your lordship, within an hour of our first meeting he began to triumph and swore by God's Blood we were all papist and lacked throughout our 'fiances;[20] and I swore by God's Heart it was not so, insomuch that I am sure he that was a stone's cast off might hear us. Notwithstanding, on my faith, he declared unto me ere we parted that he meant neither you nor me. But by God's Blood he put me in furor, I tell you.[21]

263 RICHARD LEE TO LADY LISLE *16 September 1537*

My duty remembered, it may please your good ladyship to be advertised that according to the tenour of your first letter, I was in hand with my Lord of Canterbury, who did not deny but that he had certain words to your servant, much after the rate your ladyship did write unto me. And then I showed him that your ladyship did much marvel why he should conceive such opinion in you, for I showed that there was never preacher that came thither but that

19. Vol. 4, No. 1004.
20. fyagns, ? for 'fiances' = affiances = faith *or* allegiance.
21. Vol. 4, No. 1011.

your ladyship did entertain ∧him∧ as well as lay in you to do. The which he did confess he did know by the report of them which came from thence to be true. But for all that, the report hath been made by them and other that your ladyship was given to be a little papisch. And in that he spake of it he said he did nothing but his office; that notwithstanding, he prayed me to desire your Ladyship and my Lord both that ye would be favourers of them that favour the truth. And so doing, my Lord and you both shall be assured of him to be at your commandment as any friend ye have alive. . . .

. . . As knoweth our Lord, who send your ladyship long life with the increase of honour.

At Sopewell besides Seynt albonis,[22] the xvj day of September.

By yo*ur* lovinge Cowsin duringe lyff*e* w*ith* out thret*tes*
Rychard Lee   (Vol. 4, No. 1016)

These letters from Palmer and Lee, and one from Cromwell indicating that Lady Lisle's treatment of one of his servants 'might have been better before', may have made Lisle nervous about his all-important relations with the great man and motivated the contents of Husee's next. Lisle's own letter is missing.

264   JOHN HUSEE TO LORD LISLE   *2 October 1537*

My humble and most bounden duty premised unto your lordship, these shall signify the same that my lord Privy Seal hath received the puncheon of wine, the falcon and cheeses, with the mastiff, even according unto your lordship's writing, most heartily thanking your lordship for the same. . . .

And where your lordship willeth me in your last letter to procure liberty for the advancement of your servants, if I can spy a time meet to move my lord Privy Seal in it I will open it unto him: if not, I trust ere Mr. Surveyor be furnished, your lordship shall have a stay for that matter, and whatsoever they say or do yet, your lordship should give the hearing and let it so pass. For I assure your lordship that it grieveth me not a little, that your lordship should write that you are weary of your life. For thanked be God the King is good lor[d] unto you, and I cannot see the contrary but your lordship is like to do better than ever you did. But your lordship is of so noble a nature that you show so much favour, and that maketh some to take the more upon them. . . .

For the allowance of your patent in the Court of the Augmentations, within this viij days it will be known, and then immediately I intend to depart toward Calais and then your lordship shall know all, for I have many things

22. i.e. St. Alban's.

to open which I will not declare by writing. I trust at the farthest to be with your lordship within this x days so that reserving all others thereunto I rest, praying Jhesus to send your lordship long life with much honour, and once your heart's desire.

From St. Katharine's, the ij^d of October.

By your lordship's own man,

Hol.   John Husee   (Vol. 4, No. 1022)

The following letter does not advance the Lisle story, but when we remember that Palmer was hired to execute the plot against Cardinal Pole it may give us an unusual slant on the casting and playing of the role of First Murderer in a Tudor drama.

265   SIR THOMAS PALMER   *[n.d.] October–November 1537*
        TO LORD LISLE

My lord, in my humblest manner I recommend me unto your good lordship, certifying your lordship that I have received iij letters from you, wherein I find your lordship always one man, which I rejoice much at, praising your lordship. Everybody is not of your fashion, *silentium in claustro.*[23] I beseech your lordship to have me most humbly recommended to my good lady, and I pray God send you both long life together. And albeit that I find the King's Highness very good lord unto me, and in likewise my Lord Privy Seal, yet considering the charge[24] I have I would gladly see it discharged at home. And as tomorrow I go to the Court, and God willing, not purposing to return to London until the time I have taken my leave of the King's Highness and of all the Court. I promise your lordship I have spent now fifty pound and fifty groats beside. I had need to make small banquets at Calais; and if that I should give the Ward their breakfast this year, as I have accustomed, by God's body I have ∧a∧ dozen were like to go without their dinners for it. Therefore I trust my friends will take it *ultimum posse non est esse.*[25] My lord, you must understand that I am a good scholar to learn so much Latin in so little space. This next week Mr. Treasurer shall receive our wages. I will come home with him for company sake, albeit I have nothing to receive. I promise your lordship, by the faith I owe to God, I never thought so long to be with you; and that I may be humbly recommended to all my lords and masters of the Council, trusting in God that we be all in life and charity, or else for my part, I beshrew my heart, I am at this hour clean in my

23. The monastic rule of silence from sunset to sunrise. We might say 'mum's the word', or perhaps 'don't say I said so'.

24. = expense.

25. Using *esse* as 'to eat', he means 'Do all I can, it's hardly a meal.'

soul and in my purse. . . . And where I wrote you in my last letter that I was ramplied with melancholy, at this hour Captain Reason hath subdued melancholy and all is at rest. As knoweth God, who send your good lordship good night.

            Yours,

Hol.   Palmer   (Vol. 4, No. 1025b)

266   CROMWELL TO LORD LISLE   *17 November 1537*

My very good lord, After my right hearty commendations, I am now enforced to write my mind plainly unto you, as to him the preservation of whose honour I desire, both for the discharge of my duty to the King's Highness and for the declaration of mine hearty good will which I bear unto you. And therefore I require you, my lord, to take it in good part.

First, I trust you consider what a charge you have there under the King's Majesty; and I would you should remember both what beseemeth a man to do, being in that place, and that the same containeth in it no state of inheritance ne term for life, but upon the good behaviour of the person having it. Now, if you should weigh the thing and the nature of it indifferently, would you think it meet that a man should have that charge which would bring himself to such necessity that he should be constrained to put all things to sale that be committed upon special trust to his discretion, neglecting of the one part of the King's Highness honour to be sustained in the satisfaction of his grants, of the other part as it were contemning all friendship in giving place to a little lucre. Surely, my lord, such a governor as you be should not bind himself at any man's request to perform that shall not percase lie in him, ne by any his excess in living make himself so needy that when the present thing should happen he should be forced to have more estimation of money than regard to the tale it bringeth with it.

If I were not determined to continue your lordship's assured friend I would not work thus plainly with you; neither think that I do it upon any affection, for I would that I may will honestly. One man I have oftentimes recommended, that is the Surveyor, whom the King's Majesty would have served of four men according to his grant and late commandment made for the same. But yet I write not this so much for him alone as for others, and chiefly for yourself, and after for the poor man that is bearer hereof, who hath your bond, which your honour shall be to perform and accomplish, and both mine advice and desire shall concur with the same, lest it might be taken evil where percase you did it upon an honest ground.

Finally, my lord, I remain your hearty friend, and desire you to express your friendship again towards me in your honourable proceedings, and the helping of such as the King's Majesty would should be there preferred, amongst the which the Surveyor is not the last: and yet I would he should have nothing unless his service deserve it.

Thus most heartily fare you well. From the Nete, the xvijth of November.
Signed   Yo*u*r lordshippis assuryd,
              Thom*a*s Crumwell   (Vol. 4, No. 1032a)

It is a pity that Lisle's answer has not been preserved. In essence, it is part of the perennial Calais battle over 'the gift of rooms'. Cromwell implies that Lisle's extravagant life-style makes him dependent on the sale of posts and advantages – that is, appointing any but Cromwell's own nominees, like the Surveyor Lee, though Lisle had always denied that he had made a penny out of such traffic.

More serious problems are now looming. The year 1538 forms the high ridge of Cromwell's ascendancy. The defeated Pilgrimage of Grace has shown that his enemy is the nobility heading the mass of the people in defence of their religion and in detestation of his power. In order to hold and strengthen that power he must first replace that religion. In the microcosm of Calais, where he is already all-powerful, we can see him at work. Husee, watching on behalf of his lord and lady, warns them, tackling her with tact and him more outspokenly.

267   JOHN HUSEE TO LADY LISLE   *9 March 1538*

Pleaseth it your ladyship. . . .

Your ladyship may not forget Mrs. Anne's edge of pearl. Mr. George is merry, and is a very good courtier. He goeth into the country on Monday with his master. I trust this cold weather will cease the plague, if it be God's pleasure.

I first protest with your ladyship not to be angry with me, but if it might be your pleasure to leave part of such ceremonies as you do use, as long prayers and offering of candles, and at some time to refrain and not speak, though your ladyship have cause, when you hear things spoken that liketh you not, it should sound highly to your honour and cause less speech. And though these things were right good and might be suffered, yet your ladyship of your goodness might do a very good deed to conform yourself partly to the thing that is used and to the world as it goeth now, which is undoubtedly marked above all other things. I trust your ladyship will not be miscontented, but take it even in as good part as I do mean it; for if I did not bear you my true heart and service I would not write so plain. And thus I beseech Jesu send your ladyship even as well to fare as your noble heart can wish or desire.

From London, the ixth day of March.
              By your ladyship's own man,
Hol.   John Husee   (Vol. 5, No. 1120)

A few days later he wrote to Lisle that, having found Cromwell 'in a right good mood', he had discussed their attitudes with him.

> And I said that your lordship was always indifferent; and then he asked me what my Lady was. And I shewed him, nothing so scrupulous as it hath been reported. And then he said there was no doubt but she would be won a'little and a'little.[26]

Only at the climax of the Lisle story will there emerge the importance of a throw-away line of Husee's in a letter of 15 March, all about other things:

> Here is a priest which would gladly serve my lord and your ladyship. He seemeth to be a right honest man, and I think your ladyship lacketh such one.[27]

The priest in question was Gregory Botolf.

If the politico-religious tensions were building up in Calais, at least the international ones that surrounded it would be diminished by the peace talks that Sir Francis Bryan, representing Henry, had been observing from the sidelines. George Basset, of course, was of his household, but, no doubt to his chagrin, does not seem to have been in attendance.

268   SIR FRANCIS BRYAN TO LORD LISLE   *19 June 1538*

My good Lord, after my hearty commendations to you and to my Lady your good wife: these shall be to advertise you that these Courts been so full as all the world were gathered upon a plump.[28] The Emperor's Court is great: the Bishop of Rome's less: and the French Court iij times so big as the most of them: so that with them all, the towns and villages being within iiij or five leagues of the Courts any way from them, been so full that no man passing by the way can but very hardly have lodging. And in the French Court I never saw so many women. I would I had so many sheep to find my house whilst I live! And great triumphs in all these Courts have been made, and ∧many∧ meetings of all parts but of the Emperor and the French King, for they yet met not. Nevertheless, yet have they concluded a Truce for x years, and thus been departed, the Emperor determining towards Spain, the French King homeward, and the Bishop of Rome towards Rome.

Other news know I none worth the writing; but that I trust to see you

---

26. Vol.5, No.1124.   27. Vol.5, No.1125.

28. plump *sb., arch.* and *dial.;* revived by Scott in *Marmion,* 'a plump of spears', *O.E.D.* Used here for a cluster, large number, or compact body of persons. Francis Hackett's comment on the phrase is, 'The plum was brandied and Bryan spent much time under the table' (*Henry VIII,* p. 421).

shortly. And thus fare you, my good lady, and all yours, as heartily well as I would myself.

From Antibo[29] the xix[th] of June,

Signed   Your own assured,

Francis Bryan   (Vol.5, No.1175)

The following letter is a draft, written in Sir Thomas Palmer's hand and distinctive spelling but, from other internal evidence, dictated by Lisle. The subject was so complex, official guidance so lacking, and its correct handling so literally a matter of life and death, that their joint drafting of the letter is understandable.

269   LORD LISLE TO CROMWELL   [*n.d.*] *c.6–8 July 1538*

After my most humble recommendations unto your good lordship, this shall be to advertise you that where about Easter last past I wrote unto your lordship that there were divers persons in this town, as well soldiers as commoners, which did declare divers things against the sacrament of the altar, saying it was not in a knave priest to make God and that the Mass was not made by God but by the invention of man, and that a mouse would as soon eat the body of God as a[n]other cake, with many other words which I did send unto your lordship and the information taken here before all the King's Council, and did enclose them within my letters written to your lordship. And now of late I sent your lordship a letter by Francis the post, declaring by the same that there was a young priest, a[n] Englishman, comen out of Germany, which hath ∧in his sermon∧ declared the sacrament of the altar much varying from the King's book, which hath made much people to be offended in the same, in so much that divers people say they care not for the Mass and wish they had never heard Mass in their lives, which is a great disturbance and a[n] unsurety to this the King's ∧town∧ to have any such opinions one against another and that it is clearly against the words of the King's book, which his ∧Grace∧ commands all bishops and curates to observe and keep. And further, my lord, I ensure your lordship that both in France and Flanders they do repute us but as heretics, and that we be out of the league with the Emperor and the French King, and that they trust to have war with us. I will not say that these be honest men that thus report us, nor ∧that they∧ do not know their masters' pleasure; but my lord, forasmuch as appertains to my charge, that is, the wealth and surety of this the King's town ∧I beseech your lordship∧ that I may know the King's pleasure and yours, how that I shall order this preacher, as to ∧suffer him to∧ preach still ∧or

29. Antibes.

nay∧; and in likewise how if I can take any such slanderous ∧people∧ either of France or Flanders, how ∧I shall∧ handle them.

My lord, herebefore your lordship hath written and hath ∧a∧lleged that papish dregs did remain here ∧with us of Calais∧. My lord, I dare well say, the King's Highness hath not within his realm no manner of people that favour less the traditions of popes than the King's servants and subjects do here, from the highest degree to the lowest. Wherefore I beseech your good lordship, albeit that I and others ∧here∧ have not the very knowledge and setting forward of scripture as it ought to be, but may ∧be∧ by blind guides brought out of the way contrary to the divine pleasure of ∧God∧ and the King: therefore I may know the King's pleasure and yours, which shall be obeyed to the last drop of blood in my body. For I ensure your lordship since I ∧was born∧ there was never matter went so near my heart as this does, and shall do, till I know the King's pleasure and yours in the premises. For I have written your lordship iij letters concerning this same self matter and could never hear word of answer, as knows Our Lord, who send your lordship long life with much honour.

From Calais.

My lord, because your lordship can discuss the scripture better than I can, I do send you his opinions plainly opened in the pulpit before all men, to the intent you shall know all, whether ∧they∧ be good or bad, ∧worthy∧ to be maintained or to be corrected.   (Vol.5, No.1178)

The reader who wishes to understand the end of the Lisle story will be well advised to take particular note of the letters that pass between Lisle and Cromwell concerning religious dissension in Calais, on which Husee, as usual, is invaluable for further comment and for the indications he gives of my Lord Privy Seal's attitude. Its mixed population, its trading contacts, and its outpost situation made Calais particularly susceptible to the strife between new and old, and both Retinue and townsfolk were infected with Lutheran doctrines that carried some individuals far beyond the point of the reforms that Henry was prepared to sanction. Cromwell's sympathies were Lutheran. Henry's were not. Having disposed of the papacy for dynastic and financial reasons, he remained otherwise doctrinally orthodox. Whatever their precise doctrinal convictions – if indeed they had any – the majority of the Calais Council were concerned only to do whatever was required of them by the King's injunctions, regardless of the general colour of their private beliefs. Their real difficulty was to know what was heresy and what orthodoxy, while everybody waited for the bishops to produce a settlement of religion which would satisfy the King and interpret his intentions. The only members of the Council who were in sympathy with the Lutherans were Sir Richard Grenville and Lord Grey.

The young English preacher 'comen out of Germany' (via Rome), whose sermons were causing so much trouble in Calais, was a renegade priest called Adam Damplip, alias George Bucker. He had at first been received with particular kindness by the Lisles, Honor even providing clothes for him, probably largely because he said he had been given a crown towards his journey by Arthur's cousin Cardinal Pole, which, if he had concealed his views, may even have been the case. He got permission to preach at the church of the Whitefriars, which he did at length and with great éclat several times a week, now attacking the Mass and the doctrines of Transubstantiation and the Real Presence, until the Prior objected to this being done from his pulpit. As no one else in Calais knew what exactly the new official attitude was on these points, except that the King was thought still to support Transubstantiation, and it was dangerous to be wrong, on 9 July the Council handed the problem over to the Archbishop of Canterbury's personal representative, John Butler the Commissary.

270   CROMWELL TO LORD LISLE   *16 July 1538*

After my right hearty commendations to your lordship, I have received sundry your letters and right well perused and noted the contents thereof, whereby I perceive that in the same the King's town of Calais there is some infection of certain persons denying the Holy Sacrament of Christ's blessed body and blood, of such opinion as commonly they call Sacramentaries. For remedy whereof the King's gracious pleasure is that ye shall cause the said persons suspected to be thoroughly, groundely and substantially examined, as well upon the formal as material points thereof: and well weighing their sayings, in case it shall appear unto you that they will maintain any errors against the true doctrine, ye shall not only cause them to be punished, to the example of all others, but also provide that no such errors pernicious be spread abroad there but utterly suppressed, banished and extincted as it appertaineth.

I perceive also of the variance between the friar and a preacher there, I require you likewise to cause them to be well and formally examined and their allegations heard on both parts. And thereupon [su]ch inquisition, examination, search and trial as shall be ex[pedient, of your proceed]ings therein to advertise me with convenient diligence, to the intent I may signify the same to the King's Majesty and thereupon know his further pleasure for a direction to be taken in the same. As for your desires and suits, I trust to send you shortly comfortable word of his Majesty's determinate pleasure, such as I hope shall be to the satisfaction both of you and of my lady, to whom I pray you to have me heartily commended. Thus fare ye right heartily well.

From Chelsea, this xvj[th] of July.

Signed   Y*ou*r lordshippis assuryd

Thom*a*s Crumwell   (Vol.5, No.1189)

It was presumably before this letter arrived that on 22 July Butler gave Damplip a letter to Cranmer approving his stance and recommending he be sent back to Calais with a licence to preach. Cranmer passed Damplip on to Cromwell, with the recommendation that it was the Prior who should be suspended and the Priory suppressed. Cromwell, who to an extent had also to be careful, arranged for Damplip to put his case to a bench of bishops – whereupon Damplip lost his nerve, declared that he had never said any of the things that had been imputed to him, and vanished from London. His story is important because he had amassed in a short time a considerable following, and the Calais Commission in 1540 considered that the 'great division' over religion there was 'sprung and growen' from his preaching in 1538 – he was the first there of the Sacramentaries. What we have to understand is that in 1538 (under the Ten Articles) it would be all right for him to attack Transubstantiation of the bread and wine into the Body and Blood of Christ so long as he did not deny that the Real Presence of Christ had somehow got into them; the wording of the Six Articles, subsequently established, was different again. The situation of laymen in positions of authority in such perilous times can be sympathized with. Damplip himself was arrested later in England and sent back to Calais in 1543 to be hanged, drawn, and quartered, not for heresy but for accepting that five shillings he had said Cardinal Pole contributed to his journey!

Now at last comes news of the licence to come to England for which Lisle has been asking since March.

271   JOHN HUSEE TO LORD LISLE   *26 August 1538*

Pleaseth it your lordship to be advertised that this day at one of the clock I wrote your lordship by Clare your servant with whom I sent your licence for coming to Dover. The said Clare promised me to make as much haste as was possible for the speedy delivery of the same. The King's Majesty is now minded to be at Dover on Saturday the last of this instant. It shall be necessary that your lordship come over on Friday or Saturday in the morning at the farthest. I will be there, God willing, on Friday night. The merlin that you sent my lord Privy Seal was pricked with a thorn at the first flight and thereof died, and never flew more. The Spaniel doth prove very good. And thus I beseech Jesu send your Lordship in safety to Dover.

From London the xxvjth day of August.

Your lordship's bounden man,

Hol.   John Husee   (Vol.5, No.1212)

Lady Lisle arrived at Dover with her husband, but for some reason returned almost immediately.

272   LORD LISLE TO LADY LISLE   *7 September 1538*

Mine own, In my most heartiest wise I commend me unto you, and have received your loving letter. Certifying you the King's Majesty was never better lord unto me, as will show you at my coming, which shall be on Tuesday next, God willing. My Lord Privy Seal hath promised me money, clothes, a collar and shirt, that I should not go, till the King departed, out of Calais. I pray you to send me the ij printed books which I brought over to Dover which Sterkey hath, and I pray you to have me recommended to all the Council there, and specially to Mr. Treasurer; and thus fare you well, desiring you to make much of Mr. Anthony.

ffrom Cantorbery on this *our* Lady even,

yo*ur* louyng husband

Hol.   Arthur Lyssle   (Vol.5, No.1215)

273   LORD LISLE TO LADY LISLE   *8 September 1538*

Sweetheart, In my most loving wise I commend me unto you; certifying you that this Our Ladyday the King's Majesty hath given me iiij£^{li} sterling a year during my life. I will be with you, God willing, on Tuesday next. When I come you shall know more of my mind. Commend me to all the Council, and specially to Mr. Treasurer Show him I am commissary and deputy.

at canterbery the viij day of September,

yo*ur* louyng hussband

Hol.   Arthur Lyssle[30]   (Vol.5, No.1216)

A promise from the King was one thing, its implementation, requiring my lord Privy Seal's co-operation, was another. Chapter 17, on Lisle's business affairs, shows the fate of that £400.

30. See Pl. 16.

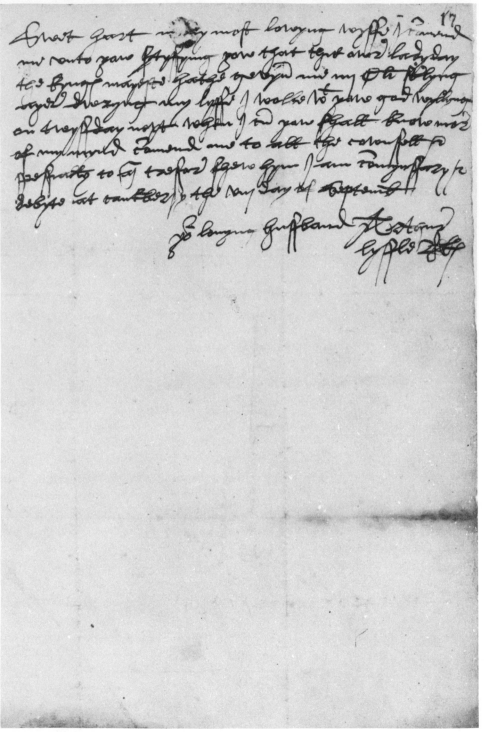

16. Lord Lisle to Lady Lisle (No. 273)

274   JOHN HUSEE TO LORD LISLE   *16 October 1538*

Pleaseth your lordship [to be] advertised that by this bearer Edmund Po[wer] I do send your lordship j dozen of the bills in articles, which shall be requisite to be set up in every place within your house: as, hall, chamber, gate, and other offices in the house; to the end that your lordship, being head, may be a light to the Inferiors. More, I do send by him vj Injunctions with the late articles added unto them, which your lordship may likewise intimate unto such spiritual persons as shall be your pleasure; and ij A B C's[31] in English, to be bestowed your pleasure.

As touching your lordship's suits, I tarry but for a good hour, which it shall please God to send when it Him liketh. The Curate of Our Lady Church[32] there is like to lose his preferment of the benefice by the Commissary's sinister and subtle suggestions, which is his back-friend to my Lord of Canterbury. It shall not be requisite other men love them when they be not uniform in themselves. God may establish his grace amongst them; which send your lordship long life, with much honour.

From London the xvj[th] of October.

   Your lordship's most bounden,

Hol.   John Husee   (Vol.5, No.1253)

On 5 September Cromwell had issued a set of Injunctions to the clergy, still famous because the final article provided for the keeping by every church of parish registers for christenings, burials, and marriages – an innovation regarded with considerable dislike in the belief that this was a device for raising taxes on these ceremonies. But in the context of the religious troubles which were developing in Calais, all these Injunctions are memorable and the first article, in particular, was to spark off an amount of trouble which has to be followed in the letters of 1539. Householders also were given the responsibility for certain religious instruction of their dependents.

A coincidence now provides us with the most delightful batch of letters from Honor Lisle to her husband and at the same time the most striking example in the collection of necessary silence in private correspondence on dangerous affairs of state. At the very time when, at the beginning of November 1538, Honor had to return to London to deal with her legal affairs, Lisle's first cousin, Margaret Pole, Countess of Salisbury, and two of her sons, and his nephew Henry Courtenay, Marquess of Exeter, were all arrested. It was common knowledge in London that they were all being questioned while Lady Lisle was visiting the King; and the real reason was that they, like her husband, were Plantagenets. The overt reason for their

31. ? used here for a catechism.   32. i.e. William Smith.

arrests was suspicion of treasonable dealings with the Countess of Salisbury's other son, Reginald Cardinal Pole, in Rome; but the Countess was the daughter of Edward IV's brother, 'false, fleeting, perjured' Clarence, and the Courtenays descended from Edward's youngest daughter, Katherine. Any of them could, in Henry's opinion, be a potential threat at any time to the Tudor succession that was his overmastering obsession. Arthur Plantagenet's bastardy protected him in this respect, but might he not be suspected of sympathy with his cousins by his nephew, the King, if a word was misplaced?

So no mention of Poles and Courtenays in these letters now – the excisions here marked in them are merely of passages concerned with legal matters transferred to the section that deals with them. It must be remembered that instructions to 'burn this' could of course be fatal if by some oversight the letter was not burned, and the absence of any at an important time could be, and was, produced as evidence of guilt in Tudor times. But letters were carried by hand, and the hand was sometimes safe enough to be trusted with a verbal message.

275   LADY LISLE TO LORD LISLE   *7 November 1538*

Mine own sweet heart, This shall be to advertise you that I have had a goodly and fair passage, but it was somewhat slow, and long ere I landed, for this night, at x of the clock, I arrived. I thank God I was but once sick in all the way; and after that I was merry and well, and should have been much merrier if I had been coming towards you, or if you had been with me. Your absence and my departure maketh heavy, also for that I departed at the stair at Calais so hastily without taking my leave of you accordingly, made me very sorry; but I assure you, my lord, that I thought you had been in the boat, and would have brought me to the ship, as you said ye would do.

And this letter I began yesternight ∧at∧ supper time, intending to have sent it to you by John Nele;[33] and at supper time, because it was in the night late, they looked not for me, so that there was no provision here ready for me; but while the supper was in dressing I told to John Nele, Markes, John Smythe, and Lamb,[34] whom I had at supper, merry tales; and then John Nele promised me to come again in the morning for a token and letter to your lordship; but contrary to his promise he went his way at iij of the clock in the morning, giving me no warning thereof, which I assure you have not made me a little sorry, for that I fear you should conceive any unkindness or displeasure towards me, thinking me so negligent that I would not write to you. The counsel and company of John Nele did me much ease, and caused us to win to land much sooner than we should have done; but he did me not

33. A member of the Calais Retinue.   34. The Captain.

so much pleasure that way but he have done me much more displeasure by this means. I beseech your lordship to be good lord to Asheton, the gunner, for I assure you he is an honest man and I think he loveth your lordship as well as any man in Calais.

Lamb had a very evil chance and ran his ship against the pier. I think John Nele have shewed you thereof, but I was out of the ship ere that time. The said Lamb will take no money of me for passage, not for the ship; but he have taken of me ij crowns for himself, which I gave him for the passage. He saith you shall agree with his owner. I gave him the ij crowns because he had loss by the breaking of his bowsprit and fore-part of his ship. And thus, good sweet heart, I bid you most heartily farewell, praying to Almighty God to send me good speed in my suit, that I may have a short end and return to you shortly again, for I shall think every hour x till I be with you again.

From Dover, the vij day of November.

I pray you shew Mistress Minshaw that William, her son, was not sick in all the way. Husee is not yet come. I intend to ride to Sittingbourne this night, if I may. Howbeit, it was very late ere I went to bed this night, and the morning boystews and windy, which causeth it to be late ere [I] do take my journey.

By her that is both your and her own,

Signed   Honor Lyssle   (Vol. 3, No. 1262)

Thus she left Dover on the 7th intending to do the thirty-one miles to Sittingbourne that day. But at Canterbury Husee met her. The Lisles would probably have known already of the arrest of Geoffrey Pole on 26 October, but the grim news Husee would now have been able to give her, of the arrests of Geoffrey's brother Lord Montague, their uncle Sir Edward Neville, and cousin the Marquess of Exeter, may have made them agree that Lisle must be informed at once. This would explain Honor's overnight stop at Canterbury, while Husee rode to Dover to send a reliable messenger, or even to cross himself on the night tide of the 7th–8th and come back on the next. Certainly by the 8th Lisle had the news. Next day Honor and Husee left for London.

276   LADY LISLE TO LORD LISLE   *8 November 1538*

Good mine own, even with whole heart and mind I have me most heartily commended unto you, and am not a little sorry that John Nele departed yesterday without my letters, which I trust ere this time are comen unto your hands. And this shall be advertising you that I have spoken with Husee, who met with me here at Canterbury. . . .

Here are no news to be written, but such as I doubt not are already comen to Calais. And at my coming to London I shall from time to time certify you how I shall prosper and proceed in all my affairs and doings, wherein I trust you shall not find me slack, but shall well know me to use such diligence as one should do whose whole heart and mind will never be settled nor 'stablished till the body be returned unto you. And thus mine own good lord, with full heart and confidence shortly to return again, I bid you most heartily farewell.

From Cawntorbury, this the viij^th daye of November.

Good my lord, I do now remember the words the King's Majesty spake ∧unto∧ you at your last being here, trusting when you shall hear of these you will utter them to no Creature, nor also be miscontent that I may write you this my poor advice; for, good my lord, you know Calais people are not all one men's childre.

> By her that is more than all your own,
Signed   Honor Lyssle   (Vol.5, No.1264)

There is no mention in the Letters of what 'the King's words' were to Lisle in September, but could they have been some hint of these troubles to come that Lisle did not then but could now interpret?

277   LORD LISLE TO LADY LISLE   *11 November 1538*

Mine own Sweetheart, in my most heartiest wise I commend me unto you, promising you I never thought so long for you, for I never sleep after ij of the clock. . . .

Touching your charges, I know well it will be costly to you. You know my riches; I am sure my receiver and yours will bring you money, and as for me, I will desire none till your coming, trusting you shall bring a m^li with you, and if you will have all my plate sent to you I will. Praying you to send me a velvet night cap and a cloth cap, and thus fare you as heartily well to fare as ever gentlewoman did, and further I pray you to take it as well as ever woman did from her husband or lover. For my part I never loved none so well, neither thought so long for none since I knew a woman; as God knoweth, to whom I put all my trust to be your aid and mine.

from callis the xj day of Nouemb*er*. . . .

> yo*ur* own assuryd louyng husband & eu*er* wolbe
Hol.   Arthur Lyssle   (Vol.5, No.1267)

When Honor reached London on the 9th she had to wait a couple of days to see Cromwell, who received her well, and was then told she could not hope to see the King until he moved to Hampton Court; but on the 13th Sir John Russell arranged for her to come to the Palace at Westminster – the very day when the climax of the interrogations of Lisle's Plantagenet kin was being reached, the King's elderly aunt proving most 'manlike in continuance'.

278   LADY LISLE TO LORD LISLE   *14 November 1538*

Mine own Sweet heart. . . .

And so I followed his counsel, and came to the Court, at the hour limited; and at my coming I was had and conveyed unto a lodging which was prepared for me, and other lodgings for my lord and lady of Suffolk, the earls of Sussex and Hertford, and their ladies, which was appointed unknowen unto me. Whereas I lay all that night, and the others, lords and ladies beforementioned; so that we were highly feasted at supper, and after banquetted,[35] and this day dined; and after dinner his Grace shewed us all the commodities of his palace, so that it was night ere we came from thence. And in this mean time I moved his Grace, and gave his Highness thanks for the great goodness he had shewed unto us and my son; so that, after much communication, his Grace was very good and gracious lord unto you, my lord, me, and my son, and willed me to resort again unto my Lord Privy Seal, which I intend to do this next morning, and incontinent thereupon to send one of my folks over unto you, by whom I shall write unto you all things at large with more leisure.

As touching Painswick, I never heard yet of it since my coming; what I shall do hereafter God knoweth, who send you, mine own good lord, as well to fare as myself, and me shortly where my heart already is.

From London, the xiiij[th] day of November.

    By her that is more yours than her own,
Signed   Honor Lyssle   (Vol.5, No.1269)

279   LADY LISLE TO LORD LISLE   *15 November 1538*

Mine own sweet good lord, Even with whole heart and mind, I have me most heartily commended unto you. And yesterday I wrote you by George Browne of the Wardrobe how the King's Highness entertained me, yet forgot I to write you that his Grace at the banquet wished you there; and I answered his Highness that you would, with all your heart, have been there, and that notwithstanding your absence it shall not be a little comfort ∧to you∧ to hear that his Grace had you in remembrance. I assure you, my lord,

35. The 'banquet' was a dessert of sweetmeats, fruit, and wine, served after the meal, usually in another room.

his Highness asked heartily for you, and wished you as heartily to have been at this banquet, which was the best that ever I was at, and was partly made for me. For at my coming to the court I thought not upon it till Mr. Grenway, the gentleman usher, met me with a wherry, and caused me to land at the privy-stairs, where Mr. Henneage received me, and so conveyed me to my chamber appointed, ∧and there Mr. Comptroller met me∧, where was a rich bed furnished, and nothing lacking for me nor my folks; where I also found his Grace most singular lord unto me in my suits; so that both the lords[36] are commanded no further to meddle with any part of my son's inheritance. . . .

I have in hope to dispatch my business ere it be long; for fain would I be with you, notwithstanding you promised me that after my departing you would dine at x of the clock every day, and keep little company, because you would mourn for mine absence. But I warrant you, I know what rule you keep and company, well enough, since my departing, and what thought you take for me, whereof you shall hear at my coming home. But now to conclude. How the King handled me, and how I was used, although I have written you part, I refer the relation of the rest till mine own coming home. And thus desiring to be heartily recommended unto my Lord Comptroller, my nephew Graynfylde and his wife, and to all others as shall please you, most heartily I bid you farewell.

From London, the xv^th of November, by her that is more yours than her own, which had much rather die with you there, than live here.
Signed   Honor Lyssle

My recommendations may not be forgotten unto Mr. Rokewood and Mr. Fowler, Mr. Scriven, Mr. Snowden, and others at your pleasure. I pray you make no man privy to my letter; for this quarrel I make you is but my fantasy.   (Vol.5, No.1270)

In spite of the King's preoccupation at this time with the remnants of what he called 'the White Rose' families, he was busy also in the religious field. On 16 November he issued an important proclamation which stressed his largely orthodox position, supporting the doctrine of Transubstantiation, forbidding the marriage of clergy, and approving several Catholic practices that the Reformers wanted abolished. At midday on the same day he staged an elaborate public debate with a Sacramentary.

280   JOHN HUSEE TO LORD LISLE   *16 November 1538*

Pleaseth your lordship to be advertised that this day, in the King's Hall of his Grace's manor of York Place, were certain scaffolds, bars and seats made ∧on∧ both sides the hall, and also a haut place for the King's Majesty where

36. i.e. the Earls of Hertford and Bridgewater.

his Grace sat at the highest end thereof, the said hall being hanged most richly: and about noon, his Grace, sitting in his Majesty, with the most parts of the lords temporal and spiritual, bishops and doctors divers, with judges, sergeants at the law, the Mayor and aldermen of London, with divers others of worshipful and honest of the Commons, was brought before his Grace one John Nycolson, clerk, otherwise called Lambert, sometime chaplain unto the English nation in Antwerp: to whom was laid certain articles of his opinions; and in especial one concerning the blessed sacrament of the altar, wherein he rested and abid by, denying the very body of God to be in the said sacrament in corporal substance as flesh and blood *realiter et effectualiter* but only to be there spiritually and mystic; and notwithstanding all scripture and authorities of the holy doctors and fathers of the Church clearly to the contrary, the King's Majesty reasoning with him in person, yea, and sundry times confounding him in his own tale, which undoubtedly his Highness handled so that his Grace alone had been sufficient to confound them, and they had been a thousand of like opinion.

It was not a little rejoicing unto all his Grace's commons, and also to all others that saw and heard, how his Grace handled and used this matter; for it shall be a precedent while the world standeth, for I think there will be none so bold hereafter to attempt any such like cause. And after his Grace had done, and confounded him by scripture, so that he had nothing to say for himself, the bishops and doctors were in hand with him, exhorting him to forsake his opinion, and to be in the number of the Catholics; which also his Grace earnestly willed him to do. He clearly refused it, and bid by his opinion, and shall have his desert according to his demerits.

They began at noon, and were there upon this matter till v of the clock; and then was he conveyed unto the Marshalsea, and there remaineth. I thought to write your lordship of this matter more distinctly, but I had no time thereto; trusting your lordship will accept my good mind in this and all other. And thus I beseech Jesu send your lordship long life, with much honour.

From London the xvj[th] of November, with most haste.

        Your lordship's bounden,

Hol.   John Husee   (Vol.5, No.1273)

Husee does not mention that it was Cromwell who, at the King's command, read out the sentence of condemnation against Lambert. In spite of his personal extreme Reformist views, perhaps this was not too difficult for him. He had already early that morning been able solemnly to assure Lady Lisle that he had no intention whatever of selling Painswick, should he acquire it, to Kingston,[37] although as time would show that was indeed his entire purpose.

37. Vol.5, No.1272.

On 21 November Lady Lisle had sent for her stepdaugher Bridget from Sir Antony Windsor's, and he presumably brought her with him when he arrived in London a few days later; but there was a child she had to see in the line of diplomatic duty, as she wrote to Lisle on the 28th:

> And this is signifying you that I have been with my Lord Prince, whose life I pray God long to prosper and continue; for his Grace is the goodliest babe that ever I set mine eye upon. I pray God make him an old man, for I think I should never be weary of looking on him. Whereas I saw also my Lady Mary and my Lady Elizabeth; my Lady Mary's grace heartily asking how you did, and even so desiring to be unto you recommended. I would not for no good but that I had been there, for it was the King's pleasure I should so do. Howbeit, it was costly unto me, for there is none cometh there but they give great rewards.[38]

Also on the 28th, she completed her side of the business deal that gave Cromwell what he wanted at great cost to the Lisles, and had to wait in London to see if it would do them any good at all, under the shadow of 'the King's weighty matters'. Montague was tried on 2 December and Exeter next day, and both were found guilty of treason; Geoffrey Pole, Edward Neville, and the others involved with them were to be tried on the 4th; and on the 3rd Honor's spirits had reached rock bottom, as she wrote to Lisle:

> And where you write that you never longed so sore for me as you now do, I assure you, my good heart root, your desire in that behalf can be no vehementer than mine is; for I know that I am here at great charge and think that small profit will rise on it, as far as I can perceive, which maketh me not a little heavy; for I can neither sleep nor eat nor drink that doth me good, my heart is so heavy and full of sorrow, which I know well will never be lightened till I be with you, which I trust shall be shortly.[39]

The others who were tried pleaded guilty, though there was not a shred of evidence of any conspiracy, and all were condemned except Geoffrey Pole, who was pardoned, having proved particularly helpful. The Countess of Salisbury was still 'held', as was Exeter's wife. By the 6th, in spite of this weight of the King's business, Cromwell had seen to the completion of all of the Lisles' affairs that were to his advantage. Lady Lisle remained on in the hope of salvaging something by another visit to the King, but by the 15th had abandoned the prospect and returned to Calais.

Although the results of this visit were so disappointing to the Lisles, when seen in relation to public events it shows most strikingly how confident the King was at this time that Arthur, in spite of his Plantagenet-Pole connections, was entirely his own man.

38. Vol.5, No.1284.   39. Vol.5, No.1298.

16

Later News of the Children

When James went to study at the University of Paris in 1537, the impression given (perhaps because he so very clearly thought so himself) is that he was taking the first steps in his career rather than completing his education. He was ten years old. He is, to the life, the precocious infant of the sixteenth century, with whom Shakespeare and the later dramatists have made us so familiar – the ideal child, from the point of view of the Tudor parent, worldly-wise, eager to study and to procure his own advancement, always ready to impress his elders with his manifold accomplishments and his pretty wit. The only person who was not favourably impressed was Husee. There is a reserve, a noticeable stiffening, as of disapproval, a lack of cordiality in his tone, whenever he mentions Master James. The impression grows that, in so far as the manners of the time permitted, little James was something of a mother's darling; and that, amongst those few thoughts which Husee did not share with his lady, there lurked the private conviction that her youngest was a spoilt brat.

James's precocity, however, was not a matter of book-learning. For that day of infant prodigies, in fact, he might almost have been described as slightly backward for his years. He was obviously unable to profit by the ordinary teaching provided in a boys' school when he was first taken over to France – hence the transfer from Paris to St. Omer, where, after three or four months of private tuition the priest reported that he had made good progress with his grammar. In December 1536 he was again sent to Paris. This time, however, he was entrusted to the personal care of Guillaume Le Gras, a substantial merchant with whom the Lisles had considerable dealings during their stay at Calais. He was a married man, with a comfortable house, and was obviously a kindly and sensible person. He did not consider that James, when he arrived, could even write French properly, but while he studied this he could learn to dance, and anything else Lady Lisle fancied. By the spring matters had improved.

281   GUILLAUME LE GRAS TO LADY LISLE   *15 March 1537*

. . .

Madame, as for Mr. James your son, I have procured for him a teacher
who cometh to my house to instruct him in the Latin tongues. As me
seemeth, madame, it cannot but profit him, and will not hinder him from
learning other things according to your desire; and as you are aware,
madame, youth comporteth itself better when employed than when idle.
Your said son hath written you a letter by Mr. Arthus of Calais, and we have
received the sprats, for the which, madame, I heartily thank you. I shall have
good use of them for your son, who cannot accustom himself to the eating of
fish: nevertheless, thanks be to God, he is in very good health this Lent, and
have ye no doubt, madame, but that I shall do all in my power for his welfare
and the profit of your said son, sparing neither money nor my own pains
therein for the honour of my lord the Deputy and yourself. And all other
things, madame, that it shall please you to command me, I shall accomplish
them right gladly.

Madame, I recommend me most humbly to your good grace and of my
lord the Deputy, praying Our Lord to keep you both in good health and to
grant you the accomplishment of your most desires.

From Paris, the xv day of March 1536.

                    Your very humble and obedient servant,
Hol.   Guillaume le Gras[1]   (Vol. 4, No. 1044)

282   JAMES BASSET TO LADY LISLE   *18 March 1537*

Madame, as humbly as I may recommend me to you, desirous that I may
be recommended to the good favour of my lord my father[2] and to my
brothers and sisters. Madame, I have received a crown that it hath pleased
you to send me, for the which I give you most hearty thanks. Monsieur
Denys Le Gras, the which hath given it me, heartily recommendeth him to
you. He would have spoken with you had it not been that he cannot speak
the English tongue. I am still at the lodging of Monsieur Le Gras where for
the most part this Lent I have been merry and in health. Further, I have sent
letters to my brother and to my sister Frances, by whom I think to be
ascertained of all news, if it be their pleasure to write to me. Madame, I have
sent letters unto you by Master Stoc[3] and others, written the xth of March,

---

1. French.
2. monsieur mon pere.
3. Probably Mr. Stokes, nephew of the Bishop of Bath and Wells.

100

Ma dame treshumblement je me recommande a vous desirant estre
recommande a la bonne grace de monsieur mon pere et de mes freres et seurs
Ma dame je recehu ung lettre lequel je vous ay plein mercye de quoy
grandement je vous remercie monsieur denys le grab le quel le ma baille
et recommande bien a vous le suis alle disner avec vous ce peust estre
quil ne pouroit parler le langage dengleterre je suis encore en logis
de monsieur le grad on je me trouve bien principalement ce karesme
amey Aux envoye des lettres a mon frere et a ma seur franchoyse je
resembles je pence estre faict certain de toutes nouvelles si leur
plaisir est de me rescrire madame je vous ay envoye des lettres par
maistre stoc et danltres escriptes du xe de mars mais pourtant que je suys
presse des messagers menz le loysir dels fermer qui firme serca pour fry priant
dieu vous donner bonne vie et longue temps a paris xviiie de mars

Vre treshumble et obeissant filz
Jacques basset

but because I was hurried by the messengers I had not leisure to close them. With which I conclude, praying God to give you good life and long.

  Written at Paris this xviiij[th] of March by

Your very humble and obedient son

Hol.   James basset[4]   (Vol. 4, No. 1045)

He sometimes, as here, signs his christian name in French, as his sister Mary did. He keeps a small initial *b* for Basset all his life. At the end of the summer Le Gras evidently thought it was time for James to have a change, and wrote to Lisle accordingly. James thought so too. He was looking for new worlds to conquer, and he knew just what arguments were likely to appeal to the recipients of his letters. The cramp rings he had asked for were for presents to grown-ups just like the ones his mother gave.

283   JAMES BASSET TO LADY LISLE   *30 September 1537*

  My most honoured Mother, I recommend me to your good grace as effectually as I can, not forgetting my lord my father, my sisters and all my friends in those parts.

  Madam, I have received your ∧letters∧ and the cramp-rings, by the which I perceive the good affection you bear me is more and more augmented. As for your wish to have me learn the Latin tongue, for that it is the thing I most desire so that I may frequent the company of those who are stranger born and not only because it is your will for me, I would for a year employ myself in the study thereof to the most of my power, if that Mons. le Gras will do for me as he hath promised. // I would fain that you should send him money for some clothes to be made for me, as well of silk as of cloth. He hath promised to place me at the College of Navarre, and my tutor with me, to take pains and to take care of me while I am there. I will advertise you how it falleth out for me and in what sort there. Also I beg of you to warn the messengers that they do not deliver your letters save to myself or to Master Bekynsaw or to my tutor. No more at this present, praying our Lord to give you in health, good life and long. Written on the last day of September by

Your most humble and obedient son,

Hol.   James basset   (Vol. 4, No. 1051)

His tutor was Claude Bunel, who also acted as his personal servant. Le Gras had urged – perhaps at James's instigation – that as the college was a long way from the house, it would not be a very good thing for such a young boy to have to make the journey to and fro every day in winter.

---

4. Written in French, as are all letters from James in this chapter. See Pl. 17.

284   JAMES BASSET TO LORD LISLE *September 1537*

My most honoured Father, I recommend me humbly to your good favour, also to my lady my Mother, and to all my brothers and sisters.

My lord my father, I have written to my lady that Monsieur le Gras had wished to place me at the College; but I perceive that he hath now for some reason changed his opinion, for the which I am sore vexed, because I should have made the acquaintance of the son of Monsieur de Vendôme and the sons of Monsieur de Guise and grown into their familiarity, and because the attachments that one forms in youth often endure to old age. If it will please you so to command Monsieur le Gras I should be well looked to for forty crowns at the President's lodging, and my tutor for xxij. If I should not be with the President, by the means of Monsieur le Gras I could be with others where I should be well entreated. If I should find I were not so entreated I should inform Monsieur le Gras, to the end that he might have me away. I could study well without removing from the lodging where I now am; but I should profit more therein in one year, being at the College, than I should here in two, seeing that I speak good French, which I did not when I was where Monsieur Poyet placed me. Also, I have a great desire to have as good a wit as any Frenchman of my own age, and to be able to show it in disputation. Monsieur le Gras will do this, and whatsoever else it shall please you to command him, as he hath a great desire that I should be well instructed. No more at this time, praying God to give you good life and long.

From your very humble and obedient son,

Hol.   James basset   (Vol. 4, No. 1052)

James's figures were a little optimistic, but the College of Navarre was every bit as grand as he claimed. Among its pupils over the years were two kings of France, Cardinal Richelieu, Henri Duc de Guise, and other princes of the houses of Bourbon, Orléans, and Lorraine, as well as, though they would not have interested James so much, many of the most distinguished French scholars. He now set about recruiting his parents' friends to his cause. The Bishop of Winchester's backing would be particularly impressive.

285   JOHN BEKYNSAW TO LADY LISLE *30 September 1537*

Right honourable and my singular good Lady, my duty humbly used, please it your good Ladyship to understand that this day Sir Wyllyam le Gras showed me a letter sent to him from my Lord your bedfellow concerning Mr. James Basset your son. Your Ladyship shall understand that my Lord of Winchester at his departing hence, was the 23rd of this month, talked with me at length what might be best devised for your son Mr. James, specially because Mr. James himself came divers times unto me, desiring me that I would speak to my Lord of Winchester to take such a way that might be for his profit, for he had a great desire to learn. And desired me to cause my Lord to speak with Sir Guyliam le Gras to put him into some college of exercise of learning. Which I did. My Lord tenderly considering the child's nature, and remembering how ill he was entered in the college when he was put thither by President Poyet, said it was not best to put him to a college, but to get an honest man, well learned, and to teach him by himself. To the which I would soon agreed if I had had any hope to get such a man at any equal price. Considering again that a child of a good nature is more pricked to learn by glory and envy to see his companion better than himself, and that in a good college he shall have of his own sort, both of birth and age, I was of the mind that it was best to put him into a college, where he might be well governed and entertained with children of his sort. And because my Lord remembered his ill entertaining when he was last in a college, I showed him the cause. President Poyet (to whom he was sent), put him to such a college as where the Principal and the Regent of his chamber would not trust the President of a penny, and he himself went out of the town the next day he had put him to the college; and when he sent to the Principal certain money for his kinsman there, he caused not once to ask how Mr. James did, trusting (as I conjecture) that he had been dead, as I think he had been, if other had not taken more heed to the child than his hope was they should.

But now it is not so, for Sir Guylyam le Gras, a substantial merchant, seeth more tenderly unto him than if he were his own son, and is as diligent to see the child profit in all things pertaining to a gentleman as can be. Here, madam, I have showed you how I reasoned with my Lord. Pity it were the child should not be put to learning, now specially considering his good will to it. To what estate soever it shall please God to call him unto, learning shall advance him in the same estate.

You have a trusty (without any flattering) and a sure friend of Sir Guylyam le Gras, and ready to show you pleasure, which way soever it shall please you to take with your son. And I would to God I could do that pleasure to your ladyship and service that my heart desireth. Your ladyship shall find me ready always to do that my little power will extend unto. This humbly I commend me to your good ladyship, desiring you I may be likewise commended to my special good lord your bedfellow. And I pray Jesus to preserve and prosper you both, with yours, to his honour and your heart's ease.

Att paris the last day off semptember 1537.
　　　　　　　by yowr one bedman
Hol.　　　　　　Joannes bekynsaw　　　　　　　　(Vol. 4, No. 1053)

At first the Lisles were adamant, but by 8 November James had won. His expenses, with his tutor-servant's, would be 64 crowns instead of the 52 crowns he had promised; but he was to share a room with the son of General Preudhomme, and his fellow students possibly included Charles, future Cardinal of Lorraine, and Louis, future Cardinal of Guise, and Charles of Vendôme, who would also be a Cardinal and uncle of Henry IV. Bills from Le Gras help to fill in some of the details for our picture of little James, as he sallies forth into the university life of Paris. Apart from the regulation scholar's cassock of frieze cloth, worn by all students at Navarre, he is handsomely if soberly clad, in velvet, satin, taffeta, and camlet. Students were not supposed to wear ornaments on their headgear, but James manages to have two velvet bonnets, one of which is fashionably trimmed with gold buttons. His violet camlet gown is furred with marten, and he has a grey satin doublet. There is black velvet to make him a coat, and for guarding his cape and a doublet, and he has several pairs of hose with pullings-out of black and violet taffeta. A dozen shirts are made for him in his first year. He has cloth slippers and shoes of leather, and a trussing coffer in which to keep his clothes.

It was presumably as a grammarian that James must have entered the College in 1537, as at ten years old he would have been over-young for the Arts course, for which the normal age was thirteen or more. This meant a tedious diet of grammatical analysis, hair-splitting logic, and disputation for its own sake. Hours were long, discipline strict, only Latin was supposed to be spoken, no one might go out unaccompanied beyond the locked college gates. However, living conditions were reasonably comfortable, in exchange for the lost freedom of the mediæval scholar's life, and James was able to stay at Le Gras's house whenever he wanted. The college authorities exercised the surveillance over the boys' correspondence usual in educational establishments. Master James managed somehow to dodge the censorship when writing to his mother on at least three occasions in the early weeks of 1538.

286   JAMES BASSET TO LADY LISLE   *28 February 1538*

Madame, This shall be to advertise you that I have written certain letters to you, but it hath been sore against my will, and because my master hath dictated them and enforced me to the writing thereof. Very sorry I am that he should have such power over me as to take and keep from me the letters you send me, so that I can neither have sight of them nor send answer, unless it so please him. If I should be ill-handled or sick I could not inform you; for here there are some with me who have been ill a month; notwithstanding, he hath compelled them to write that they are merry and in good health. Wherefore, Madame, I would have you know that all letters which I send you shall be false, and not written of my own will, if they be not closed with my seal, as you see this one is.

No more at this present, save that I may be humbly recommended to you, and to my lord my father, praying God to give you good life and long.

Written this xxviij^th of February, at Paris.

By your most humble and obedient son,

Hol.   James basset   (Vol. 4, No. 1062)

Residence at the College had evidently turned out to be not quite such a blissful experience as James had imagined, and to making himself felt and getting his own way he was now devoting the same pertinacity he had applied to these ends in the autumn. Anxious enquiries from Calais elicited a flood of replies from everyone in Paris who was either directly or indirectly in charge of him.

287   JOHN BEKYNSAW TO LADY LISLE   *4 March 1538*

Madame, this morning I received a letter from your Ladyship, by the which I understand that Mr. James hath certified you how the man in whose chamber he lieth doth lodge him with his servant and other boys. It may please you to wit that as soon as ever I knew of it, I went incontinently to the Rector of the University, in whose chamber he lieth, and was very round with him. He is a man well-learned, a good man and of a great house, and keepeth his chamber more like a prince than a scholar. He loveth your son, and studieth more to bring him up in cleanliness and good manners pertaining to a gentleman than in learning, although he doth that too very diligently. He hath with him 2 children of great houses, of his age, clean boys and prettily learned, and that boy he send ye word he was his servant is a gentleman's son, put unto him more for love than to serve him, a clean-skinned child. These iij lay in one bed big enough for 4 great men. When I came to the Rector and shewed my grudge, he shewed me both the children he lay withal, and the bed, with so honest reasons why he did it that he satisfied my mind fully.

Madame, I desire that ye will not be moved with every word your son shall send you. You be his mother; but I think it would in a manner grieve me as sore as you he should be misordered. Children complaineth otherwhile when a man doth most for their profit. I pray you quiet your mind, and let Guyllyam le Gras and me alone for the time your son shall be here. At the least, when I can I will surely certify you of all thing that is necessary. This humbly I commend me to my singular good lord and your good ladyship, whom I pray Jesus to preserve you to his honour and your heart's desire.

Att paris the iiij^th off march 1538

by yowr powr daily bedman

Hol.   Joannes bekynsaw   (Vol. 4, No. 1064)

288   JAMES BASSET TO LADY LISLE   *18 March 1538*

Madame, I have received your letters advertising me that you have had letters from my *maistre de chambre*,[5] by which he hath written you very gently of me, for the which I thank him for the honour that he hath done me in so writing and that it so pleaseth him. Nevertheless, all that I told you was true. I doubt, Madame, you do not well understand how I am placed with him; and to advertise you of the truth, so it is for a certain sum of money he keepeth me in his chamber, but yet doth he not instruct me, for each day I go to lectures with my fellows, where we have a Regent who readeth with us. After the lesson I return to our chamber, where a young man called Master Claude, who is my tutor, repeateth with me my lessons; and he doth for me whatsoever is necessary for the dressing of the chamber, to whom Monsieur Bryan hath given two crowns, of the which I was very glad. Touching your commandment that I should be obedient, I shall take therein the greatest pains that I can. Thus to conclude, praying God to give you good life and long.

From Paris, this xviij^{th} of March.

By your most humble and obedient son,

Hol.   James basset   (Vol. 4, No. 1068)

289   JAMES BASSET TO LADY LISLE   *[n.d.] ?April 1538*

Ma dame, I recommend me to your good favour, not forgetting my lord my father and all my brothers and sisters. Madame, I have sent you some gloves by one of Mr. Bryan's servants. I shall not tell you how they are made, for I fear lest they might be exchanged, for lack of care, because he has many others. In order that I may be assured, I beseech you that it may please you to write unto me how they are made. You must know, Madame, that Master Bryan hath told me that my brother George is with him. I pray you to have me heartily recommended unto him, and in likewise to the good grace of my two sisters which are at the Court. And to conclude for the present, praying God to give you good life and long.[6]

Hol.   (Vol. 4, No. 1070)

As James points out, the rest of the family are now established in their careers. Is there a hint that it is time something is done about his own? Lisle has not been idle in the matter. Since 1535, if not earlier, it has been felt that advancement through the Church offers the best prospects for James, as for many younger sons. It is unlikely that he would have been consulted, but probable that he knew about this, and hence perhaps his careful keeping in

---

5. The Rector, Pierre Du Val.   6. Subscription and signature cut off.

touch with the Bishop of Winchester. Gardiner was not only an old friend of the family, but had been Ambassador to France for some time, and that was the kind of world in which James had been preparing himself to move. A boy could be appointed to a living if he had taken the minor orders. Having installed a chaplain at a low salary to act as his substitute, he could then get leave of absence from his bishop – nominally to continue his studies for ordination, actually to live as he pleased, elsewhere, on the income derived from his prebend or his incumbency.

Lisle at first tried for an incumbency for him, but he was, after all, still only ten years old, and Cranmer objected to so young a boy having, even nominally, 'a cure of souls'. He then decided to equip James with minor orders at once, so that at least he could hold a prebend. Bekynsaw was asked to arrange this in Paris.

290   JOHN BEKYNSAW TO LORD LISLE   *19 July 1538*

Please it your Lordship to wit that on Sunday last I send your Lordship letters concerning the affairs of Mr. James your son. Since that time Sir Guyllyam le Gras and I have been with the Archdeacon of Paris, who is Vicar General under the Bishop, to have leave to a suffragan to give those orders to Mr. James. He assured us that without his letters dimissors, or dispensation of the Pope or his legate, there was no bishop out of England that dareth to give him any orders. I reasoned with him, but no reason would prevail; but knowing I was an Englishman thrust me from him and said I smelled of the fire. Howbeit, it was done laughingly and merrily. But in no manner he would not suffer no man to give him these orders without his dimissors or dispense (of whom, ye know). This I thought my duty to write unto you, and humbly commend me unto your good Lordship and my good Lady your bedfellow. Praying Jesus to send you your heart's desire.

Att paris the 19 off July 1538
        by yow*r* humble and dayly bedma*n*
Hol.   Joan*nes* bekynsaw   (Vol.4, No.1078)

The Archdeacon might treat the matter with tact and humour, but his refusal was final. There was, consequently, nothing to be gained by keeping James in Paris any longer at great expense. He spoke perfect French, had enough Latin to be going on with, and in England he could get the minor orders that would make the income from his prebend available. Whether the Lisles had made the first approach, or whether the Bishop himself offered to take the boy into his service on the strength of what he had seen and heard of him in Paris, when Gardiner and his train took ship at Calais at the end of September James Basset went with them.

It is entirely characteristic of James's story that fate should have contrived for him an opportunity to return in style to his native land in the train of an ambassador, which Wriothesley, who met them on the 27th September, described as 'very gallant'.

291   JOHN HUSEE TO LORD LISLE   *28 September 1538*

This shall be advertising your lordship that this day I received your letter of Mr. John Graynefylde concerning Mr. James Basset, whom I shall see furnished with all things according unto the contents of your lordship's letter. And as concerning his prebend, forasmuch as the half year is now past, I will defer it till Mr. Popley's coming, or else he might lose the half year's rent, which is better saved toward his installation and other charges. The Bishop of Winchester came this night. Tomorrow I will see Mr. James, who is much meeter to serve the temporal powers than the spiritual dignities. . . . As God knoweth, who send your lordship long life with much honour.

    From London, the xxviij^th of September.
           Your lordship's own man,
Hol.   John Husee   (Vol.5, No.1235)

Husee gives the first news of how James was progressing on 3 October:

Mr. James is merry, who would gladly have a chain of gold. He had been much meeter to have been in the Court, for considering the pregnancy of his wit the same should have been more for his advancement at length. Howbeit, I think he is where he shall be well seen to.[7]

He was right in his belief that James would do better at Court, but for this 'advancement' he was to wait until the accession of Queen Mary. Meanwhile, in spite of his pretty manners, he never wrote a proper letter to Guillaume Le Gras to thank him for all his kindness.

Bridget Plantagenet was still at school at St. Mary's Abbey, Winchester, at the beginning of September 1538. She was about twelve years old. The next two letters are easier to follow in this reversed order.

292   ELIZABETH SHELLEY TO LADY LISLE   *21 September 1538*

Madam, In my most lowly manner my duty remembered, this ∧is∧ to advertise your ladyship, upon a xiiij & xv day before Michaelmas,[8] Mistress Waynam and Mistress Fawkenor came to Winchester to see Mistress Brygyte lysley, with whom came two of my lord's servants, and desired to have

7. Vol.5, No.1241.   8. 29 September.

Mistress Bryggett to Sir Antony Windsor's to sport her for a week. And
because she was out of apparel, that Master Windsor might see her, I was the
better content to let her go; and since that time she came no more at
Winchester; wherein I beseech your ladyship think no unkindness in me for
my light sending of her: for if I had not esteemed her to have come again, she
should not have comen there at that time. And thus I refer me to your
ladyship, and I beseech Jesu long to preserve you and all yours.

    writtyn at wynchester the xxjth day off September

                By yo*ur* powor Bedwoman

?Hol.   Dame Elizabeth

                Shelley   (Vol.5, No.1226)

293   SIR ANTONY WINDSOR   *[n.d.] c.14 – 16 September 1538*
        TO LORD LISLE

Right honorable, after all due recommendations, my duty remembered, I
commend me unto your lordship and also to my lady. . . .

Also Mistress Bridget recommendeth her to your good lordship, and also
to my lady, beseeching you of your blessing. She is now at home with me,
because I will provide for her apparel such things as shall be necessary, for
she hath over grown all that ever she hath, except such as she hath had of
late. And I will keep her still, if it be your lordship and my lady's pleasure
that I shall so do, and she shall fare no worse than I do, for she is very spare
and hath need of cherishing, and she shall lack nothing, in learning nor
otherwise, that my wife can do for her. And thus she hath her lowly recommended unto your lordship and also to my lady. Also I wrote unto your
lordship for the stuff of your brewhouse at Soberton; now it is in such case
that a good deal a'money will not repair it and the longer it standeth, the
worse it will be. Also I have sent unto your lordship and to my lady a buck. I
trust it is so ordered that it shall come to you sweet. I would have sent your
lordship venison here-before-time if I could conveniently conveyed it to
your lordship sweet and safe. And this I beseech Almighty Jesu, to send you
both long life even to your own hearts' desire and to increase in honour.

           Yo*ur*s assuryd

Hol.   Antony Wyndesore   (Vol.5, No.1224)

At this time Pollard was in Winchester. Having removed everything that
was movable from Becket's shrine at Canterbury and Greyfriars' at Reading,
he had just dealt with St. Swithin's shrine here and wrote to Cromwell on 21
September that he proposed now to examine the abbeys of Hyde and St.
Mary's. It is not impossible that Windsor had advance knowledge of this
prospect when he sent for Bridget. One hopes that her need for 'cherishing'

was a diplomatic excuse in keeping with the discretion of the time. The Abbey was finally condemned in April and evacuated in November.

After the many years during which the Seymour-Dudley dispute had bedevilled Lisle's legal affairs, Seymour, now Lord Hertford, had on a recent visit to Calais suddenly become a friend, and his wife had offered a place in her household to Katharine Basset. As Hertford was well in favour at Court it seemed this might be a politic move in Katharine's career; but she had been very happy with Lady Rutland, and had grown up in an atmosphere in which Hertford had horns and a tail.

294   LADY LISLE TO THE EARL OF HERTFORD   *10 May 1539*

My very good Lord, In my right hearty manner I commend me unto your lordship and my good Lady your wife, thanking you for your gentle letter unto me sent, whereby I perceive your lordship's goodness towards me and my daughter, in that it would please you to accept her into your house; for the which I do thank your lordship, and knowledge myself no less bound unto you than if she had waited on my lady your wife. Nevertheless my Lord of Rutland and my Lady have by their letters desired that she may continue with them still, and even so my said daughter is willing and desirous to wait on her Ladyship still, wherefore I am very loath to take her from thence. Howbeit you and my good Lady have won my poor heart while I live.

My lord, I am sorry that the bird which was given you mischanced. Nevertheless I do send you mine own bird, which I know is the best in all this town; it shall be long ere [I] be mistress of such another. Notwithstanding I think it in my heart well bestowed; and so would I not do to never a lord in England, the King except. I doubt not but the stool that I gave to your lordship is come to your hands before this time, which was at the beginning very simple to stand in your house, and now I fear by the carriage it is much worse, for the which I am not a little sorry. . . .

. . . And thus I bid your good lordship most heartily farewell; beseeching our Lord to send you long life with increase of honour.

From Calais, the xth day of May.

> By her that shall be glad to do you such pleasure as may lie in her power,

Signed   Honor Lyssle   (Vol. 5, No. 1405)

Young James was now thirteen, and well established in the service of the Bishop of Winchester. He still writes to his mother in French, which must have been maddening as he knew she still did not speak it. Husee had clearly decided he had quite enough smart clothes to be going on with.

295   JAMES BASSET TO LADY LISLE   *16 May 1539*

Madame, I recommend me humbly to your good favour, beseeching that I may be recommended to the good favour of my lord my father, and to my brother John and to all my sisters.

Madam, I have received news whereat I am greatly rejoiced, that is to say, of the good health of my lord my father and of yours. Also I have received news of my sister Frances, that she hath a child, thanks be to God. I have always prayed to God that it should be a boy, but it is not.

Madame, I have written you by Mr. Husee that if it should be your pleasure to send me some garments that you will send them to me at Winchester. Mr. Husee hath informed me that he doth not know in any point what clothes to send me, but if it be your pleasure to send me any, I beseech you to send me un soyon of velvet or of satin, and also a doublet of silk and some hose with pullings-out of taffeta, with a pair of shoes of velvet; or, if it should be your pleasure, to write to Mr. Husee to buy them for me. My lord of Winchester recommendeth him to ∧my lord my father and to∧ you, who is in good health, thanks be to God. The eldest son of my Lord Fitzwalter is come to live with my Lord of Winchester. Madam, I beg of you to thank my Lord Bishop of Bangor who made me good cheer for love of you, and also for love of you gave me a crown. Madam, I would also pray you to give thanks to my cousin, John Grenville, and also to my cousin his wife, the which made me good cheer at their house. No more at present, praying God to grant to my lord my father and to you good life and long.

Written at London, the morrow of the Ascension, by
Your very humble and obedient son,
Hol.   James basset   (Vol.5, No.1417)

Though Anne Basset, as a sometime Maid of Honour to Jane Seymour who still had a stipend at Court, could be fairly certain to be appointed to the service of a new Queen, Katharine had only been in the household of a lady in waiting, Lady Rutland, where she still was.

296   KATHARINE BASSET   *before 19 October 1539*
       TO LADY LISLE

Madame, In my most humble wise, my duty done unto your ladyship, desiring to hear of your good health, and also desiring you of your daily blessing, the which shall be to my most comfort in this world, and thanking your ladyship for your gentle letters and for the crepine and petticoat that I received of Hussey.

Madame, the cause of my writing to your ladyship is, that we hear say that the King's Grace shall be married, and my lord and lady as yet doth hear no word of their coming up to London. Wherefore I desire your ladyship that ye will be so good lady and mother unto me as to speak that I may be one of the Queen's maids; for I have no trust in none other but your ladyship to speak for me in that cause. Moreover, shewing your ladyship that I am very sorry that I saw not my lord, my father-in-law,[9] at his being in England.

Madame, I have no news to send you here; but my lord and my lady is in good health, with all their children. And thus I pray Jesu preserve you in long life to His pleasure,

By your humble dowghter
Katherin Bassitt   (Vol.5, No.1574)

Lady Lisle continued to lobby tirelessly on Katharine's behalf, recruiting among others the Vice Chancellor of Cleves, with whom she had made friends during his stay in Calais.

297   DR. HENRY OLISLEGER TO LORD LISLE   *6 January 1540*

My Lord Deputy, as heartily as I may I recommend me to you.

My lord, very sorry at heart I am to advertise you that with the knowledge and goodwill of the Queen's Grace I have spoken with the King our master and also with my Lord Privy Seal and the other gentlemen of the Council, to have Mistress Katharine, your wife's daughter, to be of the Privy Chamber with the Queen; to the which I have had answer made me that the ladies and gentlewomen of the Privy Chamber were appointed before her Grace's coming, and that for this time patience must be had. And however much I have earnestly prayed that the gentlewoman might be taken to be of the number of the others as only for the Queen's pleasure, nevertheless I have received the same reply, for the which I am very sorry, and that I cannot at this time advertise you that I have done you pleasure in this your desire.

... Beseeching you to make my commendations to my lady your wife, your son, and other my good friends.

From Greenwich, the day of the Three Kings, January xv[th] xl.
Signed   By your very entire good friend
Henr*icus* Olis*leger* dd.[10]   (Vol.6, No.1636)

298   KATHARINE BASSET TO LADY LISLE   *17 February 1540*

Madame, In my humble wyse, my Dewtye done to your Ladyship, de-syeryng yow of your daylye Blessyng; sertifying your Ladyship, that my Lord of Rutland, and my Ladye, be in good Health, and hathe them hertelye

9. i.e. Lisle, whom we should call her stepfather.
10. French.

recommendyd to your Ladiship, thankyng yow for yowre Wyne, and your Heryng, that yow sent them. Madame, my Ladye hath gyven me a Gown of Kaffa Damask, of her own old wearyng; and that she wold in no wise that I shuld reffuse yt. And I have spoken to Mr. Husse, for a Rowle of Buckeram to new lyne yt, and Velwyt to edge it withall. Madame, I humbly besech your Ladyship to be good Ladye and Mother to me: For my Ladye of Rutland sayth, that Mother Lowe, the Mother of the Dowche[11] Maydes, maye do muche for my Preferment to the Queen's Highness; so that your Ladiship wold sende her my good Token, that she myght the better remembre me; trustyng that your Ladyship wold be good Ladye unto me in this Behalf. Madame, I have received of Ravenfford two Crownes, for the whiche I humbly thank your Ladyship. I do lake a Ke[r]tyll for every Day: I besech your Ladyship that I maye have yt; and I desyer your Ladyship, that I maye be humblye recommended to my Lorde, and to my Sisters. Madam, my Brother George is in good Helthe, and is here in the Cowrt with Sir Francis Brian. And thus the Holy Ghost have yow in his Kepyng, who send your Ladyship good Lyffe, and Length, to his Plesure. Wrytten at Yorke's Place, the 17th Daye of February,

By your humble Daughter,

Katherine Basset   (Vol.6, No.1650)

In the comparatively short time that George Basset had spent in France he had not acquired anything like James's proficiency in French. Though he had now been a good while in Sir Francis Bryan's service it was felt that his education had never been completed. In the following letter we have the first mention in the collection of the actual exchange of young people between one family and another for their mutual advantage.

299   THOMAS WARLEY TO LORD LISLE   *17 February 1540*

My bounden duty evermore most humbly remembered unto your honourable Lordship and my especial good Lady. . . .

Whereas I understand that your Lordship is minded to have Mr. George Basset from hence and to send him to Paris there to learn the language whereby he might be bounden to pray for your good lordship during his life / it fortuned me to be in company of one Mr. Thomas Tybalt[12] belonging to my Lord Privy Seal which is singular well-learned and of my said lord highly favoured: which said that a gentleman that lieth here for the Duke of Bavaria showed him that if any man of honour of England were minded to send his son into High Almayne where his friends and parents were / and

---

11. i.e. Dutch – from Cleves.   12. Thomas Theobald.

would be content to receive the son of a nobleman of his country to learn the language of England that the said child should be well entreated without any demands for his finding but only that the other said gentleman of his country might be here as well entreated /

I doubt not but that your Lordship will agree that the said language should be great preferment hereafter to them which shall have knowledge and understand the same; and specially for a gentleman being witty and toward as Mr. George Basset is / The said Mr. Tybalt highly commendeth the usage and fashion of the said country and he hath great experience as well there as in Italy: France: and for the most part of all the universities in Christendom and the famous learned men of the same / and as he saith the Lord Cobham would have sent ij of his sons there with the Chancellor of the Duke of Cleves but my Lord Privy Seal would not consent they should out of England / If it may please your lordship that I shall speak further with Mr. Tybalt in the said matter upon your lordship's commandment I will do that lieth in me. . . .

ffrom London the xvij day of februarii by your Lordshippes most bownde*n* s*er*vant

Hol.   Thomas Warley   (Vol.6, No.1651)

Husee, however, reported that Bryan was loath to part with George 'nor Mr. George would not gladly go from him', and he was left where he was.

300   ANNE BASSET TO LADY LISLE   *19 February 1540*

Madam, In my most humblest wise I commend me unto your Ladyship, desiring you of your daily blessing. Madam, I have presented your codiniac to the King's Highness, and his Grace does like it wondrous well, and gave your ladyship most hearty thanks for it. And whereas I perceived, by your ladyship's letter, that when the King's Highness had tasted of your codiniac, ye would have me ∧to∧ move his Grace for to send you some token of remembrance, that you might know the better that his Grace does like your codiniac; by my troth madam, I told his Grace that your ladyship was glad that ye could make anything that his Grace did like. And his Grace made me answer that a' did thank you with all his heart; and his Grace commanded me that Nicholas Eyre should speak with my father Heneage afore a'went; and whether a' will send your ladyship any token by him or no, I cannot tell; for, madam, I durst ∧not∧ be so bold to move his Grace for it no other wise, for fear lest how his Grace would a' takyt it. Therefore I beseech your ladyship be not discontented with me.

And whereas you do write to me that I should remember my sister, I have spoken to the King's Highness for her, and his Grace made me answer that

Master Bryan and divers other hath spoken to his Grace for their friends, but he said a'would not grant me nor them as yet; for his Grace said that a'would have them that should be fair, and as he thought meet for the room. Therefore, madam, I think if ye did send to some of your ladyship's friends that is about his Grace to speak for her, or else I cannot tell what ye are best to do in it, for I have done as much as I can. . . .

And whereas ye do write to me that I do not write with my own hand, the truth is, that I cannot write nothing myself but mine own name; and, as for that, when I had haste to go up to the Queen's chamber, my man did write it which did write my letter. No more to you at this time, but I pray God send long life, to the pleasure of Almighty God.

From York-place, the xix[th] day of February.

By your humble daughter,

Signed   Anne Basset   (Vol.6, No.1653)

17

Estate and Legal Business
1537–1539

Nothing now prevents the possession of Frithelstock but the signatures and seals that Cromwell continually promises and never provides.

301   RICHARD LEE TO LORD LISLE   *17 February 1537*

My duty as appertaineth unto your good Lordship premised, these shall be to advertise the same that I have received your letters dated at Calais the xj[th] day of February, whereby your lordship desireth me to be your solicitor concerning the Priory of Frithelstock. I assure your good lordship, therein ye put spurs to the galloping horse. I never speak seriously with my Lord Privy Seal but either head or tail toucheth your suit. And so be your lordship assured I shall not fail to do as long as I am here. My Lord Privy Seal promiseth to do it as soon as he shall have time convenient for that purpose, with as friendly words of your lordship that as ye were his brother ye could desire no more.

. . . God be with your lordship.

From London, the xvij[th] day of February.

        Your lordship's to command,

Hol.   Rychard Lee   (Vol.4, No.926)

Husee writes a few days later:

Your bill for the priory shall surely be signed as soon as the King's Grace doth next sign, or else my Lord Privy Seal bid me never trust him. Howbeit, I have made spokesmen enough unto him for the same, so that betwixt them and me he shall not forget it. If it would please your lordship to send over the ij horse, one for my lord and the other unto Mr. Richard,[1] they shall come in season, and the sooner the better, for I perceive they looketh for them.[2]

---

1. Cromwell's nephew.   2. Vol.4, No.931.

302   JOHN HUSEE TO LORD LISLE   *2 July 1537*

Pleaseth it your Lordship to be advertised that this night I came from the Court in hoping there to have been rid of my long suit, insomuch that I was so plain with my Lord Privy Seal that he said unto me, 'I am sure, Husee, my Lord Lisle putteth not so much doubt nor mistrust in the matter as you do! Set your heart at rest, my lord shall lose nothing, though the time be tracted; and you shall undelayedly be rid at the next signing.' And then he went into the King's Privy Chamber. But yet I left him not so, but at dinner I set Mr. Russell in hand with him, to whom he made this answer: 'Mr. Russell, put you no doubt, my Lord Lisle shall be no loser, and he shall have assuredly his own desire, and it shall be sooner rid than you are aware of.' This Mr. Russell shewed me at his coming down from my Lord Privy Seal's chamber; and he willed me to wait and tarry the time; so that I see no other remedy but abide [the] grace of God. Though it grieve me to see so many delays, I must take patience and tarry his courtesy; but one thing your lordship shall be assured of, that I will neither leave him till I be despatched.

Touching all other your lordship's affairs, I have written you at large, trusting the same be already come to your lordship's hands. The Earl of Northumberland is dead, and little moaned. The Lord Darcy suffered on Saturday last past. Doctor Aldrich is bishop elect of Carlisle. And thus with haste I rest, praying Jesu to send your lordship long life, with a merry heart and much honour.

From London, the ijnd of July.

Your lordship's own man bounden,

Hol.   John Husee   (Vol.4, No.974)

303   JOHN HUSEE TO LORD LISLE   *18 August 1537*

These shall signify your lordship that your long tracted suit is now finished and with no little difficulty. Howbeit, you have even ∧as∧ your own desire ∧is∧ and the best bill in fee simple signed, so that your lordship is now prior and lord of Fristock. I have already passed it the Signet and Privy Seal, and I trust within this vj days to pass the Broad Seal and to make the same sure in the Court of the Augmentations. The fees of the seals is xiiij^{li} and odd money: I mean the Signet, Privy Seal and the Broad Seal. What the other charges shall be I know not. I will tomorrow in hand with Mr. Fowler, Vice-Treasurer, to borrow xx^{li}. It shall be good your lordship write him a letter desiring him to assist me with xx^{li} allowing the same, as all my friends be in the country by reason of this plague, for if they were here I would not be in his danger. If the King had given me xl^{li} a year he should not have made me so glad. In any wise let Mr. Richard Cromwell's horse be sent with speed.

He may deserve it hereafter. Your lordship hath had a privy enemy which may be made a friend. Your lordship may not fail to write a right loving letter full of thanks to my Lord Privy Seal and that with all speed, but let it come to my hand with the copy of the same for deliverance. . . .

Your lordship may not fail to write unto my Lord Privy Seal that you will never sell nor depart from those lands the King hath given you for no good, and that it may please your lordship to make my excuse to my lady for at this time I had no leisure, as this bearer can show your lordship, to write unto her ladyship. Your lordship may give this poor man thanks, for he was glad to tarry the writing of this letter after the barge departed, but I have been so desirous to certify your lordship of this good news that in no wise I would not let this bearer depart without this my letter, which I beseech your lordship take a'worth, for I never wrote letter with more haste nor better heart. But tomorrow I will not fail to write your lordship of all things with deliberation at large, as God knoweth who send your lordship long life with much honour.

From London, the xviij^{th} day of August.

By your lordship's own man,

Hol.   John Husee   (Vol. 4, No. 1000)

The 'suit' being over did not mean that money from Frithelstock began to come in. There were minor papers, with lesser seals, still be to obtained. At the beginning of 1538, Lisle's finances were in an even worse state than usual. As Husee says, 'Ready money must do all', and there was nothing to meet the claims Lisle was facing, from £10 for which Ryngeley was suing him to his debt to Seymour. The only thing to do was to beg help from the King or borrow from Cromwell, and the man who needed help for either of these expedients was a man in Cromwell's power. Moreover, his personal affairs were complicated by the fact that somehow money must be found to redeem the Beaumont lands if John Basset's inheritance was to be secured. From March onwards he tried to get permission to go over to England, but, according to Cromwell, it was always impossible.

Hugh Yeo had been steward to Sir John Basset, and Seller was a 'privy friend' of the Lisles in the enemy camp, paid a fee to report on the finances, moods, and intentions of the malevolent Lord Daubeney.

304   HUGH YEO TO LADY LISLE   *18 May 1538*

Most honourable and my singular good Lady, my duty premised, in the most hearty manner that I can thank your good ladyship for the goshawk that it pleased you to send me and ∧that∧ your most gentlest and loving ∧heart∧ would that I should have had, as indeed she never came to my sight nor possession, for Thomas Seller delivered her to Sir William Coffyn, Knight, and he put her in mew ∧and∧ as I hear say, of the which mew, as his servants have shewed me, she broke out, and so is the hawk lost, the which is a great loss in my mind, I ensure you. God send me hereafter better fortune to them, wherein I take ∧and shall∧ great pleasure ∧to have pleased my friends∧. And over this I heartily thank your ladyship for your last gentle letter that it pleased you to send me, willing me thereby to be good among your tenants, as I will so be, with the help of Jesu, the best of my little power; and also in any other thing that your pleasure is, that I may have knowledge of that I can perceive ∧may∧ do you and yours profit or pleasure.

Good madam, so it is that your especial ∧close∧ friend and mine, John Butler, of late was at Heaunton, where I then was, and prively and secretly he desired me to speak with me there. And between him and me, ∧in a chamber there∧, he shewed unto me a letter that my Lord Daubeney had sent him, the tenor and copy thereof I have sent you in this letter closed, the which I copied out of the said letter, to the intent that ye and my Lord should secretly know what my Lord Daubeney intends to do, and that therefore there might some remedy be found to let his pre[ten]sed mind as I will advise you to do; and to keep it secret and close, for if ye ever pass it not by policy and by such discreet means, doubtless I fear me he will do to Master Basset as much displeasure as it can be devised. And therefore, for the redress of it, I remit it to you. Over this the said John Butler shewed me also in counsel that he maketh privy labour to be of the noble Order of the Garter, and would give much money to have it; and he thinketh that for lack of money it is one of the causes that he is so minded to do as afore is said to obtain the said honourable Order, as he supposeth, ∧though it cost [him . . . l . .]∧.[3] And also, as the said John hath shewed ∧me∧, he is more minded to do it away because he is disturbed and letted to sell Warham Wood. Better it were to suffer him to sell the wood, which will come again, than to put away the land, as he supposeth he may sell the land. As whether he may sell the land or not, he hath had ∧his∧ counsel viij days together upon it, that is to say, as he said, one William Portman, Mr. Willoughby, and Giles Perry, and thereupon he sent the 'foresaid letter to John Butler. And since the said ∧secret∧ conversation between John Butler and me in the Chamber at Heaunton, ∧he∧ sent me a letter, and by the same certified me that my Lord Daubeney had sent him another messenger for the same matter. The said John Butler hath letted my Lord by his counsel as much as ∧he∧ could or can∧to∧ do, because he knoweth in conscience that Mr. Basset, as he saith, should have it of right, and that my Lord had it of the title of ∧Mr∧ Master Basset, of and for nothing or little recompense ∧but∧ to the intent that if my Lord died without issue male it should come to Mr. Basset and to his heirs.

---

3. Illegible insertion, presumably referring to the money Daubeney was prepared to spend.

I have promised of my faith and poor honesty that the ∧said∧ copy and letter shall never be seen by any person living in the world but by my good lord and master your husband and you, nor never knowen that ye have any knowledge of any of the premises by him or by his means, as in performance of my promise, faith and poor honesty to him accordingly as before is said. I pray you it may be fulfilled in my lord's behalf and yours. For the truth is, ∧that his∧ very heart is to do Master Basset and you as much good in this matter as he can do or think, and that he may do ∧good∧ as long as he is great with my Lord Daubeney and advertise my Lord Daubeney to restrain his malign purpose and pretenced mind ∧in that behalf∧, and therefore always secretly to give know[le]dge to you and your friends the pretences and purposes of the said Lord Daubeney, whereupon ye may always provide remedies; where and he should be disclosed of this matter, then should he be put out of his favour and service, and then he could do you no pleasure, ∧and∧ yet parventure, after that, mischief done before ye should have knowledge. And therefore I pray you that the premises may be kept close, and the said letter burned, as soon as ye have the effect and knowledge in your heart of them, as my very trust is in you because of my ∧poor∧ promise, as knoweth God. The bearer shall shew you some credence, but he knoweth nothing of these matters comprised within this letter.

If so be that ∧it do please∧ my lord to sell Houkes Wood at Fristock, I pray you let me have it, giving as much as any stranger will do. And God send a good tassell, as your most gentle last letter did express: and also to keep my most singular good lord and you in great honour, and all yours, at your most gentle heart's desire.

ffrom hym that is all yo*ur*s att his lytell po*uer* assured the xviij day of May at london

Hol.   Hugh Yeo   (Vol.5, No.1165)

The following brief note reveals clearly enough what it was that John Butler had told Yeo. Daubeney was tired of trying to raise small amounts by wood sales and had determined to sell the Beaumonts' lands that the Lisles regarded as John Basset's rightful inheritance. And of all men with whom Lisle would have preferred to have no dealings, who but Edward Seymour should have appeared as the prospective buyer?

305   JOHN HUSEE TO LADY LISLE   *14 June 1538*

Pleaseth it your Ladyship to be advertised that as concerning such matter as hath been moved betwixt the Lord Daubeney's counsel and the Lord Beauchamp, Earl of Hertford, the matter is so sure that there shall be no farther ado therein, for both the said lords' counsel hath determined that the same is too sure for any man that wise is to meddle withal; for I know well that if the same were to do, the best learned men in England could make the same no surer. Your ladyship may set your heart at rest for that matter. The Lord Daubeney may well make offers, but there is no man will deal with him, except he be out of his wit. . . .

    From London, the xiiij[th] day of June.

                    Your ladyship's own man bounden,

Hol.   John Husee   (Vol.5, No.1174)

The following letter from Husee shows that his reassurances were premature. The Statute of Uses allowed 'the tenant in tail in possession' to lease out lands for the term of another man's life; and although at Daubeney's death John Basset could claim his right in them, this, in the opinion of all the legal talent enlisted to examine the position, would be 'a shrewd matter' – that is, difficult and vexatious – if one 'should be tangled with a great personage'. There was no need, in 1538, to point out that the late Queen's brother was already such a one, and likely to become greater. Finding no remedy in law, Husee therefore appealed to Cromwell.

306   JOHN HUSEE TO LADY LISLE   *30 June 1538*

    Pleaseth it your Ladyship to be advertised. . . .

    But when I knew the uttermost what the law might do, and that there was no other remedy but to sue by petition unto the King's Highness for stay of the recovery, I went immediately and moved my Lord Privy Seal in it; whom I found very good lord unto me in it, and said that he would move the King's Majesty therein, for he said the King was so merciful and so rightful that he would the disherison of no man.

    And so, after I had moved his lordship therein, and partly declared the matter, I departed and moved Mr. Pollard in it, desiring him to have the matter in remembrance unto my Lord, and full gently he promised so to do. And so hath done: for this day I was commanded to bring forth the book of the great Indenture, the which my Lord Privy Seal had with him into the King's Chamber; and there, before His Highness and the Council, caused Mr. Pollard to read the indenture thoroughly, so that the King's Majesty perceived the contents thereof; and the matter, by my Lord Privy Seal's preferment and Mr. Pollard's furtherance, is so taken that I put no doubts of the Lord Daubeney nor of his coadjutor, but that they shall clearly be put besides their purpose: yea, and I trust sustain both shame and rebuke.

    Madam, my Lord Privy Seal and Mr. Pollard both hath played a friendly part herein. Yea, and this matter was spied in season; but by none of those that your Ladyship will think or deem. But I thank God highly of it. At my coming, and also by my next writing your ladyship shall know more of the circumstance, which is too long now to write. The Lord Daubeney will be an earl in all haste. Whensoever he take his creation he shall lose his discretion. My Lord Privy Seal hath demerited thanks, and Mr. Pollard and Mr. Marvyn, yea and Mr. Knightley, for they would take no money; but the other had their fee, saving Mr. Yeo and Mr. Rolles. Your ladyship nor my Lord shall not be hasty in writing till the receipt of my next letters for thereby you shall perceive the whole circumstance. I doubt not but this matter is past fear. The new pretended earl will be here this week, a'Wednesday or Thursday. God send him grace to return with shame. Mr. Pollard desireth to have your house at Umberleigh this summer for vj weeks or ij months. By mine advice your ladyship shall offer it him with thanks. He shall have my heart, with the whole body, while I live, for his goodness now shewed in this cause. . . .

I assure your ladyship the canvassing of this matter hath almost spent my wits; for when I found the comfort of the law so small it struck me even to the heart. I think I should not be so sorry and I had lost all my kin! But now my heart is recovered and past fear, as God knoweth, who send your ladyship long life with much honour.

From London, the last day of June with most haste. . . .

           Your ladyship's own man bounden,

Hol.   John Husee   (Vol.5, No.1176)

Richard Pollard, the lawyer who had done most to help Lisle over Frithelstock, had been a good choice of Husee's as he was now high in favour, the King's Remembrancer and General Surveyor of the Augmentations, making a private fortune out of the confiscated monastic lands and treasure. To have got the King to sit through a reading of the interminable 'great indenture' was a considerable feat. But of course the situation was really scarcely a whit improved.

307   JOHN HUSEE TO LORD LISLE   *7 July 1538*

Pleaseth your Lordship to be advertised that since the writing of my last letters sent by Guisnes pursuivant your lordship shall understand that I never had leisure to write unto you, for where that time I thought verily, as well as other of your counsel, that the matter had been clearly stayed betwixt the Earl of Hertford and the Lord Daubeney, for the communication of the lands in Gloucestershire being part of Mr. Basset's inheritance, it was clearly the contrary; and the said Lord and Earl intended clearly to a'gone through with it, insomuch that the indentures be engrossed and all other writings made, and nothing putting the same by but only the stay of the recovery, which to suffer the Lord Daubeney is here present, and came on Wednesday night last past; and so was even wholly bent to go through with it, and came for none other purpose up but to put away the reversion of his lands from Mr. Basset, and to be created an Earl, of which his pretences I trust he shall clearly be frustrate and put by. He came up with lxxx horses, and hath made all his men new liveries of my Lord Privy Seal's servants' colour, as well gentlemen as other, with their coats guarded with velvet. And finally the saying is he shall be created Earl of Bristowe.

To write your lordship what ado hath been about the stopping of this matter it were too tedious. . . . For first, where we thought to have had remedy by the law, when the matter was debated amongst the best learned men of the realm, and that the most part of them, it was then clearly wholly by them determined that remedy was there none but at the King's hands; and that a like matter had not been seen, that the King should stop the course of his common laws. Howbeit, God wrought in it, or else it had never comen to this pass. . . .

The Earl of Hertford and his counsel thinketh yet to go through with it, but it is determined the contrary hitherto. My Lord Chancellor will surely think to have some pleasure. All the rest of the declaration of this matter I refer till my coming, which shall be after the term finished, for I will see the ending of it, for divers causes, the world is so full of falsehood. . . . I have been so troubled with this matter that I have left all other your matters sleep; but I trust to bring answer of them with me, as God knoweth, who send your lordship long life, much honour, and once your heart's desire.

From London, the vij^th of July.

Your lordship's own man bounden,

Hol.   John Husee   (Vol.5, No.1179)

So the matter was 'stayed' till the next term. Where this supposedly penniless nobleman had acquired the means to pay for his showy entry into London, with new liveries for the eighty men presumably implied by this train of eighty horses, it would be idle to inquire, as it would be to ask why he was given an earldom. Credit or Seymour could be the answer to the first: Cromwell and Seymour to the latter. Cromwell's son was married to Seymour's sister, and according to Husee it was by Seymour's means that it was 'determined and concluded' that Daubeney was to be created Earl of Bridgewater on 21 July, in return for which Seymour was to receive land to the value of £107 when the new earl died.

Lisle is with the Court at Canterbury (where the King promised him £400 a year) when Husee sends the following progress report to Lady Lisle. His comments on Pollard are in satiric vein: the latter had been too busy supervising the destruction of the shrine of St. Thomas Becket and impounding all the jewels and precious metals to have any 'idle worldly time' to peruse her book and the supplication.

308   JOHN HUSEE TO LADY LISLE   *8 September 1538*

Pleaseth it your ladyship. . . .

My lord is so entertained with the King's Majesty, and my Lord Privy Seal specially, and with all others, that he is not like to depart till the King's Highness be removed from Canterbury. His lordship hath promised to be earnest in his own cause, for if the time be now slacked it is to be doubted when such another shall succeed. I have had his lordship often enough in remembrance: I have full hope he will not be remiss in setting forth thereof. I can no more. It lieth in his lordship's own hands wholly, and standeth him also most upon. I trust the good spirit will inspire him to set forth his own cause.

As touching Mr. Pollard, he hath been so busied, both night and day, in prayer, with offering unto St. Thomas' shrine and head, with other dead relics, that he could have no idle worldly time to peruse your ladyship's book for the draft of your ladyship's letters which must be signed for the stay of your great matter. Howbeit, when his spiritual devotion is past I doubt not he will at one time or other apply his worldly causes accustomed, amongst the which I trust your ladyship's not be the last. He hath the book and supplication by my Lord's commandment. I think there be no doubt in the man. I think this late devotion hath stablished his conscience that he will use nothing but right with indifferency. I shall not fail to call diligently upon him till it be thoroughly sped.

. . . and thus I beseech Jesu to send your ladyship long life with much honour, and my lord a pension of a m^l li per annum.

From Dover, the viijth day of September.

Your ladyship's most bounden,
Hol.   John Husee   (Vol.5, No.1217)

Before the end of the month the full implication was established of the solution brought about by the King's intervention, which had held up 'the course of his common law' so that justice should be done. Daubeney could sell, but it must be to the heir's representatives, his mother and stepfather. And somehow they must find the money, and try to beat down his excessive demands.

A new complication in the Lisles' business affairs now makes them a great deal easier to follow. Lisle's suit for his £400 annuity, Lady Lisle's suit for her son's inheritance, and Lisle's pressing need for ready money are to be neatly manœuvred by Cromwell so that the success of each and all of these becomes dependent upon their willingness to sell him Lisle's life interest and her widow's interest in Painswick in Gloucestershire. In July Polstead, Cromwell's personal agent, had approached Lisle without success to sell his and his wife's life interests in the property. Cromwell has now bought the reversion of it from Lisle's stepson, John Dudley. If a man cannot borrow the money he needs, he must sell. Cromwell, the money-lender, is not going to lend money to Lisle, but will pay in money and help for the life-interest in a property of which he has bought the heir's reversionary interest, because he knows Sir William Kingston covets the property and that he can sell it to him at a good profit. If Lisle resists, all he has to do is to fall back upon the line of masterly inactivity disguised as the King's urgent business, knowing it will be simply a matter of time, and a short one at that, before the victim's necessity brings him to heel. He can afford to wait; Lisle and his wife cannot.

309   JOHN HUSEE TO LORD LISLE   *27 September 1538*

Pleaseth it your lordship to be advertised that this day I have had communication with my lord Privy Seal at leisure: and first, touching your annuity, he saith plainly that the King never made grant ne gave you more than ij^C li per annum; but my said Lord Privy Seal, before this motion made unto the King's Highness for your lordship, said that he would do his best to get you v or vj^C marks pension or annuity; wherein, as he saith, he did his best, but in nowise the King would make him farther grant them of ij^C li. I said further that forasmuch as the bruit went that the King's Grace had given you iiij^C li annuity, if your lordship should not so have, it was to be doubted you should conceive thereby some conceit that might put you in danger of life; to the which he answered, whether you died or not the King would do no notherwise. Then I desired humbly his lordship to be good in this cause and how a word of his mouth might ease this matter, so that at the last he promised to do his best, and commanded me to make ij bills, one of ij^C li, the other of iiij^C marks. The truth is, I was very plain with him. Howbeit, ere we parted, he took all in good part. . . .

. . . And thus the living God send your lordship long to live in health and with honour.

From London, the xxvijth of September.

              Your lordship's bounden man,

Hol.   John Husee   (Vol.5, No.1233)

310   JOHN HUSEE TO LORD LISLE   *12 October 1538*

Pleaseth it your lordship to be advertised that I have received your sundry letters, and these shall be answering the same: first as concerning your patent for annuity, I have moved my lord in the same, laying his promise unto him. He saith that he moved the King to have had iiijC^{li}, but he could not obtain it; so he resteth upon his first promise, saying he will do his best to get iiij$C$

marks. And this is all that I can get of him. And yet for this he saith you must take patience till the King's weighty matters be at a point. And as for the Friars, he putteth no doubts but your lordship shall have it, but the time must be tarried at his leisure. Your lordship shall not need fear but there shall be as much done to it as may be and no time lost. But your patent will bear the first payment but at Christmas next, and the gift from Michaelmas. I have made bills of iiijC^{li}. I will attempt to put them forward. I pray God they may take place. . . .

I have this day been something plain with my Lord Privy Seal for my lady's letters to the Chancellor and Justices, who saith that I shall have them stamped within this ij days at the farthest, asking of me who was in the realm that durst be so bold to meddle with those lands seeing the King had stayed the matter. I will not be slack for the obtainment of them. Mr. Treasurer is content to pay your lordship according to the King's patent as long as he shall be officer there. I find him very good unto me in all your affairs. . . .

Mr. Basset is with my Lord Privy Seal and waiteth daily by Mr. Richard's admission. Howbeit, as yet my lord never spake to him. It were good your lordship wrote some thankful letter unto my lord in his behalf. At Mr. Pollard's coming I put no doubts but he will advance the matter, as God knoweth, who send your lordship long life with much honour.

From London, the xijth day of October.

    Your lordship's own man bounden,

Hol.   John Husee   (Vol.5, No.1248)

What Cromwell is promising is to try and get £200 raised to 400 marks. £260-odd was better than £200, but a poor substitute for the £400 Lisle had imagined he was to have; moreover, anything that he now received would be at Cromwell's intercession, and what had seemed a gift had become a suit to the Lord Privy Seal, which was what that interested party had always intended. Concerning the promised letters Honor needs in the Basset-Daubeney case, on the 14th Husee writes:

> As for the King's Grace's letters, I do nothing but wait for them, nor will not, till the same be despatched. My Lord Privy Seal promiseth hourly to rid them, but as hitherto I cannot be despatched. If he tract the time ij days longer I will not fail to sue unto the King's Grace for the same. I think his Grace will not delay the matter.[4]

The risky threat of going over Cromwell's head worked; but Husee was always careful to speak well of the latter to Lisle, lest his less politic lord should force an open breach.

---

4. Vol.5, No.1251.

311   JOHN HUSEE TO LORD LISLE   *18 October 1538*

Pleaseth your Lordship to be advertised that this day, with much difficulty,
I have thoroughly despatched and delivered the King's letters unto my Lord
Chancellor and the Judges, so that there is no fear but that matter[5] is stayed
till the King's Majesty countermand or command the contrary. And being in
Westminster Hall about the premises, I received there your lordship's letter
of Holling[wor]th, the which grieved me not a little that your lordsh[ip]
should write so desperately to wish yourself where you should never be
seen, considering the King to be so good lord unto you as he is, and will in
no wise see your lordship lack: and also my Lord Privy Seal, I am sure, will
do that in him lieth for you. . . .

Alas, that your lordship, ∧which∧ can so well exhort other and give them
as good and as wholesome counsel as any man living, in any adversity, extremity or need, should now fall in this sudden agony, to the discouraging of
those which bear you their entire wit! Alas, what comfort is this to me, which
intend only the advancement of your suits and affairs here, to hear your
lordship thus agonised, as who saith that God and the world had forsaken
you, which thoroughly never more regarded you nor had you in greater
estimation! What will there be said when your lordship, being ever called the
pleasantest-witted in the world, should so suddenly be changed? There is no
doubt but your affairs shall prosper, and things shall frame as well as you can
desire it. Therefore, in the honour of God, it shall please your lordship to
extirpate these sudden desperate sorrows and fantasies out of the bottom of
your stomach, and remit all to God, and he will unfeignedly redress all things
at his pleasure. And therefore all these carnal and worldly things must be
taken as they are, and all things to be used according unto the times that doth
and shall rise which shall be healthful both for the body and soul. I have no
doubt but your lordship will pardon [my] rude writing and accept the meaning, as of him [wh]ich desireth the preservation of your health and ho[no]r
no less than his own heart blood. . . .

From London, the xviij[th] of October.
                Your lordship's bounden,
Hol.   John Husee   (Vol.5, No.1255)

Though the lands of the Basset heir were now temporarily protected, the
Lisles' own immediate needs were as great as ever, and Cromwell was quick
to remind them he still wanted Painswick. Four days later Husee writes:

As for Painswick, my Lord Privy Seal's counsel hath been in hand with

5. The Basset-Daubeney case.

me for it, saying that my lord showed them that your lordship was at a point with him at Dover and promised to get my lady's good will for the same. This Mr. Polstead shewed me. I perceive they mind to go through with it this term. Your lordship's determinate pleasure would be known, what answer I shall make them if they reason any more with me concerning the same.[6]

By the end of October it was clear to the Lisles and their advisers that Painswick was the key to everything. To achieve a permanent solution of the Daubeney case they must pay Daubeney his price now for his life-interest instead of waiting for the reversion, and for that they must have money. Because Painswick was his wife's jointure, Lisle could not sell it without her consent, and he must provide her with its true equivalent in value. If he could have the King's signature for the full promised annuity of £400 this he could do; but Cromwell would not get it unless he got Painswick. Daubeney, now Lord Bridgewater, would be in London shortly to press for the end of the King's 'stay' of his case in the next law term. The Lisles agreed with legal advice that Honor should go over to London, and this on 6 November she did.

On 14 November Husee writes that

my lady hath been both with the King's Highness and my Lord Privy Seal, of whom her ladyship hath had good words and comfort, as well of her own suit as for your lordship's annuity. . . . And hitherto my lady hath had no manner motion of Painswick: what will be hereafter, God knoweth.[7]

On the 15th, when Lady Lisle had seen the King, she wrote that Hertford and Bridgewater 'are commanded no further to meddle in my son's inheritance', but that he had referred her to Cromwell for what she needed.

And this day hath Mr. Pollard been with me, whom I find very good unto me, who hath partly broken unto me concerning Painswick, to whom I made such answer, that I trusted so to use me to my lord that he should have no cause to say that I have been ingrate, trusting farther that my lord would see me no loser.[8]

She had secured an appointment with Cromwell at six o'clock the following morning. She understood the situation perfectly well, and she had not been born a Grenville for nothing: when he still made no mention of Painswick she brought it out into the open herself.

6. Vol.5, No.1256. 8. Vol.5, No.1270.

7. Vol.5, No.1268.

312   LADY LISLE TO LORD LISLE   *16 November 1538*

Mine own good lord, With whole heart and mind I commend me unto you, not a little desirous to hear from you, but wholly and entirely to be with you. And this shall be signifying you that I was this morning with my Lord Privy Seal, to whom I declared how good and gracious the King's Majesty was unto me, and that his pleasure was that I should resort unto his lordship for the expedition of mine affairs, desiring him to be good unto you for your annuity, which he said might be no more than ijC^{li} yearly: to whom I answered, that it lay in him to obtain the iiijC^{li}, and that was his first motion and promise: whereunto he answered, that he thought you would not charge him with his promise. Finally he said that he would do the best therein for you and all others that lay in his power.

Then resumed I with him of the taking of possession of my son's lands, how the good earls had handled me; and his lordship made me answer that they should undo that was done, and that he would be in hand with them for the same within ij hours after. And forasmuch as he moved me not for Painswick, I opened the matter unto him myself; saying that Mr. Pollard had moved me in his behalf for it, and how that notwithstanding I had refused divers and sundry great offers for mine interests therein, yet forasmuch as I found him always good lord unto me, and specially now in my need, I could be content to depart with it unto him, so that he would see me no loser, as I trusted of his goodness he would not, and that this his request should not be for Mr. Kingston nor none other, but for himself; to the which he promised faithfully that it should be for no creature but himself; and thus we departed, for he had no more leisure at that time. Howbeit, I trust within a day or two I shall know further of his mind. Sir Anthony Browne hath sent me a doe, whereof I send you half by this bearer; and the other half I keep, because I think Mr. Richard Cromwell and Mr. Pollard will sup with me tomorrow night: wherewith I trust you will be content, for otherwise surely I would have sent you the whole doe. . . .

    ffrom london the xvj^th day of Novembre
             yo*urs* more then my nowne
Signed   honor lyssle   (Vol.5, No.1272)

313   LADY LISLE TO LORD LISLE   *23 November 1538*

Mine own sweet heart, Even with whole heart and mind I have me most entirely unto you ∧recommended∧, not a little desirous to be with you. Howbeit, my chance hath been such to come in such time as serveth full ill for my purpose. Howbeit, I must be and am contented, and abide the time, referring all mine affairs only unto God in whom I trust. . . .

And touching my Lord Privy Seal, he hath made plain answer that your annuity shall be no more but ij$\mathcal{C}^{li}$, yet will I not let to do my best, notwithstanding I dare not speak to the King for his displeasure. As for Painswick, I am yet at no determinate point; howbeit, Mr. Pollard hath been in hand with me, and as far as I can perceive he doth think to have the m^l li released[9] for the pleasures he hath done already to you and me, and specially now last concerning my son's inheritance. I shall be glad to accomplish my lord's mind, so ∧that∧ nor you, my good lord, nor I be no losers, which I trust, of his honour, he will not desire. You may be assured I will make as much haste as I can, that I were rid hence, for I long not a little to be ∧with∧ you. . . .

The Earl of Bridgewater[10] was this day with me at dinner, with whom I had much communication, and if he be reasonable I will do my best to make all sure ere I depart; if not, seeing the King's Highness hath been so good and gracious lord unto me, and also my Lord Privy Seal, I will let it alone; trusting in God, the King's Majesty, and him, that the said earl shall do me no wrong. Both the King and my Lord Privy Seal hath been in hand with him and the Earl of Hertford, and so shaken them up for meddling in that, ∧that∧ they both hath promised to meddle no farther therein; so that I can do no more to it than is done, unless the said earl would be content to make a surrender by fine, or part from the possession for some reasonable portion of money, wherein I shall know his mind within ij or iij days. . . .

. . . I pray you, good mine own, let me know your mind with the first; trusting you will take no unkindness for my tarrying; for surely I lose no time, but am up every day iij hours before day; and seeing I am here I would finish that I came for gladly, ere I depart, so that I might be reasonably handled; for surely I shall never be merry till I see you. By this bearer I do send you half a doe, which my Lady Sussex sent me. I have none other goodness to send you. . . .

From London, the xxiijth of November.

By her that is more than all yours,

Signed   Honor Lyssle   (Vol.5, No.1284)

314   LADY LISLE TO LORD LISLE   *28 November 1538*

Mine own good lord, even as she that is all yours I have me wholly commended unto you, being not a little desirous to see you, which I have good hope shall be shortly.

---

9. Cromwell wanted it 'clear' of the £1,000 it had supposedly to provide for the dowries of Lisle's daughters, which amounted to a gift of that figure.

10. Daubeney.

Further, I have knowledged before a Judge the surrender of my right in Painswick and Morton Valence, which was my jointure, conditionally that, at such time as the same lands shall be assured to my Lord Privy Seal, he shall assure you and me during our lives of an annual rent of vj^{xx} li by year, going out of the same, which cannot be done till the next term. Howbeit he claimeth the m^l li which was your interest after the death of your wives, as in recompense $\wedge$of$\wedge$ that which he hath done $\wedge$for$\wedge$ us in our affairs, and partly by your promise. So that, as far as I can perceive, that is past remedy. It grieveth me; for if it had not been for your displeasure, I would never have condescended thereunto. As for your annuity, he made me answer that it should be no more but ij^C li. Howbeit, I will speak with the King ere I depart, and first with my lord, and after, as I find him good to me, so will I use myself; for if it were not for his displeasure, I would move the King's Highness in it myself. You may be assured I will do what I may and rid me as shortly hence as I can, for I long not a little to be with you. . . .

. . . And thus most heartily I bid you fare well and good night, as she that shall not think the time short till I be with you.

From London, the xxviijth day of November.

By her that is more than all yours,

Signed   Honor Lyssle   (Vol.5, No.1290)

So, after all the delays and expense, once Cromwell had got what he wanted and Lady Lisle had signed an agreement to surrender her rights in Painswick and Morton Valence, as she tells Lisle in this letter she has done that very day, the necessary recognizances, binding Daubeney in the sum of £10,000 to cancel his agreement with Seymour, were signed within a week, on 6 December. It was still a bad, if necessary, bargain, including the 'gift' of £1,000.

It was evidently judged impolitic to attempt another personal approach to the King for the full annuity of £400. Lady Lisle did once, before she left England, go so far as to set out on the journey to Hampton Court, but for reasons 'too tedious' to explain she turned back – probably because she realized or was warned that the tensions over the trials of the Plantagenet connection made it a bad, conceivably a dangerous, time.

315   JOHN HUSEE TO LORD LISLE   *16 December 1538*

Pleaseth it your Lordship to be advertised that the bill of your annuity is signed, and the same must be paid for the sum of ijC^{li}, quarterly, at usual terms, by the hands of the Treasurer of the Augmentations of the revenues of the King's Crown for the time being, and the first of the said payments to commence or begin at Christmas next coming. And as far as I can see, the same shall pass the seal of the Augmentations. Howbeit, if the great seal be thought of more strength, I trust, if there be no prejudice to the high Court of the King's Augmentations, to have the same pass there. I shall all ways do my best to have the same pass for the most assurance. . . .

This journey hath been nothing pleasant nor profitable for my Lady nor your lordship, but chargeable. Howbeit, things may not be weighed as they be wished, nor times taken at pleasure, but patience must be had in all things: but undoubtedly the King is good lord unto you. . . . And thus I beseech Jesu send your lordship long life and a merry Christmas, and once your heart's desire.

From London, the xvj day of December.

Your lordship's own man bounden,

Hol.   John Husee   (Vol.5, No.1314)

It is pleasing that Lady Lisle had arranged before she left that the first £50, which was to be due at Christmas, should be earmarked for their London tailor, to whom Husee had pledged his personal credit for that sum.

Though progress in his law suits had been made by the end of the previous year, 1539 opens with Lisle deep in debt, and not least to the King. Sir Brian Tuke, the Treasurer of the Chamber, is here at pains to show he is a good friend but cannot stave off a reckoning forever. Francesco de Bardi, for whom Lisle had so fatally stood surety for a royal loan in 1528, was at one time one of the richest Florentine merchants in London.

316   SIR BRIAN TUKE TO LORD LISLE   *14 January 1539*

My lord, I humbly recommend me unto your good Lordship. My Lord, I received this Christmas holidays your gentle and kind letters of thanks for that which was not worth the xth part; but rather I am bound to give humble thanks to my good lady for her gentle and honourable entertainment of me and my poor brats, after such sort as all her virtuous doings with all other be; which on my faith, my lord, as I may say without flattery, is the best that ever I saw in any noble lady of her estate: reputing you, my lord, amongst many other great graces, that God hath sent you to have of her ladyship as great a jewel as any nobleman may wish or desire. I pray God send you both long life together, with much joy and comfort.

My lord, touching your own causes, On my faith there is no remedy but ye must write to the King's Highness or to my Lord Privy Seal in them: I mean, for your own debts, of old and new, and also for Francis de Bardi's debt. Your old debts, as far as I can now call unto remembrance, be vij[c] marks, for the which your lordship, Sir Edward Guildford and James Clare stand bounden, and was all due the xj[th] year of the King's reign: and £[li], for the which your lordship and Nicholas Maior be bounden, and was payable xvj years past, and more. Your new debt is for Mr. Basset's ward, $C\!\!\!C$ marks; for the which your lordship, Sir Thomas Arundel, Sir John Grenefeld, knights, ∧then squire∧, and John Vivyan be bounden, and was payable in iiij payments, the first beginning at All Saints, 1533. Francis de Bardi's debt is m^l li, and was due the xth day of December 1535. . . .

My lord, it becometh not me to give you counsel what you should do for discharge of these things. My counsel must be that ye send me all in ready money, without tract or delay, and I will send you your fair parchment obligations for it. But if your lordship will have or desire of the King's Highness any other favour, it must be by an earnest suit substantially to be made to his Highness and is not to be delayed, wherein letters to my Lord Privy Seal, to begin, shall much confer, alleging that ye be at point of outlawry for your debt. And my lord, if anybody show you that ye cannot be outlawed because ye be a Lord of the Parliament, or in the King's service of war and beyond the sea, Believe him not: for if extremity had been used against you, your lordship had been at outlawry vij years past and much more, but I had commandment to forbear you for a season, but not so long. This your lordship may be sure, that what I may do, playing the part of an honest man, I have done, and will do: but your lordship is so great a wise man that you know where my principal honesty resteth.

As to Francis de Bardi's debt, I think if your lordship labour in time there may be great grace showed in it, for the King's Grace hath lost by him xij m^l li more than that. And he died not worth xl li by a great deal. And his goods I have seized for the King. As to the rest, your lordship knoweth wherefore it was, and before my time, but yet I can show Mr. Heron's books of it.

So now, my good lord, set forth your suit. And if I can do you no good, for I am partial, yet will I not hinder your suit, knowing the gracious liberality that is in our great master and Sovereign Lord and the goodness of his councillors. And yet, percase, I will do you some service in your suit. But if ye slack the suit, my lord, think what I must do against you with spear and shield, as far as Westminster Hall will serve me, and all other remedies besides. And thus, my good lord, with mine humble recommendations to my good lady, I shall make an end, and shall comfort you to write to my Lord Privy Seal in these things. And let me know when ye write. And our Lord Jesu preserve you, my good lord.

At London, the xiiijth of January, 1538.

Yo*ur*s humbly at co*m*mandment,

Hol.   Brian Tuke   (Vol.5, No.1328)

Though the Basset-Daubeney dispute was officially settled, his lordship could, and did, still damage the estate by mishandling it during his life tenure.

317   JOHN HUSEE TO LORD LISLE   *22 January 1539*

This shall be advertising your Lordship that sundry persons hath shewed me that the Earl of Bridgewater should be sore sick and in danger of death. Mr. John Graynfild shewed me that he learned it of one the same Earl's servants; but I have enquired thereof at both his lodgings and can hear of no such thing. The news were too good to be true, for as it was this day shewed me at one of his lodgings, he intendeth to be here this next week. Die when he will, he shall have my good will! . . . And thus I beseech Jesu send your lordship long life with much honour.

From London, the xxij^th of January.

     Your lordship's humble most bounden

Hol.   John Husee   (Vol.5, No.1331)

From the following letter, from Cromwell to the Treasurer of the Court of Augmentations at the end of Lisle's visit to England in the autumn of 1539, we see that he has still failed to get what he has always regarded as the full annuity promised, but at least the grant is confirmed, though he has lost a year by the delays.

318   CROMWELL TO THOMAS POPE   *5 October 1539*

Mr. Pope, After my right hearty commendations, ye shall understand that whereas the King's Majesty hath given and granted unto my very good lord the Viscount Lisle, Deputy of His Grace's town and marches of Calais, an annuity of Two hundred pounds sterling by the year, to be paid by the hands of you and other Treasurers of that his Court of Augmentations for the time being, like as by his Grace's letters thereupon made it doth appear. His gracious pleasure and commandment is, that forasmuch as the said Viscount shall depart tomorrow towards the said town of Calais, ye shall, without delay, upon the receipt hereof, deliver and pay or cause to be delivered and paid unto the said Viscount or to his assign, bringer hereof, The sum of Two hundred pounds before hands, the same sum to be deducted unto him upon such payments as from time to time should be made to him for a whole year next ensuing. I pray you to despatch his p[rivy sign]et[11] this evening without any further protract. Thus fare ye right heartily well.

From London this v^th of October, The xxxj^st year of his Grace's most noble reign.

Signed   Your assuryd ffreend

                Thomas Crumwell   (Vol.5, p.668, unnumbered)

---

11. The letters within the brackets are more or less distinguishable.

Husee summarized the successes of the visit in a letter to Lady Lisle on 9 October:

> How my lord hath sped your Ladyship shall know at his coming. The commission for the Friars my lord hath with him. My Lord Privy Seal is through with my lord for Painswick, and my lord hath received iiijC^{li}. I put no doubt but your Ladyship's jointure shall be made sure this time; yet my lord hath been but meanly handled with Mr. Polstead for he will in no wise suffer my Lord Privy Seal enter any further bond than the fine, which I trust is assurance enough.[12]

The Friars was Whitefriars, the Carmelite house in Calais, for which Lisle had been negotiating since its dissolution. A commission merely confirmed a grant, and more red tape must be unwound before it would bring in any cash in hand.

Husee had recently sent an account of money he had paid in London on the family's behalf, which Lisle had said 'liked him not'; and he had then asked for a list of items to which there was objection so that he could make a detailed reply. He had had to raise the cash on his own credit.

319   JOHN HUSEE TO LORD LISLE   *14 November 1539*

Pleaseth it your Lordship to be advertised that I have received your letter of the viijth of this instant, by the which I perceive that your lordship is grieved with me, and by the same letter layeth many things to my charge, wherein I am well assured I never offended your lordship. Surely it grieveth me not a little, but I am a poor man and must take pains. And where your lordship writeth that I should be weary of you, I trust there is no such appearance. I am sure I never travailed, nor more vigilantly applied your causes, than I now do. And your lordship to conceive displeasure towards me because I wrote unto the same for such money as I have defrayed, making moan of my necessity and need, I had thought verily your lordship would not so have done. I beseech your lordship to be good lord unto me, and that none otherwise than I shall deserve. Your lordship sent me word by Warley that I have taunted you by my letters. I am well assured that I never used such things to my writing, except your lordship will misconstrue something otherwise than the same is written or meant for. I cannot tell what further to write. Your lordship hath almost made me weary of my life. . . .

As soon as the time of the Queen's coming shall be certainly knowen I will not fail to know my Lord Privy Seal's answer of the King's pleasure for your coming over. . . .

12. Vol.5, No.1562.

And thus eftsoons desiring your lordship to be good lord unto me, and not to bear me displeasure undeserved, I rest, praying God to send your lordship long life and much honour.

From London, the xiiij[th] day of November.

My lady's frontlet shall be made with all the speed possible.

Your lordship's humble most bounden,

Hol.   John Husee   (Vol.5, No.1598)

In the event, the passing of Anne of Cleves through Calais only involved Lisle in expense with no excuse to accompany her to England.

A letter from Thomas Warley to Lisle, on 17 February next, sums up for us as it must have done for him the plight of Tudor man involved in estate and legal affairs:

> As concerning my affairs I find my Lord Chancellor as good to me as any man can wish / but the search from Auditor to Auditor from Clerk to Clerk of Augmentations and daily attendance passeth the Bishop of Rome's feigned purgatory for it lighteth the purse / wearieth the legs / distempereth the body / for when upon promise the suitor thinketh him most sure he is most furthest from his desire / Yet hope assuageth great part of his pains and labour.[13]

The next letter is included for sentimental reasons: it tells the same old story, and is the last in the collection from his lordship's 'most bounden'.

320   JOHN HUSEE TO LORD LISLE   *3 March 1540*

Pleaseth your Lordship to be advertised that I have received your sundry letters by Nicholas Eyre, and for the signment of your lordship's bill my Lord Privy Seal saith the King's Highness hath it and the next time his Grace signs it shall be despatched. I will wait upon my Lord when he goeth next to the Court and I will not come thence till I bring it with me. I trust if need be Mr. Heaneage will help according to his writing. I have not seen Mr. Bonham since I received your lordship's letters. At my next meeting with him I will signify him the contents of your Lordship's writing. Your lordship hath written unto Mr. Smyth your Auditor to allow Mr. Acton his annuity according to his patent, which methinketh is not reason, seeing he hath the land in possession. Howbeit, if it be your lordship's pleasure I cannot say nay to it. Mr. Hare and Mr. Browne[14] are out of the Tower upon sureties. I have

13. Vol.6, No.1651.   14. 'Trouble makers' from Calais.

found none of them your friend hitherto. By my next letter I hope to send your lordship good news, with the help of God, who send your lordship long life and much honour.

From London the iijrd of March.

Your lordship's humble most bounden,

Hol.   John Husee   (Vol.6, No.1660)

Surely of all men he would be the least likely to have been left for long to kick his heels in some celestial waiting room when the time came.

18

Calais 1539–1540

The better accord between France and the Empire made the King nervous about his own foreign affairs. Much of his religious legislation in 1539 was designed to show, for foreign consumption, an air of orthodoxy and unity at home which would preclude foreigners finding disaffection to assist them. Calais was very much on the alert, Lisle reporting from his spies and, as in the next letter to a friend in Dieppe, guarding against any unfortunate incidents.

321   LORD LISLE TO ADRIEN REVEL   6 *February 1539*

My good friend Adrian Revel, I heartily recommend me to you. Know that I have been advertised that of late there departed from the River of Thames, which runneth by London an English pirate with a galleon of 35 tons burden, the which is an entirely new ship and hath long time been maintained in areadiness and equipped as for war save only for the fighting top that the foremast should carry. And that aboard of this said pirate there are thirty fellows, and that their intention is to go to sea in order to pillage and harm the allies and friends of the King my sovereign lord whom they may encounter. So it is that I pray you to inform Monsieur the Captain of Dieppe, so that he may warn those in his parts to keep watch the same as those who patrol the sea. And if he should fortune to have any knowledge whither these sea robbers have betaken themselves, that he should apprehend them, or at the least that it may please him to be so good as to advertise me so that I can with all diligence find means for their apprehension. And in so doing he will do also and in especial great honour to the King my sovereign liege, for that his Majesty will not permit that his good friends and allies should be in any way molested by his subjects. Fail me not in this as you would that I should do for you, and send me answer by the first that goeth. To conclude, praying God to grant you his grace

From Calais the vj^th day of February

Entirely your good friend

Of this I have similarly advertised Monsieur the Seneschal of Boulogne, so that he can be on his guard in his district.[1]   (Vol.5, No.1341)

At last something serious was to be done about the Calais defences and regular provisioning, about which Lisle had been making constant representations to Cromwell over the years. In his letter that follows he first confirms receipt and publishing of the King's orders that recall to Calais any officials and soldiers who are away, and gives him advance information of the existing supplies of food and munitions.

322   LORD LISLE TO CROMWELL   *16 February 1539*

Right honourable and my singular good lord, my humble and most hearty recommendations remembered. . . .

Furthermore, your lordship shall perceive by a letter joined to this ∧such news∧ as is brought unto me by Hugh Giles, the King's servant here, whom I did send forth along the coast of Normandy. And now I have sent one to Paris, to go the highway from hence, and shall come home then by Durlans[2] and Hesdin, and such news as he shall bring I shall not fail to advertise your lordship of. I sent Blagg, the Scottish lackey, with a letter unto your lordship to the intent he might verify his sayings that he shewed me. . . .

My good lord, I do look daily for the Surveyor, of whom we had never more need, for here may nothing be done to[3] his coming, for there is neither timber, board, planks nor other to serve, what need soever we have. . . .

From Calais, the xvj day of February.

Signed   euer at yo*ur* lordsshypis co*m*mavndment,
                    Arthur Lyssle   (Vol.5, No.1345)

So many letters about the defences of Calais are here omitted as being of more technical than general interest that the following, from the Captain of the Castle at Hammes, is included in the hope that the reader may be pleasantly puzzled by one of his requests.

323   WILLIAM LORD GREY DE WILTON   *4 May 1539*
        TO LORD LISLE

Right honourable and my singular good Lord, I commend me unto you, desiring your lordship to consider the weakness of this house, and that it will please your lordship, for the King's honour and safeguard of his house and

1. French.
2. i.e. Doullens.
3. i.e. until.

people, that I may have powder, and bows, arrows and bowstrings, and timber to stock vij organ pipes; and thus your lordship bindeth me to do you pleasure that may be in my power, by the grace of God who have your lordship in keeping.

At the Castle of Hammes, the iiij day of May.

Your own to my power,

Signed   Wyllyam Grey   (Vol.5, No.1401)

In fact, he was not aiming to soothe the spirits of 'the brutal and licentious soldiers': 'organ pipes' can be identified with the organ-gun, a piece of artillery with several charged chambers set side by side like organ pipes. He needs timber to make gun-stocks for seven of these weapons.

In London the new session of Parliament had just opened which was to discuss an act for the unifying of religion. The King had been alarmed by the Pilgrimage of Grace, and realized that, doctrinally speaking, the vast majority of his subjects were Catholic and hated the Reformers, notably Cromwell. The Duke of Norfolk was now in the ascendant again at Court and had drafted a set of 'questions' which were to result, by the end of the session, in the Act of the Six Articles. The destruction of the Pole family was a private vendetta of the King's aside from main political issues. The power struggle was not yet a survival struggle, but Cromwell could not afford to lose. Meanwhile he had to be careful.

324   CROMWELL TO LORD LISLE   *6 May 1539*

After my right hearty commendations to your lordship: Where I am advertised that of late it hath been signified from thence to my Lord of Hertford, Master Treasurer of the King's Majesty's Household, Master Browne and others, that the town of Calais should be in some misorder by certain Sacramentaries alleged to be in the same, I cannot a little marvel that your lordship, having good knowledge and experience of my good will and continual desire to the repression of errors and to the establishment of one perfect unity in opinion amongst us all, the King's Majesty's people and subjects, would not vouchsafe to give me some knowledge if there be any such lewd persons amongst you. I doubt not but your lordship knoweth both how much I do esteem that the King's Highness' town as my duty requireth, and how well I have (I thank God) hitherto considered what danger might ensue unto it by diversity of opinion, specially in matters so high and weighty, doing ever mine office as I might to quiet all things with an honest charity that have lightly insurged amongst you. But leaving this part I shall address myself to my purpose, which is to signify unto you that the King's Majesty, being desirous to know the truth of these matters, hath willed and

commanded me to write unto you and to the rest of his Council there that
you shall assemble yourselves together and make due and circumspect inquisition of this and all other such matters as do or may in anywise interrupt
the quiet and unity that should be there amongst you: And of the same to
advertise again with convenient diligence by this bearer whom I have sent
thither for that purpose, having such regard to the serious and just examination and handling thereof as his Majesty may see the perfect truth divided
from men's corrupt affections of favour, malice or displeasure. Which shall
both much advance the reformation of things if it so require, and declare
you, which be put in trust there, to be men of that sort that shall beseem you
towards the maintenance of truth and honesty and the repression of the
contrary as appertaineth. Thus fare you heartily well.

From St. James the vj of May.
Signed   Your lordshippis assuryd,
                    Thom*a*s Crumwell   (Vol.5, No.1 403)

The following letter, written on the day that the Countess of Salisbury was
attainted by act of Parliament without trial, is the only contemporary
source – apart from the official entry in the *Lords' Journals* (I 107) – for the
story about the coat-armour found in her coffer and used as evidence. The
list of those attainted by this one Act, in the Parliament of April–June 1539,
included the dead and the living – among the former, Lord Montague, the
Marquess of Exeter, Sir Edward Neville, and Sir Nicholas Carew, also Lord
Darcy, Lord Hussey, and others executed for their share in the Pilgrimage of
Grace. Among the living it included Cardinal Pole. Attainder by Act, without trial, is said to have been Cromwell's invention – a useful method when
the evidence was specious and flimsy, which became, therefore, particularly
useful when employed against himself in 1540. A person attainted of treason
was under sentence of death, to be carried out when determined by the
King.

325   JOHN WORTH TO LORD LISLE   *18 May 1539*

Pleaseth your lordship, so it is that there was a coat-armour found in the
Duchess of Salisbury's coffer, and by the one side of the coat there was the
King's Grace his arms of England, that is, the lions without the flower de
luce, and about the whole arms was made pansies for Pole, and marigolds for
my Lady Mary. This was about the coat-armour. And betwixt the marigold
and the pansy was made a tree to rise in the midst; and on the tree a coat of
purple hanging on a bough, in tokening of the coat of Christ; and on the
other side of the coat all the Passion of Christ. Pole intended to have married
my Lady Mary, and betwixt them both should again arise the old doctrine of

Christ. This was the intent that the coat was made, as it is openly known in the Parliament house, as Master Sir George Speke shewed me. And this my Lady Marquess, my Lady Salisbury, Sir Adrian Fortescue, Sir Thomas Dyngeley, with divers others are attainted today by act of Parliament. Other news here is none, but I am, as I am bound during life to be, at your lordship's commandment and my singular good lady's your wife.

at london the xviij^{th} day of may.

Y[ou]r l[or]dship's at co*m*mandyment

Hol.   [John Worth]⁴   (Vol.5, No.1419)

An important appointment in Calais was that in May of Sir George Carew as Captain of Rysbank. From then on Cromwell would have a member of the Council in his pocket. Lisle and all but two of the others were dedicated men who at all times were prepared to back whatever was the King's current orthodoxy. Carew was to protect the Reformers by reporting Council business to Cromwell, despite the fact that by the Act of 1536 all members were sworn to secrecy.

As Husee's next letter shows, the fear of buildings being bugged is not an exclusively modern phenomenon: the 'fee'd man' efficiently preceded the electronic device. But if Hertford did not trust his own household, neither did Husee trust him, although since the end of the Seymour Dudley dispute Lisle considered him his friend.

326   JOHN HUSEE TO LORD LISLE   *27 May 1539*

Pleaseth your Lordship to be advertised that I received your letter this day by Pyck, and therein closed the copy of the letter sent to my Lord Privy Seal, which shall not pass my mouth. And as concerning answer of the same letter, I cannot see that they be hasty in the despatchment of it.

Your lordship shall understand that this day I was with my Lord of Hertford in his garden, where I delivered his lordship my Lady's letter and bird; and after his Lordship had somewhat commoned with me of other matters, he fell in hand with me of news from Calais, and I shewed his Lordship that I knew none. So then he asked me what business there was ado concerning the Sacrament; and I made as though I knew nothing of it; and then his Lordship said that my Lord Privy Seal commoned with him yesterday in the matter, saying that things should be surmised and scant believed. And I shewed his Lordship that I was sure your lordship and the Council there would not write or certify anything unto the King's Highness and his Council here but that thing which might be well justified and abiden by.

4. Signature torn off; handwriting unmistakably Worth's.

Then his Lordship asked me which of the Council there, saying further, the Council there are of ij parts, and not uniform but divided, and working ij contrary ways. To the which I answered that I knew no such thing; so that after this his Lordship shewed me that this day he should see the letters, and the matter should be scanned; and further communication had his lordship not. So that by this your lordship may learn something. There are workers to the contrary, which do persuade all that they can, with their friends; which, as I suspect, may do much, and specially one of them, I will not say your lordship's fee'd man; so that by these means some are incensed, that such things as are certified are not truth but surmised, and maliciously imagined and invented: which I think is the chief cause that your sundry letters hath not been hitherto answered. This I do write your lordship of my own conjecture, and none otherwise; and all by that which I gathered of my Lord's words this day in the garden. I trust your lordship and others of my lords and masters of the King's Council there are so circumspect in such things as hath been by you hither certified that you dare at all times justify the same. I shall learn hereafter further in this matter, and thereupon to do my best in procuring answer of your former letters. And as concerning the Sacrament, I trust ere it be long your lordship's mind shall be fully certified in that behalf, and that sooner than some there would have it. This night or to-morrow my Lord of Hertford hath promised that I shall have the saddle and harness. When the same cometh to my hands it shall be sent with the first. . . .

     Your lordship's humble most bounden,
Hol.   John Husee   (Vol.5, No.1428)

Lisle's letter of the 18th is missing, but the reply to it that follows is a magnificent Tudor specimen of Civil Service fence-sitting; it is clear that Cromwell was already losing that realistic grasp of the actualities of the situation which had hitherto distinguished this perfect robot of the absolute, omnicompetent state. He was beginning to make mistakes, and his handling of the Calais crisis was one of them, in view of the fact that the state and its monarch were now one and indivisible, and that he had focussed upon himself a quite undeserved amount of popular hatred which the King had escaped.

327 CROMWELL TO LORD LISLE   *27 May 1539*

After my right hearty commendations, These shall be to signify unto you that I have received your letters of the viij^(th) of this present, with a book of such depositions as you have taken upon mine advertisement made unto you the vj^(th) of the same by the King's Majesty's commandment, And having thoroughly perused both your commune letter with the private letters of you, my Lord Deputy, and my Lord Chamberlain, and also the said depositions; forasmuch as the King's Majesty, travailing most catholicly, christianly and charitably to set a general quiet and unity in all those matters, hath not hitherto had time to read or hear your collections which, as it appeareth, you have with much travail gathered: and that I think it nevertheless to be most necessary that such slanders might be appeased as give courage to his Grace's enemies to note more division amongst us than is or can be upon any good ground thought amongst us, which may bolden them to advance evil practices against his Majesty, and enfeeble men's spirits that be of true faith and meaning towards God and his Highness: I have thought convenient not only to give you mine advice for the ordering and quieting of things till in those matters you shall know further of his Majesty's pleasure, but also to declare some part of mine opinion touching the effects of the said depositions.

And concerning the quieting of the bruits and rumours which have risen, and be spread abroad by your advertisements and earnest proceedings in those matters and examinations: I think that, like as the King's Majesty cannot better or more highly advance the honour of God, ne more prudently provide for his own surety and the tranquillity of his realm, dominions and subjects, than in the discreet and charitable punishment of such as do by any mean labour and purpose to sow sedition, division and contention, in opinion amongst his people, contrary to the truth of God's word and his Grace's most christian ordinances, so I think again, on the other side, that he or they, whatsoever they be, that would without great and substantial ground be authors or settersforth of any such rumours, may appear rather desirous of sedition than of quiet and unity, and may therein shew themselves rather devisers how to put men in trouble and despair that be peaceable, quiet, and faithful, than how to reform that is amiss, and with consideration of the matter, the time, and other circumstances meet to be pondered to preserve the number in that courage towards truth to God and their Prince that their bounden duties at all times do require. And therefore mine opinion is, that you shall by all means devise how with charity and mild handling of things to quench this slanderous bruit as much as you may, ever exhorting men discreetly, and without rigour or extreme dealing, to know and serve God truly and their Prince and Sovereign Lord with all humility and obedience.

As touching the substance of the depositions, it is sore to note any man for a Sacramentary unless he that shall be the author of the infamy know well what a Sacramentary is. And yet is it more sore to note a commune officer put in place to advise and reform others of so heinous a crime, except it might be duly and evidently proved against him. I mean this by the Commissary, the depositions against whom be not most weighty and substantial. Against the other few accused of the same crime the accusations seem to weigh somewhat deeper. And yet the small number that be accused of that offence might have been punished without a general infamy to the whole town. And as for the rest of the depositions that be made specially touching the preacher, though percase he and others might in their proceedings have done more circumspectly in some things, yet they seem to help little to fortify that there should be such a general division amongst you.

Finally, I shall advise you to use things with charity, and with such wisdom to suppress, as much as in you is, this general slander, that there may be a towardness of a quiet amongst you which the King's Majesty will shortly, I doubt not, make perfect, to the comforts of all that be well disposed and the punishment of all such as at this present appear or shall upon just and indifferent examination be found hereafter to maintain evil and corrupt opinions or to be inclined to sedition. And thus most heartily fare you well.

From St. James the xxvij^th day of May.

Signed   Your lordshippis assuryd,

                         Thom*a*s Crumwell   (Vol.5, No.1429)

If this letter and others are analysed, it can be seen that Cromwell's line of evasion remains pretty constant. Lisle and the Council are always in the wrong. If the trouble is not brought to his notice, they are negligent: if it is, then either they ought to be able to deal with it themselves without bothering the King who has given them the necessary powers; or, as here, the implication is that they themselves have been largely responsible for the situation of which they complain.

Cromwell having supported Butler, the Commissary, Lisle then sent him certain further details of the latter's support of Damplip. He had not produced this particular evidence at the time of Damplip's examination because the opinions in question had not then been condemned, as they were in the Act now before Parliament. In the next letter it becomes as usual Lisle's fault when, in the light of the Act, Cromwell has to change his tune. The reader is begged to note the second paragraph as a prize specimen of period composition.

328   CROMWELL TO LORD LISLE AND THE   *8 June 1539*
        COUNCIL OF CALAIS

After my right hearty commendations, these shall be to advertise the same that I have received your letters dated in this month, with a schedule of certain Articles preached by one Adam Damplip (as it is alleged) by the permission of the Commissary: which Damplip you judge to have been an author of the erroneous opinions which have lately appeared in Calais and those parts. Which Articles I have perused and find them very pestilent, much marvelling that the same were not presented heretofore against him, when he was accused of the matter of transubstantiation. But if it be true that he taught them, then taught he most detestable and cankered heresy. And if the Commissary consented to that doctrine, I must needs both think him unmeet for such an office and judge him also worthy great punishment. And for his examination therein and in the other matters laid to his charge by the depositions which you sent lately unto me, the King's Majesty's pleasure is that you shall deliver both the said Commissary and parish priest that hath been the preacher unto this bearer, who hath charge to see them surely and yet honestly conveyed hither.

Now, to answer to the points of your said letters; as I wrote before that I thought it necessary that, such slanders chancing to rise amongst you, the same should be rather discreetly and charitably appeased and the offenders quietly punished, than so handled as should give courage to the King's Majesty's enemies to note much division amongst us, and perchance cause them the rather to advance some evil practices: even so must I advise you again, being the same counsel that I would in like case follow myself, not seeing but offenders may as well be punished without too great a tumult as if the faults of a few, in respect of the multitude there, were bruited through an whole world. And this giveth no judgement against the truth of your advertisements but showeth a mean how, if they be good and just, by honest circumstance you may make them yet better. And as to the second point of your letters, touching the occasioners of the bruits which have been spread of these matters, I meant none other but to ascribe the same chiefly to those which were the first setters forth of any erroneous opinions. And yet to be plain with you as with my friends, many times many diseases that be of their own nature disposed to very evil effects, if it chance them to be in time espied by a good physician, his learning, wisdom, knowledge and good disposition may in such wise provide remedy, as the patient shall with little pain attain perfect health; whereas, if the same physician should upon respect wink till the infection were more deeply settled, percase all his cunning to be practised upon the sick man should not be able to help him, though he should daily rack him with medicines. And surely we be no less but more in fault which labour not to avoid evil from our neighbours where we see the same imminent, than if we should be ourselves the very authors and workers of the same evil toward them.

I have informed the King's Majesty of all your letters and of your book of depositions, whose Highness hath already taken order for the examination of all those matters, the resolution whereof shall be signified unto you. The evil (as you write therein truly) will labour to pervert the good; and even so those that be well disposed will both lament the folly of the evil and do what they can to make them better. He that either feareth not God nor esteemeth the King's Majesty's Injunctions, precepts, ordinances and commandments, is no meet herb to grow in his Majesty's most catholic and virtuous garden. If you know therefore any more of that sort to be opened than you have already revealed by such examinations as you lately sent unto me, I doubt not but, without respect, you will give the King's Majesty advertisement of them. And where I wrote the matter deposed against the Commissary not to be most heinous, now you answer that he is the maintainer and very supporter of all this evil, bringing in the foresaid matters of Damplip for a justification thereof: surely if he shall be found as great an offender as the Articles note, and as you report him to be, I will not only help to have him from thence avoided, but also do for his further punishment that shall appertain. . . .

. . . Thus most heartily fare you well.

From Saint James the viii of June.

Signed   Your lordshippis assuryd

                Thom*a*s Crumwell   (Vol.5, No.1443)

The clarity of the Act of the Six Articles, passed on 13 June, did make the work of the Council easier, and Lisle was able to get rid of Butler, Cranmer's Commissary, who had originally licenced the preaching of Damplip that was felt to be the prime cause of the present troubles. We must beware of regarding those troubles as doctrinal hairsplitting by pious afficionados of religious debate: the penalty for being on the right side at the wrong moment was death. From the point of view of the officials, the language of the Sacramentaries in particular was inflammatory enough to cause riots among the townspeople and quarrels among the soldiers of the Retinue – and this in a town maintained at the time on a war footing.

329   ARCHBISHOP CRANMER TO LORD LISLE   *13 July 1539*

My very good lord, after my right hearty commendations; these shall be to signify to you that I have received your letters dated the vij day of July, and also your other letters dated the [26] day of [June], and therewith certain depositions, the contents of the which your said letters I have thoroughly pondered and considered. And first, as touching the said depositions, process shall be made accordingly as justice shall require in that behalf; and as for to get you a discreet priest for your parish, I shall do what I can to provide you one with expedition; and likewise to provide you a learned man to be my Commissary, I will do the best that lieth in me. Howbeit, I fear me that I shall with much difficulty obtain such a one, by reason that learned men are not willing to demore continually beyond the sea and out of the realm, without great stipend, which will be to me no small charge over that it was. Nevertheless I do little pass of any charge, so that I may get one that

will mind the advancement of God's glory, the King's honour, and the quietness of your town. And as to your request that none should be suffered to
preach nor expound the holy scripture with you but such as shall be au-
thorised by the King's Majesty or by me, I shall not fail to give such a
commandment unto him that shall be my Commissary, that he shall suffer no
person to preach out of his own cure but such as shall have the said authority,
either from the King's Grace or from me. . . .

I pray yo*ur* lordeshippe to send vnto me w*ith* expedition other articles
which you haue agaynst Rauff Hare or Broke yf you haue any agaynst they*m*
specially syns y*e* Kyng*es* p*ar*don other than you haue bifore sent hither. ffor
the mo matar*es* th*at* be agaynst they*m,* the more it is to their co*nde*m*nation.

> Yo*ur* lovynge frende
> T. Cantuarien   (Vol.5, No.1489)

Hare and Broke were Sacramentaries, and the King's pardon could be
claimed for certain offences committed before the recent Act.

330   JOHN HUSEE TO LORD LISLE   *20 July 1539*

Pleaseth your Lordship to be advertised that yesterday Rauffe Hare had
his penance enjoined him, to bear a faggot at Calais, and the Fleming to bear
another at Marke; and the parish priest to preach and recant openly in the
market place all his false doctrines, knowledging his offence, and likewise to
make another sermon at Marke. And the Commissary is enjoined not to
come at Calais till after Easter without the King's special licence, so that if
[any]thing can be laid to him to make answer he must abide the trial, spite of
his teeth. I trust there will be matter enough found for him to bring him to
be in number with his fellows, or else by my faith I would be right sorry. And
as for Mr. Broke and his man, are commanded to the Fleet, there to abide
their trial further betwixt this and Christmas. . . .

> As God best knoweth, who send your lordship long life and much honour,
> From London, the xx^th day of July.
> Your lordship's humble [most bounden],

Hol.   [John Husee][5]   (Vol.5, No.1492)

Evidence against Cranmer's ex-Commissary was still being collected, such as
his keeping a 'concupyne' by whom he had 'a child or two', and that 'he had
his corn and grass brought and laid in the church there, and before the Holy
Sacrament of the Altar there he caused his threshers to thresh the same
grain, whereby all the said parish found them sore aggrieved therewith.'[6]

---

5. MS. damaged but legible.   6. S.P. 1/152, f.184.

Lisle sent copies of old letters of his to Cromwell in which he had accused him of such things as holding secret meetings with soldiers when they should have been on watch.

331   ARCHBISHOP CRANMER TO LORD LISLE   *28 July 1539*

My lord, in my right hearty wise I commend me to you. And whereas Rauf Hare with other are enjoined penance to be done in Calais according to such form and manner as I have prescribed in my late letters to you directed; forsomuch as they do fear to be imprisoned and farther corrected by you and the Council; I shall desire you, my lord, although I myself suspect no such thing by you, that they may do their penance quietly without farther let or perturbation, so that they may go and come freely; for else it may be thought that justice is not indifferently ministered. Howbeit, I know your lordship's discretion is such that there need no such monition in this behalf. Thus, my lord, right heartily fare you well. At Lambeth, the xxviij[th] day of July.

              Your lovynge frende,

Signed   T. Cantuarien   (Vol.5, No.1500)

It had been ruled that when the Bible was read aloud in churches a clear distinction was to be made between the words of the Scriptures themselves and any commentary upon them. Cranmer even advised that the Bible should be read only at such times, leaving commentary for private study. This was designed to prevent disturbances, and in Calais rabble-rousing of the Damplip kind. The following letter from one of Lisle's chaplains is chiefly of interest for the picture it gives us of a man who was to be so important in the drama of the following year, and for explaining his unpopularity with the extreme Reformist element.

332   GREGORY BOTOLF TO LORD LISLE   [*n.d.*]
        AND THE COUNCIL OF CALAIS

The true deposition of your most humble suppliant, Gregory Botolf, clerk, concerning ∧certain∧ words variably spoken between your said suppliant and one Tornaye, soldier of the King's Grace's Retinue in this town of Calais, ∧the xij[th] day of this present month∧. After evensong ∧was ended∧ in the choir I resorted into the body of Our Lady Church, where I might conveniently hear the reader of the Bible; and that which I heard him read at my first coming was the holy epistle of St. Paul to the Romans. And very shortly after he turned ∧the book and read in the prologue∧, which is an Introduction by the translator's advice, how that epistle of St. Paul should

be understood of the reader or expositor of the text, or texts, contained in the said epistle. So continued he reading therein but a small space of time and returned to the Holy Scripture again. Then upon occasion I walked up to the choir, hearing the reader reading in the said holy ∧epistle∧ to the Romans: to whom shortly after I returned again and perceived him reading of (or in) the said prologue. Then I considered secretly with myself, although I perceived the times of his digression from the Holy Scripture to the prologue and also his regression from the prologue to the Holy Scripture, yet the congregation did not; wherefor, when he next left reading of the prologue and again returned into the said holy epistle, without monition or declaring to the congregation when he read the Holy Scripture and when the exposition: I then spake, of a convenient loudness, as he might well hear, 'Torner, it shall be well done that ye declare to the hearers ∧or congregation∧ when ye end the Holy Scripture and when an exposition.' Then answered he me in grief, but I know not surely what. But certainly to his saying ∧this was maintained∧ that which ye read last was no Holy Scripture. Then in his next English he would reason with me of the King's Grace's Injunctions, and I perceiving his grief increased, and also that the congregation was disturbed, desired him briefly to read, saying, 'I pray you read somewhat, even what ye lust,' and again he reasoned with me continuously. ∧Then∧ I perceiving that, was much abashed, wherefore I came to the book offering my hand to have turned it, saying unto him, 'If ye will not read, I pray you let me.' He then answered, 'Ye shall not read here until I have done.' Then answered I him with this last answer, 'Ye do not well now, sith ye will not read yourself, neither let me, I ascertain you it would become you to let me read.' And as he continued in perverse argument I suddenly spake aloud to all the congregation, having a testament of a large volume in my hand, and turning it ∧to the said prologue saying∧, 'Friends, I shall read unto you the same ∧thing∧ wherein he left, whereby ye shall according to the translator's meaning the better understand the epistle of St. Paul to the Romans at all times hereafter when it shall be read unto you.' And then straight, without pause or speaking, I began to read the prologue, and continued, I suppose, nigh the space of an hour or iij quarters. Thus have I with all sincerity explained my fact unto you, most humbly beseeching ye will take such a direction or order for the redress of the fault as ye shall think best by your high discretions, whereunto I most heartily submit me.
Hol.   (Vol.5, No.1503)

After some of the usual delays, Lisle got a licence to cross to England, and did so on 13 September, 'not a little proud that I am become so strong a seaman'. He saw Cromwell as soon as he got to London; but there must be a letter missing, for he wrote to his wife after that meeting saying he would not describe it till his return to Calais, and yet in her next she has clearly heard some at least of what was said.

333   LADY LISLE TO LORD LISLE   *22 September 1539*

Good sweet heart, I have this hour received your letter by Nicholas Eyre, which comforteth me not a little, lauds be to Almighty God. But the one part of your letter is to me more comfort than the other, that is, where you write to me that you have been well entertained, and have good comfort, and that your journey shall be worth to you a m^{li} rejoiceth me much. But where you write that ye will trust no fair words, but at your coming to the king's highness do your own errand and trust to yourself, that rejoiceth me much more; beseeching the Holy Ghost, even as you have written, so assuredly give you grace steadfastly to continue in that mind, as I trust no persuasion shall move you from the same; wherein, if you persevere, you shall not only attain thereby much honour but also profit. I am glad ye have had so good communication with my lord Privy Seal.

. . . I thank you for your credence by John Toborow, and am very glad ye answered my lord Privy Seal as ye did. And even so I pray you to hold him, for so shall you have best of him. And whereas he sayeth that you be ruled by me, therein he taketh his pleasure; but, mine own good lord, if I had not both loved you and dread you, he should never have had of me that he hath.[7] . . .

From Calais, the xxij day of September.

I pray God your wine comen well to you, and in time
            By your true loving wife
Signed   Honor lyssle

Ye may keep both your pasties, for the ship tarried here ∧a∧ day after the receipt of your wine, and I have sent him[8] another pasty of partridges. I am glad your partridges did you so much pleasure, but I care not greatly if my lord Privy Seal had not had them. I will always send you partridges as I may have carriage, either baken or raw. And once again, sweet heart, I bid you farewell, as she that doth endure with as little sleep as any woman living, and so shall continue till your coming.   (Vol.5, No.1546)

334   LORD LISLE TO LADY LISLE   *24 September 1539*

Mine own sweetheart, after as entire recommendations as heart can think,

---

7. i.e. Painswick.   8. i.e. Cromwell.

this shall be advertising you that I have received your letters and my fur of sables, for the which I do thank you; and the same shall come right well to pass now, for I trust my gown shall be made and finished against Sunday, and then serveth the same as well my purpose as though I had brought them with me; and so did the fur of bogy[9] which I have laid in a gown of black velvet; praying you to send me the ij pieces of French wine as shortly as you conveniently may; but I will have the piece of old French wine kept for mine own drinking against my return, which I trust shall be shortly.

And in the meantime, good sweetheart, be merry and of good cheer, for I put no doubts but I shall bring you such news as shall be for both our comforts. I assure you I was never better welcome to the King's Majesty, and his Grace asked heartily how you did. I pray Jesu save his life! I was never more made of, nor better entertained than I have been since my coming. And one thing you may be assured of, that I will speak for myself, and declare unto the King's Highness my full mind; and not to trust promises and fair words, and ∧to∧ follow my suits by other men's means and mediations, for I do well know what that hath already cost me. . . .

. . . And thus desiring that I may be most heartily recommended unto my Lord Chamberlain, Mr. Wallop, Mr. Porter, Mr. Rokewood and all other my friends there, I bid you with heart and mind farewell.

From Windsor the xxiiij^tn of September

Signed   yo*ur* louyng husband for euer

Arthur Lyssle   (Vol.5, No.1547)

335   SIR THOMAS PALMER   [*n.d.*] *after 12 September 1539*
       TO LORD LISLE

Please it your good lordship to be advertised that I have spoken ∧with∧ Agar, who hath delivered me your good lordship's letter, wherefore I most heartily thank your lordship for your most gentle remembrance. My lady is merry and in good health, thanks be to God, and so is all your household. Mr Comptroller doth rejoice so much in your room that he sweareth by his faith he would give xx^li to hear that you were at Dover, coming over! My lord, it shall be well done to know my Lord Privy Seal's pleasure how that this Frenchman, Captain Andren, shall be entertained, whether that he shall come into England or whether he shall be commanded hence, or nay. No doubt of it, if he would serve the King's Highness as well as he hath served the French King, he is not a man to be cast away, for he hath the name throughout all France to be a valiant fellow, ∧and∧ of great conduct. He hath told me, since you parted, that in case the King's Highness will give him but

9. i.e. budge.

bare entertainment he is contented, whatsomever it shall please his Grace. And if it please God to give him grace to do the King service he will do that service shall be worth thanks, and will have ij thousand Frenchmen, adventurers, ready at his commandment to serve the King's Highness at all times. Wherefore, whether the King's Highness will have him or not, methinketh him unmeet to be here in this town; for a very few Frenchmen, methinks, may satisfy this town. He saith plainly he will never serve the French King, though he should beg all the days of his life. He hath slain a gentleman which longed to the Constable of France, wherefore he is but a dead man if he be taken in France. If I thought we should have war with France within this ij year I had liever pay for his abode at London or in any place of England rather than he should go his way. But yet I would not have him in Calais. But I take it good policy to cause one Frenchman destroy another.

I shall beseech your good lordship, if it shall please you, to make my most humble recommendations unto my Lord Privy Seal, and am in great doubt lest his lordship, by some evil report, should be my heavy lord, because I could have no answer of no letters sent to his lordship this twelvemonth. Say I would to God whosomever hath reported me otherwise than well, that he and I both were before my lord to be tried who were the honester man. . . .

>   yo*ur* lordcheps
Hol.   Thomas Palmer   (Vol.5, No.1556)

336   CROMWELL TO LORD LISLE AND THE   *18 October 1539*
       COUNCIL OF CALAIS

After my right hearty commendations to your Lordship, These shall be to advertise you that for certain purposes, the specialties whereof you shall further know hereafter, the King's Majesty's pleasure is that you shall view his Grace's house there called the Exchequer, that with all diligence all things therein necessary to be amended may be undelayedly repaired. For the which purpose I have by his Grace's commandment written also to his Highness's Surveyor there, who by your advice shall set in hand with the same. Furthermore, his Majesty would that you should cause the streets and lanes there to be viewed for the pavements, and where any default is, to give commandment to those which should repair the same to see it immediately amended, endeavouring yourselves to put all other things within the said town in the most honest and cleanly order you can devise; wherein you shall administer to his Majesty very thankful pleasure.

And thus fare you heartily well.

From London, the xviij^th of October.

Signed   Your good lordshippes
>   Thom*a*s Crumwell   (Vol.5, No.1571)

The object of these mysterious preparations was probably not unknown to Lisle, who had been about the Court in September when the negotiations for Cromwell's choice of a royal bride were being completed. The marriage to Anne of Cleves, daughter of an important Reformist ruling house, was to be the culmination of his power struggle with Norfolk and his party. Lisle was not to be responsible for the reception of the bride herself at Calais – his duties as commander of a frontier garrison town kept on a wartime footing were paramount. In charge of everything else was the man closer than any other of the great officials to the King, Fitzwilliam, Earl of Southampton, the Lord Admiral. From mid November, Anne, with her train of 263 attendants and 228 horses, crawled across the Low Countries at the rate of five miles a day. The English escort arrived in Calais to await her on 2 December and kicked their heels, expensively, for ten days. Cromwell's younger son, Gregory, in Southampton's suite, wrote, 'My Lord Admiral, with all other the King's Highness' servants awaiting upon him, hath been continually feasted, as well of the Lord Deputy as also other his Grace's officers here.'

The Lady Anne reached the border of the Pale early in the morning on 11 December, 'where honourably received her the Lord Deputy of Calais', accompanied by Wallop, Palmer, Richard Grenville, and George Carew, 'well appointed with great horses', and the Spears in velvet coats with gold chains, and all the Retinue in the King's livery, 'all being fresh and warlike apparelled'. The two companies rode on together, and about a mile from the town they were met by Southampton, replendent in 'a coat of purple velvet cut on cloth of gold', lavishly trimmed with aglets and trefoils of gold, wearing on a chain the badge of his office as Admiral – 'a whistle of gold set with rich stones of a great value'. With him, all attired in cloth of gold and purple velvet, with gold chains, were Lord William Howard, Sir Francis Bryan, Lord Grey of Wilton, and other lords and gentlemen to the number of four hundred, in coats of satin damask and velvet, attended by two hundred yeomen in the King's colours of red and blue cloth. At the Lantern Gate were waiting Lady Lisle and other ladies and gentlewomen, 'and there she stayed and viewed the King's ships, called the Lion and the Sweepstake, which were decked with a 100 banners of silk and gold, wherein were 200 master gunners and mariners and 31 trumpets, and a double drum that was never seen in England before, and so her Grace entered into Calais, at whose entering there was 100 and 50 pieces of ordnance let out of the foresaid 2 ships, that made such a smoke that one of her train could not see another.'[10]

There was then a considerable anticlimax, as the weather became appalling and they could not put to sea for another fifteen days. There are no letters from the Lisles during this period, and we do not know whether either of

10. S.P.1/157, f.5.

them was present on some of the occasions on which Southampton reported, such as that on which the Lady Anne begged to be taught some English card game that the King was fond of. We do know they were not when she insisted on Southampton and his gentlemen supping with her one evening, to his great embarrassment, as it was absolutely not the custom in England and he feared the King would be annoyed; but 'her manner usage and semblance', he assured him, 'was such as none might be more commendable, nor more like a princess'.[11]

And so, on a cheerful note, ends the last full year of Arthur Lisle's residence in Calais.

However, so complete was the King's disillusionment at his first sight of his bride, in spite of the loving embraces with which he greeted her in public, that he postponed the marriage ceremony for two days by insisting on a re-examination of her supposed precontract to Francis of Lorraine, in the hope that this could be taken as a lawful impediment. But there proved to be no escape this way, so with extreme reluctance Henry was married to the Lady Anne on 6 January. Cromwell was seen to have been responsible for a disastrous marriage, arranged in support of a foreign policy which he had pressed upon the King in spite of the latter's reluctance, committing him to an alliance with Lutheran implications instead of leaving him the room to manœuvre which his opportunist mind preferred, and which soon proved to have been unnecessary as there were no signs of France and the Empire combining against England. These were mistakes which played their part in enabling Cromwell's enemies to work against him, though neither in itself caused his downfall.

337   CROMWELL TO LORD LISLE   26 January 1540

After my right hearty and most affectuous commendations to your lordship, these shall be to signify unto the same the receipt of sundry your letters and therewith the book of munitions and furnitures, and also such news as ye have written unto me, whereof I have advertised the King's Majesty. . . . And his Highness willeth that ye and all other there, every man for his office, room and part, shall be so vigilant and also in so good order as it appertaineth and as the statutes of the same do require. And albeit his Majesty perceiveth no present nor imminent danger to that town, and thinketh that no prince would break the treaties so far as to invade or attempt in deed anything against the same; yet nevertheless, forasmuch as it is better to prevent than to be prevented, and to foresee that the worst may be provided for, his Grace's pleasure is that it shall be diligently foreseen there, not only that, under the colour and habit of peasants and market folks there enter not in that town by little and little a multitude of men of war disguised for to surprise the same, but also that in the carts and cars coming into the same, laden with hay, straw, wood or such other, there be not brought in weapon or other things conveyed in secretly hid in the same to the disadvantage of the town. My lord, seen that your lordship hath the chief charge and is put in the highest trust there above all other, ye ought likewise to be the more vigilant and active and timely to foresee and cause that such provisions of wine and other as may be gotten there without bruit or rumour as thereby by your good provision and industry the town may be so furnished and in that good surety that his Majesty's good expectation of you doth look for. . . . Thus fare ye right heartily well.

From London this xxvj[th] of January,

Signed   Your lordshippis assuryd

Thom*a*s Crumwell   (Vol.6, No.1639)

The following, enclosed in a letter[12] to Cromwell on 8 February, is a particularly evocative example of the minutiæ of intelligence that Lisle regularly supplied. It had been dictated more or less verbatim to his secretary by one Simon Roberghe or Rewbury of Sentercase.

Symon Roberghe of Sentercas showed unto my Lord Deputy the vj[th] day of Feb. a° xxxj° Rex. H. viij that about a month ago he commoned with one Robert Framerty of Bouchynghes besides Wast in Boullonais, which had bought one horse of the said Symon and is of his acquaintance. And in communication the said Symon asked him, 'What news in Picardy?' And the other said that there was great rumour or bruit of war. Then said Symon 'Yet I pray you, for acquaintance' sake, that if you hear of anything that it should be war, to give me knowledge of it, for I have certain horses which I would sell and if anything but good should fortune.' . . . Whereupon the said Framerty, on Thursday last was sennight, sent for the said Symon that he should meet him at Marguison on the sign of St. George, which the said Symon did so and found him there; and as soon as he had set up his horse he took Symon by the hand and led him on the back-side and said unto him, 'Symon, I have sent for you only to show you that I have enquired as far as was possible for me to enquire, and I sayeth I fear nothing ∧else∧ but war betwixt England and France. For my chance was to ride in company with ij or iij of the Dolphin's gentlemen, for I sold ij horses unto them, and they bade me to come to their lodging to recover my money at an hour that they appointed me. And when I was there they chanced to speak of the town of Calais and of Guisnes, and one said that

12. Vol.6, No.1644.

they were not so like this Ɔ years to get Calais and Guisnes as they were now, forasmuch as Flanders lieth open ∧upon∧ them, and likewise the county of Guisnes to Boullonais and Picardy; and even in one night (he said) we may burn all that country and destroy them, even to the hard gates of the said town; and so, their victuals destroyed, it was not possible for them to continue one half year's space without yielding of themselves, having also a number of ships upon the sea to stop the succour that could come from out of England, for of other parts they ∧could∧ have no favour. Then said another of the same company, 'Aye, but when the defiance shall be given between these ij kings, it will be hot for us to come there, for in the meantime they may make provision.' 'Then', quod the other, 'let us not look for any defiance.'

While the suggestions in the previous letter read far more like the product of Cromwell's mind than of Henry's, the content of this transcript would surely have gone straight to the King, in support of Cromwell's theory of danger from a Catholic power.

Though Sir John Wallop's casual opening of the next letter might suggest that its news value is slight, it is the only item in the correspondence which marks the moment when the Lord Deputy took the decision which determined the subsequent course of events. Moreover, Wallop's reason for writing calls attention to the events responsible for that decision by reminding us how fruitlessly Lisle had endeavoured to gain official support from Cromwell for dealing with contraventions of the regulations on religion that he was supposed to enforce. Wallop had been warned early in February to be ready to replace Bishop Bonner (who was of Cromwell's party) as Ambassador to France, and Norfolk passed through Calais on the 14th on a flying mission from Henry to Francis I. He wrote urgently to Cromwell and the King on the 17th imploring Henry 'for God's sake' to recall Bonner at once, as he is 'marvellously hated here', and to 'send Sir John Wallop hither'. It speaks well for the speed of the messengers that Sir John arrived at Abbeville, 'in post', on the 21st.

338   SIR JOHN WALLOP TO LORD LISLE   *27 February 1540*

My very good Lord, after my most hearty recommendations: At this time I have no other matter worthy writing, saving the good hope I have we shall live in peace for this year. Yet notwithstanding I will advise your Lordship to put all things in readiness as though ye should have war; and not to suffer Poole and Donyngton craftily to convey corn away as they did before, nor any other.

I trust if my Lord of Norfolk tarried with you one day he would so comfort you, and advise you to sequester all crafty folks – I mean those that be disobedient unto the King's Injunctions, as Poole etc. – trusting ye declared those sort according to their merits, not forgetting the flesh-eaters. Of these things I pray you make participant Mr. Comptroller, Mr. Treasurer, Mr. Porter and Mr. Rokewood, with my most hearty recommendations: ·/ with like recommendations unto the Marshal and Under-Marshal, without making them participant unto the letter. And that I may be humbly commended to my good Lady, heartily to Mistress Basset, Mistress Philippa and ∧Mary∧ etc. And thus my good lord I take my leave of you.

From Abbeville, the xxvij^ti of February.

Yours assuredly

Signed   John Wallop   (Vol.6, No.1659)

The men to whom Wallop wants his letter shown are, like Lisle, the 'King's men' on the Calais Council. Norfolk spent the 24th and 25th in Calais on his return journey. While there he stayed with Lisle, and I believe that this visit was undoubtedly responsible for bringing the relationship between the Lord Deputy and the Lord Privy Seal to its turning point. Lisle had been finding it increasingly difficult to serve two masters in Calais – the King and Cromwell; and he had realized a year ago that any help in the dispatching of private affairs through the maze of the new civil service would never be forthcoming now that Cromwell had succeeded in getting Painswick and Morton Valence from him. He now found himself with a friend and cousin who, with the King's favour, and both the old aristocracy and the vast majority of the people behind him, was bidding fair to shake Cromwell's supremacy in government. Norfolk's mission to the French King had provided him with the reassurance that the present amity between Francis and the Emperor was in no way inimical to his brother of England, and that if Henry were to discard Cromwell their relationship would again be that of perpetual allies and good friends. His brief but hitherto unnoticed stay in Calais on his return journey was, in my belief, the crucial event which gave him the cue for the kind of attack to which Cromwell would, and did, prove vulnerable within three months. Hence the dispatch of a commission to inquire into the state of Calais and its disorders within a fortnight of his return, and his reporting direct to the King the Deputy's reasons for wanting to come over which resulted in Lisle's being summoned to do so in April.

19

The Botolf Conspiracy

Lisle's last two years and two months of life and the last four months of the Letters face editor and readers with an entirely fresh problem and the consequent necessity for a different method of presentation. The letters themselves no longer provide the main thread of narrative interest. There are only forty-five of them and they cease early in April, except for one written on the 24th and the last letter of all, written on 11 May. The reader must be prepared to forgo the lively personal and social interest of the Letters, forget about the individual writers who have built up the Lisle world with its private preoccupations, and to return with the story into the larger and much less attractive world of English politics in the last months of Cromwell's final struggle to regain the power he had lost over the religious issue and the Cleves marriage. Leading to the climax of the Lisle tragedy, it has all the elements of a detective story.

The trouble started within Lisle's own household. It originated with Sir Gregory Botolf, one of his three domestic chaplains, and it involved two of his gentlemen-servitors, Clement Philpot and Edward Corbett, also John Woller, James Castyll, and Philip Herbert, and Corbett's personal servant, John Browne. Botolf was taken into Lisle's service in the middle of April 1538. From a complaint[1] made about him by a priest who had brought him up from childhood, and later from his own revelations of his past, he was obviously a bad lot – apparently the black sheep of an otherwise respectable Suffolk family. He was evidently a well-spoken, well-educated young man, with a plausible tongue and considerable charm of address, which seems to have won him the favour of his master and mistress and to have imposed upon some – though not all – of his fellow servants, especially Clement Philpot. According to the Welsh soldier-chronicler Elis Gruffudd he was known in Calais as 'Gregory Sweet-lips'. One man whom he did not deceive was Sir Oliver Browne, the oldest of Lisle's chaplains, who described him as 'the most

---

1. Vol.5, No.1625.

mischievous knave that ever was born', and prophesied he would be hanged. His religious opinions were vehemently 'papish', as Husee would have labelled them, and this no doubt helped to ingratiate him with Honor Lisle. Whether he was a genuine religious fanatic it is difficult to judge now. He probably lacked preferment commensurate with his ambitions and his own opinion of himself. A clever, irresponsible rogue, with a restless head and an itch for scheming, he reminds us of the cunning servant of ancient comedy who, like his Tudor offspring Merygreke, Brainworm, and others, revels in conspiracy for its own sake but in this case translates it into real life, with tragic results.

Clement Philpot was the young Hampshire gentleman whom Sir Antony Windsor had recommended to Lisle's service in 1538, so that he and Botolf may have been drawn together by the accident of being newcomers in the household at the same time. Husee, it may be remembered, had investigated Philpot's expectations and had recommended him as a possible husband for Philippa Basset.

At the end of January 1540 Philpot, Botolf, and John Woller all had leave from Lisle to go to England. What reasons they gave we do not know. When the trouble began, two months later, Philpot stated that he went upon business for Botolf. This, clearly, cannot have been the reason he gave to Lisle, as Botolf had leave for England at the same time. They appear to have set off on 5 February, and to have left Calais before the shutting of the gates in the evening, in order to cross by a boat that was catching the night tide at 2 A.M. Botolf took care to give everyone the impression that he was going to England and called attention to himself by spending the evening gambling in a tavern outside the gates, as Corbett, Woller, and Herbert afterwards bore witness when interrogated. Corbett insisted that 'the said Sir Gregory said to me that he would not go over that night but would tarry that night to play with men of Sussex at dice or at tables, to get his costs into England, if he could'. Woller said that he played 'unto the time it was two of the clock in the morning. And then the said Sir Gregory went up into the chamber, and so he left him behind him'. Leave to go to England, the departure before the shutting of the gates to catch a night boat, the gambling session to get money for his passage, were all cover for his real intention. When Philpot and Woller left the tavern to catch their boat, Botolf simply disappeared. How far Philpot and Woller were actively covering up for him in his getaway it would be unsafe to guess. He obviously had the charlatan's delight in mystification for its own sake and in bewildering even his own associates. Philpot certainly knew that Botolf meant to go to Rome, even if he was not then fully aware of the purpose of the journey. Woller may have been entirely in the dark.

In Calais, on 9 March there had opened the Commission set up at Norfolk's instigation immediately *post,* and probably *propter,* his meeting with Lisle there in February. This use of Calais was Norfolk's move against Cromwell. Cromwell's countermove against Norfolk, using the same weapon, will be seen shortly. Lisle himself was, most unusually, given a seat on the Commission which was to examine his own sphere of administration. Four prominent churchmen also had seats, as well as lords and lawyers, as they were to enquire into the roots of the unrest there 'as well in matters of religion as touching the observation of the laws, statutes and ordinances made for the preservation surety and defence of the said Town'. Minor offenders were to be punished or deprived of their posts and banished from the town and Pale without question or delay. Anyone found worthy of death was to be imprisoned without bail and held until the King should 'signify his resolute pleasure'. These were all measures which, where lawbreakers who were his own followers were concerned, Cromwell had made it impossible for the Lord Deputy to take.

On 31 March Sir John Wallop wrote from the French court to Lisle,[2] enclosing an extract from a letter from Norfolk which shows him jubilant at the way the King was pressing home his anti-Lutheran policy and insisting upon the establishment of unity in religion (i.e. support of opinions he approved), and at the fact that Cromwell has found it politic to have an apparent reconciliation with Bishop Gardiner of Winchester, Lisle's friend, and with Wriothesley. Wallop is clearly encouraging Lisle in his new alliance with the ascendant Norfolk, and hoping he will rally others of 'the King's party' in Calais against Cromwell's interest.

The Commissioners sent in their first report on 5 April. This, for the King, and also for Cromwell, was what had to be accepted in London as an impartial judgement of the actual state of affairs in Calais after a three weeks' investigation. It was not one of Lisle's harassed letters which Cromwell could ignore for three months and play down as unnecessarily alarmist, counselling moderation and charity. His own chickens had come home to roost. The Commissioners' attitude was entirely uncompromising and they were unanimous in support of Lisle, Sandys, and Wallop and their party on the Council. They vindicated the men on the spot, and their reports upon several of the outstanding trouble-makers and their description of the Sacramentaries as 'close, crafty and secret in all their answers' must have more than confirmed all Henry's suspicions. Moreover, they had dismissed Pelham and Stevens, two of the Retinue men whom Lisle had dismissed in the previous October, who had presumably been reinstated through Cromwell's intervention. Nothing could have been more damaging and dangerous to Cromwell than this first report. Lisle, very properly, does not sign it, as it is his complaints that have been investigated, and he has given evidence throughout.

While tensions in Calais were acute during the summoning of witnesses to

2. Vol.6, No.1663.

the Commission, and still more acute when subsequent arrests and dismissals began, events without significance in themselves, but fraught with dire consequences, had also occurred, which send us back to pick up the threads of the Gregory Botolf–Clement Philpot story where we left it, in the early hours of 5 February. Woller and Philpot went to England. The former returned to Calais on 14 March, the latter on the 24th. That Botolf actually went to Rome seems pretty certain, although at one point he denied it. He reappeared at Calais on 17 March, which means he would have had just over five weeks for his two journeys and his business there. It would have been possible: we know, for example, that Michael Throckmorton did the journey from Paris to Rome in 1537 in seventeen days, at top speed.

To accomplish it in this time, however, Botolf would have needed money for horses,[3] and Philpot, when questioned, admitted, 'I had little thought he would have gone unto Rome when he went out of Calais, for he had not passing £3 in his purse when he departed.' His own account, as given to Philpot, was that the Pope's ambassador in France gave him 'money and a guide to bring him to Rome, for immediately after he went out of Calais he went unto the said ambassador'. This he might well have done, as the French Court was in the neighbourhood of Amiens on 6 February. Accepting his story, as recounted to Philpot, he saw the Pope and Cardinal Pole,

> and when I had declared everything of my mind to them, no more but we three together in the Pope's chamber, where we reasoned on many matters, I had not a little cheer of the Pope and Cardinal Pole and all the Cardinals, as the Pope himself did command me to have. And after this at all times I might enter the Pope's chamber at my pleasure and speak with him.

'Moreover', Philpot reports, 'he said the Pope gave him in reward at his coming away from him two hundred crowns. And at his departing the Pope sang mass and prayed for him', and Pole advised him not to remain in Calais 'but to get my lord his master's licence to go to his study to the University, to Louvain'.

There is no evidence for the truth of his story beyond his own statements, as retailed by Philpot, who reports him as saying,

> And know ye for a truth what my enterprise is, with the aid of God and such ways as I shall devise. I shall get the town of Calais into the hands of the Pope and Cardinal Pole. This was the matter that I went to Rome for.[4]

Botolf's plan, as outlined to Philpot, and the behaviour of himself and his supposed accomplices, as elicited in the confessions and interrogations of those implicated, seems more wildly fantastic than any fiction. How the

3. Throckmorton had 100 crowns for his journey (*L. & P.* XII i 249).
4. Vol.6, p.75.

Commissioners could ever have thought that his crack-brained scheme represented a serious threat, or that these men were dangerous, passes belief, when we read the actual depositions. Set it all against its own background, however, and it makes contemporary sense. Philpot, with a dozen men, was to overwhelm the night watch at the Lantern Gate, while Botolf with his company scaled the twenty-foot walls with five or six hundred men, broke open the door on the leads, and entered the town by the stairs which Philpot and his troop would then be holding. No one seems to have asked what exactly the Pope and Pole were going to do with Calais when they had got it: the Papal States were one thing, but even Cesare Borgia had never thought of annexing to them a little town on the faraway Channel coast.

Botolf arrived on Wednesday 17 March at the outskirts of Calais, having come via Amiens to Boulogne where he managed to borrow a horse belonging to Sir John Wallop to ride the last twelve miles in company with Wallop's servant, Hugh Middleton. He put up at the house of one William Ashton, a gunner, and sent a message by Middleton to Edward Corbett, asking him to send him a gown. The next morning he paid his respects to the Deputy and Lady Lisle, and when Corbett asked him what he had been doing in France he told him he had been 'wind-driven out of England', implying that he had made a forced landing in France – a not-unusual occurrence in bad weather. It is at this point in the various interrogations that we begin to get discrepancies which force us to take his reported statements with reserve, as it is almost impossible to know who is lying. Philpot's account of his return was that Botolf told him he had put up at the King's Arms, a hostelry outside the gates, to wait for the return of 'his man', whom he had sent to the Pope's ambassador at the French Court before he left Boulogne. 'His man' was to bring him a hundred crowns, on the Pope's instructions, 'which appointment his man kept not, whereat Sir Gregory did not a little marvel, for the Pope's letters were that the Ambassador should give him money as he would at all times desire'. One suspects that the 'man' and the money were equally mythical, and that Philpot was credulous where Corbett was shrewd, so that Botolf was more likely to have lied to the former and the account given by the latter was therefore probably nearer the truth.

According to Corbett, when Botolf returned to the Lisle household on 18 March there was a quarrel at dinner between him and the other two chaplains about Botolf's place at table, which the elder, Sir Oliver Browne, seems to have won. It ended in Botolf telling Corbett he would 'never eat meal's meat more in this hall', and he was going to ask Lisle for a licence to go away and continue his studies. This is the first we hear of his story that he had come back determined to go to Louvain for this purpose. If he really had been to Rome, it would make some sense, if he had done so with some idea of bettering his own prospects and failed, and been advised (conceivably by Pole himself) to improve himself by further study. His story that he was going to Louvain University to do so holds the most water of the several he told. Corbett said he told him that he saw Lisle after dinner that day and asked for the licence, was told that Lisle would consider it, and thereafter asked Lady Lisle on her way to church next morning to press his request to her husband. This is in keeping with what we know of suitors to Lisle generally; but in any case he did not wait for a licence. He talked Woller into selling him 'an ambling nag' and a saddle for his journey for some damask, saying he was short of ready money: he would get the Abbess of Bourbourg, near Gravelines, to put him up till the return from England of Philpot, who alone knew where certain of his possessions were stored. It seems he needed to get out of Calais with some speed. He gave Corbett, Woller, and Bryndeholme, a priest, indications that he had some important project afoot, taking the two former outside the gates and down to a little park to show them fourteen double ducats and a single ducat that he had towards it. Just before he left Calais on the 21st he took Corbett into the chapel in Lisle's house and produced a packet in which he said there were ten crowns which he was going to get Philpot to have made into three rings for Corbett, Philpot, and himself. The fact that he said he had originally intended one of the rings for Castyll seems to indicate that Castyll had been sounded and found wanting; and Castyll was later cleared of complicity. It was all the proper stuff of high conspiracy in the manner of Tudor drama. Botolf went on foot to Gravelines, leaving his horse in the Lisle stables to save its keep till Philpot's return, and took Woller with him. When Woller returned he told Corbett that Botolf had asked him to send his own servant, Browne, with some things he had left behind. Browne evidently returned with the following letter.

339   SIR GREGORY BOTOLF   [*n.d.*] *21 March 1540*
        TO EDWARD CORBETT

First I desire pardon for my swift departing from you, so that I suppose you lost singular labour. Then desire I you to cause my gear to be trussed and sent with your servant to me at Burborow,[5] for I shall look for his coming tomorrow at night. Nevertheless, if ye think it not expedient that they be sent me before your coming, which I look undoubtedly should be on Wednesday at night, then let it be ordered as you suppose best. If Mr. Philpot come not before Wednesday, then would I that ye did but send me my raiment and tarry yourself still unto his coming. Also, if ye both come on Wednesday you shall meet me at four of the clock in the Checker in Gravelines; and there shall your servant first ask for me if he bring my clothing on Wednesday. But if Philpot

5. Bourbourg.

be home or not you nor he shall not come to me before Wednesday at night. Nevertheless, if ye think it expedient for me to have knowledge of any manner tidings or news that might be for my wealth, I most heartily beseech you fail not to send me word, either by some trusty messenger to tell it me by mouth, either else to bring me your letters. Now desire I you, if my nag tarry with you until Wednesday, fail not to see him very well fed and curried. *Hol.*   (Vol.6, No.1667)

Hearing that Philpot was expected in day or two, Corbett went to Lisle,

and desired his Lordship's licence to go to Gravelines the next day. And he asked me what I would do there, and I shewed his Lordship that I had bought Sir Gregory's bed and chest that was in his chamber, and that I had promised him to bring him his money as that day. And my Lord said, 'What doth he there so long?' And I said he tarried there for Philpot's coming home, because he knoweth not where is much of his apparel which he should have with him. And my Lord said, 'Might not the fool have tarried as well here as to spend his money there?' and so my Lord licensed me to go thither and lent me a gelding. And Wednesday before Easter I took my servant with me, and Sir Gregory's nag and his fardel, and rode to Gravelines.[6]

The dialogue rings very true; and that was the extent of Lisle's connection with the Botolf Conspiracy.

Corbett found Botolf at Bourbourg, 'sitting at dinner with the nuns'. They seem to have discussed nothing but the minor debts between them. When Corbett returned to Calais next day he left behind his servant to bring on some silk that Botolf had promised, and he returned that evening with no silk but another letter.

340   SIR GREGORY BOTOLF   [n.d.] 25 March 1540
        TO EDWARD CORBETT

I pray you remember to ask my fellow Woller [for] my shirt, which I lent him cleansed and send it me by your servant with my other gear, either clean or foul, I force not whether. Also send me my cheese with him. Also buy for me one ell of the finest and best coloured or woaded kersey in Calais and send it me. Remember well old Mercyall for my livery cloak of blue colour. Remember Sir Henry's knife and bodkin for my new scabbard. Remember that John come to me betimes on Monday so that I may return and speak with you at night except ye think it meet to send him to me with your letters for any special cause before.

6. Vol. 6, p.79.

You shall also remember and labour my good ∧lord∧ to grant me his licence, ∧sealed∧, to go to the University of Louvain, in Lombard[7] land, there to continue ∧a student∧ unto such time as it shall be his pleasure to assign my return. And no doubt if ye make the writing ready to his hand he will not fault to assign and seal it. If he suspect anything then take my lady's advice, showing her ladyship in that I most heartily besought you to procure for me of my said lord and lady that same writing. And the truth is, without feigning, during their natural lives I will never have other master and mistress but them. Remember to ask Sir Edmund if he have sent me my pillow trussed in my fardel. If not, send it.

Friend, now for a conclusion, it is past time for me to speak with my acquaintance out of Flanders until I come to Antwerp myself. Wherefore I most heartily instant you to get me all my necessaries, with my whole debt in money, so that I may the better be able to bear out my charges of my own provision until God send me more, and with his gracious help I shall in short time send you good news. So be it. All other things I put only and all to your discretion.

Hol.   Gregory Botolf

Ye can send me my monies in no better coin than groats.

(Vol.6, No.1668)

Philpot had arrived in Calais in the early hours of the day of Corbett's return, and though he had set off for Gravelines at once on hearing from Woller and Herbert that Botolf wanted him, he had not met Corbett on the way home. It is difficult to understand why this flashy, egotistical mystery-monger should have been able to induce these young men to go rushing back and forth to Flanders at his behest and deal even with his laundry; but it is to be remembered that Lady Lisle and the Abbess were also taken in by him, and that the soldiers' nickname of 'Gregory Sweetlips' would not have been bestowed for nothing.

According to Philpot's own account, he met Botolf outside the convent gates and

> he said unto me that there was no creature living so welcome as I unto him. This done, we both entered the town, he saying unto me that 'I would fain that we had a place where we might walk secretly.' We thought most best to go upon the walls about the town. And so mounted we up the walls, whereas he said unto me, 'My most joy of the world, welcome as my own heart! For you are he that I do put most trust and confidence in, that is in the world.'

Until then, Philpot had only known that his friend had been going to Rome,

7. 'Dowshe' deleted.

but Botolf now revealed the full details of his plan. Philpot protested that it seemed impossible, but Botolf explained that during the Calais herring mart, from Michaelmas (29 September) to St. Andrew tide (30 November),

'they ∧do∧ use to watch in the Lantern Gate, whereas there be in the watch-house about a dozen persons. And against the time which shall be 'pointed in the night, at a hour appointed, that you, with a dozen persons well appointed for the same purpose, shall enter the watch and destroy them. That done, ye shall recule back with your company and keep the stairs. And at the same time when you begin I with my company shall be ready to scale the walls over the gate which passeth not xviij or xx foot at the most. When we are entered the leads, there is but a little door to be broke up, which shall soon be done, where then we may enter the town easily. I will have v or vj hundred men that shall enter with me on the first brunt: the most part shall be gunners: their pieces shall shoot iiij shots: they shall be made for the purpose. And as many as will resist, shall be destroyed without mercy.' 'I do much doubt,' said I, 'that so few men shall not be able to keep the town when they be entered.' He said, 'We shall have aid, both by sea and by land, within short space. And put no mistrust, all shall be handled after the best and the politic wise that is possible to be devised by man's wit.'[8]

It was Cardinal Pole, Botolf said, who had advised him to get leave from Lisle 'to study at Louvain'. He seems to have been implying that this was to enable him to perfect the arrangements in greater safety outside the Pale. He certainly needed to keep outside it now in case Philpot should talk; but the plot would have been a more exciting reason to give his friends for giving up his place in Calais than that of simply continuing his studies. In a later statement, Philpot added that a part of the plan was to buy from Sir George Carew, who was known to be willing to sell it, the post of Captain of Rysbank for Philpot, even 'if it cost a thousand crowns'. That Botolf could in real seriousness suggest that it would be possible to purchase the reversion of one of the most important posts in the garrison for a youth who was not even a member of the Retinue seems quite incredible.

Philpot returned to Calais on Good Friday, the 26th, Botolf promising to meet him again at Gravelines at Whitsun if he could, when he would 'bring me money plenty, with silk, as damask velvet and satin'. Botolf wrote another couple of times to Corbett in the next few days, always innocuously asking for the forwarding of such things as small debts, gowns, a sarcenet tippet, his books, and a scabbard. Of this kind were all the letters from him found in Corbett's coffer when his room was searched. By Easter Monday Philpot had managed to get the three rings made for the conspirators, such essential

8. Vol.6, pp. 86–8.

prerequisites of Tudor drama, from the ten crowns Botolf must have given him at Gravelines, for Corbett, in forwarding Botolf the rest of his gear, wrote that day 'Also I have sent you a ring of gold by my servant, and there is three letters by the which ye shall know what that means; also there was much waste of the gold; also you have many foes, but I trust that they shall be overcome well enough.'[9] Browne also carried a letter which Botolf had persuaded Herbert to make out to the Captain of Gravelines and put, evidently among other papers, before Lisle to sign, authorizing him to give Botolf a passport valid in Flanders. For this service, Botolf promised Herbert a doublet of satin.

There is a nightmarish quality about the statement of John Browne which sets it apart from those of the conspirators. It is written in his own hand, in execrable phonetic spelling, on four large sheets. In it, 'so nigh as God will give me the grace', he sets down every detail, relevant or irrelevant to the purpose of the Commissioners. His style is the 'simple-continuous' of the simple man with the tape-recorder memory which plays back to perfection the very essence of his own unexplained, uncomprehended experience. He begins with an account of how he and his master rode to Bourbourg and went with Botolf to Gravelines on the Wednesday and Thursday in Holy Week to take him his nag and his fardel. At Gravelines Botolf got rid of Browne by sending him to watch the Dunkirk road for 'a man in a russet frieze cloak,' who, needless to say, never appeared. If he and Corbett discussed the plan, it was not when Browne was there to overhear them. Returning to Calais with Corbett, he left again at five in the morning of Easter Monday, with the rest of Botolf's things, the ring, and the letter for his passport.

He missed Botolf at Gravelines, his horse threw him in a ditch, when he got to Bourbourg the gates were closed, and he had to spend the night in a miller's house which cost him three groats. On Tuesday morning he found Botolf at the nunnery, where he repacked everything for Botolf, and they rode the twenty-eight miles to Nieuport, where they spent the night. He had been told to escort Botolf to Ghent, for which they set off next morning. They had passed Bruges, and Botolf was walking for a while with Browne leading his horse when Browne was presently overtaken by Francis the post, who was well known to Calais men, and John Mason, afterwards French secretary to the King, on their way to the Emperor at Ghent.

> And Francis asked me what countryman I was, and I said, 'An Englishman', and where I dwelt, and I said, 'At Calais', and he said, 'With who?' and I said 'With one of my Lord Deputy's gentlemen', and he did ask me my master's name, and I said, 'Mr. Corbett'. Then called he aloud, 'Mr. Corbett! Ho!' And I said that my master was not there, and he asked, 'Who, then?' And I said that it was a gentleman of my Lord Deputy's house. 'What call you

9. Vol.6, No.1671.

him?' And I said I did not know his name, and he asked whither he held on, and I said, 'To Louvain, to the University.' Then said he, 'Belike he is some student?' 'Yea', said I, 'he is a priest, one of my lord's chaplains'; and then they rode apace away. And he heard us and then he was angry with me because that I said I was Mr. Corbett's servant, and I said that I will never deny my master so long as I knew him for a true man. And then he was angry with me, for he would a'had me say that I had been his man.[10]

They arrived just outside Ghent on 1 April, and Botolf certainly fooled poor Browne to the top of his bent. They met a priest with whom he conversed in Latin, and then he sent Browne on ahead to find a lodging and wait at the door till he came. Browne tried all along the street Botolf indicated, but could find no lodging, so waited there for him, 'and he came not'. Then he combed the city, looking for him till five o'clock, and could find him nowhere, 'and had no money but half a groat and a styver'. Eventually he found him by chance coming out of a tailor's. Botolf abused him until Browne said that his own master never spoke to him like that and that he would tell him; whereat Botolf calmed down and asked him to drink with him in a tavern, which Browne refused. He did persuade Browne to go with him to the house of the English Ambassador, Sir Thomas Wyat (anxious again, perhaps, to look as if he had a servant of his own), to retrieve some letters he had left there for transmission to Calais, telling Browne that he had said in one to Philpot that the latter 'had been slain'. They met Francis the post, and it appeared that Rudstone, the Ambassador's servant, had the letters, so Browne was sent to find Rudstone, who said that Gresham had them, but had left for England. So Browne found Botolf again, who said he would give him another letter to Philpot very early next morning at a village nearby. So Browne left at three in the morning; but there was no sign of Botolf. He eventually materialized at two in the afternoon, by which time Browne must have been frantic, for he had now no money at all. Botolf gave him the equivalent of twenty-four pence and a few groats, and some baggage to be left for him at a certain inn in Bruges on his way home. In Bruges he spent all day trying to find the inn and had to spend the night; so he had, for the rest of his journey, only enough money for fodder for his horse 'saving that I bought some apples', until at Gravelines the Searcher for the Customs gave him some money 'for my lord's sake'.

And that was the Botolf Conspiracy, which was to prove a matter of life and death.

I do not think that the loss of Botolf's letters in Ghent was responsible for the discovery of the plot, though they may have contributed some relevant

10. Vol.6, p. 92.

evidence at a later date. Wyat, the English Ambassador, may have been alerted by John Mason and Francis the post mentioning their curious encounter with Lisle's chaplain on the road; and Rudstone had known his duty too well to forward any letters in the diplomatic bag without informing his master. Wyat opened them and must have thought they contained suspicious matter, as he confiscated them, 'and after brought them the King'. He did not reach England until early May, however; and even if he sent news of them by Gresham this would not have reached the authorities until after Browne's return to Calais on Monday, 5 April. The latter delivered to Philpot the new letter that Botolf had sent by him. This has not been preserved, but according to Philpot's deposition it concerned only the inadequacies of the horse that Woller had sold him and the usual request for items of his wardrobe to be forwarded. The two letters that Wyat said he took to England are also missing.

It would seem that it was Clement Philpot who first revealed the whole thing, taking fright and deciding to turn King's evidence in the hope of saving his own skin. In the Commissioners' memorandum it is recorded that Philpot claimed that he came forward to expose the matter immediately he heard about it from Botolf, whereas actually he had been told about it eight days earlier and had concealed this treasonable information. By the time this note was made the Commissioners knew that he had been with Botolf from Thursday 25 March to Good Friday, the 26th. This would imply that he first went to Lisle or the Commission on the 2nd or 3rd of April. In his own statement there are at least two passages in which he presents himself in the role of the would-be informer. 'Then said I, to the intent that I might know the bottom of his stomach'; 'I answered to the intent that he should not mistrust me, and that he might the boldier disclose his evil and traitorous heart'. He evidently explained his eight-day silence by the fact that he had originally intended to tell no one until he could get to England and tell the King.

From 8 April, the Commissioners started recording the depositions of all those involved, who were imprisoned in different parts of the town to ensure that there could be no collusion. The drift of the questions put in all the interrogations indicates quite clearly the attitude taken by the Commissioners. There are no emergency measures necessary: they have sized up the conspiracy at its true value, which from any practical point of view was nil. But here in the Lord Deputy's household were half a dozen young men who, together with the parish priest of Our Lady Church, had all apparently been guilty, to a greater or lesser degree, of holding treasonable communication with yet a seventh member of Lisle's establishment, one of his domestic chaplains, and of concealing treasonable information, some of them, possibly, for months. The King and Cromwell had been informed, and Henry wrote his approval of their conducting of the affair. The salutation includes Sussex and the others according to their rank.

341   HENRY VIII TO THE   *17 April 1540*
        COMMISSIONERS AT CALAIS

Right trusty and right well beloved Cousin, right trusty and well beloved, and trusty and right well beloved, we greet you well. Letting you wit that we have not only received and seen your letters of the xiij^th of this present, but also perused your others of the xiiij^th of the same, addressed to our right trusty and well beloved Councillor the Lord Privy Seal. By the first ∧letters∧, which were directed to us, we do perceive a summary repetition of our last letters unto you, with a declaration of your doings sithens your advertisement, ∧and∧ of your opinion touching the infection of the multitude there by the contagious teaching of Damplip and Smyth, of the sending hither of Sir George Carowe with the depositions against him according to our commandment. . . .

For the second, we do right thankfully take your diligence and good advisement in the matter of the said Philpot, much approving your order taken touching the persons which be also noted in the same ∧matter∧. For a due and more perfect trial whereof, our pleasure is that you shall devise among you such a letter as you shall think meet to be sent from the said Philpot unto ∧the priest Sir Gregory∧, purporting some apparent hope of a benefice to be prepared ∧for him∧ by his mean in those parts, and requiring his speedy and undelayed repair for that purpose; which ∧letter∧ you shall cause the said Philpot to write with his own hand, and ∧then∧ you to send it to the priest at Louvain by such a messenger as you shall think expedient; and yet we doubt not but you do and will ∧still∧ labour by all the means you can possible to try out more of that matter, that we may at the last receive the clearance of it; for so it behoveth us, being the thing of no small importance. Thirdly, touching your return; we weigh and consider somewhat the proceedings at Arde; and therewith do remember the great suit made by our said Cousin and Councillor the Deputy there for his repair hither, ∧both∧ to visit us and also to declare his mind and opinion in some things used in that our said town and marches, meet to be both revealed and reformed. Whereupon considering that he shall not percase have so good a time and opportunity of a long season to repair us at this present, being you, our Cousin of Sussex, there, with such other as departed hence with you, we have for that part resolved, and therefore our pleasure is, that our said Deputy shall with all diligence resort hither unto us, like as we have specially written unto him for that purpose; and that till his return thither again, you our said Cousin of

Sussex shall remain there, and take the charge of our said town for the time of his absence, and likewise you, Mr. Gage, for the ∧same∧ time to tarry there with our said Cousin, as our Commissioner, Councillor and assistant with him, to supply and help to ease him in the charge thus committed unto him. And as for you the Lord St. John, Mr. Baker, Mr. Coren, and Mr. Leighton, our pleasure is that, your things there finished, you shall return unto us with convenient diligence. And forasmuch as we consider ∧that∧ the time of the abode there of you, our said Cousin of Sussex, and of you, Mr. Gage, shall be somewhat chargeable unto you, we ∧have∧ thought meet to advise you, that we shall take such order for the ∧re∧payment of the same, as you shall have cause to be contented: heartily ∧desiring and∧ praying you to be vigilant, and with your accustomed dexterities in such substantial wise to ponder and weigh all things there, and of the parts thereabout, as we may know how the same shall from time to time proceed accordingly.

(Vol.6, No.1672)

In a letter to Lisle of the same date he tells him that Norfolk has informed him of Lisle's wish to come over to discuss the fortification of Arde and other matters, and that he has taken the opportunity of Sussex's presence in Calais to give him leave.

While the Commission continued to examine and report to the King on the troubles that had arisen since the arrival of Damplip, now known to be George Bowker, in Calais, Philpot duly wrote the letter designed to lure Botolf back into English jurisdiction.

342   CLEMENT PHILPOT TO GREGORY BOTOLF   *19 April 1540*

Brother, with a faithful heart I commend me unto you. It did not a little grieve me, the trouble and vexation that ye had in your journey towards Louvain. I received your letters sent by John, but the letter that ye sent by Mr. Wyatt's servant is not come unto my hands, wherefore I pray you, have respect in your writing unto me. Howbeit I do not greatly mistrust your wit in that behalf. I do think that ye have forgot the poor soldier of Calais, howbeit he hath not forgotten you; for through the goodness of my lord and my lady, I have gotten you a benefice here, within the Pale, called Anderne, within a mile of Arde. The parson thereof died in the Easter week, whose name was Sir Thomas Carter, sometime chaplain unto my Lord Cardinal. It is valued in the King's books at xxvj^{li} by the year. There is a fair and a pretty house, well and strongly builded, the parsonage thereof. It were too long a process to declare the whole circumstance in the obtaining of this benefice, which I shall ∧show you∧ at our next meeting. My fellow Corbet hath been much your friend herein and doth take much pain for you. He is now in

England and he shall bring your induction with him. And I cannot tell as yet what ways he hath taken for your first fruits. This matter hath made me spend my money, that I am constrained of very necessity to lay my wearing raiment unto gage, which will be a great perishment of my honesty if my friends look not upon me in haste. Ye are not a little bound unto my lord and my lady for the zeal and good will, the which they bear unto you. My lord willed me to send unto you. I did show unto my lord of the evil will of Sir Oliver[11] towards you, and my lord biddeth you not to care for that matter. Ye shall hear no more thereof, ∧for∧ my lord will have no contention in his house and specially amongst his priests, for they should give best ensample, he saith. Wherefore I do not think nor cannot perceive to be any danger unto you for that matter, for seeing that my lord biddeth ye shall not fear therefore. I would that I might shortly speak with you, not only for this cause but for other things that I must needs have your advice ∧in;∧ and that shortly as ye can possible to come unto me and in anywise look ye bring my damask and satin with you. When ye come send me word by this bearer in writing of your mind, ∧when I shall look for you and what day. I shall think the time long, for I must needs go into England. I will speak with you before I go over∧. I will be parson of Anderne until ye come and whensoever ye come I think it best that ye come unto Anderne. Ye shall find there a good fellow priest that serveth the cure in the parsonage. He hath a good bed to lodge you in, and a stable for your horse; and when ye are come send the priest unto me and he will not let to come unto me.

Hol.

(Vol.6, No.1675)

There are very minor differences between this (the original) and the corrected draft, except that in the second the value of the benefice is altered to £20, the information is added that Corbett 'went with my Lord's letters into England', for Botolf's induction, 'as soon as the parson died, and he is not returned as yet, but he hath sent word it is obtained'. At this point the corrected version introduces another appetizing morsel to bait the hook:

as it chanced, in the week after Easter, your brother John Botolf came unto Calais; and through the means of my Lord and my Lady he hath agreed, and a final end is made between him and you, and that ye shall be lovers and friends, as brethren should be. The end is this. I have received xv li. of him, sterling, and he is bound in the sum of xx^{ti} marks to pay me vij li. more at Christmas next coming. Much to do I had with him, which I shall show you when we shall meet.[12]

---

11. Oliver Browne, Lisle's senior chaplain. 12. Vol.6, p.110.

On second thoughts – Philpot's or Layton's – this was crossed out, and it was not incorporated in Layton's copy, so presumably was omitted from the letter which was actually sent. In the final passage there are two additions in the corrected version. The first informs him that Lisle has said 'as long as ye keep your study ye may be non-resident of your benefice, for I reasoned with my Lord therein, for I was in a doubt thereof. My Lord said he would save you harmless in that behalf.' The second concerns the attractions of the benefice. The 'good fellow priest' has 'a stable and hay for your horse, but one bed that is honest. Bread and drink ye shall find, cheese and eggs, but none other cates.' On second thoughts, however, the 'good fellow priest' and the 'stable and hay' are deleted. The revised draft then concludes, 'I received a packet of letters by one that came from Dr. Wotton. In haste, written the xix day of April, from Calais.' Layton's copy is signed, 'Your own Clement Philpot'.

Botolf was sought for unsuccessfully in Ghent, and then Robert Donyngton was sent to Richard Pate, who had just succeeded Wyat as Ambassador there, carrying instructions, if the device of the letter failed, to get him, though outside the King's dominion, arrested by alleging against him the robbery he had committed several years earlier when he stole the plate belonging to St. Gregory's at Canterbury when he was a canon there. Finding him in Louvain, Donyngton, perhaps with the aid of Philpot's letter, persuaded him to return with him to Calais next day; but, according to a letter from Pate to Cromwell on 1 May, 'the stay whereof came, as it is likely, more of his spotted conscience than otherwise, feigning himself sick upon a surfeit the night before taken of the good cheer they made together; whereupon he caused him to be [ar]rested by the Mayor of the town, finding the mean before wisely to know whether he were admitted scholar of the University, and found his name not registered: this doing to the intent he might work the surelier, as thanks be to God it right well hitherto hath succeeded; laying to his charge the robbery of a church, which seemed to the scholars so heinous that they, hearing of this taking, thought him worthy the gallows, whom otherwise, we judged, would have enterprised his delivery'.[13]

His extradition proved more difficult to obtain. On 16 June Cardinal Pole wrote on his behalf to Cardinal Cervini, asking that Cardinal Farnese, Ambassador to the Emperor, intercede on his behalf; and on 27 June Pate wrote to Norfolk that he was at liberty 'and highly entertained with the Bishop of Liége, sitting daily at his table, purposing furthermore to give him an honest promotion in his church'.[14] The fact of Pole's intervention at this stage is, of course, no proof of his real involvement in Botolf's fantastic story originally

13. Vol.6, pp. 112–13.   14. Vol.6, p. 114.

told to Philpot. If Botolf, in getting a message to him now, had given this story as the reason for his arrest, he might well have thought it a put-up case indeed. Botolf was attainted by act of Parliament and excluded from the general pardon in July 1540. His fate remains a mystery.

Lisle had set off immediately on receipt of the King's letter of 17 April, and arrived in London in time to be at the chapter meeting of the Order of the Garter at Westminster Palace on the 23rd (see Pl. 18). He was obviously well received, as he and Sir Thomas Cheyney were appointed to assist the Earl of Cumberland, who was to act as the King's deputy, to install the new knights then elected at the Garter feast at Windsor on 9 May. At the chapter meeting Lisle sat on the Sovereign's left, between Cromwell, newly created Earl of Essex on the 18th, and Lord Russell.

It was also on the 23rd that Botolf's accomplices were taken secretly out of Calais after the gates were closed at night (a very rare thing) to catch the two o'clock tide just as they had done on that night ten months before, and were seen safely on board by the acting Deputy and his assistant. On May Day, twelve of the 'troublemakers' who had been arrested when the Commission started its hearings, including Henry Tourney, were taken openly through the town in chains, according to Foxe's *Book of Martyrs* ill-treated on the boat, and two days later were anchored before the Tower of London. On their arrival, again according to Foxe, Cromwell commanded that their irons should be struck off, sent for them to his house, and then committed them to the Fleet Prison, bidding them 'be of good cheer, for, if God sent him life, they should shortly go home with as much honesty, as they came with shame'.

It seems clear from hints in letters that Lisle, his wife, and his friends all anticipated that he would receive preferment of some kind when recalled. We hear nothing of him after the Garter meeting on the 23rd, except that his wife had had news that he was ill.[15] We know, however, that he was present in the House of Lords on 27 and 29 April and on 1, 3, 4, 8, 10, 11 May, which means that he attended every sitting of that session from 27 April until Parliament was prorogued for the Whitsun holiday.

The Court was at Greenwich for Whitsuntide – Whit Sunday fell on 16 May – and Lisle was either with the Court or was sent for, as it was at Greenwich on the 17th that he made a 'declaration'. What he 'declared' has not been preserved; but on the 19th the blow fell. The information comes from Marillac, the French ambassador, writing from London on 21 May to Montmorency, the Constable of France.

> Two days ago, at ten o'clock at night, my lord Lisle, Deputy of Calais, uncle of this King, was led prisoner to the Tower, where before had been committed three of his servants, and similarly today a chaplain of his who

15. Vol.6, No.1677.

is come out of Flanders in a ship. The cause thereof hath not yet been so certified unto me that I can write it for truth; but it is bruited that he is accused of having had secret intelligence with the Cardinal Pole who is his near relative, and of other practices to deliver up to him the town of Calais. Howsoever it may be, the said Lord Lisle is in a very strait prison, and from the which none escape save by miracle.[16]

There was no truth in the rumour Marillac had picked up that Botolf had been brought to London.

Elis Gruffudd's account of Lisle's examination is the only one we have and must be quoted in full.[17] Though his source may only have been Calais gossip, he has proved remarkably reliable in other reports. On dates and times he clearly knows what he is talking about: Norfolk was at Court, doing his best to engineer a royal marriage for his niece Katharine Howard, and although Cromwell was in London over Whitsuntide, Greenwich is only a few miles down river. Gruffudd wrote:

At this time, the next Whitsun holiday, Lord Lisle and his friends at Calais were given to think that he would be made an earl and that he was sent to Windsor to keep the feast of St. George and that he would be the chief of the feast. The contrary indeed was true. For none of the great men of the Council looked at him save askance, for they saw that he was besmutted in some way or other, for secretly he had been before the Council once or twice, and on Whit Tuesday the Council called a meeting to discuss the matter. Here were the two dukes, the Earl of Essex, the Chancellor of the Kingdom, and others of the Council. Some say that the King was there in person, but such witnesses spoke against him [Lisle] that he was unable to go against them, for he went down on his knees and appealed to the King to help him in his righteousness. But the King told him, 'Doest thou not ask for righteousness! For I shall take trouble to hear this matter myself.' At this the lord asked the King to be merciful and righteous to him. To these words the King turned his back and went to his room without letting him answer either good or bad. The Council then sent him in the custody of Sir William Kingston, who delivered him to the Lieutenant within the walls of the Tower, around eleven at night.

The statement that Lisle had previously been before the Council in secret does not necessarily imply, as Gruffudd assumes, that he had been already interrogated about his own affairs. He could have been summoned earlier to report on any or all of the Calais troubles, and out of such questioning matter

16. French. J. Kaulek, ed., *Correspondance politique de MM. de Castillon et de Marillac ...* (1885), No.223, p. 184.
17. Mostyn MS 158 (in Welsh, translated by Prys Morgan), f. 552a, National Library of Wales. See Vol.6, p. 118.

18. Procession of the Knights of the Garter. Lord Lisle is No. 13, seventh from the left.
From J. Anstis, *The Register of the Most Noble Order of the Garter* (1724); courtesy of the Newberry Library, Chicago

could have arisen which required his 'declaration' of 17 May, which was presumably then responsible for his interrogation on the 18th in the King's presence. There is nothing, however, to indicate what was covered by the interrogation of 18 May beyond the fact that the only charge which became publicly known within twenty-four hours concerned the Botolf conspiracy, and this was treason.

Had Lisle been suspected of treasonable communications with Pole he would have been arrested on arrival and would certainly not have been allowed to see the King nor to attend either the Garter meeting or the last eight sittings of the parliamentary session. In searching for reasons for his implication in the Conspiracy, therefore, we must look for something that happened between his return and 17 May. The committal to the Tower on 24 April of Philpot and Corbett on a charge of treason and therefore subject to the use of torture evidently produced no evidence against him, and it would have contradicted essential evidence of the structure of the plot given in their already recorded statements anyway.

For clues, we must look again at the Cromwell-Norfolk power struggle. Norfolk, having talked at length to Wallop in France in February about the general situation in Calais, and visited Calais and Lisle himself on his way home, had decided to use the troubles there as a pawn in his game and had achieved the sending of the Commission and then the recall of Lisle to strengthen his arguments. Cromwell had lost ground by the Cleves marriage. His obvious remedy would have been to facilitate a royal divorce as quickly as possible after it; but this would only have been to facilitate at the same time a royal marriage – to Norfolk's own niece, Katharine Howard. The findings of the Commission on the root causes of the Calais troubles, and the sending to England on 1 May of the men he had favoured there against Lisle's advice put him himself in danger. There was too much evidence of his past support for him to disown his men, and his policy must be to discredit Lisle and reinstate them. He could use Calais to defeat Norfolk at his own game by taking the Botolf plot seriously. Nonsense it may have been, but there was no doubt of the religious disaffection of the conspirators. Cromwell could use the discovery of 'papish elements' in Calais to counterbalance Norfolk's revelation of his support for the Sacramentaries. The King was known to be fond of his uncle, Lisle, just as he had been fond of his cousin and now arch-enemy, Pole; if the one could be implicated in dealings with the other, Henry's reaction against the Catholic-conservative Norfolk-led majority party in the Council could be guaranteed.

So Cromwell had a motive, and all the opportunity required, to frame Lisle. For means, reliance could be placed on the King's suggestibility about and almost pathological hatred of one man: Reginald Cardinal Pole.

There is no other suspect.

19. Cardinal Pole, portrait at Lambeth Palace

20. Margaret Pole, Countess of Salisbury
Courtesy of the National Portrait Gallery

20

Two More Years

Elis Gruffudd's account of what happened in Calais to Lisle's family immediately after his arrest is substantially true. The King's pursuivant arrived on Thursday, 20 May, with letters to Sussex for the arrest of two soldiers who had been Lisle's servants; and

> that afternoon, in the twilight, Lord Sussex and the Council went to the Staple Inn where Lady Lisle kept house. She, after the Council had conversed a little with her, was put in prison in a room of the Palace and the girls were taken from her and put in prison in various places through the town. At this time the Treasurer took possession of all the treasure and clothes of Lord and Lady Lisle in the King's name.[1]

He says that the rumour in Calais was that it was Lady Lisle who was responsible for the whole family's downfall because 'she intended to marry her daughter to a Picard squire'. To elucidate this we have fortunately a number of formal depositions to which we can now turn.

On 24 April, a few days after Lisle's departure to England, a gentleman waited upon Lady Lisle at Calais with a letter from Monsieur de Riou, the eldest surviving brother of Madame de Bours, proposing a marriage between Mary Basset and Gabriel de Montmorency, Seigneur de Bours, who had succeeded his father on the latter's death in April 1537. A warm, mutual affection had grown up between Madame de Bours and her young English charge, and after Mary's return to Calais in March 1538 there were always messages for 'ma bien aimée fille' in Madame's letters, and requests and thanks for gifts and polite commendations from Montmorency and his married sister. The new young Seigneur spent most of his time in attendance at Court, but he had visited the Lisles twice during Lent this year. The formal courtesies of letter-writing and the normal exchanges of gifts between the families of which the correspondence informs us do not, however, prepare

---

1. Vol.6, p. 139.

us for this situation that was thrust upon Lady Lisle just after her husband's departure in April, and as will presently appear, it could not have occurred at a more unfortunate moment for Lisle's own affairs.

Mary, as we know, was a very good-looking and attractive girl, and extremely popular with the Lisles' French acquaintances. The marriage proposal, if the King's permission were granted, would have meant a very distinguished alliance for her, and Lady Lisle apparently acted both correctly and with good sense, writing immediately to Lisle and also informing the Calais Council. Lisle would not normally have approached the King on the subject until a family decision had been reached. All the letters that passed between him and his wife at this time have disappeared, and we only know of this marriage proposal and its consequences because, when orders were sent to Calais to seize his possessions, Lady Lisle and her household were interrogated and the story came to light. And the crux of the matter was – not the offer of marriage, but the fact that Gabriel de Montmorency and Mary Basset had secretly plighted their troth or made a pre-contract of marriage when he paid a second visit in Lent and stayed the night in the Lisle household on Palm Sunday Even – Saturday, 20 March, the fateful day when Botolf departed to Gravelines.

Unfortunately only abridgements of the depositions of the household have survived,[2] instead of the verbatim accounts that are so evocative in the Botolf story, so that abridging them further is not so painful. Mary said that in the second of her four-year stay in the de Bours household M. de Bours (whom we have come to know by his courtesy title of Montmorency) fell in love with her. On her return to Calais he sent her 'sleeves of yellow velvet' and she sent him 'a flower of silk'. Soon after he sent her 'a pair of linen sleeves with ruffs of gold, which she showed to her mother, and her mother to her father', and she wrote him her thanks. 'About half a year ago' he sent her a letter of commendations, and in Lent he sent her a letter and a primer with his name in it, which she showed to her mother. 'In Mid-Lent he came unto her and came with my lord her father when the keys were brought in, and dined there, and after had light words of marriage, giving her then no token at all. And at the same time had communication with her father, but what she cannot tell. And departed at the opening of the gates after one of the clock afternoon.' On the eve of Palm Sunday he brought a letter to Lisle from the Constable of France, Anne de Montmorency, and remained for the night, and 'at that time he moved her earnestly for marriage, and said he would cause his friends move it to her father and mother, and after moved it to her mother by one Wyndebanke, her servant, and of the morrow dined with her father and mother and departed his way.'

2. See Vol.6, pp. 142–7.

Wyndebanke deposed that he had indeed interpreted between Montmorency and Lady Lisle, who said that the latter 'was as welcome as her son', but no word was spoken of marriage.

Lady Lisle deposed that she had 'little communication' with Monsieur de Bours 'because she could speak no French; but as her daughter Mary did interpret his words they were in commendation of the said Mary and her daughter Anne, and no words touching marriage. . . . Mons. de Bours brought a letter to the Lord Lisle from the Constable of France, the contents whereof she knoweth not. . . . Mary told her that she durst not make her privy of the communication of marriage had between her and Mons. de Bours on Palm Sunday even, because she was young and might have time thereunto after.' She had told the messenger from de Riou that she could make him no answer in her husband's absence; and besides writing to Lisle she had written to Anne Basset, so that she could explain to the King, if he asked her, anything he wanted to know about Montmorency.

Anne Baynham, probably a member of the household, said she and Margery Lacy heard Philippa Basset say on 21 May that if Mary 'kept one thing to herself, all is well enough, but if she open that, she undoeth herself and us all; which words Mary Hussey said also, and further she saith that Mary Hussey said that she had made one thing well enough, for she had cast the letters in∧to∧ the jakes.' Mary Hussey, Lady Lisle's gentlewoman, confirmed this. Philippa also confirmed the conversation, but said she only alluded to the letters that were thrown in the jakes and knew nothing of the contract of matrimony.

There are two possible explanations of what came next. The Commissioners may have wanted clarification of the evidence of Lady Lisle and Wyndebanke and that given by Mary as to whether Lady Lisle had heard of the proposals for a marriage on Palm Sunday Even, and may therefore have questioned Mary further before sending in the report acknowledged by Cromwell on 30 May. The other alternative is that Cromwell seized on this discrepancy, and also the fact that Philippa's statement was either ambiguous or equivocal, and that he was, moreover, as he evidently said in his letter of the 30th, by no means satisfied that the matter of 'the letters cast into the jakes' had been property investigated. In any case, Mary was interrogated again, though we do not know the date, and the examiner recorded: 'The said Mary contracted matrimony with the said Mons. de Bours the said Palm Sunday even, privily, and after declared the same unto her sisters and to her mother, and whether her mother declared the same unto the Lord Lisle, or no, she knoweth not. Item, she cast all her letters in a jakes, save certain ∧letters∧ which she delivered unto Mary Hussey, who likewise did cast them in a jakes.'

There is no ambiguity about Mary's statement in her second examination that she 'contracted matrimony, privily' with Mons. de Bours on Palm Sunday Even. She means that they made a contract *per verba de praesenti* – that is, a formal troth-plight or contract of marriage by words, for which neither witnesses nor any ceremony was necessary, and which constituted a legally valid marriage. The Church did not encourage these secret betrothals, but it had to uphold them as binding. It was this same pledging of troth which had created such trouble in the Paston family in 1469, when it was discovered that Margery, the daughter of John and Margaret, had thus bound herself to Richard Calle, the bailiff, and not all the efforts of the Bishop of Norwich could undo it. Communications or discussions of a marriage were innocent enough: a pre-contract was another matter, made without the King's permission between a member of the family of the Lord Deputy of Calais and a Frenchman. It seems probable that in the conversation of 21 May Philippa had been referring to the pre-contract as the one thing Mary must keep to herself, that under interrogation she hastily pretended she had only meant the letters, and then foolishly denied knowledge of the contract, of which at that time her interrogators had never heard.

On 5 June, acknowledging Cromwell's (missing) letter of 30 May, Lord Sussex and Sir John Gage sent him Mary's new deposition and a note in her own hand of what she can 'call to her remembrance' of the destroyed letters, 'with certain other French letters found in the house'. They report having dissolved the household, paying members a quarter of the wages owed to them, committing Lady Lisle, with a gentlewoman, a chamberer, and a groom to Francis Hall (a Calais Spear) 'who is a sad man and hath a sober honest woman to his wife. . . . John Basset and his wife are departed into England. And Bridget, one of the daughters of the Lord Lisle, to whom there is no matter laid, remaineth here until we may know the King's Majesty's pleasure what shall be done for the keeping of her.'[3]

As this is the last information we have from Calais about Lady Lisle, it should perhaps be noted here that there is no confirmation whatever, in such communications as have been preserved, of Foxe's statement that, immediately upon Lisle's apprehension, she 'fell distraught of mind, and so continued many years after'. Gruffudd's report is that she lost her senses while imprisoned in the house of Francis Hall, and that he never heard if she ever completely recovered them. As there is no other evidence, one can only say that this was the rumour current in Calais, and that it is unlikely to have been entirely without foundation, nor would it have been completely improbable, in view of what we know of her temperament, of the great distress of mind she endured in 1537 when their expectation of the Plantagenet heir was so bitterly disappointed, of the intensity of her devotion to Arthur Lisle

3. Vol.6, p. 151.

and of the fact that the shock of his arrest was utterly unexpected and came when her hopes were at their highest. On the other hand, if she was really out of her mind at the time of her release, one would expect to find the Privy Council taking some steps to arrange for the control of her estates and of the money provided for her return to England. That she was, as we say, 'almost out of her mind' for a time, as the result of shock, is more than likely, and would have been quite enough to give rise to the Calais rumour and the form in which it reaches us.

As it turned out, nothing more was ever heard of the perilous de Bours contract. After his receipt of Sussex' letter of 5 June and its enclosures, Cromwell would have had only two or three days to do anything about it. On the 10th he himself was arrested.

The connections between Lisle's arrest and Cromwell's fall will be explored later. Here we are concerned only with the narrative of events and the record of fact. Lisle's arrest had been followed by that of Richard Sampson, Bishop of Chichester, within a couple of hours of his appointment as the first bishop of the new diocese of Westminster, and then by the arrest of Dr. Nicholas Wilson, chaplain to the King, both, like Lisle, accused of the treason of having communications with Rome. At the beginning of June, the French Ambassador, for one, considered Cromwell firmly in the ascendant. But he had underrated Gardiner and Norfolk. On 10 June Cromwell attended the morning session in the Lords. He dined, saw his clients as usual afterwards; and then, as he entered the Council chamber at Westminster at 3 o'clock he was arrested by order of the King on the charge of heresy and secretly working against the King's purposes in religion.

Marillac wrote on the 23rd:

As for the other prisoners, no one knows yet what to say of them, save that there is good hope in respect of the Deputy of Calais, in that this King hath said two days since that he cannot believe the said Deputy hath erred of malice, but that in those things of which he stands accused he hath proceeded rather by ignorance than otherwise.[4]

After Cromwell's arrest, proceedings for dissolving the Cleves marriage were promptly set on foot, with Gardiner, Wriothesley, and the King himself drawing up the interrogatories to be administered to all persons at Court who could give evidence to show that the King had never freely consented to the marriage and had never consummated it. Cromwell did everything required of him to help to provide evidence. The act of attainder by which he was condemned 'de crimine heresis et lese maiestatis' was passed on the 30th. Though he had renounced all hope of mercy when arrested, asking

4. Kaulek, No. 231; cf. ibid., No. 351. Vol.6, p. 154.

only that his end might be swift, he wrote an appeal to the King after his sentence, of which, according to Foxe, 'none durst take the carriage upon him'. Sadler, however, asked permission to bring it, and Henry had it 'thrice read to him' and 'seemed to be moved therewith'. If indeed he was moved it may have been by self-pity like that which drew tears from him as the cuckolded husband, but it was certainly not to mercy.

Gardiner having managed all the proceedings, and persuaded the Lady Anne to accept the jurisdiction of the clergy, her pre-contract of marriage with Francis of Lorraine (which in January had been declared no impediment as being for a marriage 'in the future') being now declared a marriage in itself, contracted, like Mary Basset's, *de præsenti*. Sentence of nullity was passed on 9 July by the clergy in full Convocation; the lady was pensioned off, and before the end of July, probably on the 28th, the day of Cromwell's execution, Henry married Katharine Howard privately at Oatlands.

Lisle must certainly have heard about Cromwell's arrest, attainder, and execution. Important prisoners of state, who paid for their board and coals, wood and candles, and had one or more servants to attend upon them, could not remain ignorant of such momentous happenings. We cannot know whether the news brought him renewed hope for himself or greater fear of a similar fate.

Meanwhile in Calais, every scrap of paper belonging to the Lisles would have already been taken to be searched for evidence, and the inventory of all their seized possessions had now been completed (Pl. 21), listed room by room as they were found. They make almost unbearable reading, these lists, stabbing the imagination with their meticulous, automatic enumerating of such things as 'two old pieces of tapestry', 'two old carpets', and 'three old worn dripping pans'. There is something at once pitiful and terrifying about their mechanical throwing open of cupboard doors upon the skeletons of ostentation and carefulness, the gay apparel and the gorgeous jewels, the poor little shifts and the worn-out splendours . . . and the memories, the standing cup with H for Henry and A for dead and forgotten Anne Boleyn on its cover, the standing cup with Henry's Tudor rose and Katharine of Aragon's pomegranate badge, those New Year's gifts from the King that Husee had received for his master with such pride. One interesting item was a set of twelve masquing gowns, with hoods and caps of buckram and twelve masquing vizards. In listing Lady Lisle's dresses and jewels, somebody had to count all the jewels sewn on to hoods and sleeves, and one billament for a hood was adorned with 203 pearls, and one pair of crimson satin sleeves with 800 pearls, and another black velvet pair with 573 pearls and 84 'paired stones' of gold. In prison, the inventory lists only that Lady Lisle had with her a taffeta cloak and gown, a kirtle of black velvet and another of tawny, and two nightgowns, one of black satin and the other of black damask.

S.P. 1/161, f.49

21. First page of the inventory of Lisle's household goods

On 2 July the patent creating Lord Maltravers Lord Deputy was delivered at Westminster. Whatever fate might yet befall, Lisle's deputyship was ended. On the 17th the bill, which was introduced in the Lords to attaint the Calais conspirators and Damplip, was headed by the names of Viscount Lisle and Lord Leonard Grey, and was read for the second time on the 19th. Then, on Wednesday the 21st, the names of Lisle and Grey were expunged before the final reading. There is no means of knowing whether this was by the King's order. On 4 August, Philpot and Bryndeholme, with eleven others including a son-in-law of Sir Thomas More and a lay brother of the London Charterhouse, were hanged, drawn, and quartered at Tyburn. Corbett, Woller, and Browne, like Lisle, were still held: they were still excluded from the general pardon. The French Ambassador wrote that 'by a law passed in the last Parliament, here they condemn men without hearing them', and once a man is a prisoner in this country, in such a place as the Tower, 'there is no one living that dare intermeddle in his affairs, nor dare ope his mouth save to speak ill of him, for dread that he himself may come under suspicion of the same crime as that of which he is accused.'

During 1541 tensions at Court became acute. In February the King began to have serious trouble with his ulcerated leg, and he suffered from what the French Ambassador called 'ung mal d'esprit', speaking bitterly of his councillors as mostly time-servers, thinking only of their own profit. His moods were unpredictable: what he said in the morning he contradicted by night time, and he had grown more and more suspicious of treason among his most trusted servants. In the country as a whole, at least as far as matters religious were concerned, things were no better. Reformists more extreme than the King were burnt for heresy, Catholics were hanged, drawn, and quartered for treason. Conspiracies by both sides were discovered in Wales and in the North of England. That in the North was founded on the hope that with the death of Cromwell a movement like the Pilgrimage of Grace might have more hope of success. Henry decided to go north with some 5,000 horse, but the abortive affair was put down before it really began, and the leaders were executed at Tyburn on 27 May. Henry had intended that before he went north the fate of all prisoners in the Tower should be decided, and now, on the same day or the next, his object-lesson in terrorism began with the execution in the Tower of the nearly seventy-year-old Margaret Pole, Countess of Salisbury. Lisle in his cell there cannot but have heard of the death of his cousin, and probably of the barbarity with which the beheading was carried out, the usual executioner being at work in the North, by an unskilled youth who literally hacked her head and shoulders to pieces. Also in the Tower was her fourteen-year-old grandson, Henry, who was expected soon to follow his dead father, Lord Montague, and his grandmother to the block. On the same day all the heads stuck on pikes on London Bridge, to remind everyone of the traitor's doom, were taken down to leave room for more.

Throughout June, as more executions followed, including that of Lord Leonard Grey, rumours were rife in London that Lisle too was to die. There is only one conclusion possible: the King did not intend, in June 1541, that he should die. His survival was not an oversight. But whether he or his unhappy wife had any idea of this is quite another matter. However, by mid July the rumour was that he was allowed more freedom of movement within the Tower, and that the King had been heard to say that his uncle had erred 'more through simplicity and ignorance than through malice'.

The projected journey north now took place, more in the form of a glorified version of one of the King's normal 'progresses' than of a punitive expedition, with the Queen and his daughter Mary and the Court accompanying him. The chief sufferers were the wild life. In one day they killed 240 stags and does, with cross-bows and long bows, and as many again the next day with greyhounds. While this was going on they took, in the King's presence, a great number of young swans, two full boat-loads of water-fowl and as much again of great pikes and other fishes. And while Henry staged this spectacular slaughter, it was here, at Hatfield in Yorkshire, that his young wife, 'the jewel of his old age' as he had termed her, 'looked out of her chamber window on Mr. Culpeper after such sort' that her waiting woman, Margaret Morton, realized for the first time 'that there was love between them'. We hear nothing of Lisle while the King was in the North. The Tower, as he intended, had been cleared of all other prisoners of importance, and it would indeed have been surprising if he had ever given a thought, during these four months, to the harmless old man. He may have intended to pardon him on his return; he could afford to be gracious, rejuvenated by his delight in his 'rose without a thorn'.

Dis aliter visum. At the beginning of October the King began his southwards journey, reaching Hampton Court at the end of the month; and on 2 November Cranmer laid before him the charges against Katharine Howard which had been communicated to him a few days before. To conceal such knowledge of the Queen's misconduct would have been treason, even though it had taken place before her marriage. She had had two lovers while living in the household of her grandmother, the dowager Duchess of Norfolk. But worse was to come, for once the interrogation started it soon became apparent that adultery must be added to the charge. By 14 November it was known in London that Thomas Culpeper, a gentleman of the King's Privy Chamber, had also been her lover during the great progress in the North.

Henry was so overcome by the discovery that he was said to have called for a sword to kill her himself. His vengeance encompassed her grand-

mother, her uncle, Lord William Howard, and his wife and sister, Lady
Bridgewater, who were indicted of misprision of treason, found guilty and
condemned to imprisonment in the Tower and the loss of their goods. All
her waiting-women and friends who knew of her 'evil life' and 'falsely and
traitorously' concealed their knowledge were similarly convicted. And Jane
Rochford, George Boleyn's widow, the guilty intermediary in the Culpeper
affair, was executed with the Queen on 13 February 1542.

Rumours that Lisle was to be set free were now growing, encouraged by
the fact that early in January his arms had been set up again in the Chapel of
the Garter Knights at Windsor. Henry was recovering his spirits: a fortnight
before his wife's execution he had entertained at his own table twenty-six
ladies and gentlemen, showing the greatest regard to Lord Cobham's sister,
according to the Imperial Ambassador, but the saying was, according to the
same authority, that he had a fancy for 'a daughter that the wife of the former
Deputy of Calais had by her first husband'. It is possible that Anne Basset,
who had been specially provided for by the King when the Queen's other
attendants were dismissed to their homes, may have been emboldened by
this mark of Henry's favour and the rumours of her stepfather's innocence to
speak on his behalf.

Elis Gruffudd tells a story which, though the dates he gives are hopelessly
muddled, could have had substance in fact at this time, when Lisle may well
have had liberty to walk upon the leads of one or other of the towers on the
waterside. He says that as 'the King's Grace moved down the river in his
barge from York Place to Greenwich', Lord Lisle 'raised his hands high, and
shouted hoarsely from the Tower where he was imprisoned for mercy and
release,' and that the King then sent his secretary to the Tower with his
pardon, promising him his release within two or three days. But there are
many arguments of time and place against this tale.

Holinshed recorded that the King sent his Secretary Wriothesley to Lisle,
and Sandford supplies the date:

> His Innocency, after much search appearing, the King sent him his Ring
> from off his own Finger, with such comfortable Expressions, that he im-
> moderately receiving so great a pressure of Joy, his Heart was over-
> charged therewith, and the Night following (viz. 3 Martii An. 33 H. 8) he
> yielded up the Ghost; which makes it observable that this King's Mercy
> was as fatal as his Judgements. His Body was honourably buried in the
> Tower of London.[5]

The great question remains: why, so long after his innocence of connection with the Botolf Conspiracy had become apparent, and, particularly, so

5. Francis Sandford, *Genealogical History of the Kings of England* (1707), p. 448.

long after the fall of Cromwell, had Lisle remained in custody? The answer lies in part in Cromwell's knowledge of the King's psychology that he had used in framing Lisle: Henry's unquenchable hatred of Pole and his ability to believe any story, however improbable, against him. This state of his mind remained constant. The very affection he had undoubtedly had for Lisle militated against him: Henry's love once turned to hatred was fatal indeed. There were Poles still unpunished, including the Cardinal himself, and Lisle had been smeared with the taint of dealings with him. It was a subject on which Henry was not altogether sane – how else was it that the fourteen-year-old son of Lord Montague, who had been a child at the time of his father's offence, was also still a prisoner? That intellectually Henry had accepted Lisle's innocence seems apparent, yet the emotional block remained, and circumstances conspired to enable him not to have to think about it. First there was the political situation that the fall of his great minister involved, at a time when he was trusting no one. Then there was the process of divorcing his Queen, and then the all-consuming triumph of a man of fifty marrying a girl some thirty years younger. The threat of a rising in the North, with its connections with the Pilgrimage of Grace, once again raised the spectre of the hated Pole; the long, joyous progress northwards with his young bride left no time for consideration of the man who must always bring Pole to the surface of his mind again; and then came immediately the trauma of the trial of his beloved Katharine Howard. We can only conjecture that by the time Lisle's pardon finally came, it was because Henry had reached a state when he needed the consolation, and the salve to his ego, of feeling that at least one of his kin had remained always faithful.

One more point must be made, the most important contribution to history of the Lisle Letters, and one so far overlooked by the historians: the light they throw on the causes for the fall of Cromwell. It was the involvement, by Norfolk, of Calais in the forefront of the political scene at the moment when he did that produced the evidence of Cromwell's support, throughout Lisle's Deputyship there, of the 'troublemakers', the extreme Lutheran opponents of the King's all-important religious policy. It was the moment when Cromwell, who had so far survived the disaster of the Cleves marriage and had indeed just been made an earl, was suddenly seen as the stumbling block to the royal divorce and the Howard marriage. Cromwell's own counter-use of Calais and its Botolf Conspiracy temporarily paid off. By throwing Lisle to the wolves the pursuit of the Sacramentaries was halted, and Lisle himself, in prison charged with popish conspiracy with Pole, was effectively discredited as a witness. It may have been when, within a week of Lisle's arrest, Cromwell removed Bishop Sampson and Dr. Wilson, that Norfolk and Gardiner realized they could not risk letting the warning go unheeded any longer, and had already closed in for the kill, putting their accusations before the King and challenging Cromwell's delay over the Cleves divorce with their own plan for the satisfaction of his desires – Katharine Howard and release from his 'Flanders mare' – to which Cromwell was the obstacle, thereby making his removal necessary. There is no record whatever of how the human drama of those three or four intervening days worked itself out, but his enemies probably used much the same methods as Cromwell had done when he turned the King against Lisle by exploiting his credulity and his increasingly suspicious temper. He had taught 'bloody instructions', and they returned to plague the inventor. In the official indictment, his enemies evidently chose the support of heretics as the major charge against him, as being easier to prove in a hurry with material to hand than that of treason, also alleged. Even Foxe, who provides all the details of how Cromwell helped the Calais Sacramentaries, has no similar accounts to give of the way in which, according to the bill of attainder, he was said to have authorized the release of those convicted of heretical opinions. It cannot be coincidence that nowhere is there more evidence to justify the charges of supporting heretics and favouring heretical opinions than in the Calais story we have been following in these Letters, and that these are the really serious counts brought against Cromwell in the bill of attainder by which he was condemned.

21

Epilogue

After the death of Lord Lisle, what became of all the people we have come to know? Elis Gruffudd believed that the news of his pardon and rumours that he was to return as Deputy reached his widow before the announcement of his death, which must have made the blow more terrible immediately after. The King sent orders for her release and that of her daughters, and she returned to England and to Devonshire about 15 March.

We hear no more of her except in certain legal transactions, including that in which in 1556, nearly twenty years after Cromwell conned Painswick and Morton Valence out of her and her husband, the final results of this sale were settled by a Chancery decree giving her arrears of rent of £900 and an annual rent of £120 from the heirs of Sir William Kingston. How pleased Husee would have been to have known it! She died at Tehidy in 1566.

Husee remained in Calais, still a member of the Retinue at 8 *d.* a day, with the office of Searcher of Mark and Oye in the Pale. During the war against France in 1544 he was in charge of supplying waggons for victuals and powder, writing from Bruges to Sir William Paget 'at the camp before Boulogne' on 4 September, still complaining of the minions of officialdom as in the old days: 'Your mastership will not believe what people they are!' He died in 1548.

Frances Plantagenet, Lisle's eldest daughter who had married her step-brother John Basset, after his death married Thomas Monk of Potheridge in Devon, a near neighbour of Frithelstock and Umberleigh. By him she was the great-grandmother of General Monk, the chief agent in the restoration of Charles II after the dictatorship of another Cromwell.

Elizabeth Plantagenet married Sir Francis Jobson, one of the Receivers in the Court of Augmentations, by whom she had four or five sons.

Bridget, the youngest of the sisters, was the child chiefly remarkable in the Letters for her requirements of lettice bonnets, and who saw practically nothing of her parents throughout her schooldays. She married, some time in the next seven years, William Carden, a gentleman with lands in Kent. She was a widow by ten years later.

John Basset had died the year before his stepfather. All the work of the Lisles and Husee to protect his inheritance paid off, for his son Arthur inherited considerable wealth. It was he who made over Tehidy in his will to his grandmother for her life, so that Honor Lisle spent her last years in the Cornwall of her Grenville childhood.

Philippa married James Pitts of Atherington in Devonshire, and six years after her stepfather's death she had a son who was christened Arthur. She died in 1582.

Katharine Basset had remained with her beloved Lady Rutland until about 1540, and after that was taken into the household of Anne of Cleves; but she never did achieve the coveted position of Maid of Honour, for by that time Anne was no longer Henry's wife but his 'dearest sister, the Lady Anne'. In 1547 she married Henry Ashley, Esquire, of Hever in Kent and later of Upper Wimborne in Dorset. He was knighted by Queen Mary the day after her coronation. They had one son, Henry, who was knighted in 1603 and was one of Queen Elizabeth's gentleman pensioners. Katharine died about 1588.

Anne Basset held her post at Court throughout the reigns of Jane Seymour, Anne of Cleves, Katharine Howard, and Katharine Parr. In the first year of Edward VI's reign she was granted an annuity for her services to Katharine Parr. With Queen Mary's succession she appears again at Court as a Lady of the Privy Chamber. By 1554 she was contracted to marry Walter Hungerford, one of the gentleman pensioners. His father, the first Baron Hungerford, had been one of Cromwell's men, beheaded when his master fell in 1540. At the time of his marriage to Anne – he was twelve years her junior – in return for a gift of 5,000 markes 'for the Queen's use' and in consideration of his marriage to one of her ladies, he was restored to his paternal lands and his father's attainder was reversed. He then owned lands in Wiltshire, Somerset, and Cornwall. This was certainly the kind of marriage that was expected to come of all the efforts that the Lisles and Husee put into obtaining her original place at Court, and it was celebrated before Queen Mary in her private chapel at Richmond Palace, with much 'mirth and pastime' afterwards. But three years later, in 1557, Anne was dead; and we do not know whether it was by her or his second wife that was born the son beside whose grave her husband wished to be buried.

Mary Basset's contract of marriage to young Gabriel de Montmorency, Seigneur de Bours, must have been accepted as having been only *de futuro,* which it certainly was, whatever she was bullied into saying by her interrogators – had she not said to her mother at the time that she was too young to take the final step? Perhaps the trauma of those terrible days proved too much for the boy-and-girl romance. In 1557 she married a Devonshire neighbour, John Wollacombe of Overcombe. Her first child was christened Honor, but lived only a few days; but she had another eight years later whom she also called Honor. She also had two sons, John and Thomas. She died in 1598.

George Basset seems to have continued to live at Umberleigh until his nephew Arthur attained his majority. He married Jacquet, the daughter of another Devonshire neighbour, John Coffin of Porthledge. They had a daughter, Blanche, and two sons, George, who died young, and James. In 1561 or 1562 George and his family moved to Tehidy, in return for which he had surrendered Umberleigh to his nephew Arthur, so that it is with him that his mother spent her declining years. He represented Launceston in Parliament for many years, and died in 1580.

James Basset had a very different career, nearer to the centre of power, as the precocious, sophisticated, and ambitious little boy we have come to know so well would have wished. He remained a faithful servant to his first patron, Gardiner, Bishop of Winchester, until the latter's fall in 1551. During those years, Gardiner had been the most influential member of the Council until 1546, when he was ousted by Edward Seymour, Earl of Hertford, and Lisle's stepson, John Dudley, now Viscount Lisle. When Seymour became Duke of Somerset and Lord Protector under Edward VI, Gardiner, for his uncompromisingly Catholic bias, was deprived of his bishopric and imprisoned in the Fleet, where James constantly visited him; and at his trial he gave evidence of his affection for him, for which, when Gardiner was imprisoned in the Tower, James was briefly immured there as well. Between 1553 and 1556 he married Mary Roper, daughter of Sir Thomas More's beloved daughter Margaret. The fact that he moved upon terms of intimacy with other members of this exclusive and devout Catholic circle in difficult times suggests that Husee may have been wrong when he cast doubts upon the sincerity of James's beliefs. His wife, Mary, had been previously married to Stephen Clarke, and like her mother was a woman of brilliance and learning. With Anne Basset she was one of the Queen's Ladies at the time of Mary Tudor's accession. James became a Gentleman of the Privy Chamber, and Philip of Spain was godfather to their eldest son, Philip. When Gardiner was released from the Tower, James immediately returned to his household, and was well placed indeed when his master was restored to his bishopric and became Lord Chancellor.

Also released at this time was Edward Courtenay, son of Lisle's nephew, the Marquess of Exeter. Now twenty-seven, he had been in the Tower since the age of twelve. He and James became friends. When Courtenay was imprisoned again two years later, wrongly suspected of complicity in Wyatt's Rebellion, and then sent into honourable exile as a potential focus of more

Plantagenet trouble, they continued to correspond; and hence a few more letters of James's have survived.

Foxe has an easily refuted story that James was involved in an improbable plot to murder Princess Elizabeth in 1555. He was advancing in favour with Mary, who would never have countenanced it. During these years he received various grants of land in the West Country forfeited to the Crown. He represented Devon County in two Parliaments. The Queen sent him to Brussels in 1555, possibly to bear to Philip of Spain the tidings of her then-supposed certain pregnancy. He died in 1558 at the age of thirty-two or thirty-three. A second son, Charles, was born posthumously.

And at the State Opening of Parliament at Westminster in 1982, one of the pages bearing the train of Queen Elizabeth II was Master James Basset, direct descendant of George Basset of Tehidy. . . .

Index

Letter-writers' names are given in capitals (LISLE). The names of people and places will usually be found under the modern spelling. Variations in spelling are given in parentheses or in cross-references only where a letter-writer's own spelling of his signature differs from that of the index entry or where difficulty locating the entry might arise.

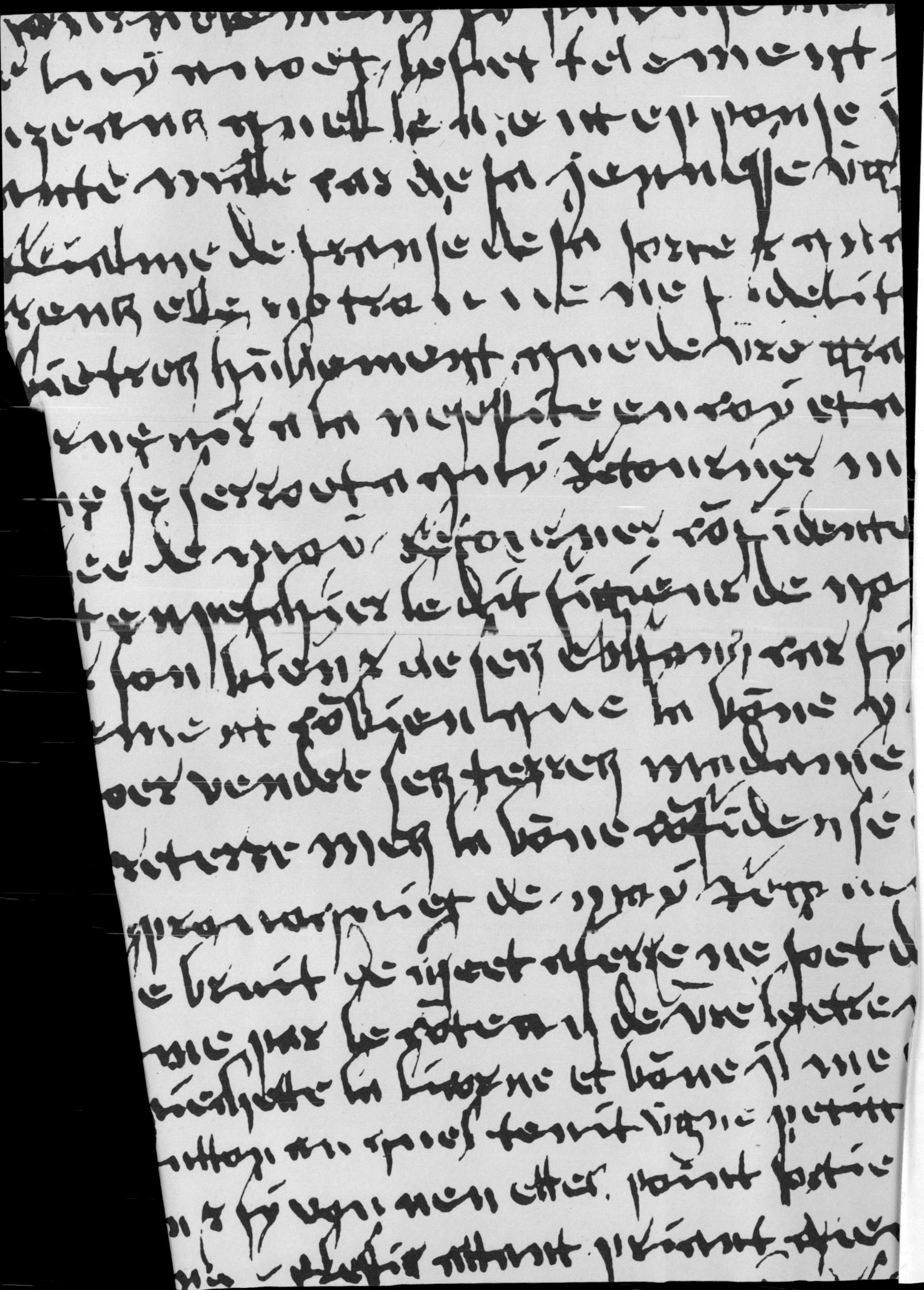